Dimensions of Transformation in the Ottoman Empire from the Late Medieval Age to Modernity

# The Ottoman Empire and Its Heritage

POLITICS, SOCIETY AND ECONOMY

*Edited by*

Suraiya Faroqhi
Boğaç Ergene

*Founding Editor*

Halil İnalcık[†]

*Advisory Board*

Fikret Adanır – Antonis Anastasopoulos – Idris Bostan
Palmira Brummett – Amnon Cohen – Jane Hathaway
Klaus Kreiser – Hans Georg Majer – Ahmet Yaşar Ocak
Abdeljelil Temimi

VOLUME 73

The titles published in this series are listed at *brill.com/oeh*

# Dimensions of Transformation in the Ottoman Empire from the Late Medieval Age to Modernity

*In Memory of Metin Kunt*

*Edited by*

Seyfi Kenan
Selçuk Akşin Somel

BRILL

LEIDEN | BOSTON

Cover illustration: "A portion of miniature where Takiyyüddin Râsıd is working, discussing and deliberating along with colleagues in his observatory in the late 16th century Ottoman Empire" (Istanbul University Library, Manuscript, FY, nr. 1404, vr.57a, modified and designed by Lâmia Kenan).

Library of Congress Cataloging-in-Publication Data

Names: Kenan, Seyfi, editor, writer of introduction. | Somel, Selçuk Akşin, editor, writer of introduction. | Kunt, İ. Metin, 1942– honouree.
Title: Dimensions of transformation in the Ottoman Empire from the late medieval age to modernity : in memoriam of Metin Kunt / edited by Seyfi Kenan and Selçuk Akşin Somel.
Description: Book edition. | Leiden : Brill, [2021] | Series: The Ottoman Empire and its heritage, 1380–6076 ; volume 73 | Includes bibliographical references and index.
Identifiers: LCCN 2021011074 (print) | LCCN 2021011075 (ebook) | ISBN 9789004409828 (hardback) | ISBN 9789004442351 (ebook)
Subjects: LCSH: Turkey—History—1453–1683. | Turkey—History—1683–1829. | Social change—Turkey—History. | Law—Turkey—History. | Turkey—Politics and government. | Turkey—History—Ottoman Empire, 1288–1918—Historiography. | Turkey—Civilization—1288–1918.
Classification: LCC DR511 .D56 2021 (print) | LCC DR511 (ebook) | DDC 956/.015—dc23
LC record available at https://lccn.loc.gov/2021011074
LC ebook record available at https://lccn.loc.gov/2021011075


Typeface for the Latin, Greek, and Cyrillic scripts: "Brill". See and download: brill.com/brill-typeface.

ISSN 1380-6076
ISBN 978-90-04-40982-8 (hardback)
ISBN 978-90-04-44235-1 (e-book)

Copyright 2021 by Koninklijke Brill NV, The Netherlands, except where stated otherwise.
Koninklijke Brill NV incorporates the imprints Brill, Brill Nijhoff, Brill Hotei, Brill Schöningh, Brill Fink, Brill mentis, Vandenhoeck & Ruprecht, Böhlau Verlag and V&R Unipress.
All rights reserved. No part of this publication may be reproduced, translated, stored in a retrieval system, or transmitted in any form or by any means, electronic, mechanical, photocopying, recording or otherwise, without prior written permission from the publisher. Requests for re-use and/or translations must be addressed to Koninklijke Brill NV via brill.com or copyright.com.

This book is printed on acid-free paper and produced in a sustainable manner.

# Contents

Acknowledgements XI
Acronyms XII
Notes on Contributors XV
Metin Kunt: Life and Work XXII
   *Selçuk Akşin Somel and Seyfi Kenan*
A Representative List of Metin Kunt's Publications XXXVII

Introduction: The Issue of Transformation within the
Ottoman Empire 1
   *Selçuk Akşin Somel and Seyfi Kenan*

### PART 1
### *Ottoman Historiography and Reflections*

1    A Firman Issued by Mustafa the Son of Bayezid I Surnamed
     Düzme (1422) 39
     *Elizabeth A. Zachariadou*

2    Imaginary Voyages, Imagined Ottomans: A Gentleman Impostor, the
     Köprülüs, and Seventeenth-Century French Oriental Romances 54
     *Tülay Artan*

3    Practices of Remembrance and Sites of Violence in Seventeenth-Century
     Istanbul: The Beheading of Şeyh İsmâil Ma'şûkî (d.1539) 97
     *Aslı Niyazioğlu*

4    Ottoman Artisans in a Changing Political Context: Debates in
     Historiography 123
     *Suraiya Faroqhi*

### PART 2
### *Ottomans – Culture and Careers*

5    *Türbedar* of the Ottoman Sultans: Şevkî Çelebi's Nostalgia for the Bursa
     of Bayezid Han and Emîr Sultan 149
     *Fatih Bayram*

6 The Personal Anthology of an Ottoman Litterateur: Celâlzâde Sâlih (d.1565) and His *Mecmua*  165
  *Cornell H. Fleischer and Kaya Şahin*

7 Transforming the Abode of War into the Abode of Islam: A Local Grandee in Ottoman Hungary, Osman Ağa, Çelebi and Bey  183
  *Pál Fodor*

8 Making Recommendations: Azmîzâde and the *Mahzar* for Vücûdî Efendi, 1608  202
  *Christine Woodhead*

9 A Poet's Warning: Veysî's Poem on the Breakdown of Ottoman Social and Political Life in the Seventeenth Century  219
  *Mehmet Kalpaklı*

10 From the 'Scribe of Satan' to the 'Master of Belâgât': Ottoman Chief Scribes and the Rhetorics of Political Survival in the Seventeenth Century  229
  *Ekin Tuşalp-Atiyas*

11 The Compass and the Astrolabe: Empiricism in the Ottoman Empire  257
  *B. Harun Küçük*

## PART 3
## *Law, Religion and Political Thought*

12 In Search of the Ancient Law or *Kānûn-i Kadîm*: Some Notes on Seventeenth-Century Ottoman Political Thought  287
  *Mehmet Öz*

13 Between a 'Brilliant Retreat' and a 'Tragic Defeat': Ottoman Narratives of the 1529 and 1683 Sieges of Vienna  305
  *N. Zeynep Yelçe*

14 *Bid'at*, Custom and the Mutability of Legal Judgments: The Debate on the Congregational Performance of Supererogatory Prayers in the Seventeenth-Century Ottoman Empire  323
  *Derin Terzioğlu*

15  The *Sicil*s of Karaferye (Veria) in the Eighteenth Century: A Case of Transformation?   367
    *Antonis Anastasopoulos*

16  Ottoman Legal Change and the *Şeriat* Courts in the Long Nineteenth Century   379
    *Iris Agmon*

17  Transformation through Constitution: Young Ottomans and the *Kānûn-i Esâsî* of 1876   399
    *Cemil Koçak*

## *In Lieu of a Conclusion*

18  Repertories of Empire: How Did the Ottomans Last So Long in a Changing World?   441
    *Karl K. Barbir*

    Glossary   455
    Index   463

# Acknowledgements

The primal idea for this book began to trickle down in the second half of 2013. In 2014, we invited Metin Kunt's colleagues and friends to offer their contributions. Time passed as ideas, analyses and essays evolved into this book in late autumn 2020. Unfortunately, Metin Hoca passed away on 3 December 2020 – a terrible loss to us while still finalizing the last touches before submission to Brill for publication. We cannot help but recall the irony of the famous Ottoman epigraph, "*Kazây-ı mübremi tedbir ile tağyîr mümkün mü?*" "Is it possible to intervene in the passage of the inexorable decree of providence by meddling?"

Metin Hoca was a genuinely kind human being, an erudite scholar and a wonderful teacher. Now it is with great difficulty that we need to make a little amendment in the title as our Festschrift turns into a memorial. We will miss him dearly.

This volume has been prepared with the magnanimous cooperation of Engin D. Akarlı. Engin Hoca took part in the conceptualization and the internal organization of the Festschrift. The editors would like to express their gratitude for his support. Another colleague to be mentioned is Tülay Artan, who contributed to this project by providing ideas that were crucial to shaping the project as well as by proof reading. We would like to thank Artan for her kind and generous assistance.

Finally, we would especially like to thank Franca de Kort and Maurits H. van den Boogert, who professionally handled the whole process of manuscript preparation at Brill with patience, and Selina Cohen of Oxford Publishing Services who meticulously read and elegantly proofread the manuscript.

In addition, we owe special thanks to Lloyd Cabasag and his team for diligently undertaking the process of the final design of this book.

# Acronyms

| | |
|---|---|
| AEK | Âtıf Efendi Kütüphanesi, Istanbul |
| AIHK | Afyon Gedik Ahmet Paşa İl Halk Kütüphanesi |
| AMKT | Ankara Milli Kütüphane |
| AO | Archivum Ottomanicum |
| AOH | Acta Orientalia Academiae Scientiarum Hungaricae |
| ATUK | Erzurum Atatürk Üniversitesi Kütüphanesi |
| AUB | American University of Beirut |
| BRL | British Library, London |
| C. DH | Cevdet Dahiliye |
| CETOBAC | Centre d'Études turques, ottomanes, balkaniques et centrasiatiques (Center for Turkish, Ottoman, Balkan and Central Asian Studies) |
| C. EV | Cevdet Evkaf |
| CFHB | Corpus Fontium Historiae (Corpus of Byzantine History Sources) |
| CNRS | Centre national de la recherche scientifique (French National Centre for Scientific Research) |
| CUP | Cambridge University Press |
| CUPR | Committee of Union and Progress |
| DIA | Türkiye Diyanet Vakfı İslam Ansiklopedisi |
| DBIA | Dünden Bugüne İstanbul Ansiklopedisi |
| DOA | Devlet Arşivleri Genel Müdürlüğü Osmanlı Arşivi |
| EBAL | Études balkaniques |
| EBR | Encyclopaedia Britannica. 11th edition |
| ECS | Evliya Çelebi Seyahatnamesi |
| EI2 | Encyclopaedia of Islam. 2nd edition |
| EIE | National Research Institute, Athens |
| EU | European Union |
| FORTH | Foundation for Research and Technology, Hellas |
| HC | History Compass |
| HR | House of Representatives |
| HUP | Harvard University Press |
| IA | İslam Ansiklopedisi |
| İE. TCT | İbnülemin Tevcihat |
| IFEA | Institut Français d'Études Anatoliennes |
| IFM | İstanbul Üniversitesi İktisat Fakültesi Mecmuası/Dergisi |
| IJMES | International Journal of Middle East Studies |
| ILS | Islamic Law and Society |

| | |
|---|---|
| IRCICA | Istanbul Research Centre for Islamic History, Art and Culture |
| ITD | İstanbul Üniversitesi Edebiyat Fakültesi Tarih Dergisi |
| IUK | İstanbul Üniversitesi Kütüphanesi |
| JAOS | Journal of the American Oriental Society |
| JESHO | Journal of the Economic and Social History of the Orient |
| JHU | Johns Hopkins University |
| JIS | Journal of Islamic Studies |
| JNES | Journal of Near Eastern Studies |
| JTS | Journal of Turkish Studies = Türklük Bilgisi Araştırmaları (Harvard University) |
| KKT | Köprülü Kütüphanesi |
| MEB | Milli Eğitim Basımevi |
| MES | Middle Eastern Studies |
| MESA | Middle East Studies Association |
| MIHK | Manisa İl Halk Kütüphanesi |
| MIKT | Millet Kütüphanesi |
| MIT | Massachusetts Institute of Technology |
| MMKY | Mevlana Müzesi Kütüphanesi Yazmaları |
| MP | member of parliament |
| MS | Historical manuscript |
| OA | Osmanlı Araştırmaları/Journal of Ottoman Studies |
| OH | Ohio |
| OLFR | Ottoman Law of Family Rights/Family Code (Hukuk-ı Aile Kanunnamesi) |
| ON | Österreichischer Nationalbibliothek, Vienna |
| OUP | Oxford University Press |
| PP | Past and Present |
| PSU | Pennysylvania State University |
| PUFR | Presses Universitaires François-Rabelais |
| ŞD | Şura-yı Devlet |
| SK | Süleymaniye Kütüphanesi |
| SOAS | School of Oriental and African Studies |
| SUNY | State University of New York |
| SUP | Stanford University Press |
| TAC | Türkiye Anıt Çevre Turizm Değerlerini Koruma Vakfı Dergisi |
| TAV | Türkiye Ekonomik ve Toplumsal Tarih Vakfı |
| TDV ISAM | Turkiye Diyanet Foundation Centre for Islamic Studies |
| TSA | Topkapı Sarayı Arşivi |
| TSMK | Topkapı Sarayı Müzesi Kütüphanesi/Topkapı Palace Library |
| TTK | Türk Tarih Kurumu Basımevi |

| | |
|---|---|
| TY | Türkçe Yazmalar |
| TYEKBY | Türkiye Yazma Eserler Kurumu Başkanlığı Yayınla |
| UNESCO | United Nations Educational, Scientific and Cultural Organization |
| USSR | Union of Soviet Socialist Republics (Soviet Union) |
| VGMA | Vakıflar Genel Müdürlüğü Arşivi |
| WIS | Die Welt des Islams |

# Notes on Contributors

*Iris Agmon*
is a historian of the Ottoman Empire. She completed her Ph.D. at the Hebrew University of Jerusalem and joined the department of Middle East Studies at Ben Gurion University. Her research interests include the Ottoman legal system, particularly the Ottoman sharia court, and legal reforms during the long nineteenth century; a socio-legal history of late- and post-Ottoman Palestine; family history; microhistory; historiography; and historical thinking. Her book, *Family and Court: Legal Culture and Modernity in Late Ottoman Palestine* (2006) explores the sharia courts of late-Ottoman Jaffa and Haifa. Her current research project focuses on the Ottoman family code (1917).

*Antonis Anastasopoulos*
is an associate professor of Ottoman History in the Department of History and Archaeology at the University of Crete and a collaborating faculty member at the Institute for Mediterranean Studies of the Foundation for Research and Technology-Hellas. He has edited or co-edited five books and has published more than thirty-five articles in academic journals and edited books with a focus on Ottoman provincial societies and their relations with the state, and on Islamic tombstones.

*Tülay Artan*
is an associate professor of history at Sabancı University, Istanbul. She works on the prosopographical networks and households of the Ottoman elite; material culture, the history of consumption and standards of living; seventeenth- and eighteenth-century Ottoman arts, architecture and literature from a comparative perspective. Her most recent publications include "Early-eighteenth Century Depictions of Women in Distress", *Journal of Medieval History* (2019); "Cosmopolitanism in the Early Eighteenth-century Ottoman Capital: The Impostor, the Alchemist, the Merchant and the Personal Dimension", in R. Gradeva (ed.) *The Balkan Provinces of the Ottoman Empire: The Personal Dimension. 1. The Agents of Faith* (Sofia: AUB Press, 2019); and "Contemplation or Amusement? The Light Shed by Ruznames on an Ottoman Spectacle of 1740–1750", in K. Fleet and E. Boyar (eds), *The Ottomans and Entertainment* (Leiden: Brill, 2019).

*Ekin Tuşalp Atiyas*
received her MA degree in History from Sabancı University in 2005. In her first year as a master's student at Sabancı, she took a course on Sources and

Methods for Ottoman History, 1450–1600 and her instructor was Metin Kunt. She received her Ph.D. degree in History and Middle Eastern Studies from Harvard University in 2014.

*Karl K. Barbir*

is professor emeritus of history at Siena College, Loudonville, New York, USA. He received his bachelor's and master's degrees from the American University of Beirut; and a master's and doctorate from Princeton University. He is the author of *Ottoman Rule in Damascus, 1708–1758*, a contributor to Jane Hathaway, *The Arab Lands Under Ottoman Rule, 1516–1800*, and co-edited (with Baki Tezcan) *Identity and Identify Formation in the Ottoman World: A Volume of Essays in Honor of Norman Itzkowitz*.

*Fatih Bayram*

was born in Samsun in 1974 and graduated from the Department of Political Science and International Relations at Boğaziçi University in 1997. In 2000, he received a Master's degree from Bilkent University for his thesis on "Ebubekir Ratib Efendi as an Ottoman Envoy of Knowledge between the East and the West" and, in 2008, a Ph.D., also from Bilkent, for his dissertation entitled "Zaviye-Khankahs and Religious Orders in the Province of Karaman: Seljukid, Karamanid and Ottoman Periods, 1200–1512". He is now assistant professor in the Department of International Relations at Istanbul Medeniyet University.

*Suraiya Faroqhi*

is a professor at the newly founded Ibn Haldun University in Başakşehir, Istanbul. She was an undergraduate at Istanbul University, but has also studied at the Indiana University in Bloomington, where she acquired an MA for teachers, and at the University of Hamburg, from where she has a Ph.D. She completed her studies in 1970. Before becoming a professor at Ludwig-Maximilians-Universität in Munich, she spent sixteen years (1971–87) at the Middle East Technical University in Ankara. She works on the Ottoman social history of the early modern period and has a special interest in merchants, as well as in artisans and their handiwork.

*Cornell H. Fleischer*

is the Kanuni Süleyman Professor of Ottoman and Modern Turkish Studies at the University of Chicago. He is the author of *Bureaucrat and Intellectual in the Ottoman Empire: The Historian Mustafa Âli* (1986; Turkish translation 1996). His recent publications include "A Mediterranean Apocalypse: Prophecies of Empire in the Fifteenth and Sixteenth Centuries" (*Journal of the Social and*

*Economic History of the Orient* 61 (1–2) 2018, 18–90). One current project, among others, is a re-evaluation of the 'Ottoman' world of the fifteenth century through the work of ʿAbd al-rahman al-Bistâmi (d.1454).

*Pál Fodor*

is director general of the Research Centre for the Humanities, Hungarian Academy of Sciences, editor of The Hungarian Historical Review (Budapest), co-editor of *Archivum Ottomanicum* (Wiesbaden), and series editor of 21st-Century Studies in Humanities and Monumenta Hungariae Historica (Budapest). He has published extensively on the military, administrative, and intellectual history of the Ottoman Empire, as well as on Ottoman politics towards central Europe. Among his many publications are *In Quest of the Golden Apple: Imperial Ideology, Politics and Military Administration in the Ottoman Empire* (Istanbul: Isis, 2000); *The Unbearable Weight of Empire: The Ottomans in Central Europe* (Budapest: Research Centre for the Humanities, Hungarian Academy of Sciences, 2015 and 2016); and *The Business of State: Ottoman Finance Administration and Ruling Elites in Transition, 1580s–1615* (Berlin: Klaus-Schwarz-Verlag, 2018).

*Mehmet Kalpaklı*

is the chair of the departments of both History and Turkish Literature at Bilkent University, Ankara, Turkey. He specializes in Ottoman literature and the cultural history of the Ottoman Empire. He is also working on several digital humanities projects. His publications include (with Walter G. Andrews) *The Age of Beloveds: Love and the Beloved in Early Modern Ottoman Turkish and European Literature, Culture, and Society* (Durham, NC: Duke University Press, 2005); an expanded edition (with Walter Andrews and Najaat Black) of *Ottoman Lyric Poetry: An Anthology* (Seattle: University of Washington Press, 2006); and *Osmanlı Divan Şiiri Üzerine Metinler* (Istanbul: Yapı Kredi Press, 1999).

*Seyfi Kenan*

completed his primary, secondary and undergraduate education in Istanbul before going to New York City in 1994 to pursue his doctoral studies at Columbia University. As research coordinator at Columbia University, he engaged in a number of research projects in both the Humanities and Middle Eastern Studies (1996–2003). He uses an interdisciplinary method with a concentration on the history of comparative intellectual thought, the educational sciences and philosophy. He returned to Istanbul in 2003, and is currently full-time professor at Marmara University in Istanbul. Dr Kenan is also managing editor of the *Journal of Ottoman Studies*. Since 1990, he has been a contributing editor to the *Encyclopedia of Islam* (44 volumes with nearly 17,000 entries) covering socio-history of the Islamic religion, culture and civilization published by ISAM Publications. He has engaged in research, overseen projects or taught classes in Cairo, New York, Beijing, Copenhagen, London and Vienna. He was awarded a Senior Fellowship at the Research Centre for Anatolian Civilizations of Koç University in Istanbul, Turkey for the autumn and spring terms of 2014/15. Among his interests are how to understand and study other cultures and societies, and realms of interactions between the Islamic world, especially the Ottomans and Europe, and the formation of modern Turkish educational thought.

*Cemil Koçak*
graduated from Ankara University with a BA in political science in 1978, an MA in 1980, and a Ph.D. in public administration and political science from the university's Social Sciences Institute in 1986. Between 1984 and 1999 he worked for the Scientific and Technical Research Council of Turkey and was appointed manager of its publications department and a member of its publications commission from 1993 to 1999. His research interests are in Turkish political history, Turkish foreign policy, historical writing and methodology. Since 1999 he has been at the Sabanci University in Istanbul/Turkey and is a founding member of the Economic and Social History Foundation of Turkey.

*Harun Küçük*
is an associate professor of History and Sociology of Science and the incoming director of the Middle East Center at the University of Pennsylvania. He holds a Ph.D. in History and Science Studies from the University of California – San Diego (2012). Küçük's recent book, *Science without Leisure: Practical Naturalism in Istanbul, 1660–1732* focuses on the relationship between science and the economy in the Ottoman Empire during the seventeenth and eighteenth centuries. Currently, he is writing a book about the temporal order of scientific labour in the modern academy. He is also part of the ERC-funded project 'Geographies and Histories of the Ottoman Supernatural Tradition Exploring Magic, the Marvelous, and the Strange in Ottoman Mentalities'. Together with Oscar Aguirre-Mandujano, he is co-editing a primary source reader on Ottoman science.

*Aslı Niyazioğlu*
is Associate Professor in Ottoman History at the University of Oxford. She is an early modern historian working on literature, Sufism and urban life. Her publications include *Dreams and Lives in Ottoman Istanbul: A Seventeenth*

*Century Biographer's Perspective* (London: Routledge, 2017) and "How to Read an Ottoman Poet's Dream? Friends, Patrons and the Execution of Figani (d.1532)", *Middle Eastern Literatures* 16 (1) 2013, 48–60. Currently, she is working on a book entitled "Early Modern Istanbul Imagined: A City of Poets, Sufis and Travellers", which aims to explore the role of imagination in the making of urban communities in early modern Istanbul.

*Mehmet Öz*
graduated from the Department of History at Hacettepe University in Ankara with a BA in 1981 and an M.Phil. in 1985. In 1991, he received a Ph.D. from the Faculty of Oriental Studies at Girton College, University of Cambridge, UK. He is currently Professor of History at Hacettepe University. He has published many articles on various aspects of Ottoman history from the fourteenth to the eighteenth centuries and is the single author of five books and editor or co-editor of a further six. He served as the vice-chairman of Turkish Historical Society between 2010 and 2012 and acted as the Dean of the Faculty of Letters at Hacettepe University between 2013 and 2016.

*Kaya Şahin*
is associate professor of history at Indiana University, with adjunct appointments in the departments of Central Eurasian Studies, and Near Eastern Languages and Cultures. He is the author of *Empire and Power in the Reign of Süleyman: Narrating the Sixteenth-Century Ottoman World* (2013; Turkish translation 2014). His recent publications include "Staging an Empire: An Ottoman Circumcision Ceremony as Cultural Performance", *American Historical Review* 123 (2) April 2018, 463–92. He is currently working on a biography of the Ottoman sultan Süleyman (r.1520–66), and a history of Ottoman public ceremonies in the fifteenth and sixteenth centuries CE.

*Selçuk Akşin Somel*
teaches history at Sabancı University, Istanbul and received his doctorate from Bamberg University, Germany, in 1993. His research interests include Ottoman education, women and gender, bureaucracy, and peripheral populations. He is author of *The Modernization of Public Education in the Ottoman Empire (1839–1908): Islamization, Autocracy and Discipline* (Brill 2001); *Historical Dictionary of the Ottoman Empire* (Scarecrow Press 2003, 2nd edn 2012); and, with co-authors Amy Singer and Christoph Neumann, *Untold Histories from the Middle East: Recovering Voices from the 19th and 20th Centuries* (Routledge 2010). Forthcoming publications include (with Mehmet Beşikçi and Alexandre Toumarkine) *Not All Quiet on the Ottoman Fronts: Neglected Perspectives on*

*a Global War, 1914–1918* (Ergon Verlag 2021) and, with Kaori Komatsu, Edhem Eldem and others, *Modernity Alla Turca: Ottoman Military, Education, and Welfare, 1826–1923* (Academic Studies Press 2022).

### Derin Terzioğlu

is an associate professor at Boğaziçi University's Department of History, and holds a Ph.D. in history and Middle Eastern studies from Harvard University (1999). Terzioğlu specializes in the history of the early modern Ottoman Empire, with research interests spanning the social and political history of religion, history of political thought, history of books and reading, and history of childhood and family. Currently, Terzioğlu, together with Tijana Krstić of the Central European University, is co-writing a book that synthesizes the findings of the ERC-funded research project, 'The Fashioning of a Sunni Orthodoxy and the Entangled Histories of Confession Building in the Ottoman Empire, 15th–17th Centuries'.

### Christine Woodhead

is Honorary Fellow in the Department of History, University of Durham, where she taught early-modern Ottoman history for several years. She is editor of *The Ottoman World* (2012) and author of several articles on Ottoman literary historiography and more recently on seventeenth-century letter collections.

### N. Zeynep Yelçe

is a researcher and instructor at the Foundations Development Directorate and coordinator for humanities courses at Sabanci University, Istanbul. She completed her MA thesis (Ideal Kingship in the Late Medieval World: The Ottoman Case, 2003) and her Ph.D. dissertation (The Making of Sultan Süleyman: A Study of Process/es of Image-Making and Reputation-Management, 2009) at Sabanci University with Metin Kunt as her adviser. Her research interests include early modern power structures, court studies, and ritual studies. She is currently working on news and information networks in the Mediterranean in the first half of sixteenth century.

### Elizabeth A. Zachariadou

As the editors of this volume, we include this chapter with deep reverence to the author, Elizabeth Zachariadou, who sadly passed away in 2018. It would be appropriate, we thought, to include a short obituary for this meticulous and fair historian who contributed significantly to Ottoman studies. Elizabeth Zachariadou (1931–2018) studied at the University of Athens and SOAS, London. She worked for many years in Montreal, Canada, before moving to the University of Crete, where she taught from 1985 to 1998; she was a member of the Institute for Mediterranean Studies/FORTH. While the main focus of Zachariadou's work was on the late Byzantine, early and 'classical' period of the Ottomans, she also wrote on the history of seventeenth-century Aegean islands, especially Crete. She received an honorary doctorate from the University of Ankara (1990) and was honoured with membership of the Academia Europaea (1993). As an acknowledgment of her contribution to the field, volume 23 of the *Archivum Ottomanicum* (2005/6) and the proceedings of the *Halcyon Days in Crete* VI symposium (2008) were dedicated to her and collections of her papers were published twice as part of the *Variorum* series – *Romania and the Turks (c.1300–c.1500)* (1985) and *Studies in pre-Ottoman Turkey and the Ottomans* (2007). We greatly appreciate Marinos Sariyannis' generous help in compiling this short obituary.

# Metin Kunt: Life and Work

*Selçuk Akşin Somel and Seyfi Kenan*

It is a great honour for us to have known Metin *Hocamız* as a dear colleague and close friend for at least fifteen years. On campus, engaged in research projects or organizing conferences, we always felt the warmth and human touch he emitted towards us and everybody in his surroundings.

At Sabancı University, over our early morning breakfasts and lunches at the campus cafeteria, we would exchange information and discuss events in Turkey and around the world. Whenever we dropped by at his office in the Faculty of Arts and Social Sciences, we would always find him immersed in his work with classical music playing in the background. Occasionally, Kunt, who lived in a faculty house, would cook dinner for his friends, which he always did with a remarkably creative flair. He was also extremely interested in Anglo-Saxon literature in general, and in crime fiction in particular.

An outstanding feature of Metin Hoca's character was his modesty. In his dealings with the university administration, colleagues or students, his approach was always kind, gentle, patient and considerate. Although a highly distinguished professor, Metin Hoca never embarrassed or put anyone down, however unimportant they may have been; on the contrary, he would spend hours with his students, and never seemed to tire of teaching them. His modest, gentle nature perhaps set him apart in a world dominated by merciless competition in the race for success and glamour, for Metin Hoca's quality-oriented, patient, slow but meticulous approach to research was unusual in the present-day academic climate.

Metin Hoca never hesitated to contribute to projects in his area of expertise and retained his modesty, care and elegance throughout. He was an ideal team member who encouraged and excited everyone around him to contribute more and, thus, tacitly to enhance the outcomes of the project. One memorable project was surely the one in which three institutions – Harvard University, Sabancı University, and the Turkiye Diyanet Foundation Centre for Islamic Studies (TDV ISAM) – together initiated a series of workshops between 2009 and 2011 on the history of Ottoman thought in which Ebussuud and his world of thought were explored. While preparing for and implementing this project, we thoroughly enjoyed working with him, Cemal Kafadar and Hülya Canbakal.

It would be appropriate here to mention an unforgettable personal anecdote, which occurred while one of us, Seyfi Kenan, was writing an introduction for a series of ISAM Papers he was putting together and editing around that time.[1] He was grappling with a paragraph about how Istanbul encapsulated the spirit of being Turkish because it was a city in which peaceful and mutually respectful coexistence was possible, and he wondered if he could make a connection between Istanbul and love. Behçet Kemal Çağlar's famous line – *İstanbul'u sevmezse gönül aşkı ne anlar* – came to mind and he wanted Metin Hoca to help him render the passage into English. However, Metin Hoca was in England awaiting surgery for a tendon, so Seyfi Kenan initially felt rather embarrassed about asking for his help at such a difficult time. However, he was happy in retrospect because he had asked for a revision from the right person. Indeed, Kunt had been taught literature by the very poet who had penned that line – *What does a heart know of love, if the heart loves not Istanbul?*

## 1    A Glimpse at His Academic Life

İbrahim Metin Kunt was born in Ankara in 1942 into an upper middle-class family of state officials with historical connections to Ottoman provincial elites from both Albania and Damascus. He attended the prestigious secondary school Maarif Koleji in Ankara before moving to Istanbul to enrol as a Robert Academy student. After graduation from the Robert Academy in 1959, he continued his undergraduate education at Robert College, from where, in 1965, he received a BA degree in comparative literature.

Kunt then became an MA student of Ottoman history in the Department of Near Eastern Studies at Princeton University. While pursuing his MA studies, he took additional Ph.D. courses that would later inspire him to write his various masterpieces, including *Sancaktan Eyalete* (From Sanjak to Eyalet) and *The Sultan's Servants*.[2] In the spring term of 1967, Norman Itzkowitz ran a seminar on nineteenth-century Ottoman history in which the works of British historian Lewis Namier were discussed. Namier's reputation as a master of prosopographical methods gave Kunt the methodological horizons he sought to approach historical figures. A second seminar was given by Halil İnalcık, who at that time was a guest professor at Princeton. As Kunt recalled, İnalcık discussed what academic tools were needed to analyse Ottoman primary sources, which he found invaluable for studying archival documents. In the autumn of 1967 he attended the seminar of another guest professor, David Ayalon, a well-known authority on Mamluk history. This gave Kunt a new insight into

---

1    Seyfi Kenan (ed.), *İSAM Konuşmaları: İSAM Papers* (Istanbul: İSAM Yayınları, 2013).
2    İ. Metin Kunt, *Sancaktan Eyalete: 1550–1650 Arasında Osmanlı Ümerası ve İl İdaresi* (İstanbul: Boğaziçi Üniversitesi Yayınları, 1978), vi–viii.

Mamluk political structures at a time when the political-military slave institution was at its most elaborate. This seminar stressed the importance of the Islamic cultural context when comparing Mamluk and Ottoman polities.[3]

In 1968, Kunt received his MA in Near Eastern studies at Princeton and pursued his Ph.D. at the same institution. His dissertation was on the period of the grand vizierate of Köprülü Mehmed Pasha, and his supervisor was Norman Itzkowitz, whose prosopographical studies on Ottoman ruling elites and *ulema* had so deeply influenced Kunt's academic interests. Kunt widened his research on Köprülü Mehmed Pasha to encompass the social background of the statesman and, through this endeavour, gained deep insights into the ethnic and regional motives of members of the Ottoman ruling class.[4]

While working on his dissertation, in November 1970 Kunt attended the fourth annual meeting of the Middle East Studies Association (MESA), in Columbus, Ohio, at which he gave a presentation on regional and ethnic solidarities within the seventeenth-century Ottoman ruling elite. An abridged version of his paper, published in 1974,[5] remains an important secondary source on the issue.

The title of Kunt's Ph.D., which he received in 1971, was "The Köprülü Years: 1656–1661". At this point, he returned to Turkey and became an instructor at Boğaziçi University, his alma mater which until then had been known as Robert College. In 1972/3 he joined the board of the newly-founded Boğaziçi University humanities journal – *Boğaziçi Üniversitesi Dergisi-Hümaniter Bilimler* – and remained an active member of its editorial board until 1980.[6]

Between 1971 and 1974 Kunt worked in the Prime Ministerial Ottoman Archives and in the Topkapı Palace Library to further his studies on late-sixteenth and seventeenth-century Ottoman history. At that time, his aim was to complete a comprehensive study of pasha and bey households within the Ottoman political and social order. During his early explorations at the archives he often cooperated with renowned Ottomanists such as Cengiz Orhonlu and Halil Sahillioğlu and with historians like Itzkowitz, İnalcık, William K. S. Tobin, Engin D. Akarlı and Mehmed Genç.[7]

---

3 Kunt, *Sancaktan Eyalete*, vii–viii; idem, *The Sultan's Servants: The Transformation of the Ottoman Provincial Government 1550–1650* (New York: Columbia University Press, 1983), ix.
4 Kunt, *Sultan's Servants*, xvi–xvii.
5 Metin Ibrahim Kunt, "Ethnic-Regional (*Cins*) Solidarity in the Seventeenth-Century Ottoman Establishment", in *IJMES* 5 (1974), 233–9.
6 *Boğaziçi Üniversitesi Dergisi: Hümaniter Bilimler* (Boğaziçi University Journal: Humanities) 1 (1973); 7 (1979).
7 Kunt, *Sancaktan Eyalete*, viii, 1; idem, *Sultan's Servants*, ix.

On 8–10 November 1973, he attended the MESA meeting in Milwaukee, Wisconsin, at which he gave a paper on "The Ottoman State and the Ottoman Household".[8] A revised and extended version of this presentation appeared in Turkish under the title "Kulların Kulları" (Servants of Servants) in 1975.[9] In autumn 1974, Kunt was given a research grant by Boğaziçi University, which enabled him to return to Princeton for an academic year as a research fellow. There, he formulated the original Turkish version of his *doçentlik* thesis. In spring 1975, during his stay in the USA, Kunt gave papers on mid-seventeenth-century grand vizier Derviş Mehmed Paşa at Princeton, at the University of Michigan and at New York University, which formed the backbone of his 1977 *Turcica* article.[10]

In April 1976, he defended the *doçentlik* thesis, titled *Sancaktan Eyalete*, and became an associate professor. According to Kunt, this study was a by-product of his more general research on the households of the Ottoman ruling elite.[11] However, as discussed below, this book is the first analytical and detailed study of the sixteenth- and seventeenth-century Ottoman provincial administration in the Turkish language and it introduces the idea of transformation into Ottoman history. This thesis was published in November 1978 by the Boğaziçi University Press.

Another by-product of Kunt's prosopographic interest in the Ottoman ruling elite in the late-sixteenth and early-seventeenth centuries was the above-mentioned article on Derviş Mehmed Paşa.[12]

Kunt aimed to make his *Sancaktan Eyalete* study accessible to a wider, more international audience and to realize this goal, he conducted further research into the relationship between a governor's official income and his administrative obligations, which he undertook during the academic year 1977/8 as a visiting associate professor at Columbia University, after which he went to Jerusalem as a fellow of the Institute for Advanced Studies at the Hebrew University. During his stay at Columbia he had benefited from fruitful discussions with numerous Ottoman and European specialists, notably T. Halasi-Kun, J. C. Hurewitz, and R. Bulliet. At the Hebrew University, he

---

8   See Jane Hathaway: *The Politics of Households in Ottoman Egypt: The Rise of the Qazdaglis* (Cambridge, UK: CUP), 186.
9   İ. Metin Kunt: "Kulların Kulları", *Boğaziçi Üniversitesi Dergisi-Hümaniter Bilimler* 3 (1975), 27–42.
10  Kunt, *Sultan's Servants*, ix; idem, "Derviş Mehmet Paşa, *Vezīr* and Entrepreneur: A Study in Ottoman Political-Economic Theory and Practice", *Turcica* IX, 1 (1977), 197.
11  Kunt, *Sancaktan Eyalete*, 1; idem, *Sultan's Servants*, ix.
12  Kunt, "Derviş Mehmet Paşa", 197–214.

enjoyed the support of Gabriel Baer and it was in Jerusalem that he completed *The Sultan's Servants*,[13] though it was not published for another few years.

Until then, Kunt's academic life was characterized by his principal attachment to Boğaziçi University, but it witnessed a notable change after 1980. In the aftermath of the military coup of 12 September 1980 and the increasingly repressive measures being imposed on universities in the subsequent years, Kunt decided to teach and continue his research at universities in the USA, UK, Canada, and the Netherlands. Before leaving Turkey, however, he published *Bir Osmanlı Valisinin Yıllık Gelir-Gideri: Diyarbekir, 1670–71* (Annual Income and Expenditure of an Ottoman Governor: Diyarbekir 1670–71).[14]

From 1982 to 1986, Kunt worked as a visiting scholar at various universities in the United States, starting at Yale in 1982/3. While there, his chapter on the "Transformation of *Zimmî* into *Askerî*" appeared in Benjamin Braude and Bernard Lewis's edited volume on *Christians and Jews in the Ottoman Empire*.[15] This was followed by *Sultan's Servants*, published by Columbia University Press, which reflected a paradigmatic shift in the approach to Ottoman history and opened very different horizons with regard to its periodization. A Greek translation of it appeared in 2001. After Yale, Kunt taught first at Fordham University in 1984, then at New York University for the academic year 1984/5, followed by Columbia University.

Although active as an academic in the USA, Kunt did not sever his ties with Turkish academia. In the early 1980s, he joined Sina Akşin's project to compile a general Turkish history. The military regime in Turkey at that time supported the existing tendency to use ancient and Ottoman Turkish history for nationalist indoctrination and inculcating an exclusivist view of Ottoman history at the level of public education. Akşin's project, by contrast, aimed to offer an alternative horizon that would present students and the general public with a more global version of Turkey's social history. As part of this project, Kunt contributed chapters on Ottoman political history from 1300 to 1789.[16]

---

13   Kunt, *Sultan's Servants*, x, xi.
14   İ. Metin Kunt, *Bir Osmanlı Valisinin Yıllık Gelir-Gideri. Diyarbekir, 1670–71* (İstanbul: Boğaziçi Üniversitesi Yayınları, 1981), viii + 102 + 26 (documents) pages.
15   İ. Metin Kunt, "Transformation of *Zimmî* into *Askerî*", in Benjamin Braude and Bernard Lewis (eds) *Christians and Jews in the Ottoman Empire: The Functioning of a Plural Society*. Vol. 1. *The Central Lands* (Teaneck, NJ: Holmes & Meier Publishers, 1982), 55–67.
16   Metin Kunt: "Siyasal Tarih (1300–1600)", in Sina Akşin (ed.) *Türkiye Tarihi 2. Osmanlı Devleti 1300–1600* (İstanbul: Cem Yayınevi, 1987), 16–143; *idem*, "Siyasal Tarih (1600–1789)", in Sina Akşin (ed.) *Türkiye Tarihi 3. Osmanlı Devleti 1600–1908* (Istanbul: Cem Yayınevi, 1988), 10–69.

In 1986, Kunt received an appointment at Cambridge University to chair the newly founded Centre for Turkish Studies as the Newton Trust Lecturer. Kunt filled this position until 1998. Meanwhile, he continued to teach as visiting professor at universities such as Simon Fraser (Vancouver, Canada, 1991), Birmingham (UK, 1992), Harvard (1993), Leiden (The Netherlands, 1993), and SOAS (1994).

At Cambridge, Kunt and Christine Woodhead together edited the first English academic volume on Süleyman the Magnificent. The chapters in this volume show Sultan Süleyman in the context of Ottoman administrative, military and cultural institutions and take the contemporary political and cultural contexts of the Renaissance and the Mamluk sultanate into consideration.[17] The book has been translated into Polish (2000) and Turkish (2002).

In 1999, Kunt joined the History Graduate Program of the newly-formed Sabancı University in Istanbul and, to a major extent, helped to shape its graduate courses, and he taught there until 2015. Among other subjects, he offered courses on Ottoman reading culture prior to the introduction of the printing press, which reflected his deepening interest in the sociology of knowledge in the sixteenth and seventeenth centuries.[18] The decades he spent at Sabancı were perhaps among the most creative periods of his academic life.

While at Sabancı, Kunt's original research interest in Ottoman households took on a comparative aspect as he started to embrace other civilizations as well. With Jeroen Duindam and Tülay Artan, he organized a major conference in Istanbul called Royal Courts and Capitals (14–16 October 2005), which received support from both Sabancı University and an EU academic programme known as 'COSTA 36: Tributary Empires Compared'. It was a first of its kind insofar as the courts, dynasties and households of diverse civilizations such as the Roman, early modern European, Ottoman, and Moghul empires were discussed in detail. This conference set a precedent for a series of similar conferences, and these in turn led to the publication of numerous volumes in the Brill series known as 'Rulers & Elites'.[19]

The organizers of the 2005 conference, including Kunt, Duindam and Artan, edited the first volume of the Rulers & Elites series, *Royal Courts in Dynastic*

---

17   Metin Kunt and Christine Woodhead (eds) *Süleyman the Magnificent and His Age: The Ottoman Empire in the Early Modern World* (London: Longman, 1995).
18   Metin Kunt, "Reading Elite, Elite Reading", in *Printing and Publishing in the Middle East: Journal of Semitic Studies*, Supplementary edn 24 (2008), 89–100.
19   Jeroen Duindam, "Introduction", in Jeroen Duindam, Tülay Artan and Metin Kunt (eds) *Royal Courts in Dynastic States and Empires. A Global Perspective* (Leiden: Brill, 2011), 3; Philip Mansel, "Conference Report: The Globalization of Court History", *The Court Historian* 11 (1), 2013, 77–80.

*States and Empires*, which appeared in 2011. This book contains comprehensive descriptions of courts, households and ceremonies from Antiquity to early modern times and it includes Kunt's chapter on "Turks in the Ottoman Imperial Palace".[20]

Kunt's other major academic contribution during his Sabancı years was his role as the founding editor of the four-volume monumental historical series called *The Cambridge History of Turkey*. Spanning the period from the Battle of Manzikert in 1071 to what is now the contemporary Republic of Turkey, it successfully synthesizes the academic achievements of researchers of pre-Ottoman, Ottoman, and Republican Turkish history over the last two decades.[21]

## 2   His Contributions to Ottoman Studies

Metin Kunt can be said to have made at least three major and lasting contributions to Ottoman historical research in the areas of the sociology of power, transformation, and periodization. As mentioned, from his graduate years onwards, Kunt has always had a strong interest in households; his earlier works, like his Ph.D. on Köprülü Mehmed Pasha, or his article on Derviş Mehmed Pasha, concentrate on specific examples. The *Sancaktan Eyalete*, then the *Sultan's Servants*, give us a more general outlook on the growing importance of households, for they expound on the structural changes of the Ottoman provincial administration in which eyalet governors and their extended households acquired unprecedented administrative autonomy. Paralleling this development were principles such as loyalty to the imperial centre and merit being increasingly replaced by patronage networks centred around households.[22]

In his post-1985 writings, Kunt seems to understand households, especially the Ottoman imperial one, in a more appreciative light and even as a stabilizing political institution that could perhaps account for the longevity of the empire. The first sentence in his chapter on 'Royal and other Households' begins with

---

20   Kunt, "Turks in the Ottoman Imperial Palace", *Royal Courts in Dynastic States and Empires* (Leiden: Brill, 2011), 289–312.
21   *The Cambridge History of Turkey*. Vol. 1, *Byzantium to Turkey, 1071–1453*, edited by Kate Fleet (Cambridge: CUP, 2009); Vol. 2, *The Ottoman Empire as a World Power, 1453–1603*, edited by Suraiya Faroqhi and Kate Fleet (Cambridge: CUP, 2013); Vol. 3, *The Later Ottoman Empire, 1603–1839*, edited by Suraiya Faroqhi (Cambridge: CUP, 2006); Vol. 4, *Turkey in the Modern World*, edited by Reşat Kasaba (Cambridge: CUP, 2008).
22   Kunt, *Sancaktan Eyalete*, 85–124; *idem*, *Sultan's Servants*, 97–9.

the statement that "households were the building blocks of the Ottoman political edifice. Therefore the basic unit for the study of the sociology of political life is the household." He also states that the formation of households was a deliberate policy of the central authority, as "he [the sultan] insisted that all his officers did the same, proportionate to their rank and allotted revenues".[23] This piece points to the wide variety of political, economic, educational, and cultural functions performed by Ottoman households. In fact, through a child levy the imperial household would recruit Christian boys from the Balkans who would then receive a comprehensive education and be assimilated into Ottoman Islamic high culture. As Kunt pointed out, there was also widespread emulation of this practice in the seventeenth and eighteenth centuries, both by the upper stratum of the *ulema* and by the civilian bureaucracy.[24]

In other studies, Kunt showed how the resilience of the household preserved the integrity of the empire for centuries. He describes the Ottoman imperial household as already highly developed during the reign of Bayezid I when Timurlenk defeated the Ottomans at the Battle of Ankara (1402), and how the extensive network of the sultan's servants played a major role in restoring the Ottoman realm following its dissolution between 1402 and 1413.[25]

At the same time, Kunt remains ambivalent about this institution because it hinders the fully-fledged institutionalization of the Ottoman state apparatus and its autonomy vis-à-vis the Ottoman royal family. His relatively recent chapter called 'A Prince Goes Forth (Perchance to Return)' elaborates on the succession processes following the deaths of Süleyman I, Selim II, Murad III, and Mehmed III, each of which was accompanied by crises arising from the fuzzy borders between the imperial household and central state institutions. In fact, he concludes the chapter by underlining the critical importance of the Ottoman imperial household for politics as late as the First Constitutional Era. According to him, even as late as 1876, "the relationship between the ruler and his government remained ambiguous".[26] It would be fair to state that, for Kunt, the imperial household, which the elite ones upheld, was one of the few

---

23  Metin Kunt, "Royal and Other Households", in Christine Woodhead (ed.) *The Ottoman World* (London: Routledge, 2012), 103.
24  Kunt, "Royal and Other Households", 107–9, 111–12; *idem*, "Sultan, Dynasty and State in the Ottoman Empire: Political Institutions in the Sixteenth Century", in *The Medieval History Journal* 6, (2), 2003, 217–30.
25  Metin Kunt, "Siyasal Tarih (1300–1600)", 55–66; *idem*, "State and Sultan up to the Age of Süleyman: Frontier Principality to World Empire", in Metin Kunt and Christine Woodhead (eds) *Süleyman the Magnificent and His Age* (Harlow, Essex: Longman, 1995), 12–14, 17.
26  Kunt, Metin, "A Prince Goes Forth (Perchance to Return)", in Karl Barbir and Baki Tezcan (eds), *Identity and Identity Formation in the Ottoman World: A Volume of Essays in Honor of Norman Itzkowitz* (Madison: Wisconsin University Press, 2007), 63–71.

institutional continuities in the Ottoman political structure from its beginnings until its demise.

Another historical continuity, which, according to Kunt defined the political culture of the Ottoman Empire was the ideology of *gaza*. In "State and Sultan up to the Age of Süleyman: Frontier Principality to World Empire", the introductory chapter to a volume he co-edited with Christine Woodhead in 1995, he underlines the resilience of *gazi* ideology from the period of the Ottoman principality until the final decades of Ottoman existence. This ideology was a driving force for the state both in the early centuries of expansion as well as during the years of trying to defend the territorial integrity of the empire until its demise, as exemplified by the *gazi* titles of Abdülhamid II and Mustafa Kemal Pasha.[27] Here, Kunt seems to pay homage to Paul Wittek's works.

Another of Metin Kunt's lasting legacies to Ottoman studies is his achievement in integrating the notion of *transformation* into Ottoman history, which has revolutionized our understanding of changes in the late sixteenth- and early-seventeenth centuries, hitherto interpreted merely as a degeneration of 'classical' institutions.

While Kunt's main interest in the early 1970s was in ruling elite households, the quality of the archival material he found and the complex aspects of household structures led him to concentrate on the 'military class' (*seyfiyye*) and its career opportunities in the century between 1550 and 1650.[28] In both *Sancaktan Eyalete* and *Sultan's Servants* he concludes that during this period continuous changes took place with respect to three aspects of provincial administration – officials from central government taking over the higher provincial posts at the expense of local functionaries; the growing importance of provinces (*beylerbeylik* gradually to be called *eyalet*) at the cost of districts (*sancak*) and the eventual substitution of the latter by the former; and the predominance of patronage and household networks over merit and loyalty to the central authority.[29] These changes emerged in the context of the loss of the military function of provincial cavalry vis-à-vis infantry equipped with firearms, the Ottoman state's growing need for cash and the capacity of *eyalet* governors to supply the central authority with the resources required to support its standing armies, and the relative efficiency of imperial and provincial households to train administrative and military personnel.[30]

---

27  Kunt, "State and Sultan up to the Age of Süleyman", 12–13.
28  Kunt, *Sancaktan Eyalete*, 4.
29  Kunt, *Sultan's Servants*, 95; *idem, Sancaktan Eyalete*, 85–124.
30  Kunt, *Sultan's Servants*, 95–7.

What makes Kunt's study on the transformation of provincial administration so crucial is his verdict that these developments *did not* constitute a decline of the Ottoman Empire, but on the contrary, a transition from a feudally-arranged prebend-based structure to a monetary-based one with powerful governors. In this regard, this transition implies a process of modernization. According to Kunt, the imperial authority expected this transition would bring about the effective centralization of the provincial administration, which, for him, was additional proof of the modernizing nature of this transition.[31] He uses the term *dönüşüm* to describe this major change in *Sancaktan Eyalete*.[32]

Kunt's interest in transformation was not confined to the provincial administration and decentralization, for he was also interested in concrete examples of individuals. In *Bir Osmanlı Valisinin Yıllık Gelir-Gideri: Diyarbekir, 1670–71* (The Annual Income and Expenditure of an Ottoman Governor-General: Diyarbekir, 1670–71), he showed that in real value in 1670/1 the annual income of a governor-general was more than three times that of a governor-general in 1550. From the local revenue that the governor-general collected, Kunt concluded that in the mid-seventeenth century the power of a provincial governor-general was immense, in fact in line with that of Istanbul, thus signifying a power shift from the centre to the provinces.[33]

Even more interesting is his article on the historical figure of Derviş Mehmed Pasha (d.1654), in which he discusses the impact of the late-sixteenth-century transformation on Ottoman political and economic thought in relation to Derviş Mehmed Pasha's ideas, as reported by the chronicler Naima. According to this form of thought, the presence of a government official as head of a powerful household ensured that significant financial resources were distributed among the people. In other words, the commercial activities of an administrator with a large household would guard against an arbitrary tax burden being imposed on the population, yet provide welfare for the region he governed. Kunt detected basic similarities between Derviş Mehmed Pasha's ideas and the socio-economic views in Ibn Khaldun's *Muqaddimah*, as well as in the works of previous classical Muslim thinkers. However, unlike Ibn Khaldun or other classical Muslim authors who considered official or government interference in economics and commerce harmful to public welfare, Derviş Mehmed Pasha saw the government's position on, for example, agriculture, handicrafts, or commerce, as a productive factor in a given economy. According to Kunt, this view constituted a major deviation from traditional Islamic political and economic

---

31   Kunt, *Sultan's Servants*, 97–8.
32   Kunt, *Sancaktan Eyalete*, 2, 5.
33   Kunt, *Bir Osmanlı Valisinin Yıllık Gelir-Gideri*, 58–60.

philosophy. Also, the notion of justice (*adl*), an indispensable principle in the ancient political treatises of people like Nasiruddin Tusi, is absent from Derviş Mehmed Pasha's views. In fact, the ancient belief that, to ensure justice, it was necessary to retain a social and political balance between groups such as agriculturalists, merchants, and artisans, is not evident in Derviş Mehmed Pasha's thought.[34] Kunt concluded his article by placing Derviş Mehmed Pasha's views in the context of the major changes of the seventeenth and eighteenth centuries and established a link between the changing political and economic conditions and the striking modifications in classical Islamic political thought as expressed by Derviş Mehmed Pasha, and formulated by Naima.

Another reflection of the overall transformation of the Ottoman social and political structure could, according to Kunt, be observed in the state's strong identification with Sunni Islam, also known as the confessionalization of the empire. His 1982 article, the "Transformation of *Zimmî* into *Askerî*", describes how the administrative transformation in the late sixteenth and throughout the seventeenth centuries included the phenomenon of Islamization at both institutional and ideological levels. In other words, the division between Muslims and non-Muslims gradually replaced the previous more or less 'secular' political and social division between the *askerî* stratum and the tax-paying *reaya* classes. This process was reinforced by the child levy used to recruit new sultanic slaves becoming obsolete, and by the gradual abandonment of expansionism leading to the disappearance of Christian members of the military elite. These factors contributed to the estrangement of non-Muslims from the now predominantly Muslim Ottoman state.[35]

A corollary to this process could also be traced, according to Kunt, to changes in Ottoman Muslim personal names among members of the ruling elite. In "Ottoman Names and Ottoman Ages", published in 1986, Kunt discusses changes in names in relation to political and ideological transitions throughout the centuries. Accordingly, in the first century of the Ottoman principality, the names of Ottoman princes were mainly of a pre-Islamic Turkic nature, which was when the Islamic character of the principality was not very pronounced. The expansion of the Ottomans in the Balkans after the 1350s, the emergence of the *ulema* influence, and the development of an Ottoman statehood in which the ascendancy of the royal household over tribal and group solidarity became pronounced, led to an increase of names of a Persian and biblical character among princes and members of the ruling elite. During this period, the Ottoman ruling establishment perceived the cultural heritage

---

34   Kunt: "Derviş Mehmet Paşa", 206–11.
35   Kunt, "Transformation of *Zimmî* into *Askerî*", 55–67.

of the empire to be mainly Persian. After 1600, the ethos and prevalence of Islamic ideology in the empire led to a notable decrease among the governing elite of Persian and biblical names in favour of Islamic ones. During this era, when stagnation replaced expansionist dynamism, a universalistic Islamic heritage replaced the perception of a Persian and pre-Islamic one.[36]

It is worth mentioning that Kunt also understood the issue of transformation at the level of the Ottoman palace. In "Royal and Other Households", he discusses certain substantial changes that took place within the Ottoman imperial household after the sixteenth century, including the gradual disappearance of the child levy and the increase of ethnic Turks among palace members. In addition, palace pages began to remain in the palace until they reached a mature age, and senior members of the inner service (*enderun*) were sent to the provinces as full provincial governor generals without previous services as junior commanders or lower-level sancak governors. Also, the black eunuchs acquired prominence in the palace and turned into major political players.[37]

Kunt's final major contribution to Ottoman historical studies relates to the periodization of Ottoman history, itself an inseparable aspect and logical outcome of his discussions on transformation. In both *Sancaktan Eyalete* and *Sultan's Servants*, Kunt demonstrates that the tremendous changes that took place between 1550 and 1650 created new structures and relations that cannot simply be seen as a degeneration of the previous institutions; indeed, as noted above, they signified a transition from a feudally-arranged prebend-based structure to a monetary-based one with powerful governors. In this regard, this transition implies a process of modernization. As a consequence of Kunt's work, historians increasingly came to view Ottoman historical eras in terms of time frameworks, each with its own specific political, economic and social institutions and relationships rather than as an organic body with periods of youth, adulthood and senescence.

Although a few authors had already questioned the decline paradigm,[38] it was Kunt who was able to demonstrate on a factual basis and in an unmistakable way the implausibility of preserving the notion of a 'decline' attributed

---

36  İbrahim Metin Kunt, "Ottoman Names and Ottoman Ages", in Bernard Lewis (ed.) *Raiyyet Rüsûmu: Essays Presented to Halil İnalcık on his Seventieth Birthday by His Colleagues and Students*, vol. I, Harvard 1986 [*Journal of Turkish Studies* x], 227–34.

37  Kunt, "Turks in the Ottoman Imperial Palace", 289–312; *idem*, "Royal and Other Households", 107–9, 103–15.

38  See Roger Owen, "The Middle East in the Eighteenth Century: An 'Islamic' Society in Decline? A Critique of Gibb and Bowen's *Islamic Society and the West*", in *Review of Middle East Studies* 1, 1975, 101–12.

to the centuries after the late-sixteenth century. Thus, the long-lasting historiographical paradigm of decline, first articulated by contemporary critics of transformation like Gelibolulu Mustafa Âli, Koçi Bey and Kâtib Çelebi, then taken over by Orientalists like Hammer-Purgstall and Jorga, and reinforced during the Cold War era by proponents of modernization theory such as Bernard Lewis and Niyazi Berkes, has itself become a subject of intellectual history.

It needs to be mentioned that Kunt should be considered one of the pioneers of the prosopographical approach to Ottoman history. In *Sancaktan Eyalete* and *Sultan's Servants* he acquired his data on the actions of provincial governors from four appointment registers located in the *Maliyeden Müdevver* and *Kâmil Kepeci* catalogues. On the basis of these sources, Kunt conducted statistical analyses of the governors' administrative ranks, career backgrounds, location or geography of their appointments, durations and intervals of their services, and their incomes, and succeeded in detecting the structural changes discussed above.[39]

Kunt has published work that is still of major importance to students of the sixteenth and seventeenth centuries, and this needs to be considered separately. In one study, "Ethnic-Regional (*Cins*) Solidarity in the Seventeenth-Century Ottoman Establishment", published in 1975, he discusses *cins* solidarity among the Ottoman ruling elite by providing intriguing examples from Ottoman historiography, the literary works of Veysî, and Evliya Çelebi's travelogue. From this highly original article, Kunt, then a Ph.D. student, acquired notable fame among contemporary Ottomanists. The main thesis of this article is that, contrary to the hitherto predominant assumption that the child levy and palace education were rather successful in at least weakening the ethno-geographical identities of Ottoman statesmen and janissary commanders, these members of the ruling elite were in fact fully aware of their early ethnic origins; in fact, the resilience of this identity could sometimes lead to factions based on ethno-geographical origins. Furthermore, the presence of such factions could shape Ottoman political decisions.[40] Though Kunt wished, as expressed in this article, further research on this issue, practically no significant academic study has yet been produced. It might be argued that, despite more than forty years having passed, this study is still the only important academic source covering ethnic connections within the seventeenth-century Ottoman ruling elite.

---

39  Kunt, *Sultan's Servants*, xviii–xxii, 127–33.
40  Kunt, "Ethnic-Regional (*Cins*) Solidarity", 233–9.

## References

*Boğaziçi Üniversitesi Dergisi: Hümaniter Bilimler* (Boğaziçi University Journal: Humanities) 1 (1973) 7 (1979).

Duindam, Jeroen. "Introduction". In Jeroen Duindam, Tülay Artan and Metin Kunt (eds) *Royal Courts in Dynastic States and Empires: A Global Perspective.* Leiden: Brill, 2011.

Faroqhi, Suraiya (ed.) *The Later Ottoman Empire, 1603–1839.* Vol. 3. *The Cambridge History of Turkey.* Cambridge: Cambridge University Press, 2006.

Faroqhi, Suraiya and Kate Fleet (eds). *The Ottoman Empire as a World Power, 1453–1603.* Vol. 2. *The Cambridge History of Turkey.* Cambridge: Cambridge University Press, 2013.

Fleet, Kate (ed.) *Byzantium to Turkey, 1071–1453.* Vol. 1. *The Cambridge History of Turkey.* Cambridge: Cambridge University Press, 2009.

Hathaway, Jane, *The Politics of Households in Ottoman Egypt: The Rise of the Qazdaglis.* Cambridge, UK: Cambridge University Press.

Kasaba, Reşat (ed.) *Turkey in the Modern World.* Vol. 4. *The Cambridge History of Turkey.* Cambridge: Cambridge University Press, 2008.

Kenan, Seyfi (ed.) *İSAM Konuşmaları: İSAM Papers.* Istanbul: İSAM Yayınları, 2013.

Kunt, İ. Metin. "Ethnic-Regional (*Cins*) Solidarity in the Seventeenth-Century Ottoman Establishment". *International Journal of Middle East Studies* 5 (1974), 233–9.

Kunt, İ. Metin. "Kulların Kulları", *Boğaziçi Üniversitesi Dergisi-Hümaniter Bilimler* 3 (1975), 27–42.

Kunt, İ. Metin. "Derviş Mehmet Paşa, *Vezīr* and Entrepreneur: A Study in Ottoman Political-Economic Theory and Practice", *Turcica* IX, 1 (1977), 197.

Kunt, İ. Metin. *Sancaktan Eyalete: 1550–1650 Arasında Osmanlı Ümerası ve İl İdaresi.* Istanbul: Boğaziçi Üniversitesi Yayınları, 1978.

Kunt, İ. Metin. *Bir Osmanlı Valisinin Yıllık Gelir-Gideri. Diyarbekir, 1670–71.* Istanbul: Boğaziçi Üniversitesi Yayınları, 1981.

Kunt, İ. Metin. "Transformation of *Zimmî* into *Askerî*". In Benjamin Braude and Bernard Lewis (eds). *Christians and Jews in the Ottoman Empire: The Functioning of a Plural Society.* Vol. 1. *The Central Lands.* Teaneck, NJ: Holmes & Meier Publishers, 1982, 55–67.

Kunt, İ. Metin. *The Sultan's Servants: The Transformation of the Ottoman Provincial Government 1550–1650.* New York: Columbia University Press, 1983.

Kunt, İ. Metin. "Ottoman Names and Ottoman Ages", in Bernard Lewis (ed.) *Raiyyet Rüsûmu: Essays Presented to Halil Inalcik on his Seventieth Birthday by His Colleagues and Students,* vol. 1, Harvard 1986 [*Journal of Turkish Studies* X], 227–34.

Kunt, İ. Metin. "Siyasal Tarih (1300–1600)". In Sina Akşin (ed.) *Türkiye Tarihi 2. Osmanlı Devleti 1300–1600.* Istanbul: Cem Yayınevi, 1987, 16–143.

Kunt, İ. Metin. "Siyasal Tarih (1600–1789)", in Sina Akşin (ed.) *Türkiye Tarihi 3. Osmanlı Devleti 1600–1908*. Istanbul: Cem Yayınevi, 1988, 10–69.

Kunt, İ. Metin. "State and Sultan up to the Age of Süleyman: Frontier Principality to World Empire". In Metin Kunt and Christine Woodhead (eds) *Süleyman the Magnificent and His Age*. Harlow: Longman, 1995.

Kunt, İ. Metin. "Sultan, Dynasty and State in the Ottoman Empire: Political Institutions in the Sixteenth Century", *The Medieval History Journal* 6, (2), 2003, 217–30.

Kunt, Metin. "A Prince Goes Forth (Perchance to Return)". In Karl Barbir and Baki Tezcan (eds). *Identity and Identity Formation in the Ottoman World: A Volume of Essays in Honor of Norman Itzkowitz*. Madison: Wisconsin University Press, 2007, 63–71.

Kunt, İ. Metin. "Turks in the Ottoman Imperial Palace". In Jeroen Duindam, Tülay Artan and Metin Kunt (eds) *Royal Courts in Dynastic States and Empires: A Global Perspective*. Leiden: Brill, 2011, 289–312.

Kunt, İ. Metin. "Reading Elite, Elite Reading". In *Printing and Publishing in the Middle East: Journal of Semitic Studies*, Supplementary edn 24 (2008), 89–100.

Kunt, İ. Metin. "Royal and Other Households". In Christine Woodhead (ed.) *The Ottoman World*. London: Routledge, 2012.

Kunt, Metin and Christine Woodhead (eds). *Süleyman the Magnificent and His Age: The Ottoman Empire in the Early Modern World*. London: Longman, 1995.

Mansel, Philip. "Conference Report: The Globalization of Court History". *The Court Historian* 11 (1), 2013, 77–80.

Owen, Roger. "The Middle East in the Eighteenth Century: An 'Islamic' Society in Decline? A Critique of Gibb and Bowen's *Islamic Society and the West*", in *Review of Middle East Studies* 1, 1975, 101–12.

# A Representative List of Metin Kunt's Publications

This volume has been edited without the knowledge of Metin Kunt. Since the editors did not ask him for a full bibliography of his works, this list of publications consist of those titles that are either widely known among the scholarly community, or have been cited in research papers, or are publicly available. The presented list has been arranged in chronological order.

"Naima, Köprülü, and the grand vezirate", *Boğaziçi Üniversitesi Dergisi-Hümaniter Bilimler* 1 (1973), 57–63.

"Ethnic-Regional (*Cins*) Solidarity in the Seventeenth-Century Ottoman Establishment", *IJMES* 5 (1974), 233–239.

"Kulların Kulları", *Boğaziçi Üniversitesi Dergisi-Hümaniter Bilimler* 3 (1975), 27–42.

"17. Yüzyılda Osmanlı Kuzey Politikası Üzerine Bir Yorum", *Boğaziçi Üniversitesi Dergisi* 4–5 (1976–77), 111–16.

"Derviş Mehmet Paşa, *Vezīr* and Entrepreneur: A Study in Ottoman Political-Economic Theory and Practice", *Turcica* 9 (1), 1977, 197–214.

Sancaktan Eyalete: 1550–1650 Arasında Osmanlı Ümerası ve İl İdaresi (Istanbul: Boğaziçi Üniversitesi Yayınları, 1978).

Bir Osmanlı Valisinin Yıllık Gelir-Gideri, Diyarbekir 1670–71 (Istanbul: Boğaziçi Üniversitesi, 1981).

"Transformation of *Zimmî* into *Askerî*", in Benjamin Braude and Bernard Lewis (eds), *Christians and Jews in the Ottoman Empire: The Functioning of a Plural Society*. Vol. 1. *The Central Lands* (Teaneck, NJ: Holmes & Meier Publishers, 1982), 55–67.

*The Sultan's Servants: The Transformation of Ottoman Provincial Government, 1550–1650* (New York: Columbia University Press, 1983).

"Türkische Beiträge zur Untersuchung der Beziehungen zwischen dem Osmanischen und dem Habsburger-Reich", in Z. Abrahamowicz, V. Kopcan, M. Kunt, E. Marosi, N. Moacanin, C. Serban, K. Teply, *Die Türkenkriege in der historischen Forschung* (Vienna: Franz Deuticke, 1983), 165–83.

"The Later Muslim Empires: Ottomans, Safavids, Mughals", in Majorie Kelly (ed.) *Islam: The Religious and Political Life of a World Community* (New York: Praeger, 1984), 113–36.

"Ottoman Names and Ottoman Ages", in Bernard Lewis (ed.), *Raiyyet Rüsûmu: Essays Presented to Halil Inalcik on his Seventieth Birthday by His Colleagues and Students*, vol. I, Harvard 1986 [*Journal of Turkish Studies* X], 227–34.

"Siyasal Tarih (1300–1600)", in Sina Akşin (ed.) *Türkiye Tarihi 2. Osmanlı Devleti 1300–1600* (Istanbul: Cem Yayınevi, 1987), 16–143.

"Siyasal Tarih (1600–1789)", in Sina Akşin (ed.), *Türkiye Tarihi 3. Osmanlı Devleti 1600–1908*. (Istanbul: Cem Yayınevi, 1988), 10–69.

(edited with Christine Woodhead), *Süleyman the Magnificent and His Age: The Ottoman Empire in the Early Modern World* (London: Longman, 1995).

"State and Sultan up to the Age of Süleyman: Frontier Principality to World Empire", in Metin Kunt and Christine Woodhead (eds), *Süleyman the Magnificent and His Age* (London: Longman, 1995), 12–17.

"Sadrazam", *Encyclopedia of Islam*. Second edn, Vol. 8 (Leiden: Brill, 1995), 751–2.

(and Jean Deny), "Sandjak", *Encyclopedia of Islam*. Second edn, Vol. 9 (Leiden: Brill, 1997), 11–13.

*The Sultan's Servants: The Transformation of Ottoman Provincial Government, 1550–1650*, Second edn (New York: Columbia University Press, 2001).

"Sancakbeyi haslarının ögeleri (1480–1540)", in Hasan Celal Güzel, Salim Koca and Kemal Çiçek (eds), *Türkler: 10. Cilt. Osmanlı* (Ankara: Yeni Türkiye Yayınları, 2002), 709–13.

(edited with Christine Woodhead), *Kanuni ve Çağı: Yeniçağda Osmanlı Dünyası*, translated by Sermet Yalçın (Istanbul: Türkiye Ekonomik ve Toplumsal Tarih Vakfı Yayınları, 2002).

"Sultan, Dynasty and State in the Ottoman Empire: Political Institutions in the 16th Century", *The Medieval History Journal/Special Issue on Tributary Empires* 6 (2) 2003, 217–30.

"Ottomans and Safavids: States, Statecraft, and Societies", in Youssef M. Choueiri (ed.) *A Companion to the History of the Middle East* (Malden, MA: Blackwell Publishing, 2005), 192–206.

"A Prince Goes Forth (Perchance to Return)", in Karl Barbir and Baki Tezcan (eds), *Identity and Identity Formation in the Ottoman World: A Volume of Essays in Honor of Norman Itzkowitz* (Madison, WI: University of Wisconsin Press 2007), 63–71.

"Sultan Süleyman ve Nikris", in Özlem Kumrular (ed.) *Muhteşem Süleyman* (Istanbul: Kitap Yayınevi, 2007).

"Reading Elite, Elite Reading", *Journal of Semitic Studies/Special issue on Printing and Publishing in the Middle East* 24 (2008), 89–100.

"Ottomans and Spain", in Lale Uluç and Ayşe Aldemir Kilercik (eds), *Ottoman Calligraphy from the Sakıp Sabancı Museum, Istanbul* (Istanbul: Sabancı Üniversitesi Sakıp Sabancı Müzesi 2008), 18–29.

"Introduccion Historica: Los Tres Grandes Imperios: Otomanos, Safavidas y Mogoles", in Sophie Makariou (ed.) *Tres Imperios del Islam: Estambul, Isfahan, Delhi. Obras Masestras de la Coleccion del Louvre* (Valencia: Bancaja Foundation, 2008), 21–8.

(as founding editor, with Kate Fleet, Suraiya Faroqhi and Reşad Kasaba), *The Cambridge History of Turkey*. Vols. I–IV (Cambridge: CUP, 2009–2013).

"Kâtip Çelebi'nin anlatımıyla Venedik = Venezia raccontata da Katip Çelebi", in Nazan Ölçer and Giampiero Bellingeri (eds), *Venezia e Istanbul in Epoca Ottomana: 18 Novembre 2009–28 Febbraio 2010, Istanbul, Università Sabancı, Museo Sakıp Sabancı= Osmanlı Döneminde Venedik ve İstanbul: 18 Kasım 2009–28 Şubat 2010: İstanbul, Sabancı Üniversitesi, Sakıp Sabancı Müzesi* (Milan: Electa 2009), 54–64.

"Osmanlı tarihçiliğinin çerçevesi: 'Türk – İran' modeli", *Doğu Batı: Osmanlılar I* 12 (51) 2010, 37–48.

(edited with Jeroen Duindam and Tülay Artan), *Royal Courts in Dynastic States and Empires: A Global Perspective* (Leiden: Brill Academic Publishers, 2011).

"Turks in the Ottoman Imperial Palace", in Jeroen Duindam, Tülay Artan and Metin Kunt (eds), *Royal Courts in Dynastic States and Empires: A Global Perspective* (Leiden: Brill Academic Publishers, 2011), 289–312.

"Characterizing Ottoman Polity: 'Turko-Persia' and the Ottomans", in İlker Evrim Binbaş and Nurten Kılıç-Schubel (eds), *Horizons of the World: Festschrift for İsenbike Togan* (Istanbul: İthaki Yayınları, 2011), 311–24.

"Royal and Other Households", in Christine Woodhead (ed.), *The Ottoman World* (London: Routledge, 2012), 103–15.

(with Zeynep Nevin Yelçe), "Divân-ı Hümâyûn: le conseil impérial Ottoman et ses conseillers, 1450–1580", in Cédric Michon (ed.), *Conseils et Conseillers dans L'Europe de la Renaissance (v.1450–v.1550)* (Rennes: PUFR, 2012), 299–339.

"An Ottoman Imperial Campaign: Suppressing the Marsh Arabs, Central Power and Peripheral Rebellion in the 1560s (Bir Osmanlı Sefer-i Hümayunu: Ceza'ir-i Arab Kalkışmasının Bastırılması, 1560'larda Merkezi Güç ve Uçlarda İsyan)", *Journal of Ottoman Studies (Osmanlı Araştırmaları Dergisi)* 43 (2014), 1–18.

(with Zeynep Nevin Yelçe), "Polonyalı İki Osmanlı" (Two Polish Ottomans), in Ayşen Anadol (ed.), *Uzak Komşu Yakın Anılar:Türkiye Polonya İlişkilerinin 600 Yılı* (Distant Neighbour Close Memories: 600 Years of Turkish – Polish Relations) (Istanbul: Sakıp Sabancı Müzesi, 2014), 50–61.

"Devolution from the Centre to the Periphery: An Overview of Ottoman Provincial Administration", in Jeroen Duindam and Sabine Dabringhaus (eds), *The Dynastic Centre and the Provinces: Agents and Interactions* (Leiden: Brill, 2014), 30–48.

"Ottoman White Eunuchs as Palace Officials and Statesmen, 1450–1600", in Juliane Schiele and Stefan Hanss (eds), *Mediterranean Slavery Revisited (500–1800)/Neue Perspektiven auf mediterrane Sklaverei (500–1800)* (Zürich: Chronos Verlag, 2014).

INTRODUCTION

# The Issue of Transformation within the Ottoman Empire

*Selçuk Akşin Somel and Seyfi Kenan*

> No man ever steps in the same river twice,
> for it's not the same river and he's not the same man
> HERACLITUS
>
> [and, more importantly perhaps, the time is not the same]

⁂

This volume is dedicated to İbrahim Metin Kunt, who made major contributions to studies on the Ottoman world of the sixteenth and seventeenth centuries throughout his four decades of research. His academic work covers the institutional changes that took the Ottoman Empire from the classical age to the era of decentralization. Considering Kunt's groundbreaking explorations into the processes of transformation, this book aims to explore the various aspects of transformation within the empire through essays that examine historical changes throughout Ottoman history, from the classical era to the age of modernizing reforms.

## 1    Transformation as a Theoretical and Historical Category

Pre-seventeenth century Ottoman works on society and history used to shun the category of transformation, which incorporates the notion of change. Within Islamic thought the rather metaphysical double notion of 'existence and disintegration' (*kevn ü fesâd*) describes a dynamic process of complete change in which *fesâd*, with its connotations of corruption, decay, and decomposition, has a negative value. This understanding ran parallel with Ottoman observers' criticisms of the structural changes taking place within the empire from the mid-sixteenth century onwards. The comparable Ottoman term for a revolution was *ihtilâl*, denoting destructive change, which again has a negative connotation. In the sixteenth century, the term *inkılâb*, meaning 'transformation' and 'reform', perhaps did not exist or was at least not commonly used. Terms such as *tagayyür*, *tebeddül* (both denoting to turn from one state into another), *tahvîl* (to change, to turn), *temessül* (the acquisition of a different form, or character) indicated changes mainly in the physical realm.[1]

The growing influence of Ibn Khaldun's philosophy of history – he will be discussed below – among Ottoman literati from the seventeenth century onwards provided a new intellectual context in which the notion of change acquired a certain degree of legitimacy. Beginning with Kâtib Çelebi (d.1657), terms such as *ıṣlāḥ* (improvement, amelioration, correction) and *tecdid* (renewal, innovation, reform) began to denote comprehensive measures to protect the Muslim community and prolong the lifespan of the empire.[2] Coming to the nineteenth century, particularly after the Rescript of Gülhane (1839), dictionaries came to include *ıṣlāḥ ve ilga* (transformation through nullification of the old), *ıṣlāḥ ve tanzim* (reform and reorganization), *tagyir ü tebdil* (continuous change), *takallüb* (change, revolution), and *inkılâb* (radical change, evolution), all of them used mostly in social and political spheres.[3]

---

1   The highly popular Arabic-Ottoman Turkish *Ahterî-i Kebîr* dictionary, completed in 1545 and having enjoyed numerous manuscript copyings and editions over the centuries, does not contain the term *inkılâb*. See Mustafa bin Şemseddin el-Akhisarî, *Ahterî-i Kebîr* (Kostantiniyye: Darü't-Tıba'atü's-Sultâniye, 1256/1840), 85, 91, 108, 116. See also İlhan Kutluer, "Fesad", DIA 12, 421–422; Kasım Turhan, "Kevn ve Fesad", DIA 25, 343–345; Süleyman Uludağ, "Kevn", DIA 25, 343. The seventeenth-century preacher-author Kadızade Mehmed İlmî used the term *ihtilâl* for revolution. See E. Ekin Tuşalp-Atiyas, "The 'Sunna-Minded' Trend", in Marinos Sariyannis, *A History of Ottoman Political Thought up to the Early Nineteenth Century* (Leiden: Brill, 2019), 255.
2   Sariyannis, *Ottoman Political Thought*, 279–325.
3   See Alexandre Handjéri, *Dictionnaire Français-Arabe-Persan et Turc*, vol. 3 (Moscow: Imprimerie de l'Université Imperiale, 1840), 332–3, 698; Muallim Naci, *Lugat-i Naci*, 4th edn. (Istanbul: Asır Matbaası, 1322/1905), 105, 233, 239, 258; Mütercim Asım, *Kamusu'l-Muhît Tercümesi*, edited by Mustafa Koç and Eyyüp Tanrıverdi, vol. 2 (Istanbul: TYEKBY, 2013), 1117–18; Sir James W. Redhouse, *A Turkish and English Lexicon* (Istanbul: Çağrı Yayınları, 2011), 129–30; idem, *Redhouse Sözlüğü: Türkçe/Osmanlıca İngilizce* (Istanbul: Redhouse Yayınevi, 1999), 528, 540; Şemseddin Sami, *Kamus-i Türkî* (Dersaadet: İkdam Matbaası, 1317/1899–1900), 122, 419, 426, 444; Şemseddin Sami, *Kamus-ı Fransevî: Dictionnaire Français-Turc*, 4th ed. (Istanbul: Mihran Matbaası, 1322/1905), 1855, 1913, 2153; Julius Theodor Zenker, *Türkisch – Arabisch – Persisches Handwörterbuch*, vol. 1 (Leipzig: Verlag von Wilhelm Engelmann, 1866), 17, 58, 108, 252, 296, 301.

A closer look at the term *transformation* shows that it includes the essential dictionary meaning of "change in form, appearance, nature, or character".[4] If we would open up this definition further, it might be stated that transformation implies a qualitative change, a kind of development that leads to a condition or conditions that are basically different from previous circumstances. Applying this concept to the more concrete dimension of the history of civilizations, societies, or political entities such as states or empires, transformation as a historical category gives researchers an analytical tool with which to describe and interpret qualitative developments in economic, political, cultural, or educational realms.

Despite the analytical importance of the category *transformation*, it has apparently still been considered too broad or ambiguous a term by mainstream social scientists to be accepted as a valid theoretical concept.[5] Instead, certain major social scientific reference sources prefer to use the term *social change* as a relatively value-free concept devoid of ideological associations because it is present in terms like 'social evolution' and 'progress'. But, as seen in these sources, even the term *social change* lacks a common definition, which implies the essential ambiguity of this concept.[6]

This ambiguity is reinforced by the fact that there are subcategories that could meaningfully be included within terms like *transformation* or *social change*. To specify these subcategories, on the other hand, might help us to

---

4  See Lesley Brown (ed.) *A New Shorter Oxford English Dictionary*, vol. 2 (Oxford: Clarendon Press, 1993), 3368; *Merriam-Webster's Collegiate Dictionary*, 10th ed. (Springfield, Massachussetts: Merriam-Webster, Incorporated, 1998), 1961–62; http://dictionary.reference.com/browse/transformation?s=t (retrieved on 27 July 2015). Della Thompson (ed.) *The Concise Oxford Dictionary of Current English*, 9th ed. (Oxford: Clarendon Press, 1995), 1481.

5  The only two exceptions in the social sciences are in economics and statistics, where the category *transformation* is used as a well-established academic term. In economics, an "historical transformation problem" denotes the Marxian question of the transformation of commodity values, based on labour values, to competitive market prices. For discussions about the issue, see M. Morishima and G. Catephores, "Is There a Historical Transformation Problem?", *The Economic Journal*, 85 ((338) 309–28) June 1975. In statistics, "transformations of data" denotes mathematical applications to simplify relationships among the data and improve further analysis. See Joseph B. Kruskal, "Statistical Analysis: Transformations of Data", in *International Encyclopedia of the Social Sciences*, edited by David L. Sills, vol. 15 (New York: The Macmillan Company and The Free Press, 1968), 182.

6  Wilbert E. Moore, "Social Change", in *International Encyclopedia of the Social Sciences*, vol. 14, 365–75; William F. Ogburn, "Change, Social", in Edwin R. A. Seligman and Alvin Johnson (eds) *Encyclopaedia of the Social Sciences*, vol. 3 (New York: The Macmillan Company, 1948), 330; Elisabetta Ruspini, "Social Change", in Jonathan Michie (ed.) *Reader's Guide to the Social Sciences*, vol. 2 (London/Chicago: Fitzroy Dearborn Publishers, 2001), 1499–1501.

establish a safer conceptual ground that enables one to understand the category of transformation in a more precise manner. These include terms such as *transition, crisis, turning point, evolution* and *revolution*. Looking more closely, the term *transition*, if used in social sciences, describes a temporal phase within a movement or development from one qualitative condition or structure to another, implying a continuous process. *Crisis* denotes a situation in which a structure becomes endangered or weakened, and cannot cope with changes of the time in question. This state of crisis leads to a *turning point*, a situation in which changes become irreversible and a qualitative condition or structure turns into a qualitatively new situation or structure. The processes of qualitative and irreversible changes from one formation to another have been described by the concepts of *evolution* and *revolution*. While *evolution* includes the meaning of a gradual and smooth process of a qualitative development, *revolution*, by contrast, contains the meaning of a radical and abrupt, even violent, qualitative rupture or change. With regard to these terms, *transformation* implies a broader category, one that embraces the above-mentioned five nouns. Thus, in this volume the category of transformation will be understood in this broad sense, in terms of the meanings of transition, crisis, turning point, evolution, and revolution, or, in terms of short- and long-term qualitative developments.

The issue of historical transformations has attracted the interest of philosophers and historians since ancient times. One of the earlier approaches is the cyclical understanding of historical events, which assumes a series of recurring happenings of similar quality or organicist life-cycles of civilizations. The writings of Herodotus, Plato and Aristotle in Ancient Greece, Sima Qian (d.86 BCE) in Ancient China, Polybius (d.118 BCE) in the Roman republic and then Machiavelli (d.1527) in Renaissance Florence reflect to a certain extent a cyclical notion of time.[7] Cyclical understanding of historical transformations has continued well into the modern era. Prior to the nineteenth century, two outstanding names were the Tunisian philosopher Ibn Khaldun (d.1406), who made a significant impact on historiography within the Ottoman Empire,

---

7  R. G. Collingwood, *The Idea of History* (Oxford: OUP, 1980), 23; Phil Harris, "Machiavelli and the Global Compass: Ends and Means in Ethics and Leadership", *Journal of Business Ethics* 93 (1) 2010, 131–8; Siep Stuurman, "Herodotus and Sima Qian: History and the Anthropological Turn in Ancient Greece and Han China", in *Journal of World History* 19 (1) 2008, 1–40; Vickie B. Sullivan, *Machiavelli, Hobbes, and the Formation of a Liberal Republicanism in England* (Cambridge: CUP, 2004), 155–6; John Van Seters, *In Search of History: Historiography in the Ancient World and the Origins of Biblical History*, reprint (Winona Lake, Indiana: Eisenbrauns, 1997).

and the Neapolitan historian Giambattista Vico (d.1725).[8] The nineteenth and twentieth centuries have observed the continuation of discussions on the cyclical approach to history. In some of these analyses, however, we see a more teleological and even a mystical approach stressing the 'doomsday' of Western civilization, represented by the Russian author N. Danilevsky, the German philosopher O. Spengler, the Russo-American sociologist P. Sorokin and the British historian A. J. Toynbee.[9]

A common problem about cyclical approaches appears to be the application of rather major historical categories and excessive generalizations that weaken one's analytical capacity to comprehend transformations. Interestingly, propositions by economists of cyclical movements based on quantitative data, such as that of the Soviet economist N. Kondratiev, might have a somewhat higher explanatory power for the historical transformations of the nineteenth- and twentieth-century industrialized societies. According to Kondratiev, there are economic ups and downs every fifty or sixty years based on the development of new technologies and succeeding depressions due to the overcapacity of production, also known as 'Kondratiev waves'. Some economic booms and depressions appear to correlate with major events such as the French Revolution, the revolutions of 1848, the Italian and German national unifications, New Imperialism, or the First and Second World Wars.[10]

An alternative to a cyclical approach for the explanation of historical changes is the idea of linear history. This concept supposes that changes in history do not reiterate themselves, but lead to transformations and produce developments and structures that are qualitatively different from those of previous ages. The origins of this type of historical perception go back to Abrahamic religions, where these traditions perceive history as a process that ultimately culminates in the Day of Judgement, albeit with some discrepancies in particulars among them. This eschatological perception of time became formalized into

---

8    Collingwood, *Idea of History*, 63–71. For a comprehensive analysis of Ibn Khaldun's impact on Ottoman political thought, see Sariyannis, *Ottoman Political Thought*, 279–325. See also Jack Kalpakian, "Ibn Khaldun's Influence on Current International Relations Theory", *Journal of North African Studies* 13 (3) 2008, 357–70.

9    Collingwood, *Idea of History*, 181–3; Oroon K. Ghosh, "Some Theories of Universal History", *Comparative Studies in Society and History* 7 (1) 1964, 1–20; Benedict Taylor, "Temporality in Nineteenth-Century Russian Music and the Notion of Development", *Music and Letters* 94 (1) 2013, 108.

10   Judy L. Klein, "The Rise of 'Non-October' Econometrics: Kondratiev and Slutsky at the Moscow Conjuncture Institute", *History of Political Economy* 31 (1) Spring 1999, 137–68; M. Z. Zgurovsky, "Metric Aspects of Periodic Processes in Economy and Society", *Cybernetics and Systems Analysis* 46 (2) 2010, 167–72.

a historical philosophy by Saint Augustine of Hippo (d.430), and reinforced by religious thinkers such as Saint Thomas Aquinas (d.1274). Eschatological approaches to history necessarily imply an element of optimism, or the view about a better future and an ultimate salvation by God. This optimistic view of history was taken over by Enlightenment thinkers and directed into a secular progressivist avenue. Philosophers like the Marquis de Condorcet (d.1794) and G. W. F. Hegel (d.1831) predicted historical development directed by universal reason and leading to the expansion of civil society and human freedom.[11]

Ironically, a progressivist historical approach, claiming the prevalence of universal reason, failed to be sufficiently universal to cover global history. Enlightenment *philosophes* were representing an intellectual reaction against anything that did not conform to their standards of reason; any historical structure falling short of universal reason was deemed unworthy of being 'historical'. 'Oriental civilizations' were basically stagnant entities living under the yoke of recurring despotic rulers, and therefore devoid of meaningful historical change, and hence unqualified for academic historical analysis. This view was even more reinforced by colonialist aspirations in the late nineteenth and early twentieth centuries, which produced Orientalist approaches that distorted academic methodology when analysing past Islamic societies.[12] In addition to this biased Western-oriented approach towards non-European civilizations, another issue to be addressed appears to be the inherent determinism and even teleology, represented by progressivism. During the Cold War era, two competing policies, namely the Marxist approach of socialist development propagated by the Soviet Bloc, and the modernization theory diffused by the liberal West, both promoting social changes, emerged as logical outcomes of the progressivist understanding of history.[13]

---

11   Collingwood, *Idea of History*, 46–55, 80, 86, 113–122; Van Seters, *In Search of History*, passim.
12   See Edward Said, *Orientalism* (New York: Pantheon Books, 1978). For postcolonial studies, see Robert J. C. Young, *Postcolonialism: A Very Short Introduction* (Oxford: Blackwell, 2001).
13   For the controversial aspects of the Enlightenment and its intellectual impact, see Daniel Carey and Lynn Festa (eds), *The Postcolonial Enlightenment: Eighteenth-Century Colonialism and Postcolonial Theory* (Oxford: OUP, 2009); Charles W. J. Withers, *Placing the Enlightenment: Thinking Geographically about the Age of Reason* (Chicago: University of Chicago Press, 2007), 136–63. See also Riad, Sally and Deborah Jones, "Invoking *Black Athena* and its Debates: Insights for Organization on Diversity, Race and Culture", *Journal of Management History* 19 (3) 2013, 394–415; Thomas R. Trautmann, "Does India Have History? Does History Have India?", *Comparative Studies in Society and History* 54 (1) 2012, 174–205. For some standard works representing liberal version of modernization theory, see S. M. Eisenstadt, *Modernization: Protest and Change* (Englewood Cliffs, NJ:

Despite these shortcomings, it was again the critical approach of the Enlightenment towards social institutions that has helped to produce a modern understanding of societies and transformations. An additional factor was the emergence of the Industrial Revolution in the West; the beginnings of modern social sciences reflect both criticisms of capitalism as well as attempts to comprehend the multiple social consequences of the industrial transformation. Notable names, among them K. Marx (d.1883), E. Durkheim (d.1917) and M. Weber (d.1920), laid the foundations of modern social sciences by conceptualizing issues such as class forces and the relationship between economic base and political superstructure, human action and the role of religion in the transformation of societies, and the introduction of empirical and quantitative methodologies to social researches.

On the basis of these foundations, we see attempts at concrete social scientific formulations on cases of historical transformations. K. Polanyi (d.1964) underlined a close relationship between political power and economics and, by rejecting the liberal belief in *laissez-faire*, he preferred to analyse the capitalization of humanity in terms of the founding of nation-states. Durkheim's application of quantitative methods to researching social structures indirectly inspired the Annales School to introduce environmental and structural factors, like geography, climate, and demography, into historical analysis. As part of this approach, time scales, such as *la longue durée*, were introduced to describe long-term structural continuities, then conjunctures, so providing a tool with which to characterize demographic or economic cycles and, finally, *événements* representing the short-term observable changes.[14]

---

Prentice-Hall, 1966); *idem, Revolution and the Transformation of Societies: A Comparative Study of Civilizations* (New York: Free Press, 1978); Samuel P. Huntington, *Political Order in Changing Societies* (New Haven: Yale University Press, 1968). Various semi-Marxist or Marxist approaches focusing on political revolutions of the modern era and social transformations from medieval Europe to modernity include Eric Hobsbawn's trilogy titled *The Age of Revolution: Europe 1789–1848* (London: Abacus 1962); *idem, The Age of Capital: 1848–1875* (London: Weidenfeld & Nicolson, 1974); *idem, The Age of Empire: 1875–1914* (London: Weidenfeld & Nicolson, 1987); Barrington Moore Jr., *Social Origins of Dictatorship and Democracy: Lord and Peasant in the Making of the Modern World* (Boston, MA: Beacon Press, 1966); Theda Skocpol, *States and Social Revolutions. A Comparative Analysis of France, Russia, and China* (Cambridge: Cambridge University Press, 1979); Immanuel Wallerstein's four-volume-series titled *The Modern World System* (published by Academic Press 1974, 1980, 1989 and University of California Press 2011).

14   Michael Bentley, *Modern Historiography. An Introduction* (London: Routledge, 1999), *passim*; Karl Polanyi, *The Great Transformation: The Political and Economic Origins of Our Time* (Boston: Beacon Press, 2001), 3–32.

In recent studies, historical transformation as a theoretical issue has been considerably expanded by the postmodern emphasis on textuality and culture that took shape in parallel with developments in the field of cultural anthropology and interpretative sociology, represented by names such as C. Lévi-Strauss (d.2009), C. Geertz (d.2006), P. Bourdieu (d.2002), M. Sahlins and A. Giddens. Their contributions towards analysing changes within a given society or demographic group in a specific time period has provided theoretical insights for historians interested in transformations. Addressing issues like structure, cultural code, mentality and individual factors, W. H. Sewell Jr has attempted to formulate a theory of qualitative historical changes through elaborating on the dynamic relationship between structures and human agency without falling into the quagmires of determinism and essentialism.

According to Sewell, happenings that can be called historical events include those that lead to the transformation of structures.[15] Thus, comprehending historical transformations requires a solid theory of structures. Before summarizing Sewell's view on structures, it should be stressed that he regards it as a necessity to undertake a synchronic analysis on structures and related developments before establishing the diachronic sequences of historical events. In effect, he attempts to overcome the conventional epistemological divide between the social sciences as disciplines with basically synchronic approaches on the one hand, and history as a discipline with an essentially diachronic methodology on the other.[16] For him, a successful historical investigation into diachronic developments needs to be based on prior synchronic research on structures.

As part of a theory of structure, Sewell adapts Giddens's 'duality of structure' approach whereby "structures shape people's practices, but it is also people's practices that constitute (and reproduce) structures." Moreover, people's innovative action can lead to changes in structures. Therefore, structures are not static beings, but themselves constitute processes. For Sewell, structures consist of *schemas* of a virtual nature, for example cultural codes and *resources* defined by space and time, such as human beings and material things. Schemas give human beings the rules with which to utilize non-human resources; thus, virtual schemas play a significant role in shaping material resources. At the same time, schemas are affected by and dependent on resources, since the sustained reproduction of schemas depends on their confirmation and promotion by the accumulation and development of the existing resources. In other

---

15   William H. Sewell Jr, *Logics of History: Social Theory and Social Transformation* (Chicago: University of Chicago Press, 2005), 218.
16   Sewell, *Logics*, 219.

words, "schemas not empowered or regenerated by resources would eventually be abandoned and forgotten, just as resources without cultural schemas to direct their use would eventually dissipate and decay."[17] The conjoint breeding of schemas and resources produces temporary structures, also termed by Bourdieu as *habitus*.[18]

These structures, or *habita*, are prone to either gradual or drastic transformations due to the presence of aspects such as (1) a multiplicity of structures existing at different layers with various modalities; (2) the transposability of schemas, or ability to generalize, export and apply them to different contexts; (3) the unpredictability of resource accumulation, namely the uncertainty of the outcomes of the enactment of schemas in terms of the varying quantities and qualities of the resources, which could lead to modifications in schemas; (4) a multiplicity of meanings (polysemy) of resources, whereby human agents can, by transposing schemas, reinterpret and use culturally coded resources in different ways; and (5) the intersection of structures as a consequence of the possibility of reinterpretations or appropriations of resources as well as transpositions and borrowings of schemas by different agents belonging to various structural complexes.[19]

The role of agency in structural changes, whether individual or collective, relates to the actor's knowledge of schemas and ability to apply some degree of control over social relations. In Sewell's words, "agency arises from the actor's control of resources, which means the capacity to reinterpret or mobilize an array of resources in terms of schemas other than those that constituted the array."[20] Actors differ significantly in their capacity to reinterpret or appropriate resources, or to adapt new schemas because of individual factors like nationality, social class, education, gender and age. People therefore display a range of transformative capacities and have different options for transformative action. A final point about agency is its social and collective nature. In other words, agents mostly act in communication and cooperation with other agents to shape and achieve collective projects while often facing opposition from those with differing and competing projects. The varying transformative capabilities of collectively acting agencies also reflect different levels of collective power.[21]

---

17   Sewell, *Logics*, 127, 136–7.
18   Sewell, *Logics*, 138.
19   Sewell, *Logics*, 140–3.
20   Sewell, *Logics*, 143–4.
21   Sewell, *Logics*, 144–5.

Sewell considers structuralist anthropologist Marshall Sahlins's study of Captain James Cook's encounter with the Hawaiians and their subsequent cultural and political changes after 1779 as a possible model for research on historical transformations. He underlines Sahlins's two basic propositions – first, people can only absorb expected or unexpected happenings through their existing cultural categories; and, second, an action in the world entails performing an act of reference, or, put differently, "human social experience is the appropriation of specific precepts by general concepts."[22] These propositions imply that, under certain changing physical circumstances or group mentalities, actors might bend the meanings or functions of cultural categories, which will eventually lead to cultural and social transformations.

On the basis of the above-mentioned discussions on structures, schemas, actors and resources, Sewell formulates his theory of historical events and transformations in the following manner. First, *"resources are produced by cultural schemas."* This means that the specific value of individuals or material items emerges from categorizations based on schemas. Second, *"resources are also governed by other dynamics than those they receive from this categorization"* because there are physical, biological and social conditions that limit the usage of resources. Third, *"the transformation of cultural schemas results from unexpected flows of resources."* In other words, while acting in the world, "cultural categories acquire new functional values," and "things marked as resources in an initial action may be subject over time to other determinations ... that will cause them to change ... in content, in quantity, in value, and in relations."[23]

So, after these elaborations, how does Sewell define a structure? Unlike classical sociologists who associate structures with material complexes, or cultural anthropologists who connect structures mainly with abstract code systems, he combines both approaches. He considers nearly everything shaped by more than one individual to be a structure, both material and virtual and varying immensely in terms of scope, ranging from an erotic couple to a means of economic production, to a civilization or even a language. He differentiates structures in terms of two main parameters – *schema dimension* or depth, and *resource dimension* or power. For him, structures with considerable depth are not easily observed; they lie beneath recognizable phenomena, and are mostly not a part of consciousness in the sense "that they are taken-for-granted mental assumptions or modes of procedure that actors normally apply without being

---

22   Sewell, *Logics*, 200, 202.
23   Sewell, *Logics*, 217.

INTRODUCTION                                                                                         11

aware that they are applying them."[24] A prime example of structures with considerable schema dimensions are linguistic structures. On the other hand, political bodies such as states represent structures that can mobilize major power resources but are relatively superficial in terms of depth. According to Sewell, the long-term durability of an institution is determined more by the depth of the structure than by its resource dimension. He gives the example of the capitalist mode of production as a centuries-long lasting structure because of its extremely transposable schema, which he describes as the commodification of things, or the conversion of use value into exchange value applicable to nearly every aspect of life through the use of money.[25]

As already mentioned above, Sewell criticizes mainstream historians' one-sided approach focusing on diachronic historical developments, and proposes a synchronic methodology for investigating in-depth changes in past societies. According to him, synchronic analyses of social changes will enable historians to engage in meaningful diachronic interpretations of historical transformations.[26]

The application of Sewell's structure theory of social transformation to concrete historical experiences for understanding the longevity of states or empires would necessitate the consideration of a variety of possible criteria such as geographic or demographic size; economic, cultural or political impact; and institutional flexibility, all of which would roughly correspond to parameters such as *resource dimension* and *schema dimension*. In this context, the political history of the Mongol Empire is an interesting example of a major political transformation, but of relatively short duration. We know that a new political structure suddenly emerged in a remote corner of eastern Central Asia around 1206, expanded as far west as Poland in 1241, and disintegrated after 1259 at an equally unexpected speed. In this example, resources such as the extraordinary agency of Genghis Khan in uniting Mongol tribes and the efficiency of the Mongol cavalry against its neighbours, played a noteworthy role in the rapid expansion of this structure. However, Mongol resources were confined mainly to agency, without other kinds of resources, such as a sizeable population or extended territorial base. Crucially, the schema dimension of the imperial structure was relatively shallow, which reflected itself in the bare existence of a Mongolian written or bureaucratic culture. The Mongols apparently lacked the necessary schemas to transform or integrate the cultures

---

24  Sewell, *Logics*, 146.
25  Sewell, *Logics*, 146–50.
26  Sewell, *Logics*, 175–96.

of occupied territories within a resilient political structure. On the contrary, nearly all the conquered populations embodied sufficient schema depth to transform and assimilate Mongol elites and their occupying forces into their respective civilizations, which also contributed to the rapid demise of this empire.

A counter-example to the Mongolian case, again using Sewell's theory of structure, could be the Ottoman Empire as an imperial structure, which is the subject of this volume. Emerging towards the end of the thirteenth century as a small principality, it reached the zenith of its territorial expansion on three continents in the late-seventeenth century, and ended after the First World War. These centuries, which include late medieval times, the early modern period, as well as modern periods and the age of colonialism, produced specific structural challenges, which the Ottomans were able to withstand and to which they were able to adapt through a series of fundamental changes. This resilience, tenacity perhaps, and adaptability were related to both the nature of the schema dimension and the quality of resource. The Ottoman political entity included an amalgam of a set of basic constitutional schemas of Iranian, Islamic, Turko-Mongol and Byzantine origins, which ensured the incorporation of different religious and ethnic people, enabled flexible policies, and achieved relative political stability. Among these, the notion of justice (*'adāle*), the concept of a universal Islamic empire and millet system, the idea of sultanic legitimation and the sultan's ability to introduce secular legislation (*ḳānūn*), the notion of reform and betterment with a view to improving things and putting them right (*ıṣlāḥ*), and the institution of caesaropapism, together with bureaucratized *ulema*, appear to be significant.[27] Except for some revisions and additions peculiar to the nineteenth century, this set of constitutional schemas did not substantially change.

A secondary level of schemas closely related to political, military, financial, and administrative resources, however, underwent notable transformations in harmony with the resource-level challenges that the military, demographic, economic, political and technological developments of the early modern age produced. The political schema devising a system of open succession and promoting pivotal agency to the first ten sultans, was replaced by agnatic seniority,

---

27    Halil İnalcık, *Ottoman Empire: The Classical Age 1300–1600*, translated by Norman Itzkowitz and Colin Imber (New Rochelle, NY: Orpheus Publishing, 1989), 65–75, 89–103; Halil İnalcık, "State and Ideology under Sultan Süleyman I", in *idem*, *The Middle East and the Balkans under the Ottoman Empire: Essays on Economy and Society* (Bloomington, IN: Indiana University Turkish Studies and Turkish Ministry of Culture Series, 1993), 70–94.

which allowed a power shift from active monarchs to a collective agency of bureaucracy, army, and *ulema*.[28] The traditional military schema of armed forces based on mounted cavalry or *timariots*, known as *sipahi*, proved to be obsolete in the face of new resources, such as an expanding firearms technology. In other words, a transformation of the military schema took place in which the role of cavalry diminished in favour of the expansion of various infantry units, namely janissaries and *sekbans* capable of using firearms. This transformation, however, put pressure on the state to create cash resources with which to remunerate its standing army and this, in turn, aggrandized tax farming practices at the expense of *tımâr* prebends. Monetary-based tax farms then replaced the former fiscal schema of the *tımâr* system, which was based on kind.

The increasing regional power of tax farmers as new local agents prompted another transformation of administrative schema leading to administrative decentralization. Crucially, the traditional schema of a "strict separation of different estates and keeping the masses (*reaya*) in their proper place"[29] became obsolete. During these developments, former actors and agencies lost their influence, while new agencies became powerful; sultanic authority was curtailed, and the state as an institutional agency, represented by the bureaucratic body of the Sublime Porte, became prominent; at the provincial level, the weight of traditional intermediary agencies such as *sipahi* fief holders shifted to tax farming *ayan* notables, many of them of common origins, with mainly market economic orientations.

A final wave of challenges to both resource and schema dimensions resulted in a new series of transformations leading the Ottoman Empire from the early modern era into the modern age. European military ventures against the empire and the expansion of the world economy constituted resource-level challenges that encouraged the imperial administration to undertake schema- and resource-level reforms towards military modernization and administrative centralization, while at the same time adopting liberal economic policies. The schema-level cultural impact of the European Enlightenment and the

---

28  According to Baki Tezcan the collective agency of scribal bureaucracy, Janissary and the *ulema* has created a constitutional system where the sultanic authority has been effectively checked by government bodies supported by segments of the imperial population. Tezcan argues that this change constitutes a major political and social transformation. See Baki Tezcan, *The Second Ottoman Empire: Political and Social Transformation in the Early Modern World* (Cambridge: CUP, 2012), *passim*.

29  Halil İnalcık, "Military and Fiscal Transformation in the Ottoman Empire, 1600–1700", *Archivum Ottomanicum* 6, 1980, 283–4.

ideological effects of the American and French revolutions posed a significant threat to the basic Ottoman constitutional schemas that had hitherto defined the political and social positions and roles of various religious communities (*millets*) within the imperial structure. The Greek War of Independence, followed by other nationalist movements, promoted schema-level measures that, while affirming the already existing constitutional schemas, nevertheless incorporated new ideological, legal and political ones that led the empire in a more secular, participatory, and pluralist direction. One of them was the policy of Ottomanism, a concept designed to integrate different religious and ethnic groups into one 'Ottoman nation' based on equal citizenship and loyal to the same sultan. During this transformative move towards modernity, collective agencies such as legislative assemblies and provincial administrative councils emerged as significant political bodies, followed by the opening of the Ottoman parliament, first in 1876 and then in 1908. Meanwhile, a new generation of actors arose, represented by diverse structures like the Young Ottomans, the Young Turks, the Internal Macedonian Revolutionary Organization, the Hunchakian Party, and the Dashnagtsutyun, all of which questioned the empire's centuries-old constitutional schemas.

The Young Turk Revolution of 1908 destabilized the constitutional schemas then defining the Ottoman structure. Fierce competition emerged between agencies with radically differing proposals for the imperial future. These included the Committee of Union and Progress (CUPR), representing a strictly centralist position, and liberal groupings of mainly non-Turkish ethnicities advocating decentralized ones. The inability to reach a viable political consensus among agencies about a new constitutional schema produced domestic instability and polarization, fomenting rebellions in Albania, Syria and Yemen. The destructive resource-based development of the Balkan Wars of 1912–13 definitely undermined the basic integrative constitutional schemas of the empire. The CUPR dictatorship, imposed through a military coup during the Balkan Wars, supported a schema combining centralization, Islamism and Turkism. This new schema, based on the transposition of the Western ones of ethnic nationalism and the nation-state, denoted both an exclusivism to Greek and Armenian populations, and containment of Arab nationalism, thus terminating certain vital schema components providing political flexibility, particularly the notion of justice, through which the imperial structure ensured its centuries-long resilience.

Following this theoretical discussion on social change and transformation, an attempt will be made to provide an overview of historiographical discussions on the issue of changes in Ottoman history before the 1980s.

## 2  Twentieth-Century Discussions on Changes in the Ottoman Empire

Prior to Metin Kunt, there were earlier discussions on the nature of political, economic and social changes in the Ottoman Empire, but, as discussed above, these remained mostly within the confines of a traditional deterministic paradigm formulated as early as Kâtip Çelebi and Naîmâ (d.1716), later followed by Ahmed Cevdet Pasha (d.1895).[30] By applying the historical theory of Ibn Khaldun, these authors formulated an organicist notion of the empire, according to which it underwent phases like birth, rise, maturity, and decline. This historiographical paradigm proved remarkably resilient, and was even reinforced in the twentieth century by the new Turkish republican intellectuals, as well as by the historiographies of new nation-states in the Balkans and Middle East, who agreed to condemn the Ottoman structure as corrupt and doomed.[31]

While remaining within this predominant paradigm, some Turkish historians also approached Ottoman history from a more dynamic viewpoint. These were among the founders of the social and economic historiography of the Ottoman Empire, namely Fuad Köprülü (d.1966), Ömer Lutfi Barkan (d.1979) and Mustafa Akdağ (d.1972). Köprülü, known as one of the precursors of academic historiography in Turkey on cultural and institutional changes during the early centuries of the Ottoman Empire, underlined the dynamic historical processes that led to the emergence of early Ottoman Turkish literature. For

---

30  Ahmed Cevdet Paşa, *Târih-i Cevdet*, 12 vols (Istanbul 1271–1301/1855–1884); Kâtib Çelebi, *Düsturü'l-Amel fî Islâhi'l-Halel* (1653), first printed version in 1863 within Ayn-i Âlî's *Kavânin-i Âl-i Osmân* (Istanbul, 1280), 119–40; Mustafa Na'îmâ, *Ravzatü'l-Hüseyn fi Hulasâti'l-Ahbâr el-Hafîkeyn*, also known as *Târih-i Na'îmâ* (1716), first printed version in Istanbul, Müteferrika Press, first two volumes in 1147/1734, the remaining part published between 1259/1843 and 1280/1863 by the Matbaa-i Âmire Press.

31  The most authoritative representatives of the Turkish official version of the organicist historiography include names like Enver Ziya Karal (*Osmanlı Tarihi*); İsmail Hakkı Uzunçarşılı (*Osmanlı Tarihi*); Yusuf Akçura (*Osmanlı Devletinin Dağılma Devri: XVIII ve XIX Asırlarda*, Ankara: TTK, 1940); and Yusuf Hikmet Bayur (*Türk İnkılabı Tarihi*). For a critical view on the prevalent orthodox-Rankean understanding of Ottoman history in Turkey, see Oktay Özel, *Dün Sancısı: Türkiye'de Geçmiş Algısı ve Akademik Tarihçilik* (Istanbul: Kitap Yayınevi, 2009); Oktay Özel and Gökhan Çetinsaya, "Türkiye'de Osmanlı tarihçiliğinin son çeyrek yüzyılı: Bir bilanço denemesi", *Toplum ve Bilim* 91 (Kış 2001/2002), 8–38. For criticisms of the nation-state focused understanding of Ottoman history, see Fikret Adanır and Suraiya Faroqhi, *The Ottomans and the Balkans: A Discussion of Historiography* (Leiden: Brill, 2002); Christine Philliou, "The Paradox of Perceptions: Interpreting the Ottoman Past through the National Present", *MES* 44, 2008, 661–75; Şuhnaz Yılmaz and İpek Yosmaoğlu, "Fighting the Spectres of the Past: Dilemmas of Ottoman Legacy in the Balkans and the Middle East", *MES* 44 (2008), 677–93.

him, the development of Ottoman poetry and prose over the centuries should be discussed by elaborating on the interactions of folk literature, *âşık* tradition and the literary traditions of various social segments and their different levels of artistic quality.[32] While writing an argumentative study on the issue of the Byzantine influence over Ottoman institutions, Köprülü emphasized the need to undertake chronological, comparative and generic studies on pre-Ottoman social and legal institutions of Iranian, Arab and Central Asian origins to comprehend the evolution of these into Ottoman structures.[33]

Barkan, while focusing on economic and specifically agricultural history, attributed the longevity of the empire to the principle of state ownership over arable land, or translated into Sewell's terminology, to a legal continuity at schema level. With an implicit etatist view, he interpreted changes with regard to the weakening of centralistic control over lands and the rise of local agents in negative terms, as a process of financial and administrative corruption, rather than a transformation from one imperial structure to another.[34] Akdağ, on the other hand, could be considered a pioneer of the 'history from below' approach to Ottoman history before the seventeenth century, in that he discussed the discontent of various population groups (such as vagrant peasants, medrese students, and *sipahi*s) as contributing to the provincial turmoil of the late-sixteenth century. While analysing the violent Jelali confrontations, he explicitly stated that these events brought a structural formation at the turn of the seventeenth century, which effectively terminated the previous, in his own words, "historically advanced imperial order".[35] In his unfinished work

---

32   M. Fuad Köprülü, *Türk Edebiyatında İlk Mutasavvıflar*, 4th edn (Istanbul: Alfa Tarih, 2014), 48–50. The original edition was published in 1919.

33   M. Fuad Köprülü, *Bizans Müesseselerinin Osmanlı Müesseselerine Tesiri*, 9th edn (Istanbul: Alfa Tarih, 2014), 33–4. The original edition appeared as an extensive article, titled "Bizans müesseselerinin Osmanlı müesseselerine tesiri hakkında bazı mülahazalar", in *Türk Hukuk ve İktisat Tarihi Mecmuası* 1 (1931), 165–313.

34   Ömer Lütfi Barkan, "Türkiye'de Toprak Meselesinin Tarihi Esasları", in idem, *Türkiye'de Toprak Meselesi: Toplu Eserleri* (Istanbul: Gözlem Yayınları, 1980) [originally published in *Ülkü Halkevleri Dergisi* 60 (1938), 63–4, 127; idem, "Şer'i Miras Hukuku ve Evlatlık Vakıflar", ibid. [originally published in *İstanbul Hukuk Fakültesi Mecmuası* 7 (1940)], 210; idem, "Türk Toprak Hukuk Tarihinde Tanzimat ve 1274 (1858) Tarihli Arazi Kanunnamesi", ibid. [originally published in *Tanzimat. 100.Yıldönümü Münasebetile* (Istanbul: Maarif Vekâleti, 1940)], 297, 324, 344–5, 367–8, 372; idem, "Osmanlı İmparatorluğu'nda Çiftçi Sınıfların Hukuki Statüsü", ibid. [originally published in *Ülkü Mecmuası* 49, 50, 53, 56, 58, 59 (1937)], 725–88.

35   Mustafa Akdağ, *Türk Halkının Dirlik ve Düzenlik Kavgası*, chapter "Celali İsyanları" (Ankara: Bilgi Yayınları, 1975), 16–20. A revised version of his habilitation thesis, titled *Celâli İsyanları (1500–1603)*, was originally published in 1963.

on the economic and social origins of the Ottoman Empire, Akdağ attempted to describe the social and economic transformation from an obscure Oghuzic principality to a cosmopolitan empire by considering not only the demographic, political, institutional, agricultural, and fiscal changes, but also the cultural impact of the admixture of Turks and Anatolian Christians such as the Greeks and Armenians.[36]

Much like the republican attitude to Ottoman history, authors like Bernard Lewis (d.2018) and Niyazi Berkes (d.1988), who adopted a modernization perspective, discussed the reform process from the late eighteenth to the twentieth century in terms of a new beginning, a departure from a traditional, decaying order towards a secular and modern political and social system, which is compatible with global developments. In Lewis's well-known *Emergence of Modern Turkey*, the period following the first ten sultans is described as a series of "breakdowns", "catastrophic falls" and "collapses" of the bureaucracy, armed forces, religious institutions and agricultural production, a process of general decline lasting for centuries.[37] It was the reformist elites who from the late eighteenth century onwards undertook modernist measures and opened the gates to Western modern influences. Facing reactions from traditionalist segments of the population against reforms and modernization, it was mostly the authoritarian and sometimes despotic governments that succeeded in undertaking modernizing measures from the top, a tendency that continued into the republican era.[38]

Inspired by the problems that twentieth-century Muslim societies faced in the process of secularization, in his *Development of Secularism in Turkey*, Berkes discusses the modernizing process in the late Ottoman Empire and early republican Turkey from the viewpoint of a struggle "between the forces of tradition, which tend to promote the domination of religion and the sacred law, and the forces of change".[39] For him, the Ottoman social order continued to be medieval and basically in order so long as the religious spirit maintained by the *ulema*, patrimonialism promoted by the absolutist sultanate, and the notion of estates more or less preserved by the state remained prevalent. Towards the end of the eighteenth century, even this structure was decaying, along with the

---

36  Mustafa Akdağ, *Türkiye'nin İktisadi ve İçtimai Tarihi*, 2 vols (Ankara: TTK, 1959, 1971), *passim*.
37  Bernard Lewis, *The Emergence of Modern Turkey*, 2nd edn (London: OUP, 1968), 22–39.
38  Lewis, *Emergence*, 74–319.
39  Niyazi Berkes, *The Development of Secularism in Turkey* (Montreal: McGill University Press, 1964), 6.

weakening of the central authority and the crumbling power of the sultans.[40] The transformation of Turkey towards modernity could take place mainly by "extricat[ing] religious values from the vicissitudes of the changing world by narrowing the scope of tradition".[41] As seen in these historiographical views of Lewis and Berkes, the notion of modernization in these narratives appears to be quite in harmony with the traditional organicist notion of Ottoman history.

One notable historian, who prior to Metin Kunt discerned the structural importance of changes in the seventeenth and eighteenth centuries and explicitly referred to them as a 'transformation', was Halil İnalcık (d.2016). In "Centralization and Decentralization in Ottoman Administration", İnalcık saw the major structural changes in the provincial administration in the seventeenth and eighteenth centuries in terms of resources and agencies, without, however, conceptualizing them or abandoning the former organic traditional notion of imperial decline.[42] In a later article, "Military and Fiscal Transformation in the Ottoman Empire 1600–1700", he spoke of the radical military and fiscal developments he conceptualized as a 'transformation'; he recognized the socio-political changes that effectively undermined status-based social differentiation among estates and altered the relationship between government and subjects. He also acknowledged the mutation of the *tımâr*-based tax system to tax farming as a change from feudal taxation to a general cash tax applicable to all imperial subjects.[43] However, even in his masterpiece, *The Ottoman Empire: The Classical Age*, İnalcık failed to step beyond a particular historiographical threshold that would have redefined Ottoman history in terms of a new periodization that abandoned the notion of decline.[44] In the 1994 volume titled *An Economic and Social History of the Ottoman Empire*, which he co-edited with Donald Quataert, however, İnalcık seemed to have adjusted to the possibility of an alternative periodization of Ottoman history.[45]

---

40   Berkes, *Secularism*, 8–19.
41   Berkes *Secularism*, 508.
42   Halil İnalcık, "Centralization and Decentralization in Ottoman Administration", in Thomas Naff and Roger Owen (eds) *Studies in Eighteenth Century Islamic History* (London: Papers on Islamic History, 1977), 27–52.
43   İnalcık, "Military and Fiscal", 283–337.
44   For a similar observation, see Suraiya Faroqhi, "Empires Before and After the Post-Colonial Turn: The Ottomans", *Osmanlı Araştırmaları: The Journal of Ottoman Studies*. Beyond Dominant Paradigms in Ottoman and Middle Eastern/North African Studies: A Tribute to Rifa'at Abou-El-Haj 36 (2010), 64.
45   Halil İnalcık and Donald Quataert (eds), *An Economic and Social History of the Ottoman Empire 1300–1914* (Cambridge: CUP, 1994), 1–7.

As already shown in the section on Metin Kunt's life and his academic contributions, it was Kunt who in the late 1970s and early 1980s proved for the first time that the history of the Ottoman Empire needed to be treated in terms of qualitatively different periods demarcated by social and political transformations. Since then, the majority of international Ottomanists have ceased to consider the notion of decline as an analytical category.

## 3   A Short Overview on Recent Discussions Concerning the Nature of the Ottoman Empire and Its Role in World History

Over the last two decades, new historiographical approaches have emerged that effectively 'emancipate' Ottoman historiography from orientalist templates by incorporating it into the broad framework of world history. The application of comparative historical approaches, in particular, makes it possible to provide new insights into the structural characteristics and transformations of the Ottoman Empire.

This recent trend displayed one of its early expressions in Rifa'at 'Ali Abou-El-Haj's seminal work, *Formation of the Modern State: The Ottoman Empire, Sixteenth to Eighteenth Centuries*. In this study, he argued for the need for a new comparative approach to Ottoman history, since the orientalist understanding of the Ottoman Empire as an abnormal phenomenon had prevented academic historiography from seeing it as part of wider historical processes or as an example of more general historical events.[46] Abou-El-Haj's exhortations have effectively opened new research paths, which, particularly after 2000, have produced a series of new studies with new insights into Ottoman society, economics, and culture. These studies have simultaneously revised the previously predominant understanding of a peripheral empire lacking internal social and economic dynamics and being shaped mainly by the forces of European economic and political penetration.

Since a considerable research literature has already emerged in diverse areas of research, including gender studies, the history of emotions, subaltern issues, the history of medicine, and cultural history, only a few examples will be highlighted.

Looking at the issue of the emergence of the Ottoman state in medieval times, Cemal Kafadar and then Heath Lowry advanced the idea of the

---

[46]   Rifa'at 'Ali Abou-El-Haj, *Formation of the Modern State: The Ottoman Empire, Sixteenth to Eighteenth Centuries* (Albany: SUNY Press, 1991).

hybridity and eclecticism of early Ottoman institutions, which gave the principality a major advantage in the post-Mongol era of chaos, thus diverting it from the *ghazi* thesis.[47] This thesis, first formulated by Paul Wittek (d.1978), claims that the early Ottoman expansionist drive towards Byzantium and the Balkans emanated mainly from the notion of the Islamic holy war, known as *ghaza*.[48] Focusing on the late-sixteenth- and seventeenth-century crisis of political and social structures, Abou-El-Haj and later Baki Tezcan argued that what had previously been considered manifestations of imperial decline were actually transformations towards popular participation and constitutional checks.[49] The late eighteenth and nineteenth centuries, when great powers imposed major political, economic, and military pressure on the empire, in fact witnessed a changing military capacity, together with a reformation of the techniques of governance and a redefinition of the methods of legitimation, as have been discussed by Carter V. Findley, Selim Deringil, and Virginia Aksan.[50]

The expansion of historiographical scope induced a new generation of Ottomanists to produce studies in diverse fields hitherto left nearly untouched. Among them, gender studies, the history of emotions, and subaltern history have provided insights into the subjective experiences of female and male individuals of modest strata. Enquiries into the actions of these agents opened up a new vista through which to understand the periods of change and transformation. For example, by utilizing the sixteenth-century court records of a provincial town in southern Anatolia, Leslie P. Peirce has shown the extent of female agency in solving family and community issues. As part of the field of nineteenth-century subaltern studies, Y. Hakan Erdem discussed the persistence of slavery in Ottoman society. Nazan Maksudyan, who concentrated on the intersection of gender studies, child history and slavery, has aimed to convey the voices of the otherwise silenced victims of Young Turk social and political measures to transform the empire radically.[51]

---

47  Cemal Kafadar, *Between Two Worlds: The Construction of the Ottoman State* (Berkeley: University of California Press, 1995); Heath W. Lowry, *The Nature of the Early Ottoman State* (Albany: SUNY Press, 2003).

48  Paul Wittek, *The Rise of Ottoman Empire: Studies in the History of Turkey, Thirteenth–Fifteenth Centuries*. London: Royal Asiatic Society, 1938.

49  Abou-El-Haj, *Formation, passim*; Tezcan, *Second Ottoman Empire, passim*.

50  Virginia Aksan, *Ottoman Wars, 1700–1870: An Empire Besieged* (Harlow: Longman/Pearson, 2007); Selim Deringil, *The Well-Protected Domains: Ideology and the Legitimation of Power in the Ottoman Empire, 1876–1909* (London: I. B. Tauris, 1998); Carter V. Findley, *Ottoman Civil Officialdom: A Social History* (Princeton: Princeton University Press, 1989).

51  Y. Hakan Erdem, *Slavery in the Ottoman Empire and its Demise 1800–1909* (Basingstoke: Palgrave Macmillan, 1996); Nazan Maksudyan, *Orphans and Destitute Children in the Late*

New approaches have also been seen in the field of economic history; in contrast to the macroeconomic perspectives or state-centred enquiries prevalent until the 1990s, we see the depictions of individuals such as merchants, artisans, and peasants as economic and cultural actors who are analysed as parts of various social networks. For example, by examining the actions of merchant families who built trade networks and accumulated political power in early modern Palestine, Beshara Doumani revealed the intertwined connections between culture, politics and economic change, while local peasants, far from being passive communities, defined their identity and shaped their understanding of justice and political authority. Artisans, who constituted a major economic sector in Ottoman urban life, have been discussed by Nelly Hanna who looked at economic life in Egypt. She revealed the artisans of Cairo in the context of their work, social relationships and interactions with guilds. According to Hanna, the European commercial impact in the late eighteenth century led artisans to adapt so that they could compete successfully and survive in a landscape of increasing European trade.[52]

A crucial component of the integration of Ottoman historiography into world history consists of the growing number of comparative studies in which the Ottoman Empire has become a major subject of analytical examination alongside certain other historic empires. While discussing the factors leading to this academic trend, Alan Mikhail and Christine Philliou state that the present post-national order is attracting growing academic and political interest in previous pre-national imperial projects.[53] Thus, there has been a rise in academic literature on historic empires in which the Ottomans are represented in a substantial manner together with other comparable bodies.

The political and psychological impact created by the termination of the Eastern Bloc, followed by the unexpected disintegration of the USSR and the accompanying international crises, has boosted new in-depth studies on Russian history in which the Habsburgs and Ottomans have come under scrutiny. An early version of such a study was edited by Karen Barkey and Mark

---

*Ottoman Empire* (Syracuse, NY: Syracuse University Press, 2014); Leslie P. Peirce, *Morality Tales: Law and Gender in the Ottoman Court of Aintab* (Berkeley: University of California Press, 2003).

52 Beshara Doumani, *Rediscovering Palestine: Merchants and Peasants in Jabal Nablus, 1700– 1900* (Berkeley: University of California Press, 1995); Nelly Hanna, *Artisan Entrepreneurs in Cairo and Early-Modern Capitalism (1600–1800)* (Syracuse: Syracuse University Press, 2011).

53 Alan Mikhail and Christine M. Philliou, "The Ottoman Empire and the Imperial Turn", *Comparative Studies in Society and History* 54 (4) October 2012, 721–4.

von Hagen. This was followed by the studies of Dominic Lieven and later of Omer Bartov and Eric D. Weitz.[54] These and similar works effectively instrumentalized the historical data of the Russian, Habsburg and Ottoman empires with a view to shedding light on contemporary geopolitical problems, but which, however, have provided a somewhat limited academic historiographical service.

On the other hand, this rising interest in empires has encouraged historians to look further east and discuss early modern Islamic empires in a comparative manner. Ali Anooshahr, for example, examined the political culture and historiography of the early Ghaznavid, Mogul and Ottoman states in an attempt to understand the legitimizing role of *ghazi* traditions for sultans like Mahmud of Ghazni, Babur, and Murad II. Stephen Frederic Dale, followed by Douglas E. Streusand, used structural approaches to discuss similarities and differences between Ottoman, Safavid and Mogul empires in terms of political, social, economic and cultural settings.[55] Such comparisons, like that of Sanjay Subrahmanyam in his comprehensive chapter comparing "Moguls, Ottomans and Habsburgs", sometimes also included the Habsburg Empire. He analysed political, economic, and cultural aspects of these bodies in a concise manner while criticizing Western historiography for its systematic downplaying of the crucial roles they played in world history down to the late eighteenth century.[56]

A different approach has been to focus on the specific monarchical institutions of various states from a range of centuries and civilizations. Here, Jeroen Duindam, Tülay Artan and Metin Kunt have edited a volume in which the royal courts of dynastic states from as early as Assyria and Seleukids down to Topkapı, Versailles and Schönbrunn have been described in depth. With these authors, Duindam developed this approach into a chronologically defined framework in which to compare major dynasties of the Old World, including the Ottoman one, by analysing the ideals of kingship, the rituals of rulership, systems of

---

54    Karen Barkey and Mark von Hagen, eds., *After Empire. Multiethnic Societies and Nation-Building. The Soviet Union and the Russian, Ottoman, and Habsburg Empires* (Boulder, CO: Westview Press, 1997); Dominic Lieven, *Empire: Russian Empire and its Rivals* (New Haven: Yale University Press, 2001); Omer Bartov and Eric D. Weitz, eds., *Shatterzone of Empires. Coexistence and Violence in the German, Habsburg, Russian, and Ottoman Borderlands* (Bloomington, IN: Indiana University Press, 2013).

55    Ali Anooshahr, *The Ghazi Sultans and the Frontiers of Islam: A Comparative Study of the Late Medieval and Early Modern Periods* (London: Routledge, 2009); Stephen Frederic Dale, *The Muslim Empires of the Ottomans, Safavids, and Mughals* (Cambridge: CUP, 2010); Douglas E. Streusand, *Islamic Gunpowder Empires: Ottomans, Safavids, and Mughals* (Boulder, CO: Westview Press, 2011).

56    Sanjay Subrahmanyam, "Mughals, Ottomans and Habsburgs: Some Comparisons", in idem, *Empires Between Islam and Christianity 1500–1800* (Albany, NY: SUNY Press, 2019), 149 85.

succession, courts and households, the political role of palace women, and the relationship between the ruler and the imperial territories. Through examining European, Middle Eastern, East Asian and African examples, he has investigated the processes behind the rise and demise of dynasties.[57]

In addition to comparative studies, we see attempts to formulate comprehensive histories of Ottoman political and economic thought prior to the nineteenth century. One of these attempts has been made by Fatih Ermiş by compiling a history of Ottoman economic thought. In this study, Ermiş elaborates on traditional Ottoman concepts of polity and society before addressing the issues of household economy, money, price ceiling, regulation, and market supervision. He then discusses the economic views of two late eighteenth-century authors, Süleyman Penah and Ebubekir Ratib.[58] The other attempt belongs to Marinos Sariyannis, who through the use of historiographical texts, philosophical tractates, mirrors for princes, moral treatises, legal documents and polemical literature, provided the reader with a dynamic panorama of changes and evolution in Ottoman political ideas from the fourteenth to the early nineteenth centuries.[59] These two attempts represent early examples of integrative studies of Ottoman intellectual history, which have clearly opened up new avenues for more exhaustive editions of a similar kind.

One study that has recently approached Ottoman history from the perspective of structural transformations has been Karen Barkey's *Empire of Difference: The Ottomans in Comparative Perspective*. Here, Barkey approaches the Ottoman centuries through the lens of institutions and social networks, whereby transformations in the episodes of imperial expansion, maintenance, decentralization and nation-state building are understood as a variety of outcomes of 'negotiations' between the elites and social classes in the centre and peripheral regions.[60]

For a full idea of the extent of the newly expanding research areas, one may consult the rather useful article by Mikhail and Philliou on recent historiographical developments.[61]

---

57  Jeroen Duindam, *Dynasties: A Global History of Power, 1300–1800* (Cambridge: CUP, 2016); Jeroen Duindam, Tülay Artan and Metin Kunt (eds), *Royal Courts in Dynastic States and Empires: A Global Perspective* (Leiden: Brill, 2011).
58  Fatih Ermiş, *A History of Ottoman Economic Thought: Developments Before the Nineteenth Century* (London: Routledge, 2014).
59  Marinos Sariyannis (with a chapter by Ekin Tuşalp Atiyas), *Ottoman Political Thought up to the Tanzimat: A Concise History* (Rethymno: FORTH, Institute for Mediterranean Studies, 2015); idem, *A History of Ottoman Political Thought up to the Early Nineteenth Century* (Leiden: Brill, 2019).
60  Karen Barkey, *Empire of Difference: The Ottomans in Comparative Perspective* (Cambridge: CUP, 2008).
61  Mikhail and Philliou, "Imperial Turn", 721–45.

4    New Insights into Transformation Processes in the Ottoman Realm

The chapters in this volume include contributions that elaborate on the cultural and social aspects of transformative developments at various periods and levels of Ottoman history. A significant number of them focus on concrete examples of actors and agents playing various roles at different stages of political, social and cultural evolution and change. Some of the contributions cover many aspects of these transformative processes and thus give the reader a broad horizon for understanding the complexities of historical transitions and transformations.

Part 1, "Ottoman Historiography and Reflections", contains discussions about how sources, historiographical issues, changing cultural and political images, and historical actors represent various kinds of embodiments of these changes. They reveal the complexities of historical research in terms of reading and interpreting Ottoman as well as international sources.

In her chapter titled "A Firman Issued by Mustafa the Son of Bayezid I Surnamed Düzme (1422)", Elizabeth Zachariadou discusses a document from the crisis era of early Ottoman statehood in which the impact of the interregnum (1402–13) lasted until as late as the accession of Murad II in 1422. Murad II's uncle, the pretender Mustafa Çelebi, had challenged his nephew and established brief rule in Rumelia before eventually being defeated and executed. Zachariadou skilfully analyses a rare text from this period, which displays multiple aspects of the Ottoman state's transition from a frontier sultanate to a well-established bureaucratic empire. As she implies, political legitimacy was precarious and prone to changes wrought by short-term events. Her study also displays the historiographical challenges that historians often face when dealing with the early centuries of Ottoman statehood.

The next contribution by Tülay Artan, "Imaginary Voyages, Imagined Ottomans: A Gentleman Impostor, the Köprülüs, and Seventeenth-Century French Oriental Romances" is a discussion about the seventeenth and early-eighteenth-century Europeans who built on each other's romantic imaginations to tell stories about Ottomans and themselves. It is about the formation and transformation of cultural and political images in time. Artan also casts light on impostors as a category of actors who emerged during the transition from the early modern era to modern times. European impostors were active when Ottoman lands were subjected to increasing contact with the West and cultural interactions between the realms of Islam (*Dârü'l-İslâm*) and the realms of Christianity (*Republica Christiana*) became more frequent. Niches of autonomous human action with deceptive goals emerged between these two realms, as the movements of individuals of all sorts across the border reflected. Impostors became rare towards the late eighteenth century when global economic dynamics and European expansionism wiped out clearly-defined civilizational spheres.

The focus of Aslı Niyazioğlu's chapter, "Practices of Remembrance and Sites of Violence in Seventeenth-Century Istanbul: The Beheading of Sheikh İsmâil Ma'şûkî (d.1539)" is on a sixteenth-century religious figure's practices of reflection and remembrance in seventeenth-century Istanbul. In the seventeenth century, Sheikh Maşuki was looked upon, depending on the political position of the observer, as either a heretic or a martyr. Niyazioğlu discusses how the sixteenth-century public monuments and landmarks in Istanbul, originally erected and shaped by ruling elites to represent imperial power, came to reflect loci of state violence and oppression in the lifeworlds of persecuted Melami-Bayrami communities of the seventeenth century. This change of perception appears to entail a transformation of the landscape of meaning among certain segments of educated strata of Istanbul towards a non-official, perhaps civilian worldview.

Suraiya Faroqhi's "Ottoman Artisans in a Changing Political Context: Debates in Historiography" is a substantial survey of the history of Ottoman artisans – a topic that enables the author to observe changes in time critically while also reviewing changes in the orientations or perspectives of modern historians. Faroqhi conveys the existence of a relatively lively artisanal life in which guilds, which are more or less autonomous from the central authority, display the ability to put considerable pressure on governments. This state of affairs perhaps began to change towards the middle of the eighteenth century when bureaucratization brought with it the expansion of *gedik*s, government intervention in guilds, and the issuing of *nizam*s, which made artisans cooperate more with the authority.

Part 2 of the volume comprises studies organized under the title "Ottomans: Culture and Careers". It concentrates on the intertwined relationship of transformations in the realms of professional careers and culture, accompanied in some cases by severe individual and social reactions. These transformations are exemplified by stories of certain historical actors, who at times encountered opportunities and often also disappointments or even dangers in their professional lives.

This part begins with Fatih Bayram's study, "*Türbedar* of the Ottoman Sultans: Şevkî Çelebi's Nostalgia for the Bursa of Bayezid Han and Emîr Sultan". It describes the tomb-keeper and antiquarian Şevkî, who felt strong nostalgia for the foundation era of the Ottoman state. Preferring to spend his life in Bursa rather than in cosmopolitan Istanbul, he was attached to the Kâzerûnî dervish order, which cherishes holy war (*ghaza*). His life, which coincided with the transformation of the Ottoman state into a bureaucratic world, in a sense symbolized the decline and disappearance of a former ethos of holy war idealism; what Şevkî could do was translate a hagiography of Sheikh Ebû İzhâk Kâzerûnî, and thus attempt to remind later generations of a forgotten ethos. Şevkî's nostalgia also called for fruitful comparisons with those historical views of the later centuries that exalted Şevkî's time as a golden era.

The next chapter, "The Personal Anthology of an Ottoman Litterateur: Celâlzâde Sâlih (d.1565) and his *Mecmua*", jointly compiled by Cornell H. Fleischer and Kaya Şahin, provides a view on the emergence of an Ottoman cultural 'renaissance' during the age of Süleyman the Magnificent. This phenomenon included the transformation of literary language into an elaborate one, as witnessed in the case of Celâlzâde Sâlih Çelebi's *mecmua*. The study emphasizes the development of a new Ottoman Turkish orthography, where Arabic words and script began to be written in a way that is more convenient for a Turkish written style. Celâlzâde Sâlih represented the transformation of Ottoman literary language from a standard chancery style to a new *belles-lettres* in the form of *münşeat*. This chapter also sheds light on the challenges and opportunities of an era as well as career lines, promoted through various patronage networks.

This study is followed by Pál Fodor's "Transformation of the Abode of War into the Abode of Islam: A Local Grandee in Ottoman Hungary, Osman Ağa, Çelebi and Bey". It discusses institutional changes in a late-sixteenth-century financial administration where financial entrepreneurs, officially known as *nazır*s, penetrated traditional military posts. This intertwining of military and fiscal spheres corresponded to the process of local administrators such as cavalrymen (*sipahi*) and *zâim*s turning into tax farmers. In this context, Fodor presents the story of Osman Ağa as a talented financial expert who proves to be an eager soldier in the 1580s and 1590s. It is shown how a local grandee far away from the border regions of the empire connects and works with the imperial centre while also acting as an intermediary between the Ottomans and the neighbouring Habsburgs.

Christine Woodhead's contribution, "Making Recommendations: Azmizade and the *Mahzar* for Vücûdî Efendi, 1608", provides an example of a provincial Ottoman scholar's career pattern, which displays development of a professional and social flexibility towards the end of the sixteenth and early-seventeenth centuries. Though being a scholar, Vücûdî Efendi served in the army and actively fought in the Caucasus, later to return to the *ilmiyye*. His career shows the gradual disappearance of the previously clearer-defined spheres of the *ilmiyye* class, military and scribal bureaucracy. Meanwhile, the mechanism of patronage became prominent as a means of moving across different career lines. Though late-sixteenth- and early seventeenth-century authors regarded such developments as corruption of the established order, this tendency on the other hand represented a growing flexibility on behalf of the career possibilities of educated individuals.

As an example for those authors who perceived this emerging social flexibility, as described by Woodhead as a threat to the existing imperial and social structure, Mehmet Kalpaklı's chapter provides a striking example. In the contribution titled "A Poet's Warning: Veysî's Poem on the Breakdown of Ottoman Social and Political Life in the Seventeenth Century", we see a poetic representation of the sense of 'decline' that numerous members of the Ottoman elite felt in this era. Veysî (d.1628), who was a *kadı*, complains about the increasing influence of new converts to Islam in the political sphere, bemoans the disappearance of the former Ottoman social order based on a supposedly moral basis, as well as the loss of the holy war (*ghaza*) spirit, replaced by the domination of women and homosexuals among the population of the capital city. The chapter reflects the deep concern of certain functionaries over transformative changes in the social and political structure in which social mobility became unprecedented.

From the second half of the seventeenth century onwards, the Ottoman scribal service began to undergo a process of transforming its political position to become a decision-taking institution, as well as the crystallization of its identity. Ekin Tuşalp Atiyas, in her study titled "From the 'Scribe of Satan' to the 'Master of *Belagat*': Ottoman Chief Scribes and the Rhetorics of Political Survival in the Seventeenth Century", discusses the career stories of Şâmîzâde Mehmed (d.1663) and Râmi Mehmed Pasha (d.1708) in terms of the transition in the political cadres "from the men of the sword/*seyfiyye* to the men of the pen/*kalemiyye*". This process was accompanied by factors such as the polarization and division of Ottoman public opinion, the increasing role of grandee households, usage of panegyric poetry (*kaside*) as a discursive tool for power contenders to secure their positions, and the emergence of the sense of a scribal community on the basis of well-defined qualifications.

While these upheavals and transformations in career patterns and sociopolitical order were taking place, a confrontation of a different kind, related to culture and careers, broke out in the realm of religion, sciences, and *ilmiyye*. This *Kulturkampf* is elaborated by B. Harun Küçük in his "The Compass and the

Astrolabe: Empiricism in the Ottoman Empire". The emergence of an orthoprax Islamic movement in the seventeenth century, known as the Kadızâdelis, constituted an intellectual reaction towards medrese scholasticism. Meanwhile, Kadızâdelis did not oppose empirical sciences, since empiricism meant recognition of the realities of nature created by God. In fact, intellectual circles of the eighteenth century close to the Kadızâdelis emerged as promoters of empirical sciences within the Ottoman Empire. However, this development did not entail a full-scale intellectual transformation, since medrese scholasticism and the *ilmiyye* class continued to exist side by side with empirical tendencies that remained devoid of institutionalization until the nineteenth century. These developments provided favourable conditions for an easier adaptation of European empirical knowledge in the subsequent centuries.

The third part of the volume, "Law, Religion, and Political Thought", includes chapters dealing less with concrete historical individuals/actors than with legal, religious and political superstructures/schemas, which underwent changes in the course of decentralization following the late-sixteenth century to centralist tendencies after the late eighteenth century. Politics became more institutionalized and less personal; Ottoman self-perception came to take the outside world into account; religion became less influenced by localism and traditionalism; legal and judicial practices underwent bureaucratization; and constitution became a means to save the empire.

The opening contribution of this part is Mehmet Öz's "In Search of the Ancient Law or *Kānûn-i kadîm*: Some Notes on Seventeenth-Century Ottoman Political Though". Here, Öz shows how political and social crises induced Ottoman administrators to bypass regulations and traditions in favour of pragmatic policies. These developments were perceived by certain bureaucrat-intellectuals as corruption of the social order (*nizam-ı alem*) and symptoms of the decline of the empire. They authored treatises that criticized changing policies and social conditions within the empire, and demanded the return to ancient rules (*kānûn-i kadîm*), which meant the return to sultanic absolutism. However, what these intellectuals perceived as institutional deterioration was actually a bureaucratization of the Ottoman state. This critical literature was an intellectual reaction to the transformations the empire was going through, as well as to the pragmatic policies pursued by the political elites of these times.

The second study of this part belongs to Zeynep Nevin Yelçe, titled "Between a 'Brilliant Retreat' and a 'Tragic Defeat': Ottoman Narratives of the 1529 and 1683 Sieges of Vienna". It discusses Ottoman discourses to legitimize the campaigns to besiege Vienna. Accordingly, the Ottomans actually did not intend to conquer and expand in Austria in 1529 and 1683; these were rather punitive actions against the Habsburgs to assert Ottoman rights over Hungarian territories. In this process, the Ottomans abandoned the principle of universal kingship, which becomes apparent when comparing the discourses against the Habsburgs in 1529 and 1683. This change entails a transformation of Ottoman understanding in international politics from a self-perception as a universal power superior to all known states to a notion of equality with Christian forces, which opened the path towards future regular diplomatic relationship with the West.

Reactions as reflected in the realm of political thought and changes in diplomatic concepts were accompanied by vivid debates on judicial-religious practices. Derin Terzioğlu in her "Bid'a, Custom and the Mutability of Shar'i Judgments: The Debate on the Congregational Performance of Supererogatory Prayers in Seventeenth-Century Ottoman Empire" reveals worries among groups of pious Muslims about the deviation from the original practices of early Islam and innovations in prayers. This phenomenon was tied to the expansion of contacts between scholars from the Ottoman central lands and the *ulema* of the recently-conquered Middle East as well as the crises of Ottoman institutions. In this context, the orthoprax Kadızadeli movement harshly criticized Islamic prayer practices popular in the central lands. The discussions on prayers during the religious Regaib, Berat and Kadir days between Kadızâdelis and their opponents were a part of a trend of similar worries that rose across the Islamic world.

Changes in the Ottoman fiscal and administrative structure from the late-sixteenth to the eighteenth century appear to have had an impact on the functions of provincial *kadı* courts. Antonis Anastasopoulos's chapter, "The *Sicil*s of Karaferye (Veroia) in the Eighteenth Century: A Case of Transformation?", analyses a collection of Islamic court records from Veroia, where he detects a weakening of the institution of *kadı* courts as deliverers of justice, which possibly reflected itself in the increasing transfer of private cases to Istanbul. Concomitantly, local *kadı*s' functions acquired a mainly administrative character. These tendencies appear to be particularly interesting, since the same century is known as 'the age of decentralization' because of the growing fiscal, administrative and military autonomy of the provincial warlords known as *ayan*s. If correct, this development might be an indicator of major judicial reforms being realized during the nineteenth century, when the functions of *kadı*s were redefined.

Resource-level developments, such as integration into world markets, the increasing presence of European merchants within the empire and administrative centralization, required modernization measures for the judicial structure.

In "Ottoman Legal Change and the *Şeriat* Courts in the Long Nineteenth Century", Iris Agmon discusses the process of transforming the Ottoman legal system and court structure while preserving certain institutional components. She shows that the foundation of modern courts did not mean the generation of an antagonistic relationship with the *ilmiyye* stratum, but the preservation and even enhancement of the sharia courts through promoting the position of the *naib*s as deputy *kadı*s and the opening of new law schools to provide institutional training for the *kadı*s and *naib*s. Similarly, Ottoman legal reforms have included the codification of certain aspects of Islamic jurisprudence to a variety of legal codes. Thus, the transformation of the Ottoman legal system contained a certain degree of structural continuity.

The Ottoman Empire during its final century of existence faced threats such as nationalist movements among its subjects and diplomatic interventions by the Great Powers on behalf of non-Muslim populations. These resource- and schema-level challenges prompted Ottoman ruling elites to promote a *Rechtsstaat* and generate the notion of citizenship among the population. These measures, known as *Tanzimat* reforms, fomented a constitutionalist opposition. Cemil Koçak, in "Transformation through Constitution: Young Ottomans and the *Kanun-i Esasi* of 1876", concentrates on the formation of the Young Ottoman movement, which fought for a constitutional regime and the opening of a parliament. Koçak shows that the Young Ottomans did not represent any significant social group within the empire. They were rather an outcome of a split within the existing ruling elite in terms of determining a political approach to saving the state and empire. Despite constitutionalist developments in 1876 and then in 1908, this elitist political direction manifested remarkable resilience at least until 1950.

The final contribution to this volume, Karl K. Barbir's "Repertories of Empire: How did the Ottomans Last so Long in a Changing World?", is a discussion of what possible factors and conditions enabled the Ottoman Empire to preserve its existence for so many centuries. According to Barbir, the Ottoman enterprise included certain features that allowed the empire to endure from the late medieval ages through to early modernity, reaching the twentieth century. These features incorporated the ability to deal with a diverse geography and a variety of ethno-religious populations by means of policies such as recognizing difference, letting local leaders administer their populations, and employing intermediaries; the impermanence of officeholding; varying and adaptable networks of governance enabled through relatively efficient communications between the centre and peripheral regions; and the ability to adjust its institutions in harmony with changing times and conditions.

## Bibliography

### Published Primary Sources

Ahmed Cevdet Pasha. *Târih-i Cevdet*, 12 vols. Istanbul 1271–1301/1855–84.

Kâtib Çelebi. *Düsturü'l-Amel fî Islâhi'l-Halel* (1653), first printed version in 1863 within Ayn-i Âlî's *Kavânin-i Âl-i Osmân* (Istanbul 1280), 119–40.

Mustafa Naîmâ. *Ravzatü'l-Hüseyn fi Hulasâti'l-Ahbâr el-Hafîkeyn*, also known as *Târih-i Naima* (1716), first printed version in Istanbul, Müteferrika Press, first two volumes in 1147/1734, the remaining part published between 1259/1843 and 1280/1863 by the Matbaa-i Âmire Press.

Yusuf Akçura. *Osmanlı Devletinin Dağılma Devri: XVIII ve XIX Asırlarda*. Ankara: TTK, 1940.

### Secondary Sources

Abou-El-Haj, Rifa'at 'Ali. *Formation of the Modern State: The Ottoman Empire, Sixteenth to Eighteenth Centuries*. Albany: State University of New York Press, 1991.

Adanır, Fikret and Suraiya Faroqhi. *The Ottomans and the Balkans: A Discussion of Historiography*. Leiden: Brill, 2002.

Akdağ, Mustafa. *Türkiye'nin İktisadi ve İçtimai Tarihi*, 2 vols. Ankara: TTK, 1959, 1971.

Akdağ, Mustafa. *Türk Halkının Dirlik ve Düzenlik Kavgası*. Ankara: Bilgi Yayınları, 1975.

el-Akhisarî, Mustafa bin Şemseddin. *Ahterî-i Kebîr*. Kostantiniyye (Istanbul): Darü't-Tıba'atü's-Sultâniye, 1256 AH/1840.

Aksan, Virginia. *Ottoman Wars, 1700–1870: An Empire Besieged*. Harlow: Longman/Pearson, 2007.

Anooshahr, Ali. *The Ghazi Sultans and the Frontiers of Islam: A Comparative Study of the Late Medieval and Early Modern Periods*. London: Routledge, 2009.

Barkan, Ömer Lütfi. *Türkiye'de Toprak Meselesi: Toplu Eserleri*. Istanbul: Gözlem Yayınları, 1980.

Barkey, Karen. *Empire of Difference: The Ottomans in Comparative Perspective*. Cambridge: Cambridge University Press, 2008.

Barkey, Karen and Mark von Hagen (eds) *After Empire. Multiethnic Societies and Nation-Building. The Soviet Union and the Russian, Ottoman, and Habsburg Empires*. Boulder CO: Westview Press, 1997.

Bartov, Omer and Eric D. Weitz (eds) *Shatterzone of Empires. Coexistence and Violence in the German, Habsburg, Russian, and Ottoman Borderlands*. Bloomington, IN: Indiana University Press, 2013.

Bayur, Yusuf Hikmet. *Türk İnkılabı Tarihi*. Vols 1–3. Ankara: TTK, 1940–1967.

Bentley, Michael. *Modern Historiography: An Introduction*. London: Routledge, 1999.

Berkes, Niyazi. *The Development of Secularism in Turkey*. Montreal: McGill University Press, 1964.

Brown, Lesley (ed.) *A New Shorter Oxford English Dictionary*, 2 vols. Oxford: Clarendon Press, 1993.

Carey, Daniel and Lynn Festa (eds) *The Postcolonial Enlightenment: Eighteenth-Century Colonialism and Postcolonial Theory*. Oxford: Oxford University Press, 2009.

Collingwood, R. G. *The Idea of History*. Oxford: Oxford University Press, 1980.

Dale, Stephen Frederic. *The Muslim Empires of the Ottomans, Safavids, and Mughals*. New York: Cambridge University Press, 2010.

Deringil, Selim. *The Well-Protected Domains: Ideology and the Legitimation of Power in the Ottoman Empire, 1876–1909*. London: I. B. Tauris, 1998.

Doumani, Beshara. *Rediscovering Palestine: Merchants and Peasants in Jabal Nablus, 1700–1900*. Berkeley: University of California Press, 1995.

Duindam, Jeroen. *Dynasties: A Global History of Power, 1300–1800*. Cambridge: Cambridge University Press, 2016.

Duindam, Jeroen, Tülay Artan and Metin Kunt (eds). *Royal Courts in Dynastic States and Empires: A Global Perspective*. Leiden: Brill, 2011.

Eisenstadt, S. M. *Modernization: Protest and Change*. Englewood Cliffs, NJ: Prentice-Hall, 1966.

Eisenstadt, S. M. *Revolution and the Transformation of Societies: A Comparative Study of Civilizations*. New York: Free Press, 1978.

Erdem, Y. Hakan. *Slavery in the Ottoman Empire and its Demise 1800–1909*. Basingstoke: Palgrave Macmillan, 1996.

Ermiş, Fatih. *A History of Ottoman Economic Thought: Developments Before the Nineteenth Century*. London: Routledge, 2014.

Faroqhi, Suraiya. "Empires Before and after the Postcolonial Turn: The Ottomans", *Osmanlı Araştırmaları: The Journal of Ottoman Studies*. Beyond Dominant Paradigms in Ottoman and Middle Eastern/North African Studies: A Tribute to Rifa'at Abou-El-Haj 36, 2010.

Findley, Carter V. *Ottoman Civil Officialdom: A Social History*. Princeton: Princeton University Press, 1989.

Ghosh, Oroon K. "Some Theories of Universal History", *Comparative Studies in Society and History* 7 (1) 1964, 1–20.

Handjéri, Alexandre. *Dictionnaire Français-Arabe-Persan et Turc*, 3 vols. Moscow: Imprimerie de l'Université Imperiale, 1840.

Hanna, Nelly. *Artisan Entrepreneurs in Cairo and Early-Modern Capitalism (1600–1800)*. Syracuse: Syracuse University Press, 2011.

Harris, Phil. "Machiavelli and the Global Compass: Ends and Means in Ethics and Leadership", *Journal of Business Ethics* 93 (1) 2010, 131–138.

Hobsbawm, Eric. *The Age of Revolution: Europe 1789–1848*. London: Abacus, 1962.

Hobsbawm, Eric. *The Age of Capital: 1848–1875*. London: Weidenfeld & Nicolson, 1975.

Hobsbawm, Eric. *The Age of Empire: 1875–1914*. London: Weidenfeld & Nicolson, 1987.

Huntington, Samuel P. *Political Order in Changing Societies*. New Haven: Yale University Press, 1968.

İnalcık, Halil. "Centralization and Decentralization in Ottoman Administration", in Thomas Naff and Roger Owen (eds) *Studies in Eighteenth Century Islamic History*. London: Papers on Islamic History, 1977.

İnalcık, Halil. "Military and Fiscal Transformation in the Ottoman Empire, 1600–1700", *Archivum Ottomanicum* 6, 1980, 283–337.

İnalcık, Halil. *The Ottoman Empire: The Classical Age 1300–1600*, translated by Norman Itzkowitz and Colin Imber. New Rochelle, NY: Orpheus Publishing, 1989.

İnalcık, Halil. "State and Ideology under Sultan Süleyman I", in Halil İnalcık, *The Middle East and the Balkans under the Ottoman Empire: Essays on Economy and Society* (Bloomington, IN: Indiana University Turkish Studies and Turkish Ministry of Culture Series, 1993), 70–94.

İnalcık, Halil and Donald Quataert (eds). *An Economic and Social History of the Ottoman Empire 1300–1914*. Cambridge: Cambridge University Press, 1994.

Kafadar, Cemal. *Between two Worlds: The Construction of the Ottoman State*. Berkeley: University of California Press, 1995.

Kalpakian, Jack. "Ibn Khaldun's Influence on Current International Relations Theory", *Journal of North African Studies* 13 (3) 2008, 357–70.

Karal, Enver Ziya. *Osmanlı Tarihi*. Vols 5–9. Ankara: TTK, 1947–1996.

Klein, Judy L. "The Rise of 'Non-October' Econometrics: Kondratiev and Slutsky at the Moscow Conjoncture Institute", *History of Political Economy* 31 (1) Spring 1999, 137–68.

Köprülü, M. Fuad. *Bizans Müesseselerinin Osmanlı Müesseselerine Tesiri*, 9th edn. Istanbul: Alfa Tarih, 2014.

Köprülü, M. Fuad. *Türk Edebiyatında İlk Mutasavvıflar*, 4th edn. Istanbul: Alfa Tarih, 2014.

Kruskal, Joseph B. "Statistical Analysis: Transformations of Data", in David L. Sills (ed.) *International Encyclopedia of the Social Sciences*, vol. 15. New York: Macmillan, 1968.

Kutluer, İlhan. "Fesad," *DIA*, vol. 12. Istanbul, 1995.

Lewis, Bernard. *The Emergence of Modern Turkey*, 2nd edn. London: Oxford University Press, 1968.

Lieven, Dominic. *Empire: Russian Empire and its Rivals*. New Haven: Yale University Press, 2001.

Lowry, Heath W. *The Nature of the Early Ottoman State*. Albany: State University of New York Press, 2003.

Maksudyan, Nazan. *Orphans and Destitute Children in the Late Ottoman Empire*. Syracuse, NY: Syracuse University Press, 2014.

Merriam-Webster Inc. *Merriam-Webster's Collegiate Dictionary*, 10th edition. Springfield, MA: Merriam-Webster, Incorporated, 1998.

Mikhail, Alan and Christine M. Philliou. "The Ottoman Empire and the Imperial Turn", *Comparative Studies in Society and History* 54 (4) October 2012, 721–45.

Moore, Barrington, Jr. *Social Origins of Dictatorship and Democracy: Lord and Peasant in the Making of the Modern World* (Boston, MA: Beacon Press, 1966).

Moore, Wilbert E. "Social Change", in David L. Sills (ed.) *International Encyclopedia of the Social Sciences*, vol. 14, New York: Macmillan, 1968.

Morishima, M. and G. Catephores. "Is There a Historical Transformation Problem?" *The Economic Journal*, 85 (338) 309–28. June 1975.

Muallim Naci. *Lugat-i Naci*, 4th edition. Istanbul: Asır Matbaası, 1322 AH/1905.

Mütercim Asım. *Kamusu'l-Muhît Tercümesi*, edited by Mustafa Koç and Eyyüp Tanrıverdi, vol. 2. Istanbul: TYEKBY, 2013.

Ogburn, William F. "Change, Social", in Edwin R. A. Seligman and Alvin Johnson (eds) *Encyclopaedia of the Social Sciences*, vol. 3. New York: The Macmillan Company, 1948.

Özel, Oktay. *Dün Sancısı: Türkiye'de Geçmiş Algısı ve Akademik Tarihçilik*. Istanbul: Kitap Yayınevi, 2009.

Özel, Oktay and Gökhan Çetinsaya. "Türkiye'de Osmanlı tarihçiliğinin son çeyrek yüzyılı: Bir bilanço denemesi", *Toplum ve Bilim* 91 (Kış 2001/2002), 8–38.

Peirce, Leslie P. *Morality Tales: Law and Gender in the Ottoman Court of Aintab*. Berkeley: University of California Press, 2003.

Philliou, Christine. "The Paradox of Perceptions: Interpreting the Ottoman Past through the National Present", *Middle Eastern Studies* 44, 2008, 661–75.

Polanyi, Karl. *The Great Transformation: The Political and Economic Origins of Our Time*. Boston: Beacon Press, 2001.

Redhouse, Sir James W. *Redhouse Sözlüğü: Türkçe/Osmanlıca İngilizce*. Edited by U. Bahadır Alkım, Sofi Huri, Andreas Tietze et al. Istanbul: Redhouse Yayınevi, 1999.

Redhouse, Sir James W. *A Turkish and English Lexicon*. Istanbul: Çağrı Yayınları, 2001 [reprint of 1890 edition].

Riad, Sally and Deborah Jones, "Invoking *Black Athena* and its Debates: Insights for Organization on Diversity, Race and Culture", *Journal of Management History* 19 (3) 2013, 394–415.

Ruspini, Elisabetta. "Social Change", in Jonathan Michie (ed.) *Reader's Guide to the Social Sciences*, vol. 2. London/Chicago: Fitzroy Dearborn Publishers, 2001.

Said, Edward. *Orientalism*. New York: Pantheon Books, 1978.

Sariyannis, Marinos (with a chapter by Ekin Tuşalp Atiyas). *Ottoman Political Thought up to the Tanzimat: A Concise History*. Rethymno: Foundation for Research and Technology-Hellas, Institute for Mediterranean Studies, 2015.

Sariyannis, Marinos. *A History of Ottoman Political Thought Up to the Early Nineteenth Century*. Leiden: Brill, 2019.

Şemseddin Sami. *Kamus-i Türkî*. Dersaadet: İkdam Matbaası, 1317 AH/1899–1900.

Şemseddin Sami. *Kamus-ı Fransevî: Dictionnaire Français-Turc*, 4th edition. Istanbul: Mihran Matbaası, 1322 AH/1905.

Sewell, William H. Jr. *Logics of History: Social Theory and Social Transformation*. Chicago: University of Chicago Press, 2005.

Skocpol, Theda. *States and Social Revolutions: A Comparative Analysis of France, Russia, and China*. Cambridge: Cambridge University Press, 1979.

Streusand, Douglas E. *Islamic Gunpowder Empires: Ottomans, Safavids, and Mughals*. Boulder, CO: Westview Press, 2011.

Stuurman, Siep. "Herodotus and Sima Qian: History and the Anthropological Turn in Ancient Greece and Han China", *Journal of World History* 19 (1) 2008, 1–40.

Subrahmanyam, Sanjay. "Mughals, Ottomans and Habsburgs: Some Comparisons", in Sanjay Subrahmanyam. *Empires Between Islam and Christianity 1500–1800*. Albany, NY: State University of New York Press, 149–85.

Sullivan, Vickie B. *Machiavelli, Hobbes, and the Formation of a Liberal Republicanism in England*. Cambridge, UK: Cambridge University Press, 2004.

Taylor, Benedict. "Temporality in Nineteenth-Century Russian Music and the Notion of Development", *Music and Letters* 94 (1) 2013, 78–118.

Tezcan, Baki. *The Second Ottoman Empire: Political and Social Transformation in the Early Modern World*. New York: Cambridge University Press, 2012.

Thompson, Della (ed.) *The Concise Oxford Dictionary of Current English*, 9th edition. Oxford: Clarendon Press, 1995.

Trautmann, Thomas R. "Does India Have History? Does History Have India?" *Comparative Studies in Society and History* 54 (1) 2012, 174–205.

Turhan, Kasım. "Kevn ve Fesad", *Türkiye Diyanet Vakfı İslam Ansiklopedisi*, vol. 25, Istanbul, 2002.

Tuşalp-Atiyas, E. Ekin. "The 'Sunna-Minded' Trend," in Marinos Sariyannis (ed.), *A History of Ottoman Political Thought up to the Early Nineteenth Century*, 233–78. Leiden: Brill, 2019.

Uludağ, Süleyman. "Kevn", *DIA*, vol. 25. Istanbul, 2002.

Uzunçarşılı, İsmail Hakkı. *Osmanlı Tarihi*. Vols 1–4. Ankara: TTK, 1947–1959.

Van Seters, John. *In Search of History: Historiography in the Ancient World and the Origins of Biblical History*. Reprint. Winona Lake, Indiana: Eisenbrauns, 1997.

Wallerstein, Immanuel. *The Modern World System*. 4 vols. Cambridge, MA: Academic Press 1974, 1980, 1989/Berkeley and Los Angeles: University of California Press, 2011.

Withers, Charles W. J. *Placing the Enlightenment: Thinking Geographically about the Age of Reason*. Chicago: University of Chicago Press, 2007.

Wittek, Paul. *The Rise of Ottoman Empire: Studies in the History of Turkey, Thirteenth–Fifteenth Centuries*. London: Royal Asiatic Society, 1938.

Yılmaz, Şuhnaz and İpek Yosmaoğlu, "Fighting the Spectres of the Past: Dilemmas of Ottoman Legacy in the Balkans and the Middle East", *Middle Eastern Studies* 44 (2008), 677–93.

Young, Robert J. C. *Postcolonialism: A Very Short Introduction.* Oxford: Blackwell, 2001.

Zenker, Julius Theodor. *Türkisch – Arabisch – Persisches Handwörterbuch*, 2 vols. Leipzig: Verlag von Wilhelm Engelmann, 1866.

Zgurovsky, M. Z. "Metric Aspects of Periodic Processes in Economy and Society", *Cybernetics and Systems Analysis* 46 (2) 2010, 167–72.

# PART 1

*Ottoman Historiography and Reflections*

CHAPTER 1

# A Firman Issued by Mustafa the Son of Bayezid I Surnamed Düzme (1422)

*Elizabeth A. Zachariadou*

The historian and linguist Evangelos Mpogkas tried to attract the interest of his contemporary scholars, especially those specializing in the history of Epirus, to a small sheet of paper on each surface of which a note was written.[1] This small sheet of paper is supposed to have its own story. The well-known amateur scholar B. D. Zotos (d.1912)[2] copied on it a short text from 'a book' belonging to the Monastery of Droviani situated in the south of Albania. The text was an agreement[3] concluded in July 1456 between the monks of the monastery and the *tımâr* holders of the neighbouring countryside. The fact would not necessarily deserve a special mention. At first sight at least an agreement of this kind was not unusual: the monks undertook the obligation to give some money and some agricultural produce every year to the *tımâr* holders in exchange for some benefits. As for Zotos's interest, he was notorious for his passion for collecting material concerning the historical past of Epirus; he was born in Droviani, a town with a good reputation for its schools,[4] and he certainly was

---

1 Evangelos Mpogkas, "Δύο ιστορικά ενθυμήματα του ΙΕ′αιώνος εκ Βορείου Ηπείρου", *Deltion Historikis kai Ethnologikis Hetereias tis Hellados* 13 (1959), 429–30.
2 B. D. Zotos composed several interesting historical and geographical studies of Epirus but not in a scholarly way; it seems that nobody has attempted a study of his life and work. Leandros I. Vranoussis, *Χρονικά της Μεσαιωνικής και Τουρκοκρατουμένης Ηπείρου* (Ioannina: Etaireia Ipeirotikon Meleton, 1962), 124–30, provides some information about Zotos's writings, but only in connection with the chronicles of Epirus.
3 According to Zotos, it was 'a treaty'. Most probably, Zotos had in mind the term *ahdname* which acquired various meanings, including agreement or pledge: Antonis Anastasopoulos, "Political Participation, Public Order, and Monetary Pledges (*Nezir*) in Ottoman Crete", in Eleni Gara et al. (eds) *Popular Protest and Political Participation in the Ottoman Empire, Studies in Honor of Suraiya Faroqhi* (eds) (Istanbul: İstanbul Bilgi Üniversitesi Yayınları, 2011), 128 fn.4.
4 Droviani is situated in the region of Delvinon (present-day Albania); it might be identified with Zuvyani, a village in the *vilâyet* of Argyrokastron, which is mentioned in the Ottoman land-census of Albania. See Halil İnalcık, *Hicrî 835 Tarihli Sûret-i Defter-i Sancak-i Arvanid* (Ankara: TTK, 1954), 2. Droviani flourished in the eighteenth and nineteenth centuries and is repeatedly mentioned as a town *philomousos*, 'loving the Muses', that is the arts, by the scholar P. Aravantinos (d.1870). See Panayiotis Aravantinos, *Βιογραφική Συλλογή Λογίων*

welcomed to the monastery in order to study the old books preserved in it. As we learn from Mpogkas's explanations, Zotos thought that the agreement was worth some attention and he sent a copy of it to Mr G. Gagari to publish it, presumably with the addition of some comments, in his Ioannina weekly newspaper of *The Voice of Epirus*. Mr G. Gagari never published Zotos's text for unknown reasons; but presumably this is the same text that was published by Mpogkas in 1959.[5]

The text written on the reverse side of the small sheet of paper is in my opinion much more interesting than the obverse. According to its first line it is a copy of a firman and, according to its date, was issued in March 1422.[6] The ruler who issued it was Mustafa the son of Bayezid – apparently the one who has passed into history as *Düzme*. The purpose of this piece is to study this firman in order to understand if it is really a firman issued by this Ottoman prince and then to collect information from its contents.

Documents issued by the early Ottoman lords are rare and therefore provoke the interest of historians. On the other hand, they often become discouraging as they present various difficulties because the early Ottoman chancery had not yet clearly established its own vocabulary and its rules in general while spelling was often casual.[7] The difficulties are of course multiplied when one has to deal with the copy of an original document and even more so when one has to deal with the translation of an original but lost document. In short, every early Ottoman document includes information which is most fascinating for an Ottomanist, but it first demands an introductory study in order to make sure that it is trustworthy.[8]

To begin with our document: most unfortunately very little is known about the fate of the copy of the original firman published by Mpogkas who did not write where he saw the copy, which he finally published, or where it could be found. Leandros Vranoussis who studied the matter suggested that the first copy perhaps is still in the Monastery of Droviani but he added that a copy probably made by Zotos was misplaced in the General Archives of Greece,

---

της Τουρκοκρατίας, edited K.Th. Dimaras (Ioannina: Ekdosis EHM, 1960). It belongs to the Greek-speaking zone of south Albania. For this, see Michalis Kokolakis, *Το Ύστερο Γιαννιωτικο Πασαλίκι* (Athens: Centre of Modern Greek Studies, EIE, 2003), 49–52.

5 Mpogas, "Δύο ιστορικά", 429–30.
6 The date of the document will be discussed at length.
7 The use of the Arabic alphabet for the Turkish language always involves difficulties in deciphering texts.
8 In recent decades a spirit of disbelief has been in the air with respect to the early Ottoman documents that are supposed to be mostly untrustworthy or fake; this spirit has not yet touched me.

where he himself found it; he also pointed out that its text shows some differences from the text published by Mpogkas; anyhow the script is that of the end of the nineteenth century.[9] Unfortunately, I have been unable to see it.

In the first line of the document under study one reads that it is a copy of a sultanic firman written in Greek. This does not answer our questions as to who was the copyist and where the original could be found.[10] At first glance one could accept that the firman was written in Greek because in the early years of the Ottoman state the Greek language was used by the sultanic chancery. Nevertheless, this occurred only in the correspondences with Western European states or when the sultans addressed their Greek Orthodox subjects to arrange matters with them.[11] But, in the present case, there was no possible reason for the sultan to write to a *kadı* in Greek. In addition to that, an odd expression in the Greek text reveals that we have to deal with a translation from Turkish into Greek. The expression occurs in the *narration* of the firman where, as usual, it is stated that the sultan is responding to a request of a petitioner who has submitted an *arzuhal* to him. However, according to our text, the petitioner "threw an *arzuhal*"[12] to the sultan. Neither in Greek nor in Turkish does this expression make any sense. The only possible explanation is that the translator misunderstood the stereotypical expression *arzuhal etdi* written in the Turkish original. More precisely, in old Ottoman texts the verb *etdi* (he made) is often written *atdı* (he threw), that is with the omission of

---

9    Vranoussis, *Χρονικά της Μεσαιωνικής*, 176–7 fn.1.
10   The firman under study is laconically mentioned by Peter Soustal, *Nicopolis und Kephallenia, Tabula Imperii Byzantini 3* (Vienna: Verlag der österreichischen Akademie der Wissenschaften, 1981), 165; Soustal mentions it in the entry regarding the Monastery of Ioannes Theologos. A less important mention of the firman has been made by Dimitris Salamagkas, "Στα πρώτα χρόνια της τουρκοκρατίας", *Epirotiki Estia*, 8 (1959), 353–6.
11   The old article by Spyridon Lampros, "Η ελληνική ως επίσημος γλώσσα των σουλτάνων", *Neos Hellenomnemon*, 5 (1908), 40–78, is still valuable; Nicholas Vatin, "L'emploi du grec comme langue diplomatique par les Ottomans (fin du XVe–début du XVIe siècle)", *Istanbul et les langues Orientales, Varia Turca*, edited by F. Hitzel (Istanbul: IFEA, 1997), 41–7; Elizabeth A. Zachariadou, *Trade and Crusade, Venetian Crete and the Emirates of Menteshe and Aydin (1300–1415)* (Venice: Hellenic Institute of Byzantine and Post-Byzantine Studies, 1983), 185–6. See also Mehemmed II's firman of the year 1451 to the authorities of Mount Athos at Stéphane Binon, *Les origines légendaires et l' histoire de Xéropotamou et de Saint-Paul de l'Athos* (Louvain: Bureaux du Muséon, 1942), 295–8. An earlier Ottoman document written in Greek and issued by Bayezid I has been also preserved in the Athonite Monastery of St Paul; unfortunately it is in a very bad condition and very little can be understood from its content. See K. Chrysochoidis, "Ιερά Μονή Αγίου Παύλου. Κατάλογος του Αρχείου", *Symmeikta*, 4 (1981), 279.
12   In Greek: έριξε αρτσιχάλι στη βασιλεία μου.

the letter *ye*, which follows the initial *alif*.[13] The omission of the letter *ye* could certainly produce some misunderstanding because *atmak* means to throw but the old scribes were used to this spelling. However, if one is finicky and sticks to a literal translation, as seems to be the case with our unknown translator, one may commit this unusual mistake, which, nevertheless, helps us to conclude that the initial document, today apparently lost, was in Turkish. Therefore, we can conclude that we have to deal with a copy of a Turkish document translated in Greek.

1      Translation of the Document

A copy of a firman of the Sultan written in Greek.

Command to the kadı of Delvinon. You must know that the Abbot of Theologos, who is mentioned in the firman, presented a petition to my sultanic court and he made a statement of his present situation: from the time of my father who left it as a testament,[14] outside the church[15] in the border[16] of Theologos certain people, who have nothing to do with the borders of it, come and cross the borders in order to take possession of it.[17] These people were earlier judged by the law court of Delvinon and their claim[18] was put aside.

In the same way you must take into consideration the judgment made by the previous kadı and you must not favour anybody and the trial

---

13   Cf. especially the entry *etmek* in J. Th. Zenker, *Türkisch-Arabisch-Persisches Handwörterbuch*, (Leipzig: Verlag von Wilhelm Engelmann, 1866. Reprinted Hildesheim: Georg Olms, 1979), 141, where several varieties of the spelling are listed.
14   In the Greek text βασιέτι, which is *vasiyet*.
15   In our text one reads church (εκκλησία) instead of monastery; as shown by documents of this historical period the Ottomans used the two terms alternatively; cf. Elizabeth A. Zachariadou, "Early Ottoman Documents of the Prodromos Monastery (Serres)", *Südost-Forschungen* 28 (1969) 5 fn.27.
16   The word σύνορον of our Greek text was certainly *sinur* in the original text, that is the Greek term σύνορον which was adopted by the Ottomans and was transformed in *sinur* according to old Turkish phonetics. The term *sinur* is often used in monastic documents in the Greek lands and according to dictionaries it means border or limit; however, it also means the land itself included within a *sinur*.
17   να το κάμουν ζάπτι is a literal translation of the Turkish expression *zabt etmek*. In our text it is followed by an additional explanation ιδικόν τους να το εξουσιάσουν. This explanation undoubtedly does not belong to the original Turkish text but was added by the Greek translator who wished to make his text absolutely clear.
18   νταβάς that is the Greek transcription of the Turkish (Arabic) *dava*.

must be carried out according to the truth and you must command that nobody can cross the border of the monastery. This is all you must know and act according to my command.

Mustafa son of Sultan Bayezid
Edirne year 825 rebîülâhir 1 first.19
Adrianoupolis 1409 month of June.20

## 2    Commentary

Two general remarks can be made. The first is that the customary expressions, or more accurately the invocations of God and his attributes, which follow the mention of a sultan dead or alive (for example, *a'azza 'llahu ansarahu*), or of a *kadı* (for example, his *elkab* and the following *dua*), or of several other important figures, are missing from the text of the document. This occurs fairly frequently in Greek translations of Ottoman documents; it seems that the translators found it difficult to translate them, probably as such expressions were written in Arabic, and consequently they omitted them; after all, such omissions did not affect the meaning of the documents.[21]

The second remark is about the category to which the document belongs. Its contents state clearly that the abbot (*hegoumenos*) of a monastery asked the sultan to confirm a previous court decision regarding its properties, which were in danger from aggressive unnamed individuals, who most probably were neighbours. In other words, the case had been already examined by the sharia court of Delvinon (Ottoman Turkish Delvine, present-day Delvinë, Albania) and a decision had been issued; the abbot asked for the confirmation of it. Therefore, our document can be classified as a *mukarrernâme*, that is a confirmation of properties and privileges.[22]

The sultan addressed the *kadı* of Delvinon with this firman and the presence of a *kadı* there around 1422 needs some comment. In the well-known *defter* of the land census of 1431–32, Delvinon is mentioned as a village of sixty houses in the *nahiye* of Vagenetia and it remained attached to that *nahiye* at least up to

---

19   πρώτη in the Greek text which will be examined together with the date of the document.
20   The date of the document will be examined in detail.
21   Zachariadou, "Early Ottoman documents", 4 fn.14.
22   The term, although not mentioned in the surviving form of our document, occurs within documents of that historical period; see Paul Wittek, "Zu einigen frühosmanischen Urkunden", part II in V. L. Ménage (ed.) *La formation de l'Empire ottoman* (London: Variorum Reprints, 1982), 245[20] and 247[22].

the end of the fifteenth century.[23] Thanks to some sources, the most trustworthy and also most lively of them being the anonymous Chronicle of the Tocco, we know the circumstances under which this region passed under Ottoman rule. In 1418, the lord of Argyrokastron (Ottoman Turkish Ergiri, present-day Gjirokastër, Albania) Gjin Zenevessi, who was a vassal of the Ottomans, died and his senior son Simon was supposed to succeed him. The Ottomans, lords of the port of Avlona (present-day Vlorë, Albania) since 1417, objected to this arrangement and profited from the circumstances concomitant with a succession; Hamza, the brother of the *uç beği* (frontier lord) of Üsküb (present-day Skopje, Macedonia) Pasha Yiğit, invaded the territories of Zenevessi and laid siege to Argyrokastron. Finally, Zenevessi's son gave up any resistance; he surrendered Argyrokastron and all his other possessions to the Ottomans and then moved to the island of Corfu.[24] After this military victory, the Ottomans obviously tried to organize their newly conquered territories and the appointment of a *kadı* in Delvinon was probably one of their first measures. Nonetheless one must not preclude the hypothesis that a *kadı* was established in Delvinon from the time when it still constituted a territory vassal to the Ottoman sultan.[25]

As already mentioned the *kadı* of Delvinon was commanded by the Sultan to protect the Monastery of the Theologos against individuals who penetrated its properties with the intention of occupying them. The monastery, mentioned in the firman just as the Monastery of the Theologos, must be the one dedicated to Saint John the Theologos, situated in the region of Delvinon, one of the most famous monastic foundations in Epirus, perhaps established as early as the seventh century.[26] It was also known as the Monastery of Droviani.

To summarize now: we have to deal with an Ottoman document translated into Greek with some purposely made omissions, which is addressed to the

---

23   Ömer L. Barkan, "894 (1488/1489) yılı Cizyesinin Tahsilâtına âit Muhâsebe Bilânçoları", *Belgeler* 1 (1964), 96; İnalcık, *Sûret-i Defter-i Sancak*, 12.
24   On these events, see Giuseppe Schirò, *Cronaca dei Tocco di Cefalonia di Anonimo* (Rome: Accademia Nazionale dei Lincei, 1975), 456–67; cf. P. Schreiner, *Die Byzantinischen Kleinchroniken*, vol. 1 (Vienna: CFHB, 1975), 452; Kenneth Meyer Setton, *The Papacy and the Levant, (1204–1571)*, vol. 1 (Philadelphia: American Philosophical Society, 1976), 404; Elizabeth A. Zachariadou, "Marginalia on the History of Epirus and Albania (1380–1418)", *Wiener Zeitschrift für die Kunde des Morgenlandes* 78 (1988), 209–10. According to the chronicle of Tocco, published by Schiro at *Cronaca*, 456, the Ottomans overran Dernopolis, that is Dryinoupolis, the ecclesiastical bishopric (*episkopi*) in which Delvinon was included: see Soustal, *Nicopolis und Kephallenia*, 139, 146–8.
25   Halil İnalcık, "Ottoman methods of conquest", *Studia Islamica* 2 (1954), 103–4.
26   B. Mparas, *Τὸ Δέλβινο τῆς Βορείου Ηπείρου καὶ οἱ γειτονικές του περιοχές*, edited by L. I. Vranoussis (Athens: Paramithias, 1966), 200–3, 321–2; Soustal, *Nicopolis und Kephallenia*, 165; Vranoussis, *Χρονικά τῆς Μεσαιωνικῆς*, 174–7.

*kadı* of Delvinon in order that he should take care of problems related to a venerable monastery situated inside his jurisdiction. Hundreds of documents of this kind have been preserved in the monastic archives of the Balkans as the monks were eager to keep their immovable possessions while they rightly considered themselves to be under the protection of the sultan. However, our document deserves some special attention because, as I wrote at the beginning of this piece, the ruler who issued it was Mustafa the son of Bayezid I, apparently the one nicknamed *Düzme*. His name followed by that of his father is written at the end of the text of the document, after the usual *corroboration*[27] and before the place of issue and the date. It is certainly well known that the name of an Ottoman lord issuing an order was never written at the end of the document, but it was included in his *tuğra* or his *pençe* at the top of the text. It is permissible to guess that the translator or the copyist of the original document took the initiative of writing the name in the place where it would have been written according to the Byzantine and in general to the European principles of chancellery. Furthermore, we can suppose that the scribe who made the translation from the original document did not necessarily decipher the *tuğra*.[28] He could have read Mustafa's name on the verso of the document: historians who have worked in archives preserved in Greek Orthodox monasteries are familiar with notes on the verso of documents written by monks who when classifying Ottoman documents used to write in Greek letters names or dates related to them.[29]

Mustafa passed into history as a controversial figure who led an active life during the chaotic period following the battle of Ankara.[30] Rumours circulated that he was not a son of Sultan Bayezid I but just an opportunistic impostor aiming to seize the Ottoman throne; these rumours, encouraged by members of the sultanic family, finally prevailed. No effort will be made here to solve the problem of Mustafa's paternity. Anyhow, it is certain that his attitudes caused considerable trouble to both the Ottomans and the Byzantines. The latter in a

---

27   In our document Ἔτσι να ξέρης και καθώς προστάζω να κάμης, which corresponds to the usual Ottoman expression şöyle bilesin mektube mütalea kılasın.

28   On the *tuğra* of Mustafa, see Wittek, "Zu einigen frühosmanischen Urkunden", (III) 135–7 [45–7]. Wittek relied on a copy of an original document issued by Mustafa.

29   Elizabeth A. Zachariadou, "Remarques sur les Notes au Verso des Documents ottomans de Patmos", *Les Archives de l'Insularité ottomane*. Documents de travail du CETOBAC, no 1 (January 2010), 10–12 (pdf document retrieved from http://cetobac.ehess.fr/docannexe/file/1353/les_archives_de_l_insularite_ottomane.pdf, accessed 5 May 2017).

30   The events of this crucial period for the Ottomans and the Byzantines in which several foreign powers were also involved, are fairly clearly known up to 1415 thanks to the book of Dimitris J. Kastritsis, *The Sons of Bayezid Empire Building and Representation in the Ottoman Civil War of 1402–13* (Leiden: Brill, 2007).

vain hope tried to use him for a while in order to break up the reunification of the Ottoman territories achieved by Mehmed I in 1413. C. Heywood rendered Mustafa's adventurous life comprehensible by publishing a special article.[31] Recently, T. Ganchou rewrote the story of Mustafa using new material found during the approximately twenty years that had elapsed since Heywood's article.[32]

One can distinguish three different periods in Mustafa's life. The first period begins before the battle of Ankara, when Mustafa was probably *sancak beği* of Hamid and Teke, and it ends with his return to Asia Minor from Samarkand, where he was taken captive by Timur. According to a document edited by Wittek, Mustafa was in Koca-ili (in Bithynia) from where he issued a *nişan* in 1405 concerning a *tımâr*; but Wittek had second thoughts later and placed the document in the year 1415.[33] I shall safely ignore the events of Mustafa's life during this early period because they are confused and anyhow irrelevant to the purpose of the present study.

The second period began in 1413,[34] that is when Mehmed I achieved supremacy over the Ottoman state after having eliminated his brother Musa Çelebi. At that point Mustafa reappeared on the scene with a claim to the Ottoman throne and with the support of the Wallachian voivode Mircea, of the Turkish independent lords of Anatolia – especially that of Cüneyd Bey of Smyrna – and of the Byzantines; all of them had become anxious as they watched the stabilization of the Ottoman power. The year 1416 was very agitated: the revolt against Mehmed I led by Şeyh Bedreddin is most probably bound up with Mustafa's activities;[35] the Venetians profited from the situation by destroying the Ottoman fleet at Gelibolu at the end of May.[36] Despite these events and others, which at first glance at least seemed to favour Mustafa, his attempt to ascend the throne failed and he himself, having been defeated near Thessaloniki, was finally forced to take refuge with the Byzantine emperor; he remained in Byzantine custody on Lemnos, in Mystras (Peloponnese) and perhaps elsewhere for some years.

---

31   Colin J. Heywood, "Mustafa Čelebi Düzme", EI2 (1993), 710–13.
32   Thierry Ganchou, "Zampia Palaiologina Doria, Epouse du Prétendant ottoman Mustafa", in E. Malamut and A. Nicolaides (eds), Impératrices, Princesses, Aristocrates et Saintes souveraines: De l'Orient chrétien et musulman au Moyen Âge et au Début des Temps modernes (Aix-en-Provence: Presses Universitaires de Provence, 2014), 133–69, mainly 139–52.
33   Wittek, "Zu einigen frühosmanischen Urkunden", (III) 135–8 [45–8] and (IV) 271[56].
34   Ganchou, "Zampia Palaiologina Doria", 141–5.
35   Heywood, "Mustafa Čelebi Düzme", 711.
36   Setton, *The Papacy and the Levant*, vol. 2 (Philadelphia 1978), 7–8.

The third period of Mustafa's life began after the death of Sultan Mehmed I, which most probably occurred on 21 May 1421. Problems of succession occurred immediately with Mustafa released by the Byzantines to succeed his brother Mehmed against his nephew Murad II. Once again, various states of the Aegean and the Balkans were involved. It is worth underlining the participation of the Genoese of New Phokaia, which was decisive as it was they who transferred Murad's army from Asia Minor to Thrace. The sequence of events that followed is already convincingly established[37] and it would be unnecessary to repeat them here. However, I must recall some dates related to the date of the firman under study.

As early as August/September of 1421, Mustafa arrived from Mystras to Gelibolu with the help of the Byzantines.[38] After establishing his power in Gelibolu and ignoring the Byzantines, he reached Edirne, the Ottoman capital in Europe, where he was enthusiastically recognized as the new sultan by the Ottoman militaries. At the beginning of 1422, Mustafa set off for an ill-fated campaign against his rival and enemy Murad, who was still in Asia Minor. Abandoned there by his ally Cüneyd of Smyrna, Mustafa crossed back to Thrace persecuted by Murad who transported his soldiers to near Gelibolu on 15 January 1422; Mustafa somehow managed to retreat to the palace (*saray*) of Edirne.

Confusion prevails about the events that followed. All the sources state clearly that Mustafa was captured by the soldiers of Murad and executed publicly by hanging in Edirne like a common criminal; but when? The sources mention several places to answer the question as to where Mustafa was arrested: on Mount Ganos (present-day Işıklar Dağı, close to Tekirdağ), in Yenice Kızıl Ağaç (a location on his way to Wallachia), or near a shore of the Danube or perhaps in Eski (present-day Babaeski) in Thrace.[39] In contrast with the perplexing answers to the question of where he was caught, no source states clearly the date of his execution. According to the chronicler Sphrantzes, he was executed

---

37   See Ganchou, "Zampia Palaiologina Doria", 147–9; Heywood, "Mustafa Čelebi Düzme", 711; cf. also Elizabeth A. Zachariadou, "Ottoman Diplomacy and the Danube Frontier (1420–1424)", in C. Mango, O. Pritsak and U. M. Pasicznyk (eds) *Okeanos: Essays Presented to Ihor Ševčenko on his Sixtieth Birthday by his Colleagues and Students* (Cambridge, MA: HUP, 1984), 686–9. Ovidiu Cristea remarked that this article "has been all but ignored in Romanian historiography despite some important conclusions". See O. Cristea, "The Friend of my Friend and the Enemy of my Enemy: Rumanian Participation in Ottoman Campaigns", in G. Kármán and L. Kunčević (eds), *The European Tributary States of the Ottoman Empire in the Sixteenth and Seventeenth Centuries* (Leiden: Brill, 2013), 257 fn.16.
38   Ganchou, "Zampia Palaiologina Doria", 148 fn.38.
39   Halil İnalcık and Mevlûd Oğuz (eds), *Gazavât-ı Sultân Murâd b. Mehemmed Hân* (Ankara: TTK, 1978), 13; Heywood, "Mustafa Čelebi Düzme", 711.

at the beginning of the year 6930, which would mean September 1421; however, it is not certain that Sphrantzes writing in the fifteenth century kept to the principal that an *annus mundi* begins in September of the previous year *annus domini*; perhaps Sphrantzes meant September 1422.[40] According to Chalkokandylas, Mustafa was executed after a reign of three years in Europe, but it is hard to understand how Chalkokandylas made this calculation, which makes the reign of Mustafa considerably longer.[41] According to the close observer, Dukas, who at that time was in the service of the Genoese of New Phokaia, Murad ascended the throne at the beginning of winter, presumably of the year 1422.[42] This sounds unlikely because Murad laid a siege to Constantinople, which lasted from June to September 1422 and one would think that he decided to begin this operation after having got rid of his troublesome uncle. Mustafa struck silver *akçe*s in Edirne and in Serres in AH 822 (1419–20), and later in AH 824 (1421–22); but these dates are not helpful in fixing the date of his demise.[43]

Ganchou meticulously re-examined all the sources, especially the Short Chronicles and the known diplomatic correspondence of that time, and he wrote with good reason that the dates mentioned in them are not always reliable; he wrote that he found it frustrating that the date of such an important event could not be fixed; but he finally guessed that Mustafa's execution took place around February of 1422.[44]

It is now necessary to examine the date of our document, but I must first recall that the Ottomans adopted the Arabic vocabulary for the reckoning of time in their calendars. Actually, there are two dates in our document; the first gives an Islamic year and also a month with a date of the Islamic calendar; the second is in Greek, it still mentions the Ottoman capital as Adrianople, and gives as the date the month of June 1409. According to Mpogkas, the second

---

40  Georgios Sphrantzes, *Memorii 1401–1477*, edited by V. Grecu (Bucharest: Academy of the Romanian People's Republic, 1966), 14. The Byzantines of the Palaeologan period had at least one different chronological system. For this, see Elizabeth A. Zachariadou, "The Conquest of Adrianople by the Turks", part XII in *Romania and the Turks (c.1300–c.1500)* (London: Variorum Reprints, 1985), 217.

41  Laonici Chalcocandylae, *Historiarum Demonstrationes*, vol. 2, edited by E. Darkó (Budapest: Academia Litterarum Hungarica, 1922), 7.

42  Ducas, *Historia Turcobyzantina (1341–1462)*, edited by V. Grecu (Bucharest: Academy of the Romanian People's Republic, 1958), 229.

43  Heywood, "Mustafa Čelebi Düzme", 712; idem, "824/'8224' = 1421: The 'False' (Düzme) Mustafa and his Ephimeral Coinage", in Abdeljelil Temimi (ed.) *Mélanges Sahillioğlu* (Zaghouan: Ceromdi)/*Arab Historical Review for Ottoman Studies* 15–16 (October–November) 1997, 159–75.

44  Ganchou, "Zampia Palaiologina Doria", 149–50, fn.43.

note was composed by Zotos who without taking into consideration the difference between the lunar year and the Christian year – perhaps he did not know it – calculated wrongly. Mpogkas corrected this mistake.[45] Let us now forget the note written by Zotos and focus on the note written by the translator who kept the Islamic date. This note has an odd addition about the day of the month: after the name of the month *Rebîülâhir* the digit 1 is written, which apparently means the first of the month (the day number 1 of the month) but immediately after the 1 there is the Greek word πρώτη, which is the feminine adjective form of πρώτος, first. The first day of a month of the lunar calendar has a special name in Arabic, *gurre* which is a feminine form in Arabic. It seems that the translator was not satisfied by the digit 1 which he wrote and he added the translation of the word *gurre* which he had read in the original. I think that this small incident testifies to the authenticity of the document in the same way as the mistake over *etmek/atmak*, which I analysed at the beginning of this article.

If we accept the authenticity of the date of our firman, Mustafa was still in Edirne on the first of the month *Rebîülâhir* of the year 825, which corresponds to 25 March of the year 1422; and he still exercised sultanic authority since he dispatched a command to the *kadı* of Delvinon. Furthermore, we cannot imagine that Mustafa was caught and executed only a few days later. All we can say is that the firman in question is one of the last documents issued by him; and that the sequence of the events of the first part of the year 1422 as described by the sources was not as rapid as has been understood.

The confusing information in the sources contemporary with the events should cause little surprise. It must be taken for certain that Thrace and northwestern Asia Minor were for a whole year in total disorder and anarchy and, as a result, all sorts of rumours circulated. On the other hand, we must remember that monks and clericals were not daunted by any social or military agitation.[46] Protected by their voluminous black cloths they walked under all kinds of circumstances to visit the sultan's court never showing any preference for any sultan; all they wanted was his protection, even that of Düzme Mustafa, for their endless affairs.

Putting aside various trivial remarks and to conclude with I believe that by using some logic we can accept that the firman is a clumsy Greek translation of a real firman issued by Mustafa. Who on earth would fabricate a fake firman

---

45   Mpogkas, "Δύο ιστορικά", 430. Unfortunately, Mpogkas did not know of the existence of Mustafa and for this reason I shall pass over his other remarks in silence.

46   Elizabeth A. Zachariadou, *Δέκα Τουρκικά Έγγραφα για την Μεγάλη Εκκλησία (1483–1567)* (Athens: National Research Center, 1996), 59.

using the name of Mustafa who twice showed himself a failure as a pretender? And who would risk appearing in the sultan's court to ask for the renewal of services or privileges granted by the miserable Mustafa? There cannot be any doubt that even the use of his name was avoided in the *saray* and by Ottoman officials in general. More than twenty years later sultan Murad II spoke bitterly about the Ottoman *beğ*s who shamelessly supported Düzme Mustafa.[47]

My colleague since our old days in SOAS, Colin Heywood, author of the now classic entry on Mustafa Çelebi in the *Encyclopaedia of Islam* wrote that "there are at least three major historical problems to be faced in any treatment of Mustafa's career." After enumerating them he concludes that "none of these problems has yet been provided with a totally watertight solution."[48] I am very much afraid that I added a fourth problem with this chapter; but I have done this because I believe that not a single early Ottoman document must be neglected. The proof of this belief of mine is that I announced my intention to study the document analysed above approximately forty-three years ago.[49] For having been so late I would add the well-known expression 'better late than never'.

"Ἴσον ἀπὸ τὸ φιρμάνι τῆς βασιλείας ᾽Ελληνιστὶ γεγραμμένον
Προσταγὴ πρὸς τὸν Κατὴν τοῦ Δελβίνου
Νὰ ξέρης ὅτι τοῦτος ὅπου εἶναι γραμμένος μέσα εἰς τὸ φιρμάνι ὁ γούμενος τοῦ Θεολόγου, ἔριξε ἀρτσιχάλι[1] στὴ βασιλεία μου καὶ κάνει ἰφαντὲν[2] τὸ χάλι του, ἀπὸ τοῦ πατέρα μου τὸν καιρὸν ὅπου μου ἀπόμεινε βασιέτι[3], εἰς τὴν ἐκκλησιὰ εἰς τὸ σύνορο τοῦ Θεολόγου ἀπόξω, κάμποσοι ἄνθρωποι, μὲ δίχως ὅπου νὰ ἔχουν νὰ κάμουν εἰς τὰ σύνορά του, ἔρχωνται καὶ μπένουν μέσα στὸ σύνορό του νὰ τὸ κάμουν ζάπτι (ἰδικό τους, νὰ τὸ ἐξουσιάσουν)[4]. αὐτοὶ ὀμπροστήτερα ἐκρίθηκαν εἰς τὴν κρίσι στὸ Δέλβινο καὶ χώρισε ὁ νταβάς[5] τους τὸ ἴδιο νὰ κυτάξης, καθὼς τὴν κρίσι ὅπου ἔκαμε ὀμπροστήτερα ὁ ἄλλος Κατῆς, καὶ νὰ μὴ κάμης χατῆρι καὶ μὲ τὴν ἀλήθεια νὰ λαβένη χώρισμα ὁ νταβάς τους, καὶ νὰ προστάξης νὰ μὴ ζυγώση κανεὶς μέσα στὸ σύνορο τοῦ Μοναστηριου, ἔτσι νὰ ξέρης καὶ καθὼς προστάζω νὰ κάμης.
Μουσταφᾶς (*a*)
υἱὸς τοῦ Σουλταν Βαγιαζὶτ
ἐντρενὲ ἔτος 825 ῥεμπιοὺλ ἀχὶρ[6] 1 πρώτη
᾽Αδριανούπολις 1409 μὴν ᾽Ιούνιος"

The firman according to Mpomgkas's publication

---

47  İnalcık and Oğuz, *Gazavât-ı Sultân Murâd*, 13–14.
48  Heywood, "Mustafa Çelebi Düzme", 710.
49  Elizabeth A. Zachariadou, "Ottoman Documents from the Archives of Dionysiou (Mount Athos) 1495–1520", *Südost-Forschungen*, 30 (1971), 2–3 fn.13.

## Acknowledgement

I am indebted to my colleague Ph. Kotzageogis for his help.

## Bibliography

### Primary Sources

Barkan, Ömer L. "894 (1488/1489) yılı Cizyesinin Tahsilâtına âit Muhâsebe Bilânçoları". *Belgeler* I (1964), 1–117.

Chalcocandylae, Laonici. *Historiarum Demonstrationes*. Vol. 2, edited by E. Darkó. Budapest: Academia Litterarum Hungarica, 1922.

Ducas. *Historia Turcobyzantina (1341–1462)*, edited by V. Grecu. Bucharest: Academy of the Romanian People's Republic, 1958.

İnalcık, Halil (ed.) *Hicrî 835 Tarihli Sûret-i Defter-i Sancak-i Arvanid*. Ankara: TTK, 1954.

İnalcık, Halil and Mevlût Oğuz (eds). *Gazavât-ı Sultân Murâd b. Mehemmed Hân*. Ankara: TTK, 1978.

Mpogkas, Ev. "Δύο ιστορικά ενθυμήματα του ΙΕ΄ αιώνος εκ Βορείου Ηπείρου." *Deltion Historikis kai Ethnologikis Hetereias tis Hellados* 13 (1959): 429–30.

Schirò, Giuseppe (ed.) *Cronaca dei Tocco di Cefalonia di Anonimo*. Rome: Accademia Nazionale dei Lincei, 1975.

Sphrantzes, Georgios. *Memorii 1401–1477*. Edited by V. Grecu. Bucharest: Academy of the Romanian People's Republic, 1966.

Zachariadou, Elizabeth A. "Early Ottoman Documents of the Prodromos Monastery (Serres)". *Südost-Forschungen* 28 (1969), 1–12.

Zachariadou, Elizabeth A. "Ottoman Documents from the Archives of Dionysiou (Mount Athos) 1495–1520". *Südost-Forschungen* 30 (1971), 1–36.

Zachariadou, Elizabeth A. *Δέκα Τουρκικά Έγγραφα για την Μεγάλη Εκκλησία (1483–1567)*. Athens: National Research Center, 1996.

### Secondary Sources

Anastasopoulos, Antonis. "Political Participation, Public Order, and Monetary Pledges (*Nezir*) in Ottoman Crete". In Eleni Gara et al. (eds) *Popular Protest and Political Participation in the Ottoman Empire, Studies in Honor of Suraiya Faroqhi*, 127–42. Istanbul: İstanbul Bilgi Üniversitesi Yayınları, 2011.

Aravantinos, Panagiotis. *Βιογραφική Συλλογή Λογίων της Τουρκοκρατίας*. Edited by Konstantinos Dimaras. Ioannina: Ekdosis EHM, 1960.

Binon, Stéphane. *Les origines légendaires et l'histoire de Xéropotamou et de Saint-Paul de l'Athos*. Louvain: Bureaux du Muséon, 1942.

Chrysochoidis, K. "Ιερά Μονή Αγίου Παύλου. Κατάλογος του Αρχείου." *Symmeikta* 4 (1981), 251–300.

Cristea, Ovidiu. "The Friend of my Friend and the Enemy of my Enemy: Rumanian Participation in Ottoman Campaigns". In G. Kármán and L. Kunčević (eds), *The European Tributary States of the Ottoman Empire in the Sixteenth and Seventeenth Centuries*. Leiden: Brill, 2013, 251–74.

Ganchou, Thierry. "Zampia Palaiologina Doria Épouse du Prétendant ottoman Mustafa". In E. Malamut and A. Nicolaides (eds), *Impératrices, Princesses, Aristocrates et Saintes souveraines: De l'Orient chrétien et musulman au Moyen Âge et au Début des Temps modernes*. Aix-en-Provence: Presses Universitaires de Provence, 2014, 133–69.

Heywood, Colin J. "Mustafa Čelebi Düzme". *Encyclopaedia of Islam*. 2nd edn, vol. 7, 1993.

Heywood, Colin J. "824/'8224' = 1421: The 'False' (Düzme) Mustafa and his Ephemeral Coinage". In Abdeljelil Temimi (ed.) *Mélanges Halil Sahillioğlu*. Zaghouan: Ceromdi/ *Arab Historical Review for Ottoman Studies* 15–16 (October–November) 1997.

İnalcık, Halil. "Ottoman Methods of Conquest". *Studia Islamica* 2 (1954), 103–29.

Kastritsis, Dimitri. J. *The Sons of Bayezid Empire Building and Representation in the Ottoman Civil War of 1402–13*. Leiden: Brill, 2007.

Kokolakis, Michalis. *Το Ύστερο Γιαννιωτικο Πασαλίκι*. Athens: Centre of Modern Greek Studies EIE, 2003.

Lampros, Spyridon. "Η ελληνική ως επίσημος γλώσσα των σουλτάνων." *Neos Hellenomnemon* 5 (1908), 40–78.

Mparas, B. *Το Δέλβινο της Βορείου Ηπείρου και οι γειτονικές του περιοχές*. Edited by Leandros I. Vranoussis. Athens: Paramithias, 1966.

Salamagkas, Dimitris. "Στα πρώτα χρόνια της τουρκοκρατίας". *Epirotiki Estia* 8 (1959), 353–6.

Schreiner, P. *Die Byzantinischen Kleinchroniken* I. Vienna: CFHB, 1975.

Setton, Kenneth Meyer. *The Papacy and the Levant (1204–1571)*, 2 vols. Philadelphia: American Philosophical Society, 1976–78.

Soustal, Peter. *Nicopolis und Kephallenia, Tabula Imperii Byzantini*, vol. 3. Vienna: Verlag der österreichischen Akademie der Wissenschaften, 1981.

Vatin, Nicholas. "L'emploi du grec comme langue diplomatique par les Ottomans (fin du XVe–début du XVIe siècle)", in *Istanbul et les langues Orientales, Varia Turca*, edited by F. Hitzel, 41–7. Istanbul: IFEA, 1997.

Vranoussis, Leandros I. *Χρονικά της Μεσαιωνικής και Τουρκοκρατουμένης Ηπείρου*. Ioannina: Etaireia Ipeirotikon Meleton, 1962.

Wittek, Paul. "Zu einigen frühosmanischen Urkunden". Part II in V. L. Ménage (ed.) *La formation de l'Empire ottoman*. London: Variorum Reprints, 1982.

Zachariadou, Elizabeth A. "Early Ottoman Documents of the Prodromos Monastery (Serres)", *Südost-Forschungen* 28, 1969.

Zachariadou, Elizabeth A. *Trade and Crusade, Venetian Crete and the Emirates of Menteshe and Aydin (1300–1415)*. Venice: Hellenic Institute of Byzantine and Post-Byzantine Studies, 1983.

Zachariadou, Elizabeth A. "Ottoman Diplomacy and the Danube Frontier (1420–1424)". In Cyril Mango, Omeljan Pritsak and Uliana M. Pasicznyk (eds) *Okeanos: Essays Presented to Ihor Ševčenko on his Sixtieth Birthday by his Colleagues and Students*. Cambridge, MA: Harvard University Press, 1984, 680–690.

Zachariadou, Elizabeth A. "The Conquest of Adrianople by the Turks." Part XII in *Romania and the Turks (c.1300–c.1500)*. London: Variorum Reprints, 1985.

Zachariadou, Elizabeth A. "Marginalia on the History of Epirus and Albania (1380–1418)". *Wiener Zeitschrift für die Kunde des Morgenlandes* 78 (1988), 195–210.

Zachariadou, Elizabeth A. "Remarques sur les Notes au verso des documents ottomans de Patmos." *Les archives de l' insularité ottomane*, Documents de travail du CETOBAC, No 1 (Janvier 2010): 9–13 (http://cetobac.ehess.fr/docannexe/file/1353/les_archives_de_linsularite_ottomane.pdf, accessed on 5 May 2017).

Zenker, J.Th. *Türkisch – Arabisch – Persisches Handwörterbuch*. Leipzig: Verlag von Wilhelm Engelmann, 1866. Reprinted Hildesheim: Georg Olms, 1979.

CHAPTER 2

# Imaginary Voyages, Imagined Ottomans: A Gentleman Impostor, the Köprülüs, and Seventeenth-Century French Oriental Romances

*Tülay Artan*

Johann Friedrich Bachstrom (1686–1742) was born in Rawitsch (today Rawicz in Poland), trained as a Lutheran theologian in Halle and Jena and learned languages and sciences as he travelled around Europe. He spent Some time in Istanbul in the late 1720s. After he left, perhaps in or around 1730, he went and settled in Leiden, where he led a quasi-scholarly life. He died in prison in Nieswiez (Nyasvizh, Belarus) in 1742.[1]

Among the various books that Bachstrom produced in Leiden is an Oriental utopia published in 1736/7.[2] For this he chose to remain anonymous, and his novel, describing a community of religious dissidents shipwrecked near a northwest African mountain range, did not receive much attention.[3] The name of the ship was the *Inqviraner*, and those who had been on board eventually

---

1  I am grateful to my colleague and friend Christoph K. Neumann for helping me with the literature in German. I thank Marloes Cornelissen for allowing me to cite Bachstrom's inventory. I am indebted to B. Harun Küçük for introducing me to the intriguing world of Johann Friedrich Bachstrom.
2  [ABC], *Bey zwei hundert Jahr lang unbekannte, nunmehro aber entdeckte vortreffliche Land der Inqviraner: Aus der Erzehlung Eines nach langwieriger Kranckheit in unsern Gegenden verstorbenen Aeltesten dieses glückseligen Landes, Nach allen seinen Sitten, Gebräuchen, Ordnungen, Gottesdienst, Wissenschafften, Künsten, Vortheilen und Einrichtung umständlich beschrieben, Und dem gemeinen Wesen zum Besten mitgetheilet* (Frankfurt and Leipzig, 1736). The second volume, appearing the following year, was subtitled *Das würckliche Land der Inquiraner*. A promised third volume never appeared.
3  It was common for early generations of Orientalists penning literary works to write under pseudonyms and to shroud their true identity in mystery so that their narratives – usually dealing with earthly paradise, Oriental wisdom, equality, and abundant sexuality, if not violence and despotism – would appear realistic and marketable. These qualities would then allow them to attract more readers to their new utopias. For a study that accounts for the fate of *Land der Inqviraner*, see Jannidis et al., "Hohe Romane und blaue Bibliotheken: Zum Forschungsprogramm einer computergestützten Buch- und Narratologiegeschichte des Romans in Deutschland (1500–1900)", in Stolz et al. *Literatur und Literaturwissenschaft auf dem Weg zu den neuen Medien* (Bern: Germanistik.Ch, 2005), 29–43. See also F. J. Lamport, "'Utopia' and 'Robinsonade': Schnabel's Insel Felsenburg and Bachstrom's Land der Inquiraner", *Oxford German Studies* 1 (1), 1966, 10–30.

set up a society of complete religious freedom. The novel drew on Bachstrom's own observations in the Ottoman capital as well as on French and British literature like Montesquieu's *Lettres persanes* or Defoe's *Robinson Crusoe*. The shipwreck, the printing equipment or the Quran (allegedly published in England) being dumped into the sea were all recurrent tropes in contemporary Orientalist literature.

## 1 A Hungarian Prince and a Köprülü Grandson?

Ottomanists learned about Johann Friedrich Bachstrom through Franz Babinger. In turn, Babinger was quoting Hermann Ullrich (d.1932), the first Robinson bibliographer, and Johann Christian Kundmann (1684–1751), a Breslau physician, numismatist and chronicler, who had reported on his friend Bachstrom's experience of attempting to establish a printing press in Istanbul in 1728/9.[4] Bachstrom was indeed planning to publish the Bible in Ottoman Turkish while he also tried to obtain support for establishing a scientific

---

4  Franz Babinger, *Stambuler Buchwesen im 18. Jahrhundert* (Leipzig: Deutscher Verein für Buchwesen und Schrifttum, 1919) [Turkish translation Franz Babinger, "18. Yüzyılda İstanbul'da Kitabiyat", in *İbrahim Müteferrika ve Matbaası* (Istanbul: Tarih Vakfı Yurt Yayınları, 2004), 11–12; 16–17; 46–48], who uses Hermann Ullrich, "Johann Friedrich Bachstrom: Ein Gelehrtenleben aus der ersten Hälfte des 18. Jahrhunderts (Mit genauem Verzeichniß von Bachstrom's Schriften)", in *Euphorion* Bd. 16, *Zeitschrift f. Literaturgeschichte* (1909/10), 320–49; and Johann Christian Kundmann, *Rariora naturae et artis item in re medica; oder, Seltenheiten der Natur und Kunst des kundmannischen Naturalien-Cabinets, wie auch in der Artzeney-Wissenschafft. Darinnen abgehandelt werden I. Examen fosilium et lapidum ... rariorum.... II. Memorabilia naturae et artis.... III. Observationes in re medica singulares* (Breslau: M. Herbert, 1737), column 710. Kundmann and Bachstrom might have known one another through Christian Thomasius, a German jurist and philosopher who taught them both. Ullrich, on the other hand, was interested in Bachstrom because of his work on Robinson Crusoe and *robinsonades*. Hermann Ullrich, *Robinson und Robinsonaden: Bibliographie, Geschichte, Kritik: Ein beitrag zur verleichenden litteraturgeschichte, im besonderen zur geschichte des romans und zur geschichte der jugendlitteratur* (Weimar: E. Felber), 1898. For Bachstrom, see also Johann Bernouillis, *Archiv zur Neueren Geschichte, Geographie, Natur-, und Menschenkenntnis VII* (Leipzig: 1787), 271–322, but 308–10 in particular; Martin Kriebel, "Das pietistische Halle und das orthodoxe Patriarchat von Konstantinopel: 1700–1730", *Jahrbücher für Geschichte Osteuropas Neue Folge* 3 (1) 1955, 50–70. Thanks to Kriebel who explored period correspondence and diaries, more is now known about Bachstrom's various missions. His given names were adjusted to Jan Fryderyk, Joannis Friderici and Jean-Frédéric, and his family name to Bachstroem, Bakstrom, Backstrom. See also Stephen Schultz, *Die Leitungen des Höchsten nach seinem Rath auf den Reisen durch Europa, Asien und Africa IV* (Halle im Magdeburgischen: Verlegt von Carl Hermann Hemmerbe, 1771), 115.

academy in Istanbul.[5] In his *Stambuler Buchwesen im 18. Jahrhundert* (1919), Babinger noted that Bachstrom's printing project had been mentioned in the European press before İbrâhim Müteferrika, a Hungarian renegade, eventually set up what came to be recognized as the first Ottoman printing house. On that basis, Babinger claimed that behind Bachstrom's enterprise was a hidden agenda of spreading Protestantism in Istanbul.[6] It is true that the printing press led to much consternation among the Ottoman elite (across all social groups), and it was perhaps just before the September 1730 revolt that Bachstrom, a restless Pietist, had to flee the capital.[7]

---

5  Babinger, "18. Yüzyılda", 16–17; 46–8. For a discussion of this (medico-physical) academy and Bachstrom's role in its establishment as reported by Kundmann, see B. Harun Küçük, "Early Enlightenment in Istanbul" (Ph.D. dissertation, University of California, San Diego, 2012), 172–8. Küçük also took note of Stephen Schultz's 1752 travelogue as an independent account of Bachstrom's visit to Istanbul, as well as the latter's projects for the Ottoman printing press and the 'academia scientarum'. See footnote 4 above.

6  Babinger, "18. Yüzyılda", 16–17; 46–8. Babinger cites many occasions in the European press, suggesting awareness of Bachstrom's endeavours in Istanbul even if his name was not mentioned. See Anon, *Die Europäische Fama, welche den gegenwärtigen Zustand der vornehmsten Höfe entdeckt* [The European Fame, which discovered the present state of the principal courts] no. 263 (1723), 991. He also noted the claim that the sultan had then allowed the publication of the Old Testament with annotations from the Quran. Babinger refers to Kundmann, Rariora naturae et artis item in re medica, column 726, as well as to the "Nationalen Gespröche", 30, in *Entrevue*, 950.

7  In a letter dated 27 July 1729, one of Bachstrom's associates said that "it is likely that he will come here (Wrocław/Breslau?) for a few days and then go back (to Istanbul)". See Kriebel, "Das pietistische Halle", 67–9. Bachstrom's visit to Istanbul has also been mentioned or discussed in two recent Ph.D. dissertations. One is B. Harun Küçük's work (footnote 5 above), while the other is Marloes Cornelissen, "The World of Ambassador Jacobus Colyer: Material Culture of the Dutch 'Nation' in Istanbul during the First Half of the Eighteenth Century" (Ph.D. dissertation, Sabancı University, 2015). Küçük has painstakingly traced such exceptional individuals through various rare publications (often in not easily accessible languages) to elucidate an impressive social network of European scientists and missionaries in the first quarter of the eighteenth century. Still, and purely with regard to Bachstrom, Küçük's work has two major flaws. One is that he takes the 1742 letter, published by Ullrich (see footnote 8 below), at face value; he does not question its most obvious fabrications. The second, partly following from the first, is that he takes the character İbrâhim, who appears and delivers a major religious sermon at one point in Bachstrom's *Bey zwei hundert Jahr lang unbekannte* book as being modelled on Grand Vizier Damad İbrâhim Pasha (see footnotes 86 and 87 below). As for Marloes Cornelissen's study, her discovery of an inventory of Bachstrom's possessions is crucial in itself (see footnote 17 below). Moreover, it suggests that Bachstrom may have left Istanbul without much preparation and could have been planning to come back. This has further helped me formulate certain hypotheses about pretenders and impostors in early-eighteenth-century Istanbul, a topic I intend to revisit in the future (see also footnote 87 below).

Towards the very end of his adventurous life, Bachstrom wrote a letter (in French, dated 27 February 1742) to Prince Michał Radziwiłł Rybenko, a descendant of an aristocratic Polish family originating from the Grand Duchy of Lithuania. He was applying for a palace job – to administer speech therapy to Radziwiłł's stammering son. It was in this letter that, by way of boosting his credentials, he laid out an astounding story of his origins. He claimed to be the son of a noble Ottoman lady – a daughter of Grand Vizier Köprülü, though he did not say which Köprülü – and also the grandson of the Prince of Translyvania, Ferenc I Rákóczi (d.1676). He further said that his mother had been captured by imperial troops in the wake of the 1683 Ottoman rout outside Vienna, and had then been rescued by Imre Thököly de Késmárk (1657–1705), a rebellious Hungarian count and Ottoman ally. Thököly had already married his grandmother, the widow of Ferenc I Rákóczi, Bachstrom remarked:

> Ma mère étoit de la Nation Turque, elle fut prise en [au?] siège de Vienne, mais comme le Comte Emeric Tökeli resçut que cette person étoit fille du Grand Vezier Kiuperli, il la racheta, voulant par là faire un service très grand à une famille assez célèbre parmi les Turcs; le Comte avoit déjà épousé ma grande mère Veuve du François I Ragozzi, qui étoit mort l'année 1681.[8]

This 'belle Turque', Bachstrom went on to say, was kept with great distinction at his grandmother's court, when his late father, then nineteen years of age (born in 1662?), became enamoured of her. At this point, let us note a few problems with this account. First, if we are to take him at all seriously, his alleged Ottoman maternal grandfather he mentioned, the Grand Vizier Köprülü, cannot have been Köprülü Mehmed Pasha (d.1661), the famous founder of this vizieral dynasty, but only his son-in-law Merzifonlu Kara Mustafa Pasha (1632–83), who was the one who was routed before Vienna in 1683 (and was then executed for it).[9] Second, Prince Ferenc I Rákóczi (Bachstrom's alleged paternal grandfather) died not in 1681 but in 1676. Third, his alleged Rákóczi father could not have been Ferenc II Rákóczi because that prince was born

---

8 Letter to Prince Michał Radziwiłł, dated 27 February 1742. See Ullrich, "Johann Friedrich Bachstrom", 336–9.

9 Babinger, in *Stambuler Buchwesen im 18. Jahrhundert*, suggested Fâzıl Ahmed Pasha, Köprülü Mehmed's elder son and his successor to office, as an alternative. Sources about Kara Mustafa Pasha's marriage to one of Köprülü's daughters are rather contradictory. For a recent treatment of Kara Mustafa Pasha's family, see Hedda Reindl-Kiel, "The Must-Haves of a Grand Vizier: Merzifonlu Kara Mustafa Pasha's Luxury Assets", *Sonderdruck aus: Wiener Zeitschrift für die Kunde des Morgenlandes* 106 (2016), 179–221.

not in 1662, as Bachstrom claimed, but just a few months before his father's death in 1676, which would make him not nineteen but only ten at the time of Bachstrom's own birth in 1686.

The rest of Bachstrom's fabrication, despite some other flaws of a more minor sort, runs relatively more smoothly. While his grandmother opposed this 'illegitimate love', he said, his father the prince declared his loyalty by promising to marry the Ottoman woman after the death of his mother, or after he became a major in 1685 (as he would then have been able to marry without his mother's consent). In the meantime, his (Köprülü) mother, said Bachstrom, was forced to live in a nearby castle where his father visited her very often under the pretext of hunting. He, that is to say Bachstrom as a Rákóczi prince, was born the day before Christmas in 1686, which he says was St Stephen's Day, which he further says gave him his name. Here, one problem is that 'Stephen' is not among his names, while another is that St Stephen's Day is not really before Christmas but is celebrated on 26 December in the Western and on 27 December in the Eastern Church. Be that as it may, his parents' secret, Bachstrom said in his letter, remained intact for another four years and more after his birth.

However, the suspicious grandmother finally found out, and threatened to kill both mother and child (who was not yet five). His father ('the prince') found no other recourse than to withdraw to Poland on the borders of Hungary, as he assured his beloved that he would remain loyal to her, that he would never take another wife, and that he would return when his mother died. The prince then left his offspring in the care of a goldsmith (jeweller?) at the court of Imre Thököly. This goldsmith was supposedly accompanying the Hungarian count when and wherever he travelled. Bachstrom claimed that it was the name of his *prétendu* father (Bachstrom) that he still carried.

Most of the characters in this fabrication are correctly positioned. Imre Thököly, a long-time ally of the Ottomans in Eastern Europe, did take part in the 1683 Vienna campaign.[10] As a displaced Hungarian notable from Árva,

---

10   Thököly was descended from a wealthy Protestant Hungarian family. After his father was executed for joining the Wesselényi conspiracy against the Holy Roman Emperor Leopold I (1670), he was elected commander in chief of the anti-Habsburg rebels and led the Hungarian Protestant resistance to the continuing repressive Catholic Habsburg policy, backed by the Ottomans, the French and the Prince of Transylvania. In 1681, the Eastern Hungarian Kingdom and the central Hungarian towns came under Thököly's authority. He was recognized as the Prince of Translyvania, and (briefly) the vassal king of Upper Hungary by Mehmed IV. In 1682, he married Ilona Zrínyi, the widow of Ferenc I Rákóczi, the Prince of Transylvania. Thököly assisted the Ottomans during the failed siege of Vienna. In the aftermath of the defeat in 1683, his rebellion was crushed, his fortresses were captured, and his wife was taken in custody to Vienna. Moreover, Grand Vizier Kara Mustafa Pasha blamed Thököly for the Ottoman defeat. He then sought to reconcile with

he had once been under the command of Ferenc I Rákóczi, the Prince of Translyvania, which was under Ottoman suzerainty.[11] Both were elected by their peers among anti-Habsburg rebels to lead the Hungarian Protestant resistance to the empire's repressive Catholic policy. In 1682, six years after (the correct date of) the death of Ferenc I Rákóczi, Thököly married the prince's widow, Jelena Zrinski (Ilona Zrínyi in Hungarian, 1643–1703), a Croatian countess whose father was the famous rebel ban Petar Zrinski. Following the Peace of Karlowitz, signed on 26 January 1699, Imre Thököly and his wife Zrínyi (who was 14 years his senior) were forced into exile first in Istanbul and then in Izmit, where both died in a few years (Ilona in 1703 and Imre in 1705). In 1717, after futile pursuit of the Hungarian cause for many years, Ferenc II Rákóczi, son of Ferenc I and Ilona Zrínyi, also took refuge in the Ottoman Empire, and lived in Tekirdağ (Rodosto) attended by a small suite until his death in 1735.[12]

---

Leopold I, but soon found himself at war with the imperial forces again. When he turned to the Ottomans for help, he was seized and imprisoned for treason. He was released in 1686 and sent to Transylvania with a small army. He failed in two expeditions, in 1686 and 1688, and he was imprisoned again. In 1690, he finally defeated the imperial forces. After this victory, Thököly was elected Prince of Transylvania. As it proved to be difficult to maintain his position against the Imperial Army, he quit Transylvania in 1691 and joined the Ottoman forces. He led the Ottoman cavalry at the battles of Slankamen (1691) and Zenta (1697) against the states of the Holy Roman Empire. After the Treaty of Karlowitz (1699), Thököly, after one more unsuccessful attempt in 1700 to recover his principality, was forced to spend his remaining years in exile first in Galata, then in İzmit. For Ottoman documents pertaining to Thököly's plight, see Ahmed Refik, *Türk Hizmetinde Kıral Tököli İmre, 1683–1705* (Istanbul: Muallim Ahmet Halit Kitaphanesi, 1932).

11  Ferenc I Rákóczi was a Hungarian aristocrat, and elected Prince of Transylvania (1652). Because of the disastrous Polish campaign of 1657, the Ottomans prohibited any Rákóczi to ascend the Transylvanian throne. He therefore withdrew to his estates in Royal Hungary. After he converted to Catholicism, Ferenc acquired favour with the Catholic Habsburg court, he was made a count in 1664. In 1666, the Prince married Ilona Zrínyi, a Croatian countess, and following her father, joined the Wesselényi conspiracy. He soon became the leader of the conspiracy, and started an armed uprising of nobles in Upper Hungary. In 1670, as the conspirators in Croatia, including his father-in-law, were suppressed, he appealed to the emperor for mercy. For a huge ransom and several castles, he was pardoned. The last ten years of his life, however, were spent in agony as the family of his wife and some other nobles involved in the conspiracy were harshly persecuted. *EBR*, s.v. "Rákóczy", 867–9.

12  Bernard Adams (ed.) *Letters From Turkey: Kelemen Mikes, Chamberlain of the Last Prince of Transylvania* (London: Kegan Paul International Limited, 2000).

## 2       What Was behind Bachstrom's Construct?

Bachstrom was certainly familiar with the late-seventeenth-century Hungarian tragedy when he claimed, in his early 1742 letter, that he had been able to approach the Ottoman court with his credentials as a descendant of the noble houses of Köprülü, Rákóczi, and Zrínyi. This, of course, is impossible to verify. We know nothing about how the Ottomans might have received the genealogical connection Bachstrom sought to establish; we do not know whether he even mentioned anything of the sort while he was still in Istanbul. It is, indeed, very unlikely that he would have dared to fabricate such a genealogy and introduce himself as a Rákóczi – especially when, since 1717, Ferenc II Rákóczi himself had been just half a day's journey away from the capital, and his agents had long been rubbing shoulders with the same people who were also supporting Bachstrom in Istanbul. How, then, could he have dared to imagine that he might be able to step into Ferenc II's shoes (or the shoes of an imagined brother of the Hungarian prince), and to go around telling this story?

Since he had studied at Collegium Orientale Theologium in Halle (founded in 1702), where the more advanced students were taught Turkish, Persian or Chinese (as well as more familiar languages such as modern Greek, Polish, Italian and Russian, in addition to Hebrew, Rabbinical Hebrew, Chaldean, Syrian, Samaritan, Arabic, and Ethiopian), he would have had an opportunity to communicate with numerous locals and adventurers in the Ottoman capital.[13] A key person in the Istanbul circles in which he found himself would have been İbrâhim Müteferrika (1674–1745), the aforementioned Hungarian-born Unitarian who converted to Islam and entered Ottoman state service.[14] Around the time of Bachstrom's arrival, he would already have been busy with the printing house for which he had received the sultan's authorization. At first glance, there would be no obvious reason for them to enter into rivalry from the start; instead, both might have benefited from a partnership. Hence, Bachstrom's sudden departure from Istanbul needs an explanation.[15]

---

13   Kriebel highlighted his language skills and said that he was fluent in French, Italian, Polish and Greek. It seems that his education in theology in Jena introduced him to Oriental studies to some extent, as well as to medicine and science. But only after he left Toruń Gymnasium, sometime in 1717, he began learning Arabic, Turkish and Russian. Meanwhile, he was practising papermaking, stamp-cutting, font casting and book printing. See Kriebel, "Das pietistische Halle", 65–6.

14   For new research on İbrâhim Müteferrika, see Orlin Sabev, *İbrahim Müteferrika ya da İlk Osmanlı Matbaa Serüveni* (Istanbul: Yeditepe Yayınları, 2006).

15   Stephen Schultz, in reference to a certain Herr Benisch, a pharmacist who mentioned Bachstrom's stay in Istanbul and his projects, tells us that when Bachstrom communicated with the sultan and grand vizier, he was 'incognito', and that he had left the Ottoman

It seems to me that, based on what he learned about exiled Hungarians (such as Thököly, Zrínyi, or Ferenc II) during his stay in Istanbul, Bachstrom fabricated his fantastic genealogy only after hearing of Ferenc II's 1735 death – and at least five years after he himself fled the Ottoman capital. This then also casts doubt on a recent argument, repeating and agreeing with Bachstrom's own claims and Kundmann's reports, that "he was well-positioned to play a key role in the establishment of the press and in the would-be academy."[16] However, when we subtract the 1742 fiction of his life, he would not necessarily be 'well-positioned' with regard to the palace and court society, though he might still have been 'well-positioned' with regard to the European and especially Protestant expatriates in Istanbul.

When he departed from Istanbul, he left his books behind in the custody of a certain Jean-Michel Hesler of Geneva who happened to be living in Pera.[17] These books were inventoried in 1733. Their titles indicate an interest in translation, and possibly in translating the Bible, as well as in medicine. Among a number of grammar books and lexicons (in Hebrew, Greek, Latin, Italian and French, as well as Arabic, Persian and Turkish), was *Institutionem Linguæ Turcicæ*, the Latin – Turkish dictionary of Hieronymus Megiser (1612). There was at least one work by Franciscus à Mesgnien Meninski, a German Orientalist attached to the Polish embassy. Meninski's *Thesaurus linguarum orientalium-Turcicae – Arabicae-Persicae* (Vienna, 1680) and *Complenaentum Thesauri linguarum orientalium, seu onomasticum Latino – Turcico – Arabico – Persicum* (Vienna, 1687) were the most reliable lexicons at the time. In the Bachstrom inventory, what is listed as Meninski's is 'folios' from *Le Grammaire Turq, Arabe, Persan et Latin*. At the same time, there is a copy of the Bible in German, an

---

capital upon the order of some scholars from the evangelical church. See Schultz, *Die Leitungen des Höchsten*, 115, after Kriebel, "Das pietistische Halle", 68. See footnote 17 below.

16  For a recent portrayal of Ahmed III and Damad İbrahim Pasha based on Bachstrom's claims of their acquaintance, see Küçük, "Early Enlightenment in İstanbul", *passim*.

17  National Archives, The Hague: Legatie Turkije 1.02.20. inv. no. 1044; 1064, in Cornelissen, "The World of Ambassador Jacobus Colyer", 140–1. Accordingly, upon the request of Jean Michel Hesler, on 20 April 1733, Rumoldus Rombouts, the Chancellor of Cornelis Calkoen, went to the house of Hesler in Pera, to inventory several goods that Bachstrom had placed in a sealed closet. The inventory was prepared in the presence of Thomas Payne, the pastor and chaplain of the English nation, and Johan Behnisch. I was unable to find more about Benisch/Behnisch who seems to have been the same person that Stephan Schultz met in Istanbul between May and September 1753. See footnote 15 above. On Jean Michel Hesler, see M. Heyer, "Genève et Constantinople. 1733 (Suite des extraits communiqués par M. Heyer)", *Bulletin de la Société de l'Histoire du Protestantisme Français (1852–1865)* 11 (1/3), 1862, 61–79.

Old Testament in Greek, plus (possibly parts of) copies of the New Testament in Modern Greek, Syriac, Arabic and Turkish. Also included are two copies of the Quran, one translated from Arabic into French by Sir Turier, and the other in Turkish. In addition, Bachstrom had a few books on Christianity, spirituality, atheism, and deism. All this suggests the possibility of him having a Protestant agenda, but there is also another, more scientific dimension. Bachstrom turns out to have possessed a number of Orientalist travel and other accounts in French. He also left with Hesler numerous medical tools and medicinal material, along with more than a dozen books on medicine, pharmacy and botany. In fact, in less than a decade, it was as a scientist that he was able to make his name in Europe.[18] He seems to have lost interest in printing altogether, and to have himself published a few scientific books on a variety of subjects. Interestingly, both Müteferrika (1732) and Bachstrom (1734) published books on magnets. Could there have been an undercurrent of rivalry between these two? Might this have had anything to do with Bachstrom's sudden departure from Istanbul? Was it more than rivalry?[19]

18   In addition to his aforementioned novel, which involves a shipwreck, Bachstrom wrote three treatises on marine sciences, on the cure of scurvy, on magnets, and on life-saving in the sea where he introduces his invention of a life-jacket made out of cork. See Johann Frederick Bachstrom, *Observationes circa scorbutum: ejusque indolem, causas, signa, et curam, institutæ, eorum præprimis in usum, qui Groenlandiam & Indiam Orientis petunt* (Leiden: Conrad Wishoff, 1734); idem, *Nova aestus marini theoria. ex principiis physico-mathematicis detecta & dilucidata. Cui accedit, Examen acus magneticae spiralis, quae a declinatione & inclinatione libera esse creditur, institutum* (Leiden: Apud Conradum Wishoff, 1734); idem, *L'Art de Nager, ou Invention à l'aide de laquelle on peut toujours se sauver du Naufrage; &, en cas de besoin, faire passer les plus larges Rivières à les Armées entières* (Amsterdam: Zacharie Chatelain, 1741).

19   Küçük has argued that it was Bachstrom who introduced a recent treatise on terrestrial magnetism to the Ottoman readership. This is a moot point, but what follows is indeed a scholarly contribution. The author of the treatise in question was Christoph Eberhard (1675–1750), a German geographer who spent the majority of his career in Halle (and possibly was Bachstrom's acquaintance). See Küçük, "Early Enlightenment in Istanbul", 178–89. See also, Christoph Eberhard, *Specimen theoriae magneticae quo ex certis principiis magneticis ostenditur vera et universalis methodus inveniendi longitudinem & latitudinem* (Leipzig: Martini, 1720). The Turkish translation of Eberhard's *Specimen* was published by İbrâhim Müteferrika in 1732 under the title *Füyûdât-ı Mıknâtısiyye*. Küçük translates the title as *Magnetic Effluvia* or the *Magnetic Counsels*, and says that "the majority of the book consisted of word-for-word translations straight out of Eberhard's *Specimen*. However, the translator had masked the original book by hiding both the author and the title. The one useful clue, namely that the book was printed in Leipzig (Lîpsîyâ) in 1721, was misleading. And the sources used in *Füyûdât* had remained a complete mystery until now. The translator removed all European references in the book. Eberhard had mentioned Descartes, Newton and Halley by name, but those had been masked with a general designation as *müte'ahhirîn* (moderns) in the Turkish edition." A serious, perhaps life-threatening

While circulating in Istanbul, probably the most crowded and culturally heterogeneous city of Europe at the time, whether he was sharing his projects with others or not, Bachstrom must have met a number of interesting people, including a few 'gentleman impostors'. Impostures and impostors featured prominently in the political, social and religious life of early modern Europe.[20] What is quite sensational about Bachstrom's story is that as he went about fabricating a lineage involving a Catholic, a Protestant and a Muslim Ottoman family, he should have chosen the Köprülüs as a fitting complement to the East European Zrínyi and Rákóczi lines. At first sight, this gives the impression that as late as the first half of the eighteenth century, the Köprülü legacy was still strongly felt in the Ottoman capital. But there could be another, more indirect explanation. Bachstrom could have been getting at least some of his ideas from an already existing literary genre. The Köprülüs were favoured figures in late-seventeenth-century French Orientalist fiction. Apart from whatever he might have heard of them during his stay in Istanbul, Bachstrom could have learned even more, and been intrigued by the possibilities of an imagined association, by reading such novellas romanticizing the East as were readily available in Leiden in a number of languages.

## 3  French Orientalist Literature

Tales of prominent Ottoman men and women in seventeenth-century French romances, including members of the Köprülü dynasty, were not fictionalized biographies of real individuals, but pure inventions for political purposes,

---

disagreement or argument about the translation and publication of Eberhard's book might have led to Bachstrom's flight from Istanbul. İbrâhim Müteferrika signed his name and gave the date of publication at the very end of the book. Accordingly, two years later, in 1734, "Bachstrom published his book on sea temperature, *Nova aestus marini theoria* (1734), and appended his own magnetic theory, which built on a Newtonian framework of forces and the inverse square law of gravitation. In this book, he used Eberhard's instruments, and also mentioned his conversations with a certain Aristotelian *molla* (teacher) in Istanbul about the direction of the flow of the Nile." See Bachstrom, *Nova aestus marini theoria, passim*; Küçük, "Early Enlightenment in Istanbul", 190.

20  Early modern Europe was indeed an 'Age of Impostors'. For an early study of this multi-faceted phenomenon, see Natalie Zemon Davis, *The Return of Martin Guerre* (Cambridge, MA: HUP, 1983). See also Miriam Eliav-Feldon, *Renaissance Impostors and Proofs of Identity* (London: Palgrave Macmillan, 2012); Tobias B. Hug, *Impostures in Early Modern England: Representations and Perceptions of Fraudulent Identities* (Manchester: Manchester University Press, 2010); Linda Woodbridge, "Imposters, Monsters, and Spies: What Rogue Literature Can Tell us about Early Modern Subjectivity", *Early Modern Literary Studies* 9 (4) January 2002, 1–11, in http://purl.oclc.org/emls/si-09/woodimpo.htm.

intended to promote interest in trade or diplomacy. While making use of existing material on the Köprülüs (and others), authors also "transformed [it] through fictionalization, embellishment, or by outright forgery".[21] The Ottomans, too, were no strangers to such political manipulation. Beginning in the late-sixteenth century, eminent Ottoman historians, such as Selânikî Mustafa Efendi (d.1600), Gelibolulu Mustafa Âlî (d.1600) and İbrâhim Peçevî (d.1650), as well as the traveller Evliya Çelebi (d.1684?), repeatedly referred to a supposed genealogical link between the Ottoman and French ruling houses to justify the enduring Ottoman alliance with the kings of France, and to legitimize the capitulations and other favours the sultans kept extending to the French. The legend of a French princess, allegedly captured either during the 1453 siege of Constantinople or at sea at a later date, who entered the harem and became the mother of a sultan, was told in multiple versions. Her alleged offspring was therefore the descendant of both the French and the Ottoman royal lines, and the ancestor of all subsequent sultans.[22]

From 1660 to 1690, that is to say at a time when the main characters in Bachstrom's story were still around, French literature started displaying a new interest in the Ottomans.[23] Voyagers like Jean-Baptiste Tavernier, Vincent de Stochove, Jean de Thevenot, Le Chevalier (Laurent) d'Arvieux, Jean Chardin, Sieur Paul Lucas and others travelled to and in the Balkans, Asia Minor, and the Middle East, and published their memoirs.[24] In addition, a number of

---

21   Christine Isom-Verhaaren, "Royal French Women in the Ottoman Sultans' Harem: The Political Uses of Fabricated Accounts from the Sixteenth to the Twenty-first Century", *Journal of World History* 17 (2) 2006, 159–96.

22   Dimitrie Cantemir, too, told another version even though he did not believe the tale. For a treatment of the versions told by Mustafa Selânikî, Gelibolulu Mustafa Âli, İbrâhim Peçevî, Evliya Çelebi and Dimitrie Cantemir, see Isom-Verhaaren, "Royal French Women", 162–70.

23   *For* a seventeenth-century French Orientalist and a summary of Oriental studies in seventeenth-century France, see Alastair Hamilton and Francis Richard, *André du Ryer and Oriental Studies in Seventeenth-Century France* (Oxford: The Arcadian Library/OUP, 2004).

24   For a comprehensive study of more than sixty seventeenth-century French travel narratives about the Levant and East Asia, including well-known accounts such as those by Chardin and Tavernier, as well as lesser studied and anonymously published works, see Michael Harrigan, *Veiled Encounters: Representing the Orient in seventeenth-century French Travel Literature* (Amsterdam: Rodopi, 2008). It also includes an extensive bibliography of primary and secondary sources. For a thorough literary analysis of French *récits de voyage* as a genre, see Sophie Linon-Chipon, *Gallia orientalis: Voyages aux Indes orientales, 1529–1722* (Paris: Presses de l'Université de Paris-Sorbonne, 2003). See also footnote 29 of this chapter.

seventeenth-century French authors like François Eudes de Mézeray,[25] Gilbert Saulnier du Verdier[26] or Louis du May[27] kept producing popular histories of the Ottoman dynasty or more episodic accounts of their recent exploits.[28] All these texts testify to the increasing French presence and interest in diplomatic contacts and trade with the Ottomans. Along with them, Orientalizing novellas, too, became quite popular in Europe. They included dramatic details of the (real or alleged) travellers' adventures, while also representing the physical and cultural peculiarities of the Ottomans, and offering gossip and other juicy stuff.[29]

Translations into English and Italian, as well as some original work in these languages, quickly followed. Not only the contemporary Sultan Mehmed IV (r.1648–87) or his harem, but Ottoman dignitaries, too, loomed large in these

---

25   François Eudes De Mezeray, *Histoire des Turcs, depuis 1612 jusqu'à 1649* (1650, in-folio).
26   Gilbert Saulnier du Verdier, *Abbrégé de l'histoire des Turcs: Contenant tout ce qui s'est passé de plus remarquable sous le regne de vingt-trois empereurs. Recueilly tres-soigneusement par le sieur Du Verdier, historiographe de France. Enrichy en cette dernière édition de leurs Portraits en Taille-douce; Et augmenté de plusieurs belles Remarques Curieuses, qui n'ont point esté insérées dans les autres* (Paris: Théodore Girard, 1665).
27   Louis Du May, *Discours historiques et politiques sur les causes de la Guerre de Hongrie et sur les causes de la paix. Entre Leopold I. Empereur des romains et Mahomet IV Sultan de Turquie. Par Louis du May, Chevalier, Sieur de Sallettes, Conseiller de son Altesse de Wirtemberg* (Lyon: Barthelemy Riviere, rue Merciere, à l'Image S. Augustin, 1665). The contemporary English translation is called *A Discourse. Historical and Political of the War of Hungary, and of the Causes of the Peace between Leopold the First Emperor of the Romans, and Mahomet the Fourth Sultan of Turkey. By Louis du May of Sallettes, Knight, and Counsellor of His Highness the Duke of Wirtemberg* (Glasgow: Printed by Robert Sanders, 1669). It includes a description of the Ottoman military procession on 11–18 June 1663 (81–3). His treatment of the Hungarian war, written as a dialogue between "G" and "P", mixes history with current politics.
28   Some were compiled by anonymous authors, such as *A Relation of the siege of Candia: From the First Expedition of the French Forces under the Command of M. de la Fucillade, Duke of Roannez, to it Surrender, the 27th of September, 1669. Written in French by a gentleman who was a voluntier in that service, and faithfully Englished* (London: Printed for T. Williams and I. Starkey, and to be sold in their shops, at the Bible in Little Brittain, and the Miter in Fleet-Street near Temple Barr, 1670). Translation of *Journal de l'expédition de Monsieur de la Fueillade*, pour le secours de Candie.
29   Ina Baghdiantz McCabe, *Orientalism in Early Modern France. Eurasian Trade, Exoticism, and the Ancien Régime* (Oxford: Berg, 2008); Nicholas Dew, *Orientalism in Louis XIV's France* (Oxford: OUP, 2009); Michael Harrigan, *Veiled Encounters*; Desmond Hosford and Chong J. Wojtkowski (eds), *French Orientalism: Culture, Politics, and the Imagined Other* (Cambridge: Cambridge Scholars Publishing, 2010); Michèle Longino, *Orientalism in French Classical Drama* (Cambridge: CUP, 2002).

accounts mostly by writers who had never set foot on Ottoman soil.[30] For the later part of Mehmed IV's life, it was his love affairs and hunting parties that were highlighted. Such Oriental romances often incorporated statesmen of the Köprülü family, too, into their story lines. The reverse was also the case: sometimes the Köprülü viziers occupied centre stage. In 1676, François de Chassepol (whose date of death is unknown) published his *Histoire des grands vizirs Mahomet Coprogli Pacha et Achmet Coprogli Pacha*. John Evelyn's (d.1699 or 1706) English translation of it followed immediately in 1677 (four parts in one volume).[31] Almost twenty years later Eustache Le Noble (d.1711) wrote *Abra-Mulé* (1695), a romance woven around the dethronement of Mehmed IV, which highlighted the Köprülü dynasty.[32] Several other titles cannot be classified as romances.[33] *An Account of a Late Voyage to Athens*, penned by André

---

[30] These accounts often give a detailed physical and psychological portrait of the people in question. Mehmed IV's hunting craze was frequently mentioned by Eustache Le Noble, in *Abra-Mulé*: "Mahomet, for stature, was somewhat taller than the ordinary height, well proportion'd, black hair, little eyes, but quick, more ill favour'd then comely; nimble in all the exercises of the body, valiant, courtly, profuse, magnificent, passionate in his amours, a lover of hunting even to excess; an extraordinary discerner of merit; but rash, obstinate, ingrateful, and one that suffer'd himself to be very much govern'd by the ministers of the Seraglio" (3); "he quietly enjoy'd the fruits of his victories which had acquir'd him Candie, Kaminice, and some places in Hungary; so that he abandon'd himself to the sports of hunting, and the pleasures of love", (7); "Would you, Madam, carry her back to Mahomet whom she avoids, and who without question hunts after her in a thousand disguises of mind?" (109). See Eustache Le Noble, *Abra-Mulé, ou l'Histoire du Déthronement de Mahomet IV: Troisiéme Nouvelle historique* (Amsterdam: André de Hoogenhuysen, 1695). Another edition appeared in France (Paris: M. et G. Jouvenel, 1696). An English version appeared as Eustache Le Noble, *Abra-Mulé, or a True History of the Dethronement of Mahomet IV*, translated by John Philips (London: R. Clavel, 1696).

[31] François de Chassepol, *Histoire des grands vizirs Mahomet Coprogli Pacha et Achmet Coprogli Pacha: Celle des trios derniers Grands Seigneurs, de leurs sultanes, principales favorites avec les plus secretes intrigues du serrail. Et plusieurs autres particularitez des guerres de dalmatie, Transilvanie, Hongrie, Candie, & Pologne. Avec l'histoiere de grand Sobieski, roy de Pologne. Et le plan de la bataille de Cotzchin* (Paris: E. Michallet, 1676). The English version appeared as François de Chassepol, *The history of the grand visiers, Mahomet and Achmet Coprogli, of the three last grand signiors, their Sultana's and chief favourites, with the most secret intrigues of the seraglio besides several other particulars of the wars of Dalmatia, Transylvania, Hungary, Candia, and Poland/Englished by John Evelyn, Junior* (London: Printed for H. Brome, at the Gun at the West-end of St. Pauls, 1677).

[32] See footnote 30 above. Le Noble likely drew information from Donneau de Visé, *Histoire du Mahomet IV, depossedé* (Lyon: Chez Thomas Amaulry, 1688). Years later, Joseph Trapp staged a play based on it. See Joseph Trapp, *Abra Mulé, or Love and Empire: A Tragedy* (London: Printed for Jacob Tonson, 1704). It was released in several editions throughout the eighteenth century.

[33] For other genres, see Baghdiantz McCabe, Orientalism in Early Modern France, *passim*. See also Nicholas Dew, "Reading Travels in the Culture of Curiosity: Thévénot's Collection of Voyages", *Journal of Early Modern History* 10 (1–2) 2006, 39–59.

Georges Guillet de Saint-George (d.1705) in 1675, is basically a quest for Classical Greece, but also reflects on the life of the reigning sultan, Mehmed IV, and his Köprülü grand viziers.[34] There is also the very curious *L'Espion du Grand Seigneur* in no fewer than eight volumes (644 letters). As the title suggests, this is a collection of fictional letters by an imaginary Ottoman spy named Mahmut, the Arabian at the court of Louis XIV, from 1637 to 1682. Furthermore, it also incorporates visions of the Ottoman court. The first volume (102 letters) was written by Giovanni Paolo Marana (d.1693), a Genoese political refugee who had in fact joined Louis XIV's entourage (1682 to 1689). Published in both Italian and French between 1684 and 1686, it was translated into English in 1687 (*Letters writ by a Turkish spy*).[35] The remaining seven volumes appeared

---

[34] Georges Guillet de Saint-Georges, *Athènes ancienne et nouvelle et l'estat present de l'empire des turcs: contenant la vie du Sultan Mahomet IV. Le ministere de Guillet de Saint-Georges, Georges, Coprogli Achmet Pacha, G. Vizir, & son Campement devant Candie. Avec le plan de la Ville d'Athenes*, 2nd edn (Paris: Chez Estienne Michallet, M.DC.LXXV [1675]). The English version is known as Georges Guillet de Saint-George, *An Account of a Late Voyage to Athens, Containing the Estate Both Ancient and Modern of that Famous City and of the Present Empire of the Turks: The Life of the Now Sultan Mahomet the IV, with the Ministry of the Grand Vizier Coprogli Achmet Pacha. Also the most remarkable passages in the Turkish camp at the siege of Candia and divers other particularities of the affairs of the port by Monsieur de La Guillatiere, a French gentleman; now Englished* (London: Printed by J. M. for H. Herringman, 1676). He called himself de la Guillatière. He had never been to Athens, and his vivid descriptions of the physical features of the city was based on a variety of eye-witness accounts provided by the French Capuchins who had settled in Athens.

[35] Giovanni Paolo Marana, *L'Esploratore turco, e le di lui relazioni segrete alla Porta ottomana, scoperte in Parigi nel regno di Luiggi il Grande. Tradotte dall'Arabo in Italiano, da Gian-Paolo Marana, e dall'Italiano in Francese da \*\*\*. Contengono le più nobili azioni della Francia e della Christianità, dall' anno 1637. fino al 1682. Tomo primo* (Paris: Claude Barbin, 1684); idem, *L'Espion du Grand-Seigneur, et ses relations secrètes, envoyées au Divan de Constantinople. Découvertes à Paris, pendant le règne de Louys le Grand. Traduites de l'Arabe en Italien Par le Sieur Jean-Paul Marana, Et de l'Italien en François par \*\*\*. Ces Relations contiennent les Evenemens les plus considerables de la Chrestienté & de la France, depuis l'Année 1637. jusques en l'Année 1682. Tome premier* (Paris: Claude Barbin, 1684). See also C. J. Betts, *Early Deism in France: From the So-called 'déistes' of Lyon (1564) to Voltaire's "Lettres philosophiques" (1734)* (The Hague: M. Nijhoff Publishers, 1984) 97–8; Béatrice Guion, "L'Espion du Grand Seigneur, ou l'invention du roman épistolaire oriental", *Littératures classiques* 1 (2010), 187–202; Aleksandra Porada, "Giovanni Paolo Marana's Turkish Spy and the Police of Louis XIV: the Fear of Being Secretly Observed by Trained Agents in Early Modern Europe", *Altre Modernità/Otras Modernidades/Autres Modernités/Other Modernities, Saggi/Ensayos/Essais/Essays* 11 (2014), 96–110. Mahmut "sends reports from Paris to Constantinople on politics and current events in France, but corresponds privately on other subjects including religion, and adds stories and anecdotes for diversion". We are told that his observations range from "those on political figures such as Richelieu and Mazarin to speculations on the status of women, advice about state policy, and major interventions in controversies about religious doctrine and their consequences". His political

first in English between 1691 and 1694, prefaced with a letter claiming that they were translated from a manuscript in Italian. A French edition of the last seven volumes was published in 1696/7, under the title *L'Espion dans les cours des princes Chrétiens*.

## 4 Köprülü's Alleged Origins: A Patchwork

Fascinating as all these are, here I will be limiting myself to the two texts by de Chassepol and Le Noble, especially since both asserted that Köprülü Mehmed was born a Frenchman. Of the reign of Murad IV, Chassepol says that

> the Empire never enjoyed a greater calm, and nothing was thought of in Constantinople, but feasting and rejoicing. The Grand Signior's court since the peace concluded with the Persian, was crowded with idle officers, who waited there in expectation of some recompense for their services.

He then remarks that

> Mahomet Coprogli Pacha was one of this number, his father was named Coprogly, whom some affirmed to be the son of a mariner, others of a gentleman, who by some concerns of his family, being obliged to quit France, and settle himself in Italy, was in his voyage thither assaulted, and slain by a Turkish pirate, by whom his son then about ten or twelve years old, was made a slave, and carried into Cyprus. The Bassa Barac Bey,

---

position in the letters changes from that of liberal Catholic to that of a rationalistic Deist. The work was popular throughout the eighteenth century and went through fifteen complete editions by 1801. Daniel Defoe is said to be attracted to the deist rationalist sympathies of "Mahmut". On Oriental fantasies in English novels, see Srinivas Aravamudan, *Enlightenment Orientalism: Resisting the Rise of the Novel: Narratives about the Rise of the Novel* (Chicago: University of Chicago Press, 2011). Aravamudan explores how Oriental tales, sexual fantasies, and political satires became popular in eighteenth century Europe; he poses a range of urgent questions that uncover the interdependence of Oriental tales and domestic fiction, thereby challenging standard scholarly narratives about the rise of the novel. Paula R. Backscheider and Catherine Ingrassia (eds), *A Companion to the Eighteenth-Century English Novel and Culture* (London: Wiley-Blackwell, 2005); Rosalind Ballaster (ed.), *Fables of the East: Selected Tales, 1662–1785* (Oxford: OUP, 2005); *idem*, *Fabulous Orients: Fictions of the East in England, 1662–1785* (Oxford: OUP, 2005); Martha Pike Conant, *The Oriental Tale in England in the Eighteenth Century* (London: Forgotten Books, 2013, reprint of 1908 edn).

governor of this island, taking notice of the gallant spirit of the young Coprogli and his inclination to arms, educated him [with] great care, and when he went to the Persian war took him along with him, where he behaved himself so well, that he obtained a Timariots Place for him of the Emperor Achmet, and another very considerable charge in the army, in which afterwards his son Mehmet Coprogli, notwithstanding his youth and the contrary custom of the Turks, succeeded him: He acquired himself in his employment with great reputation, and by his merit and good mind, advantageously maintained that credit which his valor had gained in the war.[36]

On the same point of origins, this is Le Noble's version:

His father was a French Renegade, born in Champagne, near Chalons, in a Village call'd Cuperli, from whence he took his Name, being a Serjeant in a Foot Company, and which he left to his Posterity. A certain Murder which he committed, enforc'd him to fly his Country, and the Bark which he took himself being taken by the *Turkish* Corsairs, he thought it more convenient to wear a Turbant, then to see himself chain'd to the Oar, and being a handsome person, he was soon enroll'd among the *janissaries*, among whom, having rais'd himself by Valour to signal Employments, he obtain'd a *Timar*, or a proportion of Lands for Life, and spun so fair a Thread for himself, that by degrees he arriv'd to the highest place of the Empire. This is the truth, both of the Original and Name of the Cuproli's, and whatever is aver'd to the contrary is mere Fiction.[37]

Thus, both accounts agree on his having been a renegade – but from where? Is there any room at all for a French insertion at this point? Köprülü Mehmed's origins and his early career are indeed vague, which is common enough for a *devşirme*, but perhaps not so vague as to be entirely unknowable. Thus it was noted by his contemporaries that he was from Ruznik (Rudnik, Roshnik or Roşnik) of Berat. Furthermore, he actually built a mosque and a school in the village of Ruznik, which in one of his endowment deeds was specified as his motherland (*vatan-ı aslî*).[38] Such evidence notwithstanding, for some like the

---

36   De Chassepol, *Histoire*, 12–13.
37   Le Noble, *Abra-Mulé*, 5–6.
38   Metin Kunt, "The Köprülü Years: 1656–1661" (Ph.D. dissertation, Princeton University, 1971); idem, "Na'îmâ, Köprülü and Grand Vizieriate", *Boğaziçi Üniversitesi Dergisi. Hümaniter Bilimler* 1 (1973), 57–64; idem, "Ethnic-Regional (cins) Solidarity in the Seventeenth-Century Ottoman Establishment", *IJMES* 5 (1974), 233–9; idem, "The Waqf as an Instrument of Public

Moldavian chronicler Ion Neculce (d.1745), his Albanian origins rested on a legend "full of Oriental charm, historical inaccuracies and anachronisms", so that by the mid-eighteenth century doubts had been cast on it. Neculce, for his part, claimed that two poor Albanian boys had met on the road to Istanbul, and promised to support one another in the future. One, he said, was an 'Arbëreshë', which could be either an 'Albanian' or a 'speaker of Albanian' who went on to become Gheorghe Ghica, while the other was a 'Turk from Cyprus'; this is how he referred to Mehmed, the founder of the Köprülü (Chiprului) dynasty.[39]

It is unclear how this is supposed to refute the main narrative tradition, which other accounts tend to reinforce, although it is also clear that, after a point, many authors are reading and borrowing rather fancifully from each other, so that story lines keep criss-crossing all the time. As the Prince of Moldavia (1658–59) and Wallachia (1659–60), Gheorghe (Georgios) Ghica is – in some of the relevant scholarly literature – thought to have suppressed his Albanian origins. He is identified as a native of Veles (Köprülü), a town on the Vardar River (in today's North Macedonia), who was born to Albanian parents. During Ottoman times Veles was a township (*kaza*) in the *sancak* of Üsküb (modern-day Skopje). It was actually called Köprü (Kiupru) in Turkish.

Policy: Notes on the Köprülü Family Endowments", in Colin Heywood and Colin Imber (eds) *Studies in Ottoman History in Honor of Professor V. L. Ménage* (Istanbul: Isis Press, 1994), 189–98. Since then a number of articles, theses and dissertations have been written especially on the military accomplishments of the Köprülü viziers. For primary sources, see Ahmed Refik, *Köprülüler* (Istanbul: Kitaphane-i Hilmi-İbrâhim Hilmi, 1331/1915), republished as Ahmed Refik Altınay, *Köprülüler* (Istanbul: Tarih Vakfı Yurt Yayınları, 2012); Mehmet Arslan (ed.) *Hadîkatü'l-Vüzerâ ve Zeylleri: Osmanlı Sadrazamları* (Istanbul: Kitabevi, 2013), 118–20; Behçet-i İbrâhim, *Tarih-i Sülâle-i Köprülü (Silsiletü'l Asafiyyeti fî Devleti'l-Hakaniyyeti'l- Osmaniyye)*, KKT, Ahmed Pasha no. 212. For the Ottoman chronicles, see Defterdar Sarı Mehmed Pasha, *Zübde-i Vekayiât: Tahlil ve Metin (1066–1116/1656–1704)*, edited by Abdülkadir Özcan (Ankara: TTK, 1995); M. Tayyib Gökbilgin, "Köprülüler", *ISA* 6, 892–908; Mücteba İlgürel, "Köprülü Mehmed Paşa", *DIA* 26, 258–60; Nacire Karaçay-Türkal, "Silâhdar Fındıklılı Mehmed Ağa. Zeyl-i Fezleke, (1065–22 c.1106/1654–7 Şubat 1695) (Tahlil ve Metin)" (Ph.D. dissertation, Marmara University, 2012); Na'îmâ Mustafa Efendi. *Târih-i Na'îmâ*, 4 vols edited by Mehmet İpşirli (Ankara: TTK, 2007); Râşid Mehmed Efendi, *Çelebizâde İsmaîl Âsım Efendi. Târîh-i Râşid ve Zeyli (1071–1114/1660–1703)*, edited by Abdülkadir Özcan, Yunus Uğur, Baki Çakır et al. (Istanbul: Klasik, 2013); R. C. Repp, "Köprülü Mehmed Paşa", *EI*² 5, 256–9; Mehmet Topal, *Nusretnâme; Inceleme-Metin (1106–1133/1695–1721)* (Ankara: Türkiye Bilimler Akademisi, 2018); Sultan Murat Topçu, *Gücün Mimariye Yansıması: Köprülüler* (Ankara: TTK, 2015); İ. H. Uzunçarşılı, *Osmanlı Tarihi* III/2 (Ankara: TTK, 1988, first published 1954), 414–18.

39    Legend 37 from Ion Neculce, *Letopisețul Țării Moldovei* (București: Editura Litera International, 2001), 28–30. Ion Neculce went to Russia alongside Dimitrie Cantemir and spent a few years there before his return to Moldavia in 1719. http://www.ghika.net/Divers/Articles/Famille%20Ghika.htm.

A biographer of the Ghica family has suggested that Georgios joined Köprülü Mehmed's faction in Istanbul in 1653 and achieved commercial and political successes with the latter's support, implying that their childhood friendship and Albanian solidarity had withstood the test of time.[40] In another version, Mehmed is said to have recognized Gheorghe while he was selling melons in the streets of Istanbul and helped him on to high positions.[41] It has been proposed, somewhat speculatively, that the Albanian form of Mehmed's name was *Qyprilliu* or *Qypëelliu*, and *Qyprillinjte e beratit* still stands for the Köprülüs in Albanian secondary literature. An alternative version is that his nickname derived from Köprü (later Vezirköprü) near Amasya where he was sent from the Topkapı Palace treasury because of his difficult personality. Perhaps a more truthful explanation is the very opposite – that he actually gave his already existing nickname, Köprülü, to the town, which thereby became Köprü. In any case, there he is said to have married the daughter of the town's *voyvoda* to resume his quick rise through the ranks. As his former mentor, Grand Vizier Hüsrev Pasha kept climbing in imperial service, so did Köprülü, who was promoted to increasingly important offices, and was eventually appointed grand vizier in 1656.[42]

At the time of these French reconstructions, Köprülü Mehmed Pasha had been dead for at least fifteen years. A few bits and pieces of information they contain, such as his father gaining a *tımâr* during the reign of Ahmed I (1603–17), appear as if they could have derived from some Ottoman sources (though that does not make them automatically reliable). At the same time, his connection to Cyprus remains most unfounded and needs an explanation.

Then there is also the story of his rise to power. Chassepol claims that Mehmed gained the esteem and friendship of the chief of the Black Eunuchs (*Kisler Agasi*, named 'Uglan'), who further trained, educated, and introduced him to court dignitaries, topped by the grand vizier and the sultan's confidant.[43] Uglan as such is impossible to identify or to assimilate to any known

---

40  Christine Philliou, *Biography of an Empire: Governing Ottomans in an Age of Revolution* (Berkeley: University of California Press, 2011), 16. Philliou's footnote 32 refers to Kunt's 1974 article, which actually does not contain this information. See Kunt, "Ethnic-Regional (cins) Solidarity", *passim*.
41  *EBR*, 11th edn, s.v. "Ghica".
42  İlgürel, "Köprülü", 258; Na'îmâ, *Târîh* 4, 1697.
43  De Chassepol, *Histoire*, 14–15: "This Eunuch was so favourable to Mahomet Coprogli that he promised to second him in all occasions that might serve to raise his fortune. He was a man of great address, had experience in all the intrigues of the court in which he was grown old." The chronology of the Chief Black Eunuchs in this period is as follows: Reyhan (1603), Hacı Mustafa (1604–20 and 1623–24), Süleyman Ağa (1620–22), İsmail (1622–23), Hacı Mustafa again (1623–24), İdris (1624–39?), İbrahim (1639), Sünbül (1640), Taşyatur

Ottoman character, but if there is any truth to this whole construct, the Black Eunuch in question may have been (Hacı) Mustafa Ağa, who was notorious for his interventions in court politics under Ahmed I and Mustafa I. De Chassepol presents him as an ally of Murad IV's mother Kiozem (Kösem) Sultan, saying that he became the sultan's mother's ally after the death of Roxana (la Rosso, Russo), Murad's favourite. At first sight this looks very anachronistic, giving one to think that de Chassepol might have got his centuries hopelessly confused (Süleyman I's Roxelana died in 1558). At the same time, Murad IV is said to have had a son from the sister, allegedly called Rachima, of the defeated governor of Yerevan, Mirgune (Emir Gûne) Tahmasp Quli Khan. Furthermore, the boy is said to have been called Soliman Amurath (Süleyman Murad).[44] I cannot decide whether this explains or further complicates the situation.

To proceed, de Chassepol recounts how the courtiers of Murad IV grew jealous of Köprülü Mehmed as the sultan came to favour him. The author introduces Zaime, a young woman brought from Circassia to the palace by the grand admiral in the absence of Murad IV. Zaime is cast as Hadice Turhan Sultan, mother of Mehmed IV. De Chassepol also introduces Zaime's slave woman, Fatima, who is said to have caught the eyes of the sultan's courtiers including (Köprülü) Mehmed and Zalim Achmed, Mehmed's rival who appears to have been modelled on Hafız Ahmed Pasha (d.1632). The sultan, too, is reported to have fallen in love with Fatima.[45] However, Zaime manages to marry Fatima to Köprülü Mehmed, and to send the couple off to Beirut; simultaneously, Zalim Achmed (cast as the nephew of Grand Vizier Receb Pasha, d.1632) was made governor of Syria and posted to Aleppo.[46]

---

Ali (1644), Celâli İbrahim (1645), İshak (1647), for a few days Musahib Mehmed, then İshak again, Mesud, and Celâli İbrahim once more (1648), Mehmed (1649), Süleyman (1651), Behram (1652), Dilâver (1656), Solak Mehmed (1658). See Ahmet Resmî Efendi, *Hamîletü'l-Küberâ*, edited by Ahmet Nezihi Turan (Istanbul: Kitabevi, 2000).

44  No hasekis (favourite consort in the imperial harem who mothered the sultan's child) of Murad IV are recorded. De Chassepol mentions Roxana as accompanying Murad IV during the campaign to Iran; she was extremely jealous when Rachima became his lover. De Chassepol also notes that although the sultan had many women in the harem, he had no children. So Rachima, says Chassepol, was left in Damascus and gave birth to a son. See de Chassepol, *Histoire*, 118. It should be noted that the Ottoman army did not make a stop in Damascus; and Naîmâ records the birth of Prince Alaüddin on the way from Revan at Bakû/Makû Suyu (12 Rebîyülevvel 1045/26 August 1635). See Na'îmâ, *Târîh* 4, 252.

45  De Chassepol, *Histoire*, 19–25. Hafız Ahmed Pasha was appointed twice as the grand vizier: February 1625–December 1626 and October 1631–February 1632. He was brutally murdered during a revolt when the janissaries attempted to overthrow Sultan Murad IV. See İsmail Hami Danişmend, *Osmanlı Devlet Erkânı* (Istanbul: Türkiye Yayınevi, 1971), 33–4.

46  De Chassepol, *Histoire*, 29. We do not know whether Köprülü Mehmed was married to a certain Fatima. His wife Ayşe Hatun, on the other hand, is well-documented. She was the

## 5 Seductive, Sequestered Women

Travellers to the Levant have said and imagined much about lust in the harem. Chapters on royal ladies and the harem were part and parcel of their narratives. De Chassepol says that Zaime was pregnant when Murad IV died (February 1640). Both Murad IV's mother Kiozem and Zaime feared that the new sultan İbrâhim would sacrifice Murad's child for his own safety, and they called Fatima, Köprülü Mehmed's wife, to help take the child out of the palace. Fatima herself was about to give birth, and this served as a pretext for her coming to Istanbul. In the meantime, Köprülü indeed had a son (Fâzıl Ahmed b.1635), and Zaime, we are told, gave birth to Murad IV's daughter, Iohaime (Rachima?), who, according to de Chassepol, was also raised by Köprülü Mehmed and Fatima.

It was around this time, in de Chassepol's account, that the chief of the Black Eunuchs Süleyman Ağa replaced Uglan;[47] and both Zaime (for the second time) and Bassée, a handsome Georgian who had then become Sultan İbrâhim's favourite, gave birth to sons. Bassée's son was called Osman. This Osman is then conflated with Padre Ottomano, a famous figure in the Turkish lore and legend of the 1650s. This pretender, who claimed to be a son of İbrâhim, was said to have found himself in Europe as a result of a series of unfortunate events.

Such pretenders were common phenomena in medieval and early modern times, and are also occasionally mentioned in Ottoman chronicles. In *Nusretnâme*, for example, Fındıklılı Silahdâr Mehmed Ağa narrates the 1708 story of one who arrived in Chios, claiming that his pregnant mother had been sent to Egypt, and that he had taken refuge first in Morocco and then in Algeria.[48]

---

daughter of a certain Yusuf Ağa, a notable originally from the Kayacık (village) of Havza (town) at Amasya (administrative district). Yusuf Ağa was the voyvod[a] of Kadegra, a district of Amasya, where Mehmed was the sancakbey in 1634. Kadegra was named Köprü after a bridge that Yusuf Ağa constructed and Vezirköprü after his daughter Ayşe was united with Mehmed Pasha. Not only Ayşe Hatun's identity as Köprülü Mehmed's wife and mother of his children, but also her patronage in her home town and elsewhere, are supported by documentary evidence. See Sultan Murat Topçu, "Osmanlılar Döneminde Güçlü Bir Kadın Bani: Köprülü Ayşe Hanım", *Kadın/Woman 2000 Kadın Araştırmaları Dergisi* 10 (2) 2009, 45–84.

47 See de Chassepol, *Histoire*, 76–7 on Uglan's murder and Süleyman succeeding Uglan.
48 "Def'-i fitne-i 'azîme: Bu vaķitde Cezâ'îr'den bir şehzâde ẓuhûr eyleyüb Saķız Adası'na gelmiş, 'ben Sulṭân Meḥmed evlâdındanım, vâlidem ḥâmile iken maġdûben Mıṣır'a sürülmüş, giderken kâfir eline düşmüş, kendüyü bildirmiş, i'tibâr edib İspanya ķralına getürmüşler, vaķti geldikde beni doğurmuş, az zamânda fevt olub beni ḥadd-i bulûġa irdüğümde beni Fas pâdişâhına gönderdiler. Bir taķrîb ile Rûm diyârına ulaşdırabildiniz deyü tenbîh eylediler. Ol daḫî beni Cezâ'îr'e gönderib ândan işbu maḥalle geldim. Türkçe bilmez, Frengî ve 'Arabî tekellüm ider, tercümân lisânıyla bî-pervâ böyle sözler

Back to Osman who becomes Padre Ottomano. There are different variants of his story, and the earliest seems to have been published in 1669 by John Evelyn (also de Chassepol's translator). In *The History of the Three Late, Famous Impostors, viz. Padre Ottomano, Mahomed Bei and Sabatai Sevi*, Evelyn claimed that his stories were "of 'undoubted Verity', having been obtained from eyewitnesses, whose names are suppressed lest they should be exposed thereby to inconvenience."[49] The narrator of the first two impostures, 'a Persian stranger', is easily identified as a Safavid Jew. At the beginning of the first story a beautiful slave is obtained by Kesler Ağa, the chief of the Black Eunuchs, through a merchant called Jacobo Cesii. A study on John Evelyn has revealed that the

söylemiş. Ben ḫaṭṭ-ı hümâyûn ve fermân ile geldim deyü yanında sâḫte fermânlar ve ḫaṭṭ-ı hümâyûna taḳlîd ba'żı kâġadlar bulunmuş, ḳapucubaşı nâmıyla Rûmlu bir münşî ḥerîfi vezîr idinmek fikriyle bile uydurup bir taḳrîb ile Anadolu'ya geçüb sâde-dil bir alay eşḳiyâyı başına cem' eyleyüb Burusa'da taḫta geçmek fikrinde olduğu şâyi' olmağla Sakız Muḥâfıẓı Ṣadr-ı sâbıḳ Bâlṭacı Meḥmed Paşa ikisini de giriftâr idüb Rikâb-ı hümâyûna 'arż-ı i'lâm eyledi. Der-'aḳab fermân-ı vâcibü'l-îẕân ile vezîr-i a'ẓam ḳapıcılar ketḫüdâsı gönderilüb başların kesüb getürdü ve Bâb-ı hümâyûna bırakıldı (early Zilkade 1119/late January 1708)'". See Topal, "Silahdar Fındıklılı Mehmed Ağa", 698.

49 John Evelyn, *The history of the three late, famous impostors, viz. Padre Ottomano, Mahomed Bei and Sabatai Sevi. The one, pretended son and heir to the late Grand Signior, the other, a prince of the Ottoman family, but in truth, a Valachian counterfeit, and the last, the suppos'd Messiah of the Jews, in the year of the true Messiah, 1666: with a brief account of the ground and occasion of the present war between the Turk and the Venetian: together with the cause of the final extirpation, destruction and exile of the Jews out of the Empire of Persia* (In the Savoy [London]: Printed for Henry Herringman, 1669). See also "Padre Ottomano: The Supposed Heir of Sultan Ibrahim", in Anon. *Celebrated Claimants from Perkin Warbeck to Arthur Orton* (London: Chatto and Windus, Piccadilly, 1874), 42–5: "In the miscellaneous writings of John Evelyn, the diary-writer, there is an account of this extraordinary impostor, whose narration of his own adventures outshines [46] that of Munchausen, and whose experiences, according to his own showing, were more remarkable than those of Gulliver. In 1668 this marvellous personage published a book entitled the 'History of Mohammed Bey; or, John Michel de Cigala, Prince of the Imperial Blood of the Ottomans.' This work he dedicated to the French King, who was disposed to favour his pretensions." The author of this compilation of interesting stories remains anonymous. For Padre Ottomano, see also Vincenzo Abbondanza, *Dizionario storico delle vite di tutti i monarchi ottomani; fino al regnante ignore Achmet IV., e delle piu riguardevoli cose appartenenti a quella Monarchia. Dato alla luce da Vincenzo Abbondanza* ... (Rome: Per Luigi Vescovi, a Filippo Neri, 1786), 81–3; and Robert Southey and Samuel Taylor Coleridge, *Omniana, or Horae Otiosiores* 1–2 (London: Printed for Longman, Hurst, Rees et al., 1812), 60–9. For a recent study that claims to sort out the many facts from fiction, see Thomas Freller and Dolores Campoy, *Padre Ottomano and Malta: A Story of the 1001 Nights* (Santa Venera: Midsea Books, 2006). For a Wallachian pretender, see Gábor Kármán, "The Networks of a Wallachian Pretender in Constantinople: The Contacts of the Future Voivode Mihail Radu 1654–1657", in Gábor Kármán and Radu G. Păun (eds) *Europe and the 'Ottoman World': Exchanges and Conflicts (Sixteenth to Seventeenth Centuries)* (Istanbul: Isis Press, 2013), 119–39.

corresponding entry in the author's *Diary* under 29 September 1668 reads: "I had much discourse with Sig. Pietro Cesij, a Persian gent., about the affaires of Turkey to my great satisfaction."[50]

In a 1689 Italian account, entitled *Vita del padre maestro f. Domenico di S. Tomaso dell'Ordine de' Predicatori, detto prima Sultan Osinan Ottomano, figlio d'Ibraim imperador de' Turchi*, Osman was identified as the first-born son of Sultan İbrâhim from Mehmed IV's milk mother Zarife (or Sultana Zafira), a Georgian slave procured by Sünbül Ağa.[51] In another version, we are told that İbrâhim had developed a particular affection for Zarife's son Osman, to the extent that he injured his crown prince (Mehmed) by throwing him into a pool after getting into a quarrel with jealous Zaime (Hatice Turhan Sultan) over 'Sultana Zafira'. In de Chassepol's account of the clash between İbrâhim's two women, "out of sorrow and anger", we are told, "he had the thrust of his dagger in to her (Hatice Turhan's) breast, if young Mahomet had not staid his hand, and received the stroke which he intended to have given his mother." Then thrown away, the young prince was hurt above the right eye.[52] After this incident, we are told, Sünbül, the chief of the Black Eunuchs (who had presented Zarife to the sultan) decided to save his own life, together with those of the milk mother and her son Osman. The three left on the pretext of going to Hajj. They were allegedly captured by the Knights of Malta (or by the pirates) in a giant galleon on 28 September 1644, and Sünbül Ağa was murdered. The young boy was raised as Padre Domenico Ottomano, and the Maltese claimed him to be an Ottoman prince and took him around Europe. He was kept as a secret weapon to be made operational if the need arose; this was common practice at the time. It has been claimed that it was this incident that led İbrâhim to declare war on the Venetians, whom he accused of collaborating with the Knights of Malta. All along, one also keeps reading about how Zalim Achmed, who had become grand vizier, wanted to take revenge on both Köprülü Mehmed and Zaime (Hatice Turhan) (for sending him away to Aleppo?).[53] In the European literature of the time, there are several other accounts of Osman who is said to

---

50   Geoffrey Keynes, "John Evelyn: A Study in Bibliophily", Sandars Lectures, 1933–34 (Cambridge: CUP Archive, 1934), 194. Evelyn (d.1706) was a writer, a diarist whose memoirs cast considerable light on the art, culture and politics of the time in England.

51   Ottaviano Bulgarini, *Vita del padre maestro f. Domenico di S. Tomaso dell'Ordine de' Predicatori, detto prima Sultan Osinan Ottomano, figlio d'Ibraim imperador de' Turchi. Disposta in dieci libri dal padre baccelliere f. Ottaviano Bulgarini ... Con una breve geneologia di tutti l'imperadori ottomani sino al presente regnante per introduzione dell'opera* (Naples: Presso Giuseppe Roselli, 1689), *passim*.

52   De Chassepol, *Histoire*, 52–3.

53   De Chassepol, *Histoire*, 58. See footnote 46 above.

have been educated in Malta and taken the vows of a Dominican friar before becoming known as Padre Ottomano.

## 6  Sex, Lies, and Grand Viziers

De Chassepol's version, however, is perhaps even more convoluted. It was İbrâhim's decision to secure himself on the throne by ensuring the death of one of his own children and leaving only the other as his heir. For this he tried to use the pretext of a vow about sending one to Mecca. He did not want to send his eldest son Osman by Basseé, but Zaime was once more pregnant and she could not be allowed to accompany her son, Mehmed (IV). Then Basseé, as soon as she found out about İbrâhim's plan, managed to set off (with Sünbül) for Alexandria, but this was when they were captured by the Knights of Malta. Later, after much-publicized sojourns in Naples, Rome and Paris and, according to de Chassepol, Padre Ottomano participated in an expedition to relieve Crete from the long Ottoman campaign to capture the island. European rulers, including Louis XIV who embraced him as the heir of the Ottoman dynasty, sent letters to Fâzıl Ahmed Pasha (Köprülü Mehmed's son and successor as grand vizier) to have Osman installed on the throne. When this scheme failed, Osman stepped back from European politics and settled in Malta as a prior of Porto Salvo in Valletta and the vicar general of the Dominicans.[54]

All these were recounted in de Chassepol's first book. His second book is entirely on Köprülü Mehmed's military and political achievements. The grand vizier's cruelty and bloodshed are attributed to his desire to raise and train the young sultan (Mehmed IV).[55] There is also the end to the story of Soliman Amurath, who is said to be the son of Murad IV and Rachima, Mirgune's (Emir Gûne) sister. He marches from Aleppo to Istanbul in order to win the Ottoman throne. Köprülü Mehmed sends his own son Ahmed (Fâzıl Ahmed Pasha) to crush him, and restrains Mehmed IV, who wants to go with Ahmed. Soliman Amurath, the other 'illegitimate' Ottoman prince, is defeated, captured and executed.[56]

In the third and fourth books by de Chassepol, it is Köprülüzâde Fâzıl Ahmed Pasha who looms large over a number of complicated and quite dramatic love stories involving long-held stereotypes such as the Circassian slave girl. Fâzıl Ahmed falls in love with Murad IV's daughter Iohaima; Mehmed IV

---

54  De Chassepol, *Histoire*, 59–60.
55  De Chassepol, *Histoire*, 73–4.
56  De Chassepol, *Histoire*, 109–22.

is also said to have fallen in love with her without knowing that she happened to be his half-sister (as their mother is Zaime).[57] Then somebody called Eugeni is introduced, and is said to have changed her name to Zachi. This has to be the real-life Gülnuş Emetullah, mother of Mehmed IV's two princes (the future Mustafa II and Ahmed III). There is also Maiama, Prince Süleyman II's mother.[58] Another intricate subplot involves a Zizim Morat Pasha who receives a slave woman called *Zulemai*, as a gift from Izmir's *sancak beyi* Sinan. (It should be noted that Mehmed II's son Cem, the first Ottoman prince who sought refuge in Europe, was called Zizim by the French.) While *Zulemai* is kept in Zizim Murat's country house, Mehmed IV comes visiting, meets the gardener's daughter Abdima, and has an affair with her. As Gülnuş (Zachi, Eugenia) suspects not Abdima but *Zulemai*, the story gets even more entangled. This is no surprise: de Chassepol's book was written as a novel, and he even wanted to write a sequel in the future.[59]

Like de Chassepol's love tragedy, the final story of Eustache Le Noble's *Abra-Mulé* (1695) revolves around two Süleymans, the prince (later Süleyman II) and the vizier (Sarı Süleyman Pasha), as well as Mehmed IV.[60] Le Noble accounts for the 1687 deposition of the Ottoman sultan as the product of rivalries among these three over the love of an alluring slave in the harem. The main character, Abra-Mulé, is a Muscovite, the daughter of a boyar (Mulé-Alexowitz). The vizier, Süleyman, is the first to fall in love with her.[61] When she is brought to the palace, both the sultan, Mehmed IV, and the prince, Süleyman II, also fall in love with her. A number of letters are exchanged. In the end, following a number of dramatic events, including an accident at sea and a fire at the palace, Abra-Mulé commits suicide.[62] Süleyman the vizier is strangled, Süleyman the prince falls into melancholy, and Mehmed IV loses his empire. Other than the sultan and the prince, all the other main characters – such as Marama, Prince Süleyman's confidant; Sarai, Abra-Mulé's slave; Zaid, Sarai's niece – are fictional. As for the vizier named Süleyman, I believe him to have been modelled on Sarı Süleyman Pasha, who acted as grand vizier from 18 November 1685 to 18 September 1687. He was executed in October 1687 after the Ottoman defeat at the battle of Mohács.[63] Among the secondary cast are

---

57  De Chassepol, *Histoire*, 169. Ahmed and Iohaima unites, 178.
58  De Chassepol, *Histoire*, 86–8, 233.
59  De Chassepol, *Histoire*, 237–41.
60  De Chassepol, *Histoire*, 235–45; Le Noble, *Abra-Mulé, passim*.
61  Le Noble, *Abra-Mulé*, 14.
62  Le Noble, *Abra-Mulé*, 73, 105.
63  After the defeat, the Ottoman army started a rebellion against the grand vizier. Süleyman Pasha escaped first to Belgrade and then to Istanbul. At the beginning of September 1687,

some other real people who appear to have been included just to enhance the realistic flavour of Le Noble's novel. As Imre Thököly, too, is mentioned several times,[64] it should be noted that among Le Noble's many publications there is also a volume on *François Ragotzi, Prince Souverain de Transslyvanie*, which includes the prince's engraved portrait.[65]

## 7  Where Did These Stories Come From?

There are numerous similarities between de Chassepol's and Le Noble's accounts, as well as a few others from the same period. In some of these novellas, correct place names are given, or flora and fauna, or a hut in the forest, or a hunting party are described quite realistically (to the extent of becoming informative to the modern researcher). Certain architectural features or aspects of material culture often seem to reflect eye-witness accounts. Many characters, including their physical features or character traits, also appear to be based on observation.[66] How were such true-to-life reconstructions possible?

In *The Whispers of Cities*, John-Paul A. Ghobrial has recently focused on Istanbul, Paris and London to explore information flows between early modern Europe and the Ottoman Empire. He sheds light on the transmission of news and knowledge involving real people and real events.[67] He presents a

---

news about his defeat and escape arrived in Istanbul. Mehmed IV proclaimed Abaza Siyavuş Pasha as the new commander of the army, Süleyman Pasha was executed. Two months later, the sultan himself was also removed from power as the result of the defeat in the Battle of Mohács, and was replaced by Sultan Süleyman II. İsmail Hami Danişmend, *İzahlı Osmanlı Tarihi Kronolojisi* 3 (Istanbul: Türkiye Yayınevi, 1972), 462–5.

64   Le Noble, *Abra-Mulé*, 45–7, 81.
65   Eustache Le Noble, *Histoire du prince Ragotzi: ou La guerre des mécontents sous son commandement* (Paris: Chez J. de Nully, 1707).
66   "This Prince [Mehmed IV] is capable of being strongly ingaged, and his conduct has manifested that he is very constant in love, his soul is great and royal, his humor is chearful, sociable, and familiar, but not indifferently with everybody, for he can be grave on occasion, and that with so much majesty, as imprints an universal awe: his shape is not very advantageous, but it was straight, before he fell from his horse one day in leaping a ditch in hunting, which hurt him on the left side, and makes him a little crooked. He has the finest eyes that a man can have; his mouth is good, his complexion is a little gross, and not very smooth, since he had the Small Pox; his beard is of Chesnut colour, like as his hair; his-gate is grave, and though his constitution be somewhat tender, yet he is very vigorous: he is very skilful in the use of the Bow, and the Musquet; he is exceeding generous, and when he has any War in hand, lays aside all his plaesures, though he loves them excessively" (de Chassepol, *Histoire*, 163–4).
67   John-Paul Ghobrial, *The Whispers of Cities: Information Flows in Istanbul, London, and Paris in the Age of William Trumbull* (Oxford: OUP, 2013).

well-documented case on the role that Sir William Trumbull, the English ambassador at the Porte from 1686 to 1691, played, through his personal connections in Istanbul, in the 'information flow' about the dethronement of Mehmed IV to audiences in Europe. The private papers of Trumbull, compiled in forty volumes and including all his notes and letters from Istanbul, have enabled Ghobrial to reconstruct the ambassador's social circle. Diplomats, dragomans, renegades, merchants, doctors, and Ottoman officials turn out to have provided Trumbull with information on a variety of topics. Some of these people, moving from one distinguished house to the other, often changed their identities to hide their shady backgrounds. This leads us to the question of impostors, a curious crowd of people in the Ottoman capital. Aubry de la Motraye, for example, mentions an Italian who was pretending to be a doctor at the court of Imre Thököly in Izmit when he last saw him.[68] Previously, they had met in salons in Milan and Istanbul. While such people easily found patrons in Europe as well as in the Ottoman capital, there were also Ottoman subjects travelling and finding benefactors in Europe.[69]

---

68  Aubry de La Motraye's travels was first printed in English in London in 1723. See Aubry de La Motraye. *A. de La Motraye's Travels Through Europe, Asia, And Into Parts Of Africa: With Proper Cutts And Maps. Containing A Great Variety Of Geographical, Topographical, And Political Observations On Those Parts Of The World; especially on Italy, Turky, Greece, Crim and Noghaina Tartaries, Circassa, Sweden, and Lapland. A Curious Collection Of Things particularly Rare, both in Nature and Antiquity; such as Remains of ancient Cities and Colonies, Inscriptions, Idols, Medals, &c.* (London: Printed for the Author, 1723). The French version is A. de la Motraye's *Voyage du Sr.A. De La Motraye, en Europe, Asie & Afrique. Où l'on trouve une grande varieté de recherches geographiques, historiques & politiques, sur l'Italie, la Grèce, la Turquie, la Tartarie Crimée, & Nogaye, la Circassie, la Suède, la Laponie, &c. Avec des remarques instructives sur les moeurs, coutumes, opinions &c. des peuples & des Païs où l'auteur a voyagé; & des particularitez remarquables touchant les personnes & les auteurs distingués d'Angleterre, de France, d'Italie, de Suede, &c.* (The Hague: Chez T. Johnson & J. van Duren, 1727, 1–2).

69  John-Paul Ghobrial, "The Secret Life of Elias of Babylon and the Uses of Global Microhistory", *Past and Present* 222 (1) 2014, 51–93. On Dom Philippe, from Tunis, and Jean Bonnet, his slave from Cassis near Marseilles, see Baghdiantz McCabe, *Orientalism in Early Modern France* (Oxford: Berg, 2008), 142. There were lesser adventurers as well. On İsmail Beşe, allegedly a janissary turned merchant from Edirne who ended up England under the name Ismael James Bashaw, see Aykut Kansu, "18. Yüzyılda İngiltere'de bir Yeniçeri ya da Yasalara Bağlı bir Serseri'nin Yaşamından Kesitler", in Hamdi Can Tuncer (ed.) *Osmanlı'dan Cumhuriyet'e Problemler, Araştırmalar, Tartışmalar* (Istanbul: Tarih Vakfı Yurt Yayınları, 1998), 166–83. It is based on a short book, anonymously published in 1797, called *The Turkish refugee: being a narrative of the life, sufferings, deliverances, and conversion, of Ishmael Bashaw, a Mahometan merchant, from Constantinople, who was taken prisoner by the Spaniards, and made a wonderful escape to England, where, having become a convert to the Christian faith, he was publicly baptized, with the approbation of the Right Reverend the Lord Bishop of Lincoln* (London: printed by the family, 1797). Here

In addition to Trumbull's personal archive, now deposited in the British Library as "Memorials of My Embassy in Constantinople", there are his letters at the Public Record Office, reports of his expenditures in the Calendars of Treasury Books, and his official dispatches in the National Archives in London. Venetian diplomats, too, sent regular dispatches, *Dispacci*, to Venice that included immediate information with personal touches, intimate details, and gossip, plus more comprehensive official accounts, *Relazioni*, after the termination of their term in Istanbul. After all, the embassies (the Dutch, the German and the French too) did not get the bulk of their information from subscriptions to *nouvelles* or through their correspondence with the centre, but by connecting with locals.[70]

The news about Mehmed IV's abdication in favour of his brother Süleyman II (r.1687–91) was circulated both orally, and in scribal and printed texts. As Ghobrial notes, "some stories about Mehmed's deposition circulating in Europe were the product of pure speculation, and many writers used the event of Mehmed's deposition simply as a frame for telling more fanciful stories about politics in Istanbul."[71]

In 1689, John Phillips (1631–1706), a (rather scandalous) nephew of the celebrated poet John Milton, who is said to have visited the Ottoman capital in the aftermath of the 1683 Ottoman defeat at Vienna, highlighted the severity of the 1687 deposition of Mehmed IV in his *The Dilucidation of the Late Commotions of Turkey*, which he claimed to have translated from Italian:

---

we learn that "Ishmael James Bashaw was buried in 1815 at the burial ground of the Gildencroft Quaker Meeting House in Norwich. However, the register records that he was a non-member, that is not a Quaker. Other records here and there show his marriage to Elizabeth Fornish in Stamford in 1776, and the births of (some of) their children, George, Ann, Esther, James, Charlotte and John, between 1777 and 1795. The pattern of births shows the family moving from Wisbech to Spalding to Norwich to Framlingham to Colchester. They appear to have been mobile if not itinerant, and not wealthy – indeed, the parish authorities in Framlingham conducted a settlement examination in September 1788 to establish whether Bashaw and his family could claim relief in the parish, or could be lawfully palmed off on to a different parish." (http://www.bluebirdresearch.com/2013/06/bashaw-pasha/ Retrieved 28 September 2015.)

70   See also Rosanne Baars, "Constantinople Confidential: News and Information in the Diary of Jean-Louis Rigo (c.1686–1756), Secretary of the Dutch Embassy in Istanbul", *Lias* 41 (2) (2014), 143–171; Hannah Neudecker, "From Istanbul to London? Albertus Bobovius' Appeal to Isaac Basire", in A. Hamilton, M. van den Boogert and B. Westerweel (eds), *The Republic of Letters and the Levant* (Leiden: Brill, 2005), 173–96; R. Zaimova, "L'Espace culturel de Constantinople: Temoignages des Ambassedeurs de France à Constantinople (XVIIe–XVIIIe siècle)", *EBAL* 38 (1) 2002, 86–95.

71   Ghobrial, *Whispers*, 126.

It is thought that the deposed's life will be but very short, by reason of it's being the usual custom of that nation to step out of prisons into the grave, as also because that Mahomet being for so many years accustomed to pastimes, to the exercises of hunting, and to riding daily, and what is more to government, could very ill brook to see himself clapt-up in a chamber, deprived of all the recreation and authority, whence he must in a short time be conveyed to his tomb, although his death should not be hastned by the new Grand Signiors command.[72]

Ghobrial emphasizes that the period's more fanciful stories (such as, I would say, those told by de Chassepol or Le Noble, though he himself does not mention them explicitly), also constituted an important link in 'information flow' in a number of directions. Thus, for a start, Le Noble seems to have fed on Donneau de Visé's *Histoire du Mahomet IV* (1688).[73] Le Noble's account was then almost immediately translated into English, again by John Phillips, and published in 1696 as *Abra-Mulé, or a True History of the Dethronement of Mahomet IV*.[74] Years later, Joseph Trapp breathed new life into the tale when he wrote and staged a play based on it, entitled *Abra Mulé, or Love and Empire: A Tragedy*. It was first published in London in 1704, and several new editions were released throughout the eighteenth century. Ghobrial, noting that certain stories acquired a long and complex European genealogy, argues that they go back "to rumours that first circulated orally among the residents of the

---

72  I was unable to locate the original in Italian. See John Phillips, *The Dilucidation of the Late Commotions of Turkey: Containing an Exact and Distinct Account of all the Causes and Motives of the deposing of Mahomet, and of the advancing of Soliman to the Imperial Throne of Constantinople. Gather'd from the Letters of a person dwelling in, and Minutely infor'd of the Affairs that City, and Consecrated to the ever August Merit of the most Serene Elector of Bavaria. Printed in Italian at Venice, and translated into English by the Author of the Monthly Account. To be Annex'd to Numb. 10 of the Monthly Account* (London: printed by J. B. and are to be sold by Randall Taylor, near Stationers-Hall, 1689), 15–16. As noted in the title, it was part of his *Modern History, or Monethly Account of All Considerable Occurrences*, 1687–90. He had also (translated and) published *The Six Voyages of John Baptista Tavernier, Baron of Aubonne*, 1677; *A Late Voyage to Turkey*, 1683; *The Turkish Secretary*, 1688. Some sources of reference to his works in book catalogues of the period include a title "Jo. Phillip's Late Voyages to Constantinople, with Cuts 1683". See John T. Shawcross, *The Arms of the Family: The Significance of John Milton's Relatives and Associates* (Lexington, Kentucky: University Press of Kentucky, 2004), 245, footnote 23. For a long list and discussion of the books he published, see 95–33.
73  De Visé, *Histoire du Mahomet IV*.
74  John Phillips [translator], *Abra-Mulé, or a True History of the Dethronement of Mahomet IV* (London: R. Clavel, 1696).

Ottoman capital."[75] Once they were developed into preposterous stories about Istanbulite politics, they acquired a life of their own in the hands of adventurers, impostors or pretenders, many of whom were chasing their own fortunes. Another scholar comments:

> Not surprisingly, the sultan's seraglio, which was routinely represented as a microcosm of Ottoman society for its inversion on 'natural' principles, aroused particular interest. There, enveloped in unimaginable luxury and attended by a strange cast of black and white eunuchs, dwarfs, and mutes, the sultan was depicted as administering through subalterns, who were subject to immediate strangulation if they incurred the slightest disfavour. So, too, was the sultan served by hordes of captive women of Christian origin, selected to satisfy his lusts but inclined out of sexual frustration to engage in much discussed 'unnatural' practices. Further inciting French curiosity in the seraglio was the mystery that surrounded it due to a partial blackout of information. For unlike the personal affairs of French kings, which were largely a matter of public knowledge, the romances of the sultan were shrouded in secrecy. One frustrated seventeenth-century chronicler of the Turkish court despaired that so little reliable information was available regarding the internal affairs of the Seraglio that one could not describe them 'without … writing a novel', which is just what many novelists would do in the next century.[76]

That the Köprülüs should have loomed so large in European accounts of the late-seventeenth and early-eighteenth centuries comes as no surprise. In January 1691, as he was about to leave Istanbul, Trumbull met the newly appointed Köprülüzâde Fâzıl Mustafa Pasha. The ambassador referred to the grand vizier's father Mehmed and older brother Ahmed, and the protection and favours they had extended to his predecessors and himself as a reminder of his personal connections.[77] It was truly an impressive longevity, which, after the most illustrious first three of Mehmed, Ahmed, and Mustafa, would keep extending into the future. All in all, seven Köprülü grand viziers came to rule from 1656 to 1735, though not consecutively, while several other family

---

75  Ghobrial, *Whispers*, 126.
76  T. Kaiser, "The Evil Empire? The Debate on Turkish Despotism in Eighteenth-Century French Political Culture", in James B. Collins and Karen T. Taylor (eds), *Early Modern Europe: Issues and Interpretations* (Oxford: Blackwell, 2006), 81. The frustrated French traveller was Jean-Baptiste Tavernier, *Nouvelle relation de l'intérieur du serail du Grand Seigneur* (Paris, 1681), 312.
77  Ghobrial, *Whispers*, 75–77.

members, including those married to Köprülü women, also rose to high office. The founding patriarch attracted particular attention, frequently with overtones of a horrified fascination. On the one hand, Köprülü Mehmed Pasha's power, authority and military prowess continued to be appreciated. On the other hand, he was quite notorious for his brutality, and many Ottoman authors did not mince their words. Evliya Çelebi, for example, depicted Köprülü Mehmed very negatively, especially because of the resentment he felt at the exclusion of his patron Melek Ahmed Pasha in 1656. A leading specialist on the subject has written that

> Evliya's views, however, have a depth and complexity that go beyond mere sycophantic praise of his patron, matched by undiscriminating condemnation of that benefactor's rivals. In point of fact, contemporary opinion was deeply divided in its assesment of Köprülü Mehmed Pasha's vezirate (1565–1661). Some authors, in particular the historian Silahdar (d.1136/1723), were in essential agreement with Evliya and characterized the vezirate of the founding member of the Köprülü dynasty as a 'reign of terror'.[78]

In contrast, others such as Mehmed Halîfe, Abdurrahman Abdi, Mustafa Naîmâ, and Râşid Mehmed have drawn a positive portrait of the vizier while acknowledging that the methods he used to suppress rebels were cruel and excessive. Still others, like Tayyarzâde Atâ, have made more of an effort to excuse his high-handed methods on the grounds that they were necessary and unavoidable.[79]

## 8    Bachstrom as a Gentleman Impostor, and His Sources of Inspiration

So how might all this tie in with Bachstrom and his real as well as assumed 1742 identity? In particular, when, where, and to what extent might he have come

---

[78]    Robert Dankoff, *The Intimate Life of an Ottoman Statesman: Melek Ahmed Pasha (1588–1662) as Portrayed in Evliya Çelebi's Book of Travels, With an Historical Introduction by Rhoads Murphey* (Albany, NY: SUNY, 1991), 23.

[79]    Abdurraḥman Abdi, *Abdurrahman Abdi Paşa Vekâyi' nâmesi: Osmanlı Tarihi (1648–1682)* edited by Fahri Çetin Derin (Istanbul: Çamlıca, 2008); Mehmet Halife, *Târih-i Gılmânî* (Istanbul: Kültür Bakanlığı Yayınları, 1976); Na'îmâ, *Târîh 1–4, passim*; Râşid Mehmed, *Çelebizâde İsmaîl Âsım: Târih-i Râşid ve Zeyli, passim*; Tayyâr-zâde Atâ, *Osmanlı Saray Tarihi: Tarih-i Enderun*, edited by Mehmet Arslan (Istanbul: Kitabevi, 2010).

into contact with French Enlightenment Orientalism, to the point of starting him to think about directly inserting himself into a comparable romance?

From the list of books that he left in Istanbul, we understand that in Bachstrom's possession were a few Orientalist works in French, which, however, would not qualify as fiction or romance. Joseph Pitton de Tournefort (d.1708) was a botanist educated in classical languages and science (chemistry, medicine, and botany), who undertook long herborizing expeditions first in Europe and then in the Levant (1700–02). Clearly, Bachstrom would have purchased his books in pursuit of his own scientific projects, or at least to present himself to possible patrons as an up-to-date and hence reliable scientist. De Tournefort's *Contractus Tournefortii, de Ré Herbaria et materia Metica* (London, 1708) was translated from his lectures at the Jardin des Plantes, and was published in English before appearing in French. His *Relation d'un Voyage du Levant*, published posthumously in 1717, provided systematic information on the history (from ancient to current time, citing and comparing the corresponding myths and legends with the information provided by coinage), topography, economy, administration, ethnic composition, and the customs and habits of everyday life of the places he visited, as well as particular events he witnessed and his encounters with locals. De Tournefort also commented on caves, mosques, monasteries and churches as well as residential architecture. The *Relation* includes engravings of city views, ports, fortresses and other architectural monuments, as well as plants, instruments and costumes, drawn by the artists in his retinue. To document his research, de Tournefort cited numerous texts by Greek and Latin authors, as well as by Byzantine writers, Renaissance humanists, and earlier travel accounts.[80]

Bachstorm also had a copy of *Voyage de Mr Wheler de la Grace*. This is a work by George Wheeler, who travelled accompanied by Mr Jacob Spon (d.1685), a medical doctor and archaeologist. Their travel account was first published in French as *Voyage d'Italie, de Dalmatie, de Grèce et du Levant fait aux années 1675 & 1676 par Jacob Spon ... et George Wheler* (Lyon, 1677).[81] In the later English

---

80  Joseph Pitton de Tournefort, *Relation d'un voyage du Levant. Fait par ordre du Roi: contenant l'histoire ancienne & moderne de plusieurs isles de l'Archipel, de Constantinople, des Côtes de la Mer Noire, de l'Armenie, de la Georgie, des frontières de Perse & de l'Asie Mineure ... enrichie de descriptions ... d'un grand nombre des plantes rares, de divers animaux et de plusieurs observations touchant l'histoire naturelle* (Lyon: Chez Anisson et Posuel, 1717).

81  Jacob Spon and George Wheeler, *Voyage d'Italie, de Dalmatie, de Grèce et du Levant, fait aux années 1675 & 1676 par Jacob Spon, Docteur Medicin Aggregé & George Wheler, Gentilhomme Anglois* (Lyon: Chez Antoine Cellier le fils, 1678/Amsterdam: Chez Henry & Theodore Boom, 1679).

version, *A Journey into Greece in Company of Dr Spons of Lyons* (London, 1682), Wheeler added his own observations about some further curiosities that had escaped the more academic Spon during their joint voyage. The most recent book of this kind in Bachstrom's library was Charles César Baudelot de Dairval's *De L'utilité des Voyages, et de l'Avantage que la Recherche des Antiquités procure aux Sçavans* (Paris, 1727).[82] Baudelot de Dairval was an antiquarian given to mixing studies of manuscripts, talismans, gems and medals.

In the light of the travelogues he brought with him to Istanbul and later left in the custody of Jean-Michel Hesler, Bachstrom seems not to have been interested in 'light' reading at that time. On the other hand, he may have had easier access to Oriental romances after he settled in Leiden where, as in The Hague or Amsterdam, many such works were actually published or republished.[83] I have noted above that it would have been quite risky for Bachstrom to step into Ferenc II Rákóczi's shoes as long as the prince was living not far from Istanbul; hence, it is quite unlikely that he would have been going around touting the genealogy that he had constructed for himself – or even that he might

---

82   Charles César Baudelot de Dairval, *De l'Utilité des voyages, et de l'avantage que la recherche des antiquités procure aux sçavans* (Paris: Emery, 1727). De Dairval was an antiquarian and gemmologist, collected antiquities, statues, medallions and books. He had acquired the library of Jean de Thévenot, the botanist-traveller, and the marbles of Marquis de Nointel, the French ambassador to the Ottoman court, 1670–1679, which are now in the Louvre Museum collections. See Jörn Lang, "Baudelot de Dairval, Charles César", in Peter Kuhlmann, Helmuth Schneider and Brigitte Egger (eds), *Brill's New Pauly Supplements I – Volume 6: History of Classical Scholarship: A Biographical Dictionary* (https://reference works.brillonline.com/browse/ brill-s-new-pauly-supplements-i-6/alphaRange/Ko%20-%20Ku/K.) Consulted 8 August 2016.

83   As stated above, Bachstrom was certainly familiar with the late-seventeenth century Hungarian tragedy. For the European interest in the Hungarian uprisings, see Humberto Garcia, "A Hungarian Revolution in Restoration England: Henry Stubbe, Radical Islam, and the Rye House Plot", *Eighteenth Century: Theory and Interpretation* 51 (1–2) 2010, 1–25. "As Matthew Birchwood and Nabil Matar have consistently shown, images of Islam and the dreaded Ottoman Turk have played a crucial role in the formation of national identity and religious difference in Restoration England. At the height of the Exclusion Crisis (1679–81), Catholic France was not England's only worry; the rise of Islamic Ottoman power in Hungary and other parts of eastern Europe took centre stage in English national debates about monarchical succession and religious authority, even as the cultures of this remote geographical region might initially appear entirely alien to the concerns of late Stuart England. Back in 1978, Daniel Clarke Waugh, by analysing one genre of Muscovite turcica, namely the apocryphal letters of the sultan, proved conclusively that all the Muscovite variants are translations from European prototypes." See Daniel C. Waugh, *The Great Turkes Defience: On the History of the Apocryphal Correspondence of the Ottoman Sultan in Its Muscovite and Russian Variants* (Columbus, OH: Slavica Publishers, 1978).

have at all constructed it while he was in Istanbul.[84] His claim of descent from the Köprülüs would have been equally improbable and dangerous because in 1729–30 there were many family members who were still in positions of power. In 1742, however, when he approached Prince Michel Radziwiłł for a job, he had nothing to fear.

His Istanbulite acquaintances might have constituted a starting point. Did these connections include İbrâhim Müteferrika? We do not really know. Babinger, with reference to another Hungarian traveller in Ottoman lands by the name of Caesar de Saussure Czészarnak, says that, following the Peace of Passarowitz, Müteferrika was assigned to the service of Ferenc II Rákóczi, and that he helped Hungarian exiles in Tekirdağ as their middleman in the Ottoman capital.[85] Babinger's account of Müteferrika is now being revisited in the light of new findings that might eventually hit upon a Bachstrom connection. However, unless and until they do so, we can only speculate about a possible partnership (or alternatively or simultaneously a rivalry) between the two men. Müteferrika might have benefited from Bachstrom's expertise and international connections. Certainly, Müteferrika would have been able to provide Bachstrom with first-hand information about the various people that he would later incorporate into his fabricated family history. These would have comprised the Rákóczi family, Zrínyi and Thököly, as well as their connections with Köprülü Mehmed Pasha. It could have been this initial bedrock that, using Orientalist novellas as a model, he might have built on and embellished in Leiden.

Ultimately, however, Bachstrom was one whose ambition "o'erleapt itself and fell on the other side," though on a much more mundane level than Macbeth. Among his publications, all of which came out after he left the Ottoman capital, is the aforementioned Oriental utopia. In *Land der Inqviraner*, published

---

84   The literature popularizing the Hungarian struggle against the Habsburgs is monumental. The European interest in the Rákóczi and Thököly families was manifested in texts ranging from *memoires* to historical accounts. See Imre Thököly, *Nova vera, e distinta relatione della segnalata vittoria ottenuta Dall'armi imperiali. Con la Rotta, e fuga al Ribelle Techeli, e con la morte di quantità de fuoi feguaci, oltre prigioni, e con l'acquisto di Bandiere Cavalli, e Monitioni, cosida Bocca come da Guerra. Sotto il Comando del General Haisler* (Venice: Batti, 1688). For an anonymous text that discusses Imre Thököly in 1681, see Anon. *The Intreigues of the French King at Constantinople to embroil Christendom: discovered in several dispatches past betwixt him and the late Grand Seignior, Grand Vizier and Count Teckily: all of them found among that Count's papers seiz'd in December last: with some reflections upon them* (London: Printed for Dorman Newman, 1689). See also Jean de Préchac, *Le Comte Tekely: Nouvelle historique* (Amsterdam: Chez Henry Desbordes, 1686).

85   Babinger, "18. Yüzyılda", 16. However, Mikes Kelemen, the Chamberlain of Ferenc II Rákóczi, does not mention İbrâhim Müteferrika (see footnote 12 above).

under the pseudonym ABC in 1736/7, a shepherd and cottage-builder by the name of İbrâhim plays a part.[86] Müteferrika İbrâhim could have been an attractive and accessible candidate for Bachstrom to bring into his story at this point.[87]

## Bibliography

### Primary Sources

Abbondanza, Vincenzo. *Dizionario storico delle vite di tutti i monarchi ottomani; fino al regnante ignore Achmet IV., e delle piu riguardevoli cose appartenenti a quella Monarchia. Dato alla luce da Vincenzo Abbondanza ...* Rome: Per Luigi Vescovi, a Filippo Neri, 1786.

[ABC]. *Bey zwei hundert Jahr lang unbekannte, nunmehro aber entdeckte vortreffliche Land der Inqviraner: Aus der Erzehlung Eines nach langwieriger Kranckheit in unsern Gegenden verstorbenen Aeltesten dieses glückseligen Landes, Nach allen seinen Sitten, Gebräuchen, Ordnungen, Gottesdienst, Wissenschafften, Künsten, Vortheilen und Einrichtung umständlich beschrieben, Und dem gemeinen Wesen zum Besten mitgetheilet. Franckfurt und Leipzig, 1736.*

Abdi, Abdurrahman. *Abdurrahman Abdi Paşa Vekâyi nâmesi: Osmanlı Tarihi (1648–1682)*. Edited by Fahri Çetin Derin. Istanbul: Çamlıca, 2008.

Adams, Bernard (ed.) *Letters from Turkey: Kelemen Mikes, Chamberlain of the Last Prince of Transylvania.* London: Kegan Paul International, 2000.

Ahmed Resmî Efendi. *Hamîletü'l-Küberâ*, edited by Ahmet Nezihi Turan. Istanbul: Kitabevi, 2000.

Anon. *Die Europäische Fama, welche den gegenwärtigen Zustand der vornehmsten Höfe entdeckt.* No. 263, 1723.

---

86  For partial translations from Bachstrom's religious utopia *Land der Inqviraner*, see Küçük, "Early Enlightenment in İstanbul", 23–5. At this point, I must repeat that I do not agree with Küçük's identification of the real-life model for Bachstrom's İbrahim as Damad / Nevşehirli İbrahim Pasha who was brutally murdered during the 1730 rebellion. For a version of my interpretation. see Tülay Artan, "Cosmopolitanism in the Early 18th-Century Ottoman Capital: The Impostor, the Alchemist, the Merchant and the Personal Dimension", *The Balkan Provinces of the Ottoman Empire: the Personal Dimension. I. The Agents of Faith* (Sofia: AUB Press, forthcoming).

87  Damad İbrahim Pasha was not popularized later either. For the eighteenth-century changes in French Orientalist literature, see Irini Apostolou, *L'orientalisme des voyageurs français au XVIIIe siècle: Une Iconographie de l'Orient méditerranéen* (Paris: Presses de l'Université Paris-Sorbonne, 2009). For the French images of the Turk, which evolved from being nearly entirely allegorical in the seventeenth century to more ethnographic in the eighteenth, see Julia Landweber, "Celebrating Identity: Charting the History of Turkish Masquerade in Early Modern France", *Romance Studies* 23 (3) November 2005, 175–89.

Anon. *The Intreigues of the French King at Constantinople to embroil Christendom: discovered in several dispatches past betwixt him and the late Grand Seignior, Grand Vizier and Count Teckily: all of them found among that Count's papers seiz'd in December last: with some reflections upon them.* London: Printed for Dorman Newman, 1689.

Anon. *Celebrated Claimants from Perkin Warbeck to Arthur Orton* (London: Chatto and Windus, Piccadilly, 1874).

Anon. *A Relation of the siege of Candia: from the first expedition of the French forces under the command of M. de la Fucillade, Duke of Roannez, to it surrender, the 27th of September, 1669. Written in French by a gentleman who was a voluntier in that service, and faithfully Englished.* London: Printed for T. Williams and I. Starkey, and to be sold in their shops, at the Bible in Little Brittain, and the Miter in Fleet-Street near Temple Barr, 1670. Translation of *Journal de l'expédition de Monsieur de la Fueillade, pour le secours de Candie.*

Anon. *The Turkish refugee: being a narrative of the life, sufferings, deliverances, and conversion, of Ishmael Bashaw, a Mahometan merchant, from Constantinople, who was taken prisoner by the Spaniards, and made a wonderful escape to England, where, having become a convert to the Christian faith, he was publicly baptized, with the approbation of the Right Reverend the Lord Bishop of Lincoln.* London: printed by the family, 1797.

Arslan, Mehmet (ed.) *Hadîkatü'l-Vüzerâ ve Zeylleri: Osmanlı Sadrazamları.* Istanbul: Kitabevi, 2013.

Bachstrom, Johann Frederick. *Nova aestus marini theoria. ex principiis physico-mathematicis detecta & dilucidata. Cui accedit, Examen acus magneticae spiralis, quae a declinatione & inclinatione libera esse creditur, institutum.* Leiden: Apud Conradum Wishoff 1734.

Bachstrom, Johann Frederick. *Observationes circa scorbutum: ejusque indolem, causas, signa, et curam, institutæ, eorum præprimis in usum, qui Groenlandiam & Indiam Orientis petunt.* Leiden: Conrad Wishoff, 1734.

Bachstrom, Johann Frederick. *L'Art de Nager, ou Invention à l'aide de laquelle on peut toujours se sauver du Naufrage; &, en cas de besoin, fair passer les plus larges Rivières à les Armées entières.* Amsterdam: Zacharie Chatelain, 1741.

Behçet-i İbrahim. *Tarih-i Sülâle-i Köprülü (Silsiletü'l Asafiyyeti fî Devleti'l-Hakaniyyeti'l-Osmaniyye).* MS no. 212. Ahmed Paşa, Köprülü Kütüphanesi.

Bernouillis, Johann. *Archiv zur Neueren Geschichte, Geographie, Natur, und Menschenkenntnis VII.* Leipzig, 1787.

Bulgarini, Ottaviano. *Vita del padre maestro f. Domenico di S. Tomaso dell'Ordine de' Predicatori, detto prima Sultan Osinan Ottomano, figlio d'Ibraim imperador de' Turchi. Disposta in dieci libri dal padre baccelliere f. Ottaviano Bulgarini ... Con una breve geneologia di tutti l'imperadori ottomani sino al presente regnante per introduzione dell'opera.* Naples: Presso Giuseppe Roselli, 1689.

de Chassepol, François. *Histoire des grands vizirs Mahomet Coprogli Pacha et Achmet Coprogli Pacha: Celle des trios derniers Grands Seigneurs, de leurs sultanes, principales favorites avec les plus secretes intrigues du serrail. Et plusieurs autres particularitez des guerres de dalmatie, Transilvanie, Hongrie, Candie, & Pologne. Avec l'histoiere de grand Sobieski, roy de Pologne. Et le plan de la bataille de Cotzchin*. Paris: E. Michallet, 1676.

de Chassepol, François. *The history of the grand visiers, Mahomet and Achmet Coprogli, of the three last grand signiors, their Sultana's and chief favourites, with the most secret intrigues of the seraglio besides several other particulars of the wars of Dalmatia, Transylvania, Hungary, Candia, and Poland/Englished by John Evelyn Junior*. London: Printed for H. Brome, at the Gun at the West-end of St Pauls, 1677.

de Dairval, Charles César Baudelot. *De l'Utilité des voyages, et de l'avantage que la recherche des antiquités procure aux sçavans*. Paris, Emery, 1727.

de La Motraye, A. *A. de La Motraye's Travels Through Europe, Asia, And Into Parts Of Africa: With Proper Cutts And Maps. Containing A Great Variety Of Geographical, Topographical, And Political Observations On Those Parts Of The World; especially on Italy, Turky, Greece, Crim and Noghaina Tartaries, Circassa, Sweden, and Lapland. A Curious Collection Of Things particularly Rare, both in Nature and Antiquity; such as Remains of ancient Cities and Colonies, Inscriptions, Idols, Medals, &c*. London: Printed for the Author, 1723.

de La Motraye, A. *Voyage du Sr. A. De La Motraye, en Europe, Asie & Afrique. Où l'on trouve une grande varieté de recherches geographiques, historiques & politiques, sur l'Italie, la Grèce, la Turquie, la Tartarie Crimée, & Nogaye, la Circassie, la Suède, la Laponie, &c. Avec des remarques instructives sur les moeurs, coutumes, opinions &c. des peuples & des Païs où l'auteur a voyagé; & des particularitez remarquables touchant les personnes & les auteurs distingués d'Angleterre, de France, d'Italie, de Suede, &c. 1–2*. The Hague: T. Johnson & J. van Duren, 1727.

de Mezeray, François Eudes. *Histoire des Turcs, depuis 1612 jusqu'à 1649* (1650, in-folio).

de Préchac, Jean. *Le Comte Tekely: Nouvelle historique*. Amsterdam: Chez Henry Desbordes, 1686.

de Saint-George, Georges Guillet. *Athènes ancienne et nouvelle et l'estat present de l'empire des turcs: contenant la vie du Sultan Mahomet IV. Le ministere de Guillet de Saint-Georges, Georges, Coprogli Achmet Pacha, G. Vizir, & son Campement devant Candie. Avec le plan de la Ville d'Athenes*. 2nd edn. Paris: Chez Estienne Michallet, 1675.

de Saint-George, Georges Guillet. *An Account of a Late Voyage to Athens, Containing the Estate Both Ancient and Modern of that Famous City and of the Present Empire of the Turks: The Life of the Now Sultan Mahomet the IV, with the Ministry of the Grand Vizier Coprogli Achmet Pacha. Also the most remarkable passages in the Turkish camp at the siege of Candia and divers other particularities of the affairs of the port. by Monsieur de La Guillatiere, a French gentleman; now Englished.* London: Printed by J. M. for H. Herringman, 1676.

de Tournefort, Joseph Pitton. *Relation d'un voyage du Levant. Fait par ordre du Roi: contenant l'histoire ancienne & moderne de plusieurs isles de l'Archipel, de Constantinople, des Côtes de la Mer Noire, de l'Armenie, de la Georgie, des frontières de Perse & de l'Asie Mineure ... enrichie de descriptions ... d'un grand nombre des plantes rares, de divers animaux et de plusieurs observations touchant l'histoire naturelle.* Lyon: Anisson et Posuel/Paris: Imprimerie Royale, 1717.

de Visé, Jeanne Donneau. *Histoire du Mahomet IV, depossedé.* Lyon: Thomas Amaulry, 1688.

Defterdar Sarı Mehmed Paşa. *Zübde-i Vekayiât: Tahlil ve Metin (1066–1116/1656–1704)*, edited by Abdülkadir Özcan. Ankara: TTK, 1995.

Du May, Louis. *Discours historiques et politiques sur les causes de la Guerre de Hongrie et sur les causes de la paix. Entre Leopold I. Empereur des romains et Mahomet IV Sultan de Turquie. Par Louis Du May, Chevalier, Sieur de Sallettes, Conseiller de son Altesse de Wirtemberg.* Lyon: Barthelemy Riviere, rue Merciere, à l'Image S. Augustin, 1665.

Du May, Louis. *A Discourse. Historical and Political of the War of Hungary, and of the Causes of the Peace between Leopold the First Emperor of the Romans, and Mahomet the Fourth Sultan of Turkey. By Louis du May of Sallettes, Knight, and Counsellor of His Highness the Duke of Wirtemberg.* Glasgow: Printed by Robert Sanders, 1669.

Du Verdier, Gilbert Saulnier. *Abbrégé de l'histoire des Turcs. Contenant tout ce qui s'est passé de plus remarquable sous le regne de vingt-trois empereurs. Recueilly tres-soigneusement par le sieur Du Verdier, historiographe de France. Enrichy en cette dernière édition de leurs Portraits en Taille-douce; Et augmenté de plusieurs belles Remarques Curieuses, qui n'ont point esté insérées dans les autres.* Paris: Théodore Girard, 1665.

Eberhard, Christoph. *Specimen theoriae magneticae quo ex certis principiis magneticis ostenditur vera et universalis methodus inveniendi longitudinem & latitudinem.* Leipzig: Martini, 1720.

Evelyn, John, *The history of the three late, famous impostors, viz. Padre Ottomano, Mahomed Bei and Sabatai Sevi. The one, pretended son and heir to the late Grand Signior, the other, a prince of the Ottoman family, but in truth, a Valachian counterfeit, and the last, the suppos'd Messiah of the Jews, in the year of the true Messiah, 1666: with a brief account of the ground and occasion of the present war between the Turk and the Venetian: together with the cause of the final extirpation, destruction and exile of the Jews out of the Empire of Persia.* Savoy: Printed for Henry Herringman, 1669.

Halife, Mehmet. *Târih-i Gılmânî.* Istanbul: Kültür Bakanlığı Yayınları, 1976.

Kundmann, Johann Christian. *Rariora naturae et artis*. Breslau: M. Herbert, 1737.

Le Noble, Eustache. *Abra-Mulé, ou l'Histoire du Déthronement de Mahomet IV: Troisiéme Nouvelle historique*. Amsterdam: André de Hoogenhuysen, 1695.

Le Noble, Eustache. *Abra-Mulé, or a True History of the Dethronement of Mahomet IV*. London: R. Clavel, 1696.

Le Noble, Eustache. *Abra-Mulé, ou l'Histoire du Déthronement de Mahomet IV: Troisiéme Nouvelle historique*. Paris: M. and G. Jouvenel, 1696.

Le Noble, Eustache. *Histoire du prince Ragotzi: ou La guerre des mécontents sous son commandement*. Paris: J. de Nully, 1707.

Marana, Giovanni Paolo. *L'Esploratore turco, e le di lui relazioni segrete alla Porta ottomana, scoperte in Parigi nel regno di Luiggi il Grande. Tradotte dall'Arabo in Italiano, da Gian-Paolo Marana, e dall'Italiano in Francese da \*\*\*. Contengono le più nobili azioni della Francia e della Christianità, dall' anno 1637. fino al 1682. Tomo primo*. Paris: Claude Barbin, 1684.

Marana, Giovanni Paolo. *L'Espion du Grand-Seigneur, et ses relations secrètes, envoyées au Divan de Constantinople. Découvertes à Paris, pendant le règne de Louys le Grand. Traduites de l'Arabe en Italien Par le Sieur Jean-Paul Marana, Et de l'Italien en François par \*\*\*. Ces Relations contiennent les Evenemens les plus considerables de la Chrestienté & de la France, depuis l'Année 1637. jusques en l'Année 1682. Tome premier*. Paris: Claude Barbin, 1684.

Na'îmâ Mustafa Efendi. *Târih-i Na'îmâ*, 4 vols edited by Mehmet İpşirli. Ankara: TTK, 2007.

Phillips, John (ed.) *Modern History, or Monethly Account of All Considerable Occurrences* 1–2 (1687–90).

Phillips, John. *The Dilucidation of the Late Commotions of Turkey: Containing an Exact and Distinct Account of all the Causes and Motives of the deposing of Mahomet, and of the advancing of Soliman to the Imperial Throne of Constantinople. Gather'd from the Letters of a person dwelling in, and Minutely infor'd of the Affairs that City, and Consecrated to the ever August Merit of the most Serene Elector of Bavaria. Printed in Italian at Venice, and translated into English by the Author of the Monthly Account. To be Annex'd to Numb. 10 of the Monthly Account*. London: printed by J. B. and are to be sold by Randall Taylor, 1689.

Phillips, John. *Abra-Mulé, or a True History of the Dethronement of Mahomet IV*. London: R. Clavel, 1696.

Râşid Mehmed Efendi. *Çelebizâde İsmaîl Âsım Efendi: Târîh-i Râşid ve Zeyli (1071–1114/1660–1703)*, edited by Abdülkadir Özcan, Yunus Uğur, Baki Çakır et al. Istanbul: Klasik, 2013.

Schultz, Stephen. *Die Leitungen des Höchsten nach seinem Rath auf den Reisen durch Europa, Asien und Africa IV*. Halle im Magdeburgischen: Verlegt von Carl Hermann Hemmerbe, 1771.

Southey, Robert and Samuel Taylor Coleridge. *Omniana, or Horae Otiosiores* 1–2. London: Printed for Longman, Hurst, Rees et al., 1812.

Spon, Jacob and George Wheeler. *Voyage d'Italie, de Dalmatie, de Grèce et du Levant, fait aux années 1675 & 1676 par Jacob Spon, Docteur Medicin Aggregé & George Wheler, Gentilhomme Anglois*. Lyon: Antoine Cellier le fils, 1678.

Tavernier, Jean-Baptiste. *Nouvelle relation de l'intérieur du serail du Grand Seigneur*. Paris, 1681.

Tayyâr-zâde Atâ, *Osmanlı Saray Tarihi: Tarih-i Enderun*, edited by Mehmet Arslan. Istanbul: Kitabevi, 2010.

Thököly, Imre. *Nova vera, e distinta relatione della segnalata vittoria ottenuta Dall'armi imperiali. Con la Rotta, e fuga al Ribelle Techeli, e con la morte di quantità de fuoi feguaci, oltre prigioni, e con l'acquisto di Bandiere Cavalli, e Monitioni, cosida Bocca come da Guerra. Sotto il Comando del General Haisler*. Venice: Batti, 1688.

Trapp, Joseph. *Abra Mulé, or Love and Empire: A Tragedy*. London: Printed for Jacob Tonson, 1704.

Waugh, Daniel C. *The Great Turkes Defience: On the History of the Apocryphal Correspondence of the Ottoman Sultan in its Muscovite and Russian Variants*. Columbus, OH: Slavica Publishers, 1978.

### Secondary Sources

Ahmed Refik (Altınay). *Köprülüler*. Istanbul: Kitaphane-i Hilmi-İbrahim Hilmi, 1331 (1915) [republished Istanbul: Tarih Vakfı Yurt Yayınları, 2012.]

Ahmed Refik (Altınay). *Türk Hizmetinde Kıral Tököli İmre, 1683–1705*. Istanbul: Muallim Ahmet Halit Kitaphanesi, 1932.

Apostolou, Irini. *L'Orientalisme des voyageurs français au XVIIIe siècle: Une Iconographie de l'Orient méditerranéen*. Paris: Presses de l'Université Paris-Sorbonne, 2009.

Aravamudan, Srinivas. *Enlightenment Orientalism: Resisting the Rise of the Novel: Narratives about the Rise of the Novel*. Chicago: University of Chicago Press, 2011.

Artan, Tülay. "Cosmopolitanism in the Early 18th-Century Ottoman Capital: The Impostor, the Alchemist, the Merchant and the Personal Dimension". *The Balkan Provinces of the Ottoman Empire: the Personal Dimension. I. The Agents of Faith*. Sofia: American University of Beirut Press, forthcoming.

Baars, Rosanne. "Constantinople Confidential: News and Information in the Diary of Jean-Louis Rigo (c.1686–1756), Secretary of the Dutch Embassy in Istanbul". *Lias* 41 (2) 2014, 143–171.

Babinger, Franz. *Stambuler Buchwesen im 18. Jahrhundert*. Leipzig: Deutscher Verein für Buchwesen und Schrifttum, 1919. [Turkish version: Franz Babinger, "18. Yüzyılda İstanbul'da Kitabiyat". In *İbrahim Müteferrika ve Matbaası*. Translated by Nedret Kuran Burçoğlu. Istanbul: Tarih Vakfı Yurt Yayınları, 2004, 1–58.

Backscheider, Paula R. and Catherine Ingrassia (eds). *A Companion to the Eighteenth-Century English Novel and Culture*. London: Wiley-Blackwell, 2005.

Baghdiantz McCabe, Ina. *Orientalism in Early Modern France: Eurasian Trade, Exoticism, and the Ancien Régime*. Oxford: Berg, 2008.

Ballaster, Rosalind (ed.) *Fables of the East: Selected Tales, 1662–1785*. Oxford: Oxford University Press, 2005.

Ballaster, Rosalind (ed.) *Fabulous Orients: Fictions of the East in England, 1662–1785*. Oxford: Oxford University Press, 2005.

Betts, C. J. *Early Deism in France: From the So-called 'déistes' of Lyon (1564) to Voltaire's "Lettres philosophiques" (1734)*. The Hague: M. Nijhoff Publishers, 1984.

Conant, Martha Pike. *The Oriental Tale in England in the Eighteenth Century*. London: Forgotten Books, 2013, reprint of 1908 edition.

Cornelissen, Marloes. "The World of Ambassador Jacobus Colyer: Material Culture of the Dutch 'Nation' in Istanbul During the First Half of the 18th Century". Ph.D. dissertation, Sabancı University, 2015.

Danişmend, İsmail Hami. *Osmanlı Devlet Erkânı*. Istanbul: Türkiye Yayınevi, 1971.

Danişmend, İsmail Hami. *İzahlı Osmanlı Tarihi Kronolojisi* 3. Istanbul: Türkiye Yayınevi, 1972.

Dankoff, Robert. *The Intimate Life of an Ottoman Statesman: Melek Ahmed Pasha (1588–1662) as Portrayed in Evliya Çelebi's Book of Travels. With an Historical Introduction by Rhoads Murphey*. Albany, NY: State University of New York Press, 1991.

Davis, Natalie Zemon. *The Return of Martin Guerre*. Cambridge, MA: Harvard University Press, 1983.

Dew, Nicholas. *Orientalism in Louis XIV's France*. Oxford: Oxford University Press, 2009.

Dew, Nicholas. "Reading Travels in the Culture of Curiosity: Thévenot's Collection of Voyages". *Journal of Early Modern History* 10 (1–2) 2006, 39–59.

Eliav-Feldon, Miriam. *Renaissance Impostors and Proofs of Identity*. London: Palgrave Macmillan, 2012.

Freller, Thomas and Dolores Campoy. *Padre Ottomano and Malta: A Story of the 1001 Nights*. Santa Venera: Midsea Books, 2006.

Garcia, Humberto. "A Hungarian Revolution in Restoration England: Henry Stubbe, Radical Islam, and the Rye House Plot". *Eighteenth Century: Theory and Interpretation* 51 (1–2) 2010, 1–25.

Ghobrial, John-Paul. *The Whispers of Cities: Information Flows in Istanbul, London, and Paris in the Age of William Trumbull*. Oxford: Oxford University Press, 2013.

Ghobrial, John-Paul. "The Secret Life of Elias of Babylon and the Uses of Global Microhistory". *Past and Present* 222 (1) 2014, 51–93.

Gökbilgin, M. Tayyib. "Köprülüler". *İslâm Ansiklopedisi*, vol. 6. Istanbul, 1977.

Guion, Béatrice. "L'Espion du Grand Seigneur, ou l'invention du roman épistolaire oriental". *Littératures classiques* 1 (2010), 187–202.

Hamilton, Alastair and Francis Richard. *André du Ryer and Oriental Studies in Seventeenth-Century France*. Oxford: Oxford University Press, 2004.

Harrigan, Michael. *Veiled Encounters: Representing the Orient in 17th-century French Travel Literature*. Amsterdam: Rodopi, 2008.

Heyer, M. "Genève et Constantinople: 1733 (Suite des Extraits Communiqués par M. Heyer)". *Bulletin de la Société de l'Histoire du Protestantisme Français (1852–1865)* 11 (1/3) 1862, 61–79.

Hosford, Desmond and Chong J. Wojtkowski (eds). *French Orientalism: Culture, Politics, and the Imagined Other*. Cambridge: Cambridge Scholars Publishing, 2010.

Hug, Tobias B. *Impostures in Early Modern England: Representations and Perceptions of Fraudulent Identities*. Manchester: Manchester University Press, 2010.

İlgürel, Mücteba. "Köprülü Mehmed Paşa". *Türkiye Diyanet Vakfı İslam Ansiklopedisi*, vol. 26. Ankara, 2002.

Isom-Verhaaren, Christine. "Royal French Women in the Ottoman Sultans' Harem: The Political Uses of Fabricated Accounts from the Sixteenth to the Twenty-first Century". *Journal of World History* 17 (2) 2006, 159–96.

Jannidis, Gerhard Lauer and Andrea Rapp. "Hohe Romane und blaue Bibliotheken. Zum Forschungsprogramm einer computergestützten Buch- und Narratologiegeschichte des Romans in Deutschland (1500–1900)". In Michael Stolz, Lucas Marco Gisi and Jan Loop (eds) *Literatur und Literaturwissenschaft auf dem Weg zu den neuen Medien*. Bern: Germanistik.Ch, 2005, 29–43.

Kaiser, Thomas. "The Evil Empire? The Debate on Turkish Despotism in Eighteenth-Century French Political Culture". In James B. Collins and Karen T. Taylor (eds), *Early Modern Europe: Issues and Interpretations*. Oxford: Blackwell, 2006, 69–81.

Kansu, Aykut. "18. Yüzyılda İngiltere'de bir Yeniçeri ya da Yasalara Bağlı bir Serseri'nin Yaşamından Kesitler". In Hamdi Can Tuncer (ed.) *Osmanlı'dan Cumhuriyet'e Problemler, Araştırmalar, Tartışmalar*. Istanbul: Tarih Vakfı Yurt Yayınları, 1998.

Karaçay-Türkal, Nazire. "Silâhdar Fındıklılı Mehmed Ağa. Zeyl-i Fezleke, (1065–22 ca.1106/1654-7 Şubat 1695) (Tahlil ve Metin)". Ph.D. dissertation, Marmara University, 2012.

Kármán, Gábor. "The Networks of a Wallachian Pretender in Constantinople: The Contacts of the Future Voivode Mihail Radu 1654–1657". In Gábor Kármán and Radu G. Păun (eds) *Europe and the "Ottoman World": Exchanges and Conflicts (Sixteenth to Seventeenth Centuries)*. Istanbul: Isis Press, 2013, 119–139.

Keynes, Geoffrey. "John Evelyn: A Study in Bibliophily". *Sandars Lectures, 1933–34*. Cambridge: CUP Archive, 1934.

Kriebel, Martin. "Das pietistische Halle und das orthodoxe Patriarchat von Konstantinopel: 1700–1730". *Jahrbücher für Geschichte Osteuropas*. Neue Folge 3 (1) 1955, 50–70.

Küçük, Bekir Harun. "Early Enlightenment in Istanbul". Ph.D. dissertation, University of California, San Diego, 2012.

Kunt, Metin. "Ethnic-Regional (cins) Solidarity in the Seventeenth-Century Ottoman Establishment". *International Journal of Middle East Studies* 5 (3) 1974, 233–9.

Kunt, Metin. "The Köprülü Years: 1656–1661". PhD diss., Princeton University, 1971.

Kunt, Metin. "Naima, Köprülü and Grand Veziriate". *Boğaziçi Üniversitesi Dergisi. Hümaniter Bilimler* 1 (1973), 57–64.

Kunt, Metin. "The Waqf as an Instrument of Public Policy: Notes on the Köprülü Family Endowments". *Studies in Ottoman History in Honor of Professor V. L. Ménage*, edited by Colin Heywood and Colin Imber, 189–98. Istanbul: Isis Press, 1994.

Lamport, F. J. "Utopia and 'Robinsonade': Schnabel's Insel Felsenburg and Bachstrom's Land der Inquiraner". *Oxford German Studies* 1 (1) 1966, 10–30.

Landweber, Julia. "Celebrating Identity: Charting the History of Turkish Masquerade in Early Modern France". *Romance Studies* 23 (3) November 2005, 175–89.

Lang, Jörn. "Baudelot de Dairval, Charles César". In Peter Kuhlmann, Helmuth Schneider and Brigitte Egger (eds), *Brill's New Pauly Supplements I – Volume 6: History of Classical Scholarship: A Biographical Dictionary* (https://referenceworks.brillonline.com/browse/brill-s-new-pauly-supplements-i-6/alphaRange/Ko%20-%20Ku/K). Consulted 8 August 2016.

Linon-Chipon, Sophie. *Gallia orientalis: Voyages aux Indes orientales, 1529–1722*. Paris: Presses de l'Université de Paris-Sorbonne, 2003.

Longino, Michèle. *Orientalism in French Classical Drama*. Cambridge: Cambridge University Press, 2002.

Neculce, Ion. *Letopisețul Țării Moldovei*. Bucharest: Editura Litera International, 2001.

Neudecker, Hannah. "From Istanbul to London? Albertus Bobovius' Appeal to Isaac Basire". In A. Hamilton, M. van den Boogert and B. Westerweel (eds). *The Republic of Letters and the Levant* (Leiden: Brill, 2005), 173–96.

Philliou, Christine. *Biography of an Empire: Governing Ottomans in an Age of Revolution*. Berkeley: University of California Press, 2011.

Porada, Aleksandra. "Giovanni Paolo Marana's Turkish Spy and the Police of Louis XIV: the Fear of Being Secretly Observed by Trained Agents in Early Modern Europe". *Altre Modernità/Otras Modernidades/Autres Modernités/Other Modernities, Saggi/Ensayos/Essais/Essays* 11 (2014): 96–110.

Reindl-Kiel, Hedda. "The Must-Haves of a Grand Vizier: Merzifonlu Kara Mustafa Pasha's Luxury Assets". Reprint from *Wiener Zeitschrift für die Kunde des Morgenlandes* 106 (2016), 179–221.

Repp, Richard C. "Köprülü Mehmed Paşa". *Encyclopedia of Islam*. 2nd edn, vol. 5. Leiden, 1986.

Rose, Hugh James. "Bachstrom, John Frederic". In E. Hogson et al., *A New General Biographical Dictionary*, vol. 2. London: T. Fellowes/F. & J. Rivington, 1857.

Sabev, Orlin. *İbrahim Müteferrika ya da İlk Osmanlı Matbaa Serüveni*. Istanbul: Yeditepe Yayınları, 2006.

Shawcross, John T. *The Arms of the Family: The Significance of John Milton's Relatives and Associates*. Lexington, Kentucy: University Press of Kentucky, 2004.

Topal, Mehmet. *Nusretnâme: Inceleme-Metin (1106–1133/1695–1721)*. Ankara: Türkiye Bilimler Akademisi, 2018.

Topçu, Sultan Murat. *Gücün Mimariye Yansıması: Köprülüler*. Ankara: TTK, 2015.

Topçu, Sultan Murat. "Osmanlılar Döneminde Güçlü Bir Kadın Bani: Köprülü Ayşe Hanım". *Kadın/Woman 2000 Kadın Araştırmaları Dergisi* 10 (2) 2009, 45–84.

Ullrich, Hermann. "Johann Friedrich Bachstrom: Ein Gelehrtenleben aus der ersten Hälfte des 18. Jahrhunderts. (Mit genauem Verzeichniß von Bachstrom's Schriften)". *Euphorion Bd.16, Zeitschrift f. Literaturgeschichte* (1909/1910), 320–49.

Ullrich, Hermann. *Robinson und Robinsonaden: Bibliographie, Geschichte, Kritik. Ein beitrag zur verleichenden litteraturgeschichte, im besonderen zur geschichte des romans und zur geschichte der jugendlitteratur*. Weimar: E. Felber, 1898.

Uzunçarşılı, İsmail Hakkı. *Osmanlı Tarihi* III/2. 2nd edn. Ankara: TTK, 1988, first published 1954.

Woodbridge, Linda. "Imposters, Monsters, and Spies: What Rogue Literature Can Tell us about Early Modern Subjectivity". *Early Modern Literary Studies* 9 (4) January 2002, 1–11, in http://purl.oclc.org/emls/si-09/woodimpo.htm.

Zaimova, Raïa. "L'Espace culturel de Constantinople: Temoignages des Ambassedeurs de France à Constantinople (XVIIe–XVIIIe siècle)". *Études Balkaniques* 38 (1) 2002, 86–95.

CHAPTER 3

# Practices of Remembrance and Sites of Violence in Seventeenth-Century Istanbul: The Beheading of Şeyh İsmâil Ma'şûkî (d.1539)

*Aslı Niyazioğlu*

How did seventeenth-century Istanbulites understand the past? And what did they want to write about the history of their city? My article addresses these questions by focusing on the case of a controversial beheading, or more precisely, the revisionist discourse it generated a century later. In 1539, the Melâmî-Bayramî Şeyh İsmâil Ma'şûkî was executed for heresy in At Meydanı with his ten disciples and thrown into the sea at Ahırkapı. In the 1620s, defenders of the sheikh began to circulate written accounts of how his severed head and headless corpse moved upstream on the Bosphorus and reached Rumeli Hisarı to be buried together (Map 1). Thus, about a century after the execution, Melâmî-Bayramî supporters summoned the beheaded sheikh into their lives and commemorated the sites of violence as a part of the historical landscape of Istanbul.

Early modern martyrdom narratives, such as that of İsmâil Ma'şûkî, are rich sources for observing power and dissent displayed on the urban landscape.[1] While state authorities attempted to eliminate those they perceive as heretics at public spectacles, followers of the executed tried to safeguard their memory by establishing sites of commemoration. In the case of the history of Istanbul, a systematic examination of such accounts is especially needed. Although we have begun to study how empire-building projects shaped early modern Istanbul, we still know very little about the ways Istanbulites experienced

---

1  The scholarship on the impact of violent pasts on the construction of landscape and memory in early modern Europe is vast. For a review of historiography, see Katharina Schramm, "Landscapes of Violence: Memory and Sacred Space", *History & Memory* 23, (1) 2011, 5–22. See also, Christopher R. Friedrichs, *The Early Modern City 1450–1750* (Abingdon: Routledge, 2003), 243–303; Brad S. Gregory, *Salvation at Stake, Christian Martyrdom in Early Modern Europe* (Cambridge, MA: HUP, 2001); Julius Ruff, *Violence in Early Modern Europe* (Cambridge: CUP, 2004), 100–15; Alexandra Walsham, "Sacred Topography and Social Memory: Religious Change and the Landscape in Early Modern Britain and Ireland", *Journal of Religious History* 36 (1) 2012, 31–51.

and discussed the political history of their city.[2] A beheaded sheikh on the Bosphorus, I argue, can show us the diverse ways early modern Ottomans wrote this history and reflected on their city's violent imperial past, turning what had been the sultan's assertion of power into a site of critical reflection of Ottoman history.

My aim here is not to discuss the reasons for İsmâil Maş'ûkî's execution or what happened in 1539. Thanks to meticulous research on archival and narrative material, we now have a detailed factual account of the sheikh's life: Abdülbaki Gölpınarlı gathered İsmâil Ma'şûkî's poetry from miscellanea; İsmail Erünsal discovered the earliest Melâmî-Bayramî source on İsmâil Ma'şûkî's life; Ahmet Yaşar Ocak established the detailed analysis of the execution, which is now our main reference source; Betül Yavuz and Ali Erken discussed the sheikh's life in the context of intra-community rivalries.[3] From these studies, we learn that Melâmî-Bayramîs were a splinter group of the Bayramî order, who practiced the principle of self-blame and believed that being held in good esteem would lead to worldly attachment. In their struggle with worldly ties, they shunned some practices typical of other Sufi groups. Unlike other Sufis, they did not have a distinctive litany, wear identifying clothing, or live from endowments. They also held particular visions about the spiritual power of their sheikhs and in the sixteenth and seventeenth centuries were persecuted

---

2 For the early modern Ottoman experiences of Istanbul, see the pioneering work of Tülay Artan, "Architecture as a Theater of Life: Profile of the Eighteenth Century Bosphorus" (Ph.D. dissertation, MIT, 1989); Shirine Hamadeh, *City's Pleasures: Istanbul in the Eighteenth Century* (Seattle: University of Washington Press, 2007); Çiğdem Kafesçioğlu, *Constantinopolis/Istanbul: Cultural Encounter, Imperial Vision, and the Construction of the Ottoman Capital* (University Park, PA: PSU Press, 2009); Gülru Necipoğlu, *Age of Sinan: Architectural Culture in the Age of Sinan* (London: Reaktion Books, 2005).

3 Nathalie Clayer, Alexandre Popovic and Thierry Zarcone(eds) *Melâmis-Bayrâmîs: Études sur Trois Mouvements Mystiques Musulmans* (Istanbul: Les Éditions Isis, 1998), 179–205; Ali Erken, "A Historical Analysis of Melami Bayramî Hagiographies" (master's thesis, Boğaziçi University, 2009); İsmail Erünsal, "Abdurrahman el-Askerî's Mir'âtü'l-Işk: A New Source for the Melâmî Movement in the Ottoman Empire During the 15th and 16th Centuries", *Wiener Zeitschrift für die kunde des Morgenlandes* 84 (1994), 95–15; idem, *XV–XVI. Asır Bayrâmî-Melâmîliği'nin Kaynaklarından Abdurrahman el Askerî'nin Mir'âtü'l-Işk'ı* (Ankara: TTK, 2003); Abdülbaki Gölpınarlı, *Melâmilik ve Melâmiler* (Istanbul: Milenyum Yayınları, 2013 reprint), 48–54; Ahmet Yaşar Ocak, "Kanuni Sultan Süleyman Devrinde Osmanlı Resmi Düşüncesine Karşı Bir Tepki Hareketi: Oğlan Şeyh İsmail-i Maşukî", *Osmanlı Araştırmaları* 10 (1990), 49–58; idem, "XVI–XVII Yüzyıllarda Bayramî Melâmîleri ve Osmanlı Yönetimi", *Belleten* 61 (1997), 93–110; idem, *Osmanlı Toplumunda Zındıklar ve Mülhidler: 15–17. Yüzyıllar* (Istanbul: Türkiye Ekonomik ve Toplumsal Tarih Vakfı, 1998, 274–90; Reşat Öngören, "Şeriatın Kestiği Parmak: Kanuni Sultan Süleyman Devrinde İdam Edilen Tarikat Şeyhleri", *İlam Araştırma Dergisi* 1 (1996), 123–40; Betül Yavuz, "The Making of a Sufi Order Between Hersey and Legitimacy: Bayrami-Malâmis in the Ottoman Empire" (master's thesis, Rice University, 2013), 101–19.

for their messianic claims. İsmâil Ma'şûkî was one of the persecuted. He was the son of the Melâmî-Bayramî Sheikh Pîr Ali Aksarâyî (d.1539) from Aksaray in Central Anatolia. He arrived in Istanbul as a young man and gained immense popularity. The state authorities, however, found his teachings heretical and ordered his execution in 1539.[4]

Unfortunately, available contemporaneous sources neither present us with a satisfactory understanding of İsmâil Ma'şûkî's teachings nor an explanation of why he was so severely persecuted. Yet, they offer interesting insights into so-far little explored Ottoman views on political dissent. In his study of dissonant voices and conflicting opinion in seventeenth-century Ottoman history-writing, Rhoads Murphey suggests that his intention was "not so much to reconcile differences or discover the correct version, but to assess the whole range of opinions expressed in the sources [and] to add new dimensions to our understanding of the past."[5] I find his approach particularly helpful for understanding the accounts of İsmâil Ma'şûkî's execution. In my reading, rather than bringing the available information together to establish a coherent factual account, as is often done, I focus on differences. These differences, I argue, reveals what each author chose to say about a controversial execution in a medium of debate.

When seventeenth-century writers narrated İsmâil Ma'şûkî's martyrdom in their works, they engaged in a conversation with a diverse group of adversaries and defenders. The Halvetî-Sivâsî sheikh Sivâsî (d.1639), for instance, was a staunch opponent of the Melâmî-Bayramîs and advocated their persecution.[6] These were important threats because the executions did not end with İsmâil Ma'şûkî – sheikhs Hamza Bâlî (d.1572/3) and Beşir Ağa (d.1683) were also put to death in Istanbul.[7] In response, the Melâmî-Bayramîs sought the protection of the ruling circles and built alliances with the *ulema*, Sufi sheikhs from

---

4  For the correct date of the execution as 1539, see Ocak, *Osmanlı Toplumunda Zındıklar*, 279–80 and Betül Yavuz, "The Making of a Sufi Order", 110.

5  Rhoads Murphey, "Ottoman historical writing in the seventeenth-century: a survey of the general development of the genre after the reign of Sultan Ahmed I (1603–1617)", *Essays on Ottoman Historians and Historiography* (Istanbul: Eren, 2009), 100–1.

6  Abdülmecid Sivâsî, *Dürer-i Akā'id*, fol.68a, MS 300, Mihrişah Sultan, SK. See also Cengiz Gündoğdu, "XVII: Yüzyıl Osmanlısında İki Farklı Sufi Tipi, Abdülmecid Sivâsî ve İdris-i Muhtefî", *İlam Araştırma Dergisi* 2 (1997), 21–39; and Derin Terzioğlu, "Sufi and Dissident in the Ottoman Empire: Niyāzī-i Mıṣrī, 1618–1694" (Ph.D. dissertation, Harvard University, 1999), 236–43.

7  For Hamza Bâlî and Beşir Ağa, see Hamid Algar, "Hamzaviye: A Deviant Movement in Bosnian Sufism", *Islamic Studies* 36 (2–3) 1997, 243–61; Nihat Azamat, "Hamza Bâlî", *DIA* 15, 502–5; and Ocak, *Osmanlı Toplumunda Zındıklar*, 290–306.

different orders, and high-ranking bureaucrats.[8] This new alliance produced Melâmî sympathizers who wanted to re-evaluate the sixteenth-century clash between İsmâil Ma'şûkî and the state authorities. Among them were the scribe Sarı Abdullah Efendi (d.1660), the âlim Nev'îzâde Atâî (d.1635), and traveller Evliya Çelebi (d.c.1684), who wanted to present defensive views of the sheikh that at the same time did not undermine the imperial power.

In her study of seventeenth-century Chinese ghost stories surrounding the fall of the Ming dynasty, Judith T. Zeitlin argues that the memory of the violent end of Ming was still alive and sometimes painful for the early Qing dynasty. By comparing different versions of a historical ghost story, she shows how each version presents the political position of its author and the particular way in which he pacified a painful memory.[9] Like the stories studied by Zeitlin, three versions of İsmâil Ma'şûkî's martyrdom present three different ways of voicing dissent, each more outspoken than the other. Each author offered his view of a controversial beheading through the way he presented, or avoided, the sites of execution and burial. While Sarı Abdullah omitted the execution to amend the conflict between the sheikh and the sultan, Atâî emphasized the community's survival by saying how they established sites of remembrance, and Evliya Çelebi presented the criticism of the sultan at a garden at Kandilli. All, however, shared a similar purpose; they raised a traumatic event of the past to put it to rest. When doing so, they offered a revisionist account. They transformed the execution from a display of imperial power as it originally was to a contested site of imperial authority.

1      At Meydanı and an Execution Untold

The topography of Istanbul plays a crucial role in these three authors' reconciliations of İsmâil Ma'şûkî's memory. By organizing my chapter around the sites of execution, burial, and the miraculous spectacle, I examine the diverse ways these three seventeenth-century Istanbulites wrote the violent history of their city. Let us begin with the site of execution and the exclusion of its depiction in the first defensive portrait of İsmâil Ma'şûkî. In her study of social meanings of violence in early modern England, Susan Dwyer Amussen argues that corporal punishment performed at public spectacles was central to power maintenance

---

8  See Terzioğlu, "Sufi and Dissident", 241–2; Yavuz, "The Making of a Sufi Order", 131–4.
9  Judith T. Zeitlin, "The Return of the Palace Lady: The Historical Ghost Story and Dynastic Fall", in David Der-wei Wang and Shang Wei (eds) *Dynastic Crisis and Cultural Innovation from Late Ming to the Late Qing and Beyond* (Cambridge, MA: HUP, 2005), 151–99.

MAP 1   Sites in Istanbul depicted in İsmail Maşuki's
        hagiographies
        MAP PREPARED BY GİZEM DÖRTER

of the early modern state.[10] She discusses how the spectators watched mutilation and burning, rituals that obliterated the criminal and inscribed the power of the ruling elite on the body of the executed.

In the case of İsmâil Ma'şûkî's beheading, we also observe how Ottoman authorities aimed to display state power, staging the execution at a site associated with imperial ceremonies and executions.[11] As Çiğdem Kafescioğlu shows, At Meydanı, the Byzantine Hippodrome, was among the execution spots of

---

10   Susan Dwyer Amussen, "Punishment, Discipline, and Power: The Social Meanings of Violence in Early Modern England", *Journal of British Studies* 34 (1) 1995, 1–34.
11   Kaya Şahin, *Empire and Power in the Reign of Süleyman Narrating the Sixteenth-Century Ottoman World* (New York: CUP, 2013), 50–3.

late-fifteenth-century Istanbul. A hagiography completed in 1484, for instance, depicts how dervish Otman Baba and his followers save themselves from the stakes and hooks awaiting them in At Meydanı.[12] During the reign of Sultan Süleyman (r.1520–66), At Meydanı emerged as one of the main locations for imperial weddings and circumcisions, as well as executions. In 1539, crowds gathered in At Meydanı to watch festivities organized for the circumcisions of the princes Bayezid and Cihangir.[13] They were probably the same crowds that gathered there to watch the execution of İsmâil Ma'şûkî, which took place at Çukurçeşme, facing the Egyptian obelisk near İbrahim Pasha Palace the same year.[14] By choosing such a central location for the beheading, the state authorities must have aimed to impress a large audience, much like in their imperial festivals.

As the public executions in At Meydanı for heresy were rare, İsmâil Ma'şûkî's beheading must have had an exceptional impact on its audience.[15] Yet, this is not to say that the spectators who gathered were universally scandalized by the offenses and edified by the punishments. As discussed by a number of early modern historians, many in the crowd came to support rather than condemn the victims, who were seen as martyrs. Followers and sympathizers showed their solidarity with the executed through the circulation of stories and poems soon after the executions. Patricia Palmer, for instance, discusses how early modern Irish poets elegized their patrons killed by the English by writing poems about the severed heads; "some howl, some curse, and some remain silent but all were openmouthed to offer rival narratives of resistance among the early modern Irish."[16]

---

12   Kafescioğlu, *Constantinople/Istanbul*, 136. See also Küçük Abdal, *Vilāyetnāme-i Sultan Otmān*, microfilm no A22, 94v–97r and 117–v118v, AMKT.

13   For an imperial wedding in 1524 and circumcision festival of princes in 1530 and 1539, see Özdemir Nutku, "At Meydanında Düzenlenen Şenlikler", in Ekrem Işın (ed.) *Hippodrom/At Meydanı* (Istanbul: Pera Müzesi, 2010), vol. 2, 71–95.

14   On Çukurçeşme, see Baha Tanman and Vefa Çobanoğlu, "At Meydanı ve Çevresinde Osmanlı Mimarisi", in Ekrem Işın (ed.), *Hippodrom*, 39. See also "At Meydanında İki Mezar ve Kaybolan bir Eski Esarın Hikayesi". *DIA* 1 (4) 1986, 7–12; and Baha Tanman, "Çukur Çeşme", *DBIA* 2, 53.

15   For a brief survey of the use of At Meydanı as a site for executions during the Ottoman and Byzantine periods, see Seza Sinanlar, *Bizans Araba Yarışlarından Osmanlı Şenliklerine At Meydanı* (Istanbul: Kitap Yayınevi, 2005), 35–7, 64–7.

16   Patricia Palmer, "'An headless Ladie' and 'a horses loade of heads': Writing the Beheading", *Renaissance Quarterly* 60 (2007), 25–57. The particular power of İsmâil Ma'şûkî's story comes from the severed head as the memento vitae. According to Patricia Palmer, the wrenching quality of still-life death and animation abruptly arrested both mesmerizes and repels us. She writes that "there is a potent difference between a severed head and a skull. If a skull is a *memento mori*, the severed is a *memento vitae*. It is its resemblance

Similarly, Ottoman writers used the powerful image of the severed head and circulated stories of what they perceived as unjust executions. An interesting example is the biographer Taşköprizâde Ahmed Efendi's (d.1561) account of Molla Lutfi's (d.1494) beheading in At Meydanı. According to Taşköprizâde, Molla Lutfi was a pious Muslim, not a heretic as he was condemned to be. He described how Molla Lutfi repeatedly confessed his faith while at the galleys, "[t]o the extent that", wrote Taşköprizâde, "it is narrated that his head continued to pronounce the unity of God after it fell on the ground."[17]

Were such stories also circulated about İsmâil Ma'şûkî in the immediate aftermath of his death? Our sources are conspicuously silent. We do not encounter voices of dissent except implicitly in a legal opinion cited by Ahmet Yaşar Ocak and issued by the chief mufti Ebüssuûd Efendi (d.1574) to address the question of what should be done to those who say İsmâil Ma'şûkî was executed unjustly.[18] The need for such a legal opinion suggests that Melâmî-Bayramîs criticized the execution and raised doubts about its justice. It is possible that they also circulated martyrdom stories in defence of their sheikh. Unfortunately, we do not know of any written account of these pro-İsmâil Ma'şûkî voices from the late-sixteenth century. If they had been written down, we are yet to discover them in our various collections.

Significantly, the first written account of the sheikh's life we now have is not a defence produced by his close followers. On the contrary, it presents the views of his opponents among the Melâmî-Bayramîs. The contemporary biographer Askerî, who was a follower of an adversary of İsmâil Ma'şûkî's, presents him as an arrogant youth who harmed his community.[19] Later biographers did not attack the sheikh as he did, but they were also not interested in defending him by circulating narratives about his martyrdom. They chose silence instead. While *ulema* biographers Taşköprizâde and Mehmed Mecdî (d.1591) did not

---

to the living, while being utterly drained of life that disturbs". See Palmer, "'An headless Ladic'", 41.

17  Taşköprizâde Ahmed Efendi, *Eş-Şekā'iku n-nu'mānīye fī 'ulemā'i'd-Devleti'l-'Oşmānīye*, edited by Ahmed Subhi Furat (Istanbul: İstanbul Üniversitesi Edebiyat Fakültesi Yayınları, 1985), 280. See also Orhan Şaik Gökyay and Şükrü Özen, "Molla Lutfî", *DIA* 30, 255–8; Şükrü Özen, "Molla Lutfî'nin İdamına Karşı Çıkan Hamlidüddin Efendi'nin Ahkâmü'z-zındîk Risalesi", *İslam Araştırmaları Dergisi* 4 (2000), 7–16; *idem* "İslâm Hukukunda Zındıklık Suçu ve Molla Lutfî'nin idamının Fıkhîliği", *İslam Araştırmaları Dergisi* 4 (2001), 17–62.

18  His response was severe – "they should also be executed if they follow his path." See Ertuğrul Düzdağ, *Şeyhülislam Ebussud Efendi'nin Fetvaları ışığında 16.Asır Türk Hayatı* (Istanbul: Enderun Kitabevi, 1972), 196; Ocak, *Osmanlı Toplumunda Zındıklar*, 284.

19  İsmail Erünsal (ed.) *XV–XVI: Asır Bayrâmî-Melâmîliği'nin Kaynaklarından Abdurrahman el Askerî'nin Mir'âtü'l-Işk'ı* (Ankara: TTK, 2003), 230.

include İsmâil Ma'şûkî in their collective lives, Münîrî Belgradî (d.1619–20), who was a Melâmî-Bayramî follower, only wrote "what he did, what he said is unknown" (ne eylemişdir, ne demişdir ma'lûm degildir).[20]

As discussed by Carl Ernst, Sufi martyrdom narratives are often written down only after the establishment of an alliance between the persecuted Sufi order and the ruling elite.[21] In the case of İsmâil Ma'şûkî, the author of the first defensive account of his career and spiritual pursuits shows the spread of Melâmî-Bayramî teaching among different members of the ruling circles.[22] Sarı Abdullah was a high-ranking bureaucrat who presented himself "as a Bayramî in his origin, Celvetî in his path, and Mevlevî in his education".[23] He shared his interest in Sufism by composing the Semerātü'l Fu'ād fi'l- mebde' ve'l-me'ād' (Fruits of the Heart in the Beginning and the End) (c.1624), a collection of teachings and biographies from different orders including Nakşibendîs and Halvetîs, as well as the Melâmî-Bayramîs. Our knowledge of the contemporary readers of the Semerāt is inadequate as the surviving dated manuscripts do not present much information.[24] Yet, we may assume that in the Semerāt, Sarı Abdullah shared İsmâil Ma'şûkî's life with a mixed audience that probably included Sufis from different orders and bureaucrats among the ruling elite.

---

20  MS Belgradi, *Silsiletü'l-Mukarrabin*, Şehid Ali Paşa 2819/3, fol. 141a, SK.

21  Carl Ernst, "From Hagiography to Martyrology: Conflicting Testimonies to a Sufi Martry of the Delhi Sultanate", *History of Religions* 24 (1985), 308–27.

22  The history of early modern Ottoman executions is yet to be written. Yet, we also observe how learned circles chose to neglect to mention the executions of their contemporaries. See for instance, the case of the chief mufti Ahîzâde Efendi (d.1634) in Nev'îzâde Atâî, *Ḥadā'iḳü'l-Ḥaḳā'iḳ fi Tekmiletü'ş-Şaḳā'iḳ*, published as vol. 2 of eş Şakâik-i Nu'mâniyye ve zeyilleri edited by Abdülkadir Özcan (Istanbul: Çağrı Yayınları, 1989), 755–7.

23  On Sarı Abdullah's life and works, see Nihat Azamat, "Sarı Abdullah", *DIA* 36, 145–7. See also MS Sarı Abdullah, *Naṣiḥatü'l-Mülûk*, Ty 09625, fol. 263b, IUK. This statement reflects his training from Melâmî-Bayramî sheikhs İdris-i Muhtefî (d.1615) and Hacı Kabayi (d.1627) as well as his possible relationship with Celvetî sheikh Hüdâyî (d.1628) and Mevlevî sheikh Ankaravî (d.1631). He held the post of *reîsülküttâb* in 1626 and 1638.

24  Although the number of surviving *Semerāt* copies is small (six are recorded in the Turkish manuscript sources database), they seem to have been considered important among the learned elite in Melâmî-Bayramî circles. The prominent poet Cevrî (d.1654) who was famous for his calligraphy prepared a *Semerāt* copy in 1661. See the copy MS Ty 01619 at IUK. None of the *Semerāt* copies I examined had any marginal notes about İsmâil Ma'şûkî. An undated copy of MS 2344 at Esad Efendi, SK was owned by a certain Mustafa Efendi, the head physician (*re'isü'l-eṭṭibā*). For the *Semerāt* copies from the eighteenth and nineteenth centuries, which do not have records of ownership, see MS Ty 00074, Ty 01473, Ty 01758 and Ty 01258 at IUK. The eighteenth-century copy, MS 45 Ak Ze 199/1 at MIHK was endowed by a certain Zeynel b. Hacı Aliye.

According to the introduction, Sarı Abdullah began the project because of a request from the Sufi brethren at the Mevlevî lodge at Galata. This group of readers might have included his patron, the Grand Vizier Kayserili Halil Pasha (d.1629) because Sarı Abdullah began his book at the beginning of one of Halil Pasha's campaigns and ended it with its end.[25]

What did readers and listeners learn in the pages of the Semerāt about İsmâil Ma'şûkî's execution in At Meydanı? They found a humble young man who sought martyrdom. Although they are presented İsmâil Ma'şûkî as a martyr, they would not have come across any information about the beheading itself. This absence might have been surprising for some because Sarı Abdullah described lengthy martyrdom accounts. For instance, we learn how Hallâc's limbs, eyes, and tongue were cut one by one at a public execution, which he endured with great patience. These passages present the readers with the ordeals of the respected martyrs of Islamic history who were accepted by the seventeenth century. While Sarı Abdullah wanted his readers to imagine painful executions through the cases of renowned martyrs from the non-Ottoman past, he excluded İsmâil Ma'şûkî's execution in At Meydanı in 1539.

Thus, interestingly, the first defensive portrait of the sheikh we have is silent about the execution in At Meydanı. Although Sarı Abdullah presents İsmâil Ma'şûkî as a martyr in response to critics like Askerî, he does not state where and how the martyrdom took place. This absence must be related to Sarı Abdullah's social position vis-à-vis the state authorities and his aim to amend the sheikh's controversial life for the *ulema*, Sufi sheikhs, and the bureaucrats among the seventeenth-century ruling elite who might have found the memory of the conflict problematic. In other parts of the sheikh's life, Sarı Abdullah again overlooks the struggle between the sheikh and the sultan. He emphasizes an alliance instead. He writes, for instance, how the sultan warned the sheikh against his adversaries and advised him to return to his hometown.

---

25  Sarı Abdullah Efendi, *Semerâtü'l-Fuâd*, in Tek, *Melâmet Risaleleri*, 63–120, recorded the beginning and ending of his work as, respectively, 17 July and 15 September in 1624. Halil Pasha left for a campaign on 17 July and ended it upon his arrival on 15 September. For the dates of the campaigns, see Alexander H. de Groot, *The Ottoman Empire and the Dutch Republic* (Istanbul: Uitgaven van het Nederlands Historisch-Archaeologisch Instituut, 1978), 76. For Halil Pasha and his Sufi interests, see also A. H. de Groot, "Halil Paşa, Kayserili", *DIA* 15, 324–6.

The sheikh, however, convinces his followers that he would like to follow his fate. The biography ends here and does not include a depiction of the beheading.[26]

This exclusion shows how Sarı Abdullah attempts to revise the controversial aspects of İsmâil Ma'şûkî's life. On the one hand, he breaches the silence on the sheikh and presents him as a part of the Melâmî-Bayramî genealogy, as well as a member of Ottoman Sufi circles. Yet, on the other hand, he recalls this life without any mention of dissent and persecution. To do so, he omits the public execution in At Meydanı. His contemporaries Atâî and Evliya Çelebi, however, commented more directly on the relationship between the sheikh, his community, and state authorities by depicting the miraculous deeds of a martyr on the Bosphorus.

## 2    Rumeli Hisarı and a Beheaded Body United

Atâî narrates a brief but powerful story of the disposal of the sheikh's dismembered body into the sea and its miraculous union at the burial site. By including this story in his work, Atâî shows how the Melâmî-Bayramîs ensured community solidarity and established sites of remembrance. Atâî writes,

> It has been narrated that when he was beheaded, his remains were thrown into the sea. His body emerged in this area of Kayalar at Rumeli Hisarı. His people wanted to bury it. İsmâîl, however, had willed them not to separate his head from his body, which caused puzzlement and curiosity. At this moment, his head also landed at the seashore revolving just like his body. Thus they were able to carry out his will and bury him.[27]

Atâî's account presents a persecuted community's response to a precarious political landscape. In his study of exemplary deaths in early modern Spain, Carlos Eire has argued that Spanish writers did not include posthumous

---

26   Sarı Abdullah, *Semerātü'l Fu'ād fi'l-mebdā' ve'l-me'ād*, MS Ty 01619, fol. 158a–161a at IUK. Its transliteration has been provided by Abdurrezzak Tek, *Bayrâmî Melâmiliği'ne Dâir Melâmet Risâleleri* (Bursa: Emin Yayınları, 2007), 63–120.

27   "Mesmū'dur ki boynu uruldukdan sonra deryāya atılup bedeni Rumili Ḥisārında olan Kayalar nām maḥale gelüp muta'alaḳātı defn itmek istediklerinde başımı bedenimden cüdā etmeyesiz diyü tavṣiye itmegin bā'is-i tevaḳḳuf ve tecessüs olur. Ol esnāda farḳ-ı seri kendi gibi dönerek sāḥile gelüp emr-i tavṣiye ve defni yerine getirürler". *Ḥadā'iḳü'l-Ḥaḳā'iḳ fī Tekmiletü'ş-Şaḳā'iḳ*, MS 2341, fol. 824b, Esad Efendi, SK (autograph copy). See also the other seventeenth century MS 2309, fol. 53b at Esad Efendi and MS 1671, fol. 46b, at Beşir Ağa, SK, as well as the facsimile with index published by Özcan, *eş-Şakâik-i Nu'mâniyye* 2, 89.

miracles randomly in their works but narrated them to address specific issues of their milieu. Hagiographers at the time of Saint Teresa of Avila (d.1582), for instance, related reports about the incorruptibility of her flesh as a reflection of their concern with the corruptibility of the world at a time when the Spanish state and society were experiencing drastic transformations.[28] In the case of Atâî, we also observe how a biographer responds to specific anxieties of his period. Atâî wrote this story at a time when prominent learned men – including those whom he personally knew – were executed and their bodies annihilated. In 1634, the Chief Mufti Ahîzâde Hüseyin Efendi, to whom Atâî dedicated one of his mesnevîs, was sent to exile, stopped before leaving Istanbul and executed on the shore of the Marmara Sea. In 1635, the poet Nefʿî, with whom Atâî had a poetry exchange, was hanged, put into a sack, and thrown into the Bosphorus. Both bodies were never recovered.[29]

In response to the attempts of state authorities to annihilate the executed, families, friends, and communities fought back. In a few cases, they managed to bring back the mutilated body, ensure proper burial, and establish marked burial sites. The family of the executed finance director Mehmed Pasha (d.1589), for instance, bought the severed head from rebels and buried it in his shrine in Eyüp.[30] The Melâmî-Bayramî followers also faced a similar ordeal after the execution of their sheikh Hamza Bâlî. Their biographer Lâʿlîzâde Abdülbâki (d.1746) writes how the followers of the sheikh bribed executioners, reclaimed the body and the head, and buried their sheikh secretly at a location known only to the community.[31]

---

28   Carlos Eire, *From Madrid to Purgatory: The Art and Craft of Dying in Sixteenth-Century Spain* (Cambridge: CUP, 1995), 371–502.
29   On Nefʿî, see Metin Akkuş, "Nefʿî", *DIA* 32, 523–5. On Ahîzâde's execution, see İsmail Katgı, *Maktul Şeyhülislamlar* (Istanbul: İz, 2013), 125–207.
30   For the murder of Mehmed Pasha, see Günhan Börekçi, "Factions and Favorites at the Courts of Sultan Ahmed I (r. 1603–17) and his Immediate Predecessors" (Ph.D. dissertation, Ohio State University, 2010), 190–5. Börekçi also provides us with the translation of an interesting anonymous account where the author writes, "thereafter the soldiers praised the sultan highly and left with great satisfaction, taking the governor-general's head with them. They practised all kinds of mischief with it: throwing balls at it, hitting the mouth with their fists, tramping through the most important streets with the head set on a high pole so that everyone could see it. They mocked, cursed, and spoke all kinds of evil against him." Quotation from Anon. *Warhafftige und gar auszfierliche Newer Zeyttung, Ausz Constantinopel, Welcher massen die Türckische Kriegsleut ein Erschröckliche Auffruhr angerichtet halben, Auch fast die halbe Statt Angezündet und in Brand gestecket* (Augsburg: Wöhrlin, 1589), 4–6. Also see Börekçi, "Factions and Favorites", 191.
31   Lâʿlîzâde Abdülbaki, *Sergüzeşt*, MS 1274 at TSEH. A transliteration of the manuscript provided by Tek, *Melâmet Risaleleri*, 132.

Safeguarding the body and the memory of an executed sheikh must have been crucial for a persecuted community's survival. Lâ'lîzâde describes the challenges faced by Melâmî-Bayramîs to maintain solidarity after İsmâil Ma'şûkî's execution by writing, "as fear and hate appeared in the hearts of the lovers of God, previous companionship and community became hidden. Companions were scattered around."[32] Like the sheikh's body facing obliteration, disciples were executed along with their sheikh and other disciples were persecuted in the following decades. And even within the Melâmî-Bayramî community itself, there was division and difference of opinion. Adversaries like Askerî found the punishment appropriate and wrote claiming that İsmâil Ma'şûkî disappeared from the pages of time without a trace.[33]

Atâî's account is a response to critics like Askerî and it illustrates how the sheikh was not forgotten. He narrates this account in his biographical collection Ḥada'iķü'l-Ḥaḳā'iḳ (Gardens of Truths) (c.1635), which gathers about one thousand *ulema* and Sufi sheikhs from 1558 to 1634.[34] Having died in 1539, İsmâil Ma'şûkî should not have been included in the Ḥada'iḳ, but covered in the previous biographical compilation. This book, Taşköprizâde's Şaḳā'iḳ, however, did not include the sheikh. This was a gap Atâî intended to fill. Unlike the biographer Taşköprizâde, who showed little interest in the Melâmî-Bayramîs, he was committed to record their lives in his work and often presented defensive portraits of them. His readers noticed these Melâmî-Bayramî sympathies. The Halvetî-Sivâsî sheikh Mehmed Nazmi Efendi (d.1701), for instance, accused him of being a follower of the sheikh İdrîs-i Muhtefî (d.1615) and presenting false information in support of the Melâmî-Bayramîs.[35] We do not know whether Nazmi's claims were true or whether Atâî was indeed a Melâmî-Bayramî follower himself, but his brief story in the Ḥada'iḳ shows his Melâmî-Bayramî sympathies. By deciding to include İsmâil Ma'şûkî in his collection, he presented him as a revered martyr to his *ulema* readers.[36]

The inclusion of İsmâil Ma'şûkî's martyrdom story in the Ḥada'iḳ shows how the sheikhs' sympathizers were able to circulate stories in defence of

---

32  "Uşşāk-ı ilāhī kulūbunda vahşet ve nefret ārız olmakla evvelki sohbet ü cemiyet butūna vardı. Ahbāb u fukarā etraf u eknāfa dağıldı." See Tek, *Melâmet Risaleleri*, 134.

33  "Ve naḳş-ı vücūdını şaḥife-i rūzgārdan tīġ-ı celāl ile ḥakk itdiler ve nā-būd u nā-peydā eylediler". Askerî, 237.

34  For Atâî's life and works, see Haluk İpekten, "Atâî", *DIA* 4, 40–2.

35  Mehmed Nazmi Efendi, *Osmanlılarda Tasavvufi Hayat. Hediyyetü'l-İḫvān: Halvetilik Örneği* (Istanbul: İnsan Yayınları, 2005), 174.

36  For the owners of the *Ḥada'iḳ* manuscript copies mainly among the *ulema*, see Güvemli Zahir Sıdkı, "İstanbul Kütüphanelerinde *Ḥada'iḳü'l-Haḳā'iḳ* Nüshaları", *Yeni Türk Dergisi* 66 (1938), 214–20 and 75–6 (1939), 125–9.

their sheikh in seventeenth-century learned circles. Atâî did not specify his sources but he probably heard the sheikh's story from the Melâmî-Bayramîs themselves at gatherings they frequented together. The Halvetî-Celvetî Sheikh Aziz Mahmud Hüdâyî's lodge at Üsküdar, for instance, provided a common social space. It brought together members of the learned elite like Atâî, as well as Sarı Abdullah and Evliya Çelebi, with the Melâmî-Bayramîs for whom it provided shelter. Such shared social landscapes must have contributed to the remembrance of İsmâil Ma'şûkî among the learned circles and his inclusion in a prominent biographical collection.

Like its circulation, the story's theme reveals to us the community's efforts to safeguard the memory of their sheikh. The narrative is structured around the theme of a martyr seeking his burial place, a common motif in Ottoman folk tales also popular in the seventeenth century.[37] These were warriors who continued to fight after death, carrying their heads under their arms, until they fell at sites later memorialized with shrines. Our knowledge of the circulation of these stories is meager, but we may assume that they were narrated to boost the morale of the fellow fighters and make the selected landmarks sacred. Following this topos, Atâî also presented İsmâil Ma'şûkî as a martyr and displayed the locations associated with his death as sacred sites. But here, he also emphasized the significance of the community ties for the Melâmî-Bayramîs. In his narrative, İsmâil Ma'şûkî's miracle was to take his head and body to the same site but it was actually his disciples who realized his last wish, brought his remains together, and marked the sites of execution and burial.

The emphasis on the sites of remembrance in this account raises the question of whether the Melâmî-Bayramîs aimed to bring their community together at their sheikhs' tombs. In her seminal work on sixteenth-century Bektaşî shrines, Zeynep Yürekli has shown how a persecuted sixteenth-century Sufi order ensured community solidarity through writing life stories and building shrines.[38] Do we observe similar uses of shrine-building in the case of the Melâmî-Bayramîs? Although we know too little about Melâmî-Bayramî commemoration practices to be able to address this question, we may assume that the followers of İsmâil Ma'şûkî might have considered building a shrine as it was a common practice in the sixteenth century. İsmâil Ma'şûkî's father Pîr Ali Aksarâyî (d.1532–33), his adversary Pîr Ahmed Edirnevî, and successor

---

[37] Ahmet Yaşar Ocak, *Türk Folkloründe Kesik Baş: Tarih-Folklor İlişkisinden Bir Kesit* (Ankara: Dergah, 2013). For seventeenth-century accounts of the beheaded martyrs, see Ocak, *Türk Folkloründe*, 25, 97–103.

[38] Zeynep Yürekli, *Architecture and Hagiography in the Ottoman Empire: The Politics of Bektashi Shrines in the Classical Age* (Surrey: Ashgate, 2012).

Sârbân Ahmed (d.1545) all had shrines built for them.[39] In the 1630s when Atâî wrote his biography, however, Melâmî-Bayramîs had gone underground to avoid persecution and changed their burial practices. Şeyh İdrîs-i Muhtefî, for instance, was buried at the public cemetery of Kasımpaşa without any mark of his Melâmî-Bayramî affiliation.[40] Others did not even have tombstones, like the Melâmî-Bayramî sympathizer Cevrî İbrâhim Çelebi (d.1654), who had two trees to mark his tomb.[41]

This is not to say that Melâmî-Bayramî tombs were not sites of visit. Although we do not observe shrine-building as in the case of the Bektaşîs, tombs of Melâmî-Bayramîs occasionally became meeting points for the community. Lâ'lîzâde, for instance, records how Sarı Abdullah met his future sheikh Beşir Ağa the first time during a visit to the tomb of Hamza Bâlî.[42] Yet, such encounters must have been difficult. Without clearly marked sites, these graves depended on their visitors to transmit knowledge about their location from one generation to another. As the eighteenth-century Melâmî-Bayramî biographer Müstakimzâde Süleyman Sâdeddin wrote, for Cevrî, "because his tomb is hidden, only the brethren know about it."[43] These tombs depended on the transmission of communal knowledge about their place to bring the community together.

Thus, location in the city, another theme that Atâî emphasizes in his narrative, plays a crucial role in ensuring visits to these 'hidden' sites. When Atâî wrote the Ḥadā'iḳ, both the mescid erected at the execution site in At Meydanı and the tomb at Rumeli Hisar were located at the well-known excursion sites of seventeenth-century Istanbulites. The centrality of the mescid in At Meydanı is especially striking.[44] The area was a fashionable promenade site in the late-sixteenth century.[45] The poet Taşlıcalı Yahyâ Bey (d.1582) described its popularity and how it was a beloved site for a promenade after Friday prayers at the nearby Ayasofya. In the 1610s, visitors might have included Melâmî-Bayramîs like İdrîs-i Muhtefî and Sarı Abdullah, who first met at Ayasofya after a Friday prayer.[46] After the building of the Sultan Ahmed Mosque in 1616, the use of At

---

39  Gölpınarlı, Melâmilik, 44, 46, 55, 68; Ḥadā'iḳ, 65–70.
40  Gölpınarlı, Melâmilik, 124, 138.
41  Gölpınarlı, Melâmilik, 140.
42  Tek, Melâmet Risâleleri, 44–5.
43  Müstakîmzâde Süleyman Sâdeddin, Risâle-i Melâmiyye-i Şuttâriyye, which was published in Tek's Melâmet Risâleleri, 258–9.
44  For the mescid in At Meydanı, see Eyice, "At Meydanında", 7–12.
45  For Yahya Bey's in At Meydanı, see Asaf Hâlet Çelebi, Dîvân Şiirinde İstanbul (Ankara: Hece Yayınları, 2002), 57–8. See also Deniz Çalış Kural, Şehrengiz, Urban Rituals and Deviant Sufi Mysticism in Ottoman Istanbul (Farnham: Ashgate, 2014).
46  Tek, Melâmet Risaleleri, 141.

Meydanı for such Friday strolls must have increased. In the early-seventeenth century, Evliya Çelebi describes the obelisk facing the execution spot as a temâşâgâh-ı cihân, a place of promenade for the world. Thus, when Atâî noted the mescid at the site of execution, he was not referring to a secluded spot. On the contrary, it was centrally located, popular and easily accessible for the visits of his readers.

Compared with the mescid in At Meydanı, the tomb was located in a relatively secluded area in the sixteenth century.[47] The burial of the sheikh close to a major urban centre would have been problematic in 1539, so the persecuted Melâmî-Bayramîs sought protection from another order in a safe location. The Halvetî-Gülşenî lodge built at Rumeli Hisarı by Zarîfî (d.1569–70) provided them with that shelter.[48] The Rumeli Hisarı neighbourhood would also have been suitable because of its location, which was far from the centre but still reachable in a day.[49] In the early-seventeenth century, however, the neighbour-

---

[47] For the Kayalar Mescidi at Rumeli Hisarı, see Esra Dişören, "Kayalar Mescidi ve Tekkesi", DBIA 4, 498–9; and Hafız Hüseyin and Howard Crane (translator and editor), *The Garden of Mosques: Hafız Hüseyin Al-Ayvansarayi's Guide to the Muslim Monuments of Ottoman Istanbul* (Leiden: Brill, 2000), 436. The current tombstone, marked with a Kâdirî headgear, is probably from the nineteenth century when the lodge was rebuilt by the Kâdirî sheikh Niyâzî Efendi buried now next to İsmâil Ma'şûkî. The inscription reads "Yā hu/Ṭarīḳ-ı 'ulya-yı Bayrāmiye ricālinden/Aksaraylı pīr 'Alī Efendinüñ maḥdūmı/ḳuṭbu'l-'ārifīn ve ġavsü'l-vāsīlīn/şehīd İsmāil Ma'şūkī/ḥażretlerinüñ rūḥ-ı sa'ādetlerine/lillah el-fātiḥa/935 sene". For the tombstone, see Gölpınarlı, *Melâmilik*, 49–50.

[48] Zarîfî was a disciple of Gülşenî, another persecuted sheikh, who chose this lodge at Rumeli Hisarı as his burial place. The biographer Muhyi claimed that he had enjoyed good relations with the chief mufti of the time. If this was the case, it must have helped the Melâmî-Bayramîs to ensure the establishment of the tomb using these connections. See Reşat Öngören, *Osmanlılar'da Tasavvuf Anadolu'da Sûfîler, Devlet ve Ulemâ, (XVI. Yüzyıl)* (İstanbul: İz Yayıncılık, 2000); and Baha Tanman, "Muhsine Hatun", 495. Another interesting site around Rumeli Hisarı is the "cemetery of the martyrs". As studied in-depth by Edhem Eldem and Günay Kut, the identification of the cemetery on top of the hill near the fortress as "the cemetery of the martyrs" was probably a nineteenth-century development. Evliya Çelebi and Eremya Çelebi as well as Atâî are silent about this cemetery. Even if the cemetery were revered for its martyrs in the seventeenth century, it is notable that these authors did not emphasize a possible connection with İsmâil Ma'şûkî. See Edhem Eldem and Günay Kut, *Rumeli Hisarı Şehidlik Dergâhı Mezar Taşları*, (İstanbul: Boğaziçi Üniversitesi Yayınevi, 2011).

[49] Similarly, in the 1530s, Yahya Efendi, an Üveysi sheikh frustrated with the state authorities, sought confinement at the nearby Bosphorus town of Beşiktaş. We are yet to study the spiritual landscape of the Bosphorus systematically. Today, it hosts a variety of holy sites, including the mosque-lodge complex of Sheikh Yahya Efendi in Beşiktaş, Telli Baba in Sarıyer and Yuşa in Beykoz. See M. Tayyib Gökbilgin, "Boğaziçi", DIA 6, 251–62.

hood emerged as a popular pleasure spot. Thus, the tomb's relative isolation in the sixteenth century changed and its visibility increased.[50]

Atâî could not have been indifferent to the area. Having grown up in the neighbourhood of Anadolu Hisarı on the other shore, he spent his early years with views of the neighbourhood. In 1617, he included its lengthy depiction in his first mesnevî 'Alemnümā, where he described the beauties of the Rumeli Hisarı, and its visitors. These visitors included Gülşenîs, Mevlevîs and Abdals, who visited Rumeli Hisarı on their boats, playing music and singing mystical songs. Some also visited the holy sites in the neighbourhood such as the tombs of Durmuş Dede and Akbaba Sultan.[51] What about the tomb of İsmâil Ma'şûkî? The Ḥadā'iḳ entry presents how the Melâmî-Bayramîs survived the persecution and safeguarded the memory of their sheikh. However, were the Melâmî-Bayramîs also successful in marking the tomb as a place for seventeenth-century Istanbulites to visit? Atâî is silent. His contemporary Evliya Çelebi, however, called it a ziyâretgâh (a place to visit) and narrated his version of its establishment, focusing on what Atâî overlooks, to which we now turn.[52]

## 3   The Bosphorus and Criticism of the Sultan

When we look at the Bosphorus from the neighbourhood of Rumeli Hisarı today, it is hard to imagine beheaded corpses and severed heads swirling upstream to present their petition about an unjust execution. Yet, it was this story that Evliya Çelebi wanted to share with his readers when describing the Rumeli Hisarı neighbourhood in his Seyahatnâme. In this account, he presents a spectacle of semâ, the whirling dance, of the sheikh and his disciples in front of the sultan, whose name he leaves blank. After providing brief information about the sheikh and his execution in At Meydanı, he writes,

---

50   Tülay Artan, "Boğaziçi", DBIA 2, 282–6.
51   In his book on Rumeli Hisarı, İhsan Keseder, mentions the shrine of "Kesikbaş Dede" ("severed headed holy man") on Kara Koyun Caddesi in his *Rumeli Hisar Köyü* (Istanbul: Günlük Ticaret Gazetesi, 1983), 72, 115. A tombstone without any inscription, known as Kesikbaş Dede, still exists. Today, the site is venerated as the burial place of an Ottoman Muslim shepherd who resisted the Byzantines and was martyred by beheading. I thank İlham Khuri-Makdisi for her assistance in locating the tomb.
52   Lâ'lîzâde in his *Sergüzeşt* (Tek, *Melâmet Risaleleri*, 134) mentions being unable to find the tombstone. The current tombstone with its Kâdirî headgear in the courtyard of Kayalar Mescidi must be from the nineteenth century when Kayalar mescidi was rebuilt by the Kâdirî sheikh Niyâzî Efendi in 1877. See Dişören, "Kayalar Mescidi", 498.

They threw the blessed bodies of the sheikh and his disciples into the sea from Ahırkapı. At the time, the sultan was at Kandilli garden of Hisar. The sheikh and his ten disciples emerged in front of the sultan and performed semâ on the sea carrying their heads on their hands. Waves rushed violently. It is known that a corpse remains underwater for three days before it comes out. These bodies did not sink. They moved against the current in the middle of a severe winter and reached Kandilli garden. Such a wonder. When ... Ḫān and others saw this, they cried out. One of them said, "my padişah, they came to submit a petition because you executed them unjustly." The sultan cried. After an hour of semâ, the sheikh and his disciples left. They moved against the current, doing semâ and reached Durmuş Dede lodge where they were buried. I was honoured to meet those who have seen the light over their tombs for ten days.[53]

At first glance, Evliya Çelebi's account is very similar to that of Atâî. Both begin with the severed head and headless body moving upstream on the Bosphorus and end with the body and the head buried at Rumeli Hisarı. Yet, there is an important difference. Like Sarı 'Abdullah, Atâî presents cooperation rather than conflict with the state authorities. When he describes the events that led to the execution, he writes how İsmâil Ma'şûkî sought the help of the chief mufti Çivizâde Efendi, and thus overlooks the strife between them. When Evliya Çelebi narrates the beheading, however, he emphasizes the struggle. This difference is interesting because the Ḥada'iḳ is among Evliya Çelebi's main sources for the first volume of the Seyahatnâme. Although Evliya Çelebi uses some factual information about the biography of İsmâil Ma'şûkî from the Ḥada'iḳ,[54] he does not follow the Ḥada'iḳ in his account of the sheikh's

---

53 "Menâkıb-ı kerâmet-i Şeyh İsmâ'îl: Kaçan kim bu azîz hazretlerinin halîfeleriyle cesed-i mübâreklerin deryâya Âhûrkapu'dan bırakdıklarında meğer pâdişâh Hisâr'da Kandîlli bâğçede imiş. Anı görseler rû-yı deryâda azîz on halîfesiyle Kandîlli Bâğçe önünde Hünkâr huzûrunda başları ellerinde semâ' edüp deryâ cûş [u] hurûşa gelir. Hikmet bu kim bir âdem na'şı deryâda üç gün durup sonra zâhir olur. Bunlar gark olmadan İslâmbol'dan o şiddet-i akındıyı kesüp Kandîlli bâğçesine varalar, aceb hikmetdir. (...) Hân ve gayrı cân bu hâli görüp gırîv [u] feryâd edüp, 'Pâdişâhım bunları nâ-hak katl etdiğine arzuhâle geldiler' deyince Hünkâr giryeler eyler. Kâmil bir sâ'at semâ'dan sonra yine akındıya karşu semâ' ederek kayalar dibinde Durmuş Dede tekyesi önüne varup anda defn etdiklerinde kâmil on gece üzerlerine nûr yağdığın müşâhede etmiş cânlar ile müşerref olmuşuz. Rahmetullâh". See Evliya Çelebi, *Evliya Çelebi Seyahatnâmesi: 1.Kitap: Topkapı Sarayı Bağdat 304 Yazmasının Transkripsyonu-Dizini*, edited by Orhan Şaik Gökyay (Istanbul: Yapı Kredi Yayınları, 1996), 195.

54 Hatice Aynur, "Seyahatname'de Türkçe Edebi ve Biyografik Eserler" in Hatice Aynur and Hakan Karateke (eds), *Evliya Çelebi Seyahatnamesi'nin Yazılı Kaynakları* (Ankara: TTK,

post-mortem miracle. He narrates what Atâî omits and presents his message directly using reported speech: "'they came to present a petition about their unjust death', says a witness to the crying sultan."[55] This is a unique voice; there are no other known accounts of this story in our sources before or after the Seyahatnâme.

We still know too little about Evliya Çelebi's political position vis-à-vis the state authorities to understand why he departed from his main source to present such a critical voice.[56] Yet, the author's Melâmî-Bayramî sympathies must have played an important role in the inclusion of this unique story in his work. Like Atâî, Evliya Çelebi presents his support for the Melâmî-Bayramîs in different parts of his ten-volume travelogue. For him, Hamza Bâlî was the pole (kutb), one of the highest stations in the Sufi path, and İdrîs-i Muhtefî was a sheikh who performed many hundred miraculous deeds.[57] Evliya Çelebi also praised the Melâmî-Bayramîs for following a noble path originating from the Prophet himself and grieved their persecution despite having done nothing against the sharia.[58] His account of İsmâil Ma'şûkî's post-mortem miracle supports these points and condemns the persecution of a Melâmî-Bayramî sheikh. Here he narrates how the sheikh fights back the state's display of power at a public execution.

By setting the story at an imperial garden, presenting it as a public spectacle, and depicting an astonishing semâ performance, Evliya Çelebi presents the executed sheikh's power over the sultan. Each one of these three elements of İsmâil Ma'şûkî's miraculous deed plays an important role in his critical account of an unjust execution. First, the setting of the petition at an imperial garden is noteworthy. Suraiya Faroqhi has shown how Evliya Çelebi often recorded

---

2012), 249–50; Meşkure Eren, *Evliya Çelebi Seyahatnâmesi Birinci Cildinin Kaynakları Üzerine Bir Araştırma* (Istanbul: Nurgök Matbaası, 1960), 83–7.

55  Evliya, *Seyahatnâme 1*, 195.
56  On Evliya Çelebi's life and his work, see the seminal study of Robert Dankoff, *An Ottoman Mentality: The World of Evliya Çelebi* (Leiden: Brill, 2004), 1–47. For his political views on rebels and their clash with state authorities, see Görkem Özizmirli, "Fear in Evliya Çelebi's Seyahatnâme: Politics and Historiography in a Seventeenth Century Ottoman Travelogue" (Master's thesis, Koç University, 2014), 52–82. For his views on the dynasty, See Yahya Kemal Taştan, "Evliyâ Çelebi'nin Osmanlı Hanedanına Bakışı" in Nuran Tezcan and Semih Tezcan (eds), *Doğumunun 400. Yılında Evliyâ Çelebi* (Ankara: Kültür ve Turizm Bakanlığı, 2011), 356–90.
57  Evliya Çelebi, *Evliya Çelebi Seyahatnâmesi: Topkapı Sarayı Bağdat 305 Yazmasının Transkripsiyonu*, vol. 3, edited by Seyit Ali Kahraman and Yücel Dağlı (Istanbul: Yapı Kredi Yayınları, 1999), 118; idem, *Seyahatnâme 1*, 181.
58  Evliya Çelebi, *Evliya Çelebi Seyahatnâmesi: Topkapı Sarayı Bağdat 304 Yazmasının Transkripsiyonu*, vol. 2, edited by Zekeriya Kurşun, Seyit Ali Kahraman and Yücel Dağlı (Istanbul: Yapı Kredi Yayınları, 1999), 225.

the history of Bosphorus gardens as a history of imperial wrath and violence. While Çubuklu was the garden where Sultan Bayezid II (r.1481–1512) beat his son Selim (r.1512–20) with a stick, Kuleli was the garden where Sultan Selim tried to kill his son Süleyman.[59] Thus, according to Evliya Çelebi, Çubuklu takes its name from the trees that sprang forth from Bayezid's stick (çubuk) and Kuleli is the tower (kule) where Süleyman hid from his father. We know from Gülru Necipoğlu's work that a number of imperial gardens were established on the shores of the Bosphorus in the sixteenth century.[60] What is interesting here is how a seventeenth-century Istanbulite like Evliya Çelebi presented his city's history. For him, imperial gardens on the Bosphorus, like the garden at Kandilli, were sites for the violent struggles of the sixteenth century.[61]

Second, the public spectacle on the Bosphorus has an important role in the story. Like the execution, where the state inscribes its power on the body of the executed in a public square, here the sheikh presents his power over currents of the Bosphorus in front of an imperial gathering. Akıntı Burnu, close to Rumeli Hisarı and Kandilli, is famous for the strength of its currents.[62] Evliya Çelebi, like other travel writers since antiquity, also notes their power when describing the area. In this account, he presents his surprise that the sheikh was able to move upstream against violent waves and forceful currents. Significantly, he sets this spectacle on the two shores of the Bosphorus. Tülay Artan has argued that the eighteenth-century Bosphorus could be seen as a theatre where each shore watched the other.[63] In this seventeenth-century account, Evliya Çelebi establishes a similar connection; the court at Kandilli watches the sheikh and his dervishes until they leave for Rumeli Hisarı on the other shore.

---

59  Evliya, *Seyahatnâme* 1, 229–31; Suraiya Faroqhi, "What happened in Istanbul Gardens and Beauty Spots? Evliya Çelebi on Religion, Communication and Entertainment", unpublished paper presented at Boğaziçi University Symposium, September 2011, 6–7, 11. For a survey of Evliya Çelebi's depictions of gardens throughout his work, see also Nurhan Atasoy, "Evliyâ Çelebi ve Matrakçı Nasuh: Osmanlı Bahçelerine Yönelik Bakış Açıları (1534–1682)", in Tezcan and Tezcan, *Doğumunun 400. Yılında*, 500–27.

60  Gülru Necipoğlu, "The Suburban Landscape of Sixteenth-Century in Istanbul as a Mirror of Classical Ottoman Garden Culture", in Attilio Petruccioli (ed.) *Gardens in the Time of Great Muslim Empires: Theory and Design* (Leiden: Brill, 1997), 32–71.

61  We do not know about the tension between Selim and his only son Süleyman, but the clash between Bayezid and his son Selim is well-documented. Selim revolted against his father, abducted him from his throne, and sent him to a forced retirement on the way to which Bayezid died. See Erdem Çıpa, *Yavuz'un Kavgası* (Istanbul: Yapı Kredi Yayınları, 2013).

62  On Akıntı burnu, see Dionysios Byzantios, *Boğaziçi'nde bir Gezinti*, translated by Mehmet Fatih Yavuz (Istanbul: Yapı Kredi, 2010), 8, 61, 96; Evliya, *Seyahatnâme* 1, 194.

63  Artan, "Boğaziçi", 283.

Finally, it is interesting that the sheikh presents his petition to the sultan not through words but with a semâ performance. This is noteworthy because the Melâmî-Bayramîs did not generally practise semâ in their rituals and not all agreed about its permissibility. Still, as Terzioğlu noted, the court records of İsmâil Ma'şûkî's trial suggest that he held a favourable view of the practice.[64] Although we do not know whether he actually included it in his rituals, stories of his practice of semâ might have been circulating in Evliya Çelebi's circles. For example, Lâmekânî Hüseyin Efendi (d.1625), whom Evliya Çelebi claimed to have met as a young boy, composed a treatise in defence of semâ and might have narrated just such a miraculous semâ of İsmâil Ma'şûkî at his gatherings.[65]

Evliya Çelebi was not partial to the early-seventeenth-century debates on the semâ. At the time he wrote the first volume of his Seyahatnâme, Kadızâde Mehmed Efendi (d.1635) and his followers secured imperial support to banish semâ rituals and close down some of the Mevlevî lodges.[66] Evliya Çelebi, who had had close ties with the Mevlevîs since his youth, condemned these prohibitions in different parts of his work. When he visited a deserted Mevlevî lodge at Aydın, for instance, he inscribed his critique on the wall with a couplet.[67] He also wrote how Kadızâde Mehmed broke his leg when he refused to attend a semâ gathering in Konya.[68] The story of İsmâil Ma'şûkî's spectacular semâ performance must have also appealed to Evliya Çelebi as an opportunity to criticize the suppression of the semâ in his time.

Thus, through his focus on the semâ performance in front of an imperial garden, Evliya Çelebi connects sixteenth-century grievances about imperial policies with those of his seventeenth century. Evliya Çelebi ends his account by establishing a personal connection in time. "I was honoured to meet those who have seen light over their tombs for ten days," he wrote. While it is highly unlikely that witnesses of the miracle in 1539 could have met Evliya Çelebi in the 1630s, it is important to note that Evliya Çelebi wanted to establish such a

---

64  Ocak, *Osmanlı Toplumunda Zındıklar*, 285 and Terzioğlu, "Sufi and Dissident", 222–3.
65  Evliya, *Seyahatnâme* 1, 161: "Hamd-ı Hüda bu azizin şeref-i sohbetleri ile müşerref olmuşuzdur."
66  Alberto Fabio Ambrosio, *Bir Mevlevî'nin Hayatı, 17. Yüzyılda Sufilik Öğretisi ve Ayinleri*, translated by Ayşe Meral (Istanbul: Kitap Yayınevi, 2012), 175–285; and Terzioğlu, "Sufi and Dissident", 227–33.
67  Evliya Çelebi, *Evliya Çelebi Seyahatnâmesi: Topkapı Sarayı Kütüphanesi Bağdat 306, Süleymaniye Kütüphanesi Pertev Paşa 462, Süleymaniye Kütüphanesi Hacı Beşir Ağa 452 Numaralı Yazmaların Mukayeseli Transkripsiyonu-Dizini*, vol. 9, edited by Yücel Dağlı, Seyit Ali Kahraman and Robert Dankoff (Istanbul: Yapı Kredi Yayınları, 2005), 84.
68  Evliya, *Seyahatnâme* 1, 164–5.

personal connection and presented his account as a living memory rather than being in the distant past.[69]

To conclude, seventeenth-century Istanbulites lived in a city in which the sixteenth-century Ottoman ruling elite had inscribed its power with building projects and public ceremonies. The monumental architecture shaped the Istanbul skyline and lavishly illustrated manuscripts memorialized imperial ceremonies. Compared with these marks of imperial history, the sites of remembrance of persecuted communities are difficult to see. Yet, they are not invisible. İsmâil Ma'şûkî's martyrdom account is an example. It displays the ways in which persecuted communities shaped their own spaces and wrote their history. In Evliya Çelebi's account, the tomb at Rumeli Hisarı connects the sheikh's tomb to the imperial garden on the opposite shore and presents him with a medium through which to criticize the state violence. In Atâî's account, the site of the execution and the tomb brings together the Melâmî-Bayramîs and thus allows him to display how a community ensures the remembrance of its executed sheikh. In these practices of commemoration, the sites of violence play a crucial role. By uniting the past and the present, the stories about the sites of violence offered seventeenth-century Istanbulites a medium with which to reflect on the history of a persecuted order and the imperial past of Istanbul. While the state inscribed its power over a persecuted community at a public execution in the sixteenth century, seventeenth-century Istanbulites began to circulate a revisionist account and contested the display of imperial power in their city. Their accounts of a public execution show how they contested the display of imperial power at a major public space of the city.[70]

## Acknowledgements

I would like to thank Ilham-Khuri Makdisi, Görkem Özizmirli, Derin Terzioğlu and Rossen Djagalov for their many insightful comments and suggestions. I am also grateful for the Bagep award from the Bilim Akademisi, which provided me with support during the research for and writing of this chapter.

---

69  For other examples of his ways of establishing connections with the mid-sixteenth century, see Dankoff, *An Ottoman Mentality*, 159–64. Also see Robert Dankoff, "Daily Life in the Seyahatname, A Party in Istanbul", *JTS* 27 (1) 2003, 1–8; and Aslı Niyazioğlu, "Babalar ve Oğullar: Evliya Çelebi Babasını Neden Sözlü Kaynak Olarak Kullandı?", *Evliya Çelebi ve Sözlü Kaynakları* (Ankara: UNESCO, 2012), 107–14.

70  I would like to thank Ilham-Khuri Makdisi, Görkem Özizmirli, Derin Terzioğlu and Rossen Djagalov for their many insightful comments and suggestions. I am also grateful to the Bagep award of Bilim Akademisi for their support for this article's research and writing.

## Bibliography

### Primary Sources
Süleymaniye Kütüphanesi Library (SK)
Abdülmecid Sivâsî. Dürer-i Akā'id. MS 300, Mihrişah Sultan, Süleymaniye Kütüphanesi.
Nev'îzâde Atâî. Ḥada'iḳü'l-Ḥaḳā'iḳ fī Tekmiletü'ş-Şaḳā'iḳ. MS 2341, Esad Efendi, Süleymaniye Kütüphanesi.

İstanbul Üniversitesi Kütüphanesi Library
Sarı Abdullah. Semerātü'l Fu'ād fi'l- mebdā' ve'l-me'ād. MS TY 01619, İstanbul Üniversitesi Kütüphanesi.

Ankara Milli Kütüphane Library
Küçük Abdal. Vilāyetnāme-i Sultan Otmān. MS microfilm no A22. Ankara Milli Kütüphane.

### Published Primary Sources
Anon. *Warhafttige und gar auszfierliche Newer Zeyttung, Ausz Constantinopel, Welcher massen die Türckische Kriegsleut ein Erschröckliche Auffruhr angerichtet halben, Auch fast die halbe Statt Angezündet und in Brand gestecket*. Augsburg: Wöhrlin, 1589.
Dionysios Byzantios. *Boğaziçi'nde bir Gezinti*, translated by Mehmet Fatih Yavuz. Istanbul: Yapı Kredi, 2010.
Erünsal, İsmail (ed). *XV–XVI: Asır Bayrâmî-Melâmîliği'nin Kaynaklarından Abdurrahman el-Askerî'nin Mir'âtü'l-Işk'ı*. Ankara: TTK, 2003.
Evliya Çelebi. *Evliya Çelebi Seyahatnâmesi: 1.Kitap: İstanbul: Topkapı Sarayı Bağdat 304 Yazmasının Transkripsiyonu-Dizini*, edited by Orhan Şaik Gökyay. Istanbul: Yapı Kredi Yayınları, 1996.
Evliya Çelebi. *Evliya Çelebi Seyahatnâmesi: 2.Kitap: İstanbul: Topkapı Sarayı Bağdat 304 Yazmasının Transkripsiyonu-Dizini*, edited by Zekeriya Kurşun, Seyit Ali Kahraman and Yücel Dağlı. Istanbul: Yapı Kredi Yayınları, 1999.
Evliya Çelebi. *Evliya Çelebi Seyahatnâmesi: 3.Kitap: İstanbul: Topkapı Sarayı Bağdat 305 Yazmasının Transkripsiyonu-Dizini*, edited by Seyit Ali Kahraman and Yücel Dağlı. Istanbul: Yapı Kredi Yayınları, 1999.
Evliya Çelebi. *Evliya Çelebi Seyahatnâmesi: 9.Kitap: İstanbul: Topkapı Sarayı Kütüphanesi Bağdat 306, Süleymaniye Kütüphanesi Pertev Paşa 462, Süleymaniye Kütüphanesi Hacı Beşir Ağa 452 Numaralı Yazmaların Mukayeseli Transkripsiyonu-Dizini*, edited by Yücel Dağlı, Seyit Ali Kahraman and Robert Dankoff. Istanbul: Yapı Kredi Yayınları, 2005.

La'lîzâde Abdülbaki. *Sergüzeşt*. In Tek, Melâmet Risaleleri, 121–210.

Mehmed Nazmi Efendi. *Osmanlılarda Tasavvufi Hayat. Hediyyetü'l-İḫvān: Halvetilik Örneği*. Transliterated by Osman Türer. Istanbul: İnsan Yayınları, 2005.

Müstakîmzâde Süleyman Sâdeddin. Risâle-i Melâmiyye-i Şuttâriyye. In Abdurrezzak Tek (ed.). *Bayrâmî Melâmiliği'ne Dâir Melâmet Risâleleri*. Bursa: Emin Yayınları, 2007, 211–342.

Sarı Abdullah Efendi. *Semerâtü'l-Fuâd*. In Tek, *Melâmet Risaleleri*, 63–120.

Taşköprizâde Ahmed Efendi. *Eş-Şeḳā'iḳu n-nu'mānīye fī 'ulemā'i'd-Devleti'l-'Osmānīye*, edited by Ahmed Subhi Furat. Istanbul: İstanbul Üniversitesi Edebiyat Fakültesi Yayınları, 1985.

Tek, Abdurrezzak (ed.) *Bayrâmî Melâmiliği'ne Dâir Melâmet Risâleleri*. Bursa: Emin Yayınları, 2007.

## Secondary Sources

Akkuş, Metin. "Nef'î". *DIA*, vol. 32. Ankara, 2006.

Algar, Hamid. "Hamzaviye: A Deviant Movement in Bosnian Sufism". *Islamic Studies* 36 (2–3) 1997, 243–61.

Ambrosio, Alberto Fabio. *Bir Mevlevî'nin Hayatı, 17. Yüzyılda Sufilik Öğretisi ve Ayinleri*. Translated by Ayşe Meral. Istanbul: Kitap Yayınevi, 2012.

Amussen, Susan Dwyer. "Punishment, Discipline, and Power: The Social Meanings of Violence in Early Modern England". *Journal of British Studies* 34 (1) 1995, 1–34.

Artan, Tülay. "Architecture as a Theater of Life: Profile of the Eighteenth Century Bosphorus". Ph.D. dissertation, Massachusettes Institute of Technology, 1989.

Artan, Tülay. "Boğaziçi". *Dünden Bugüne İstanbul Ansiklopedisi*, vol. 2. Istanbul, 1994.

Asaf Hâlet Çelebi, *Dîvân Şiirinde İstanbul*. Ankara: Hece Yayınları. 2002.

Atasoy, Nuran. "Evliyâ Çelebi ve Matrakçı Nasuh: Osmanlı Bahçelerine Yönelik Bakış Açıları (1534–1682)". In Tezcan and Tezcan, *Evliyâ Çelebi*, 500–27.

Aynur, Hatice. "Seyāḥatnāme'de Türkçe Edebi ve Biyografik Eserler". In Hatice Aynur and Hakan Karateke (eds). *Evliya Çelebi Seyahatnamesi'nin Yazılı Kaynakları*. Ankara: TTK, 2012, 245–8.

Azamat, Nihat. "Hamza Balî". *DIA*, vol. 15. Istanbul, 1997.

Azamat, Nihat. "Sarı Abdullah". *DIA*, vol. 36. Istanbul, 2009.

Börekçi, Günhan. "Factions and Favorites at the Courts of Sultan Ahmed I (r.1603–17) and his Immediate Predecessors". Ph.D. dissertation, Ohio State University, 2010.

Çalış Kural, Deniz. *Şehrengiz, Urban Rituals and Deviant Sufi Mysticism in Ottoman Istanbul*. Farnham: Ashgate, 2014.

Çıpa, Erdem. *Yavuz'un Kavgası*. Istanbul: Yapı Kredi Yayınları, 2013.

Clayer, Nathalie, Alexandre Popovic and Thierry Zarcone (eds). *Melamis-Bayramis: Études sur Trois Mouvements mystiques musulmans*. Istanbul: Les Éditions Isis, 1998.

Dankoff, Robert. "Daily Life in the Seyahatname, A Party in Istanbul". *Journal of Turkish Studies* 27 (1) 2003, 1–8.

Dankoff, Robert. *An Ottoman Mentality: The World of Evliya Çelebi*. Leiden: E. J. Brill, 2004.

Dişören, Esra. "Kayalar Mescidi ve Tekkesi". *Dünden Bugüne İstanbul Ansiklopedisi*, vol. 4. Istanbul, 1994.

Düzdağ, Ertuğrul. *Şeyhülislam Ebussud Efendi'nin Fetvaları ışığında 16. Asır Türk Hayatı*. Istanbul: Enderun Kitabevi, 1972.

Eire, Carlos. *From Madrid to Purgatory: The Art and Craft of Dying in Sixteenth-Century Spain*. Cambridge: Cambridge University Press, 1995.

Eldem, Edhem and Günay Kut. *Rumeli Hisarı Şehidlik Dergâhı Mezar Taşları*. Istanbul: Boğaziçi Üniversitesi Yayınevi, 2011.

Eren, Meşkure. *Evliya Çelebi Seyahatnâmesi Birinci Cildinin Kaynakları Üzerine Bir Araştırma*. Istanbul: Nurgök Matbaası, 1960.

Erken, Ali. "A Historical Analysis of Melâmî Bayramî Hagiographies". Master's thesis, Boğaziçi University, 2009.

Ernst, Carl. "From Hagiography to Martyrology: Conflicting Testimonies to a Sufi Martry of the Delhi Sultanate". *History of Religions* 24 (1985), 308–27.

Erünsal, İsmail. "Abdurrahman el-Askerî's Mir'âtü'l-Işk: A New Source for the Melâmî Movement in the Ottoman Empire During the 15th and 16th Centuries". *Wiener Zeitschrift für die kunde des Morgenlandes* 84 (1994), 95–115.

Eyice, Semavi. "At Meydanında İki Mezar ve Kaybolan bir Eski Esarın Hikayesi". *Türkiye Anıt Çevre Turizm Değerlerini Koruma Vakfı Dergisi* 1 (4) 1986, 7–12.

Faroqhi, Suraiya. "What Happened in Istanbul Gardens and Beauty Spots? Evliya Çelebi on Religion, Communication and Entertainment". Paper presented at Boğazici University Symposium, September 2011.

Friedrichs, Christopher R. *The Early Modern City 1450–1750*. Abingdon: Routledge, 2003.

Gökyay, Orhan Şaik and Şükrü Özen. "Molla Lutfî". *DIA*, vol. 30. Istanbul, 2005.

Gölpınarlı, Abdülbaki. *Melâmilik ve Melâmiler*. Istanbul: Milenyum Yayınları, 2013.

Gregory, Brad S. *Salvation at Stake: Christian Martyrdom in Early Modern Europe*. Cambridge, MA: Harvard University press, 2001.

de Groot, Alexander H. *The Ottoman Empire and the Dutch Republic*. Istanbul: Nederlands Historisch-Archaelogisch Instituut, 1978.

de Groot, Alexander H. "Halil Paşa, Kayserili". *DIA*, vol. 15. Istanbul, 1997.

Gündoğdu, Cengiz. "XVII: Yüzyıl Osmanlısında İki Farklı Sûfî Tipi, Abdülmecîd-î Sîvâsî ve İdris-i Muhtefî". *İlâm Araştırma Dergisi* 2 (1997), 21–39.

Hafız Hüseyin and Howard Crane (translator and editor), *The Garden of Mosques: Hafız Hüseyin Al-Ayvansarayi's Guide to the Muslim Monuments of Ottoman Istanbul*. Leiden: Brill, 2000.

Hamadeh, Shirine. *City's Pleasures: Istanbul in the Eighteenth Century*. Seattle: University of Washington Press, 2007.

İpekten, Haluk. "Atâî", *DIA*, vol. 4, Ankara, 1991.

Kafesçioğlu, Çiğdem. *Constantinople/Istanbul: Cultural Encounter, Imperial Vision, and the Construction of the Ottoman Capital*. Pennsylvania: Pennsylvania State University Press, 2009.

Katgı, İsmail. *Maktul Şeyhülislamlar*. Istanbul: İz, 2013.

Keseder, İhsan. *Rumeli Hisar Köyü*. Istanbul: Günlük Ticaret Gazetesi, 1983.

Murphey, Rhoads. "Ottoman Historical Writing in the Seventeenth-Century: A Survey of the General Development of the Genre after the Reign of Sultan Ahmed I (1603–1617)". *Essays on Ottoman Historians and Historiography*. Istanbul: Eren, 2009, 95–112.

Necipoğlu, Gülru. "The Suburban Landscape of Sixteenth-Century in Istanbul as a Mirror of Classical Ottoman Garden Culture". In Attilio Petruccioli (ed.) *Gardens in the Time of Great Muslim Empires: Theory and Design*. Leiden: Brill, 1997, 32–71.

Necipoğlu, Gülru. *Age of Sinan: Architectural Culture in the Age of Sinan*. London: Reaktion Books, 2005.

Nev'îzâde Atâî. Ḥadā'iḳü'l-Ḥaḳā'iḳ fî Tekmiletü'ş-Şaḳā'iḳ, published as vol. 2 of *eş-Şakâik-i Nu'mâniyye* edited by Abdülkadir Özcan (Istanbul: Çağrı Yayınları, 1989).

Niyazioğlu, Aslı. "Babalar ve Oğullar: Evliya Çelebi Babasını Neden Sözlü Kaynak Olarak Kullandı?" *Evliya Çelebi ve Sözlü Kaynakları*. Ankara: UNESCO, 2012, 107–14.

Nutku, Özdemir. "At Meydanında Düzenlenen Şenlikler". In Ekrem Işın (ed.), *Hippodrom/At Meydanı II*. Istanbul: Pera Müzesi Yayınları, 2010, 71–95.

Ocak, Ahmet Yaşar. "Kanunî Sultan Süleyman Devrinde Osmanlı Resmî Düşüncesine Karşı Bir Tepki Hareketi: Oğlan Şeyh İsmail-i Ma'şukî". *Osmanlı Araştırmaları* 10 (1990) 49–58.

Ocak, Ahmet Yaşar. "XVI–XVII Yüzyıllarda Bayramî Melâmîleri ve Osmanlı Yönetimi". *Belleten* 61 (1997), 93–110.

Ocak, Ahmet Yaşar. *Osmanlı Toplumunda Zındıklar ve Mülhidler: 15–17. Yüzyıllar*. Istanbul: Türkiye Ekonomik ve Toplumsal Tarih Vakfı, 1998.

Ocak, Ahmet Yaşar. *Türk Folklöründe Kesik Baş: Tarih-Folklor İlişkisinden Bir Kesit*. Ankara: Dergâh, 2013.

Öngören, Reşat. "Şeriatın Kestiği Parmak: Kanuni Sultan Süleyman Devrinde İdam Edilen Tarikat Şeyhleri". *İlâm Araştırma Dergisi* (1996), 123–41.

Öngören, Reşat. *Osmanlılar'da Tasavvuf: Anadolu'da Sûfîler, Devlet ve Ulema (XVI. Yüzyıl)*. Istanbul: İz Yayıncılık, 2000.

Özen, Şükrü. "Molla Lutfî'nin İdamına Karşı Çıkan Hamîdüddin Efendi'nin Ahkâmü'z-zındîk Risalesi". *İslam Araştırmaları Dergisi* 4 (2000), 7–16.

Özen, Şükrü. "İslâm Hukukunda Zındıklık Suçu ve Molla Lutfî'nin idamının Fıkhîliği". *İslam Araştırmaları Dergisi* 4 (2001), 17–62.

Özizmirli, Görkem. "Fear in Evliya Çelebi's Seyahatnâme: Politics and Historiography in a Seventeenth-Century Ottoman Travelogue". Master's thesis, Koç University, Istanbul, 2014.

Palmer, Patricia. "'An Headless Ladie' and 'a Horses Loade of Heads': Writing the Beheading". *Renaissance Quarterly* 60 (2007), 25–57.

Ruff, Julius. *Violence in Early Modern Europe*. Cambridge: Cambridge University Press, 2004.

Şahin, Kaya. *Empire and Power in the Reign of Süleyman: Narrating the Sixteenth-Century Ottoman World*. New York: Cambridge University Press, 2013.

Schramm, Katharina. "Landscapes of Violence: Memory and Sacred Space". *History & Memory* 23 (1) (2011): 5–22.

Sinanlar, Seza. *Bizans Araba Yarışlarından Osmanlı Şenliklerine At Meydanı*. Istanbul: Kitap Yayınevi, 2005.

Tanman, Baha. "Muhsine Hatun Mescidi ve Tekkesi". *Dünden Bugüne İstanbul Ansiklopedisi*, vol. 5. Istanbul, 1994.

Taştan, Yahya Kemal. "Evliya Çelebi'nin Osmanlı Hanedanına Bakışı". In Nuran Tezcan and Semih Tezcan (eds), *Doğumunun 400. Yılında Evliyâ Çelebi*. Ankara: Kültür ve Turizm Bakanlığı, 2011, 356–90.

Terzioğlu, Derin. "Sufi and Dissident in the Ottoman Empire: Niyāzī-ı Mıṣrī, 1618–1694". Ph.D. dissertation, Harvard University, 1999.

Tezcan, Nuran and Semih Tezcan (eds). *Doğumunun 400. Yılında Evliyâ Çelebi*. Ankara: Kültür ve Turizm Bakanlığı, 2011.

Walsham, Alexandra. "Sacred Topography and Social Memory: Religious Change and the Landscape in Early Modern Britain and Ireland". *Journal of Religious History* 36 (1) 2012, 31–51.

Yavuz, Betül. "The Making of a Sufi Order Between Hersey and Legitimacy: Bayrami-Malāmīs in the Ottoman Empire". Master's thesis, Rice University, 2013.

Yürekli, Zeynep. *Architecture and Hagiography in the Ottoman Empire: The Politics of Bektashi Shrines in the Classical Age*. Surrey: Ashgate, 2012.

Zahir Sıdkı, Güvemli. "İstanbul Kütüphanelerinde Ḥadā'iḳü'l-Ḥaḳā'iḳ Nüshaları", *Yeni Türk Dergisi* vol. 66, 1938 and 1939.

Zeitlin, Judith T. "The Return of the Palace Lady: The Historical Ghost Story and Dynastic Fall". In David Der-wei Wang and Shang Wei (eds). *Dynastic Crisis and Cultural Innovation from Late Ming to the Late Qing and Beyond*. Cambridge, MA: Harvard University Press, 2005, 156–99.

CHAPTER 4

# Ottoman Artisans in a Changing Political Context: Debates in Historiography

*Suraiya Faroqhi*

Historians of the Ottoman craft world have developed two different interpretations of the relationship between artisans and the sultans' officials. On the one hand are scholars who believe that, by definition, the sultan – or in practical terms, his bureaucrats – represented the interests of the Islamic community and even, to an extent, those of the sultans' subjects at large. If this claim was justified, any dissent was ipso facto both illegal and immoral. On the other hand, some researchers assume that while the sultans' Islamic legitimacy was never in doubt, there was scope for ordinary subjects, including craftsmen, to develop initiatives that were legitimate, at least in their own eyes, but also in those of certain literati. If their demands were not met, artisans might participate in rebellions, which some authors of the eighteenth century recorded with a degree of sympathy. As a contribution to this ongoing debate, I discuss why artisans apparently thought that compliance with officialdom was the royal road to success – especially in the 1700s, but also earlier – and why, such conformity notwithstanding, Ottoman guilds often successfully defended master craftsmen's interests.

## 1   Emergent Guilds: Between the Demands of Officeholders and the Exigencies of the Market

Due to the peculiarities of our documentation, it is easy to view the world of working people all but exclusively through the lenses of the sultans' officials. Some forty years ago, few people objected to such a perspective, and there were Ottomanist scholars who thought that artisans' organizations were merely an arm of the state apparatus to provide goods needed by the sultan's court and his army and navy.[1] The craft organizations had to provide

---

1   My thanks go to Engin Akarlı for his thoughtful comments before publication. When referring to the Ottoman world, I try to avoid using the term 'Ottoman state' (*devlet, devlet-i aliyye*) because, in some Ottomanist historiography, it is surrounded by a quasi-numinous aura.

artisans to accompany soldiers on campaigns and to produce whatever manufactured goods were required. Moreover, until the 1600s, Istanbul boatsmen's associations had to supply rowers for the navy – an obligation that ended only after the Mediterranean navies had switched to sailing ships. Thus, it is impossible to deny that service to the sultans and their armed forces was a major obligation of urban artisans and working people in general.

However, once Ottomanist historians began to delve more deeply into the documentation on craftsmen in the empire's larger cities, including Sarajevo, Istanbul, Bursa, Ankara, Aleppo, Jerusalem, Damascus and Cairo, the notion that these associations had no other role but to serve the sultans' servitors became increasingly dubious. One of the first authors to show that artisans were quite capable of using their organizations to promote their own interests was Haim Gerber, in his now classical book on seventeenth-century Bursa.[2] Later studies, particularly of Istanbul, have confirmed this view: with more or less success, artisans tried to balance their own interests against the demands of the administration and the requirements of the market.[3]

As for the market, for historians working in the 1980s it was, so to speak, a new factor in the game. In the earliest work on the artisanal relationship with the sultanic bureaucracy, the emphasis was on prices decreed by officialdom (*narh*); the market did not seem to play any role at all. Moreover, in a setting where the customer had no choice but to buy the often inferior goods available in the shops, as was true in Turkey in the 1960s and 1970s, the idea that customer preferences might have an impact on production was not even a possible topic of discussion. However, as the role of the Turkish state in the late-twentieth-century economy receded, historians became increasingly aware that at least the better-off among Ottoman urban dwellers did not simply buy

---

Instead, it seems better to employ relatively neutral terms, such as 'central administration/government', 'sultans' officials', or 'Ottoman officialdom'. Analogous to terms like 'numismatist', the word 'Ottomanist' will refer to scholars who from the end of the First World War onwards, studied the Ottoman Empire, as opposed to 'Ottoman authors' who worked when the empire was still functioning.

2   Haim Gerber, *Economy and Society in an Ottoman City: Bursa, 1600–1700* (Jerusalem: The Hebrew University, 1988). Gerber's teacher Gabriel Baer had been the principal proponent of the view that Ottoman craft associations were no more than 'arms of the state'. However, after reading Gerber's work when it was still a thesis in the late 1970s, he had the moral courage to say that he had changed his mind. See Gabriel Baer, "Ottoman Guilds: A Reassessment", in Halil İnalcık and Osman Okyar (eds), *Türkiye'nin Sosyal ve Ekonomik Tarihi (1071–1920), Social and Economic History of Turkey (1071–1920)* (Ankara: Meteksan, 1980), 95–102.

3   Suraiya Faroqhi, "Urban Space as Disputed Grounds: Territorial Aspects to Artisan Conflict in Sixteenth to Eighteenth-Century Istanbul", in *idem. Stories of Ottoman Men and Women: Establishing Status, Establishing Control*, (Istanbul: Eren, 2002), 219–34.

whatever the artisans of their respective towns might offer, but had tastes of their own and the ability to secure goods conforming to those preferences. They might for instance favour Indian cotton over the local product, no matter how much Sultan Selim III (r.1789–1807) fulminated against the practice. In the mid-1700s, moreover, manufacturers of the region now divided between southeast Turkey and northern Syria, successfully began to produce imitations of these textiles.[4]

Although few seventeenth- or eighteenth-century Ottoman luxury goods have survived the wars and migrations of the 1800s and the first half of the twentieth century, written sources such as post-mortem inventories tell us that they did exist: and it is hard to imagine that a family that bought an engagement gift of a mirror, embroidered shoes and other small luxuries for a bride, as was common in Istanbul in the early 1800s, did not tell the manufacturing artisans exactly what they wanted.[5] In fact, when the shoemakers who had branched out into manufacturing mirrors were challenged for transgressing the borders between craft guilds, their defence was that customers wanted to buy these presents as a set, in other words from a single source. It does not really matter whether this excuse had any validity, but it is worth noting that these modest artisans invoked the demands of their customers as a justification for their behaviour.

## 2   Towards a History of Guilds

To complicate matters yet further, it has emerged that Ottoman craft organization had a history, and that arrangements prevailing in the sixteenth century were rather different from those observable around the year 1800. This understanding has only emerged in the last twenty-five or so years, for in the 1950s and 1960s, before the topic totally dropped out of sight for a decade or two, scholars tended to assume that Ottoman institutions, guilds included, changed very little from their emergence in the later 1400s to the overall reconstruction of the years after 1840, which Ottomanist historians call the *Tanzimat*, and which resulted in an assertively 'modern' state.

---

[4]  Katsumi Fukasawa, *Toilerie et commerce du Levant, d'Alep à Marseille* (Paris: Editions du CNRS, 1987).

[5]  Nalan Turna, "The Shoe Guilds of Istanbul in the Early Nineteenth Century: A Case Study", in Suraiya Faroqhi (ed.) *Bread from the Lion's Mouth: Artisans Struggling for a Livelihood in Ottoman Cities* (New York: Berghahn Books, 2015), 157–71.

To put it in a nutshell, in the larger cities, from the late-sixteenth century and perhaps in some cases from an even earlier date, artisans typically organized by craft specialties, and from now on we will call these associations guilds (*esnaf, hirfet*). Over time, guilds acquired leaders, known as sheikh, *kethüda*, or *kâhya*, which the local Islamic judge or *kadı* needed to recognize, although the elaborate appointment process documented for eighteenth-century Istanbul seems to have been part of the bureaucratization that, by this later period, we can observe in other walks of life as well.[6] In earlier periods, matters were handled in a more informal manner and, around 1500, when dealing with the central administration many artisans apparently relied on the mediations of a few experienced masters (*ehl-i hibre*) who enjoyed the trust of their colleagues.[7]

Given this situation, we must avoid defining the term 'craft guild' in too narrow a fashion: rather, we will assume that such an organization existed whenever its members initiated court cases as a group, and under the responsibility of some kind of leader, who might – or might not – have received an official appointment. Or else, once again through the mediation of recognized leaders, guildsmen might address their petitions to the central administration directly. These artisan organizations normally would have formed more or less spontaneously, with central or local administrators intervening only in case of complaints. There were thus some guilds, especially among the non-Muslims, that seem to have rarely if ever applied to officialdom; therefore they very seldom appear in archival documents. For the most part, these artisans and their associations are known from inscriptions, produced for instance when they made a donation as a group to a sanctuary, as was common among Orthodox craftsmen of the eighteenth and early-nineteenth centuries.[8] Well documented or not, presumably all craft or shop-keeping guilds tried to control access to the relevant trades, although quite obviously they did not always succeed. As for the Ottoman government, before the late-eighteenth century it always operated on the assumption that the monopolies of craft guilds were an advantage and

---

6 Halil İnalcık, "The Appointment Procedure of a Guild Warden (Kethudâ)", in *Festschrift für Andreas Tietze, Wiener Zeitschrift für die Kunde des Morgenlandes* 76 (1986), 135–42.
7 Ömer Lütfi Barkan, "Bazı Büyük Şehirlerde Eşya ve Yiyecek Fiyatlarının Tesbit ve Teftişi Hususlarını Tanzim Eden Kanunlar", *Tarih Vesikaları* 1 (1942), 5, 326–40; 2 (1942), 7, 15–40; 2 (1942), 9, 168–77.
8 Anna Ballian, "Karamanlı Patronage in the Eighteenth and Nineteenth Centuries: The Case of the Village of Germir/Kermira", in Evangelia Balta and Matthias Kappler (eds) *Cries and Whispers in Karamanlidika Books: Proceedings of the First International Conference on Karamanlidika Studies (Nicosia, 11th–13th September 2008)* (Wiesbaden: Harrassowitz Verlag, 2010), 45–62.

should enjoy the sultan's protection. Only around 1800 do we encounter some officials disagreeing with these views and inclined to dismantle monopolies.

For the most part, the emergence of the guilds remains unrecorded and thus rather obscure. But, by the sixteenth century, this type of organization seems to have become a hallmark of Ottoman governance. While historians generally agree that no guilds existed in Egypt or Syria under the Mamluk sultans (1250–1517), once the Ottoman administration was in place, local artisans soon joined such organizations, which, by the seventeenth century, had become all but ubiquitous in many of the Arab provinces as well. However, we must admit that much of our information comes from a rather limited number of cities. Even from this sample, it has become clear that while 'general trends' probably covered all the major cities of the empire, there remained plenty of room for regional variations. Thus, an important book on the town of Mosul in today's Iraq deals quite extensively with questions concerning the local marketplace; however, the author has concluded that, for the sixteenth century, there is so little evidence that we cannot be sure that craft guilds even existed.[9] By the 1700s they certainly had appeared, as was true in other regions of the empire as well; but, an increase of demand for craft products and the domination of a magnate family over the Mosul market made it difficult for guildsmen to gain or retain the monopolistic restrictions by which they normally controlled their respective trades. Some artisans prospered, particularly by branching out into commerce, but others were completely disenfranchised.

Furthermore, we know very little about the organization and marketing of rural craft production. For the 1500s, there are some tantalizing references in the tax registers (*tahrir defteri*), usually brief notes about taxes payable from such products. The economic historian Huri Islamoğlu has suggested that, by 1600, rural crafts allowed certain peasants to eke out their incomes and thus survive rapid population growth. After all, in early modern times, whenever the number of people increased, the available grain supply lagged behind, a universal phenomenon well reflected in the Ottoman tax registers of the time.[10] However, as the author has pointed out, these records say too little about rural crafts for any hypothesis on this subject to be amenable to proof.

At the present stage of research, it is unclear how large a given town needed to be before the local artisans began to form guilds. To date, we have little evidence of rural craft associations: a recently-documented exception concerns, a rarity of rarities, namely female textile artisans active in eighteenth-century

---

9   Dina Khoury, *State and Provincial Society in the Ottoman Empire: Mosul, 1540–1834* (Cambridge: CUP, 2002), 36, 133–41.
10  Huri Islamoğlu, *State and Peasant in the Ottoman Empire* (Leiden: Brill, 1994), 167–71.

Thessaly, a province of villages and small towns where cotton fabrics were an important craft product. The women in question manufactured soap, probably needed for washing the finished cloth. As for their organization, it straddled the boundary between family and guild because new members had to be the daughters or daughters-in-law of women already active in the organization.[11] In the surviving document, the women asked the local bishop (metropolitan) to record that no men could become members; and this dignitary complied. Presumably, this request reflects the efforts of male craftsmen to push the women out of the market. Unfortunately, we have no idea how this all-female grouping emerged and for how long it remained active.

## 3    Eighteenth-Century Novelties

During and after the war of 1683–99 against the Habsburgs, the first to result in territorial losses, the Ottoman administration began a hunt for revenues that, in different forms, was to continue for as long as the empire existed. There were attempts to collect more money from existing taxes and, in addition, institute lifetime tax farms. The latter would, it was hoped, yield more money – in the short run because the incumbents paid heavy initiation fees and in the long run because, as lifetime holders, the personages receiving these awards should take an interest in the continued productivity of 'their' sources of income.

In addition, the administration encouraged military men and other recipients of state grants to forego their pay and instead accept positions as guild heads, thus effectively selling these offices.[12] In consequence, by the eighteenth century at least, guild headmen must have collected dues from the artisans whose interests they supposedly represented; for, if this custom had not existed, the recipients of payment from official sources would have had no interest in giving up their grants. We do not know how widespread this set of practices was outside Istanbul, but in the capital multiple sales of guild

---

11   Spyros I. Asdrachas, *Greek Economic History: 15th–19th Centuries*, 2 vols (Athens: Piraeus Bank Group Cultural Foundation, 2007), vol. 2, 284. I thank Olga Katsiardi Hering and Eleni Gara for directing me to this publication. As the text in question is in Greek, it is only due to the kindness of Anna Vlachopoulou that I have become acquainted with its contents.

12   Suraiya Faroqhi, "Purchasing Guild- and Craft-Based Offices in the Ottoman Central Lands", *Turcica* 39 (2007), 123–46; Mehmet Genç, "Ottoman Industry in the Eighteenth Century: General Framework, Characteristics and Main Trends", in Donald Quataert (ed.) *Manufacturing in the Ottoman Empire and Turkey 1500–1950* (Albany: SUNY Press, 1994), 59–86.

headships were common enough. In the course of these transactions, prices increased progressively, as each new incumbent had to compensate the previous holders.

On the face of it, the sultans' treasury benefited only from the original sale. However, since the *kadı*s and a slew of bureaucrats making a living out of the fees they collected had to confirm and record every transfer, indirectly the Ottoman governing apparatus derived revenues from the later transactions as well.

In Ottoman towns, many craftsmen did not own their shops, but rented them from pious foundations (waqf, *vakıf, evkâf*); for these institutions, artisan tenants were significant sources of income. By the eighteenth century, generations of urbanites desiring to do something for the good of their souls had turned much of the real estate available in Istanbul and other large cities into *vakıf* land; and quite a few artisans had acquired everlasting leases to their shops, which their children could inherit. However, although according to Islamic law, monarchs and princes could not appropriate the incomes of pious foundations, by the 1700s the official hunt for revenues certainly did not bypass these institutions. On the contrary, by various juridical devices, the sultans' treasury began to collect money from *vakıf*s as well, losses for which the latter sought compensation from their craftsmen tenants.

The people thus affected seem to have responded by claiming that the usufruct rights they had acquired were akin to property and that alienation was only possible within the craft guild at issue.[13] Such arrangements, known as *gedik*, had very occasionally also existed in the seventeenth century. However, by the mid-1700s, as we shall see, the Ottoman administration and the artisans concerned, cooperated in extending the requirement that to exercise a given craft legitimately, an artisan must own the relevant *gedik*. The details are not always clear, but by the century's end, the *gedik* was no longer as closely related to permanent tenancy as it had been in the past; and, even a man who operated in the public street or market, needed a *gedik* if he wanted to be a legitimate artisan rather than an interloper.

At first glance, the spread of the *gedik* might seem to be a development that tied the artisan very closely to his fellows, who could supervise and judge his every move. But, remarkably, Ottomanist scholars have discovered that, in real life, the consequences differed from case to case; in fact, some craftsmen seemingly regarded the *gedik* as their private property, which they could buy and

---

13  Engin Akarlı, "*Gedik*: A Bundle of Rights and Obligations for Istanbul Artisans and Traders, 1750–1840", in Alain Pottage and Martha Mundy (eds) *Law, Anthropology and the Constitution of the Social: Making Persons and Things* (Cambridge: CUP, 2004), 166–200.

sell without much reference to the guild, no matter the penalties with which officialdom might threaten them. Historians thus have detected a 'secondary market in *gediks*' at least in certain craft specialties and at certain times, but research into these processes is still very much a work in progress.[14]

## 4  Outside History: Glimpses of Non-guild Labour

However, before further discussing the relationship between guildsmen and the Ottoman government apparatus, we need to insert some qualifications. For, to be realistic, it is important not to confuse 'guildsmen' and 'people working as artisans', as some Ottomanist scholars have been inclined to do because of the very limited documentation on non-guild workpeople. As for the journeymen, who comprised a significant part of the labour force, at least in certain fields, they could make their voices heard only in a few – and very exceptional – cases.[15] We also know very little about apprentices, as it was rare for parents to have apprenticeship contracts recorded in the judges' registers, the only place where such material might have been preserved. Some guilds decided on the length of time that an apprentice would have to serve before he could operate a shop independently, but since most of the surviving evidence comes from the eighteenth and nineteenth centuries, we do not know how apprenticeship rules had operated in earlier times.

In addition, some artisans employed labourers, who presumably were not in line for a position as master. In seventeenth-century Bursa, there was a market where such people assembled and waited for employers to hire them.[16] It does not seem that in the normal run of things, the sultans' officials tried to control this process, except when they tried to limit migration into Istanbul, a matter much discussed by present-day Ottomanists.[17] Occasionally, the registers of the *kadıs* note contracts in which a man pledged to render service, or in which a father committed his son or daughter to a master or mistress. But, in these cases, with the service remaining mostly unspecified, we do not know whether

---

14  Onur Yıldırım and Seven Ağır, "*Gedik*: What's in a Name?", in Suraiya Faroqui (ed.) *Bread from the Lion's Mouth* (New York: Berghahn Books, 2015), 217–36.

15  Sherry Vatter, "Journeymen Textile Weavers in Nineteenth-Century Damascus: A Collective Biography", in Edmund Burke III and David N. Yaghubian (eds), *Struggle and Survival in the Modern Middle East* (Berkeley: University of California Press, 2006), 64–79.

16  Fahri Dalsar, *Türk Sanayi ve Ticaret Tarihinde Bursa 'da İpekçilik* (Istanbul: İstanbul Üniversitesi İktisat Fakültesi, 1960), 114.

17  This issue is so complex that I have excluded it for reasons of space.

there was any connection to the craft world; in many cases, the young people in question may have been domestic servants.

Last, but not least, there were some women who worked in jobs requiring skills, for instance midwives; however, for the period with which we are concerned, not much information has come to light. Women who taught religion to other females, another activity demanding skills, in this case intellectual ones, also show up very rarely in our documents.[18] Some Orthodox women seem to have worked as embroiderers and examples of their work, embellished with names and dates, have survived, one of the earliest dating to the last years of the sixteenth century. However, the problem is that the female names appearing on these items could also have belonged to wealthy women who sponsored the liturgical textiles in question, although the lack of honorific titles makes it seem likely that the names are in fact those of the embroiderers.[19] Most documents concerning women in crafts relate to the silk industry of Bursa, where the preparation of silk for weaving was often a female activity. Thus, quite a few non-guild members made contributions to skilled craft production; but it is safe to say that when major decisions were at issue, they had no role to play. Only masters had a claim to the benefits that guild organization was likely to yield.

## 5    Artisans and the Ottoman Bureaucracy: The Question of Sultanic Legitimacy

Given our more or less recently acquired knowledge of the historicity of Ottoman guilds, the old question of relations between artisans and the bureaucratic apparatus has taken on new dimensions. In the decade following Gabriel Baer's articles, the debate was between those Ottomanists who regarded all artisanal activity as dominated by the sultans' officials and those who wished to dwell on artisans' initiatives.[20] Since the 1990s, the discussion has focused on the question of whether Ottoman artisans could even have conceived that rejecting demands emitted in the sultans' names might be legitimate, or whether such behaviour had always been viewed as unacceptable, or even outright criminal.

---

18   For an exceptional case, see Leslie Peirce, *Morality Tales: Law and Gender in the Ottoman Court of Aintab* (Berkeley: University of California Press, 2003), 251–75.

19   For examples, see Dionissis Fotopoulos and Angelos Delivorrias, *Greece at the Benaki Museum* (Athens: Benaki Museum, 1997), 298, 302–7.

20   Cf. footnote 2 above.

An outside observer may regard the idea that artisans always willingly submitted to officialdom as a value judgement resulting from a confluence of two assumptions. On the one hand, it is worth stressing that 'the state' – and here the term is appropriate – in the political ideology of the late Ottoman Empire and of the Turkish Republic by now nearly a century old, has taken on a quasi-religious connotation. This emphasis on the 'survival of the state' has served to justify all sorts of actions, including warfare against those members of the subject population whom the military governments running the empire during its closing years had declared to be dangerous.[21] Conditioning the thinking of Ottomanists who assume that the Ottoman government always defended the best interests of the Muslim population, there is a second assumption, namely that the sultans' legitimacy in religious terms was so powerful that, for a believing Muslim, it was impossible to conceive that the ruler might be in the wrong. Therefore, only morally deficient, 'corrupt' persons would have opposed the demands emitted in the sultan's name.[22]

A scholar sceptical about the validity of this model may by contrast point out that no fewer than seven of the fourteen sultans who occupied the throne between 1603 and 1807 – put differently, one half – suffered deposition.[23] Three sultans, namely Osman II (d.1622), İbrâhim (d.1648), and Selim III (d.1808), were even murdered. The reigns of these monarchs ended not through any outside force, but due to the opposition of palace factions together with urban groupings such as janissaries doubling as artisans and – usually lower-level – men of religion. At some stage of the movement, these rebels normally obtained legal opinions from a representative of the religious cum scholarly hierarchy, to the effect that the current ruler had neglected his duties and therefore lost his right to remain in power; sometimes military defeat occasioned the discontent that preceded the depositions.[24] Such events occasioned considerable disagreement, with partisans of the soon-to-be deposed sultan on the one hand and his opponents on the other.

We may well wonder when – if representing the interests of the Islamic community was the major issue – the incumbent sultan ceased to represent these interests and his successor took over this particular source of legitimacy; and,

---

21   Ryan Gingeras, *Sorrowful Shores: Violence, Ethnicity, and the End of the Ottoman Empire 1912–1923* (New York: OUP, 2011), 37–52.
22   Mehmet Demirtaş, *Osmanlı Esnafında Suç ve Ceza: İstanbul örneği H 1100–1200/1688–1786* (Ankara: Birleşik Yayınevi, 2010).
23   Mustafa I ruled twice, in both instances briefly, as he was deemed of unsound mind. There, were thus fifteen reigns but only fourteen rulers.
24   Rifa'at A. Abou-El-Haj, "Ottoman Attitudes Toward Peace-Making: The Karlowitz Case", *Der Islam* 51 (1) 1974, 131–7.

as a strong moral component was involved, we may also ask ourselves whether deposition by a crowd of discontented officeholders, rebellious soldiers-cum-artisans and lower-level men of religion, sufficed to deprive a given ruler of his moral qualities.

## 6  Inculcating 'Desirable Moral Qualities'

At this point, we need to insert a short digression into political ideology because, quite frequently, scholars who subscribe to the idea that the sultan or the 'state' is ipso facto always right, will also often invoke the moral principles inculcated in aspiring craftsmen by training in fütüvvet/futuwwa. These virtues of 'young-manhood' involved abnegation, modesty, self-control, obedience, and a lack of interest in material gain.[25] Education in moral values is often linked to the *ahis*, the urban groupings that the Moroccan traveller Ibn Battuta had observed during his mid-fourteenth-century travels in Anatolia. As in many towns, Ibn Battuta was lavishly hosted by such *ahis*, he was quite favourably impressed. But we should not forget that the author knew no Turkish, as he has stressed many times over.[26]

*Ahis* are documented for the fifteenth century as well; and some scholars think that their organizations were at the root of the craft guilds that we observe from the sixteenth century onwards. Perhaps such a connection existed, but hard evidence is lacking and sceptics, the present author included, may suspect that in today's Turkey the current vogue of the *ahis* has political reasons. Conservative ideologues posit the *ahis* as 'domestically-grown good guys', with trade unions as the 'baddies'.

While treatises incorporating *fütüvvet* principles were in fact copied out – and presumably read – in artisan circles throughout the early modern period, and at least in Sarajevo, young men wishing to become masters had to be knowledgeable in this respect, there are reasons to doubt that all artisans were steeped in fütüvvet ideology. First of all, at least in Istanbul, many guilds

---

25  Inez Aščerić-Todd, "The Noble Traders: The Islamic Tradition of 'Spiritual Chivalry' (*futuwwa*) in Bosnian Trade Guilds (16th–19th Centuries)", *The Muslim World* 97 (April 2007), 159–73; Deodaat Anne Breebaart, "Fütüvvetname-i Kebir: A Manual on Turkish Guilds", *JESHO* 15 (1972), 203–15; Abdülbaki Gölpınarlı, "Burgâzî ve Fütüvvet Nâmesi", *IFM* 11 (1–4) 1949–50, 3–354; idem, "İslâm ve Türk İllerinde Fütüvvet Teşkilâtı ve Kaynakları", *IFM* 15 (1–4) 1953–54, 76–153.

26  Ibn Battuta, *Voyages d'Ibn Batoutah, Texte arabe, accompagné d'une Traduction*, edited and translated by C. Defrémery and B. R. Sanguinetti (Paris: Imprimerie Impériale, 1854), vol. 2, 302, 326–7, 334–5.

contained both Muslim and non-Muslim masters and, as fütüvvet appealed to Muslims exclusively, it is difficult to imagine that all guildsmen were equally committed to this set of ideas.[27] Moreover, recent research has shown that in Istanbul at least, seventeenth-century artisans were quite adept at circumventing assorted guild rules in pursuit of material gain.[28] As long as these people were generous to their fellow artisans and gave ample alms to the poor, they seemingly continued to be acceptable members of their respective guilds.[29]

## 7 Formulating a Counter Argument

### 7.1 *Working Hard for Children and Wife*[30]

Given current research, I find it a bit difficult to assume that all craftsmen regarded those of their fellows who aimed at larger profits as ipso facto corrupt, for it is worth remembering that non-profit-seeking and thus submissive artisans greatly facilitated the exploitation of crafts for fiscal purposes. In consequence, the sultans' officeholders should have found such artisan attitudes worth promoting, especially since they adhered to the notion that prices should be kept low so as to make the sultans' wars and building projects more affordable.[31] Sociologists of the early republican period have sometimes commented on the lack of interest that the artisans of their time showed in expanding their markets and increasing their profits.[32] But, it is possible and even likely that this world view gained increased currency due to the massive impoverishment that ordinary people in Turkey suffered because of the almost uninterrupted wars of 1912–23, the economic crisis of the 1930s, and military mobilization during the Second World War. Put differently, some Ottomanist historians, including the present author, do not believe in a kind

---

[27] This objection has been already been made in the old but still valuable study by Robert Mantran, *Istanbul dans la seconde moitié du dix-septième siècle: Essai d'histoire institutionelle, économique et sociale* (Istanbul: Institut français d'Archéologie d'Istanbul and Adrien Maisonneuve, 1962), 364.

[28] Eunjeong Yi, *Guild Dynamics in Seventeenth-Century Istanbul: Fluidity and Leverage* (Leiden: Brill, 2004).

[29] Eunjeong Yi, "Rich Artisans and Poor Merchants: A Critical Look at the Supposed Egalitarianism in Ottoman Guilds", in Suraiya Faroqhi (ed.) *Bread from the Lion's Mouth* (New York: Berghahn Books, 2015), 194–216.

[30] This line is based on an American trade-union song.

[31] Murat Çizakça, "The Ottoman government and economic life", in Suraiya Faroqhi and Kate Fleet (eds) *The Cambridge History of Turkey* (Cambridge: CUP, 2013), vol. 2, 241–75.

[32] Sabri Ülgener, *İktisadi Çözülmenin Ahlak ve Zihniyet Dünyası* (Istanbul: Der Yayınları, 1981).

of 'pre-established harmony' between artisans and 'the state', and suspect that the sultans' bureaucrats defended above all their own material and political interests.

However, if we assume the existence of at least potential tensions between artisans and officialdom, we have to come to terms with two difficulties: first, writing texts that had a chance to be preserved, in the registers of local judges or in those of the central administration, was an almost exclusive privilege of officialdom. 'Dissidents' thus had only very limited chances to write texts that have come down to us; and when we try to interpret extant texts 'against the grain', as the saying goes, we need to take care that we do not make them say something that their authors never meant to say. Second, Ottoman artisans, especially those in Istanbul, often invoked regulation by the central authorities even in cases, which at least from an outsider's perspective, they might have decided within their own craft organizations.[33]

## 8 Archive Documents, Decisive as Always: Establishing Craft Regulations

However, this dependence on officialdom is the source of much of our knowledge; most of our sources on relations between artisans and members of the sultan's bureaucracy have come into being because of disputes, which the parties had taken either to the local Islamic judge or else directly to the central administration. The judges had no written sources from which to derive information about artisan practices, unless a previous dispute had left a 'paper trail' in the registers of their town. Therefore, they needed to hear the testimonies of guild masters concerning 'traditional' practices; if the *kadıs* endorsed the latter by committing them to writing, these rules became enforceable as 'custom', for the authorities were always much concerned about repressing anything contrary to 'what had been done [in the past]' (*olagelene muhalif*).[34]

In the sixteenth and seventeenth centuries, most craft regulations must have been transmitted by word of mouth, but after 1700, recording these rules, now called nizam, in official registers became a widespread practice, at least in Istanbul.[35] Based on a record dated 1746, we will discuss a dispute between

---

33   For an example, cf. Ahmet Kal'a et al. (eds), *İstanbul Külliyatı: İstanbul Ahkâm Defterleri*, 10 vols. (Istanbul: İstanbul Araştırmaları Merkezi, 1997–98), vol. 1, *İstanbul Esnaf Tarihi* 1, 63. The dispute was between cooks selling prepared food and men who served dishes made of tripe.
34   Genç, "Ottoman Industry", 59–86.
35   Kal'a et al., *İstanbul Esnaf* 1, 49–50.

the manufacturers of fine cottons (*tülbend*) and the cotton printers working for them. The latter complained that, over the course of time, their expenses for labour and raw materials had increased, so they needed to renegotiate the prices for the finished product as well.

In addition, the *tülbendcis* supposedly had agreed among themselves to form a group that would attempt to 'corner the market'. Apparently, members of this group, a cabal at least in the eyes of their accusers, collected the fabrics produced by their fellow guildsmen and brought them to the cotton printers in large bundles, claiming preferential access to the services of the latter. Given the establishment of an oligopoly with tendencies towards monopolization, 'outsiders', if they managed to have their fabrics printed at all, would have to pay the prices determined by the 'insiders'.

Apparently, the matter was of some seriousness, for most if not all the artisans involved – Muslims and Christians belonging to both trades – appeared in the reception room of the palace of the grand vizier. Presumably, there was heated bargaining, but our document only records the results, namely an increase in the sum of money to be paid to the cotton printers and the dissolution of the group of tülbendcis who had attempted to dominate the trade: as of now, every master was to see only to the printing of his own fabrics.

However, perhaps for the historian, the recording process was even more interesting. Two highly placed dignitaries, namely the *kadı* of Istanbul and the inspector of the two Holy Cities (*Haremeyn müfettişi*), reported to the sultan on the agreement, although the text does not say whether these two scholar-bureaucrats had been present in person or had merely received the information from their subordinates. Consequently, the relevant scribes issued a command in the name of the sultan, addressed to the judge and the inspector, which was entered into the Vilayet Ahkâm Defterleri (registers of commands sent to the provinces), a form of record-keeping that was still a relative novelty in the mid-1700s. In addition, both parties to the dispute received copies of their own, which they may have retained until the documents were destroyed in the next fire, a common fate of any items kept in the city's wooden houses.

As both the grand vizier and the local judge were in charge of deciding disputes among Istanbul guildsmen, we occasionally encounter the latter engaging in a bit of 'forum shopping'. In other words, some of these men might prefer the *kadı*'s court over the council room of the grand vizier, as was true of the defendants in a case dated 1759, which we will analyse next. However, all the same, going to the *kadı* rather than to the grand vizier did not mean that the parties to the dispute avoided all contact with the central administration, as the latter always had to issue the document that finally settled the case.[36]

That the dispute occurred at all must have been a surprise for many of the people involved because the 'inhabitants of the Tophane [district] and the shopkeepers of the surrounding area' had already agreed that a shop selling copper goods did not exist in this area but would be convenient to the inhabitants.[37] Thus, the opening of a new shop for copperware seemed unproblematic, until two people protested and refused to have the matter decided in the council of the grand vizier, as we have seen. Unfortunately, we do not know the considerations prompting this decision; perhaps, the two complainants felt that the judge would call a larger number of people than the secretaries of the vizier, and that whatever decision he made would therefore be fairer. In fact, the judge did call a large number of witnesses, all Muslims, who testified that the new shop would be useful to the locals. In so doing, the witnesses used a formula current at the time, saying that the new establishment would make life easier for old people, women living alone and especially old women, who would have difficulty covering long distances, especially in winter and at times of high wind – in this context, it is worth noting that whoever drafted the text anticipated that women would need to go to a copper shop, presumably to replace damaged cooking pots.

In this case, resistance to increasing the number of shops was the work of just two people, who lost out against the majority. However, in the normal course of things, guildsmen attempting to control entry into their specialties were quite selective about who they were willing to admit. In this endeavour, they could count on the support of the central administration with its enduring commitment to 'tradition'. However, in the mid-eighteenth century, when for a few decades the empire was not involved in any lengthy wars, Istanbul experienced a building boom: in addition to mosques and other charities, the city's better-off inhabitants had larger and/or more elaborate houses constructed. These buildings contained many windows, which, given the cold and humidity of the Istanbul winter, those who could afford to do so closed with glass panes. Some builders achieved a decorative 'jewelled' effect by setting small pieces of coloured glass in frames made of white plaster of Paris; as these arrangements were quite fragile only a few original examples survive to the present day.

---

36   Kal'a et al., *İstanbul Esnafı* 1, 245–6.
37   The Istanbul district of Tophane, named after a cannon foundry that is now an exhibition hall, is still extant and located to the east of Galata, roughly where the Bosporus meets the Golden Horn.

Now the glaziers, a guild that contained only Muslims, or else sent only its Muslim members to the *kadı*'s court, litigated against the plaster manufacturers of the Ottoman capital.[38] Up to this time, November–December 1757, there had been eight such plaster-producing establishments spread over the city, all operated by Christians except for one man who may have been Jewish. In court, the glaziers accused the plaster manufacturers of artificially increasing the price of their product by preventing outsiders from even delivering the stone from which the plaster was made, which came from a town some distance away, on the Sea of Marmara. As a result, the owners of buildings to be erected suffered unnecessary delays, while artisans – like the complainants – who needed plaster could not find work.

In the *kadı*'s court, the plaintiffs demanded and received permission to open nine further workshops producing plaster of Paris; as a result, the supply should have more than doubled, particularly since anybody who wished to do so, could now bring the stone needed by the manufacturers into the capital and its suburbs.

However, we are left to wonder if religiously-based animosities were partially responsible for the conflict, for the operators of the nine new manufactories were Muslims to a man. During the 1700s, court cases involving the attempts of Muslim artisans to push non-Muslims out of their trades occasionally occurred, although the central administration did not necessarily support such ventures: although the officials were all Muslims, they often acted on the principle that every legally established artisan had the right to earn a living.[39] In some cases, given the interest of wealthy Istanbulites of the mid-1700s in decorative stonework, the administration even permitted non-Muslim stone cutters who had previously worked exclusively for Muslim employers, to set up on their own. Generalizations are thus risky; and it is not a good idea to project backwards in time the ambition of early twentieth-century governments dominated by the Committee of Union and Progress to create a 'Turkish and Muslim economy' and force non-Muslims out of business. However, in the case of the plaster manufacturers, it does seem that officialdom used the occasion of increasing demand for the finished product to promote Muslim manufacturers, perhaps – but that is not certain – at the expense of their non-Muslim competitors.

---

38  Kal'a et al., *İstanbul Esnafı* 1, 161.

39  Suraiya Faroqhi, "Did Cosmopolitanism Exist in Eighteenth-Century Istanbul: Stories of Christian and Jewish Artisans", in Ulrike Freitag and Nora Lafi (eds), *Urban Governance under the Ottomans: Between Cosmopolitanism and Conflict* (London: Routledge, 2014), 33–48.

As our documentation mostly concerns Istanbul, occasional information on the practices then current in provincial towns are of special interest. For that purpose we will take a close look at a regulation (*nizam*) concerning the barbers of Edirne, an important Balkan city, which in the 1600s had for about fifty years served as a subsidiary capital.[40] These artisans complained that, while in the past the permission of the guild headman (*kethüda*) and his aides had been necessary when a man wished to open a barbershop, or to sell or rent his equipment to a newcomer. However, many people had recently disobeyed that rule and, in a discourse 'hallowed by centuries-long use', the guildsmen complained that customers suffered from incompetent treatment while their own regulations had fallen into disuse.

In this context, it is noteworthy that the barbers failed to mention the term *gedik*, although in later decades they would probably have viewed this transaction as connected with the possession or non-possession of a *gedik*. Probably, 'institutionalization' of this sort had not yet reached Edirne, though once again, it is hard to be sure.

Up to this point, the document conformed to a well-established pattern, but there was one remarkable variant feature: the barbers wanted the customs of Istanbul to become applicable in their own city. While on today's highways, the distance between the two cities is less than 220 kilometres, the trip took several days before the advent of the railways; and, while this distance did not prevent travel, it was still quite rare for Ottoman guildsmen to refer to regulations current in another city, much less to ask for their adoption. Probably, Edirne's past role as an 'almost capital' had strengthened its connections to Istanbul, even insofar as relatively poor artisans were concerned. Whatever the situation, adopting the regulations of another city required the support of the central administration, for the barbers first needed to obtain the support of the local *kadı*, who petitioned on their behalf. Then, officials in Istanbul had to look up their records on what practices were current in their own city. Thus, the adoption of the Istanbul regulations by the barbers of Edirne would have been impossible without high-level administrators in both cities being willing to cooperate.

The enforcement of all these rules and regulations was the job of the market inspector (*muhtesib*) and his servants, who were apparently much feared by the townspeople; at least in the 1600s, this office was a tax farm, with the incumbent receiving payment from dues paid by artisans and traders – presumably in addition to any fines he might impose. Evliya Çelebi, the seventeenth-century author of a massive travelogue covering many Ottoman provinces

---

40   Kal'a et al., *İstanbul Esnafı* 1, 56.

and a few foreign cities, has pointed to the grave responsibility of the market inspector, presumably because it was so difficult to be fair to both producers and consumers.[41] Moreover, this official imposed penalties such as beatings, although it was sometimes claimed that to do so was illegal without the *kadı*'s permission. The market inspector also might impose punishments that were repulsive in themselves, such as wrapping the innards of slaughtered animals around the head of an artisan or trader who had cheated on the weight of the goods that he had sold. Such penalties were widely visible and, presumably, many potential customers avoided making purchases from a man who had recently suffered that humiliating punishment. Thus, the market supervisor and his men could determine who might survive in the urban market and who would have to find another job.

For the purposes of this chapter, we will take these four texts to represent the numerous published and unpublished nizam texts that a historian of crafts might consult. We have encountered the attempted formation of cabals by which a group of prosperous artisans at least attempted to limit the access of outsiders to their suppliers. If all went well according to their plans, they might ultimately have monopolized access to the finishing processes through which their products needed to pass before they reached the customers. In addition, we have seen how the involvement of both the *kadı* and grand vizier in fairly mundane artisan conflicts permitted astute complainants to choose the venue that best suited their interests. It has also become clear that religious conflicts might become intertwined with run-of-the-mill disputes in the marketplace; and the central administration, while strongly committed to 'tradition' and the right of all established artisans to make a living, might occasionally be inclined to place Muslims in lines of work previously dominated by their non-Muslim competitors. Last, but not least, the relative closeness of Istanbul and Edirne might prompt a guild from the latter city to adopt regulations current in Istanbul, either for some practical advantage remaining unknown today, or else because the prestige of the capital encouraged provincials to imitate its customs as well as they could.

---

[41] Evliya Çelebi, *Evliya Çelebi Seyahatnâmesi: 1.Kitap: Topkapı Sarayı Bağdat 304 Yazmasının Transkripsyonu-Dizini* (ed.) Orhan Şaik Gökyay (Istanbul: Yapı Kredi Yayınları, 1996), 296, 301.

## 9 In Conclusion

It would be good to say that at least some of these tendencies were a novelty of the eighteenth century. Unfortunately, in many if not most cases, such claims would be imprudent. The increasing bureaucratization of Ottoman government, along with official attempts to control closely those parts of the empire that had not fallen under the sway of local notables, has left us with a mass of documentation for the 1700s that is simply unavailable for earlier periods. We thus need to avoid drawing the facile conclusion that the imitation of Istanbul rules by provincial guilds was a new tendency resulting from increased commercial communication between the empire's major cities. Perhaps such an increase did occur, but to date we have no way of proving it; and, it is a thoroughly bad idea to explain one unknown with another.

Unfortunately, where relationships between artisans and officialdom are concerned, seventeenth-century documentation is not very ample and, therefore, we cannot really tell when the Ottoman bureaucracy came to be as intrusive in artisan affairs as it was to be in the middle of the eighteenth century. The reign of Ahmed III (r.1703–30) was certainly a period in which the central administration consolidated its hold over the artisan world.[42] However, we still do not know what exactly motivated the sultans' bureaucrats to choose just those years for aggressively 'putting people in their places' by promoting *gediks* where they had not previously existed. At least we know that such a drive did really occur, because the *kadıs* of Istanbul and their scribes in the 1720s and 1730s filled pages and pages of their registers with decisions concerning newly instituted *gediks*.[43] Given the present state of our knowledge, we can only venture to guess that the somewhat precarious position of Sultan Ahmed III, after a series of less than successful wars, induced him to accommodate the demand of Istanbul's artisans, so often eager to close ranks against outsiders. While I think that more serious reasons were involved, at present they remain unknown.

Yet, there is one difference we can clearly envisage: in the 1700s, the complainants – and thus the documents emitted – are not greatly concerned with the methods of manufacturing. As a result, they do not often tell us – for instance – which ingredients should go into the preparation of baklava

---

[42] Onur Yıldırım, "Osmanlı Esnafında Uyum ve Dönüşüm", *Toplum ve Bilim* 83 (Winter 1999–2000), 146–77.

[43] Suraiya Faroqhi, "Surviving in Difficult Times: The Cotton and Silk Trades in Bursa around 1800", in Suraiya Faroqhi (ed.) *Bread from the Lion's Mouth* (New York: Berghahn Books, 2015), 136–56.

or tripe soup, although such matters did occur in the lists of administratively determined prices (narh) emitted during the 1500s and 1600s.[44] By contrast, in eighteenth-century documents, the focus is on questions related to the division of the urban market among competing artisans and shopkeepers, including servitors of the sultan who frequently used their privileges to control the craft activities of 'ordinary' people.[45]

In this context, it is worth noting that the prevention of harm to the customers on account of bad workmanship, which in older times had often served as a justification for regulation, was not a major reason to request nizams; this statement is not invalidated by the fact that the Edirne barbers did refer to possible harm to their customers. After all, had the demands and complaints of clients played a major role in this process, we would have expected them to occur more often in the surviving texts.

Among the questions that to date remain unanswered, there is one that is particularly intriguing: did the emphasis on markets, privileges, and distribution as opposed to the humdrum realities of production reflect a change of orientation in the artisan world, or was it an artefact of the officials who have produced our documentation?

Returning to the question posed at the outset, what do we know about artisan attitudes towards the sultan and his elite? It is hard to deny that most of the surviving documents show the craftsmen to be quiescent; or, if they take the initiative, it is to demand more and not less regulation. We get the impression that at least those artisans about whom something is known were inclined to 'play the system', frequently asking for the support of the administration against those whom they perceived as competitors. But, at least during the 1600s and 1700s, Istanbul craftsmen, through their close links with the janissaries and other military men stationed in the capital, participated more or less visibly in quite a few rebellions, demanding the execution/exile of dignitaries whom they perceived as their enemies, and sometimes even the dethronement of a sultan. Certainly in Istanbul, the guilds as organizations did not participate in these events, but guild members in their 'second identities' as military men certainly did so.[46]

---

44  Barkan, "Bazı Büyük Şehirlerde", I, 5 (1942), 326–40; II, 7 (1942), 15–40; II, 9 (1942), 168–77; Mübahat Kütükoğlu (ed.), "1009 (1600) tarihli Narh Defterine göre İstanbul'da çeşidli Eşya ve Hizmet Fiyatları", *Tarih Enstitüsü Dergisi* 9 (1978), 1–86; *idem* (ed.), *Osmanlılarda Narh Müessesesi ve 1640 Tarihli Narh Defteri* (Istanbul: Enderun Kitabevi, 1983).
45  Kal'a et al., *İstanbul Esnafı* 1, 57–8.
46  Suraiya Faroqhi, *Artisans of Empire: Crafts and Craftspeople under the Ottomans* (London: I. B. Tauris, 2009), 142–59.

Although the participants in such rebellions did not in every case directly address the problems of artisans trying to make a living, these uprisings must be viewed as another means by which these men expressed their attitude to the government; I would plead for viewing eighteenth-century Istanbul craftsmen as cooperating, and even submissively cooperating, with the sultans' bureaucracy under normal circumstances. But in times of crisis, they aggressively aimed to punish the men they regarded as being responsible for the misery of Istanbul's petit people.[47]

## Bibliography

### *Primary Sources*

Barkan, Ömer Lütfi (ed.) "Bazı Büyük Şehirlerde Eşya ve Yiyecek Fiyatlarının Tesbit ve Teftişi Hususlarını Tanzim Eden Kanunlar". *Tarih Vesikaları* I, 5 (1942), 326–340; II, 7 (1942), 15–40; II, 9 (1942), 168–177.

Evliya Çelebi. *Evliya Çelebi Seyahatnâmesi: 1.Kitap: Topkapı Sarayı Bağdat 304 Yazmasının Transkripsyonu-Dizini*, edited by Orhan Şaik Gökyay. Istanbul: Yapı Kredi Yayınları, 1996.

Fotopoulos, Dionissis and Angelos Delivorrias. *Greece at the Benaki Museum*. Athens: Benaki Museum, 1997.

Gölpınarlı, Abdülbaki. "Burgâzî ve Fütüvvet Nâmesi". *İstanbul Üniversitesi İktisat Fakültesi Mecmuası/Dergisi* 11 (1–4) 1949–50, 3–54.

Gölpınarlı, Abdülbaki. "İslâm ve Türk İllerinde Fütüvvet Teşkilâtı ve Kaynakları". *İstanbul Üniversitesi İktisat Fakültesi Mecmuası/Dergisi* 15 (1–4) 1953/4, 76–153.

Ibn Battuta. *Voyages d'Ibn Batoutah, Texte arabe, accompagné d'une Traduction*. Vol. 2, edited and translated by C. Defrémery and B. R. Sanguinetti. Paris: Imprimerie Impériale, 1854.

Kal'a, Ahmet et al. (eds). *İstanbul Külliyatı: İstanbul Ahkâm Defterleri. 10 vols. Istanbul: İstanbul Araştırmaları Merkezi, 1997–98*, vol. 1: İstanbul Esnaf Tarihi. Istanbul, 1997.

Kütükoğlu, Mübahat (ed.) "1009 (1600) tarihli Narh Defterine göre İstanbul'da çeşidli Eşya ve Hizmet Fiyatları". *Tarih Enstitüsü Dergisi* 9 (1978), 1–86.

Kütükoğlu, Mübahat (ed.) *Osmanlılarda Narh Müessesesi ve 1640 Tarihli Narh Defteri*. Istanbul: Enderun Kitabevi, 1983.

---

47  Annemarike Stremmelaar, *Justice and Revenge in the Ottoman Rebellion of 1703* (Leiden: PrintPartners Ipskamp, 2007).

## Secondary Sources

Abou-El-Haj, Rifaʿat A. "Ottoman Attitudes Toward Peace-Making: The Karlowitz Case". *Der Islam* 51 (1) 1974, 131–7.

Akarlı, Engin. "*Gedik*: A Bundle of Rights and Obligations for Istanbul Artisans and Traders, 1750–1840". In Alain Pottage and Martha Mundy (eds). *Law, Anthropology and the Constitution of the Social: Making Persons and Things*. Cambridge: Cambridge University Press, 2004, 166–200.

Aščerić-Todd, Inez. "The Noble Traders: The Islamic Tradition of 'Spiritual Chivalry' (futuwwa) in Bosnian Trade Guilds (16th–19th Centuries)". *The Muslim World* 97 (April 2007), 159–73.

Asdrachas, Spyros I. *Greek Economic History: 15th–19th Centuries*. 2 vols. Athens: Piraeus Bank Group Cultural Foundation, 2007.

Baer, Gabriel. "Ottoman Guilds: A Reassessment". In Halil İnalcık and Osman Okyar (eds). *Türkiye'nin Sosyal ve Ekonomik Tarihi (1071–1920), Social and Economic History of Turkey (1071–1920)*. Ankara: Meteksan Limited, 1980, 95–102.

Ballian, Anna. "Karamanlı Patronage in the Eighteenth and Nineteenth Centuries: The Case of the Village of Germir/Kermira". In Evangelia Balta and Matthias Kappler (eds). *Cries and Whispers in Karamanlidika Books: Proceedings of the First International Conference on Karamanlidika Studies (Nicosia, 11th–13th September 2008)*. Wiesbaden: Harrassowitz Verlag, 2010, 45–62.

Breebaart, Deodaat Anne. "Fütüvvetname-i Kebir: A Manual on Turkish Guilds". *Journal of the Economic and Social History of the Orient* 15 (1972), 203–15.

Çizakça, Murat. "The Ottoman Government and Economic Life". In Suraiya Faroqhi and Kate Fleet (eds) *The Cambridge History of Turkey*. Cambridge: Cambridge University Press, 2013, vol. 2, 241–75.

Dalsar, Fahri. *Türk Sanayi ve Ticaret Tarihinde Bursa 'da İpekçilik*. Istanbul: İstanbul Üniversitesi İktisat Fakültesi, 1960.

Demirtaş, Mehmet. *Osmanlı Esnafında Suç ve Ceza: İstanbul örneği H 1100–1200/1688–1786*. Ankara: Birleşik Yayınevi, 2010.

Faroqhi, Suraiya. "Urban Space as Disputed Grounds: Territorial Aspects to Artisan Conflict in Sixteenth to Eighteenth-Century Istanbul". In *idem. Stories of Ottoman Men and Women: Establishing Status, Establishing Control*. Istanbul: Eren, 2002, 219–234.

Faroqhi, Suraiya "Purchasing Guild- and Craft-Based Offices in the Ottoman Central Lands". *Turcica* 39 (2007), 123–46.

Faroqhi, Suraiya. *Artisans of Empire: Crafts and Craftspeople under the Ottomans*. London: I. B. Tauris, 2009.

Faroqhi, Suraiya "Did Cosmopolitanism Exist in Eighteenth-Century Istanbul: Stories of Christian and Jewish Artisans". In Ulrike Freitag and Nora Lafi (eds). *Urban*

Government under the Ottomans: Between Cosmopolitanism and Conflict. London: Routledge, 2014, 33–48.

Faroqhi, Suraiya. "Surviving in Difficult Times: The Cotton and Silk Trades in Bursa around 1800". In idem. (ed.) *Bread from the Lion's Mouth: Artisans Struggling for a Livelihood in Ottoman Cities*. New York: Berghahn Books, 2015.

Fukasawa, Katsumi. *Toilerie et Commerce du Levant, d'Alep à Marseille*. Paris: Editions du CNRS, 1987.

Genç, Mehmet. "Ottoman Industry in the Eighteenth Century: General Framework, Characteristics and Main Trends". In Donald Quataert (ed.) *Manufacturing in the Ottoman Empire and Turkey 1500–1950* (Albany: SUNY Press, 1994), 59–86.

Gerber, Haim. *Economy and Society in an Ottoman City: Bursa, 1600–1700*. Jerusalem: The Hebrew University, 1988.

Gingeras, Ryan. *Sorrowful Shores: Violence, Ethnicity, and the End of the Ottoman Empire 1912–1923*. New York: Oxford University Press, 2011.

İnalcık, Halil. "The Appointment Procedure of a Guild Warden (Kethudâ)". In *Festschrift für Andreas Tietze: Wiener Zeitschrift für die Kunde des Morgenlandes* 76 (1986), 135–42.

İslamoğlu, Huri. *State and Peasant in the Ottoman Empire*. Leiden: Brill, 1994.

Kal'a, Ahmet et al. (eds). *İstanbul Külliyatı: İstanbul Ahkâm Defterleri, 10 vols*. (Istanbul: İstanbul Arastırmaları Merkezi, 1997–98), vol. 1, İstanbul Esnaf Tarihi 1.

Khoury, Dina. *State and Provincial Society in the Ottoman Empire: Mosul, 1540–1834*. Cambridge: Cambridge University Press, 2002.

Mantran, Robert. *Istanbul dans la seconde moitié du dix-septième siècle: Essai d'histoire institutionelle, économique et sociale*. Istanbul: Institut Français d'Archéologie d'Istanbul and Adrien Maisonneuve, 1962.

Peirce, Leslie. *Morality Tales: Law and Gender in the Ottoman Court of Aintab*. Berkeley: University of California Press, 2003.

Stremmelaar, Annemarieke. *Justice and Revenge in the Ottoman Rebellion of 1703*. Leiden: PrintPartners Ipskamp, 2007.

Turna, Nalan. "The Shoe Guilds of Istanbul in the Early Nineteenth Century: A Case Study". In Suraıya Faroqhi (ed.) *Bread from the Lion's Mouth*. New York: Berghahn Books, 2015, 157–71.

Ülgener, Sabri. *İktisadi Çözülmenin Ahlak ve Zihniyet Dünyası*. Istanbul: Der Yayınları, 1981.

Vatter, Sherry. "Journeymen Textile Weavers in Nineteenth-Century Damascus: A Collective Biography". In Edmund Burke III and David N. Yaghubian (eds). *Struggle and Survival in the Modern Middle East*. Berkeley: University of California Press, 2006, 64–79.

Yi, Eunjeong. *Guild Dynamics in Seventeenth-Century Istanbul: Fluidity and Leverage*. Leiden: Brill, 2004.

Yi, Eunjeong. "Rich Artisans and Poor Merchants: A Critical Look at the Supposed Egalitarianism in Ottoman Guilds". In Suraıya Faroqhi (ed.) *Bread from the Lion's Mouth*. New York: Berghahn Books, 2015, 194–216.

Yıldırım, Onur. "Osmanlı Esnafında Uyum ve Dönüşüm". *Toplum ve Bilim* 83 (Winter 1999–2000), 146–77.

Yıldırım, Onur and Seven Ağır. "*Gedik*: What's in a Name?" In Suraiya Faroqhi (ed.) *Bread from the Lion's Mouth*. New York: Berghahn Books, 2015, 217–36.

**PART 2**

*Ottomans – Culture and Careers*

∴

CHAPTER 5

# *Türbedar* of the Ottoman Sultans: Şevkî Çelebi's Nostalgia for the Bursa of Bayezid Han and Emîr Sultan

*Fatih Bayram*

> He is an outstanding watchman of the land of Rûm – And the gatekeeper of the Ottoman cities
> By his favour the city of Bursa – Always flourishes with clemency[1]

∴

In Acquaintances, the British historian Arnold J. Toynbee devotes a chapter to his patron at Chatham House for International Affairs, Lionel Curtis.[2] They were travelling together to the United States in the summer of 1925 for a conference in Michigan. The subject of Curtis's lecture was: "If Christ were to come back to Earth, where, in the present-day world, would he find that his precepts were being best practised?"[3] When Curtis asked Toynbee for his answer to that question, Toynbee replied: "Well, not, I take it, in the churches. No, not there, of course. Well, perhaps, then, in the lives of humble people who have never been heard of."[4] Arnold Toynbee's answer reflects his respect for the authentic lives of 'humble people' and, luckily, such people have left written sources so that later generations can remember them in their prayers.

---

1 Şevkî, *Menâkıb-ı Emîr Sultan*, Mevlânâ Müzesi Kütüphanesi Yazmaları, no. 4940, folio 9a. Translation of "Husûsâ milk-i Rûm'un bekcisüdür – Ki Osman illerinün gözcisüdür. Burusa şehri ânun himmetiyle – Olur ma'mûr dâyim re'fet ile".
2 Arnold J. Toynbee, *Acquaintances* (London: OUP, 1967), 129–48.
3 Toynbee, *Acquaintances*, 146.
4 Toynbee, *Acquaintances*, 146. When Toynbee asked Curtis for his own answer to that question, Curtis said: "The answer is: 'In the British Commonwealth' ... The relation between the peoples of the Commonwealth is the best attempt to carry out Christ's teaching that the present-day world has to show". Toynbee (*Acquaintances*, 146) adds: "Obviously Lionel was surprised at my stupidity at not having seen this obvious answer for myself".

One such person was Şevkî Çelebi of Bursa, whose name, despite being the first Turkish translator of Kâzerûnî hagiography, has been forgotten in the Kâzerûnî literature.[5] Sources are silent about Şevkî's childhood, but from a story about a 'Lamb Spring and Walnut Tree' (*Kuzulu Pınar ve Koz Ağacı*) in Emîr Sultan's hagiography, henceforth cited in this chapter as *Menâkıb-ı Emîr Sultan*, it can be assumed that he spent his childhood (*sabâvet zamanında*) in Bursa.[6] Mehmed Şevkî b. Ahmed's patron was Fenârîzâde Şemsi Beg, who was the tutor (*lala*) of Şehzâde ('prince') Selim, the future Selim I, in Trabzon.[7] Sources are silent about whether Şevkî Efendi accompanied Selim when he became the Ottoman sultan in 1512. Nevertheless, Âşık Çelebi, who served as the trustee (*mütevelli*) for Emîr Sultan's waqfs (*vakıfs*) in Bursa between 1541 and 1546, gives the most authentic information about the life of a person who viewed Bursa as a place of ideal sultans and of 'the perfect man' (*insân al-kâmil*).[8]

Like Şevkî of Bursa, whom Âşık Çelebi calls Şevkî-i Sânî (the Second Şevkî) not to be confused with Şevkî of Edirne,[9] Âşık Çelebi himself was related to both Emîr Sultan and Ebû İshâk-ı Kâzerûnî (d.1035). Apart from being a trustee for Emîr Sultan's *vakıfs*, Âşık Çelebi was also a great-grandson of Seyyid Ali

---

5    Biographies of poets, known as *şuarâ tezkires*, give different names to Şevkî. I have preferred Mehmed Süreyya's usage: Şevkî Çelebi. See Mehmed Süreyya, *Sicill-i Osmanî, Osmanlı Ünlüleri*, edited by Nuri Akbayar and Seyit Ali Kahraman, vol. 5 (Istanbul: Tarih Vakfı Yurt Yayınları, 1996), 1595. The most detailed account of Şevkî's life can be found in the tezkire of Âşık Çelebi. See Âşık Çelebi, *Meşâ'irü'ş-Şu'arâ*, vol.3, edited by Filiz Kılıç (Istanbul: İstanbul Araştırmaları Enstitüsü, 2010), 1450. For further information, see also Kınalızade Hasan Çelebi, *Tezkiretü'ş-Şuarâ*, edited by İbrahim Kutluk, vol. 1 (Ankara: TTK, 1989), 537–8. Bursalı Mehmed Tahir confuses Şevkî Efendi of the sixteenth century with Çömezzâde Şevkî (d.1100/1688). See Bursalı Mehmed Tâhir, *Osmanlı Müellifleri*, edited by Mustafa Tatcı and Cemâl Kurnaz, vol. 3 (Ankara: Bizim Büro, 2000), 72, 73.

6    "Günlerden bir gün.... Emîr Sultân 'aleyhi'r-rahmetü ve'l-ğufrân sa'âdethânelerinden taşra gelüb der-i devlet-me'âblarınun öninde mübârek 'aşâlarına dayanub dururlardı. Dervîşlerinden ba'zı kimse tażarru' idüb eyitdiler: 'Sulṭânum! n'olaydı şol yirde vużû' itmek icün âb-ı revân olaydı. Müslümânlar gelüb âbdest alalardı'.... Bir su ẓâhir oldı, aḳdı. Ol zamândan berü ol su cârî olub aḳar. Ba'zı kimse ol suya Ḳuzulı Pınar dirler. Ol zamân ol yirde bir ḳoz ağacı varıdı. Faḳîr ya'nî Şevḳî daḫî ṣabâvet zamânında ol ḳoz ağacını ol yirde görmişümdür. Sonra ḳurıdı". Şevkî, *Menâḳıb-ı Emîr Sulṭân*, fol. 38b–39a, MS 4940, MMKY.

7    Âşık Çelebi, *Meşâ'ir*, 1450. For a list of Selim's *lalas*, see Feridun M. Emecen, *Zamanın İskenderi, Şarkın Fatihi Yavuz Sultan Selim* (Istanbul: Yitik Hazine Yayınları, 2010), 41. Emecen points out that Şehzâde Selim sent a number of his men from Trabzon to Bursa to find money for his expenses in the year 1507. The reason for his need for extra money was attributed to the limited amount of revenue in the Trabzon region in one of Selim's letters. See Emecen, *Yavuz*, 42. Perhaps Şevkî Çelebi and his patron Şemsi Beg were among those men sent from Trabzon to Bursa.

8    Günay Kut, "Âşık Çelebi", DIA 3, 549–50.

9    Âşık Çelebi, *Meşâ'ir*, 1448–9.

Nattâ b. Muhammed, the first sheikh of the Kâzerûnî lodge in Bursa. When Seyyid Ali Nattâ Bagdadî came to Bursa with Emîr Sultan, Bayezid I appointed him the first *nakîbüleşraf* (person in charge of sayyids or descendants of the Prophet) in the Ottoman Empire.[10]

Âşık Çelebi met Şevkî Çelebi during his stay in Bursa. At that time, Şevkî seemed to be quite old, for the author mentioned "his stature [as] being bent double with age".[11] Compared with the other tezkires, Âşık Çelebi's book gives valuable insights into the hidden life of Şevkî, who was mostly reluctant to reveal personal information about himself. The exact dates of his birth and death are unknown. Nevertheless, it is evident that Şevkî, whom Âşık Çelebi referred to as 'deceased' (*merhûm*), died before 1568, the year in which Âşık Çelebi presented his biographies of poets, titled *Meşâirü'ş-şuarâ*, to the Ottoman sultan Selim II (r.1566–74).[12] According to Âşık Çelebi, Şevkî served his patron Fenârîzâde Şemsi Beg in Istanbul, and later became Sultan Selim I's finance officer (*defterdar*).[13] After Şemsi Beg died, Şevkî returned to Bursa and worked as an antiquarian (*sahaf*). The good old days had passed and he began to live a life devoid of material wealth.[14] If that story is true, it is amazing that the reader of Şevkî's works cannot find any word about his sojourn in Istanbul.

The greatest honour in Şevkî's life was being recognized by the Ottoman sultan, Selim I, when he came to Bursa. Şevkî felt proud that Selim had remembered his face after such a long time. When the sultan was meeting the residents of Bursa, he suddenly recognized Şevkî, who felt honoured to have caught the sultan's gaze (*şâhâne nigâh*). Selim asked his vizier, Zeynel Pasha,

---

10   Ş. Tufan Buzpınar, "Nakîbüleşraf", *DIA* 32, 322–4.
11   "Burusa'da şu'arâ tekyesinün iḥtiyârı idi, bâ-vücûd ki pîrlik ḳāmetin iki ḳāt itmiş idi". Âşık Çelebi, *Meşâ'ir*, 1450.
12   Kut, "Âşık Çelebi", 549.
13   Şemsi Beg became *defterdar* in 1514 and was dismissed from the office in 1516. For further information about Şemsi Beg, see İsmail Hami Danişmend, *Osmanlı Devlet Erkânı* (Istanbul: Türkiye Yayınevi, 1971), 416–7.
14   "Şâh Selîm Dırabzın'da şehzâde iken defterdâr u lâlâ ve zemân-ı salṭanatlarında ḳadri vâlâ olub ba'dehû defterdâr-ı ḫazîne vü ṣāḥib-i livâ olan Fenârî Şems Beg-i merḥûmun yanında neşv ü nemâ bulmış, ânun ḫıdmetinde olmış kimesnedür. Ol devr döndükden ve sâḳî-i devr ânlara ecel ayağın ṣundukdan ṣonra Burûsa'da ṣaḥḥâf dükkânı açmış". Âşık Çelebi, *Meşâ'ir*, 1450. Şevkî's patron Şemsi Beg became governor of Teke *sancağı* on 28 Muharrem 925/30 January 1519. After serving as the governor of Teke province (present-day Antalya), Şemsi Beg was appointed as governor of Safed *sancağı* (present-day northern Israel) in 1521. See Abdüllatif Armağan, "XVI. Yüzyılda Teke Sancağı'nın Yönetimi ve Yöneticileri", *Ankara Üniversitesi Dil ve Tarih-Coğrafya Fakültesi Türkoloji Dergisi* 18 (1) 2011, 277 ff. It seems that Şemsi's post as governor of Safed sancağı did not last long because in the year 1522 the governor of Safed was Çavuş Sinan Bey. See Enver Çakar, "XVI. Yüzyılda Şam Beylerbeyliğinin İdarî Taksimatı", *Fırat Üniversitesi Sosyal Bilimler Dergisi* 3 (1) (2003) 359.

if this was 'our Şevkî' (*Zeynel Pâşâ'ya bizüm Şevkî degül mi diyü gösterdi*),[15] but Zeynel Pasha erroneously told the sultan that he had died. Şevkî later met Zeynel Pasha and told him that he was indeed still alive. Zeynel Pasha's reply to Şevkî Çelebi is reminiscent of Arnold Toynbee's summing up of a humble person: "You wretched, are you still alive?" (*Miskîn dahı sağ mısın?*)[16] In fact, *miskîn* (wretched) Şevkî encapsulated the humble person of his time.

Şevkî longed for the good old days of the reign of Bayezid I (1389–1402), when the first Ottoman Kâzerûnî lodge opened and he, Şevkî, undertook the first Turkish translation of Kâzerûnî hagiography. He decided to translate the Persian original into the Turkish language at a 'sorrowful time', namely when he was trying to win the hearts of Kâzerûnî dervishes.[17] I myself have recently produced a new version of Şevkî's translation of Kâzerûnî *menâkıbnâme*.[18] It was in honour of Bayezid's son-in-law Emîr Sultan, that Şevkî recorded the latter's miraculous deeds. One section of the menâkıb hagiography describes the building of the Ulucami, or 'Grand Mosque' of Bursa,[19] with booty (*gazâ mâlı ile*) seized from Nicopolis (Ott. Niğbolu). Like his father-in-law, Emîr Sultan was also a ghazi, and took part in the siege of Constantinople with his 500 disciples in the year 1422, which was during the reign of Murad II (r.1421–44 and

---

15 "Merhûmun her zemânda 'unvân-ı hikâyâtı ve mefhar u mübâhâtı buydı ki Sultân Selîm-i merhûm Drabzın'dan beni bilürdi. Niçe yıldan şonra Burûsa'ya şikâre geldiler. Şehr halkı ile istikbâle çıkduk. Zeynel Pâşâ ile yanaşmışlardı. Çûn hażret-i pâdşâh selâm yirine geldi nâ-gâh bana şâhâne nigâh kıldı, teşhîş idüp ism ü resmümi bildi. Zeynel Pâşâ'ya bizüm Şevkî degül mi diyü gösterdi". Âşık Çelebi, *Meşâ'ir*, 1450.

16 "Zeynel Pâşâ dahı bu ol degüldür, ol ölmişdür diyü pâdşâha şübhe virdi. Hattâ birer kozı üç itmişler. Çünki [çûnki] otaklarına nüzûl idüp âsâyiş itmişler. Zeynel Pâşâ'ya vardum, beni görüb miskîn dahı sağ mısın diyü hâlüm hâtırum şordı, gâyet ri'âyet itdi, ba'dehû vech-i mestûr üzre mâ-cerâyı hikâyet itdi". Âşık Çelebi, *Meşâ'ir*, 1450.

17 Şevkî described his reason for translating the *menâkıb* of Kâzerûnî from Persian to Turkish as follows: "Nekebât-ı zamândan hazîn ve nekebât-ı cihândan ğamgîn olub kûşe-i hasretde sâkin ve hâne-i mihnetde mütemekkin iken nâgâh takdîr-i Rabbânî ber-mûcib-i emr-i Yezdânî ilhâm-ı Şamedânî irişüb hâtır-ı şikeste-bâl ve dil-i âşufte-hâle şöyle hutûr itdi kim menâkıb-ı sultânî'l-evliyâî'l- 'ârifîn kutb-ı ekâbir-i aşfıyâî'l-vâşılîn şeyhü'ş-şuyûhı's-sâlikin sultân-ı selâtîn-i dîn şâhenşâh-ı pîşvâ-yı ehl-i yakîn kıdvetü evliyâî'l-muhakkikîn zübdetü'l-etkıyâî'l-müdakkıkîn kutbü'l-âfâk Şeyh Ebû İshak İbrâhîm bin Şehriyârı'l-Kâzurûnî kaddesellahu rûhahu'l-'azîz ki defter-i meşâyıhda sultânî'l-evliyâ okurlar ve kutbü'l-aktâb yazarlar ve şeyhü'l-mürşid eydürler; menâkıb-ı şerîfini ve siyer-i latîfini zebân-ı Fârsî'den lisân-ı Türkî'ye tercüme idem; tâ kim aşhâb-ı şeyhü'l-âfâk ve ahbâb-ı Şeyh Ebû İshak hazz-ı evferle mahzûz olub bu fakîri hayır du'â' ile zikr ideler". Şevkî, *Menâkıb-ı Ebû İshak Kâzerûnî*, fol. 5b–6a, MS 2429, Esad Efendi, SK.

18 Şevkî Çelebi, *Menâkıb-ı Ebû İshâk-ı Kâzerûnî. Ebû İshâk İbrâhîm Kâzerûnî'nin Menâkıbı*, edited by Fatih Bayram (Istanbul: TYEKBY, 2016).

19 "Yıldırım Bâyezîd Hân 'aleyhi'l-mağfiretü ve'l-ğufrân câmi'-i kebîrün binâsında Emîr Sultân'la vâki' olan ahvâl beyânındadır". Şevkî, *Menâkıb-ı Emîr Sultân*, fol. 26b.

1446–51).[20] However, there is no mention of events related to Constantinople in Şevkî's works, and it is difficult to know whether or not that was a deliberate choice. However, we do know that he was unhappy about the status quo at the time and complained about ignorant people being highly esteemed while knowledgeable men were suffering.[21]

Şevkî's love for the old Ottoman capital is what led him to record the deeds of Emîr Sultan, "with whose blessing (*baraka*) Bursa always flourishes."[22] Rather than squabbling over acquiring highly paid positions in the Ottoman bureaucracy, Şevkî busied himself as a *türbedar* (the keeper of a mausoleum), which involved safeguarding the tombs of the founders of the Ottoman state, Osman and Orhan Gazi. He also protected old books by working as an antiquarian (*sahaf*) and, like others of his time, suffered financial hardship.[23] Although Şevkî was not particularly interested in earning money, he needed enough time to enable him to finish his books.[24]

Şevkî Çelebi's view of the Ottoman dynasty was reminiscent of Âşıkpaşazâde's stance towards the sultans: "This Ottoman dynasty is such a family that their miraculous deeds are apparent."[25] Şevkî Çelebi presented his hagiography on Emîr Sultan to Süleyman I's son, Şehzâde (Prince) Bayezid in 1553. At that time, Bayezid (d.1561) was staying in Bursa.[26]

Şevkî and Âşıkpaşazâde were not alone in elevating Ottoman sultans to the status of 'saints' (*velîs*). In the eyes of the Ottoman public, some like Murad I and Bayezid II were considered to be *velîs* and their miracles (*keramât*) were announced at public gatherings. One Ottoman sultan, Süleyman, was believed

---

20  Hüseyin Algül and Nihat Azamat, "Emîr Sultan", *DIA* 11, 147; Osman Turan, *Türk Cihân Hâkimiyeti Mefkûresi Tarihi. Türk Dünya Nizâmının Millî, İslâmî ve İnsanî Esasları* (Istanbul: Ötüken Yayınları, 2006), 272.
21  "Câhil olanlar katı 'izzetdedir – Ma'rifet ehli bugün zellettedür". Şevkî, *Menâkıb-ı Kâzerûnî*, fol. 59b.
22  "*Burusa şehri ânun himmetiyle – Olur ma'mûr dâyim re'fet ile*". Şevki, *Menâkıb-ı Emîr Sultân*, fol. 9a.
23  İsmail E. Erünsal, *Osmanlılarda Sahaflık ve Sahaflar* (Istanbul: Timaş Yayınları, 2013), 56.
24  "Burûsa'da ṣaḥḥâf dükkânı açmış, sedd-i ramak içün ḳūt-ı lâ-yemûtla ve ba'żı ḫurde cihetle ḳanâ'at idüb sâ'ir sevdâdan geçmiş idi". Âşık Çelebi, *Meşâ'ir*, 1450.
25  Halil İnalcık, "How to Read Âşıkpaşazâde's History", in *Essays in Ottoman History* (Istanbul: Eren Yayınları, 1998), 36.
26  There are different opinions about the dates of *Menâkıb-ı Emîr Sultan* and *Menâkıb-ı Kâzerûnî*. Nevertheless, it can safely be argued that both works were written before the death of Süleyman the Magnificent. For possible dates of both works, see Mustafa Okan Baba, "Menâkıb-ı Emîr Sultan (Metin-İnceleme-Gramer-İndeks)" (Ph.D. dissertation, Marmara University, 1991), xv–xvii.

to be "master in the manifest as well as in the unseen world" (*zâhirde ve bâtında ânun hükmi revândur*).[27]

Apart from being the sultans' *türbedâr*, Şevkî was also an extensive reader of extraordinary stories about saints and sultans. One saint whose stories were of interest to him was Ebû İshâk İbrâhim b. Şehriyâr el-Kâzerûnî, known as the sheikh of the ghazis (*şeyh-i gaziyân*). Şevkî Çelebi's last great task was to present a summary of Firdevsî-i Rûmî's *Süleymannâme* to Süleyman the Magnificent, but his death at an old age prevented him from fulfilling that ambition.[28]

## 1   Hagiography of Emîr Sultan (*Menâkıb-ı Emîr Sultan*)

Şevkî explained that his main reason for writing a hagiography of Emîr Sultan was to prepare himself for the afterworld. He claimed to have undertaken the task at the suggestion of one of his friends, but failed to provide the name of that friend.[29]

The sources tell us that Emîr Sultan was born in Bukhara and, after a pilgrimage to Mecca, had come to Bursa with a number of disciples. His original name had been Şemseddin Muhammed b. Ali el-Huseynî.[30] According to the sixteenth-century Ottoman historian Gelibolulu Mustafa Âlî, Emîr was not only a saint endowed with "limitless miracles" (*kerâmât-ı bî-ğâyât ile mevşûf olan 'azîzdir*),[31] but also a man of great learning and enthusiasm. He had also studied Sadreddin Konevî's *Miftâhu'l-ğayb* ("Key to the Invisible World") – the classification of the sciences – under the guidance of Molla Fenârî.[32]

As Şevkî explained, there are numerous different versions of Emîr Sultan's *menâkıb*, from which he selected eighteen.[33] In his work, Şevkî omitted stories

---

27   Halil İnalcık, "State, Sovereignty and Law during the Reign of Süleyman", in *Süleyman the Second and His Time*, edited by Halil İnalcık and Cemal Kafadar (Istanbul: Isis Press, 1993), 71.

28   "Firdevsî'nün üç yüz altmış mücelled *Süleymân nâme*'sin telḫîṣe başın aşağa egüp niçe yıl tażyî'-i evḳāt itmiş idi. Ol müsvedde beyâża çıkmadın dest-i ecel bunun ismin ḥayât defterinden terâş itdi, dîvân-ḫâne-i maḥşerde ḳıṣṣa-i a'mâlin okumağa gitdi". Âşık Çelebi, *Meşâ'ir*, 1450. For an analysis of the Ottoman literature about the life of the Prophet Solomon, see Hüseyin Akkaya, *The Prophet Solomon in Ottoman Turkish Literature and the Süleymâniye of Şemseddin Sivasî, Textual Analysis, Critical Edition and Facsimile* [Part I: Textual Analysis], (Cambridge, MA: Harvard University, 1997), 29–49.

29   Baba, "Menâkıb-ı Emîr Sultan", 8.

30   Mustafa Âlî, *Künhü'l-Ahbâr: Dördüncü Rükn: Osmanlı tarihi: Tıpkıbasım*, vol. 1 (Ankara: TTK, 2009), 43–4.

31   Âlî, *Künhü'l-Ahbâr*, 44.

32   Âlî, *Künhü'l-Ahbâr*, 44.

33   Baba, "Menâkıb-ı Emîr Sultan", 18.

about Bayezid I's wine drinking and about Emîr Sultan's criticism of the sultan. It thus seems that he respected the *velî* status of Ottoman sultans and saw it as a great honour to serve the sultans, whom he regarded as friends of God. In Şevkî's world, there was little difference between being *türbedar* of the Ottoman sultans and recording the deeds of Muslim saints.

Linda T. Darling saw Bayezid I's defeat by Timur at the Battle of Ankara (1402) as "the death of a cosmopolitan identity".[34] Bayezid I had formed his empire with the help of not only his Muslim subjects but also his Christian vassals, who took part in the Siege of Constantinople (1394–1402) and in the conquest of the Anatolian principalities.[35] Bayezid had been on the point of conquering the Byzantine capital and the residents of Constantinople were planning to surrender the city to him.[36] Bayezid's empire was, in Darling's words, "a hybrid, multi-religious and multi-cultural state", but both Muslim and Christian men of religion harshly criticized his policies.[37] Having been educated in Kütahya, 'the cultural capital of Anatolia',[38] Bayezid was regarded as an intellectual figure. Darling argues that he adopted a "ghazi rhetoric" as a result of "the legitimacy contest with Timur".[39] Bayezid had also supported the opening of a Kâzerûnî lodge in the Ottoman capital in the period between the Battle of Nicopolis (1396) and the Battle of Ankara (1402). This event can be viewed as a symbolic gesture to those dervishes who devoted themselves to the service of the sheikh of the ghazis, Ebû İshâk-ı Kâzerûnî, and to the sultan of the ghazis, Yıldırım Bayezid Han.

Not only dervishes but also historians took part in Bayezid's 'legitimacy contest with Timur'. According to Mehmed Neşrî, Timur was "the most evil person" (*Timur a'zam-ı eşirrâ idi*) in the world.[40] However, in the eyes of the

---

34   Linda T. Darling, "Reformulating the Ghazi Narrative: When was the Ottoman State a Ghazi State", *Turcica*, 43 2011 41. Although I appreciate Darling's point about Bayezid's cosmopolitanism, I think that Bayezid was a forerunner to Mehmed II in establishing a cosmopolitan identity in the Ottoman Empire. The efforts of Bayezid I and Mehmed II can be compared with Jalaluddin Muhammad Akbar's policies in India in terms of listening and appealing to the different voices throughout their empires but without losing their ghazi spirit.
35   Darling, "Reformulating", 41.
36   Nevra Necipoğlu, *Byzantium between the Ottomans and the Latins: Politics and Society in the Late Empire* (New York: CUP, 2009), 182.
37   Darling, "Reformulating", 41.
38   Darling, "Reformulating", 41.
39   Darling, "Reformulating", 41.
40   Mehmed Neşrî, *Kitâb-ı Cihan-nümâ: Neşrî Tarihi*, edited by Faik Reşit Unat and Mehmed A. Köymen, vol.1 (Ankara: TTK, 1995), 347. Like Şevkî Çelebi, Neşrî also lived in Bursa and pursued "a quiet and obscure life". For more information about Neşrî, see V. L. Ménage, *Neshrî's History of the Ottomans: The Sources and Development of the Text* (London: OUP, 1964), 4–5.

Anatolian principalities, he was a saviour. Following Bayezid's 1398 invasion of the Karamanid principality, the Karamanids perceived Timur as their liberator from Ottoman rule.[41] Perhaps, not surprisingly, the Karamanid dervishes also took Timur's side against Bayezid. For instance, a Karamanid sheikh, Seyyid Ali Semerkandî (d.860/1455–56), is said to have asked one of his disciples, Evhadüddin-i Horasanî, to help Timur against Bayezid I.[42]

Fifteenth-century Ottoman historians disapproved both of Bayezid I's marriage to a Serbian princess, 'Despina Hatun' (Olivera Despina Lazarević), and of his drinking habits.[43] According to other historians, however, Bayezid was "not corrupt and did not consume wine" and was a true ghazi.[44] Şevkî's approach to Bayezid was closer to the latter position.

As Şevkî saw it, there was not much difference between his world and that of Bayezid I, who built the first dervish lodge in honour of Kâzerûnî and Şehzâde Bayezid, the son of Süleyman the Magnificent, to whom he presented the *Menâkıb-ı Emîr Sultan*. In the 1550s, Şehzâde Bayezid and his brother Selim were competing candidates to succeed their father to the Ottoman throne. Şevkî thought that Bayezid deserved to be the sultan of the Ottoman throne (*sezâvâr-ı tâc u taht*),[45] especially since his contemporaries regarded him as a "pious, generous and benevolent governor".[46] In fact, when he was serving as governor of Kütahya, he was surrounded by the scholars and poets of the time[47] and Şevkî may well have visited him there at that time. In Şevkî's words,

---

41  For more information about the Karamanids' view of Timur, see Fatih Bayram, "Zâviye-Khankâhs and -Religious Orders in the Province of Karaman: The Seljukid, Karamanoğlu and the Ottoman Periods, 1200–1512" (Ph.D. dissertation, Bilkent University, 2008), 160–2.

42  "Ḥażret-i Ḳuṭb [Seyyid Ali Semerkandî] beni ... nuṣret-i cüyûş ḫıdmetine ḳodı.... Ḥattâ Tîmûr Sulṭân Yıldırım'ı aḫẕ eyledi ki Tîmûr Ḫân'ın nuṣretine me'mûl olmuşdum". See Seyyid Nizam Bedahşî, *Menâkıb-i Seyyid Ali Semerkandî*, fol. 97a, MS 4603, Hacı Mahmud Efendi, SK. For more information about Seyyid Ali Semerkandî and his works, see Fatih Bayram, "Timur İstilasına Beylikler Dünyasından Bakış: Karaman Diyarı'nda Cennet Bahçeleri", in *Prof. Dr Erdoğan Merçil'e Armağan*, eds. Emine Uyumaz, Muharrem Kesik, Aydın Usta et al. (Istanbul: Bilge Kültür Sanat, 2013), 308–16.

43  Darling, "Reformulating", 41.

44  Darling, "Reformulating", 43.

45  Baba, "Menâkıb-ı Emîr Sultan ", 14–16. One of the poets who sought the patronage of Şehzâde Bayezid was Emre, who used similar words to praise Bayezid: "Şâh-ı 'âdil kâm-bahş ü dest-gîr/Lâyık-ı tâc u sezâ olur serîr". See Filiz Kılıç, *Şehzade Bayezid "Şâhî", Hayatı ve Divanı* (Ankara: Kültür Bakanlığı Yayınları, 2000), 35.

46  Halil İnalcık, "Sen Olasan Kaleme İ'tibar İçün Hâmî: Fuzûlî ve Patronaj", in *Cultural Horizons: A Festschrift in honor of Talat S. Halman*, edited by Jayne L. Warner (Syracuse, NY: Syracuse University Press, 2001), 310.

47  Şerafettin Turan, "Bayezid, Şehzâde (ö. 969/1562)", *DIA* 5, 231.

Prince Bayezid was far more generous than Hâtim et-Tâ'î.[48] Similarly, Bayezid's justice was much like that of the Sasanian emperor Khosrow I Anushirvan (*Cihanda 'adl ile Nûşirevandur*).[49]

Şevkî saw both Şehzâde Bayezid and Emîr Sultan as representing the gate of felicity. According to a story about Emîr's spiritual successor (*halîfe*), Şeyh Sinan, he reached "the gate of felicity" when he found the house of his future sheikh in Bursa.[50]

There is an interesting story in Emîr Sultan's menâkıb about his marriage to Bayezid I's daughter, in which two subjects – a dream and a ghaza (a military expedition to promote Islam) – feature. Bayezid's daughter had a dream that led to her decision to marry Emîr Sultan. At that time, Bayezid I was engaged in a ghaza. When Bayezid heard the news of this marriage he became very angry.[51] According to the story, he sent his vizier Süleyman Pasha to punish Emîr Sultan.[52] However, all the vizier's attempts to punish Emîr Sultan proved futile. Eventually, the sultan regretted what he did to prevent the marriage.[53] It was the *kadı* of Bursa, Molla Fenârî, who persuaded the sultan to accept the inevitable.[54]

## 2   Hagiography of Ebû İshâk-ı Kâzerûnî (*Menâkıb-ı Ebû İshâk-ı Kâzerûnî*)

As far as we know, Şevkî undertook the first Turkish translation of the Persian hagiography of Ebû İshâk-ı Kâzerûnî. The translation is not an exact one, since Şevkî left out some parts of the Persian version titled Ferdous al-Morşediyya, which is in turn a translation by Maḥmūd bin 'Uthmān of an original Arabic text.

---

48  "Seḥâ'da Ḥâtem-i Ṭâ'î bendesidür – 'Aṭâ' itmekde ḫalḳ efkendesidür". Şevkî, *Menâkıb-ı Emîr Sulṭân*, fol. 5b.

49  Şevkî, *Menâkıb-ı Emîr Sulṭân*, fol. 6a.

50  "Bir ḳapuya irdük. Ne ḳapu! Der-i devlet ve âsitâne-i sa'âdet imiş". Şevkî, *Menâkıb-ı Emîr Sulṭân*, fol. 34a.

51  "Yıldırım Bâyezîd Ḫân ziyâde ġażûb idi, dirler". Baba, "Menâkıb-ı Emîr Sultan", 77.

52  Süleyman Pasha was criticized for his severity and merciless behaviour. For example, "when this news reached Süleyman Pasha, it did not soften his heart, being harder than stone and firmer than iron" (*Bu haber Süleyman Paşa'ya vardı. Taşdan katı ve demürden muhkem gönline eser itmedi*). See Baba, "Menâkıb-ı Emîr Sultan", 85–6.

53  "Yıldırım Padişah itdügi fiile nedâmet idüb peşiman olub istiğfâr itdi". Baba, "Menâkıb-ı Emîr Sultan", 89.

54  Considering Emîr Sultan's *sayyid* status, Molla Fenârî thought that his marriage to Bayezid's daughter was a divine blessing to the Ottoman house: "*Bir hümâ-yı devlet ve hümâ-yı saâdetdür kim başumuza kondı*". Baba, "Menâkıb-ı Emîr Sultan", 92.

Ottoman sultans rated the Kâzerûnî order very highly.[55] Bayezid I built the first dervish lodge (*zâviye*) in honour of Kâzerûnî, and Mehmed II (r.1444–46; 1451–81) renewed the deed of trust of the pious endowment (*vakfiye*) of this lodge. It is no coincidence that Bayezid, who was known as 'the sultan of the ghazis',[56] built a *zâviye* to honour the sheikh of the ghazis, Ebû İshâk-ı Kâzerûnî, in the then Ottoman capital, Bursa.[57] In the *vakfiye*, dated 802/1399, the *zâviye* is described as "the house of Ebû İshâk" (*Ebû İshâkhâne*).[58]

Later, Ottoman sultans continued to respect the Kâzerûnî order, whose sheikh presided over both ghazis and sailors at sea. For instance, Süleyman I visited the dervish lodge of Kâzerûnî in Erzurum during his campaign against the Safavid state.[59]

Ebû İshâk İbrahim bin Şehriyâr (d.426/1035) was born in Kâzerûn, a town close to Shiraz, Iran, in 352/963. Over the centuries, many dervish lodges were built to commemorate the Kâzerûnî in Islamic lands stretching from the Balkans to China. Most of their *zâviye*s were built in port cities[60] and, compared with other lodges, these dervish ones were also centres of material wealth. Nearly three centuries after the death of Kâzerûnî, Ibn Battuta visited his tomb and explained why the Kâzerûnî lodges amassed such great wealth:

> I left Shiraz to visit the tomb of pious Sheikh Abu Ishak al-Kazerunî at Kazerun, which lies two days' journey [west] from Shiraz. This Sheikh is held in high honour by the inhabitants of India and China. Travellers on the Sea of China, when the wind turns against them and they fear pirates, usually made vows to Abu Ishak, each one setting down in writing what he has vowed.[61]

There is also a chapter on the importance of vows in the hagiography; thus, "the vowings of the sheikh (his excellency) were fruitful and of special virtue."[62] According to the author of the *menâkıb*, a vow is a miracle (*kerâmet*) on the

---

55    Turan, *Türk Cihan Hakimiyeti*, 122.

56    Halil İnalcık, *Devlet-i 'Aliyye-Osmanlı İmparatorluğu Üzerine Araştırmalar-I* (Istanbul: Türkiye İş Bankası Kültür Yayınları, 2010), 68.

57    Mustafa Kara, *Bursa'da Tarikatlar ve Tekkeler* (Bursa: Sır Yayıncılık, 2001), 99.

58    Adnan Erzi, "Bursa'da İshakî Dervişlerine Mahsus Zaviyenin Vakfiyesi", *Vakıflar Dergisi* 2 (1942) 423.

59    Turan, *Türk Cihan Hakimiyeti*, 122.

60    Kara, *Bursa'da Tarikatlar*, 95.

61    Ibn Battuta, *Travels in Asia and Africa, 1325–1354*, translated by H. A. R. Gibb (London: Darf Publishers, 1983), 97.

62    "Şeyḫ ḥażretlerinün nüzūrınun semeresini ve ḫāṣıyetini beyān ider". Şevkî, *Menâkıb-ı Kâzerûnî*, fol. 98a–102b.

part of the sheikh insofar as when someone expresses a desire for something, it is thanks to the sheikh's *baraka* (blessing) that God fulfils that person's wish.[63]

The life story of Ebû İshâk-ı Kâzerûni has been written in its original form by Abū Bakr Muḥammad al-Khaṭīb (d.502/1108–9), who was the third sheikh of the central lodge in Kâzerûn after the death of Ebû İshâk.[64] This Arabic hagiography, unfortunately lost, was translated into Persian by Maḥmūd bin 'Uthmān in the year 728/1327–28 under the title Ferdous al-Moršediyya.[65] Fritz Meier published a German version of the Persian translation of Kâzerûni's hagiography under the title *Die Vita des Scheich Ebû Ishaq al-Kâzarûnî*.[66] A. J. Arberry points out another Persian translation of the Arabic original, titled "Remarks of the Noble Persons on the Life of the Sheikh" (*Marṣad al-aḥrâr ilâ siyar al-muršid*). In the words of Arberry, *Marṣad* was an "inflated translation of Abū Bakr al-Khaṭīb's Arabic original."[67] According to Arberry, *Marṣad* was completed around the year 750/1349.[68] Its author was Rajā' Muhammad al-Kâzarûnî, nicknamed 'Alā.[69] It should be noted that there is no mention of 'Alā's *Marṣad* in Şevkî's Turkish translation.

Not only did the Ottoman sultans venerate the name of Kâzerûnî, but so too did the pre-Ottoman Anatolian principalities. In the *Dânişmendnâme*, an epic work depicting the collective memory of the Anatolian Turks during the Crusades, there is a reference to Ebû İshak's banner (*'alem*). The relevant passage explains how the regiments were organized in the dervish army. At the front were the *sayyids*, the Prophet's descendants, followed by the sons of sheikhs and dervishes. Bare-headed, barefooted dervishes bearing

---

63 "Bil ve âgâh ol ki Ḥaḳ Te'âlâ sana raḥmet eylesün. Şeyḫün ḳaddesellahu rûḥahu'l-'azîzü cümle kerâmetinden biri nezirdür. Her kimse ki bir niyetün ḫuşûliçün nezr itmiş ola. Şeyḫün himmeti berekâtında nezrini edâ itdükden ṣonra ber-murâd olur ve maḳṣūdı her neyise ḥâṣıl olur. Ḥaḳ Te'âlâ bu ḫâṣṣai hemân şeyḫ ḥażretlerine virmişdür". Şevkî, *Menâḳıb-ı Kâzerûnî*, fol. 98b.

64 Kara, *Bursa'da Tarikatlar*, 87 ff. b. 'Utman, *Die Vita des Scheich Ebû Ishaq al-Kâzarûnî*, edited by Fritz Meier (Leipzig: Deutsche Morgenländische Gesellschaft, 1948), 1. Şevkî also refers to Ebûbekir Muhammed as follows: "*Ḫaṭîb-i İmâm-ı Ebûbekr-i Muḥammed ibni 'Abdü'l-kerîm raḥmetullahi 'aleyh ki Ḥażret-i Şeyḫün ḫulefâsındandur. Ḥattâ şeyḫün siyerini ve menâḳıbını cem' idüb bir kitâb-ı 'Arabî idendür. Beyne'n-nâs meşhûr ve müte'ârefdür*". Şevkî, *Menâḳıb-ı Kâzerûnî*, fol. 10b.

65 Fritz Meier, "The Sumâdiyya: A Branch Order of the Qâdiriyya in Damascus", in Fritz Meier, *Essays on Islamic Piety and Mysticism*, edited by Bernd Radtke, translated by John O'Kane (Leiden: Brill, 1999), 304.

66 'Utman, *Die Vita des Scheich*, passim.

67 A. J. Arberry, "The Biography of Shaikh Ebû İshaq al-Kâzarûnî", *Oriens* 3 (2) (1950), 164.

68 Arberry, "The Biography of Shaikh", 177.

69 Arberry, "The Biography of Shaikh", 164.

golden-headed Ebû İshak banners would walk along, as their tongues busily praised God and recited verses from the Quran foretelling victory for the Muslims.[70]

It is possible that Kâzerûnî dervishes began to enter Anatolia following the Battle of Manzikert (1071).[71] According to Osman Turan, the Kâzerunî order began to expand in the Saltuk lands, another Turkoman principality in eastern Anatolia, in the twelfth century. The reason behind the spread of Kâzerûnî dervishes in eastern Anatolia might be attributed to the Saltukids' ghaza raids into Georgia.[72] We know that Ebû İshâk-ı Kâzerûnî himself was sending his disciples to the ghaza raids in the Byzantine lands.[73] Nevertheless, the ultimate institutionalization of the order became possible under the patronage of the Ottoman sultans, particularly Bayezid I and Mehmed II.

There was also a Kâzerûnî lodge in the Karamanoğlu principality. Karamanoğlu Mehmet Beg II built the Kâzerûnî zâviye in Konya in 821/1418. Yet, the *vakfiye* was, on the instruction of the same ruler, written two years before the completion of the *zâviye* building. Interestingly, in the inscription on the building, Karamanoğlu Mehmed Beg is described as a ghazi sultan. In this *vakfiye*, Ebû İshâk-ı Kâzerûnî is called "the master of the poles and of the followers of the spiritual path" (*seyyidu'l-aktâb ve's-sâlikîn*).[74] It was the Ottoman sultan Mehmed II who renewed the *vakıf* following the incorporation of the Karamanid principality into Ottoman lands.

---

70   "Gâzîler kamu işlerin kolaylar/İşit nicesi düzüldi alaylar
Pes evvel yürüdi Seyyid ü sâdât/Meşâyih-zâde vü ehl-i sa'âdât
Dahî berehne ser pâ nice derviş/Yürürdi anlarunla yâd ü biliş
Başı altun 'alemler ellerinde/Huda'nun zikri dâyim dillerinde
Bu âyet yazılubdı her 'alemde/Ki gören okuyan ola selemde
Abū İshak'ın idi ol 'alemler/ İşit altunla ne yazmış kalemler
Pes-oku sen dahī: 'Nasrun min' Allah'/Ki nusret vire mü'minlere Allah
Hem okı ba 'dehû: 'Fethun karîb'i/Ki kahr ide Hudā Ehl-i Salībi
Pes ol cemiyyet ile ehl-i İslam/Yüridiler çalub zil dühlile bâm".
Melik Danişmend, *La Geste de Melik Dânişmend: Étude Critique du Dânişmendnâme*, edited by Irène Mélikoff, vol. 2 (Paris: Librairie Adrien Maisonneuve, 1960), 157–8. For the French translation of this passage see *La Geste de Melik Dânişmend* 1, 342–3. See also M. Fuad Köprülü, "Anadolu Selçukluları Tarihi'nin Yerli Kaynakları", *Belleten* 7 no. 27 (1943), 379–458. According to the Kâzerûnî sources, the banner of Ebû İshak was also highly esteemed by the Mamluk sultans. For further information, see Şevkî, *Menâkıb-ı Kâzerûnî*, fol. 85a–85b.

71   There is a Kâzerûnî *makâm* (station) in Malazgird. See Kamil Uğurlu, *Konya Şehrengizi* (Konya: Konya Büyükşehir Belediyesi, 2005), 63–4.

72   Osman Turan, *Doğu Anadolu Türk Devletleri Tarihi* (Istanbul: Turan Neşriyat Yurdu, 1973), 122.

73   Hamid Algar, "Kâzerûnî", *DIA* 25, 145.

74   İbrahim Hakkı Konyalı, *Âbideleri ve Kitabeleri ile Konya Tarihi* (Konya: Enes Kitap Sarayı, 1997), 915–916.

The first registers of pious foundations (*evkaf defteri*), compiled for the province of Karaman in 881/1476 after the Ottoman conquest, mentions the Kâzerûnî lodge, and states that it was still functioning".[75] The *evkaf defteri* of 888/1483 also confirms the presence of the Kâzerûnî lodge in Konya, and states that the *vakıf* of the *zâviye* had been acknowledged by the imperial edict of the then deceased sultan Mehmed II (*be-berât-i Sulṭân Meḥmed ṭâbe serâhu*).[76] This register also venerates Kâzerûnî as the "spiritual master of the horizons" (*vakf-ı zâviye-i mürşid-i âfâk Şeyḫ Ebû İshâḳ-ı Kâzerûnî raḥmetullahi ʿaleyh*).[77] The same words are repeated in the *evkaf defteri* of 992/1582.[78] There were also other Kâzerûnî *zâviyes* in Ottoman Turkish cities such as Bursa, Edirne and Erzurum.[79]

Instead of using the word convent (*tekke*) or lodge (*zâviye*), Kâzerûnî authors like Şevkî preferred to use the word *ribat* (frontier military station) when referring to their dervish lodges. According to the text that Şevkî translated, there were sixty *ribat*s when the founder sheikh was alive. The central dervish lodge was located at Kazerun and the second largest one was at Nishapur in northeastern Iran.[80] Each day food was served to 400 dervishes in the central lodge at Kazerun.[81] As the name implies, the Kâzerûnî *ribat*s served not only as dervish lodges, but also as military garrisons organizing *ghaza* raids into 'infidel lands', including the land of Rûm, namely Anatolia.[82] If Şevkî's text is true, the Kâzerûnî raids into Anatolia began when Sheikh Kâzerûnî was still alive. It was thus likely that the Kâzerûnî *ghazi*s were active in Anatolia even before the arrival of Seljuks into the land of Rûm.

Şevkî Çelebi's life story is typical of that of an Ottoman man of learning, as are his works. To the Ottomans, *ghaza*, in the words of Metin Kunt, was "the

---

75  Konyalı, *Konya Tarihi*, 916.
76  Fahri Coşkun, "888/1483 Tarihli Karaman Eyaleti Vakf Tahrir Defteri (Tanıtım, Tahlil ve Metin)", *Vakıflar Dergisi* 33 (2010) 47.
77  Coşkun, "888/1483 Tarihli", 47.
78  Konyalı, *Konya Tarihi*, 916.
79  Konyalı, *Konya Tarihi*, 919.
80  "Ḫaṭîb-i İmâm Ebûbekir eydür: "İşitdüm Şeyḫ Ebû Caʿfer-i Enṣâr'den, didi kim: Şeyḫün altmış ribâṭı var idi. Şeyḫ aḥbâbını ol ribâṭlara ḳısmet itmiş idi. Her fütûḥ ki vâḳiʿ olurdı, ol ribâṭlara ḳısmet iderdi. İki ribâṭ şeyḫ-i mürşidün idi. Biri şehr-i Nîşâbûr'da ve biri ḳarye-i Sîrân'da idi". Şevkî, *Menâḳıb-ı Kâzerûnî*, fol. 34b.
81  "Ol vaktin her gün dört yüz kimse ṣûfîlerden ḥâẓır olub ṭaʿâm yirlerdi". Şevkî, *Menâḳıb-ı Kâzerûnî*, fol. 77a.
82  "Râvî-yi ṣâdıḳu'l-aḳvâlden menḳûldür ki bir gün şeyḫ ḥażretleri İslâm leşkerini cemʿ idüb Rûm'a gönderdi". Şevkî, *Menâḳıb-ı Kâzerûnî*, fol. 36b. Şevkî does not explain the *ghaza* raids into Anatolia in detail. Instead, he refers the reader to *Ferdous al-Morşediyya* of Mahmud b. Osman: "Bâḳî ḥikâyet-i ġazâ ve rivâyet-i mücâhede-i nefs-i emmâre Kitâbü'l-Mürşidî'de mesṭûrdur". Şevkî, *Menâḳıb-ı Kâzerûnî*, fol. 37a.

greatest virtue".[83] Şevkî looked after the tombs of *ghazi* sultans and kept his position as the *türbedar* of Osman Gazi and Orhan Gazi until his death, the date of which is not exactly known. He was a compiler of the miraculous deeds of the *ghazis*' sheikhs, Emîr Sultan and Ebû İshâk-ı Kâzerûnî.

Şevkî lived a humble lifestyle in Bursa, preferring not to be heard of in the new Ottoman capital. For him, Bursa was not only the city of Osman Gazi, Orhan Gazi, Murad I Hüdâvendigâr, Bayezid Han, Kâzerûnî and Emîr Sultan, but it was also where the then sultan, Selim, recognized his face in a huge crowd. When the sultan went to the new Ottoman capital, he left the old capital in the custody of 'his' Şevkî.

## Bibliography

### *Primary Sources*
Süleymaniye Kütüphanesi Library (SK)

Şevkî, *Menâkıb-ı Ebû İshak Kâzerûnî*. MS no. 2429. Esad Efendi, Süleymaniye Kütüphanesi.

Seyyid Nizam Bedahşî, *Menâkıb-i Seyyid Ali Semerkandî*, MS no. 4603, Hacı Mahmud Efendi.

Konya Mevlânâ Müzesi Kütüphanesi Library

Şevkî. *Menâkıb-ı Emîr Sultan*. MS no. 4940. Mevlânâ Müzesi Kütüphanesi Yazmaları.

### *Published Primary Sources*
Âşık Çelebi. *Meşâ'irü'ş-Şu'arâ*, edited by Filiz Kılıç. 3 vols. Istanbul: İstanbul Araştırmaları Enstitüsü, 2010.

Kınalızade Hasan Çelebi. *Tezkiretü'ş-Şuarâ*, edited by İbrahim Kutluk. 2 vols. Ankara: TTK, 1989.

Mehmed Neşrî. *Kitâb-ı Cihan-nümâ: Neşrî Tarihi*, edited by Faik Reşit Unat and Mehmed A. Köymen, 3rd edition. 2 vols. Ankara: TTK, 1995.

Mustafa Âlî. *Künhü'l-Ahbâr: Dördüncü Rükn: Osmanlı Tarihi: Tıpkıbasım*, vol. 1. Ankara: TTK, 2009.

Şevkî Çelebi. *Menâkıb-ı Ebû İshâk-ı Kâzerûnî. Ebû İshâk İbrâhîm Kâzerûnî'nin Menâkıbı*, edited by Fatih Bayram. Istanbul: TYEKBY, 2016.

---

83  Metin Kunt, "State and Sultan up to the Age of Süleyman: Frontier Principality to World Empire", in *Süleyman the Magnificent and His Age*, edited by Metin Kunt and Christine Woodhead (London: Longman, 2001), 12.

'Utman, Mahmud b. *Die Vita des Scheich Abû Ishâq al-Kâzarûnî (Firdevsü'l-Mürşidiyye fî esrâri's-samediyye)*, edited by Fritz Meier. Leipzig: Deutsche Morgenländische Gesellschaft, 1948.

### Secondary Sources

Akkaya, Hüseyin. *The Prophet Solomon in Ottoman Turkish Literature and the Süleymâniye of Şemseddin Sivasî, Textual Analysis, Critical Edition and Facsimile* [Part I: Textual Analysis]. Cambridge, MA: Harvard University, 1997.

Algar, Hamid. "Kâzerûnî." In *DIA*, vol. 25. Ankara, 2002.

Algül, Hüseyin and Nihat Azamat. "Emîr Sultan." In *DIA*, vol. 11. Istanbul, 1995.

Arberry, A. J. "The Biography of Shaikh Abû İshaq al-Kâzarûnî." *Oriens* 3 (2) 1950, 163–82.

Armağan, Abdüllatif. "XVI. Yüzyılda Teke Sancağı'nın Yönetimi ve Yöneticileri." *Ankara Üniversitesi Dil ve Tarih-Coğrafya Fakültesi Türkoloji Dergisi* 18 (1) 2011, 273–93.

Baba, Mustafa Okan. "Menâkıb-ı Emîr Sultan (Metin-İnceleme-Gramer-İndeks)". Ph.D. dissertation, Marmara University, 1991.

Bayram, Fatih. "Zâviye-Khankâhs and -Religious Orders in the Province of Karaman: The Seljukid, Karamanoğlu and the Ottoman Periods, 1200–1512". Ph.D. dissertation, Bilkent University, 2008.

Bayram, Fatih. "Timur İstilasına Beylikler Dünyasından Bakış: Karaman Diyarı'nda Cennet Bahçeleri". *Prof. Dr Erdoğan Merçil'e Armağan*, edited by Emine Uyumaz, Muharrem Kesik, Aydın Usta et al., 308–16. Istanbul: Bilge Kültür Sanat, 2013.

Bursalı Mehmed Tâhir. *Osmanlı Müellifleri*. Edited by Mustafa Tatcı and Cemâl Kurnaz, 3 vols. Ankara: Bizim Büro, 2000.

Buzpınar, Ş. Tufan. "Nakîbüleşraf." *DIA*, vol. 32. Istanbul, 2006.

Çakar, Enver. "XVI. Yüzyılda Şam Beylerbeyiliğinin İdarî Taksimatı." *Fırat Üniversitesi Sosyal Bilimler Dergisi* 3 (1) 2003, 351–74.

Coşkun, Fahri. "888/1483 Tarihli Karaman Eyaleti Vakıf Tahrir Defteri (Tanıtım, Tahlil ve Metin)." *Vakıflar Dergisi* 33 (2010).

Danişmend, İsmail Hami. *Osmanlı Devlet Erkânı*. Istanbul: Türkiye Yayınevi, 1971.

Danişmend, Melik. *La Geste de Melik Dânişmend, Étude Critique du Dânişmendnâme*, edited and translated by Irène Mélikoff. 2 vols. Paris: Librairie Adrien Maisonneuve, 1960.

Darling, Linda T. "Reformulating the Ghazi Narrative: When was the Ottoman State a Ghazi State." *Turcica* 43 (2011) 13–53.

Emecen, Feridun M. *Zamanın İskenderi, Şarkın Fatihi Yavuz Sultan Selim*. Istanbul: Yitik Hazine Yayınları, 2010.

Erünsal, İsmail E. *Osmanlılarda Sahaflık ve Sahaflar*. Istanbul: Timaş Yayınları, 2013.

Erzi, Adnan. "Bursa'da İshakî Dervişlerine mahsus Zâviyenin Vakfiyesi," *Vakıflar Dergisi* 2 (1942) 423–9.

Ibn Battuta. *Travels in Asia and Africa, 1325–1354*. Translated and compiled by H. A. R. Gibb. London: Darf Publishers, 1983.

İnalcık, Halil. "State, Sovereignty and Law during the Reign of Süleyman." In *Süleyman the Second and His Time*, edited by Halil İnalcık and Cemal Kafadar, 59–92. Istanbul: Isis Press, 1993.

İnalcık, Halil. "How to Read Âşıkpaşazâde's History." In *Essays in Ottoman History*, 31–50. Istanbul: Eren Yayınları, 1998.

İnalcık, Halil. "Sen Olasan Kaleme İ'tibar İçün Hâmî: Fuzûlî ve Patronaj." In *Cultural Horizons: A Festschrift in Honor of Talat S. Halman*, edited by Jayne L. Warner, 308–15. Syracuse, NY: Syracuse University Press, 2001.

İnalcık, Halil. *Devlet-i 'Aliyye-Osmanlı İmparatorluğu Üzerine Araştırmalar-I*. Istanbul: Türkiye İş Bankası Kültür Yayınları, 2010.

Kara, Mustafa. *Bursa'da Tarikatlar ve Tekkeler*. Bursa: Sır Yayıncılık, 2001.

Kılıç, Filiz. *Şehzade Bayezid "Şâhî", Hayatı ve Divanı*. Ankara: Kültür Bakanlığı Yayınları, 2000.

Konyalı, İ. Hakkı. *Âbideleri ve Kitabeleriyle Konya Tarihi*. Konya: Enes Kitap Sarayı, 1997.

Köprülü, M. Fuad. "Anadolu Selçukluları Tarihi'nin Yerli Kaynakları." *Belleten* 7 (27) July 1943, 379–458.

Kunt, Metin. "State and Sultan up to the Age of Süleyman: Frontier Principality to World Empire." In Metin Kunt and Christine Woodhead (eds) *Süleyman the Magnificent and His Age*. London: Longman, 2001, 3–29.

Kut, Günay. "Âşık Çelebi (ö. 979/1572)". In *DIA*, vol. 3. Istanbul, 1991.

Mehmed Süreyya. *Sicill-i Osmanî, Osmanlı Ünlüleri*. 6 vols. Edited by Nuri Akbayar and Seyit Ali Kahraman. Istanbul: Tarih Vakfı Yurt Yayınları, 1996. First published 1308/189–91 by Matbaa-i Âmire.

Meier, Fritz. *Essays on Islamic Piety and Mysticism*, edited by Bernd Radtke, translated by John O'Kane. Leiden: Brill, 1999.

Ménage, V. L. *Neshrî's History of the Ottomans: The Sources and Development of the Text*. London: Oxford University Press, 1964.

Necipoğlu, Nevra. *Byzantium between the Ottomans and the Latins: Politics and Society in the Late Empire*. New York: Cambridge University Press, 2009.

Toynbee, Arnold J. *Acquaintances*. London: Oxford University Press, 1967.

Turan, Osman. *Doğu Anadolu Türk Devletleri Tarihi*. Istanbul: Turan Neşriyat Yurdu, 1973.

Turan, Osman. *Türk Cihân Hâkimiyeti Mefkûresi Tarihi. Türk Dünya Nizâmının Millî, İslâmî ve İnsanî Esasları*. Istanbul: Ötüken Yayınları, 2006.

Turan, Şerafettin. "Bayezid, Şehzâde (ö. 969/1562)," *DIA*, vol. 5, 231.

Uğurlu, Kamil. *Konya Şehrengizi*. Konya: Konya Büyükşehir Belediyesi, 2005.

CHAPTER 6

# The Personal Anthology of an Ottoman Litterateur: Celâlzâde Sâlih (d.1565) and His *Mecmua*

*Cornell H. Fleischer and Kaya Şahin*

This chapter revolves around the autograph *mecmua* of Celâlzâde Sâlih (*c*.1495–1565), compiled by the author towards the end of his life as a selection from his own writings, both literary and epistolary.[1] The Süleymaniye manuscript (called as such to differentiate it from another copy, as discussed below), meant to be a representative summary of the author/compiler's œuvre, begins with letters sent by Sâlih to the sultan, various officials, and acquaintances (1b–21b; another letter is appended at the end of the following section, in 34a). It continues with a few panegyrics offered to grandees, and a selection of poetry (21b–33a). Next comes an account of the 1532–33 campaign against the Habsburgs, the so-called *Alaman seferi* (35a–82a). The Süleymaniye manuscript ends with a group of letters sent by Sâlih to Prince Bayezid (d.1561) and two members of his household concerning a translation project commissioned by the prince (82b–88b). Here, we will present preliminary findings and initial impressions that stem from a joint reading of the manuscript between the fall of 2013 and the fall of 2014. We will eventually publish the manuscript in a facsimile edition, with a critical and historical introduction. Because the *mecmua* affords testimony to themes dear to Metin Kunt's scholarly heart – such as the large-scale institutional and cultural transformations of the sixteenth century, the ideological and cultural functions of history-writing, and networks of patronage and solidarity – we have found the occasion of commemorating our common mentor and friend as an appropriate one to discuss this manuscript.

## 1   Celâlzâde Sâlih: A Biographical Sketch[2]

The life of Celâlzâde Sâlih reflects the tensions, challenges and opportunities of the Süleymanic era. Sâlih was born in Vushtrri/Vučitrn (O. Vulçıtrın, town in

---

1  Celâlzâde Sâlih, *Münşe'ât*, MS 557, Kadızâde Mehmed, SK.
2  Our summary of Sâlih's life is based on Zehra Toska, *Sâlih Çelebi and Mecnûn u Leylâ Mesnevisi*, Department of Near Eastern Languages and Literatures, Harvard University, 2007, 1–27.

present-day Kosovo), during his father Celâl's tenure there as a judge, c.1490–95. His elder brother Mustafa (c. 1490–1567), who served Selim I (r.1512–1520) and, most notably, Süleyman (r.1520–1566) as a secretary of the Imperial Council, chief secretary, and eventually chancellor between 1516 and 1557, would distinguish himself as the most prominent bureaucrat of the Süleymanic period.[3] The presence of his brother in the highest echelons of the central administration must have provided Sâlih with a critical level of access, as it will be seen below. After living in the Balkans for a time, and spending more than ten years in Amasya where he studied under his father's supervision,[4] Sâlih attended the lectures of Kemalpaşazâde Ahmed (c.1470–1534), one of the most prominent scholars, history writers and statesmen of the early sixteenth century.

Several sources mention the warm personal relationship between master and student, a closeness corroborated by a poem Sâlih personally submitted to Kemalpaşazâde while the latter was on his deathbed.[5] Despite this long and close relationship, Sâlih would receive his first appointment in 1520 at the hands of Hayreddin Efendi (d. 1543). When Süleyman came to the Ottoman throne, his tutor Hayreddin was given the right to select, from among his advanced students (*dânişmend*), those eligible (*mülâzım*) for a position as a teacher or a judge. Sâlih's move from Kemalpaşazâde Ahmed to Hayreddin, whose pragmatic bent was recognized and commented upon by his contemporaries, led to his appointment to a teaching position in Edirne's Saraciyye medrese in 1520. Sâlih's *mecmua* contains a letter dictated by Hayreddin (called Hâce Efendi in the letter's title) to Sâlih, and a letter sent by Sâlih to his old master on the occasion of his recovery from an illness.[6] The inclusion of these texts in his *mecmua* may be interpreted as Sâlih's urge to salute his teachers at the end of his life, as well as his desire to reply to the criticisms about his pragmatic move by emphasizing his close relationship with both masters.

---

3   On Celâlzâde Mustafa, see Kaya Şahin, *Empire and Power in the Reign of Süleyman: Narrating the Sixteenth-Century Ottoman World* (New York: Cambridge University Press, 2013); Mehmet Şakir Yılmaz, "'Koca Nişancı' of Kanuni: Celâlzâde Mustafa Çelebi, Bureaucracy and 'Kanun' in the Reign of Süleyman the Magnificent" (Ph.D. dissertation, Bilkent University, 2006).

4   See Celâlzâde Sâlih, *Münşe'ât*, fol. 88a: "Ve dâ'î-i fakīr ve bende-i hakīrleri eyyâm-ı şabâ ve evvel-i neşv ü nemâ on yıldan ziyâde ol zevâyâtda atamuz merhûm yanında tahṣîl-i 'ulûm iderdük."

5   Celâlzâde Sâlih, *Münşe'ât*, fol. 26a–27a. In 26a, Sâlih introduces his poem as follows: "Fâżıl-ı Rûm ve bahr-ı 'ulûm merhûm Kemâlpâşâoğlı'na denilmişdi. Maraż-ı mevte yatdukları esnâda iletdüm. Bu fakīrin kelimâtına mâ'ilidi. Kendü mübârek elleriyile elümden alub firâş üzre yaturken hem okurlar hem rikkatle ağlarlardı. Rahmetullahi 'aleyh." For other references to Kemalpaşazâde Ahmed in Sâlih's works, see Toska, *Sâlih Çelebi*, 3–4.

6   Celâlzâde Sâlih, *Münşe'ât*, fols. 10b–11b, and 11b–12b, respectively.

Sâlih was soon transferred to the capital, after submitting a poem to the new grand vizier İbrâhim Pasha (appointed in 1523) on the occasion of his inspection visit to Egypt in 1524–25. His brother Mustafa, who had become one of the grand vizier's closest collaborators and accompanied him to Egypt, must have been instrumental in securing a poem from his younger brother and presenting it to the grand vizier. As a teacher at the Murad Pasha medrese, and perhaps earlier, Sâlih began to try his hand at writing histories of Süleyman's military campaigns, which led to the capture of Belgrade (1521) and Rhodes (1522), and resulted in the destruction of the Hungarian kingdom and Süleyman's entry into Buda and Pest in 1526. It seems that Sâlih, at some point, developed the intention of gathering these individual texts within a larger history of Süleyman's reign.[7] He continued to write narratives on individual campaigns, as shown by his work on the *Alaman seferi* of 1532–33, included in the *mecmua*. Ottoman history writing, relatively few examples of which were composed in the reigns of Mehmed II (r.1444–46, 1451–81) and Bayezid II (r.1481–1512), developed after Süleyman's arrival to the throne to become a rich and varied field. This was partly due to new levels of palace patronage, and the keen interest (and acute anxiety) on the part of Süleyman and İbrâhim to explicate and legitimize an imperial venture that increasingly relied on (and promoted) ideas of messianic kingship and universal monarchy. Perhaps more importantly, the cataclysmic events that signalled the dawn of a global early modernity, such as the rise of several rival imperial/royal polities in the post-Mongol/post-medieval periods, and the expansion and popularization of debates about temporal and spiritual leadership, gave to the historical assessment of current events a particular urgency and promoted what may be called a Cinquecento *Zeitgeschichte*.

Sâlih continued his progress through the ranks of the medrese system, and became a teacher at the Atik Ali Pasha medrese (located in Istanbul) in 1535. Thanks to the positive reception of a *kaside* presented to grand vizier Ayas (which is reproduced in the *mecmua*, in 23a–24a), he was promoted, in 1536–37, to a teaching position at the then highest layer of the Ottoman medrese system, the Sahn-ı Seman in the capital. There, he translated into Ottoman Turkish, at the sultan's request, a Persian collection of moral stories and pseudo-historical

---

[7] We agree with Fatma Kaytaz's argument that Sâlih wrote individual campaign narratives first, and developed the intention of incorporating these within a larger history of Süleyman later. See Fatma Kaytaz, "*Târih-i Sefer-i Zafer-Rehber-i Alaman* Adlı Eserinin Tanıtımı Dolayısıyla Celâlzâde Sâlih'in *Süleymannâme*'si Hakkında Bazı Yeni Çıkarımlar", *OA* 43 (2014), 155–61.

anecdotes as *Kıssa-i Firuz Şah*. This translation earned Sâlih a move to a higher-paid position in Edirne, at the Sultan Bayezid medrese, in 1542–43. He continued to seek royal favour from this new position as well, as shown by a letter to the sultan, included in the *mecmua* (1b–4a). The sultan granted Sâlih's request for another promotion, and Sâlih transferred from the professorial to the legal-administrative branch with his appointment to Aleppo as judge (*kadı*). This posting formally lasted from December 1544 to February 1545, when he was replaced by Arabzâde Abdülbaki Efendi (d. 1564). Sâlih was instead sent to Cairo to help the governor-general inspect the province's endowments. His stay in Egypt inspired him to write a history of Egypt from Antiquity to the present: *Târîh-i Mısr-i Cedîd*. This interesting work, which incorporates local lore, the author's own observations, and a few Mamluk histories, was finished in Istanbul around December 1546–January 1547. After refusing an offer of reappointment to Aleppo as *kadı*, he briefly worked at the Sultan Bayezid medrese in Istanbul, before being sent first to Damascus (1547), and then Cairo (1547–48) as *kadı*. He retired from this position in 1550 and relocated to Istanbul, to the neighbourhood of Eyüp where his brother Mustafa lived.

Despite having personally requested a transfer from the professorial to the judicial career, Sâlih would come to regret the few years he spent as a *kadı*, as his remarks in two of his prefaces and a letter to his younger brother Celâlzâde Atâullah show.[8] During his retirement, he devoted himself to a compilation of his life's work. He continued to enjoy the patronage of the dynasty, as evidenced by the translation request he received from Prince Bayezid. For the prince, he translated Muḥammad 'Awfī's (1171–1242) Persian *Jawāmi' al-ḥikāyāt wa lawāmi' al-riwāyāt*, an early thirteenth-century collection of historical, moral and political anecdotes produced in the lands of the Delhi Sultanate. Through the prince's intercession, he received the last teaching position of his life in Eyüp, in November/December 1558. His increasing eye problems, which plagued him throughout his retirement and eventually resulted in blindness, led to Sâlih's second and definitive retirement in October 1561. He passed away in September/October 1565, and was buried in the courtyard of the small mosque his older brother Mustafa had built. His tomb, with the epitaph composed by his brother Mustafa, still stands there. The penultimate diptych mentions Mustafa's pen name, and the final line of the last diptych is a chronogram that gives the year of Sâlih's passing, AH 973:

> In order to make known the date of his passing/The sinful Nişânî sought God's help

---

8  See Toska, *Sâlih Çelebi*, 5–6. The letter to Atâullah is in Celâlzâde Sâlih, *Münşe'ât*, fol. 16a–18a.

A voice said: This prayer contains the date/"May God make Sâlih's tomb a part of Heaven."[9]

## 2  The Compilation and Contents of the *Mecmua*

A note on the first page of the Süleymaniye manuscript provides a list of its contents, briefly describes its nature, and asserts that this is an autograph copy:

This *mecmua* contains, in prose, reproductions of certain letters, and the history of the Alaman campaign; in verse, some odes and *gazel*s; and a tale of Leyla and Mecnun. These are selections from Ṣâliḥ bin Celâl's literary compositions, and they are written in his own humble hand (1a).[10]

The extant manuscript differs from the author's description. It lacks the story of Leyla and Mecnun, which is found in the only other copy, preserved today at the Erzurum Atatürk University Library.[11] Following Zehra Toska's suggestion, we assume that this particular section was separated from the Süleymaniye manuscript at a later date, possibly after the author's passing.[12] More interestingly, the Süleymaniye manuscript includes a group of letters sent by Sâlih to Prince Bayezid. These letters are not found in the Erzurum manuscript, which indicates that, after a copy of the Süleymaniye manuscript was made, possibly by an acquaintance of Sâlih or a family member, Sâlih added these letters to the Süleymaniye manuscript, almost out of a sense of urgency. Compared with the rest of the Süleymaniye manuscript, these letters are written in a less careful manner and do not share several of its common features, such as the use of seventeen lines to a page, and the consistent use of red ink for headings, subheadings and Arabic quotations. The inclusion of these letters is not the only editorial act on the part of Sâlih, however; the frequent marginal notes, additions and corrections display the ongoing relationship between the author and his *mecmua*, and Sâlih's urge to create and leave behind a definitive version of his writings.

---

9   "Rıḥleti sâlini ma'lûm etmege/İstedi Ḥaḳḳ'dan Nişânî-i pür-günâh//Dedi hâtif bu du'â' târîḫdir/Ḳabr-i Ṣâliḥ cennet ola yâ İlah".
10  "Neşr-i ba'żı mekâtîb ṣûretlerini ve Aleman seferi târîḫini ve naẓm-ı ba'żı ḳaṣâ'id ve gazeliyyâtı ve bir Leylî ve Mecnûn ḥikâyetini câmi' mecmû'adır ki Ṣâliḥ bin Celâl-i faḳīrün münşe'âtındandır ve kendü dest-i ḫaṭṭ-ı ḥaḳīrânesidir".
11  This copy is registered at MS 523–25, Agâh Sırrı Levend Yazmaları, Seyfeddin Özege Bölümü, ATUK. We are grateful to Dr Fatma Kaytaz for sharing sections of this manuscript with us. A critical edition of the Leyla and Mecnun story on the basis of the Erzurum manuscript is in Toska, *Sâlih Çelebi*, 127–285 (translit.), 289–340 (reproduction of the original).
12  Toska, *Sâlih Çelebi*, 26.

While the Süleymaniye manuscript includes pieces of writing gathered from Sâlih's long literary career, the majority of it must have been compiled and rewritten during his retirement. Like his brother Mustafa, who produced several of his works and incorporated the historical writings of his youth into his expansive *Tabakâtü'l-memâlik ve derecâtü'l-mesâlik*, Sâlih saw his years of *retraite* as a propitious time for the compilation of his œuvre.[13] The Süleymaniye manuscript must have taken its final shape sometime after 1558; the latest additions to the *mecmua*, the letters sent to Prince Bayezid, can be dated to late in that year. Sâlih finished the translation commissioned by the prince in 1558, and came out of retirement to obtain a teaching post, which he would hold until 1561. References in the last group of letters to the death of Bayezid's mother Hürrem (in May 1558) and the relocation of the prince's governorship from Kütahya to Amasya (in September 1558) indicate that these later additions must have followed these events. Sâlih's loss of eyesight, and his definitive retirement for health reasons in 1561, would preclude any editing work after that date. A chronogram on the inside cover, written in a different hand and commemorating the renovation of a mosque carrying the name of Sâlih and Mustafa's father, offers further clues to the terminal date for the Süleymaniye manuscript:

> The masjid of Kadı Celâl has been restored/After it had become old and decrepit
> As for the date of this renewal/Calculate the letters of 'Hayr-ı mesacidu'l-hayy' [The best of God's masjids] 967.[14]

The year 967 of the Hijri calendar corresponds to October 1559–September 1560. While the chronogram refers to a building project, most likely financed by the Celâlzâde brothers to honour their father's memory, its placement inside the Süleymaniye manuscript implies that Sâlih's final touches to the manuscript coincided with the end of the mosque renovations.

The act of compilation was clearly related to Sâlih's desire to leave behind a representative body of what he saw as his best work. Compilations of miscellany and anthologies would eventually become very popular with Ottoman readers, but these are usually, although not exclusively, prepared by readers anthologizing the works of others. (There were notable exceptions to this: Sâlih's near-contemporary Lâmiî Çelebi (1473–1532) prepared a selection from

---

13  For Mustafa's activities during his retirement, see Şahin, *Empire and Power*, 149–54.
14  "Tâ ki yenilendi bu mescid-i Ḳāḍı Celâl/Eski esâsı gidüb resmi olıcak ḫarab//Eyle bu tecdîd içün bilmeğe târîḫini/Ḫayr-ı mesâcidu'l-ḥayy lafẓı ḥurûfın ḥisâb 967".

his own prolific correspondence under the title of *Münşeat*.[15] In the next generation, Gelibolulu Mustafa Âlî, a literary disciple of Celâlzâde Mustafa, would anthologize and publish not only his first two poetic *dîvân*s, but also his own notable correspondence as *Menşeü'l-inşâ*.)[16] In Sâlih's case, in the first half of the sixteenth century, the preparation of the *mecmua* is an act of self-anthologizing that compactly displays the personal image and cultural reputation he wanted to construct and bequeath. At the beginning of the *mecmua*, Sâlih qualifies its contents as part of his *münşeat*, a term that could be translated here, at this early point in the development of literary Ottoman Turkish, as 'literary compositions'.

The title of *münşeat* is typically used for collections of official letters that were written in accordance with the linguistic and cultural frames of the chancery prose (*inşâ*), or for collections of letters addressed to various officials, both in actual and ideal forms. In Sâlih's case, however (and possibly in the case of other Ottoman literati, such as Lâmiî Çelebi as mentioned above), *münşeat* also took on a meaning that implied a new Ottoman belles-lettres in the first half of the sixteenth century. Sâlih's urge to create a representative body of his life's work, and his notion of *münşeat*, are illustrated by another work he rewrote during this period, his *Târîh-i Feth-i Budun*, housed today in the Topkapı Palace Library. A quick comparison of this work with the Süleymaniye manuscript reveals several commonalities that suggest that they were reproduced around the same time – the author's handwriting itself, the use of a very similar type of paper, seventeen-line pages, and the use of red ink to highlight headings, subheadings and Arabic quotations. On the title page of *Târîh-i Feth-i Budun*, presenting his work and announcing his authorship, Sâlih qualifies this work of history as part of his *münşeat* as well.[17] Another outcome of Sâlih's project of gathering and rewriting his life's work is his *dîvân*, which was not written by Sâlih himself due to his eye problems, but rather dictated during the last few years of his life.[18]

The *mecmua* opens with a section that includes seventeen letters. The first one (1b–4a) is addressed to Sultan Süleyman. As its title indicates,[19] the letter must have been penned around 1542–43, and before the end of 1544, during

---

15  For a critical edition, see Lâmiî Çelebi, *Münşeât-ı Lâmiî*, edited by Hasan Ali Esir (Trabzon: Karadeniz Teknik Üniversitesi Rektörlüğü, Rize Fen-Edebiyat Fakültesi, 2006).
16  Cornell H. Fleischer, *Bureaucrat and Intellectual in the Ottoman Empire: The Historian Mustafa 'Ali (1541–1600)* (Princeton, NJ: Princeton University Press, 1986), 68, 129.
17  Celâlzâde Sâlih, "Târîh-i feth-i Budun ez münşe'ât bi-dest-i ḫaṭṭ-ı Ṣâlih bin Celâl 'afa 'anhumâ", at MS R.1280, fol.1a, TSMK.
18  Celâlzâde Sâlih, *Dîvân*, MS 3846, Nuruosmaniye, SK; Toska, *Sâlih Çelebi*, 25–6.
19  "Pâdişâh-ı 'âlempenâha idilen 'arż-ı ḥâl ṣûretidir Edirnede müderrisken".

Sâlih's tenure at the Sultan Bayezid medrese in Edirne. While Sâlih does not present the sultan with a specific request in the letter, his subsequent appointment as a judge to Aleppo in December 1544 indicates that the letter played a role in one of the important turning points in the author's professional life, one that he would eventually regret. The next few letters are directed to various notables, only some of whom are named by the author. These congratulate a pasha on the occasion of a series of conquests on the European front (4a–7b),[20] a vizier on his promotion to the grand vizierate (7b–9a),[21] and another vizier on his success in the battlefield (9a–10a).[22] A letter, addressed to the Khan of Crimea Saadet Giray (r. 1524–1532), expresses Sâlih's gratitude for gifts received (10a–10b).[23] In these letters, Sâlih expands his network of patronage (or possible clientage) into the regime's grandees, possibly with the help of his brother Mustafa, and presents himself as a scholarly voice that further promotes and frames military victories with religious and cultural references. The fairly simple and didactic tone of the letters addressed to various viziers shows that these were meant to be read and understood, rather than dazzling the recipient through a shower of Perso-Arabic metaphors and quotations, of which Sâlih was clearly capable; Quranic citations, for example, are followed by Turkish translations.

The next twelve letters offer further information about Sâlih's circles of acquaintance, association, and friendship. The sixth letter of the *mecmua* reproduces a text dictated by Hayreddin Efendi, Süleyman's tutor and Sâlih's teacher (10b–11b).[24] In the following eleven letters, Sâlih sends greetings to the same Hayreddin Efendi (identified as Hâce Efendi in the letter's title) on the occasion of a recovery from illness (11b–12b);[25] vouches for an advanced

---

20  "Pâşâlardan birisi Rûm iline küffârla cihâda müteveccih olub elinde feth ü fütûhlar müyesser oldukda anlara tehniye-i gazâ' içün gönderdiğümüz mektûb sûretidir".

21  "Yine vüzerâdan birisine vezîr-i a'zam olduklarında tehniye-i vizâret içün gönderdiğimüz mektûb sûretidir".

22  "Bir âhar vezîre dahı sefer-i cihâda müteveccih olub 'asker-i küffârı basub gazâ'-yı ekber itdüklerinde tehniye-i fethi içün gönderdiğimüz mektûb sûretidir".

23  "Tatâr Hânı Sa'âdet Gîrây Hân'a gönderdiğimüz muhabbetnâme sûretidir".

24  The original letter was dictated as a reply to an Ottoman prince who, after reaching the location of his first posting as provincial governor (*sancak beyi*), had informed Hayreddin of his safe arrival: "Merhûm u mağfûr lehü Hʷâce Efendi'ye şehzâdelerden birisi sancağa çıkub sancaklarına vuṣûl bulduklarını i'lâm içün mektûb-i şerîflerin gönderdüklerinde ânın cevâbında Hʷâce Efendi yazdırdıkları mektûb sûretidir".

25  "Merhûm Hʷâce Efendi'nin marażdan şifâ' bulduklarında tehniye-i şıhhat içün gönderdüğimüz mektûb sûretidir."

student of his (12b–13a);[26] seeks solace in an old friend's confidence (13a–13b);[27] consoles another friend who was made to suffer by his detractors (13b–16a);[28] announces to his brother Ataullah that he misses him (16a–18a);[29] and addresses other acquaintances to offer condolences, congratulate on a promotion, ask for a favour, and simply remind them of his presence.[30] These letters help us chart the contours of Sâlih's social network, which includes family members, students, friends in the same line of work who sound like old acquaintances, as well as colleagues with whom he has a more reserved relationship. The letters also offer a glimpse into the author's emotions or, rather, the performance of emotions on the written page. These extend from statements of sadness and sympathy to outbursts of joy; an imaginary dialogue with a close friend navigates from feelings of anger directed to common rivals to the sharing of jokes and puns. We also see the tensions of Sâlih's professional life within the Ottoman scholarly and legal establishment: there are references to low salaries, professional rivals attacking hard-built reputations, the psychological strains of serving in faraway cities away from relatives. Put together, these letters constitute the most interesting section of the collection, since they allow us to see the various ways in which an Ottoman litterateur presented himself to benefactors, official figures, close friends and family members.

These letters are followed by five odes. The first one (21b–23a) was offered to İbrâhîm Pasha on his return from the fateful Two Iraqs campaign of 1533–36.[31] Sâlih's emphasis, in the ode, on the perfect harmony between Süleyman and

---

26  "Ḳāḍıaskerlerden birine mu'îdimüz Ṣâliḥ Çelebi içün gönderdüğimüz şefâ'atnâme ṣûretidir."
27  "Ḳudemâ'-ı eḥibbâdan birinin mektûbı cevâbında kendüye gönderdüğimüz mektûb ṣûretidir."
28  "Faḳīr maḥrûse-yi ma'mûre-yi Edirne'de merḥûm Sulṭân Bâyezîd medresesinde müderrisken eḥibbâdan biri ḥüssâd-ı aḳrânından kendü ḥaḳḳında ba'żı nâ-sezâ kelimât istimâ' idüb andan şikâyet-gûne bize mektûb gönderib istinsâḫ itdüğinde ana gönderilen mektûbımız ṣûretidir."
29  "Karındâşım 'Aṭâ'î Beğ ḥażretlerine gönderdüğimüz firḳatnâme ṣûretidir ki Ḥaleb'e teveccühümüz zemânında mâ-beynimüzde niçe sâl müfâraḳat elemine ibtilâ' esnâ'sında gönderilmişidi."
30  These are listed as the following: "eḥibbâ'dan biri re'îs-i küttâb-ı dîvân-ı 'âlî-şân olıcaḳ ana gönderilen mübârek-bâd mektûbı ṣûretidir" (18a–18b); "eḥibbâ'dan birine gönderilen mektûb ṣûretidir" (18b–19a); "Tatâr Ḫânı'nın ḳâḍı 'askeri olan Tatâr dânişmendi Mevlânâ Tâcüddîn'e gönderdüğimüz mektûb ṣûretidir" (19a–20a); "eḥibbâ'dan birinin ḳarındâşı vefât itdükde ana gönderilen ta'ziye mektûbı ṣûretidir" (20a–20b); "ṣûret-i ta'ziyenâme" (20b); "ṣâḥib-devletlerden birine ki mâ-beynde ḥuḳûḳ-ı sâbıḳa varidi, ba'żı murâdımuz ḳażâ'sı içün gönderdüğimüz mektûb ṣûretidir" (20b–21b).
31  "'Acem seferinden geldüklerinde vezîr-i 'âlî-câh merḥûm İbrâhîm Pâşâya denilen ḳaṣîdelerden birisidir."

his grand vizier would soon be rendered awry by the pasha's execution on the sultan's orders. It is meaningful that the next three odes address Ayas Pasha, who succeeded İbrâhim as grand vizier. In the first ode to Ayas (the second of five odes, located in 23a–24a), Sâlih asks for a promotion;[32] in the second one (24a–25b), he congratulates the pasha on his sons' circumcision;[33] in the third one (25b–26a), he celebrates Ayas's return from a campaign.[34] (As grand vizier, Ayas participated in two major campaigns – the Korfos campaign of 1537, and the Karaboğdan campaign of 1538.) Significantly enough, this section does not include any other odes addressed to individuals who occupied the position of grand vizier after Ayas's passing away in 1539. As seen in his letter to Süleyman, and his correspondence with Prince Bayezid, it is likely that Sâlih had access to the members of the dynasty, particularly through the agency of his brother Mustafa, who had become *nişancı* in 1534. The final ode in this section (26a–27a) addresses Sâlih's teacher Kemalpaşazâde.[35] Sâlih presents these odes with a slight tone of regret, and blames his youth, poetic temperament and ardour for the existence of these pleas to the officials of the day.[36] The odes are followed by a selection of twenty-six *gazel* (lyric poems) (27a–33a), and a *nazire* (imitative piece of poetry) to a *gazel* by Prince Bayezid. (The prince's original is also reproduced on the margin, in 33a.) This section ends with the copy of a letter, added at a later date in a less careful hand, in which Sâlih tells a friend that he is unable to write, at apparently short notice, an introduction to his poetry collection.[37]

Next comes the longest section of the *mecmua* (35a–82a), which contains Sâlih's narrative of the anti-Habsburg campaign of 1532–33, *Târîḫ-i sefer-i ẓafer-rehber-i Alaman* (The History of the Campaign of Germany, the Bringer of Victories).[38] This interesting work, until now largely unstudied but for a recent article by Fatma Kaytaz, reflects various dynamics of İbrâhim Pasha's grand vizierate (1523–36). Writing shortly after the campaign was completed, Sâlih gives a panoramic view of a grand imperialist venture commanded by

---

32  Sâlih presents this ode as "vezîr-i bî-naẓîr-i revşen-żamîr merḥûm Âyâs Pâşâ'ya didüğimüz ḳaṣîdelerdendir."
33  "Bu daḫı yine merḥûm Âyâs Pâşâ'ya denilmişdi ebnâ'sına sünnet düğüni itdüklerinde."
34  "Gazâ' seferinden geldüklerinde bu daḫı merḥûm Âyâs Pâşâ'ya denilmişidi."
35  "Fâżıl-i Rûm ve baḥr-ı 'ulûm merḥûm Kemâlpâşâoğlı'na denilmişdi."
36  This is how he presents the odes to his readers: "Ḥadâşet-i sinn eṣnâ'sında ṭab'ın ḥiddeti ve ẕihnin germiyyeti taḳāżâsıyle eş'âra rağbet iş'âr iden dil-âgâh ve süḫan-şinâs ba'żı ṣâḥib-devletlerile müşâḥabet ve istînâs içün didüğimüz ḳaṣâ'id ṣûretleri cümlesindendir" (21b).
37  This letter is in 34a, with the following title: "erbâb-ı fażldan bizden dîvân-ı eş'ârıma dîbâce inşâ' idivirmek iltimâs etdükde âna beyân-ı i'tiżârda gönderdiğimiz mektûb ṣûretidir."
38  For a concise discussion of this work, see Kaytaz, "*Târih-i Sefer*", 147–55.

Süleyman and assisted by İbrâhim. The political as well as politico – religious conflict between the Ottomans and the Habsburgs is referenced throughout the work, which incorporates Sâlih's own observations (while he did not himself participate, he was present during the elaborate ceremonies organized in Istanbul at the beginning of the campaign) with the testimonies of several individuals who participated in the 'German travels', including Sâlih's brother Mustafa. The narrative opens with a eulogy to the sultan, and continues with a brief reflection on the collaboration and achievements of Süleyman and İbrâhim. After a summary of the sultan's earlier conquests, which promotes İbrâhim's role in these military ventures, Sâlih explains the reasons behind the *Alaman seferi*. The narrative then proceeds through detailed accounts of the campaign preparations, the departure ceremonies, the march of the army to Edirne and then Sofia, the reception of French and Habsburg ambassadors in Niş, and the details of the military campaign, which ravaged a large area extending from Graz in southeast Austria to Požega in northeast Croatia in a massive show of force that was meant to demonstrate beyond question Ottoman superiority in central Europe. The narrative ends with the sultan's return to Belgrade after having received the submission of a variety of cities and fortresses.

The final section of the *mecmua*, which is not found in the Erzurum manuscript, includes a series of letters sent by Sâlih to Prince Bayezid (twelve in total) and members of his household (two letters).[39] The first nine letters (82b–86a) concern Sâlih's translation of *Jawāmiʿ al-ḥikāyāt wa lawāmiʿ*

---

39   These letters are listed with the following titles: "Şehzâde Sulṭân Bâyezîd ḥażretlerine gönderilen mektûb ṣûretidir emr-i şerîfleri cevâbında" (82b–83a); "yine meẕkûr şehzâde-i civân-baḫtın bu faḳîrlerine gönderdikleri nâme-i nâmîlerinin cevâbında gönderilen mektûbımız ṣûretidir" (83a–83b); "yine meẕkûr şehzâde-i civân-baḫta yazılan mektûb ṣûretidir *Câmiʾüʾl-ḥikâyât* kitâbınıñ cild-i evveli terceme olınub âsitâne-i saʿâdetlerine gönderildükde" (83b–84a); "yine meẕkûr şehzâde-i civân-baḫt âsitânesine gönderilen mektûb ṣûretidir, mevsim-i bahârda" (84a); "bu da yine meẕkûr şehzâde-i civân-baḫt âsitânesine gönderilen mektûb ṣûretidir, bendelerine gelen kitâb-ı müsteṭâbları cevâbından" (84a–84b); "bu mektûb dahi keẕalik ânların âsitânesine gönderilmişdir" (84b–85a); "meẕkûr kitâb terceme olınub âsitâne-i saʿâdetlerine gönderildükde gönderilen mektûb ṣûretidir" (85a–85b); "meẕkûr şehzâde-i civân-baḫt-ı âsitân-taḫt bendelerine câʾize-i firâvân ve iḥsân-ı bî-pâyân irsâl buyurdukda âsitânelerine gönderilan duʿâʾnâme ṣûretidir" (85b); "meẕkûr şehzâde-i ʿâlem-penâhın ḫazînedârbaşıları Ḥasan Aġaʾya gönderilen duʿâʾnâme ṣûretidir ki bize gönderdikleri mektûb-ı şerîfleri cevâbında yazıldı" (85b–86a); "meẕkûr şehzâde-i civân-baḫta gönderilen taʿziyenâme ṣûretidir vâlide-i cennet-mekânları vefât itdükde" (86a–86b); "yine meẕkûr şehzâde-i ʿâlem-penâha bu mektûbımuz cevâbında bize gönderdükleri nâme-i nâmîleri cevâbında yazılan mektûb ṣûretidir" (86b–87a); "yine meẕkûr şehzâde-i dil-âgâha gönderilen mektûb ṣûretidir mektûb-ı şerîfleri cevâbında" (87a); "meẕkûr şehzâde-i ʿâlem-penâh Kütâhiyeʾden Âmâsiye sancaġı virildükde tehniye

*al-riwāyāt* on Bayezid's request; these letters provide a detailed account of the commission of the work, the unfolding and completion of the translation, and Sâlih's remuneration. The first eight letters reflect the exchange between Sâlih and the prince, while the ninth (in 85b–86a) is addressed to the prince's chief treasurer Hasan Ağa, whom Sâlih thanks for not deducting the customary treasurer's share from the prince's payment for the translation. Beyond the work on the translation, this section displays the intensification of the personal and, indeed, political ties between Sâlih and the prince's household. As a testimony to his continuing communication with the prince's retinue, in 88a–88b, Sâlih congratulates an unnamed *ağa* on his promotion to the position of the prince's chancellor (*nişancı*). In 86a–87a, there are three letters that revolve around the passing away of the prince's mother Hürrem in 1558. The first is the letter of condolence from Sâlih to the prince, and the following two are replies to the prince's answers; it is significant that, even in the midst of a personally and politically troubling period, the prince would take the time to reply twice to Sâlih. The affinity between Sâlih and the prince is further illustrated in a letter sent on the occasion of the prince's transfer, on his father's orders and in anticipation of a struggle between Bayezid and his brother Selim, from Kütahya to Amasya (87a–88a). In this final correspondence between the two, Sâlih consoles the prince and predicts, erroneously as it would soon become apparent, his eventual accession to the Ottoman throne.

## 3  Preliminary Observations on the Contents of the *Mecmua*

What follows is a series of preliminary observations that stem from notes we have taken while reading the Süleymaniye manuscript. These reflect our initial reactions to specific passages, and the results of our informal discussions. While we will develop and expand them further when we publish the manuscript with a critical introduction, we are pleased to use this occasion to offer them to a larger group of readers.

One of the first general impressions afforded by a thorough reading of the *mecmua* is that, through the agency of his act of compilation, Sâlih manufactures a self that involves several personae: an accomplished scholar, a pious Muslim, a loyal subject of the sultan, an acquaintance of several grandees, a student of two great masters, an affectionate friend, a witness of the achievements of Ottoman imperialism, a passionate poet in his youth and, finally, a

---

içün gönderilen mektûb ṣûretidir" (87a–88a); "meẕkûr şehzâde-i dil-âgâhın ağalarından birisine nişâncıları olıcak mübârek-bâd içün gönderilen mektûb ṣûretidir" (88a–88b).

humble man between his sixth and seventh decades who devotes himself to literary pursuits. In this, he is very similar to his peers in early modern Eurasia who, through references to classical cultures (in Sâlih's case, the Arabo-Persian legacy in the form of its classical and Timurid variants) and an intense discussion of the events they witnessed during their lifetimes, used the agency of writing to establish their *auctoritas*. While Sâlih deserves to be viewed within a more expansive discussion of Ottoman letters in the sixteenth century, he can as easily be placed within an even more comprehensive framework that would bring and tie together the Renaissances of the sixteenth century and its practitioners, on an axis that extends from Tudor England to Mughal India. In any case, Sâlih can be squarely situated within an Ottoman Renaissance in political thought, literature, arts, and administration. In this new cultural environment, new forms of writing in new idioms blossomed in diverse genres, and emphatically individualized approaches to the recording of cultural and political life emerged. Individual authors tried to reconcile imperial political agendas and cultural ideals, while also trying to establish their literary and scholarly reputations. Sâlih's *mecmua* is a telling testimony to this new cultural environment.

Another general impression that strikes the reader is the author's acute consciousness of writing in Ottoman, which appears in these pages as a language that is constantly developing its orthography and vocabulary. The word *gıda*, for instance, is written without the *hemze* that follows the *elif* in the Arabic original (10a); the verb *başlamak* omits the *elif* between *be* and *şin* (6b); or the word *merteben* skips the last *he* between *be* and *nun* (27a). Sâlih is careful and deliberate in writing a new language; he applies these orthographical rules consistently throughout the *mecmua*. His mixture of the Anatolian colloquial Turkish with Arabic and Persian, his use of a *dîvânî* orthography for certain words, and the Arabo-Persianate themes and tropes that he endows with new meanings to convey the experiences of an Ottoman litterateur, eventually converge towards a distinctly Rumi expression. This Rumi expression is spread across different registers, and Sâlih's stylistic and linguistic dynamism manifests itself in the contents of his letters and poems. When he congratulates a victorious pasha (4a–7b) or a new grand vizier (7b–9a), he opens his letter with Quranic verses, which he then carefully translates into idiomatic Turkish, as if to teach these members of the military class the transcendental meanings of their acts; he does this in a manner that is at once clear, pedantic, and perhaps also patronizing. The tone he adopts in his letter to the sultan is suitably lofty and deferential, but his correspondence with friends and close acquaintances offers a veritable private universe of sentiments that range from joy to commiseration, and from expressions of sympathy for friends to frustration with rivals. Puns and popular stories lighten the nostalgic and anxious overtones, and establish an intimate, and at times irreverent, connection between Sâlih and his interlocutors.[40]

Several passages in the *mecmua* reflect the increasing exaltation of the figure of the sultan through claims to both temporal and spiritual authority. The image of Süleyman oscillates between the figure of a messianic conqueror (in the account of the *Alaman seferi*), and that of the purveyor of peace and justice (in the first letter of the *mecmua*). Equally significantly, the figure of the grand vizier is ubiquitous in these texts, not only as a high-ranking official, but also as a veritable partner of the sultan who is endowed with various powers and responsibilities. This applies to İbrâhim Pasha, in the pages that narrate the *Alaman seferi*, but also to Ayas Pasha and the unspecified viziers of the letters. The vizier not only supports the sultan through consultation, which increasingly becomes a formal duty, but is also charged, even under Süleyman, with supplementing and indeed correcting the sultan's actions. The visibility and prominence, even indispensability, of the viziers beyond the grand vizier is observed through the passages on the *Alaman seferi*, where the second and third viziers Ayas and Kasım's actions are celebrated, together with those of the sultan and the grand vizier (51b–52a).

Other passages provide a different set of cues about the life of a member of the Ottoman elite. Individuals like Sâlih dwelled in a very status-conscious environment, and had to compete with others for promotions and offices. The anxieties provoked by these rivalries surface in a few places in the correspondence.[41] In his letter to an old friend who has received a significant promotion to become *reîsülküttâb*, Sâlih ends with a congratulatory tone that refers to the joy of the new appointee's friends and acquaintances, and suggests that the appointee has prevailed over rivals and detractors.[42] These anonymous yet potent detractors re-emerge in two letters to medrese colleagues, where Sâlih complains about those who continue to assail his reputation following his

---

40  For instance, see Celâlzâde Sâlih, *Münşe'ât*, fol. 15b: "ol size bûn diyen nâdâna ki ağzından çıkan lafzın nûnını kâf idüb yüzine urmalu ve ağzına çalmalıdur." Here, Sâlih turns the final consonant of '*bûn*' (idiot) from *kef* to *nun*, and then suggests that the *nun* be made *kaf*, thus obtaining 'bok', that is faeces, which he suggests should be thrust into the rival's face and jammed into his mouth.

41  Cf. Cornell H. Fleischer, "Secretaries' Dreams: Augury and Angst in the Ottoman Scribal Service", in Ingeborg Baldauf et al. (eds) *Armağan: Festschrift für Andreas Tietze* (Prague: Enigma, 1994), 77–88.

42  Celâlzâde Sâlih, *Münşe'ât*, fol. 18b: "Ümîddir hemîşe cûy-bâr-ı ref'etinüz ter u tâze ve makām-ı 'izz u devletiniz bülend-âvâze olub dûstân-ı bî-'illet ve du'â'-gûyân-ı bî-minnetinüz istimâ' itmekle ferah u hemdân ve mübtehic u şâdân olmakdan zâ'il olmıyalar."

move from Istanbul to Edirne in 1542/3,[43] and he consoles another colleague by arguing that aversion and antipathy have plagued humanity since Creation and that one cannot escape from their effects.[44]

Sâlih's work on the *Alaman seferi* draws attention to several issues related to the first decades of Süleyman's rule, and deserves further study. Here, we will again offer a few points that were inspired by our initial reading of the text. First of all, the campaign preparations, and the campaign itself, come across as profoundly performative processes through which the sultan and his elite project, to audiences in Istanbul as well as those encountered throughout the campaign, specific images of the might of the Ottoman armies and the politico-religious authority of the Ottoman sultan. From the beginning of Sâlih's narrative, the campaign unfolds as a series of movements the chief aim of which is to serve Ottoman anti-Habsburg propaganda, rather than to achieve specific military objectives, which remain fairly vague.[45] War, with its prospect of enslaved women and children, is described with erotic overtones, where the author's fascination for the destructive capacities of the new gunpowder weapons and his obsession with the humiliation of the enemy often culminate in striking scenes of rhetorical violence, which might seem to be in contrast with the scholarly ruminations of a retired medrese teacher found in other parts of the *mecmua*. The natural attributes of the invaded territories and the built environment encountered by the Ottomans (mountains, fortresses, castles, dungeons, cities, bridges) constitute another source of fascination for Sâlih, whose cosmological imagination of the Ottoman realm incorporates these foreign lands by describing them in detail within a narrative that emphasizes their surrender to the Ottomans.

The group of letters that charts the progress of the translation commissioned by Prince Bayezid is quite significant for the history of literature, since the letters describe the various stages of translation, an activity that would

---

43   Celâlzâde Sâlih, *Münşe'ât*, fol. 13b: "İşidirüz tâ'ife-yi hussâd hanzalahumullah yine hakkımızda neçe şerr-âmîz remzler ve fitne-engîz gamzlardan hâlî değillerimiş."

44   Celâlzâde Sâlih, *Münşe'ât*, fol. 14a–14b: "Ma'lûm-ı râ-yı enverdir tebâyün-i ahlâk cihetinden meyân-ı halâ'ikde olan bu tenâfür ve tenâkür belâsı bize tâ zemân-ı kâl ü belâda takdîr olınub tebdîl u tagyîre kâbil-i ibtilâ' değildir. Ânunçündir ki olur olmaz her dûnın elinden dünyâda kişinin bağrı başı hûn, gözleri yaşı Ceyhûn olur."

45   The performative dimension of the campaign has been noted, on the basis of other sources, in Özlem Kumrular, "Campaña de Alemania: Rito, arte y demostración", in Ramón Puig de la Bellacasa and Alain Servantie (eds), *L'Empire ottoman dans l'Europe de la Renaissance* (Leuven: Leuven University Press, 2005), 191–214; Gülru Necipoğlu, "Süleymân the Magnificent and the Representation of Power in the Context of Ottoman-Habsburg-Papal Rivalry", *Art Bulletin* 71 (3) 1989, 401–27. Also see Şahin, *Empire and Power*, 81–6.

become particularly significant by the late-sixteenth century – from initial commission to the securing of copies of the original; to the preparation of sample translations for the patron's scrutiny; to the submission of the final draft and eventual remuneration. These letters also establish the high level of political speculation surrounding an Ottoman prince, and display at least one of the ways in which a prince secured the loyalty and support of prominent literati. Sâlih clearly addresses Prince Bayezid as a sultan in the making, calling him *padişah* on a number of occasions. When the prince is relocated by his father to Amasya from Kütahya, a move we know the prince resented, Sâlih reminds Bayezid that former princely residents of Amasya (notably his great-grandfather Bayezid II) eventually reached the Ottoman throne, which would thus be Bayezid's lot as well.[46] Given the tragic turn of events that would pit Bayezid against the forces of his father and brother shortly after Sâlih's letter, this correspondence is also a reminder of the sometimes rapidly shifting nature of political alliances and fortunes. This may partly explain why Sâlih's brother Mustafa, who wrote for his fellow bureaucrats and literati, would hastily devote his last work, an Ottoman translation from Arabic of the story of Prophet Joseph, to Prince Selim, the heir apparent of the Ottoman throne after Bayezid's strangling in Iran in 1561.[47]

Taken as a whole, the *mecmua* is an eloquent illustration of the ways in which a medrese graduate was pulled into the orbit of Ottoman imperialism in the sixteenth century, and was made a member of an ever-expanding ruling elite. The adventures of Ottoman imperialism in the first half of the sixteenth century provided Sâlih and others with a series of events on a global scale, and Sâlih attempted to memorialize them on the written page, and that with the new, Ottoman Turkish, language of empire. He did this, it seems clear, not only to seek patronage, but also because he identified with the objectives of Ottoman imperialism, and felt he had a creative, perhaps formative, role to play in this new environment.

---

46  About Amasya and its princely residents in the fifteenth and sixteenth centuries, see Petra Kappert, *Die osmanischen Prinzen und ihre Residenz Amasya im 15. und 16. Jahrhundert* (Istanbul: Nederlands Historisch-Archaeologisch Instituut, 1976).

47  Celâlzâde Mustafa, *Cevâhiru'l-aḫbâr fî ḥaṣâ'ili'l-aḫyâr*, fol. 4a–5a, MS 2356, Nuruosmaniye, SK. Also see Şahin, *Empire and Power*, 177–8.

## Acknowledgement

The authors met Metin Kunt while they were graduate students (at different times and in different institutions), and they have been inspired, ever since, by his synthesis of meticulous research and innovative thinking. To those fortunate enough to take courses with him, and to many others who read his work, Metin Kunt offered a well-articulated view of Ottoman history that seamlessly conjoined larger historical narratives with the finer points of administrative and cultural history. He was also among the pioneers of a new, less insular Ottoman history that would be studied and researched within the broader context of the early modern world. We offer this chapter as a token of our own gratitude and appreciation, and as testimony to a profoundly humanistic influence that spans multiple generations.

## Bibliography

### *Primary Sources*

Süleymaniye Kütüphanesi Library (SK)

Celâlzâde Mustafa. *Cevâhiru'l-ahbar fi hasâ'ili'l-ahyâr*. MS no. 2356. Nuruosmaniye, Süleymaniye Kütüphanesi.

Celâlzâde Sâlih. *Dîvân*. MS no. 3846. Nuruosmaniye, Süleymaniye Kütüphanesi.

Celâlzâde Sâlih. *Münşe'ât*. MS no. 557. Kadızâde Mehmed, Süleymaniye Kütüphanesi.

Topkapı Sarayı Müzesi Kütüphanesi Library (TSMK)

Celâlzâde Sâlih. *Târîh-i Feth-i Budun*. MS no. 1280. Revan, Topkapı Sarayı Müzesi Kütüphanesi.

Erzurum Atatürk Üniversitesi Kütüphanesi Library

Celâlzâde Sâlih. *Münşe'ât*. MS no. 523-5. Agâh Sırrı Levend Yazmaları, Seyfeddin Özege Bölümü, Atatürk Üniversitesi Kütüphanesi.

### *Published Primary Sources*

Lâmiî Çelebi. *Münşeât-ı Lâmiî*, edited by Hasan Ali Esir. Trabzon: Karadeniz Teknik Üniversitesi, Trabzon Rektörlüğü, Rize Fen-Edebiyat Fakültesi, 2006.

### *Secondary Sources*

Fleischer, Cornell H. *Bureaucrat and Intellectual in the Ottoman Empire: The Historian Mustafa 'Ali (1541–1600)*. Princeton, NJ: Princeton University Press, 1986.

Fleischer, Cornell H. "Secretaries' Dreams: Augury and Angst in the Ottoman Scribal Service". In Ingeborg Baldauf et al. (eds) *Armağan: Festschrift für Andreas Tietze*. Prague: Enigma, 1994, 77–88.

Kappert, Petra. *Die osmanischen Prinzen und ihre Residenz Amasya im 15. und 16. Jahrhundert*. Istanbul: Nederlands Historisch-Archaeologisch Instituut, 1976.

Kaytaz, Fatma. "*Târih-i Sefer-i Zafer-Rehber-i Alaman* Adlı Eserinin Tanıtımı Dolayısıyla Celâlzâde Sâlih'in *Süleymannâme*'si Hakkında Bazı Yeni Çıkarımlar". *Osmanlı Araştırmaları/Journal of Ottoman Studies* 43 (2014), 145–63.

Kumrular, Özlem. "Campaña de Alemania: Rito, arte y demostración". In Ramón Puig de la Bellacasa and Alain Servantie (eds), *L'Empire ottoman dans l'Europe de la Renaissance: idées et imaginaires d'intellectuels, de diplomates et de l'opinion publique dans les anciens Pays-Bas et le monde hispanique aux XV$^e$, XVI$^e$ et début du XVII$^e$ siècles: actes du programme organisé par l'Instituto Cervantes de Bruxelles (Bruxelles, novembre-décembre 2003)* = *El Imperio Otomano en la Europa renacentista: ideas e imaginarios de intelectuales, diplomáticos y opinión pública del siglo XV, XVI y principios del siglo XVII en los antiguos Países Bajos y el Mundo Hispánico*. Leuven: Leuven University Press, 2005, 191–214.

Necipoğlu, Gülru. "Süleymân the Magnificent and the Representation of Power in the Context of Ottoman – Habsburg – Papal Rivalry". *Art Bulletin* 71 (3) 1989, 401–27.

Şahin, Kaya. *Empire and Power in the Reign of Süleyman: Narrating the Sixteenth-Century Ottoman World*. New York: Cambridge University Press, 2013.

Toska, Zehra. *Sâlih Çelebi and Mecnûn u Leylâ Mesnevisi*. Cambridge, MA: Department of Near Eastern Languages and Literatures, Harvard University, 2007.

Yılmaz, Mehmet Şakir. "'Koca Nişancı' of Kanuni: Celâlzâde Mustafa Çelebi, Bureaucracy and 'Kanun' in the Reign of Süleyman the Magnificent". Ph.D. dissertation, Bilkent University, 2006.

CHAPTER 7

# Transforming the Abode of War into the Abode of Islam: A Local Grandee in Ottoman Hungary, Osman Ağa, Çelebi and Bey

*Pál Fodor*

In my book published a few years ago, I wrote at length about the institutional changes that took place in the Ottoman state administration – in particular the financial administration – from the last third of the sixteenth century onwards.[1] I found that one of the major innovations incurring numerous negative consequences was that the holders of military-administrative high offices gradually became tax farmers, who paid money for their posts and functioned primarily as money and tax collectors. I also revealed the manner in which traditional military positions were penetrated by financial entrepreneurs who, in return for services to the state, demanded and received high offices from the Imperial Council. The intertwining of the two formerly distinct spheres is best demonstrated by the rise of the *nazır*s – state 'inspectors' of tax farms. Originally, the *nazır*s had been paid by the state to supervise tax farms in minor areas, but in the period under discussion a growing number of them became major entrepreneurs who sometimes took under their charge all the tax farms in an entire province or even larger region. Over time, the composite income sources under their control became separated in an organizational sense, becoming – around the turn of the century – separate financial administrative units (*nezaret*s) subordinated to the provincial finance directors (*defterdar*s). In return for revenue bids made to the Ottoman treasury, the *nazır*s obtained many posts for themselves and their men. Increasingly, such posts included the office of district governor. Around the turn of the century, this new structure

---

1  Pál Fodor, *Vállalkozásra kényszerítve: Az oszmán pénzügyigazgatás és hatalmi elit változásai a 16–17. század fordulóján* [Unwilling Entrepreneurs: Changes in Ottoman Financial Administration and the Ruling Elite at the Turn of the Seventeenth Century] (Budapest: MTA Történettudományi Intézete, Magyar-Török Baráti Társaság, 2006). The English version is *idem, The Business of State: Ottoman Finance Administration and Ruling Elites in Transition* (Berlin: Klaus Schwarz Verlag, 2018). I owe special thanks to Géza Dávid, Balázs Sudár, and Klára Hegyi for their help in preparing this essay.

also appeared in Ottoman Hungary, in the form of the *nezaret*s of Belgrade and Vác (O. Vaç).[2]

At the time I wrote my book, the first piece of data relating to the new *nezaret* of Vác, referred to as a 'thirtieth' (*harmincad*) or 'head thirtieth' (*főharmincad*) in Hungarian sources,[3] was from 1612/13, but I already suspected that the *nezaret* had come into being well before this time.[4] My hunch was proven right by the following entry in an Ottoman *defter*, which has since come to light. Incidentally, the entry vividly shows the genesis of the new model in Ottoman Hungary:

> 23 February 1586. The *sancak* of Szécsény (O. Seçen): Yûsuf, governor-general of Buda (O. Budin), and Seyyid Mehmed,[5] finance director of Buda, presented the following in their report [sent to the Porte]. Previously, the *mukataa*[6] of Vác in the cited province had been leased out to treasury commissioners and tax farmers for a projected revenue amount of 14,900,000 *akçe*s, but they had proved incapable of fulfilling their assignment. The actual inspector of the *mukataa* in question, the *zeâmet* holder Osman, through whose efforts the revenues have increased on several occasions by [in total] 6,000,000 *akçe*s, recently contracted out the *mukataa* for a period of three years to tax farmers for the sum of 20,700,000 *akçe*s. A year and a half of their term has passed, and the revenue for the first year, according to the daily instalment,[7] amounts to 6,900,000 *akçe*s, a sum that they have paid in full to the Buda treasury. When Osman made a bid for the

---

2  On the historical geography and administrative division of Ottoman Hungary (with an exceptionally correct rendering of Hungarian place names both in their Ottoman and Hungarian versions), see Sadık Müfit Bilge, *Osmanlı'nın Macaristanı: Osmanlı Hâkimiyetindeki Macaristan'ın Tarihî Coğrafyası ve İdarî Taksimâtı (1526–1718)* (Istanbul: Kitabevi, 2010).

3  The *harmincad* (*tricesima*) was a Hungarian term denoting customs duty levied *ad valorem* on foreign trade. Due to an increase in its rate in the second half of the fifteenth century, it was thirtieth only by name, and in effect it meant 5 per cent, that is a twentieth. Cf. Zsigmond Pál Pach, "Hogyan lett a harmincadvámból huszad? [How the Thirtieth Customs Duty Became Twentieth?]", *Történelmi Szemle* 37 (3) 1995, 257–76.

4  Fodor, *The Business of State*, 115.

5  Frenk Yûsuf (also known as Sinan Pasha) resided in Buda from 29 September 1583 until 17 April 1586. See Géza Dávid, *Török közigazgatás Magyarországon* [Ottoman Public Administration in Hungary], D.Sc. dissertation, Budapest, 1995, 214–15. Mehmed, whose surname Seyyid appears in the document given here and who had been a *tımâr defterdarı* in Bosnia, was appointed as head of the treasury in Buda on 1 April 1584. See MS Kepeci 262, 24, DOA; here his name is also given as Seyyid Mehmed; Fodor, *The Business of State*, 171–2. He certainly remained in the post until April 1586. See also Lajos Fekete, *Budapest a törökkorban* [Budapest in the Ottoman Era] (Budapest: Királyi Magyar Egyetemi Nyomda, 1944), 212.

6  Separate section of revenue, income management unit, tax farm.

7  The 'daily instalment' was the share of the annual payable amount due for a single day. Despite the inference from the term, such payments were often made every three or six months or according to some other (probably shorter) time interval. See Fodor, *The Business*

tax farm, one of his conditions was that he should be appointed as district governor. Earlier, the commissioners, who had farmed out the *mukataa*, had been granted the district of Nógrád (O. Novigrad). [Since the *beylerbeyi* and the finance director] have sent information that the Osman in question is extraordinarily diligent and suitable, the finance director Burhan Efendi issued a sealed memorandum on 19 February 1586 proposing that he should receive the district of Szécsény. Thus, [the grand vizier] has ordered that this be so recorded [in the *ruûs defteri*].[8]

As we attempt to understand the new facts contained in the text, it is worth noting that the *mukataa* of Vác, the most valuable element in the nascent *nezaret*, had long counted as the 'jewel' of the Ottoman treasury in Hungary and as its most important source of revenue. This was particularly so because, as time passed, an increasing number of formerly separate income management units had been attached to it (including, from 1559, such lucrative cattle customs stations as those of Ráckeve, Paks, Földvár, Tolna and Báta).[9] Around 1580, under dozens of legal titles, representatives of the *mukataa* of Vác were collecting revenue in almost half of Ottoman Hungary.[10] Accordingly, the amount of revenue increased dramatically. An increase in efficiency and a willingness to take risks

---

*of State*, 111, fn.198; and Gyula Káldy-Nagy, *Magyarországi török adóösszeírások* [Ottoman Survey Registers in Hungary] (Budapest: Akadémiai Kiadó, 1970), 60–1.

8  MS Kepeci 246, 162, DOA. In the period, these registers contained mostly short extracts of the decrees of the Imperial Council relating to the assignments of state offices and revenue grants. See Nejat Göyünç, "X V I . yüzyılda ruûs ve önemi", *Tarih Dergisi* 17 (22) 1967, 17–34. The original Ottoman Turkish version of this text is as follows: "4 Rebî'ü'l-evvel 994. Livâ'-i Seçen: Budun beğlerbeğisi Yûsuf pâşâ ve defterdârı Seyyid Meḥmed 'arż gönderüb vilâyet-i mezbûrede vâḳi' Vaç muḳâṭa'ası bundan akdem ümenâ ve 'ummâl üzerinde 149 yük akçede olub maṣlaḥatda küllî iẓhâr-i 'acz ederlerdi bi'l-fi'il muḳâṭa'a-i mezbûre nâẓırı olan zâ'im 'Oṣmân bi'd-defa'at 60 yük akçenün izdiyâdına bâ'iṣ olub ḥâlen üç yıla 207 yük akçeye yarar mültezimlere der'uhde edüb bir buçuk senesi geçüb bir yıllık kıste'l-yevmi 69 yük akçe olur Budun ḫazînesine bî-ḳusûr edâ' edüb iltizâm olundukda şurûṭında kendüye sancâḳ verilmek muḳayyed olub muḳaddemân muḳâṭa'a-i mezbûreyi iltizâm eden emînlere Novigrâd sancâğı verildi mezbûr 'Oṣmân zikr olunduğı üzere küllî sâ'î olub yarardür deyü bildirdükleri [ecilden] 994 ṣaferinün yiğirmi doḳuzuncı güni Seçen sancâğı verilmek fermân olunduğına bâş defterdâr Burhân efendi mümżâ tezkire vermeğin ḳayd olunmaḳ buyuruldı."

9  Gyula Káldy-Nagy, "Statisztikai adatok a török hódoltsági terület nyugat felé irányuló áruforgalmáról [Statistical Data on Ottoman Hungary's Trade Towards the West]", *Történeti Statisztikai Szemle* 11 (1) 1968, 29; Káldy-Nagy, *Magyarországi*, 66, fn.42; Előd Vass, "Éléments pour compléter l'histoire de l'administration des finances du vilayet de Buda au XVIe siècle", in Lajos Ligeti (ed.), *Studia Turcica* (Budapest: Akadémiai Kiadó, 1971), 486.

10  MS Mxt 613, 3v, 5v, Türk. Hss., ON. Vass, "Éléments", 489; Antal Velics and Ernő Kammerer, *Magyarországi török kincstári defterek* [Ottoman Treasury Registers from Hungary], vol. 2 (Budapest, 1890), 522–3, 556–7.

on the part of the tax farmers were contributory factors in this development. Still, the most significant factor was clearly an economic and trade boom, which saw an unprecedented increase in the export of livestock from Hungary. Tens of thousands of Hungarian grey cattle and sheep, as well as thousands of horses, left the Ottoman part of Hungary by way of Vác and the branch customs houses subordinated to it.[11] This explains why, in the late 1560s, the tax farm of Vác, with its annual starting price of more than five million *akçe*s, lay well ahead of the other forty-five tax farms of the *vilayet* of Buda.[12]

The beneficiary of the cited petition and resolution, Osman, who was a revenue grant-holder of higher income, wrote the following to Archduke Ernst of Habsburg on 20 August 1581:

> For 12 years I have been faithfully serving my merciful master in the matter of the thirtieth, and now, once again, those living in Transylvania and in Hungary wrote to me, requesting that I should not give [the thirtieth] to other unknown parties, and so I had to take charge of the thirtieth once again.[13]

Our hero, who signed his name as Osman Ağa, wrote the truth: in the late 1560s he did indeed come into contact with the *mukataa* of Vác, which the Ottoman officials also referred to as a *harmincad* ('thirtieth') in their letters in Hungarian. The earliest surviving piece of data on Osman is from 23 April 1564: at the time, he was serving as the commander (*ağa*) of the cavalrymen (*faris*, or *beşli*) of the Castle of Fülek (O. Filek, present-day Fiľakovo, southern Slovakia). If not before, it was around this time that he began thinking of trying his luck in financial

---

11  Káldy-Nagy, "Statisztikai"; Káldy-Nagy, *Harácsszedők és ráják. Török világ a XVI. századi Magyarországon* [*Harac*-Collectors and *Reaya*s: The Ottoman World in Sixteenth-Century Hungary] (Budapest: Akadémiai Kiadó, 1970), 122–9; Vera Zimányi, "Gazdasági és társadalmi fejlődés Mohácstól a 16. század végéig [Economic and Social Development from the Battle of Mohács to the End of the Sixteenth Century]", in Zsigmond Pál Pach and Ágnes R. Várkonyi (eds), *Magyarország története 1526–1686. 1. kötet* [The History of Hungary, 1526–1686, vol. 1] (Budapest: Akadémiai Kiadó, 1985), 313–16. For a vivid and comprehensive portrayal of life in Vác under Ottoman rule, including a brief account of Osman, see Klára Hegyi, "Vác a törökkorban [Vác in the Ottoman Period]", in M. Ferenc Horváth (ed.), *Vác: A Dunakanyar szíve. Történelmi kalauz helybelieknek és világcsavargóknak* [Vác: The Heart of the Danube Bend. A Historical Guide for Locals and World Travellers] (Vác: Vác Város Önkormányzata, 2009), 89–105.

12  Pál Fodor, "Some Notes on Ottoman Tax Farming in Hungary", *AOH* 54 (4), 2001, 432.

13  Sándor Takáts, Ferenc Eckhart and Gyula Szekfű (eds), *A budai basák magyar nyelvű levelezése. I. 1553–1589* [Correspondence in the Hungarian Language of the Pashas of Buda. Part 1, 1553–1589] (Budapest: Magyar Tudományos Akadémia, 1915), 228, no. 196.

administration, for on this date he and a fellow cavalryman named Mustafa jointly leased out the tax farms of the towns of Rimaszombat (Rimavská Sobota, present-day southern Slovakia), Szikszó and Sajószentpéter (both in northern Hungary) for a term of three years.[14] It seems Osman soon acquired an appetite for such ventures, because on completion of the three-year term for the tax farm he set his sights on the crown lands (*has*) of Fülek. According to a *defter* entry of 7 February 1568, he succeeded in acquiring the right to tax farm these revenues by pledging to pay 5000 *akçes* more than the amount paid by the previous tax farmer (in connection with the new appointment, he is referred to as the 'earlier tax farmer', which may indicate that he had already been involved in the administration of the imperial *has* estates of Fülek).[15]

Three months later (on 18 May 1568), he commenced an even bigger venture: together with Mehmed, the former vice-commander (*kethüda*) of the garrison troops of Visegrád (O. Vişegrad, present-day northern Hungary), and apparently while retaining his post in Fülek, Osman took control of the *mukataa* of Vác from the previous tax farmers, whose contract had been due to run for another year. Instead of his predecessors' revenue bid of 14,900,000 *akçes*, which they had failed to pay, Osman and his associates undertook to collect a sum of 15,800,000 *akçes* in the next three years. However, after no more than a year, a five-member consortium (supervised and warranted by Ferhad, the *ağa* of the *azab* infantry of Pest, and including an *azab* from Pest, a *tımâr*-holder from Semendire [present-day Smederevo, Serbia] and two Jews from Buda) succeeded in having Osman and his associates ousted – for undisclosed reasons and on an unknown pretext. The consortium achieved this without outbidding the original amount of money due for the three-year term of tenure.[16]

Thereafter, Osman Ağa temporarily disappears from our view. Based on the aforementioned letter, however, we may conclude that by around 1570 he had managed, after a struggle, to regain what was possibly the most lucrative post in Ottoman Hungary.[17] There is, however, a further piece of evidence of Osman's interest in Vác and his possible residency there: according to a 1570 census of houses in the town, he owned a house in the vicinity of the Hasan Voyvoda mosque and had previously sold a plot of land in the Kasım Bey

---

14   MS Mxt 609, 3a, at Türk. Hss., ON; Velics and Kammerer, *Defterek*, II, 313.
15   MS Mxt 609, 3a, at Türk. Hss., ON; Velics and Kammerer, *Defterek*, II, 378 (erroneously dated 20 October 1577).
16   MS Mxt 609, 2b, at Türk. Hss., ON; Vass, "Éléments", 488; Velics-Kammerer, *Defterek*, II, 350.
17   It seems that it was based on an extract from this letter that Előd Vass thought that Osman had been the commissioner (*emin*) of the *mukataa* of Vác for a twenty-year period as of 1570 (Vass, "Éléments", 489), for he does not provide any other evidence.

mosque quarter.[18] For the years 1578–93, we have at our disposal a series of data that indicate almost conclusively that Osman worked throughout the period at the *mukataa* of Vác.

Such continuity, however, does not mean there were no changes in Osman's position and rank. In the period 1578–81, Osman Ağa administered the *mukataa* as a 'simple' tax farmer (*mültezim*), together with his colleague Mustafa, a *sipahi*. The tax farm had previously been held by a certain Mehmed Ağa and the inhabitants of the town of Vác, who had promised to pay 17,100,000 *akçes* over three years. Osman and Mustafa offered an extra 1,400,000 *akçes*, and in this way they won the right to operate the *mukataa* for a three-year term for the sum of 18,500,000 *akçes*.[19] The accounts register containing these figures also tells us that by this time Osman Ağa had become the holder of a larger prebend (*zeâmet*) in Fülek, his 'mother *sancak*'. In broad terms, we know how he acquired the estate. Concerning the beginnings of the process, we are informed that by the first half of 1579, in place of receiving his earlier pay, Osman had come into possession of a *tımâr* estate worth 12,922 *akçes* (comprising six villages and three to four separate portions of income). However, he had renounced this holding sometime before 9 September 1579 because, according to a *rûznâmçe defteri* entry made on that day, a part of the prebend worth 6000 *akçes* was received by the Receb, son of Abdullah, a mounted soldier in the fortress of Szabadka (O. Sobotka, present-day Rimavská Sobota in Slovakia), who had been waiting for five years for his initial *tımâr*, which he had earned on account of his bravery, while the other half was granted to Yûsuf, son of Abdullah.[20] Osman doubtless had good reason to renounce the estate: it was probably around this time that he obtained the *zeâmet* holding in the *nahiye* of Fülek and the *sancak* of Nógrád, which provided revenue of 37,000 *akçes*. The first definite information on his ownership of this estate stems from 8 January 1580. On this day, the registrar of Fülek – evidently under an agreement signed with Osman – completely reorganized the estate: he exchanged parts of it that were unwanted by the *ağa* for new settlements, and he then increased the value of the grant by 3000 *akçes*, arguing that the *ağa* "had brought villages lying on the abode of war for registration". This means that Osman had subjugated villages in Royal Hungary and forced them to pay

---

18  Balázs Sudár, "Vác városának török házösszeírása 1570-ből [The Ottoman Housing Census in Vác from 1570]", *Századok* 138 (4), 2005, 831, 835.

19  MS Mxt 613, 3b, at Türk. Hss., ON; cf. Velics and Kammerer, *Defterek*, II, 522–3 (in a poor translation that distorts important aspects).

20  MS Mxt 579, 64, at Türk. Hss., ON. The *tımâr rûznâmçe defteri*s "registered the changes among the timariots". See Géza Dávid, "The Sancakbegis of Arad and Gyula", *AOH* 46 (2–3) 1992–93, 144.

taxes.[21] On 12 August of the same year, he managed to have the value of the *zeâmet* estate increased from 40,000 to 48,000 *akçe*s: it was at this point that he was able to transfer to himself the four times 2000 *akçe*s reward ('increase') he had been granted in recognition of his brave fighting in 1579/80. The entries for this development are particularly interesting, as they reveal that, in addition to being a responsible finance official, Osman Ağa had also shown himself to be a brave soldier. He had initially taken part in the defeat of the 'infidels' in the Szécsény marches (consequently receiving an increase dated 28 April–7 May 1579). Thereafter, in the *sancak* of Esztergom (O. Estergon), he had helped defeat an invading force from Komárom (leading to an increase dated 17–26 February 1580). Then, in the Nógrád borderlands, he had proven his valiance by defeating the 'giaours' of three enemy fortresses (the increase of 16–25 April 1580). Finally, he had excelled himself in the battle against the fortress soldiers of Csábrág (present-day Čabraď, southern Slovakia), who were advancing against the Castle of Kékkő (O. Kekköy, present-day Modrý Kameň, southern Slovakia) (the increase of 12–21 August 1580).[22] Since the aforequoted document from 1586 also refers to him as a *zeâmet* holder, Osman Ağa evidently retained his large revenue grant in the intervening years and perhaps supplemented it with further acquisitions.

This comes as no surprise, given that he had strong ties to the Vác 'thirtieth' and had risen ever higher in its administration. In 1581, when his three-year term of tenure as tax farmer ended, a new role appeared: from then on, Osman was the inspector (*nazır*) of the *mukataa*, and he also became the guarantor (*kefil*) of the whole enterprise, while the tasks of tax farmer were formally performed by Süleyman Hoca, a resident of Vác. In the light of the proposal of 1586, there is barely any doubt that the contractor was one of Osman Ağa's men, who, having been inspired by his boss, raised the revenue amount by 1,800,000 akçes, whereby in the following three years (1581–84) it increased to 20,300,000 akçes.[23] A similar change must have taken place at the start of the following period when *nazır* Osman Ağa and the bidders presented by him offered 20,700,000 *akçe*s for the *mukataa* of Vác for the period 1584–87 (see the document quoted above). If we compare this sum with the offer made by Osman and his associate for the year 1568 (15,800,000 *akçe*s for three years, instead of the preceding amount of 14,900,000), then we see that the

---

21   MS Mxt 579, 192, at Türk. Hss, ON.
22   MS Mxt 579, 192, at Türk. Hss, ON. The increase of 8000 *akçe*s was transferred to him from a 15,000 *akçe*s *tımâr*-estate in Nógrád, the beneficiary of which had recently died.
23   MS Mxt 613, 5b at Türk. Hss, ON; cf. Velics and Kammerer, *Defterek*, II, 556–7 (in a poor translation that distorts important aspects).

document presented at the beginning of this chapter is roughly correct in stating that Osman – in a series of increases – pushed up the revenues in Vác by some 6,000,000 *akçes*. (The great leap in the price offers occurred in the mid-1560s, when there was an increase from 5,000,000 to almost 15,000,000 *akçes*.) Osman Ağa differed from his predecessors in that he paid in more of the pledged sums than they had done (it is no accident that this fact was emphasized in the document ordering his appointment as *sancakbeyi*).[24]

If our hero was capable of providing the financial backing for such a serious enterprise (and unless this had been so, he would hardly have become a *nazır*), then this was because he had grown rather wealthy over the preceding decade. An evident measure of his prestige was his success in retaining his post in Vác without any great struggle. Moreover, all the pashas of Buda during this period had acknowledged his strengths in their reports to the Porte. In addition to the titles of *ağa* and *zâim*, on several occasions his name is accompanied by the title of *çelebi*. The Vác census of 1570 is the first occasion when this epithet is placed by his name, and the same byname features in two letters in Hungarian from 1583 (the first written by Osman himself and the second by Kalaylıkoz Ali, governor-general of Buda).[25] In Osman's case, the title of *çelebi* – normally reserved for literate, educated men – was probably used in recognition of his financial acumen. We know, for instance, that the *defterdar*s and other financial officials of various ranks often bore this title.[26]

After these successes, it was natural for Osman Ağa to perceive the status of *zeâmet* holder as less than what he was rightly due. Accordingly, at the beginning of the entrepreneurial period in 1584, he demanded the status of district governor (*sancakbeyi*) in return for pledging to provide much higher revenues (the text cited above shows that even prior to this the Ottoman 'thirtieth holders' of Vác had received a *sancak* as remuneration, namely the post of *bey* of Nógrád.) It is not surprising that his demand was warmly supported by the

---

24  Unless the drafters of the memorandum were exaggerating, then it seems Osman and his associates did manage to pay in full the revenues undertaken for 1584/5. This was a significant feat. In the period 1578–81, they already achieved similar success: against a total sum of 18,500,000, they remained indebted to a sum of 293,709 *akçes* (MS Mxt 613, 3b–4a, at Türk. Hss, ON). In the imperial accounts relating to the *mukataa*s, I have rarely found such a positive performance ratio.
25  Takáts et. al., *A budai basák*, 94, no. 266, 303, no. 274.
26  For instance, Ali Çelebi, who died in Buda in 1587, leaving behind substantial libraries; see Balázs Sudár, "Egy budai török értelmiségi könyvtára a 16. században [The Library of an Ottoman Intellectual from Buda in the Sixteenth Century]", *Történelmi Szemle* 47 (3–4) 2005, 315–31.

governor-general and finance director of Buda. In recognition of his work and connections, and in line with the chief *defterdar*'s suggestion, Osman was granted the *sancak* of Szécsény on the same day (19 February 1586). From then onwards, Osman was entitled to refer to himself as *bey*.[27] Serious difficulties arose, however, when he took action to obtain the revenue grants accompanying his new status. Three years later, in the spring of 1589 (before 27 April–6 May), he complained through one of his men to the Porte that the taking over of the fixed-amount *has* estates (*icmallü haslar*) of the *sancak* of Szécsény had 'failed' because the relevant decree of transfer had been lost prior to the issuing of the appointment diploma (*berat*). He therefore requested that he might receive the decree of assignment once more, based on the entry record found in the central *defter*. The Ottoman court first ordered the *beylerbeyi* of Buda to take such a step (between 27 April and 6 May 1589), but after a decree was issued by the ruler or the grand vizier, the competent department of the Imperial Council took charge of the matter. The memorandum (*tezkire*) required for the issuing of an appointment diploma was produced on 3 August 1589. On 29 August, a detailed record of the villages and revenue grants that were due to Osman was included in the *rûznâmçe defteri*. (These income sources were situated in four *nahiye*s of four different districts – Szécsény, Fülek, Nógrád and Vác.) Thus, finally, more than three years after his appointment, Osman Bey was retroactively granted his prebend worth 240,238 *akçes*.[28] At first sight, it appears that the delay in gaining possession of the *has* estates was due in part to an unfortunate coincidence (the loss of a document) and in part to the slow working pace of Ottoman bureaucracy. In reality, however, during the preceding three years, Osman Ağa had spent little time in the *sancak* of Szécsény. Rather, he had kept several irons in the fire, burning his fingers as a result.

He had only just taken on his first post as district governor when, on 5 May 1586, he managed to have himself transferred to the head of the more prestigious *sancak* of Esztergom.[29] We can only guess the reasons for this rapid change. A possible explanation is that on 17 April of the year in question Kalaylıkoz Ali Pasha – elevated to the rank of vizier – had been reinstalled in his former position of governor-general of Buda and Ali Pasha was – at least according to an undocumented claim by Sándor Takáts[30] – the brother of Osman. The familial relationship may have given a new impetus to Osman's

---

27  MS Kepeci 262, 23, DOA; Kepeci 246, 172; MS Ruznamçe 107, chapter on Szécsény, 4, DOA.
28  MS Ruznamçe 107, chapter on Szécsény, 3–4, DOA.
29  MS Kepeci 262, 20, DOA. The abandoned Szécsény was given on the same day to Ali Bey of Koppány (O. Kopan), MS Kepeci 262, 23, DOA.
30  Sándor Takáts, "Vezír Kalajkiloz [sic!] Ali basa [Vizier Kalaylıkoz Ali Pasha]", in *idem*, *A török hódoltság korából* [From the Era of Ottoman Hungary] (Budapest: Genius, 1927), 169.

career, but this is no more than a possibility. Further, we cannot be sure how long he remained in Esztergom. According to an entry in the repeatedly cited central register, Osman would seem to have been replaced by Memi Bey of Kirka on 25 May 1587.[31] Yet, in connection with a further transfer in the early autumn of 1588, the same list – in contradiction to the above assertion – indicates that Osman was still the *bey* of Esztergom at that point.[32] Since, however, an entry in the *rûznâmçe defteri* referring to a reward also indicates that Osman was still stationed in Esztergom in the spring and early summer of 1588,[33] we must accept that Osman headed the district of Esztergom throughout the more than two-year period (if this is so, then either the keepers of the central records made an error or the change in personnel of 1587 did not actually take place, despite this having been recorded in the registers). At any rate, there is no sign that Osman took on the *has* estates accompanying the post, a development that may be linked with the complications surrounding the holding assigned to him in Szécsény. On 5 September 1588, he was then appointed as *sancakbeyi* of the district of Hatvan, the *has* estates of which were equivalent to those of Szécsény.[34] Thereafter, we see a continuation of the oddities in Osman's career: according to one entry in the records, here too he 'failed' to establish himself properly in the post and was unable, once again, to obtain the appointment diploma – this time for the Hatvan post.[35] In the meantime, however, he administered with full powers the affairs of the district.[36] Ultimately, it seems Osman grew rather tired of the confusion surrounding his holdings. In the spring of 1589, in the manner presented above, he contacted the Porte with a view to securing the allocation of the *has* estates in the *sancak* of Szécsény, which had been assigned to him three years earlier. Obviously, for such a course of action to be open to him, he must have been reinstated as the *sancakbeyi* of Szécsény. We have no exact knowledge of when this took place (possibly in the spring of 1589). At any rate, the entry in the *rûznâmçe defteri* for 3 August mentions him as the "present *sancakbeyi* of Szécsény" when summarizing the events that led to his request.[37]

---

31  MS Kepeci 262, 20, DOA.
32  MS Kepeci 262, 20, DOA.
33  MS Ruznamçe 131, chapter on Szolnok, 15–16, DOA.
34  MS Kepeci 262, 20, DOA.
35  MS Ruznamçe 131, chapter on Szolnok, 16, DOA.
36  On 22 May 1589, Stephen Báthory (István Báthory) sent him a letter, addressing him as follows: "Az Nagos Ozmán bégnek Hatvanban Török császárnak fő szandzsák bégjének." [To the Great Osman Bey, head sancakbeyi in Hatvan of the Turkish Emperor]. See Takáts et al., *A budai basák*, 489–90, no. 418.
37  MS Ruznamçe 107, chapter on Szécsény, 4, DOA.

He did not enjoy for long the hard-won fruits of his return to the initial *sancak*. The ambitious Osman seems to have considered this post to be beneath him. A good year or so later, he scored a 'big hit': on 29 October 1590 he obtained Szolnok (O. Solnok), one of the most important and highest-ranking districts in Hungary.[38] In theory, he was entitled to the same amount of *has* estates as in his previous post. However, when mapping out his prebend, he was able to apply the increases he had acquired through his recent battlefield achievements. The first increase – worth 20,000 *akçes* and implemented during his tenure in Esztergom – was approved between 26 June and 5 July 1588 on the basis of a proposal by Sinan/Yûsuf Pasha of Buda (Osman was rewarded for having dealt successfully with the roaming 'infidels'); the second increase, also worth 20,000 *akçes*, was received at the time of his appointment as *bey* of Szolnok; this had been proposed by Ferhad Pasha of Buda – prior to his murder in mid-September 1590 – on the grounds of Osman's excellent performance under the Castle of Eger (O. Eğri). This amount of 40,000 *akçes* was then increased by 10,000 *akçes* (with reference to the fact that this part holding could not be detached from the revenues assigned as *has*), and so, together with the 240,238 *akçes* received as a base income in Szécsény and received here too, he was allocated in total 290,238 *akçes* of *has* estates. Since in the course of the procedure it was noted by the central authorities that in 1588, after having been granted the *sancak* of Hatvan, Osman had not taken out his appointment diploma, for the sake of caution an order was issued that before the estates might be granted to him, he should be required to pay the "treasury fee" (*resm-i miri*).[39]

---

38   MS Ruznamçe 131, chapter on Szolnok, 15, DOA. Interestingly, but not unusually in the Ottoman bureaucracy, even before his actual appointment as *bey* of Szolnok, Osman received a command from the Imperial Council addressing him as such. See MS Mühimme defteri 73, 333, no. 736, DOA. The command, dated 14 October 1590, was also cited in Viktor Tomkó, "Török közigazgatás Magyarországon: a szolnoki szandzsákbégek története II [Ottoman Public Administration in Hungary: History of the *Sancakbeyi*s of Szolnok II]", *Zounuk. A Jász–Nagykun–Szolnok Megyei Levéltár Évkönyve* 19 (2005), 9 and 9, fn.2. However, he converted the date of 14 Zilhicce 998 (which is far from certain) to 9 September on one occasion and to 14 September on another.

39   The recipients had to pay three kinds of fee for their prebends: 1. a fee for the memorandum (*resm-i tezkire*), 2. a fee for the appointment diploma (*resm-i berat*), comprising two parts: the treasury fee (*resm-i miri*) and the fee due to the *çavuş*es and the gate-keepers (*resm-i çavuşan ve bevvaban*), and finally 3. the fee due to the standard bearer (*adet-i rüsum-i mir-i alem*). The treasury fee of the district governors was 1200 *akçe* (the full *berat*-fee amounted to 2700 *akçe*) in the latter half of the sixteenth century. See Douglas A. Howard, "Ottoman Administration and the Tîmâr System: Sûret-i Kânûnnâme-i 'Osmânî Berây-i Tîmâr Dâden", *JTS* 20 (1996), 99; author unknown, untitled, MS 1734, fol. 202b, Atıf Efendi Kütüphanesi; cf. Géza Dávid, "A 16–17. századi oszmán közigazgatás működése: a beglerbégek és szandzsákbégek kiválasztása és kinevezése [The Operation of the Ottoman Public

After this had taken place, a memorandum was submitted on 7 November 1590 authorizing the issuing of the appointment diploma (*berat*). As a final step, on 5 December 1590, his estates were noted down in the *tımâr rûznâmçe defteri*, whereupon Osman could take up office as *sancakbeyi* of Szolnok with all the trappings of that post.

Osman seems to have liked being in Szolnok and successfully held on to the office for some time, despite rival bids by members of various cliques. As late as mid-1594, he was still stationed there. In the meantime, another census of the *sancak* took place under the auspices of a general imperial survey,[40] and the *tımâr defteri* drawn up by the end of 1592 included a considerably increased *has* estate belonging to Osman: the projected revenues had risen from 290,238 to 385,000 *akçes*. The change was not, however, a source of unclouded delight for Osman, for in the course of the rearrangement there had been a decrease in the share of more certain revenues, and the surplus transferred to him came mostly from areas along the border or under partial Ottoman rule (for example, the area near Nagykálló).[41]

Even so, with his appointment as *sancakbeyi* of Szolnok and given that he appears to have retained control of the *nezaret* in Vác,[42] Osman became one of the most distinguished lords of the frontier zone. Indicative of the high esteem in which he was held, between late January and April 1593 and until the arrival of the official successor to the dismissed governor-general of Buda, Osman ran the affairs of the *vilayet* in his role as deputy.[43] During the diplomatic tug-of-war that preceded the so-called Long War of 1593–1606 (or, the Fifteen Years' War, as the Hungarians called it) he mediated between the Porte and the Viennese court on several occasions. On the outbreak of war, he immediately entered the battle with his troops, participating in numerous

---

Administration in the Sixteenth and Seventeenth Centuries: Selection and Appointment of the *Beylerbeyi*s and the *Sancakbeyi*s]", in Pál Fodor, Géza Pálffy and István György Tóth (eds), *Tanulmányok Szakály Ferenc emlékére* [Studies in Memory of Ferenc Szakály] (Budapest: MTA TKI Gazdaság-és Társadalomtudományi Kutatócsoportja, 2002), 111–13.

40  For a Hungarian translation of the larger part of the resultant detailed register, see Gábor Ágoston, "A szolnoki szandzsák 1591–92. évi összeírása I–II", *Zounuk. A Szolnok Megyei Levéltár Évkönyve* 3 (1988), 221–94; *Zounuk* 4 (1989), 191–287.

41  MS Tapu Tahrir Defterleri 658, 3–4, DOA.

42  In his letter in Hungarian dated 4 March 1593, Osman Bey describes himself as follows: "török császárnak fő szandzsákbégje Szolnok várában és váczi harmincadjának fő gondviselője" [the head *sancakbeyi* of the Ottoman emperor in the castle of Szolnok and the main caretaker of the thirtieth of Vác]. See Gustav Bayerle, *Ottoman Diplomacy in Hungary. Letters from the Pashas of Buda 1590–1593* (Bloomington: Indiana University, 1972), 172, no. 39.

43  Tomkó, "Török közigazgatás", 11.

engagements, including the military advance in October against Nagykálló as well as the battles of Székesfehérvár (O. İstolni Belgrad) on 3 November 1593, Romhány on 21 November, and Tura on 1 May 1594.[44] He then rushed to the defence of Esztergom, which had fallen under siege shortly before.[45] After a series of defeats, it was here that he tasted victory for the first time. Indeed, it was thanks in part to his efforts that the Christian troops withdrew from Esztergom by 29 June. Subsequently, he travelled home to Szolnok for a brief period, whence he sought (in vain) to persuade the Transylvanian leaders to enter the war. Then, in early August, he and the Tatar auxiliary troops joined the grand vizier's army and fought throughout the campaign that ended with the occupation of Győr (O. Yanık). Thereafter, however, he completely disappears from our view. Viktor Tomkó claimed that Osman lost the *sancak* of Szolnok in the autumn of that year (1594). His successor is not known either. One thing is certain, namely that the *sancak* was headed by Bektaş Bey at the time of the sultan's campaign of 1596. It seems, however, that when Bektaş was appointed as governor-general of Eger on 17 August 1598, his vacated seat was once again occupied by Osman. Several sources state, for instance, that he took part in this capacity and with his troops in the rescue of Buda and Pest, which a Christian army had lain siege to between 3 October and 2 November 1598.[46] During these difficult years, it seems likely that he also lost control of the *mukataa* of Vác. We know, for instance, that a decree of the ruler issued on 18 February 1597 mentions a certain Arslan as commissioner (*emin*) of the *mukataa*.[47]

Since biographical reports about Osman end at this point, the final years in the life of the man whom the Ottoman chronicler Kâtib Çelebi called 'Earless' are shrouded in mystery. Thus, the dates of both his birth and death

---

44  Câfer Iyânî, *Tevârîh-i Cedîd-i Vilâyet-i Üngürüs* (*Osmanlı-Macar Mücadelesi Tarihi, 1585–1595*) transliterated by Mehmet Kirişçioğlu (Istanbul: Kitabevi, 2001), 66; Tomkó, "Török közigazgatás", 11–12; Sándor László Tóth, *A mezőkeresztesi csata és a tizenöt éves háború* [The Battle of Mezőkeresztes and the Fifteen Years' War] (Szeged: Belvedere Meridionale, 2000), 151–2.

45  Sarhoş 'Abdî, *Zafernâme*, fol.5a, MS 1328, Manzum, Ali Emiri, SK. On the author and on another work describing in critical terms the situation in the Hungarian borderlands, see Balázs Sudár, "A tizenöt éves háború török költői [Ottoman Poets of the Fifteen Years' War]", *Hadtörténelmi Közlemények* 117 (4), 2004, 1147–8, 1154–7.

46  Tomkó, "Török közigazgatás", 22; *Török történetírók. III. kötet. 1566–1659* [Ottoman Chroniclers. Vol. III: 1566–1659], translated and annotated by Imre Karácson (Budapest: Magyar Tudományos Akadémia, 1916), 285; Tóth, *A mezőkeresztesi csata*, 291–2.

47  Lajos Fekete, "Debrecen város levéltárának török oklevelei [Ottoman Documents in the Municipal Archives of Debrecen]", *Levéltári Közlemények* 3 (1925), 55, no. 49. Obviously, one can easily imagine that this *emin* functioned merely as a subordinated official (a subcontractor) in Vác, rather than as the director of the entire organization.

are unknown to us. Even so, his personality shines through his deeds and his achievements, and it is also revealed in some of his personal statements that have come down to us. Above all, we must conclude that he was a talented financial expert. This is demonstrated not only by the length of his term in the Vác post and by the enduring trust placed in him by successive and everchanging leaderships in Buda. A further proof is his success – far above the average – in achieving better income collection results. Working busily, he sought to satisfy both Habsburg-Hungarian and Ottoman sides, with a view to upholding and increasing trade between the two parts of the country as well as custom turnover in Vác.[48] At the same time, he could be quite ruthless when trying to persuade or intimidate tax payers, when unpaid custom fees had be recovered, or when he felt his personal material interests were at stake.[49] In one sense, he differed greatly from his fellows, who achieved high office mainly through their financial capabilities and who, because of their activities in the business field, neglected their traditional military-administrative duties (usually leaving such duties to their deputies). Osman, who began his life in Hungary as a mounted soldier, always attempted to fulfil or even exceed the expectations placed on men in such positions. As the principal administrator of the Vác *mukataa*, he might easily have evaded military service, but it seems he actually enjoyed going to war and seeking military adventures. It was not only at times of peace that he wielded his sword in defence of his territories or even to expand them. Rather, he excelled himself on several occasions during the Long (Fifteen Years') War. In Kâtib Çelebi's view, it was Osman who kept spirits high among the Ottoman soldiers at Fülek in the autumn of 1593. And, according to the same author, Osman also played a critical role in the defence of Pest in 1598.[50] We know that this is not merely the opinion of a later, possibly prejudiced chronicler, because there is also evidence from Sarhoş Abdi, who

---

48  See his letters to the King of Hungary and to other authorities in Takáts et al., *A budai basák*, 227–28, no. 196, 265–6, no. 238, 280–1, no. 255 (cf. 281–2, no. 256), 293–4, no. 266 (cf. 303, no. 274 and 304–5, no. 276). Cf. Sándor Takáts, "A budai basák emlékezete [The Memory of the Pashas of Buda]", in *idem, Rajzok a török világból* (Budapest: n.p., 1915), I, 144–6.

49  Fekete, "Debrecen", 51, no. 32, 54, no. 42, 55, no. 47; Takáts et al., *A budai basák*, 426, no. 378, 483, no. 414; Tomkó, "Török közigazgatás", 9, fn.2 (cf. Bayerle, *Ottoman Diplomacy*, 82–3 no. 39).

50  "Osman Bey conducted himself very bravely and brought about the liberation of the soldiers, although several of his men fell in battle" (*Török történetírók*, III, 211); "After this unwise decision, 'Earless' Osman Bey, who had shown to some extent his excellence at the Iron Gate, spoiled this plan, on arriving in the morning with the border troops of Szolnok. Taking the Pest soldiers at his side, he made many cannon strikes from Pest against the enemy, chasing them from street to street. Other soldiers also arrived there and descended on the enemy, which then withdrew" (*Török történetírók*, III, 285).

fought throughout the 1594 campaign and was very familiar with conditions in Ottoman Hungary. In a poem, Abdi, who later became *defterdar* of Eger, praised Osman for the bravery he had shown at Esztergom: "Among the *bey*s, he is the most excellent now/the giaour is petrified of his sword."[51]

Osman Bey differed in another respect from the parvenu entrepreneurial elite of the period: although during the years spent in the financial administration and high offices of the marches, he evidently amassed great wealth, this did not only serve his own comfort or that of his family. We can agree with Lajos Fekete, who argued that the builder of the mosque in the Víziváros (Watertown) area of Buda near the 'Cock Gate' (in what is today Fő Street near the Danube) – a mosque named after Osman Bey – "was probably the sultan's man Osman, who worked in Vác for a long time around 1580".[52] For my part, I would add the quite plausible supposition that Osman also founded the school in Buda that features on a list from the 1660s as Osman Bey *medresesi*,[53] and that this school perhaps formed part of a complex of buildings constructed around the mosque in Víziváros bearing his name. Thus, Osman Bey was one of several local Ottoman grandees who – like Kasım Voyvoda, Bey and Pasha, whom we know from Géza Dávid's research work[54] – contributed greatly to the expansion and consolidation of Ottoman rule in Hungary, both in the economic and in the intellectual and cultural field. In this way, the man who had been an *ağa* of the fortress cavalry and then a *nazır* and *sancakbeyi* proved that he might rightly call himself a *çelebi*, that is, an educated gentleman.

---

51  Sarhoş 'Abdî, *Zafernâme*, fol.5a: "Ümerâ içre odur şimdi yarar/Havf iderdi kılıcından küffâr."
52  Fekete, *Budapest a törökkorban*, 93; cf. *ibid.*, 116, 263. For a recent localization and description of the mosque with illustrations (seventeenth to eighteenth-century European paintings and drawings), see Balázs Sudár, *Dzsámik és mecsetek a hódolt Magyarországon* [Djamis and Mosques in Ottoman Hungary] (Budapest: MTA Bölcsészettudományi Kutatóközpont, Történettudományi Intézet, 2014), 210–14.
53  M. Kemal Özergin, "Eski bir Rûznâme'ye Göre İstanbul ve Rumeli Medreseleri", *İstanbul Üniversitesi Edebiyat Fakültesi Tarih Enstitüsü Dergisi* 4–5 (1973–74), 281. This evidence has already been cited by Gábor Ágoston, "Muslim Cultural Enclaves in Hungary under Ottoman Rule", AOH 44 (2–3) 1991, 189. The teacher of the medrese received 25 *akçe*s a day.
54  Géza Dávid, "An Ottoman Military Career on the Hungarian Borders: Kasım *Voyvoda*, Bey and Pasha", in Géza Dávid and Pál Fodor (eds), *Ottomans, Hungarians, and Habsburgs in Central Europe: The Military Confines in the Era of Ottoman Conquest* (Leiden: Brill, 2000), 265–97.

## Acknowledgement

Presenting the career and personality of an Ottoman figuring prominently in a remote frontier province of the empire, I would like to pay tribute to Metin Kunt who made tremendous efforts to bring the issue of Ottoman provincial societies to the fore of Ottoman studies. For his original essay on the provincial administration, see "Devolution from the Centre to the Periphery: An Overview of Ottoman Provincial Administration", in Jeroen Duindam and Sabine Dabringhaus (eds), *The Dynastic Centre and the Provinces: Agents and Interactions* (Leiden: Brill, 2014), 30–48.

## Bibliography

### *Primary Sources*
Âtıf Efendi Kütüphanesi Library
[author unknown, untitled], MS 1734, fol. 202b. Âtıf Efendi Kütüphanesi, Istanbul.

Devlet Arşivleri Genel Müdürlüğü Osmanlı Arşivi (DOA)
Kepeci 246. Devlet Arşivleri Genel Müdürlüğü Osmanlı Arşivi, Istanbul.
Kepeci 262. Devlet Arşivleri Genel Müdürlüğü Osmanlı Arşivi, Istanbul.
Mühimme Defteri 73. Devlet Arşivleri Genel Müdürlüğü Osmanlı Arşivi, Istanbul.
Ruznamçe 107. Devlet Arşivleri Genel Müdürlüğü Osmanlı Arşivi, Istanbul.
Ruznamçe 131. Devlet Arşivleri Genel Müdürlüğü Osmanlı Arşivi, Istanbul.
Tapu Tahrir Defterleri 658. Devlet Arşivleri Genel Müdürlüğü Osmanlı Arşivi, Istanbul.

Österreichische Nationalbibliothek (ON)
Türk. Hss. Mxt 579. Österreichische Nationalbibliothek, Vienna.
Türk. Hss. Mxt 609. Österreichische Nationalbibliothek, Vienna.
Türk. Hss. Mxt 613. Österreichische Nationalbibliothek, Vienna.

Süleymaniye Kütüphanesi Library
Sarhoş Abdî. *Zafernâme*. Manzum 1328. Ali Emiri. Süleymaniye Kütüphanesi, Istanbul.

### *Published Primary Sources*
Câfer Iyânî. *Tevârîh-i Cedîd-i Vilâyet-i Üngürüs (Osmanlı-Macar Mücadelesi Tarihi, 1585–1595)*. Transliterated by Mehmet Kirişçioğlu. Istanbul: Kitabevi, 2001.
Takáts, Sándor, Ferenc Eckhart and Gyula Szekfű (eds). *A budai basák magyar nyelvű levelezése. I. 1553–1589* [Correspondence in the Hungarian Language of the Pashas of Buda. Part 1, 1553–1589]. Budapest: Magyar Tudományos Akadémia, 1915.

*Török történetírók. III. kötet. 1566–1659* [Ottoman Chroniclers. Vol. III: 1566–1659], translated and annotated by Imre Karácson. Budapest: Magyar Tudományos Akadémia, 1916.

## Secondary Sources

Ágoston, Gábor. "A szolnoki szandzsák 1591–92. évi összeírása I–II [The Cadastral Survey of 1591–92 of the Sanjak of Solnok]". *Zounuk. A Szolnok Megyei Levéltár Évkönyve* 3 (1988), 221–94; 4 (1989), 191–287.

Ágoston, Gábor. "Muslim Cultural Enclaves in Hungary under Ottoman Rule". *Acta Orientalia Academiae Scientiarum Hungaricae* 44 (2–3) 1991, 181–204.

Bayerle, Gustav. *Ottoman Diplomacy in Hungary. Letters from the Pashas of Buda 1590–1593*. Bloomington: Indiana University, 1972.

Bilge, Sadık Müfit. *Osmanlı'nın Macaristanı: Osmanlı Hâkimiyetindeki Macaristan'ın Tarihî Coğrafyası ve İdarî Taksimâtı (1526–1718)*. Istanbul: Kitabevi, 2010.

Dávid, Géza. "The Sancakbegis of Arad and Gyula". *Acta Orientalia Academiae Scientiarum Hungaricae* 46 (2–3) 1992–93, 143–62.

Dávid, Géza. *Török közigazgatás Magyarországon* [Ottoman Public Administration in Hungary] D.Sc. dissertation, Hungarian Academy of Sciences, Budapest, 1995.

Dávid, Géza. "An Ottoman Military Career on the Hungarian Borders: Kasım Voyvoda, Bey and Pasha." In Géza Dávid and Pál Fodor (eds), *Ottomans, Hungarians, and Habsburgs in Central Europe: The Military Confines in the Era of Ottoman Conquest*. Leiden: Brill, 2000, 265–97.

Dávid, Géza. "A 16–17. századi oszmán közigazgatás működése: a beglerbégek és szandzsákbégek kiválasztása és kinevezése [The Operation of the Ottoman Public Administration in the Sixteenth and Seventeenth Centuries: Selection and Appointment of the *Beylerbeyi*s and the *Sancakbeyi*s]". In Pál Fodor, Géza Pálffy and István György Tóth (eds), *Tanulmányok Szakály Ferenc emlékére* [Studies in Memory of Ferenc Szakály]. Budapest: MTA TKI Gazdaság-és Társadalomtudományi Kutatócsoportja, 2002, 111–13.

Fekete, Lajos. "Debrecen város levéltárának török oklevelei [Ottoman Documents in the Municipal Archives of Debrecen]". *Levéltári Közlemények* 3 (1925), 42–67.

Fekete, Lajos. *Budapest a törökkorban* [Budapest in the Ottoman Era]. Budapest: Királyi Magyar Egyetemi Nyomda, 1944.

Fodor, Pál. "Some Notes on Ottoman Tax Farming in Hungary". *Acta Orientalia Academiae Scientiarum Hungaricae* 54 (4), 2001, 427–35.

Fodor, Pál. *Vállalkozásra kényszerítve: Az oszmán pénzügyigazgatás és hatalmi elit változásai a 16–17. század fordulóján* [Unwilling Entrepreneurs: Changes in Ottoman Financial Administration and the Ruling Elite at the Turn of the Seventeenth Century]. Budapest: MTA Történettudományi Intézete, Magyar-Török Baráti Társaság, 2006.

Fodor, Pál. *The Business of State: Ottoman Finance Administration and Ruling Elites in Transition*. (Studien zur Sprache, Geschichte und Kultur der Türkvölker, 28.) Berlin: Klaus Schwarz Verlag, 2018.

Göyünç, Nejat. "XVI. yüzyılda ruûs ve önemi". *Tarih Dergisi* 17 (22) 1967, 17–34.

Hegyi, Klára. "Vác a törökkorban [Vác in the Ottoman Period]." In M. Ferenc Horváth (ed.), *Vác: A Dunakanyar szíve. Történelmi kalauz helybelieknek és világcsavargóknak* [Vác: The Heart of the Danube Bend. A Historical Guide for Locals and World Travellers]. Vác: Vác Város Önkormányzata, 2009.

Howard, Douglas A. "Ottoman Administration and the Tîmâr System: Sûret-i Kânûnnâme-i 'Osmânî Berây-i Tîmâr Dâden". *Journal of Turkish Studies* 20 (1996), 46–124.

Káldy-Nagy, Gyula. "Statisztikai adatok a török hódoltsági terület nyugat felé irányuló áruforgalmáról [Statistical Data on Ottoman Hungary's Trade Towards the West]". *Történeti Statisztikai Szemle* 11 (1) 1968, 27–97.

Káldy-Nagy, Gyula. *Harácsszedők és ráják. Török világ a XVI. századi Magyarországon* [*Harac*-Collectors and *Reaya*s: The Ottoman World in Sixteenth-Century Hungary]. Budapest: Akadémiai Kiadó, 1970.

Káldy-Nagy, Gyula. *Magyarországi török adóösszeírások* [Ottoman Survey Registers in Hungary]. Budapest: Akadémiai Kiadó, 1970.

Kunt, Metin. "Devolution from the Centre to the Periphery: an Overview of Ottoman Provincial Administration". In Jeroen Duindam and Sabine Dabringhaus (eds), *The Dynastic Centre and the Provinces: Agents and Interactions*. Leiden: Brill, 2014, 30–48.

Özergin, M. Kemal. "Eski bir Rûznâme'ye Göre İstanbul ve Rumeli Medreseleri". *İstanbul Üniversitesi Edebiyat Fakültesi Tarih Enstitüsü Dergisi* 4–5 (1973–1974): 263–90.

Pach, Zsigmond Pál. "Hogyan lett a harmincadvámból huszad? [How the Thirtieth Customs Duty Became Twentieth?]". *Történelmi Szemle* 37 (3) 1995, 257–76.

Sudár, Balázs. "A tizenöt éves háború török költői [Ottoman Poets of the Fifteen Years' War]". *Hadtörténelmi Közlemények* 117 (4) 2004, 1146–65.

Sudár, Balázs. "Egy budai török értelmiségi könyvtára a 16. században [The Library of an Ottoman Intellectual from Buda in the Sixteenth Century]". *Történelmi Szemle* 47 (3–4) 2005, 315–31.

Sudár, Balázs. "Vác városának török házösszeírása 1570-ből [The Ottoman Housing Census in Vác from 1570]". *Századok* 138 (4), 2005, 791–853.

Sudár, Balázs. *Dzsámik és mecsetek a hódolt Magyarországon* [Djamis and Mosques in Ottoman Hungary]. Budapest: MTA Bölcsészettudományi Kutatóközpont, Történettudományi Intézet, 2014.

Takáts, Sándor. "A budai basák emlékezete [The Memory of the Pashas of Buda]". In idem, *Rajzok a török világból*, vol I. Budapest: n.p., 1915. 105–159.

Takáts, Sándor. "Vezír Kalajkiloz [sic!] Ali basa [Vizier Kalaylıkoz Ali Pasha]". In *idem*, *A török hódoltság korából* [From the Era of Ottoman Hungary]. Budapest: Genius, 1927, 151–79.

Takáts, Sándor, Ferenc Eckhart and Gyula Szekfű (eds). *A budai basák magyar nyelvű levelezése. I. 1553–1589* [Correspondence in the Hungarian Language of the Pashas of Buda. Part 1, 1553–1589] (Budapest: Magyar Tudományos Akadémia, 1915), 105–59.

Tomkó, Viktor. "Török közigazgatás Magyarországon: a szolnoki szandzsákbégek története II [Ottoman Public Administration in Hungary: History of the *Sancakbeyi*s of Szolnok II]". *Zounuk. A Jász-Nagykun-Szolnok Megyei Levéltár Évkönyve* 20 (2005), 9–59.

Tóth, Sándor László. *A mezőkeresztesi csata és a tizenöt éves háború* [The Battle of Mezőkeresztes and the Fifteen Years' War]. Szeged: Belvedere Meridionale, 2000.

Vass, Előd. "Éléments pour compléter l'histoire de l'administration des finances du vilayet de Buda au XVIe siècle". In Lajos Ligeti (ed.), *Studia Turcica*. Budapest: Akadémiai Kiadó, 1971, 483–490.

Velics, Antal and Ernő Kammerer. *Magyarországi török kincstári defterek* [Ottoman Treasury Registers from Hungary], 2 vols. Budapest: Athenaeum, 1886–90.

Zimányi, Vera. "Gazdasági és társadalmi fejlődés Mohácstól a 16. század végéig [Economic and Social Development from the Battle of Mohács to the End of the Sixteenth Century]". In Zsigmond Pál Pach and Ágnes R. Várkonyi (eds). *Magyarország története 1526–1686. 1. kötet* [The History of Hungary, 1526–1686, vol. 1] (Budapest: Akadémiai Kiadó, 1985), 285–391.

CHAPTER 8

# Making Recommendations: Azmîzâde and the *Mahzar* for Vücûdî Efendi, 1608

*Christine Woodhead*

Among the various letters to friends, colleagues and men of influence in the *münşeat* of Azmîzâde Mustafa Hâletî Efendi (d.1631) is a short item headed "written for the petition in support of Vücûdî Efendi".[1] In format, style and length it is very similar to a *takriz*, a brief document recommending a particular literary or historical work and its author, written to support a bid made by the latter for reward or promotion.[2] However, the recommendation for Vücûdî Efendi appears slightly unusual, both in its description as *mahzar*[3] rather than *takriz*, and with regard to the flexible career of its subject. Over the course of four decades, Vücûdî alternated between two distinct career paths. Having begun as a *müderris* in the mid-1570s, he subsequently transferred to a military role and spent several years on campaign. In mid-1006/early 1598 he re-entered the scholarly profession as teacher and mufti in a *medrese* in his home region of Larende (present-day Karaman). Following the *mahzar* of 1608 he was also appointed *kadı* and elevated to *mevleviyet* status on an *ad hominem* basis.

While Vücûdî's varying career may be specific in some of its details, it was not unusual, certainly in its earlier stages. It nevertheless serves as a useful example of the kind of professional and social flexibility possible for some in the late-sixteenth and early-seventeenth centuries, and contributes to knowledge of the broader context in which the well-known concerns of conservative Ottoman writers about irregularities and falling standards should be set. Vücûdî's career advanced through carefully cultivated patronage links, with members primarily of the *ulema*, in particular the Kınalızâde family, but also of

---

1 "Vücûdî Efendinün mahżarına yazılmışdur" (entitled by the contemporary compiler, possibly by Azmîzâde himself), *Münşe'ât-i 'Azmîzâde*, fol. 15b, MS Or. 1169, BRL.
2 On a set of six *takriz* written for a historical work c.1620, see Christine Woodhead, "Puff and Patronage: Ottoman *Takriz*-Writing and Literary Recommendation in the 17th Century", in Çiğdem Balım-Harding and Colin Imber (eds), *The Balance of Truth: Essays in Honour of Professor Geoffrey Lewis* (Istanbul: Isis Press, 2000), 395–406.
3 Defined in Redhouse as "petition, round robin", which could be either positive or negative in nature; *takriz* carries the notion more of an encomium or glowing reference. Cf. Mehmet İpşirli, "Mahzar", *DIA* 27, 398–401.

the *ümerâ*. The *mahzar* itself raises certain questions about how *ulema* patronage of mid-ranking scholars functioned, not least that of why Azmîzâde's text is headed *mahzar* rather than *takriz*. This chapter therefore uses the vagaries of Vücûdî's career to indicate some of the options open to a provincial scholar, and to discuss aspects of the ease (or otherwise) and acceptability of crossing career lines in this era, and of the use of patronage relationships. It concludes with a transcription and an English translation of Azmîzâde's contribution to the *mahzar* of 1608.

## 1   The Careers and Patrons of Vücûdî Efendi

When, some time around 1608, Vücûdî Mehmed Efendi journeyed to Istanbul to seek advancement, he was probably in his late sixties and was not seeking a higher post elsewhere. Instead, he sought recognition of his learned and literary status as a means of achieving *mevleviyet* rank and a greater income in his home area in his final years. He died shortly afterwards, in 1612.

Much of what is known about Vücûdî derives from the autobiographical sections in his *mesnevi*, *Hayâl u Yâr*. The following biographical discussion is based largely on the online edition of the two manuscripts of this text published by Yaşar Aydemir.[4] The work is essentially in three parts. The first part, containing the allegorical tale to which the title refers, concludes in both manuscripts on folio 76b, with a chronogram stating that this part of the text was completed in 981/1573–74.[5] It was a work originally of Vücûdî's youth, a proof of his literary ability and cultural understanding.[6] The introduction to this first part contains some sketchy biographical information, comparable in extent to that found in many Ottoman texts of the period. However, the second part of the text is a further thirty folios (to folio 106 in both manuscripts) of mainly autobiographical material – equivalent to almost a third of the complete work – which has little connection with the story of *Hayâl u Yâr*. Entitled *telimme*, 'supplement', and

---

4  Yaşar Aydemir (ed.), *Vücûdî: Hayâl u Yâr* (Ankara: T. C. Kültür ve Turizm Bakanlığı, 2009), http://ekitap.kulturturizm.gov.tr/TR,78446/Vücûdî-hayal-u-yar.html). Apart from autobiographical details in *Hayâl u Yâr*, the principal Ottoman sources are Kınalızâde Hasan Çelebi, *Tezkiretü'ş-Şuarâ* (ed.) İbrahim Kutluk, vol.2 (Ankara: TTK, 1981), henceforth Kınalızâde, *Tezkiretü'ş-Şuarâ*, 1035–8; and Nev'îzâde Atâ'î, *Hadâ'ikü'l-hakâ'ik fî tekmileti'ş-şakâ'ik: zeyl-i şakâ'ik* (Istanbul: Matbaa-i Âmire, 1268/1852), henceforth 'Atâ'î, *Zeyl-i Şakâ'ik*, 559–60.
5  Aydemir, *Hayâl u Yâr*, 163: verse 2449, Didi târîh-i hatmi hayr makâl.
6  On the contents and style of *Hayâl u Yâr*, see Aydemir's introduction, xxv–lxvii.

added around 1593,[7] this section plays down the years Vücûdî had spent as a *zeâmet* holder on campaign and expands considerably upon his education and his *ulema* patrons. It was clearly intended to support his subsequent request for a non-military post. The third part is appended to only one of the two manuscripts (ff. 106–8) and contains two *kaside*s, one addressed to the Khan of the Crimea, Gazi Giray II (r.1588–1607), and one to the *reîsülküttâb* Yahyâ Efendi. Both addressees were prominent figures when Vücûdî made his first appeal to the Imperial Council in 1006/1597–98, and were presumably considered by him as potential patrons.

Vücûdî was born in Larende, the son of a certain Abdülaziz Efendi, probably some time in the 1540s.[8] Entry into the service of Kınalızâde Ali Efendi is the first event of note recorded in *Hayâl u Yâr*. This association appears to have begun around 1563, at the time of Kınalızâde's appointment as *kadı* of Damascus, his first judgeship after several years' teaching at the Süleymaniye *medrese*. Vücûdî seems to have entered Kınalızâde's service almost by chance. As he gives no indication of having left Larende to study in Istanbul, Vücûdî is unlikely to have been previously a student of Kınalızâde. His early education was probably at home and then in a local *medrese* or *medreses*. Among these would have been the Emir Musa *medrese* in Larende, to which he was later appointed *müderris*. Verses in *Hayâl u Yâr* suggest that, as an aimless and despairing young man – presumably having exhausted the educational opportunities available in and around Larende – Vücûdî decided to go on pilgrimage but that on the way he met Kınalızâde while the latter was en route to Damascus, was offered employment, and his plans changed.[9] He remained in Kınalızâde's household for eight years, as his master's personal servant (*bende-i has*), "like a shadow, constantly at his side",[10] and accompanied him to postings around the empire, in Cairo (1566), Aleppo (1567), Bursa and Edirne (both 1569). *Hayâl u Yâr* contains several verses describing each city.

On appointment as *kadı* of Istanbul in 1570, Kınalızâde presented Vücûdî 'according to custom' as a *dânişmend* to his next patron, the *şeyhülislâm*

---

[7] See below, p. 207. An early section in part one in praise of Murad III (date of accession mid-982/December 1574) and "the şehzade" (subsequently Mehmed III) on ff. 6b–10b (*Hayâl u Yâr*, 14–22) must also have been added or amended later, before Murad III's death in January 1595.

[8] Aydemir, *Hayâl u Yâr*, introduction, xiv.

[9] Aydemir, *Hayâl u Yâr*, 24: verses 328–31; 25: 346–50. Cf. Cornell H. Fleischer, *Bureaucrat and Intellectual in the Ottoman Empire: The Historian Mustafa Âli (1540–1600)* (Princeton, NJ: Princeton University Press 1986), 43, for Âli also joining Kınalızâde's household in Damascus.

[10] Aydemir, *Hayâl u Yâr*, 176: verses 2626–7; 181: 2709.

Ebüssuûd Efendi.[11] Almost one-sixth of the revised version of *Hayâl u Yâr* (around 600 verses, or 18 folios) is devoted to Vücûdî's time with Ebüssuûd. He studied in particular Arabic grammar and syntax, logic, lexicology and the Quran; he also discovered that, contrary to what he had been told, Ebüssuûd was not averse to poetry *per se* but that he preferred Arabic verse to Turkish. Vücûdî presented work to Ebüssuûd which was well received, and at an appropriate *nevbet* (rotation period) gained his *mülâzemet*. So far, so good. The provincial student from central Anatolia had studied with, and gained the support of, two of the most highly regarded members of the *ulema* of the time and was well placed for a successful scholarly/judicial career.

However, both his patrons died within little more than two years of each other, Kınalızâde in early 1572 while serving as *kazasker* of Anatolia, and Ebüssuûd in summer 1574, shortly after Vücûdî became a *mülâzim*. These losses probably contributed to Vücûdî's subsequent career change, if only in the sense that he no longer had strong support to gain *ilmiyye* appointments. Initially, he did attempt to maintain scholarly standing, and obtained from Kadızâde Ahmed Şemseddin, *kazasker* of Rumeli 1575–77, appointment as *müderris* at the Şah Kulu *medrese* in the Parmakkapı district of Istanbul, with a daily stipend of 30 *akçe*.[12] However, enthusiasm for the life of a *müderris* clearly waned: "years passed lethargically; the post became the bane of my life".[13]

Vücûdî then acquired a third major patron, from a different direction. Another significant meeting in Damascus in the mid-1560s had been with Lala Mustafa Pasha, governor of the province from 1564 to 1567.[14] According to Atâî, after dismissal from a 30-*akçe* teaching post Vücûdî entered the household of Lala Mustafa when the latter was appointed *serdar* on the 1578 eastern campaign, and became his *musâhib*, a close companion. What this role comprised and whether it had any legal or religious aspect is unclear. In *Hayâl u Yâr* Vücûdî says little about what became a purely military career, implying that he changed course on a whim, which he later regretted. However, given that it was twenty years before he finally returned to a learned career, such regrets seem to have taken some time to appear.

As *musâhib* to Lala Mustafa Pasha, Vücûdî was enrolled in the *müteferrika* corps and given a 40,000-*akçe zeâmet*, which, according to Kınalızâde Hasan,

---

11  Aydemir, *Hayâl u Yâr*, 187: 'âdet-i mu'tâde üzre.
12  Aydemir, *Hayâl u Yâr*, 225–7, esp. verses 3373, 3392. For this *medrese*, see Cahid Baltacı, *XV–XVI. Asırlarda Osmanlı Medreseleri: Teşkilat, Tarih* (Istanbul: İrfan Matbaası 1976), 435–6. 'Atâ'î, *Zeyl-i Şakâ'iḳ*, 560, notes appointment to the Şah Kulu as a 30-*akçe medrese*, though according to Baltacı this *medrese* later rose to 40, and by 1585 to 50 *akçe* per day.
13  Aydemir, *Hayâl u Yâr*, 227: verse 3406, and the following *ḥasbiḥâl*.
14  Aydemir, *Hayâl u Yâr*, 27–8: verses 382 ff.

was in the province of Damascus.[15] Its value would have compared well with the remuneration offered to some of the secretarial staff appointed to the campaign,[16] but not with that of a financial bureaucrat such as Gelibolulu Mustafa Âlî, whose appointment in 1578 to the post of *tımar defterdarı* for the province of Aleppo brought him a *zeâmet* worth 80,000 *akçes*.[17] The value of Vücûdî's grant was possibly calculated by analogy with the 40-*akçe* salary he would have received had he remained a *müderris*. Although Lala Mustafa Pasha's death in 1580 soon deprived Vücûdî of his third patron, he remained in military service in the Caucasus, through the conquest of Şirvan (eastern Caucasus, present-day Azerbaijan) and the occupation of Demirkapı (Derbend, present-day Dagestan, Russian Federation) by Özdemiroğlu Osman Pasha in the early 1580s. As a *zeâmet* holder, Vücûdî would have been regularly called upon to campaign during the 1580s. Atâî notes that he became well known for his excellent swordsmanship, which suggests that he was more enthusiastic and competent militarily than he later wished to emphasize.[18] Vücûdî is credited by late Ottoman sources with having composed a *gazânâme* (or possibly two) on the campaigns of Lala Mustafa Pasha and Özdemiroğlu Osman Pasha. However, neither *Hayâl u Yâr* nor any of the contemporary sources mention these. If such *gazânâmes* existed, Vücûdî would have been just one of several participants who composed similar works on the exploits of the viziers commanding the campaigns of 1578–85.[19] He would also have been one of several hopefuls left bereft of potential patronage once again when Osman Pasha – by then grand vizier – died near Tabriz in 1585, shortly after capturing the city.

A brief introduction to the second part of *Hayâl u Yâr* concludes with a single verse stating that at the time of writing Vücûdî had settled in Aleppo, living off the income from his *zeâmet*.[20] His choice of Aleppo was clearly

---

15  ʿAṭâʾî, *Ẕeyl-i Şaḳâʾiḳ*, 560: hem-rikāb ve muṣāḥib-i vezîr-i âṣaf-cenâb olub, 40,000 akçe zeʾâmetle müteferrika olmış idi; Kınalızâde, *Tezkiretüʾş-Şuarâ*, v. 2, 1036.

16  Compare this to the 5000-*akçe tımâr* awarded by Özdemiroğlu Osman Pasha in 1585 to Taʿlîkîzâde Mehmed Efendi, one of his secretaries (noted in the latter's *Tebrîziye*, fol. 10a, MS 1299, Revan 1299, TSMK).

17  Fleischer, *Bureaucrat and Intellectual*, 82, 90–91, 115.

18  ʿAṭâʾî, *Ẕeyl-i Şaḳâʾiḳ*, 560.

19  Cf. Agâh Sırrı Levend, *Ġazavāt-nāmeler ve Mihaloğlu Ali Beyʾin Ġazavāt-nāmesi* (Ankara: TTK, 1956), 85, 89, 175. Levend lists but had not seen either of these works. The list of contemporary sources in Bekir Kütükoğlu, *Osmanlı-İran Siyâsî Münâsebetleri, I: 1578–1590* (Istanbul: Edebiyat Fakültesi, 1962) does not include anything by Vücûdî.

20  Aydemir, *Hayâl u yâr*, 165: verse 2471.

determined by the posting there as *kadı* in 1591 of Kınalızâde Hasan, the son of his first patron, and someone of sufficient learned and literary standing to be a useful patron himself. Vücûdî makes particular note of certain members of the scholarly circle around Kınalızâde Hasan in Aleppo.[21] These included Dukaginzâde Osman Efendi, the descendant of a wealthy and prestigious *ümerâ* family; Ömer Efendi, the current *defterdar* of Aleppo and son of the poet Hayâlî; and Tab'i Süleyman Efendi, a former *kadı* turned finance official and former *defterdar* of Baghdad. To these men Vücûdî read *Hayâl u Yâr*, and in his supplementary text reports Tab'i's favourable comments on it. Given that Kınalızâde Hasan remained in Aleppo for two years, from 1591 to 1593, and that for personal reasons Dukaginzâde Osman probably spent some time in Aleppo between dismissal from the post of *kadı* of Mecca in 1592 and appointment to Cairo in 1594, Vücûdî's reading and revision of *Hayâl u Yâr* can be dated to late 1592 or 1593.[22]

Participation in the *meclis* of Kınalızâde Hasan probably prompted Vücûdî to consider seriously a return to *medrese* teaching, and would account for the long encomia on Kınalızâde Ali and Ebüssuûd in the second part of *Hayâl u Yâr*, with only passing mention of his military service. Nevertheless, for the time being Vücûdî remained bound by his status as a *zeâmet* holder and was therefore obliged to attend the Hungarian campaign of 1594, which resulted in the capture of the fortress of Yanık (present-day Győr, Hungary), possibly that of 1595, and certainly that of 1596. The two *kasides* in the third part of *Hayâl u Yâr* refer to this period and were probably composed in 1597. The first *kaside* is addressed to Gazi Giray Han II. Although Vücûdî possibly met the khan during the eastern campaigns of the early 1580s, the latter and his Tatar forces made a considerable contribution to the 1594 campaign and the *kaside* refers specifically to the capture of Yanık.[23] The second *kaside*, addressed to the *reîsülküttâb* Yahyâ Efendi – who was also present on the 1594 campaign – has

---

21  Halil Çeltik, "Halep'te Kınalızâde Hasan Çelebi'nin Şairler Meclisi", *Gazi Türkiyat* 1 (2007), 139–45 (but note misidentification of Dukaginzâde Osman, d.1603; cf. 'Atâ'î, *Zeyl-i Şakâ'ik*, 460).

22  On *mevleviyet* appointments in the late-sixteenth century, see Abdurrahman Atçıl, "The Route to the Top in the Ottoman *İlmiye* Hierarchy of the Sixteenth Century", *Bulletin of the School of Oriental and African Studies* 72 (2009), 506. On the Dukaginzâde family *evkaf* in Aleppo, see Heghnar Zeitlian Watenpaugh, *The Image of an Ottoman City: Imperial Architecture and Urban Experience in Aleppo in the 16th and 17th Centuries* (Leiden: Brill, 2004), 77–9.

23  Aydemir, *Hayâl u Yâr*, 165: verse 247. Cf. Halil İnalcık, "Gazi Giray Han II: Kırım hanı (1588–1607)", *DIA* 13, 451–2.

a much darker tone and contains a catalogue of woes.[24] In short, Vücûdî had been summoned to attend the 1596 Hungarian campaign but had suffered one calamity after another: his horse died, his money ran out, he had to proceed on foot and arrived at Belgrade neither in time nor properly equipped to join the army; as a result, his *dirlik* was confiscated (probably in the aftermath of the Battle of Haçova in October 1596).[25] Atâî corroborates this collapse into poverty, stating that Vücûdî had become destitute due to the fact that *"Celâlîs* destroyed the villages of his *zeâmet* and his personal livelihood was plundered by unruly troops."[26]

A combination of genuine rekindling of enthusiasm for a learned, literary environment together with the loss of military status and income made a return to teaching both attractive and financially necessary. Following the 1594 campaign, Vücûdî had spent some time in Buda composing a second literary work, a didactic *mesnevi* entitled *Şâhid ü Ma'nâ*.[27] By 1597, he therefore had at least two literary works to his credit, and could call upon a sound educational background with Kınalızâde Ali and Ebüssuûd, and some teaching experience. Atâî notes that Vücûdî "was received at the sultan's court and entered the feverish throng of petitioners" for office. In January 1598 he received brief appointment to the Osman Pasha *medrese* in Istanbul, as a stepping stone to his desired post as *müderris* at the Emir Musa *medrese* in Larende.[28]

It is at this point – his return to a *medrese* post – that Vücûdî's career becomes more unusual. There are innumerable examples in the late-fifteenth and sixteenth centuries of *medrese* graduates, *müderris*es and *kadı*s at virtually all levels who for various reasons chose other careers. The expanding bureaucracy, both central and provincial, could not have functioned without such recruits. The careers of men such as Celâlzâde Mustafa and Mustafa Âlî

---

24  On Yahyâ Efendi, see Christine Woodhead, "Scribal Chaos? Observations on the Post of *Reîsülküttâb* in the Late Sixteenth Century", in Eugenia Kermeli and Oktay Özel (eds), *The Ottoman Empire: Myths, Realities and 'Black Holes': Contributions in Honour of Colin Imber* (Istanbul: Isis Press, 2006), 155–72.

25  The word in Aydemir, *Hayâl u Yâr*, 232, verse 3472 which Aydemir reads tentatively as 'serem' is probably Srem/Sirem, the region to the west of Belgrade where the Ottoman army began operations in August 1596: cf. Selânikî, *Tarih-i Selânikî*, edited by Mehmet İpşirli, vol. 2 (Ankara: TTK, 1989), 625.

26  'Atâ'î, *Zeyl-i Şakâ'ik*, 560. Cf. Sam White, *The Climate of Rebellion in the Early Modern Ottoman Empire* (Cambridge: CUP, 2011), 142, 207 on famine and *Celalis* in the Damascus region, where Vücûdî's *zeâmet* was probably still located.

27  For summary of contents, see Aydemir, *Hayâl u Yâr*, introduction, xl–xlii.

28  Cf. Baltacı, *XV–XVI. Asırlarda Osmanlı Medreseleri*, 190–1 for "Emîr Musa medresesi (Karaman)"; 330–2 for "Osman Paşa medresesi, Istanbul". This must have been the Emir Musa *medrese* in the city of Larende/Karaman, and not the *medrese* of the same name in Ermenek, Karaman province; cf. İsmail Çiftçioğlu, "Ermenek'te Emir Musa Bey medresesi (Tol medrese) ve vakfiyesi", *İlmî Araştırmalar* 12 (2001), 73–82.

are just the most well known in a pattern recognized and widely accepted by their contemporaries. Tab'i Süleyman Efendi, mentioned above, is typical of a lower-level transfer. However, to *return* to a scholarly or judicial career later in life appears much less usual. This impression may be misleading, partly because those reverting to their original profession would have been mostly low or mid-ranking men for whom evidence is difficult to find. The present discussion of why and how Vücûdî did so is based on the fortuitous survival of autobiographical details. There certainly were other cases. One is that of a poet known as Meylî. As recorded in the *tezkire* of Beyânî, Meylî Mustafa was a native of Kayseri, gained his *mülâzemet* from Ebüssuûd, and chose to become a provincial *kadı*. He then made almost the same career change as Vücûdî, at almost the same time.

> With a reversal of fortune and a change of circumstances, he joined Özdemiroğlu Osman Pasha's Şirvan campaign and served for a while as *defterdar* and then as *mirliva*. On his return he accepted a *kadılık* for a while, then became *müderris* and *müfti* in Kayseri.[29] When the medrese was given *dahil* status, he sought [and presumably received] the *kaza* of Kayseri with *mevleviyet* rank.[30]

Vücûdî and Meylî would certainly have been known to each other. As Beyânî completed his *tezkire* shortly before his death in 1597, Meylî's successful return to scholarly status must have occurred only a few years before Vücûdî's first appeal, and would have been an encouraging precedent. On the whole, however, given the increasing competition for scholarly-judicial appointments in the 1590s, the cases of successful reversion by those in military or bureaucratic service were probably relatively few.

## 2  *Ulema* Patronage

Atâî does not identify the patrons who assisted Vücûdî in 1597/8 but, given the hiatus in the latter's scholarly career, he is unlikely to have succeeded in gaining appointment without very strong support. Vücûdî's heartfelt plea to Yahyâ Efendi (*reîsülküttâb* for a third time from September 1597 to late 1598) could

---

29   Possibly the Handi (or Huand) Hatun *medrese*: cf. Baltacı, *XV–XVI. Asırlarda Osmanlı Medreseleri*, 249, for a previous *müderris* of this college also acting as *müfti*.
30   Beyânî, *Tezkiretü'ş-Şu'ara*, edited by Aysun Sungurhan Eyduran (Ankara: T. C. Kültür ve Turizm Bakanlığı, 2008), 202: "Meylî-i diger". Beyânî also includes a short entry on Vücûdî, 227–8: "Vücûdî-i diger".

have paid dividends, but a continuing association with Kınalızâde Hasan was probably more important. It is worth noting that Vücûdî was appointed to the Osman Pasha *medrese* in Cemâziyelâhir 1006/January 1598, in the same month as Kınalızâde was reappointed *kadı* of Egypt. His appointment may have been granted as a form of *teşrif* ('promotion gift/honour') for Kınalızâde.[31] It is also tempting to speculate that Vücûdî had some connection with the administrators or patrons of the Osman Pasha *medrese*, a college founded under the terms of a bequest by one of Vücûdî's previous actual or potential patrons, Özdemiroğlu Osman Pasha, and completed in 1588.

Vücûdî may also have been very fortunate in the timing of his first petition, in two respects. First is that he presented his case just before the promulgation in Ramazan 1006/April 1598 of a new *ilmiyye kânûnnâmesi*. This regulation had the express purpose of controlling admission to the learned careers by enforcing stricter rules on the granting of *mülâzemet*. One clause stated that members and protégés of military and other *kul* groups would no longer be granted *mülâzim* status without evidence of sufficient previous education.[32] Even though Vücûdî had technically passed the *mülâzim* stage twenty years previously, a stricter code of practice designed to keep numbers down and standards up could have worked against him. In any case, he was required to accept a token appointment to the 50-*akçe* Osman Pasha *medrese* as a formality, "to pass through the ranks", before gaining appointment in Larende.[33] Second, it has been assumed so far that Vücûdî actively requested the post in Larende because it was his home area. However, he may not have had much alternative. In the late 1590s, the province of Karaman was dominated by *Celâlîs*. Assignment to Larende – which has been described as the 'epicentre' of the rebellion[34] – is unlikely to have been popular among petitioners for teaching posts. Because of his early background, Vücûdî may have been considered a prime candidate for a position that no one else would take, and one that

---

31  On *teşrif* grants of *mülâzemet* on the promotion of a senior *kadı*, see Yasemin Beyazıt, "Efforts to Reform Entry into the Ottoman *İlmiyye* Career Towards the End of the 16th Century: The 1598 Ottoman *İlmiyye Kanunnamesi*", *Turcica* 44 (2012–13), 201–18; Mehmet İpşirli, "Osmanlı İlmiye Teşkilatında Mülazemet Sisteminin Önemi ve Rumeli Kadıaskeri Mehmed Efendi Zamanına Ait Mülazemet Kayıtları", *Güneydoğu Avrupa Araştırmaları Dergisi* 10–11 (1981–82), 224.

32  Beyazıt, "Efforts to Reform Entry", 203, 211.

33  'Atâ'î, *Zeyl-i Şakâ'ik*, 461: *mahzan kat'-i pâye içün medrese-i mezbûra hakk-ı meşrûtî olmak üzre*, in his entry on Zuhûrî Efendi, who had to make way temporarily for Vücûdî to fulfil this requirement. In his entry on Vücûdî, 'Atâ'î uses the phrase *meşrutiyet davası ile*.

34  White, *Climate of Rebellion*, 113, and chapter 7 on the rebellion itself.

he was unable to refuse. As was the case with Meylî's appointment to Kayseri noted above, with the post of *müderris* also went that of mufti.[35]

In 1016/1607–8, Vücûdî returned to Istanbul and petitioned the Imperial Council a second time.[36] Again, he would have needed strong support to succeed, especially given his ten-year absence from the capital. However, in the interim all those who could have assisted him in 1597/8 had either died – Kınalızâde Hasan in 1604, Gazi Giray Han in 1607, and (a possible patron) Dukaginzâde Osman, in 1603 – or, in the case of Yahyâ Efendi, were no longer influential. The *mahzar* to which Azmîzâde contributed was probably the best – perhaps the only? – alternative to individual patronage for a provincial scholar without recent connections. It also catered for a situation where a petitioner was offering more than one work for consideration. How usual was such an individual petition, and what rules applied? The heading for a different item in his *münşeat* referring to *infisalimüz*, 'my dismissal' indicates that Azmîzâde compiled the collection and wrote the headings himself.[37] His choice of the term *mahzar* clearly differentiates this item from two subsequent *takriz*, and suggests a specific procedure.

According to Atâî, Vücûdî "presented several of his writings and works to the sultan and to several leading members of the Imperial Council, and received the inestimable honour of the rank of *mevleviyet*." As he was neither resigning from his teaching post nor had he been dismissed from it, the usual procedure of registering with a *kazasker* for a new appointment was not relevant. Azmîzâde describes Vücûdî as having "built up a strong case with the help of the leading *ulema*", which suggests that the petitioner presented himself and his works to a wide circle of scholar-judges, and not just to the *kazasker*s and other members of the *Dîvân-ı Hümâyûn*. Receiving requests for recommendation would have been a regular occurrence for senior *ulema* present in Istanbul but not in post. Azmîzâde was out of office at the time he wrote his contribution, having been dismissed as *kadı* of Bursa in Şevval 1016/January–February 1608. Similarly, five of the six *takriz* appended c.1620 to a world history by a secretary of the *Dîvân*, Mehmed b. Mehmed, were written by retired *kazasker*s; the sixth was by the preacher Şeyh Sivâsî.[38] None of these six writers was currently responsible for making teaching or judicial appointments. There

---

35   On joint *müderrislik/müftilik* appointments, see R. C. Repp, *The Müfti of Istanbul: A Study in the Development of the Ottoman Learned Hierarchy* (London: Ithaca Press 1986), 64–8, including Larende, 66.
36   1016 given in ʿAṭâʾî, *Zeyl-i Şaḳâʾiḳ*, 460.
37   *Münşeʾât-i ʿAẓmîzâde*, fol. 51b.
38   Woodhead, "Puff and Patronage", 398–406.

is no indication of how many recommendations were sought for the *mahzar* of 1608 but use of the term *mahzar* suggests a considerable number.

The principal scholarly works attributed to Vücûdî by Atâî and subsequent sources are his translations into Turkish of al-Jawzî (d.1256)'s *Mir'ât al-Zamân*,[39] a general history from the creation to the author's own time, and of el-Ghazzâlî's *Naṣâ'iḥ al-Mulûk*.[40] As neither of these is mentioned in *Hayâl u Yâr*, they must have been products of his later period as *müderris*, from 1598 to 1608. While Vücûdî's interest in ethics and advice literature such as el-Ghazzâlî's text had probably been inspired much earlier by his studies with Kınalızâde Ali, his translation of *Naṣâ'iḥ al-Mulûk* contributed to a genre particularly popular around 1600, as seen in the 'mirrors for princes' produced by writers such as Hasan Kâfî Akhisârî (c.1596–97) and Veysî (c.1608).[41] The chief works upon which Vücûdî was judged in 1608 therefore comprised two new translations of significant works and his two previous *mesnevi*s. None of these were *medrese* teaching materials, but must have fitted into an acceptable range of *ulema* literary activity.[42]

Examples of *takriz* writing sometimes appear in *münşeat* collections or appended to the particular work to which they refer, but the majority probably remained as uncopied texts on loose sheets of paper. Azmîzâde's *münşeat* includes a *takriz* also written around 1608 for a *risâle* by Tabîb Beyzâde[43] and signed by him as "former *kadı* of Bursa", and another for the *münşeat* of Ganîzâde Mehmed Nâdirî.[44] However, there must have been many more, as Atâî notes that "[Azmîzâde's] *takriz* written for the works of contemporaries

---

39    Cf. Ali Sevim, "Sıbt Ibnü'l-Cevzi", *DIA* 37, 86–7.

40    Cf. Casım Avcı, "Nasihatü'l-müluk", *DIA* 32, 411, which also refers to a translation of this by Kınalızâde Ali. If this attribution is correct, it would be interesting to compare these two texts to see how Vücûdî's translation differed from that of his master. Bursalı Tâhir in *Osmanlı Müellifleri* 3, 158–9, also credits Vücûdî with translating a work by Ibn Qayyim (d.1350), but contemporary sources do not mention this.

41    Pál Fodor, "State and Society, Crisis and Reform in 15th–17th Century Ottoman Mirrors for Princes", *AOH* 40 (1986), 225–9.

42    Cf. Suraiya Faroqhi, "Social Mobility among the Ottoman 'Ulemâ in the Late Sixteenth Century", *IJMES* 4 (1973), 207–8 on literary genres favoured by *ulema* writers.

43    Cf. 'Aṭâ'î, *Zeyl-i Şaḳâ'iḳ*, 638–9, "El-molla Meḥmed", d.1029/1620; Kâtib Çelebi, *Fezleke-i Kâtib Çelebi*, vol. 1 (Istanbul: Ceride-i Havadis Matbaası, 1286/1869), 402, "El-molla Meḥmed Ṭabîb Beyzâde", and idem, *Keşf-el-Zünun*, edited by Şerefeddin Yaltkaya, vol. 1 (Istanbul: Maarif Matbaası, 1941), 924, as "Meḥmed b. İbrâhim eş-şehîr bi-Beyzâde", physician to Ahmed I.

44    *Münşe'ât-i 'Aẓmîzâde*, fol. 18a–b (24 lines), 18b–19a (8 lines). Both *takriz* are in Arabic. Cf. Woodhead, "Puff and Patronage", 399 fn.1, for another *takriz* for the *risâle* of Tabib Beyzâde composed by Zekeriyazâde Yahyâ; 'Aṭâ'î, *Zeyl-i Şaḳâ'iḳ*, 639, comments specifically on appreciation of this *risâle*: *'ulemâ-yı 'aṣr takrîz-ü-imżâ … itmişler idi*.

are, like the coins struck by the imperial mint, productive of demand and of joy."[45] His *takriz* for the *münşeat* of Nergisî, written c.1627, is a fine example.[46] It may be that Azmîzâde's *takriz* writing was undertaken mainly during the 1620s and therefore after the compilation of the version of his *münşeat* used here, in which the majority of items can be dated between 1602 and 1614. It would certainly be the case that the more senior he became and the more time he spent in Istanbul but out of office, the more *takriz* requests he would receive. As with most items within a *münşeat* collection, the reasons why the *mahzar* text for Vücûdî was selected for inclusion cannot be ascertained. Although intriguing in other senses, in literary terms it does not seem to be a particularly remarkable composition. The text is a workmanlike composition of thirteen manuscript lines, generally formulaic in tone. Its main distinguishing features are a play on the word *vücud* and acknowledgement of the petitioner being far from home and in need. Azmîzâde's rather conventional concluding statement – that since everyone was agreed on the outcome, he need write no more – suggests that he felt little need to make a particularly strong case.

Nevertheless, both the term *mahzar* and the format of Azmîzâde's text deserve further comment. In other contexts, a *mahzar* is usually described as a petition or *arzuhal*-type document containing a single text to which any number of supporters would add their signatures. A 'political' *mahzar* seems to have been mostly (though not always) a petition against something or somebody, seeking removal of a tax imposition or an oppressive official.[47] However, the *mahzar* for Vücûdî was clearly a positive petition, and if testimonials were sought from a number of leading *ulema* it must have been a much more elaborate document or collection of documents. It would be good to find other contributions to this *mahzar*. With regard to internal format, in a typical, early-seventeenth-century *takriz* written for a single work, between half and two-thirds of the assessment would relate to the text concerned, and the rest of the *takriz* to the merits of its author and how he clearly deserved financial reward or professional advancement.[48] However, in contrast to a *takriz*, Azmîzâde's contribution to the *mahzar* of 1608 contains no mention of any specific work and is primarily a general recommendation of Vücûdî as an accomplished scholar.

The text does not indicate conclusively why Vücûdî petitioned the *Dîvân* in 1608. Given that the outcome was promotion to *mevleviyet* rank and, according

---

45  'Atâ'î, *Zeyl-i Şakâ'ik*, 560.
46  Printed in J. R. Walsh (ed.), "The *Esālībü'l-mekātīb* (*Münşe'āt*) of Mehmed Nergīsī Efendi", *Archivum Ottomanicum* 1 (1969), 305.
47  Halil İnalcık, "Şikayet Hakkı: 'Arz-ı Hal ve 'Arz-ı Mahzar", *OA* 7–8 (1988), 55–70; İpşirli, "Mahzar", 398–401.
48  See the six examples in Woodhead, "Puff and Patronage", 398–406.

to Atâî, addition of the post of *kadı* of Larende to that of *müderris* and mufti,[49] the principal reason may have been simply financial, buttressed by a desire for recognition of his personal status. The Emir Musa *medrese* carried a notional daily salary of 50 *akçe*, a standard rate for the principal *medreses* in the cities of central Anatolia. However, as a pre-Ottoman, Karamanid foundation (c.1340) it may be that the *vakıf* properties supporting this *medrese* were no longer adequate; any accrued shortfall might also have been exacerbated by pillage and population movement during the *Celâlî* era.[50] By adding to this the daily salary of 300 *akçe* for a *mevleviyet kadılık*, any financial difficulties should have been solved, even allowing for a local shortfall on this amount too. On the other hand, such a combination of offices went against contemporary concern for maintaining the integrity of individual *kadılık*s, as seen in a petition by a group of provincial *kadı*s to the sultan, c.1602, stressing *inter alia* the need for properly regulated appointment procedures.[51] *Ad hominem* arrangements such as that made for Vücûdî can be found in the late-sixteenth century but clearly drew increasing criticism in the early-seventeenth, if not from those like Azmîzâde at the top of the *ulema* hierarchy then certainly from lower-ranking competitors.[52] Whether or not the *mahzar* of 1608 was an unusual procedure, it was probably essential for Vücûdî to achieve his aim. The question of how long he might have been able to hold on to his portfolio of posts in Larende was solved, perhaps fortunately, by his death in 1612.

### Appendix: Azmîzâde's Contribution to the Mahzar[53]

[15b/17] Vücûdî Efendinün maḥżarına yazılmışdur
[16a/1] Mezbûr dâʾîleri
  ʿulemâʾ-i ʿiẓâmun hidmetleriyle iktisâb-ı bihbûd
  ve ḥalḳa-ı ifâdelerine düḫûlle istîḥâb-ı vücûd ḳıldugından mâʿadâ
  kendü daḫi beżâʿa-ı ʿömrden iżâʿe itmeyüb
  taḥṣîl-i cevâhir-i ʿirfâna naḳd-ı vaḳtin dâʾimâ maṣrûf

---

49  ʿAṭâʾî, *Ẕeyl-i Şaḳâʾiḳ*, 560: *ḳażâ-ı Lârende żamîme-i manṣıb-ı tedrîs-ü-iftâʾolınub*. For a similar example in Kütahya c.1562–3, see Repp, *Müfti of Istanbul*, 48.
50  Baltacı, *XV–XVI. Asırlarda Osmanlı Medreseleri*, 190–1, lists the *vakıf* properties.
51  Halil İnalcık, "The *Rūznāmče* Registers of the *Kadiasker* of Rumeli as Preserved in the Istanbul *Müftülük* Archives", *Turcica* 22 (1988), 267–9.
52  Cf. Repp, *Müfti of Istanbul*, 37–8, 47–9 on specially-created *mevleviyet*s.
53  *Münşeat-i ʿAzmi-zade*, fol. 15b–16a.

ve baḥreyn-i ʿilm-ü-maʿrifet cânibine ʿinân-ı ʿazîmetin hemvâra maʿṭûf
  ḳılmak üzredür.
Ḥaḳḳâ ki ẓihn-i vücûdi beynü'l-ʿulemâ' müsellem
  belki vücûd-ı ẓihnî-miṣâl maʿlûm-ı ʿâlemdur.

El-ḥâletü hâzihi, nevâle-i ʿâṭifet-i şehinşâhîye gülû-yı ricâsın âmâde
  ve niṣâr-ı ʿaṭîye-i ḫüsrevânîye dâmen-i ümîdin güşâde ḳılub
  dâr-u-diyârından dûr ve ehl-u-ʿiyâlinden mehcûr olmışdur.

Şâyeste-i resm-i şehriyârî ve bâyeste-i ḳânûn-ı merevvet-kârî
  bâb-ı ʿinâyeti bi-tamâma bâz
  ve heybetle rücûʿından kemâ yenbagî iḥtirâz ḳılmakdur.
  *beyt*  ez lutf-ı nigehdâr dil-haste dilân-râ
       tâ lutf-ı Ḫüdâvend nigehdâr-ı tû bâşed

Çûnki garaż-ı enẓâr vifâḳ
  ve zümre-i sâbiḳîne ḳaṣd-i iltiḥâḳdur
  bu miḳdârla iktifâ olındı.

### *Written for the Petition in Support of Vücûdî Efendi*

The petitioner, the aforesaid [Vücûdî Efendi], has built up a strong case with the help of the leading *ulema* and has requested the favour of his entry and inclusion in the circle of *ulema* benefits.

He himself has not neglected the management of his life's stock of ability. He has always spent the small change of his days on acquisition of the jewels of learning and has guided the reins of his determination continually towards the two seas of learning and knowledge.

In fact, his understanding of existence/existing intelligence [*zihn-i vücûdi*] is recognized among the *ulema*, and is perhaps even, like the existence of intelligence [*vücûd-i ẓihnî-miṣâl*], known among the people.

This being the case, he has prepared his throat to receive a morsel of imperial favour and has spread wide the skirt of his hopes [to await] the scattering of royal gifts. He is far from his home and country and separated from his family and household.

It is fitting according to imperial regulations and appropriate in terms of the munificent *kanun* that the sultan should open fully the door of his favour and thereby prevent Vücûdî Efendi's returning [home] in despair.

  *verse*  with the kindness of the guardian to those sick at heart
        until the favour of God becomes guardian over you

Because opinions are agreed and [Vücûdî Efendi's] inclusion in the aforementioned group is the intention, this much will suffice.

## Bibliography

### Primary Sources
British Library
Azmîzâde Hâletî. *Münşeat-i Azmî-zade*. MS no. Or. 1169. British Library.

Topkapı Sarayı Müzesi Kütüphanesi Library (TSMK)
Ta'lîkîzâde Mehmed. *Tebrîziye*. MS no. Revan 1299, Topkapı Sarayı Müzesi Kütüphanesi.

### Published Primary Sources
Aydemir. Yaşar (ed.) *Vücûdî Mehmed: Hayâl u Yâr*. Ankara: T. C. Kültür ve Turizm Bakanlığı, 2009. [http://ekitap.kulturturizm.gov.tr/TR,78446/Vücûdî---hayal-u-yar.html].

Beyânî. *Tezkiretü'ş-Şu'ara*, edited by Aysun Sungurhan Eyduran. Ankara: T. C. Kültür ve Turizm Bakanlığı, 2008 [http://ekitap.kulturturizm.gov.tr/TR,78462/beyani----tezkiretus-suara.html].

Kâtib Çelebi. *Fezleke-i Kâtib Çelebi*, vol. 1. Istanbul: Ceride-i Havadis Matbaası, 1286/1869.

Kınalızâde Hasan. *Tezkiretü'ş-Şuarâ*, edited by İbrahim Kutluk, vol. 2. Ankara: TTK, 1981.

Nev'îzâde Aṭâ'î. *Ḥadâ'iḳü'l-ḥaḳâ'iḳ fî tekmileti'ş-şaḳâ'iḳ: zeyl-i şaḳâ'iḳ*. Istanbul: Matbaa-i Âmire, 1268/1852.

Selânikî Mustafa. *Tarih-i Selânikî*, edited by Mehmet İpşirli, vol. 2. Istanbul: TTK, 1989.

### Secondary Sources
Atçıl, Abdurrahman. "The Route to the Top in the Ottoman *İlmiye* Hierarchy of the Sixteenth Century". *Bulletin of the School of Oriental and African Studies* 72 (2009), 489–512.

Avcı, Casim. "Nasihatü'l-Müluk". *DIA*, vol. 32. Istanbul, 2006.

Baltacı, Cahid. *XV–XVI. Asırlarda Osmanlı Medreseleri: Teşkilat, Tarih*. Istanbul: İrfan Matbaası, 1976.

Beyazıt, Yasemin. "Efforts to Reform Entry into the Ottoman *İlmiyye* Career Towards the End of the 16th Century: The 1598 Ottoman İlmiyye Kanunnamesi". *Turcica* 44 (2012–13), 201–18.

Bursalı Mehmed Tâhir. *Osmanlı Müellifleri* (Istanbul 1333–42), v. 3, 158–9.

Çeltik, Halil. "Halep'te Kınalızâde Hasan Çelebi'nin Şairler Meclisi". *Gazi Türkiyat* 1 (2007), 137–47.
Çiftçioğlu, İsmail. "Ermenek'te Emir Musa Bey medresesi (Tol medrese) ve vakfiyesi". *İlmî Araştırmalar* 12 (2001), 73–82.
Faroqhi, Suraiya. "Social Mobility among the Ottoman *'Ulema* in the Late Sixteenth Century". *International Journal of Middle East Studies* 4 (1973), 204–18.
Fleischer, Cornell H. *Bureaucrat and Intellectual in the Ottoman Empire: The Historian Mustafa Ali (1540–1600)*. Princeton, NJ: Princeton University Press, 1986.
Fodor, Pál. "State and Society, Crisis and Reform in 15th–17th Century Ottoman Mirrors for Princes." *Acta Orientalia Academiae Scientiarum Hungaricae* 40 (1986): 217–40.
İnalcık, Halil. "Gazi Giray Han II: Kırım hanı (1588–1607)", *DIA*, vol. 13. Istanbul, 2003, 451–2.
İnalcık, Halil. "Şikayet Hakkı: 'Arz-ı Hal ve 'Arz-ı Mahzar". *Osmanlı Araştırmaları* 7–8 (1988), 55–70.
İnalcık, Halil. "The *Rūznāmče* Registers of the *Kadiasker* of Rumeli as Preserved in the Istanbul *Müftülük* Archives". *Turcica* 22 (1988), 251–75.
İpşirli, Mehmet. "Osmanlı İlmiye Teşkilatında Mülazemet Sisteminin Önemi ve Rumeli Kadıaskeri Mehmed Efendi Zamanına Ait Mülazemet Kayıtları". *Güneydoğu Avrupa Araştırmaları Dergisi* 10–11 (1981–82), 221–31.
İpşirli, Mehmet. "Mahzar". *DIA*, vol. 27. Istanbul, 2003.
Kütükoğlu, Bekir. *Osmanlı-İran Siyâsî Münâsebetleri, I: 1578–1590*. Istanbul: Edebiyat Fakültesi, 1962.
Levend, Agâh Sırrı. *Ġazavāt-nāmeler ve Mihaloğlu Ali Bey'in Ġazavāt-nāmesi*. Ankara: TTK, 1956.
Ocak, Ahmet Yaşar. *Osmanlı Toplumunda Zındıklar ve Mülhidler: 15–17. Yüzyıllar*. Istanbul: Türkiye Ekonomik ve Toplumsal Tarih Vakfı, 1998.
Repp, R. C. *The Müfti of Istanbul: A Study in the Development of the Ottoman Learned Hierarchy*. London: Ithaca Press 1986.
Sevim, Ali. "Sıbt İbnü'l-Cevzi". *DIA*, vol. 37. Istanbul, 2009.
Walsh, J. R. (ed.) "The *Esālībü'l-mekātīb* (*Münşe'āt*) of Mehmed Nergīsī Efendi". *Archivum Ottomanicum* 1 (1969), 213–302.
Watenpaugh, Heghnar Zeitlian. *The Image of an Ottoman City: Imperial Architecture and Urban Experience in Aleppo in the 16th and 17th Centuries*. Leiden: Brill, 2004.
White, Sam. *The Climate of Rebellion in the Early Modern Ottoman Empire*. New York: Cambridge University Press, 2011.
Woodhead, Christine. "Puff and Patronage: Ottoman *Takriz*-Writing and Literary Recommendation in the 17th Century." In Ciğdem Balım-Harding and Colin Imber (eds), *The Balance of Truth: Essays in Honour of Professor Geoffrey Lewis*. Istanbul: Isis Press, 2000, 395–406.

Woodhead, Christine. "Scribal Chaos? Observations on the Post of *Reîsülküttâb* in the Late Sixteenth Century". In Eugenia Kermeli and Oktay Özel (eds), *The Ottoman Empire: Myths, Realities and 'Black Holes': Contributions in Honour of Colin Imber.* Istanbul: Isis Press, 2006, 155–72.

CHAPTER 9

# A Poet's Warning: Veysî's Poem on the Breakdown of Ottoman Social and Political Life in the Seventeenth Century

*Mehmet Kalpaklı*

The changes or 'breakdowns' in the Ottoman state and society observed from the late-sixteenth century onwards brought into Ottoman political and cultural life the tradition of 'letters of advice' (*nasihatnâme*) written in particular by intellectuals belonging to the ruling class.

Works of this genre, usually written in prose, generally describe the structural breakdown of Ottoman society and politics, and propose ways in which proper order could be restored.[1]

However, the Ottoman poets of this age also composed poems addressing the same themes and with the same goals, which may be considered poetic representatives of a more inclusive 'advice' genre.

I will examine the corruption perceived in Ottoman life during the post-classical age within the framework of a little-known poem by the seventeenth-century poet Veysî (d.1628). This text also demonstrates the pitfalls of relying solely on archival documents and prose essays as sources for Ottoman history and points to the necessity of paying more attention to poetic sources as well.[2]

Uveys bin Mehmed is usually known by his *mahlas* (pen name) as Veysî. He was the son of a judge of Alaşehir, western Anatolia, and died in 1628 in Skopje (O. Üsküp, present-day North Macedonia). He was a noted poet who earned a living also as a *kadı* (judge) in various parts of the Ottoman Empire. Veysî was one of the best prose writers, and his works, such as *Siyer-i Veysî* (Life of the Prophet Muhammed), *Münşeat* (Writings and Letters) and *Hâbnâme* (The Vision) were considered among the finest examples of the Ottoman prose genre.[3] His *nasihatnâme* (*Hâbnâme*), composed in 1608 and presented to the reigning sultan Ahmed I (r.1603–17), was written in plain Turkish unlike his other prose works. In this work, Veysî describes a dream. He overhears a

---

1 For an overview on Ottoman advice literature, see Mehmet Öz, *Osmanlı'da 'Çözülme' ve Gelenekçi Yorumcuları* (Istanbul: Dergâh Yayınları, 1997).
2 For Veysî's poem, see E. J. W. Gibb, *A History of Ottoman Poetry*, vol. 3 (London: Lusac, 1904; reprint 1965), 205–18; and Günay Kut [Alpay], "Veysi'nin Divanında Bulunmayan Bir Kasidesi Üzerine", *Türk Dili Araştırmaları Yıllığı-Belleten* 18 (1970), 169–78.
3 For Veysî's life and works, see Bayram Ali Kaya, "Veysî", *DIA* 43, 2013, 76–7.

conversation between the reigning Sultan Ahmed I and Alexander the Great. Ahmed I bemoans the ruined condition of the country at the time of his accession and its disorder and moral collapse. Alexander replies by saying "since when was this world, which we call a ruins, ever not ruined?" and cites examples from Adam on words to show that these kinds of social disorder had happened in every age.

In addition to his prose advice, Veysî wrote a long poem, found not in his *Dîvân* but only in many private poetry anthologies (*mecmua*s).[4] We can adduce a number of reasons for accepting this text as having been written by Veysî, although in the text the poet gives some information that does not match the story of Veysî's life.

First, several *mecmua*s, including some written in Veysî's own time, attribute the text to him. Moreover, Veysî himself may have included misleading information in order to disguise his authorship because of the difficulties and dangers of that time of expressing such critical and accusatory sentiments. In any case, no matter who the author might have been, it is a significant text insofar as it reflects Ottoman social and political life in the period of its writing, points out a series of problems, and expresses one person's opinion as to their solutions.

In this sixty-seven-couplet poem, Veysî addresses the people of Istanbul, or, more correctly, Istanbul's ruling elites, and points to them as the reason for the evils that had befallen the Ottomans. And, throughout the poem, Veysî discusses the role played by members of the ruling classes (for example, judges, counsellors, viziers, pashas, and *ağa*s) in the breakdown of Ottoman society. In addition, he addresses the Ottoman sultan and indicates ways in which he could solve these problems.

In the first couplet, the poet speaks to the people of Istanbul and the administrative elites:

*Eyâ ey ḳavm-i İstanbul bilin taḥḳîḳ olun âgâh*
*İrişir nâgehân bir gün size ḳahr ile ḫışmullâh*

Oh people of Istanbul, know well and be certain
One day the wrath of God will come and overwhelm you.

He then goes on to criticize the sumptuous buildings being constructed in Istanbul:

---

4 Some of the *mecmua*s containing Veysî's poem include MS 617, fol. 28a–29a, Yeni Yazmalar, TSMK; MS Ty 264, fol.105a, IUK; MS 3409, fol.189b, Esad Efendi, SK; MS 6334, fol.44b, Hacı Mahmud, SK; MS 235, fol. 50a, Muallim Cevdet, ATUK.

*Yapıp dünyâ evin vîrân edersiz ḫâne-i dîni*
*Ne Firʾavn yapdı ne Şeddâd binâlar bu şekil billâh*

You are building worldly houses and ruining the house of faith
Neither Pharaoh nor Sheddad built such edifices

Later he criticizes the judges:

*Ḳużât aḥvâlini dersen ne mümkündür beyân etmek*
*Eger ḫaṣmun ise ḳâḍı efendi yarıcın Allâh*
*Ḳurub bir dâm-ı tezvîri demişler mahkeme adın*
*Ḥani seccâde-i Aḥmed ḥani aḥkâm-ı şerʾullâh*

If you mention the state of judges, what can one say?
If a judge bears a grudge against you, God help you!
They have set a snare of deceit and called it a court of justice.
Where is the prayer rug of Muhammed, where the law of God?

This is followed by "becoming the slave of women" and "becoming besotted by young boys".

*Zamâne uydu nisvâna, döşendi ekser oğlana*
*Ekâbir tapdı hemyâna olup yâr-ı ʿaduvvullâh*

This age is enslaved by women and addicted to boys
The great worship their purses and befriend the enemies of God

And, "the cruelty and bad morals of Istanbul people have surpassed all bounds"; he fears that "soon a sudden punishment/curse will fall on them":

*Stanbul ḳavminin ẓulm ü fesâdı ḥadden aşmışdır*
*Budur ḳorḳum yaḳınlarda irişe bir belâ nâgâh*

The people of Istanbul are boundless in their cruelty and immorality
My fear is this that soon there will befall a sudden calamity

After this couplet, Veysî begins his critique of the administration of the state. Here the poet criticizes the rise of converts (*dönme*) to high positions in the Ottoman government. According to him, it is not right that people born as non-Muslims should be given positions in the administrative apparatus of the state.

> *Yahûdî gibi mel'ûnlar geçerler ṣadra bî-teklîf*
> *Ḳapıdan baḳsa bir mü'min ederler andan istikrâh*
> *Nedendir böyle ḫâ'inler emânet ṣâḥibi olmak*
> *'Aceb hîç ehl-i İslâmda bulunmaz mı emînullâh*

> Without trouble accursed ones such a Jews become leaders
> If a believer looks in the door they regard him with loathing.
> Why should such traitors be in positions of trust?
> Are there none among the Muslims who are trustworthy?

In this section of the poem, Veysî turns to the sultan and urges him to be just:

> *Ḫudâ ṣaḳlar ḫaṭâlardan 'adâlet eyleyen şâhı*
> *Ve hem dünyâ ve 'uḳbâda olurlar fî-emânillâh*

> God shields the just Shah from committing error
> For he is under the surety of God in this world and the next

Then he addresses the sultan himself and complains about the viziers:

> *Vezîre i'timâd etme benim devletli ḥünkârım*
> *Olardır düşmeni dînin, olardır devlete bed-ḫʷâh*
> *Vezâret ṣadrına geçmiş oturmuş bir bölük ḥayvân*
> *Bu dîn ü devlete ḥizmet eder yoḳdur âh vâh*

> Do not rely on your viziers oh fortunate monarch
> They are enemies of the religion who wish the state ill.
> A drove of animals have come and sat in the vizirial seats;
> But there is not one to serve the faith and state, ah ...

After these harsh words for those who constituted the highest administrative class in the empire, he turns his attention to the insincerely religious and ascetic. He says that they have strayed far from the truth of the faith with their ostentatious prayers and that, unless they receive money, they refuse to perform sermons and lessons, nor lead prayers, nor even recite the Quran.

> *Hemân bir hây u hûy ile yıḳar câmi'leri ṣûfî*
> *Ḥani evrâd ile esmâ hani tevḥîd-i ẕikrullâh*

The 'Sufis' level the mosques with their clamour
But where are the holy verses, the holy names, where praise
   of God's unity?

*Gerek va'ż u ḫiṭâbetler, gerek ders ü imâmetler*
*Verilmez olsa ücretler okunmazdı Kelâmullâh*

Neither sermons nor homilies, nor lessons nor leading prayers
They will do nothing without a wage, not even recite the Words
   of God.

Among those who get their share of criticism are also the sheikhs (religious heads):

*Ṣırâṭ-ı müstaḳîm üzre değildir şeyḫ ü vâ'iẓler*
*Ṣapınca reh-nümâ yoldan nice ḫalḳ olmasın güm-râh*

Sheikhs and preachers have fallen from the straight and
   narrow way
When the guide has strayed how can the people not go awry?

According to Veysî, people have lost interest in religion because of religious leaders who are preoccupied with the affairs of this world and look only for monetary gain.

*Anınçün dinlemez vâ'iẓ sözin ḳoymaz ḳulaga ḫalḳ*
*Mü'essir mi olur pendi gönülde olsa gayrullâh*

For this reason the people pay no heed to the preacher's words
If in his heart he opposes God, how can his words be effective?

In the time of the foundation and rise of the Ottoman Empire, the most important factor was the spirit of *ghaza* (holy war), which united the country and supported its conquests. A number of works written about the Ottoman decline criticize the disappearance of this spirit, especially during the seventeenth century, and the loss of this motivation in the Ottoman army and administration. The loss of this *ghazi* spirit is given as a reason for the cessation of conquest. In his poem, Veysî too touches upon this subject.

*Çalışır bir tarîḳ ile seferden kalmaga herkes*
*Ḳanı bir atlanır gider gazâya fî-sebîlillâh*

> Everyone strives one way or another to avoid campaigns
> Where is one who mounts his horse and rides to ghaza?

In many of the Ottoman *nasihatnâme*s, the reason given for the breakdown in wages and order is the waywardness of the janissaries and *sipahi*s. For his part, Veysî seems to defend these two institutions:

> *Beş on akça ulûfeyle sipâhî neylesin nitsin*
> *Eger Yeniçeri dersen ne kadir söylemek billâh*

> What is a *sipahi* to do on a wage of five or ten aspers
> If you ask about janissaries, how can I describe them for God's sake?

He then goes on to say that it is not the janissaries and *sipahi*s but the pashas and *ağa*s who are the real cause of decline.

> *Bozulmasına dünyânın sebeb paşalar ağalar*
> *Fesâd u fitneye bâ'iş bulardır şübhesiz vallâh*

> The reason for this disruption of the world is the Pashas and Aghas
> Without doubt they are the source of corruption and sedition, by God.

However, he claims that the pashas and *ağa*s are not solely to blame and that the disruptions are also caused by ill-intentioned persons at the top of the Ottoman administration. In particular, Veysî blames the *defterdar* who was responsible for the fiscal policies of the empire and the *reîsülküttâb* who was responsible for foreign policy:

> *İdinmiş kalfa iblîsi Re'îs-i küttâb u Defterdâr*
> *Tarîk-i şeytânetde ol değil mi bunlara hem-râh*

> The Reîsülküttab and Defterdar have made the devil their
>     apprentice
> Is it not he who has become their companion on the path
>     of wickedness.

After taking to task those in the general administration of the state, he gets around to the local officials, especially *asesbaşı* and the *subaşı* (local police officials).

> *Cihânda ḫırsız u hemyânkesici kim durur dersen*
> *'Asesbaşı ile taḥḳîḳ Subaşıdır inan billâh*

> In this world, you ask, who is the thief and cut-purse?
> Be assured it is certainly the Asesbaşı and Subaşı, by God.

Then the discussion turns to the learned class. Above all, he criticizes the *kadiaskers* (*kazaskers*) who occupy the highest rank of this class and brings up the subject of bribery which we see in almost all the *nasihatnâme*s.

> *Bulardan dahi aẓlemdir efendim Ḳāḍî'askerler*
> *Cihânı irtişâ birle ḫarâba verdiler vallâh*

> More tyrannical than all of these, sir, are the Kadiaskers
> By God, they have ruined this world with bribery.

This text also emphasizes that bribery has brought about the destruction of the school (medrese) system:

> *Faḳîr 'âlimlerin 'ömrü geçer 'azl ile ẓılletde*
> *Olursan mürteşî câhil bulursun 'izzet ü hem câh*

> Poor scholars' lives pass in joblessness and wretchedness
> But if you are an ignorant briber, you will find fame and glory.

In his critiques, Veysî also mentions several ethnic groups that could rise to the highest positions in the state. He points especially to Albanians and Bosnians, and criticizes their involvement in the administration of the empire.

> *'Acebdir 'izz ü devletde cem'en Arnavud, Boşnaḳ*
> *Çeker devrinde ẓılletler şehâ Âl-i Resûlullâh*

> It is odd that those of fame and fortune are all Albanian and Bosnian
> The people descended from the Prophet of God all suffer misery in
>     their time.

After Veysî has listed all the things that have contributed to the decline of the Ottoman Empire, addressing the sultan directly, he even warns him and reminds him of his responsibilities. He says that God has put the world under the care of the sultans and that it is necessary for them to be aware of their responsibilities. He even makes a veiled threat by saying that this responsibility will be called into account in the next world.

> *Ḥużûr-ı Ḥaḳḳ'a vardıḳda olursuz evvelâ mes'ûl*
> *Size tefvîż olunmuşdur, emânetdir 'ibâdullâh*

> When you come into the presence of God you will first, be questioned about your responsibility towards the people of God.

By referring to the succession of earlier sultans, Veysî emphasizes the transitory nature of this world:

> *Süleymânlar gelib gitdi niçe bu fânî dünyâya*
> *Ḥani cedd-i 'iẓâmın pes kime ḳaldı bu mülkullâh*

> How many Süleymans came and went from this fleeting world?
> How many of your glorious ancestors retained anything of this
>     God's Earth?

Finally, he tells the sultan how he should behave, and what he should do to save society from this terrible situation:

> *Bugün 'adl eyleyib ḫalḳa edersen lutf u iḥsânı*
> *Yüzün ag olısar yarın maḳâmın ẓıll-ı 'arşullâh*
> *Bir alay mużḥik u dilsiz cücelere ḳarîn olma*
> *Şeyâṭîn ḳavmine uyma değillerdir fî-ẓıllullâh*

> Today if you do justice and are beneficent and generous to the people
> Your face will be white tomorrow and your place will be the
>     shadow of the throne of God.
> Do not be the companion of a troop of jesters and dumb voiceless
>     dwarves
> Do not bend to the tribe of Satan, they are not in the shadow of God.

We have no certain knowledge who the sultan addressed by Veysî might have been. We only know from the following couplet that the text was written before the conquest of Baghdad and therefore probably at a time when the conquest was on the Ottoman agenda.

*Nice feth olısar Bağdâd imâmlar eylemez imdâd*
*Bulardan yüz çevirmişdir 'azîzim evliyâullâh*

How will Baghdad be conquered when the imams will not help
My lord, the saints of God have turned their faces away from these (administratives).

Judging from this couplet, it seems likely that the poem was composed in the time of Mustafa I or, even more probably, that of Murad IV.

Towards the end of the text, Veysî gives the reasons for this work. While he and the other intellectuals were 'sleeping' he, by the grace of God, saw the light and was able to distinguish the truth from falsehood:

*Uyurdum Ḥaḳḳ naẓar itdi gözümden perdeler gitdi*
*Ağ u ḳarayı farḳ itdi bi-ḥamdillâh bi-ḥamdillâh*

As I slept, God looked and the veils fell from my eyes
I could distinguish the light from the dark, God be praised, be praised.

He then says that he is not afraid about having given these proofs and warnings and that he did out of the sole desire to win the approval of God in both worlds:

*Ne ḫavf u ne murâdım var beg ü paşa agalardan*
*İki 'âlemde maḳṣûdum hemân ancak rıżâullâh*

I have no fear or wish of bey or pasha or ağa
My only goal in two worlds is the approval of God.

Veysî's poem is not alone in relating the breakdown in social life and the disorder and changes seen in the structure of Ottoman society towards the end of the sixteenth century. It is possible to find in the *dîvâns* of Ottoman poets couplets in which social criticisms are couched in the form of 'complaints about the spheres' or 'the seditious nature of the beloved' or more generally complaints about 'fate'. Numbers of poems were composed about the collapse of the order of this world, about the deleterious effects of hypocrisy and bribery. For this reason it seems right to include this kind of literary work within the *nasihatnâme* tradition.

## Bibliography

### Primary Sources
Süleymaniye Kütüphanesi Library
Veysî [Uveys bin Mehmed]. *Hâbnâme.* MS no. 3409. Esad Efendi, Süleymaniye Kütüphanesi.
Veysî [Uveys bin Mehmed]. *Hâbnâme.* MS no. 6334. Hacı Mahmud, Süleymaniye Kütüphanesi.

Topkapı Sarayı Müzesi Kütüphanesi Library
Veysî [Uveys bin Mehmed]. *Hâbnâme.* MS no. 617. Yeni Yazmalar, Topkapı Saray Müzesi Kütüphanesi.

İstanbul Üniversitesi Kütüphanesi Library
Veysî [Uveys bin Mehmed]. *Hâbnâme.* MS Ty 264. İstanbul Üniversitesi Kütüphanesi.

Erzurum Atatürk Üniversitesi Kütüphanesi Library
Veysî [Uveys bin Mehmed]. *Hâbnâme.* MS no. 235. Muallim Cevdet, Erzurum Atatürk Üniversitesi Kütüphanesi.

### Secondary Sources
Gibb, E. J. W. *A History of Ottoman Poetry,* vol. 3. London, Lusac, 1904. Reprint London: Lusac and Company Ltd, 1965.
Kaya, Bayram Ali. "Veysî". In *DIA*, vol. 43. Istanbul, 2013.
Kunt, Metin Ibrahim. "Ethnic-Regional (Cins) Solidarity in the Seventeenth-Century Ottoman Establishment." *International Journal of Middle East Studies* 5 (1974), 233–9.
Kut, Günay [Alpay]. "Veysi'nin Divanında Bulunmayan Bir Kasidesi Üzerine." *Türk Dili Araştırmaları Yıllığı-Belleten* 18 (1970): 169–178.
Öz, Mehmet. *Osmanlı'da 'Çözülme' ve Gelenekçi Yorumcuları.* Istanbul: Dergâh Yayınları, 1997.

CHAPTER 10

# From the 'Scribe of Satan' to the 'Master of Belâgât': Ottoman Chief Scribes and the Rhetorics of Political Survival in the Seventeenth Century

*Ekin Tuşalp-Atiyas*

This chapter follows the careers of two Ottoman chief scribes – Şâmîzâde Mehmed (d.1663) and Râmi Mehmed (d.1708). With only a few decades separating them, the two Mehmeds occupied the post of the chief scribe (*reîsülküttâb*) which began gaining more relevance in Ottoman politics from the second half of the seventeenth century onwards.[1] Both Şâmîzâde and Râmi have been noted as critical figures in this transition.[2] A perhaps less obvious thing they had in common was their extraordinary political resilience: Şâmîzâde Mehmed and Râmi Mehmed were among the few bureaucrats who steered through the muddy waters of seventeenth-century Ottoman politics and managed – at least for a while – to avoid the political executions that many of their bureaucrat peers faced at the time.[3] Even when they were swept away by

---

[1] *Reîsülküttâb*, literally the chief of the scribes, is the most senior official among the chancellery scribes. See Recep Ahıskalı, *Osmanlı Devlet Teşkilatında Reisülküttablık (XVIII. yüzyıl)* (Istanbul: Tarih ve Tabiat Vakfı Yayınları, 2001); Halil İnalcık, "Reîsülküttâb", *IA* 9, 671–83.

[2] See İnalcık, "Reîsülküttâb", 682.

[3] The end of Ahmed I's rule (1617) started one of the most dramatic periods of Ottoman history. Sultan Osman's murder in 1622, the urban and military revolts that jeopardized and abrogated sultans' rules, and the dearth of mature and sane heirs to take up the throne manifested the vulnerability of the Sultanic charisma when faced with an increasingly disgruntled population at the centre and in the provinces. In the meantime, two female members of the dynasty, Kösem Sultan (Sultan Ahmed I's favourite concubine and mother of Sultan İbrâhim and Murad IV) and later Turhan Sultan (Sultan İbrâhim's concubine and Mehmed IV's mother, d.1683) became powerful political figures through the coalitions they formed and the immense personal wealth they used to boost their political alliances. The provincial military governors, who undertook uprisings in the provinces, constantly opted in and out of the political system. Istanbul had its own share of these disturbed times, and witnessed a series of urban riots undertaken by different combinations of guildsmen, merchants, janissaries, cavalrymen and *ulemâ*. Chronic budget deficits, urban and provincial populations strained by increasingly extractive economic policies and the prolonged conflicts with the Safavids and the Venetians dramatically shortened the careers of the Ottoman political elite. The seventeenth-century grand viziers would occupy their seats for much shorter periods than their predecessors and were often executed or disgraced at the hands of

hostile political coalitions, they found a way to come back and resumed their posts in the Ottoman administration. This brings us to the third and the most important feature that they had in common. The stories of their political survival fed a variety of political narratives and created a unique rhetorical world that presented their political rise (and subsequent demise) as the rise of the Ottoman scribal community. The narratives about the two Mehmeds – both critical and praiseful – took their patronage and fame as the subject matter. More importantly, however, they captured the development of the Ottoman scribal community at different stages and documented its self-proclaimed political credentials and claims in detail.[4]

I survey the 'scribal rhetorics' that materialized in different primary sources from the 1640s onwards when Şâmîzâde Mehmed first appeared on the political-administrative scene. I study the period until the early 1700s when Râmi Mehmed was dismissed from his post as the grand vizier. In the approximately half a century that saw Şâmîzâde Mehmed's fall from grace and Râmi Mehmed's rise to power, the arguments about what qualified people coming from scribal backgrounds to assume political power became clearer, more mature and more confidently expressed by the members of the Ottoman scribal community. Şâmîzâde Mehmed's success in surviving the mid-century political crises was the product of complex patronage relations that guaranteed him a secure financial base that none of his scribal peers enjoyed at the time. However, it was not only his wealth that distinguished Şâmîzâde Mehmed from the other occupants of the Ottoman political space. One particular genre that had a strong rhetorical standing at the time is panegyric poetry (*kaside*). The panegyrics written to honour Şâmîzâde Mehmed contrasted his knowledge of what they called 'the language of the state' with the 'ignorance' of the others, although in Şâmîzâde Mehmed's case it is not clear what this knowledge entailed in the actual world of Ottoman politics.

The conditions under which Râmi Mehmed arrived on the political scene were different from those in Şâmîzâde Mehmed's time. Both the political stability under the relatively long reign of Mehmed IV (r.1648–87) and the increasingly independent tenure of the Köprülü grand viziers saved the lesser members of the Ottoman bureaucracy the troubles of the former times. In this

---

the disgruntled coalitions. See Stanford J. Shaw, *History of the Ottoman Empire and Modern Turkey*, vol.1 (New York: CUP, 1976), *passim*.

4    For a wider discussion of this transformation, see Ekin Tuşalp-Atiyas, "Political Literacy and the Politics of Eloquence: Ottoman Scribal Community in the Seventeenth Century" (Ph.D. dissertation, Harvard University, 2014).

environment, the scribal community had not only strengthened its dealings within the existing patronage system but also matured its political discourses. By the time Râmi Mehmed was granted the seal of the grand vizier, he was already surrounded by a scribal community that would see his rise to the grand vizierate as the long-awaited reversal of their fortune, the awakening of their long dormant potential and the realization of their claims to political power. Râmi Mehmed Efendi's tenure as the chief scribe and later his appointment as the grand vizier provided the occasion for scribes to express themselves as the most eloquent (*belîg*) and the most articulate (*fasîh*) contenders for political power.[5] Their most reiterated claim was that political power was unfairly held by people whom they considered illiterate, ignorant and unworthy.

The aim here is to give a sense of how political communities came into being and how they achieved a sense of 'political worth' in the early modern era. It is also to touch on wider questions about political mobility and the transformation of political elites in the seventeenth century, issues about which Professor Metin Kunt has made many valuable observations over the years.

## 1    The Rise and Demise of Şâmîzâde Mehmed

In his biographical dictionary of poets, Mustafa Safâyî wrote that the chief scribe Şâmîzâde Mehmed was the 'chief satan' (*reîs-i iblis*) and an 'uncouth fool' (*hammâlü'l-hattâb*).[6] The pretext for Safâyî's accusation was Şâmîzâde Mehmed's alleged involvement in the execution of the poet Vecdî who was a possible contender for the post of the chief scribe.[7] Another Ottoman biographer Ahmed Resmî, in his account of Şâmîzâde's life, denounced excessive

---

5  The basic concepts of Perso-Arabic literary criticism, eloquence (*belâgat*) and subtlety of meaning/articulateness (*fasâhat*) had already been in circulation in Ottoman literary texts prior to the seventeenth century. In the second half of the seventeenth century, we see that the Ottoman scribal community resorted to these twin concepts with full force in order to underline their intellectual superiority. For a more detailed discussion of the employment of these concepts in seventeenth-century Ottoman scribal literature, see Tuşalp-Atiyas, "Political Literacy", 161–85.

6  Mustafa Safâyî, *Tezkire-i Safâyî (Nuhbetü'l-Asar Min Feva'idi'l-Eş'ar) İnceleme-Metin-İndeks*, edited by Pervin Çapan (Ankara: Atatürk Kültür Merkezi Yayınları, 2005), 684.

7  According to different sources, threatened by the prospect of Vecdî replacing him, Şâmîzâde had him executed by accusing him of taking part in a plot against the grand vizier Köprülü Mehmed Pasha. See İsazade, *İsazade Tarihi (Metin ve Tahlil)*, edited by Ziya Yılmazer (Istanbul: İstanbul Fetih Cemiyeti İstanbul Enstitüsü Yayınları, 1996), 68 fn.1. The event is also in Safâyî's biography of Rûhî's; see Safâyî, *Tezkire-i Safâyî*, 202.

ambition and claimed that it was high status that really tested men.[8] According to Ahmed Resmî, when something significant – like appointment to a significant post – happened to a man, if he were sturdy in character and close to God, he would do his best to serve the public and therefore God. If not, death would befall on him just as it did Şâmîzâde Mehmed.

According to Ahmed Resmî, Şâmîzâde first appeared on the political scene as the secretary of the eminent political figure of the time, Hezarpâre Ahmed Pasha (d.1648). According to another Ottoman chronicler Mustafa Naîmâ, Şâmîzâde was already an important member of Hezarpâre's entourage even before the latter became grand vizier in 1647.[9] Hezarpâre Ahmed rose to power from within the bureaucracy and it is possible that he recruited Şâmîzâde earlier in his career in the financial bureaucracy.[10] Once he became the grand vizier, Hezarpâre instructed his secretary Şâmîzâde, whom he appointed as *reîsülküttâb*, not to accept any bribes, to follow the law and the *şeriat* and to prioritize the issues that could improve the plight of the treasury.[11] The relationship between the secretary and the patron indicates that patronage mechanisms were perfectly at work inside the bureaucracy. Like many of his peers at the time, Hezarpâre could not escape execution when the janissaries and some members of the *ulema* moved to depose Sultan İbrâhim (1615–48). At the end of the rebellion, Mehmed IV was instated as the sultan, and Hezarpâre was strangled and torn to pieces (hence the name!) on 18 Receb 1058 (8 August 1648). Despite his patron's gory demise, Şâmîzâde Mehmed remained in his post as the chief scribe until 1065 (1654/5).[12]

The period from 1648 until 1654 witnessed the emergence of a new coalition of forces formed by Turhan Sultan and her main political ally, the chief black eunuch Süleyman Ağa, replacing Kösem and her cronies in the palace. The first incident that put Şâmîzâde on the narrative map of the Ottoman chroniclers occurred at this time. The issue was the selection of a new grand vizier

---

8     Ahmed Resmî, *Sefînetü'r-Rü'esâ*, fol.32, MS 720, Ali Emiri, MIKT.

9     Mustafa Na'îmâ, *Tarih-i Naîma: Ravzatü'l-Hüseyn fî Hulâsati Ahbâri'l-Hâfikayn*, edited by Mehmet İpşirli, vol. 3 (Ankara: TTK, 2007), 1142.

10    Resmî, *Sefînetü'r-Rü'esâ*, 27. Hezarpâre Ahmed was a man from within the bureaucracy. Son of a cavalryman (*sipahi*) and talented in calligraphy, he entered the financial bureaucracy at an early age. He was initially a petition writer (*tezkireci*) for Kemankeş Mustafa Pasha. He later became the director of the bureau of retained revenues (*mevkufatçı*) and the keeper of registers (*defterdar*) in 1646.

11    Osmanzade Ahmed Taib, *Hadîkatü'l-Vüzerâ* (Istanbul: Cerîde-i Havâdis Matbaası, 1271/1854), 87, 88; Şeyhî Mehmed Efendi, *Veka'yü'l-Fudâlâ, Şâkâyık-i Numâniye ve Zeyilleri*, edited by Abdülkadir Özcan, vol. 5 (Istanbul: Çağrı Yayınları, 1989), 154–6.

12    Resmî, *Sefînetü'r-Rüesâ*, 27.

following the deposition of Grand Vizier Derviş Pasha in 1654. Among the contenders for Derviş Pasha's seat were İbşir Pasha, who was supported by the Chief Mufti Hoca Mesud, and the director of finances Moralı Defterdar, who was backed by Şâmîzâde Mehmed. Eventually, the chief mufti put his weight behind İbşir Pasha, arguing that the vizierial seal was too much for a director of finances to bear. This statement is crucial since, first, it delineates what was off-limits to a mid-ranking bureaucrat and, second, it shows that Şâmîzâde was soon to become the target of the newly instated grand vizier İbşir Pasha's hostility. After he was appointed as the grand vizier, İbşir Pasha continued to carry a grudge against his rival Moralı Defterdar and his main supporter Şâmîzâde. He moved on to execute Moralı Defterdar, who at the time of his execution, made a confession that further exposed Şâmîzâde's connivance. Moralı Defterdar swore that it was upon Şâmîzâde's compulsion that he decided to compete against İbşir Pasha.[13] According to Ahmed Resmî, the pretext for Şâmîzâde's detention and imprisonment by İbşir Pasha was that he penned an imperial order banishing İbşir and his men from arriving at the capital to claim the vizierial seal. Şâmîzâde's life was spared thanks to the intervention of his adherents within İbşir Pasha's household, who convinced the grand vizier of Şâmîzâde's innocence. The ex-chief of the scribes had previously won hearts by having others' business done at his chancellery for free.[14]

The story of Şâmîzâde's first fall from grace manifests the extent of his fortune and entourage.[15] Continually forced by İbşir Pasha to give more to the treasury, Şâmîzâde was obliged to sell his precious horses, sable furs, saddles, and gold and silver belongings. He took all his property to brokers to be sold at auctions. His 180 bags of gold were all confiscated. Even after all that he possessed was taken away, his entourage and friends still owed 30,000 *guruş* to the treasury. However, those who had previously enjoyed Şâmîzâde's favours intervened once again to soothe Grand Vizier İbşir Pasha. They argued that there was no point in hassling Şâmîzâde to give more and that he would have to sell his most indispensable possessions. The grand vizier was finally persuaded to allow Şâmîzâde to bequest all the cash he would get by auctioning this property. Şâmîzâde first retreated to his house in Üsküdar and later moved to Tosya where he had a land grant (*zeâmet*). He stayed there for a year until Mimar Kasım Ağa, the chief instigator of the rise of Köprülü Mehmed Pasha to power,

---

13   Naîmâ, *Târîh* 4, 1588.
14   Naîmâ, *Târîh* 4, 1594.
15   Naîmâ, *Târîh* 4, 1594, 1595.

recalled him.[16] It was through his mediation that Şâmîzâde was readmitted into administration as the *reîsülküttâb*, this time for a much longer period, between 1066 (1655/6) and 1074 (1663).[17]

Ahmed Çelebi, known by the penname Tıflî composed a *kaside* to celebrate Şâmîzâde's second appointment.[18]

By the glad tidings arrived at the heart
News from the genie of the unknown

Found his place one more time,
Arrived the former master of favours

It is again the old pleasing spring,
Arrived again the crystalline sun

His highness, the jewel Chief of the time,
Arrived as the world-conquering khedive

---

16  The new coalition that Turhan Sultan masterminded following the elimination of her archrival Kösem, could not avert yet another riot in the capital, which was undertaken by the dangerously unforeseen coalition of janissaries and cavalrymen. The Platanus Incident (*Vaka-yı Vakvakiye* or *Çınar Vakası*) of 1656 erased the remaining tier of harem eunuchs and their collaborators from the political scene. The erosion of the eunuchs' political power cleared the space for Köprülü Mehmed Pasha, who in 1656 persuaded Turhan Sultan and her entourage that they had no choice other than surrendering him the vizierial seal. Turhan Sultan, who was then acting as the regent for her adolescent son Mehmed IV and weary of the factitious politics of the last fifty years, agreed to Köprülü's grand vizierate and to his unusual preconditions for a hands-off approach to his tenure. Professor Kunt regards the oft-quoted deal that Köprülü Mehmed allegedly made with the palace as a slightly exaggerated narrative. According to Kunt, Köprülü Mehmed's coming to power was the product of an era of a greater grand vizierial autonomy that had previously resulted in Tarhuncu Ahmed's and Derviş Mehmed's attempted, yet failed budgetary reforms. See Metin Kunt, "The Köprülü Years 1656–1661" (Ph.D. dissertation, Princeton University, 1971); idem, "Na'îmâ, Köprülü, and the Grand Vezirate", *Bosphorus University Journal-Humanities* 1 (1973), 57–64.

17  Evliya Çelebi dates his execution to 9 Safer 1074/12 September 1663. See Evliya Çelebi, *Evliya Çelebi Seyahatnâmesi: 6. Kitap: Topkapı Sarayı Kütüphanesi Revan 1457Numaralı Yazmanın Transkripsiyonu-Dizini*, edited by Seyit Ali Kahraman and Yücel Dağlı (Istanbul: Yapı Kredi Yayınları, 2002), 201.

18  The *kaside* is entitled "Berây-ı Re'îs Efendi". See Bekir Çınar, "Tıflî Ahmed Çelebi. Hayatı, Edebi Kişiliği, Eserleri ve Dîvânının Tenkitli Metni" (Ph.D. dissertation, Fırat University, 2000), 186, 187.

No need to worry even when it brings winter cold,
Arrived at his doorstep the face of delight

Spring has arrived in wintertime,
Arrived the eloquent nightingale

Ending the chilliness of the world,
Arrived the cure at the ailing state.[19]

The real significance of the *kaside* lies in the way it 'remembered' the enmity between Şâmîzâde and İbşir Pasha. In the remainder of his *kaside*, Tıflî describes or rather deplores the situation before Şâmîzâde was reappointed and portrays a grand vizier who in the poem is pictured as coming from Üsküdar along with 'begetters of sedition'.[20] Tıflî describes him as the omen of doomsday and as undeserving as Timur (*Tîmûr-ı nâ-sezâ*). According to Tıflî, the grand vizier left an ailing world behind him when he left office.[21] This grand vizier is most likely İbşir Pasha, who had taken over the seat of the grand-vizierate after governing Aleppo and – according to Ahmed Resmî – whose arrival at the capital was unsuccessfully blocked by Şâmîzâde.[22] The terms of İbşir Pasha's arrival in Istanbul, accompanied by a large militia of cavalrymen from Anatolia, were hastily negotiated on account of the threats he made about an Anatolian uprising that he would lead unless his demands were met. As mentioned above, upon his arrival, he got rid of all top-ranking officials, including Şâmîzâde.

---

19   "Müjde-i luṭf ile derûn-ı dile/Hâtif-i gaybdan nidâ geldi/Yine evvelki menzîlin buldı/ Geldi evvel ṣâḥib-i 'aṭâ' geldi/Yine evvel bahâr-ı şâdîdür/Yine ḫurşîd-i rûşenâ geldi/Zât-ı 'âlî güher-i re'îs-i zamân/Ol ḫıdîv-i cihân-güşâ geldi/Dem-i serd-i şitâ getürse ne gam/ Âsitânında yüz ṣafâ' geldi/Vaḳt-i sermâda nev-bahâr oldı/'Andelîb-i süḫan-sezâ geldi/ 'Âlemün ref' idüp bürûdetini/Maraż-ı devlete devâ geldi." In Çınar, "Tıflî", 186, 187.
20   "Cânib-i Üsküdârdan yana/Yine berâber fitne-zâ geldi/Bir 'alâmet idi ḳıyâmetden/ Çeşmine 'âlemün bükâ' geldi." Çınar, "Tıflî", 187.
21   "Mûr itmiş pâ-şikeste bilmez idün/Şûreta gerçi ejderhâ geldi/Pây-ı keçe gören o bedrî /Didi Tîmûr-ı nâ-sezâ geldi/Geldi ṣadr-ı sa'âdete geçdi/Eceli tîg der-i ḳafâ' geldi." Çınar, "Tıflî", 187.
22   İbşir Mustafa Pasha, who was the governor of Sivas at the time, occupied Ankara in 1651 declaring himself as the leader of the sultan's cavalry regiments against the janissaries. He demanded the suppression of the Druzes of Lebanon who had a monopoly over the tax farms in Aleppo. He was soon appointed as the governor of Aleppo. His harsh government and the threats he made to march to the capital to depose the government alarmed those in the capital and they hastily proposed the vizierial seal to him and arranged his betrothal to Ayşe Sultan, the widowed daughter of Ahmed I. See İsmail Hakkı Uzunçarşılı, *Osmanlı Tarihi*, vol. 3 part 1 (Ankara: TTK, 1995; reprint of 1951 edn), 272–4.

Tıflî in his *kaside*, continued to depict the events of the time and wrote that İbşir Pasha's post was later occupied by "one or two helpless people" whom he described as "a gang with no religion and no language skills."[23] He complains of what he calls "people of the peasant sort", who came to the city and bought and sold posts upon request. After the rule of these "unworthy men", Şâmîzâde's arrival was very fortunate and hence became the central action – *redif* – in the *kaside*. Tıflî portrayed Şâmîzâde as the only one capable of cleaning up the mess left over by the previous grand viziers.

Şâmîzâde Mehmed's involvement in the running of the daily business of Ottoman politics as the chief scribe from 1655/6 onwards until his death was not documented in the chronicles at all. Yet, when it comes to his second fall from grace, the sources come up with multiple versions of the events leading to his demise.[24] Evliya Çelebi told his version of Şâmîzâde's demise in the *Seyahatnâme*. Evliya Çelebi served Şâmîzâde's son-in-law Kadızâde İbrâhim Pasha during the Uyvar campaign of 1663.[25] He claimed that Grand Vizier Köprülüzâde Fâzıl Ahmed Pasha (1635–76) summoned Şâmîzâde and İbrâhim Pasha to his tent and accused Şâmîzâde of making plans to depose him and to instate İbrâhim Pasha in his place. It was later claimed that when Grand Vizier Fâzıl Ahmed met the sultan to be presented with the imperial banner to lead the Uyvar campaign, he was instructed by the sultan to consult Reîsülküttâb Şâmîzâde on important policy matters. The grand vizier allegedly resented this warning, which he saw as upsetting the traditional political hierarchies and hence as humiliating. Evliya Çelebi, never unassuming about his prescience, claims that he had always been aware of the grand vizier's hostility and was not surprised by his decision to execute Şâmîzâde and his son-in-law, which he thought was unfair.[26] According to a different version reported by the chron-

---

23  "Ruḫṣat-ı çarḫ-ile anuñ yerine/Bir iki şaḫṣ-ı bî-nevâ geldi/Bir alây dîni yol lisân bilmez/ Şehre ecnâs-ı rüstâ geldi/Aldılar ṣatdılar murâd üzre/Dehre ser-mâye-i şifâ' geldi." Çınar, "Tıflî", 188.
24  See Evliya, *Seyahatnâme* 6, 201, 202; İsazade, *İsazade Tarihi*, 79.
25  The Ottoman intervention in Transylvania increased the tensions with the Habsburgs whose candidate to succeed György II Rákóczi as the Prince of Transylvania, Yanos Kemény was driven out by the Ottoman forces. On 14 April 1663 Fâzıl Ahmed left Edirne for Belgrade at the head of the imperial army. Negotiations between the two imperial delegations failed and the Ottoman forces moved north, crossing the Danube and faced the Habsburg army led by general Raimondo Montecucolli. The castle of Uyvar (Nové Zámky) was besieged for five weeks and the Habsburg defenders finally surrendered. See Uzunçarşılı, *Osmanlı* 3 part 1, 402–7.
26  According to Evliya, during the siege of Yanık, İbrâhim bravely fought the enemy for five hours. However, nobody from the grand vizier's compound, which was only half an hour away, came to help him and his forces. Evliya, *Seyahatnâme* 6, 202.

icler İsâzâde, grand vizier Fâzıl Ahmed got an order from the sultan for the execution of Kadızâde İbrâhim Pasha, and showed the order to Şâmîzâde.[27] Şâmîzâde asked the grand vizier to seek pardon from the sultan claiming that those with vizierial titles like Kadızâde İbrâhim must be given three chances to be pardoned before being executed. Fâzıl Ahmed Pasha distorted Şâmîzâde's words on purpose and misled the sultan into believing that Şâmîzâde was contesting the sultanic order. The sultan found Şâmîzâde's opposition unacceptable and ordered his and his son-in-law İbrâhim Pasha's execution.

Another version of the story of Şâmîzâde's demise is worth mentioning here since it relates the chief scribe's execution to differences over matters of actual policy. During the negotiations that predated the Uyvar campaign, the chief scribe was reported to have favoured the option of securing a peace deal with the Habsburgs while the more bellicose grand vizier Fâzıl Ahmed Pasha was eager to go on a campaign and saw Şâmîzâde's opposition as an obstacle to be staved off.[28] So in any case it seems that while Tıflî structured his panegyric poem on the possibility of Şâmîzâde becoming grand vizier, others like Fâzıl Ahmed Pasha were actually threatened by the same prospect.

What allowed a scribe like Şâmîzâde to acquire such power, both financially and politically, seems to be his connections. The best gates for upward mobility were the households of the grand viziers of the early-seventeenth century like that of Hezarpâre Ahmed Pasha who not only acquired their seats through their access to the capital but also maintained their power base through their financial power.[29] As chief of the Imperial Council scribes, Şâmîzâde must have had some monopoly over the production of imperial documents. By helping the petitioners at the Imperial Council with their cases, he must have made life easy for them in a bureaucratic system that was otherwise complicated and difficult to deal with. According to the chroniclers, it was these people who intervened on his behalf during the crises of the seventeenth century. When he regained the favour of the Köprülü regime, Şâmîzâde seemed to have

---

27  İsazade, *İsazade Tarihi*, 79.
28  J. de Hammer, *Histoire de l'Empire ottoman depuis son origine jusqu'à nos jours; ouvrage puisé aux sources les plus authentiques et rédigé sur des documents et des manuscrits la plupart inconnus en Europe*, translated by J. J. Hellert, vol. 2 (Paris: Béthune et Plon, 1835), 81.
29  For a study that underlines the importance of the socio-economic assets that the civilian power holders mobilized to overcome the obstacles deriving from their more modest political backgrounds, see Baki Tezcan, *The Second Ottoman Empire: Political and Social Transformation in the Early Modern World* (New York: CUP, 2010).

retrieved both his wealth and influence.[30] Given the broader socio-economic background in which the scribal profession evolved in this period, Şâmîzâde's wealth appears even more extraordinary.[31]

The *kasides* written to celebrate Şâmîzâde Mehmed by the seventeenth-century Ottoman poets reflect his influence as a major patron of the period's political and literary circles. Nâilî-i Kadîm (d.1077/1666), Neşâtî (d.1085/1674), Tıflî (d.1070/1659-60) and Vecdî (d.1661 or 1663), who not only had collections of poetry but were also all from scribal backgrounds, all wrote *kasides* praising Şâmîzâde.[32] Among these panegyrists, it was Tıflî, who pulled the most critical string and emphasized his patron's uniqueness in a world characterized by

---

30   Some brief research at the Public Endowment Archives turned out the copies of the deeds of the public endowments (*vakıf*) registered under Şâmîzâde Mehmed's name. In Istanbul, two undefined *vakıf*s, one in Küçük Ayasofya, the other one in the vicinity of the Kadırga harbour; in Tosya a house with two rooms, a jewellery store with eight rooms and three vineyards; a *vakıf* in the Ilgın district of Konya; and three more unnamed *vakıf* properties are registered as Şâmîzâde endowments. Evliya Çelebi in his account on Edirne, listed his palace '*Reîsülküttâb Şâmîzâde Sarayı*', among the palatial residences that prominent public figures embarked on building once the sultan had decided to take permanent residence in the city. See Evliya Çelebi, *Evliya Çelebi Seyahatnâmesi: 3.Kitap: Topkapı Sarayı Bağdat 305 Yazmasının Transkripsiyonu-Dizini*, edited by Seyit Ali Kahraman and Yücel Dağlı (Istanbul: Yapı Kredi Yayınları. 1999), 257.

31   The seventeenth-century archival sources offer us a picture, albeit an incomplete one, about the number of scribes in different administrative divisions, their economic well-being and their social backgrounds. The consolidation of the territorial and political integrity of the empire during the sixteenth century necessitated the intake of an increasing number of scribes into the central bureaucracy. However, on account of the nature and the current state of the archival sources, the total population of the scribal body at the beginning of the seventeenth century cannot be precisely estimated. For estimates on the sixteenth- and the early-seventeenth-century scribal populations, see Ömer Lütfi Barkan, "H.933-934 (M.1527-28) Mali Yılına Ait Bütçe Örneği", *IFM* 15 (1–4), 1953/4, 238–329; and Christine Woodhead, "Research on the Ottoman Scribal Service, c.1574-1630", in Christa Fragner and Klaus Schwarz (eds). *Festgabe an Josef Matuz: Osmanistik-Turkologie-Diplomatik* (Berlin: Klaus Schwarz Verlag, 1992), 311–28. Some information about the material conditions of scribal existence has nevertheless surfaced. For example, based on my study of the petitions submitted by scribes in the seventeenth century, it becomes evident that many scribes or apprentices, worked without any income, either prebendal or cash (*timarsız ve ulûfesiz*), and asked to be assigned one. It is also clear that while the numbers of *dirlikli* (with prebend) and *ulûfeli* (with cash) scribes were increasing, many were still working without any compensation and that there was fierce competition for the income of the retired or deceased scribes. For a discussion of these sources see Tuşalp-Atiyas, "Political Literacy", 91–103.

32   Haluk İpekten, *Naili-i Kadim Divânı* (Istanbul: MEB, 1970), 168, 169; Mahmut Kaplan, *Neşati Divânı* (Izmir: Akademi Kitabevi, 1996), 48–53; Ahmed Mermer, *XVII.yy, Divân Şairi Vecdi ve Divânçesi* (Ankara: MEB, 2002), 97–100.

ignorance. It was Şâmîzâde's experience and knowledge of the affairs of the state that distinguished him from others. Among the reports of his scandalous acts and deeds, only Tıflî and to a certain extent Evliya touched on the tension between Şâmîzâde and others who resented his knowledge of the inner workings of imperial politics. However, while Tıflî stopped short of explaining what 'knowing the language of the state' meant, Evliya framed this tension as an infraction of the hierarchy between the grand vizier and the chief scribe.

## 2  The Secretary-Grand Vizier, Râmi Mehmed

Twice the *reîsülküttâb* and then the grand vizier of the seventeenth-century *fin-de-siècle*, Râmi Mehmed was the least anonymous of the Ottoman scribes. In Ottoman history he epitomizes the transition in the political cadres 'from the men of the sword/*seyfiyye* to the men of the pen/*kalemiyye*' as the first chief scribe to be appointed as the grand vizier. The scholarly consensus is that, beginning with Râmi Mehmed's rise, the position of the *reîsülküttâb* became a stepping-stone for higher political posts that previously excluded people from a civilian bureaucratic background.[33]

Râmi Mehmed was recruited as an apprentice to the office of the chief scribe and then taken into the household (*kapı*) of Musâhib Mustafa Pasha (d.1685/6), the vizier and companion to Mehmed IV.[34] After serving as the master scribe of Musâhib Mustafa Pasha's vizierial council (*dîvân efendisi*), Râmi Mehmed began to rise within the imperial administration.[35] He first served six years

---

33  In the eighteenth century, from among the forty-three chief scribes, six would become grand viziers, while seven attained the rank of vizier. Some of the most important Ottoman political figures of the eighteenth century would begin their careers as scribes in the imperial council. See Christoph K. Neumann, "Political and Diplomatic Developments", in Suraiya N. Faroqhi (ed.) *The Cambridge History of Turkey*, vol. 3: *The Later Ottoman Empire, 1603–1839* (New York: CUP, 2006), 54.

34  On the structure of Ottoman households, see Rifa'at Abou El-Haj, "The Ottoman Vezir and Pasha Households 1683–1703: A Preliminary Report", *JAOS* 94 (4), 1974), 438–447; Robert Dankoff, *The Intimate Life of an Ottoman Statesman: Melek Ahmed Pasha (1588–1662), As Portrayed in Evliya Çelebi's Book of Travels (Seyahatname)* (Albany: State University of New York Press, 1991); Carter V. Findley, "Patrimonial Household Organization and Factional Activity in the Ottoman Ruling Class", in Halil İnalcık and Osman Okyar (eds). *Türkiye'nin Sosyal ve Ekonomik Tarihi 1071–1920* (Ankara: Meteksan Limited, 1980), 227–35; Jane Hathaway, "The Military Household in Ottoman Egypt", *IJMES* 27 (1) 1995, 39–52.

35  Mirzazâde Sâlim Mehmed Emin Efendi, *Tezkiretü'ş-Şu'arâ Sâlim Efendi*, edited by Adnan İnce (Ankara: Atatürk Kültür Merkezi Yayınları, 2005), 313.

as assistant to the chief scribe (*beylikçi*), and later was appointed as the chief scribe in 1106/1694. His outstanding secretarial skills in editing the imperial edicts that addressed the viziers were mentioned in the sources as the cause of the envy and resentment of his peers.[36] He was dismissed at the beginning of 1697 following an altercation with Grand Vizier Elmas Mehmed Pasha, but shortly afterwards was reinstated into his former post as the chief scribe.

The most noteworthy episode of his service as the chief scribe was his appointment to the town of Karlowitz following the wars on the Western front, as the head of the Ottoman delegation along with the chief dragoman Alexandros Mavrokordatos (1636–1709).[37] By negotiating individual peace treaties with Austria, Venice, Poland and Moscow, Râmi Mehmed was said to have secured the wellbeing of 'the people of God' (*ibâdullah*), who suffered greatly as a result of the warfare on the Western front.[38] He even wrote a long account of the negotiations, known as the 'Report on Peace' (*Sulhnâme*).[39]

Following the conclusion of the Karlowitz negotiations in 1699, Râmi Mehmed was twice offered the title of the vizier of the dome but each time provided an excuse to decline.[40] He eventually attained the status of a vizier upon the recommendation of the chief mufti (*şeyhülislâm*) Seyyid Feyzullah Efendi (1639–1703), who had secured himself a powerful position as Sultan

---

36   One such agitated party was Grand Vizier Elmas Mehmed Pasha (d.1697), who allegedly saw Râmi Mehmed's editing as an act of transgression. See Abdülkadir Özcan (ed.), *Anonim Osmanlı tarihi*, 1099–1116 (1688–1704) (Ankara: TTK, 2000), 125.

37   See Nestor Camariano, *Alexandre Mavrocordato: Le Grand Dragoman, Son Activité diplomatique (1673–1709)* (Thessaloniki: Institute for Balkan Studies, 1970).

38   On the Treaty of Karlowitz, see Rifa'at Abou-El-Haj, "The Reisü'l-küttab and Ottoman Diplomacy at Karlowitz", Ph.D. dissertation, Princeton University, 1963; idem., "The Formal Closure of the Ottoman Frontier in Europe: 1699–1703", *JAOS* 89 (3) 1969, 467–75; Monika Molnar, "Karlofça Antlaşması'ndan sonra Osmanlı-Habsburg Sınırı 1699–1701", in Güler Eren(ed.), *Osmanlı*, vol. 1 (Ankara: Yeni Türkiye Yayınları, 1999), 472–79; idem, "Venezia e la questione turca nella prima metà della guerra dei quindici anni secondo i memoriali romani di un diplomatico veneziano", *Nuova Corvina* 6 (1999), 167–76; William Bruce Munson, "The Peace of Karlowitz", Ph.D. dissertation, University of Illinois, 1940; Abdülkadir Özcan, "300.yılında Karlofça Antlaşması", *Akademik Araştırmalar Dergisi* 2 (4–5), 2000, 250–1; Michajlo R. Popović, *Der Friede von Karlowitz* (Paderborn: EGV, 2012; reprint of 1893 edn).

39   [Râmi Mehmed Pasha], *Ṣulḥnâme*, MS 685, Reşid Efendi, SK. Also see Ali Canib Yöntem, "Rami Mehmed Paşa'nın Sulhnâmesi", in *IV. Türk Tarih Kongresi: Kongreye Sunulan Tebliğler [Türk Tarih Kongresi (IV: 1948: Ankara)]* (Ankara: TTK, 1952), 346–53.

40   Dimitrie Cantemir, The history of the growth and decay of the Othman Empire. Part I. Containing the growth of the Othman Empire, from the reign of Othman the founder, to the Reign of Mahomet IV. Translated by N. Tindal (London: Printed for James, John, and Paul Knapton, MDCCXXXIV [1734]), 418.

Mustafa II's counsellor at his Edirne court.[41] Râmi Mehmed's initial reluctance to take on a vizierial appointment is interesting, for we do not know what exactly made him change his mind. Chronicles depict Feyzullah Efendi as the main character behind Râmi Mehmed's rise to the grand vizierate. However, because most accounts of the period are heavily polarized either for or against Feyzullah Efendi, the real nature of his influence remains unknown. Was Feyzullah Efendi an influential mentor for Râmi Mehmed as he was for Mustafa II, or did he simply promise Râmi other gains and benefits to lure him into political office? What changed Râmi Mehmed's mind must be a combination of all these factors.

After his predecessor Daltaban Mustafa was executed for charges of treason, Râmi Mehmed Efendi was swiftly appointed as the grand vizier.[42] He occupied the seat for a mere eight months until he was toppled by a disgruntled group of medrese graduates, janissaries, and craftsmen who marched to Edirne in August 1703 and ended the reign of Mustafa II (d.1703) by forcing the court to move back to Istanbul with Ahmed III (d.1736) as the new sultan.[43] There are different versions of the story of his flight from the scene of the rebellion. Yet, it is certain that he remained in hiding until some friends intervened on his behalf and convinced the new grand vizier Moralı Hasan Pasha (d.1713) to pardon him. Only then was he admitted back into the system, first as the governor of Cyprus and later of Egypt.[44] His final fall from grace took place

---

41   Feyzullah Efendi penned an autobiography, introduced by Ahmet Turek and F. Çetin Derin, "Feyzullah Efendi'nin Kendi Kaleminden Hal Tercümesi", *ITD* 23 (1969), 205–18. For secondary sources on the life and career of Feyzullah Efendi, see Sabra Meservey, "An Ottoman Şeyhülislam" (Ph.D. dissertation, Princeton University, 1965); Michael Nizri, "The Kapı in Ottoman Society: The Household of Şeyhülislam Feyzullah Efendi, 1695–1703" (Ph.D. dissertation [in Hebrew], Tel-Aviv University, 2009); idem, "The Memoirs of Şeyhülislam Feyzullah Efendi (1638–1703), Self, Family and Household", in Yavuz Köse and Ralf Elger (eds) *Ego-Documents: Arabic, Persian, Turkish (14th–20th Century)*, (Wiesbaden: Harrassowitz Verlag, 2010), 29–38.

42   Daltaban became increasingly unpopular since he kept provoking warfare against the stipulations of the Treaty of Karlowitz and ignited unrest among the Tartars. There were bribery charges against him as well. See Cantemir, *History*, 417; Özcan, *Anonim*, 193.

43   For contemporary accounts of the Edirne Incident, see Hrand Andreasyan, "Balatlı Georg'a göre Edirne Vak'ası", *ITD* 11 (15) 1960, 47–64; Masrafzâde Şefik Mehmed Efendi, *Kitâb-ı Şefîknâme-i 'İbret-me'âl ve Mâfîh mine'l-Makalât ve'l-Emsâl*, known as the *Şefîknâme*; the earliest manuscript is dated 1707, located at MS 2307, Esad Efendi, SK. Naîmâ devoted the last volume of his history to the Edirne Uprising. See Naîmâ, *Târîh* 4, passim.

44   A MS from DOA (iE. TCT. 2141) dated 4 Receb 1116/2 November 1704, recorded Râmi Mehmed's appointment to Cyprus. Two DOA MS describe the people in Râmi Mehmed's entourage in Egypt, after Râmi Mehmed's dismissal from the post of governor. C. DH 7226,

when he was dismissed from his post in Egypt in 1705 for having fallen out with the local notables. He was banished to Rhodes, where he died in March 1708 (15 Zilhicce 1119).

The biographical information about Râmi Mehmed in late-seventeenth and eighteenth-century sources conveys the polarization that divided Ottoman public opinion in this period. During and in the immediate aftermath of the Edirne Incident, Râmi Mehmed became the subject of both praise and calumny. The eighteenth-century chronicles depict either a treacherous and despotic vizier or a wise and skilled scribe holding the provision of the public good above all else.[45] In his history of the Ottoman Empire, Dimitrie Cantemir claimed that the people of Istanbul and the janissaries were very much dissatisfied to see a man raised from a scribe to a grand vizier; "a good scribe indeed but unfit for that office".[46] A palace insider and later chronicler, Fındıklılı Silâhdar Mehmed Ağa, described Râmi Mehmed as "a carefree and bohemian city boy" (*bir rind-i cihan şehir oğlanı*) who failed to appreciate the gravity of the situation before the Edirne Incident and lost its control.[47] However, for many others who witnessed his rise and fall, Râmi Mehmed was known for his literary and intellectual skills and was depicted as an expert on the affairs of the Ottoman State.[48] In fact, a cursory look at the biographical dictionary of poets written at the beginning of the eighteenth century will reveal that Râmi Mehmed had built an impressive household that employed many scribe-cum-poets as political auxiliaries.[49] It was these scribes who produced the bulk of the panegyric literature to honour him.

---

dated 29 Safer 1119/1 June 1707, concerns the dispatch to Istanbul of people, who were previously in the service of the dismissed ex-governor of Egypt, Râmi Mehmed Pasha. C. EV 12988, dated 29 Cemâziyelâhir 1117/18 October 1705, is on the particular case of İbrâhim Efendi, the preacher (imam) of the governor of Egypt Râmi Mehmed. The document stipulates that İbrâhim Efendi be spared a certain amount of income from the Istanbul customs and that he be given his father's post of the sayer of prayers (*duâgû*).

45  Two histories that were openly hostile to Râmi Mehmed were written by two members of the religious establishment who were close to the Chief Mufti Feyzullah Efendi. See Müminzade Seyyid Ahmed Hasib Efendi, *Ravzâtü'l-Küberâ: Tahlil ve Metin*, edited by Mesut Aydıner (Ankara: TTK, 2003); Uşşakizade İbrâhim Efendi, *Uşşakizade Tarihi*, edited by Raşit Gündoğdu (Istanbul: Çamlıca Basım Yayın A. Ş., 2005).

46  Cantemir, *History*, 420.

47  Silahdar Fındıklılı Mehmed Ağa, *Nusretname*, edited by İsmet Parmaksızoğlu, vol. 2 (Ankara: MEB, 1962), 141.

48  See Defterdar Sarı Mehmed Pasha, *Zübde-i Vekayiât: Tahlil ve Metin (1066–1116/1656–1704)*, edited by Abdülkadir Özcan (Ankara: TTK, 1995), *passim*; Özcan, *Anonim, passim*.

49  See Mirzazâde Sâlim, *Tezkiretü'ş-Şu'arâ, passim*; Safâyî, *Tezkire-i Safâyî, passim*.

To understand the emphasis cast on Râmi Mehmed's literary and intellectual skills, we need to examine how his appointment respectively as the chief scribe and the grand vizier was received in the panegyric space. What needs to be underlined here is that Râmi Mehmed's success was celebrated by a unique panegyric vocabulary that prioritized different aspects of the patron's praiseworthy qualities.[50] In a chronogram setting the date for 1106, the year when Râmi Mehmed was appointed as the *reîsülküttâb* for the first time, poet Nâzım Mehmed, who would later become the secretary of the Crimean Khan Selim Giray, makes a rhetorical enquiry in verse.[51]

> Good news O the people of the pen, exalted Râmi Efendi has virtuously set out in the chamber of chiefdom.
> Who is the master of difficult endeavors, the composer of the unique?
> Only Vassaf is worthy of [him] in qualities.
> Who is always the centre of the sphere of meaning and discourse?
> Through the abundant blessing of his invocations prospers exquisite poetry.
> On his reed of magic duties is dependent nice prose.
> His fluent poems merit the munificient's memory.[52]

In another *kaside*, he wrote upon Râmi's accession to the grand vizierate that Nâzım had constructed the panegyric as a celebration and had announced

---

50   Saadettin Nüzhet Ergun in his 1933 biography of Râmi Mehmed, gathered the panegyrics and the chronograms, which dated and celebrated these new appointments. See Saadettin Nüzhet Ergun, *Rami Paşa hayatı ve eserleri* (Istanbul: Kanaat Kütüphanesi, 1933).

51   In Safâyî's biographical dictionary, Nâzım Mehmed appears as a poet from Istanbul, known as Kirli Nâzım. According to Safâyî, he served some "genteel people" as secretary and later became a tutor for the sons of the Crimean Khan Selim Giray. Safâyî also mentions that he composed a *divan* of poems. He died in 1116 /1704–5 in Çatalca. See Safâyî, *Tezkire-l Safâyî*, 619. Nâzım is mentioned in Sâlim's biographical dictionary as Nâzım-ı diğer. According to Sâlim he was known as Kara Nâzım Mehmed Efendi among the learned men of the time. Sâlim mentions that he completed his studies with Şeyhülislâm Feyzullah Efendi. After his dismissal from his teaching job in a forty-*akçe* medrese, he became secretary to various people, including Selim Giray Khan. He died in Selim Giray's farm in Çatalca. See Mirzazâde Sâlim, *Tezkiretü'ş-Şu'arâ*, 641.

52   "Ḥażret-i Râmî Efendi müjde ey ehl-i ḳalem/Oldu eyvân-ı riyâsetde şerefle hem celîs/ Ḫvâce-i müşkîl küşâ münşî-i yektâ kim/Rûḥ-i Vaṣṣâf olsa lâyıḳ bezm-i vaṣfında/Isî-i çerḫ-i ma'ânî vü beyân kim dembedem/Feyż-i enfâsiyle iḥyâ' olmada şi'r-i nefîs/Kilk-i siḥr-âşârına vâbeste inşâ'-yi laṭîf/Ḫâṭır-ı feyyâżına şâyeste eş'âr-ı selîs." Nâzım 1106. See Ergun, *Rami Paşa*, 8, 9.

Râmi Mehmed's grand vizierate as glad tidings (*müjde*). The arrival sequence that we saw in Tıflî's praise of Şâmîzâde is replicated here as well. Nâzım stamps on Râmi the conventional political virtues as the owner of the sword and pen, the one who hoists the flags of the Islamic community (*ümmet*), the undoer of oppression and animadversion, the just shelter for the weak, the protector of the state and religion (*dîn ü düvel*), the overrider of every trickery and scam, the overseer of property and communities (*mülk ü milel*), and the assurance for the deprived.[53] Rüşdü from Sarajevo, known as Rüşdü the bouquiniste (Rüşdü-i Sahhaf), also praised Râmi when he occupied the seat of the *reîsülküttâb*.[54] Rüşdü points to written histories and the records of his predecessors as proof of his unprecedented wisdom and perfection:

> The world has not seen, since the universe has started turning, such
>   graceful person, let him be the ideal for the men
> Râmi Efendi, the chief of the refined people
> If Mercury saw his works, it would persevere
> No such *reîsülküttâb* has served in the state before
> Here are the works of the predecessors here are the old histories
> Drops of sweat from his pen are from the water of the river of paradise
> His grace is soft like the bellies of gentle youths
> His prose and writing is admired by people of perfection
> His beautiful poetry would make Selmān and Selīm jealous
> May God bless his verses that are of a new kind
> Every verse of it became the pearl of the pearls of poetry.

The historian Râşid Mehmed (d.1735), who composed a *kaside* for Râmi Mehmed, praises his prescience, his knowledge of the language of the age and declares him unequalled in writing, and specifically in his practice of different calligraphic scripts.[55] According to Râşid, if there were a science that Râmi was oblivious to that would be the science of stupidity.[56] The poet Nâbî (d.1712) develops the scribal theme further and uses it as an allegory to praise Râmi's

---

53   "Ṣâḥib-i tîg u ḳalem râfi'-i râyât-ı himem/Râfi'-i ẓulm ü sitem dâdpenâh-ı żu'afâ/Ḥâmî-i dîn ü düvel mâḫî-i her mekr ü ḥiyel/Nâẓır-ı mülk ü milel kehf-i emân-ı fuḳarâ'." Ergun, *Râmi Paşa*, 13; Mirzazâde Sâlim, *Tezkiretü'ş-Şu'arâ*, 641.
54   Mirzazâde Sâlim, *Tezkiretü'ş-Şu'arâ*, 354–9.
55   "Lisân-ı 'aṣrı gâyet iyi bilür ṣâḥib-i firâsetdir"./Kitâbetde naẓîri yoḳdur envâ'ın bilür anın/ Agarr-ı ta'lîḳ u dîvânî agarr-ı nesḫ ü siyâḳatdir." Ergun, *Râmi Paşa*, 61.
56   "Fünûn-ı ḳâbiliyyât-ı cihân ma'lûmudur cümle/Eğer mechûlü bir fenn varsa fenn-i belâhetdir." Ergun, *Râmi Paşa*, 62.

unerrability. He addresses him "you are the pure copy, with no misplaced mutation marks, no mistaken letters, and with no tangled expressions."[57] In his *kaside*, Râşid also claimed that Râmi was the favourite among the political grandees of the time since he increased the value of the "bazaar of eloquence".[58] On his knowledge of the affairs of the state and his skills in peace-making – alluding to his role at the Karlowitz negotiations – Nâbî claimed that a variety of people from 'noble predecessors' to 'different classes of the public' used to consult him on the difficult affairs of the state. According to Nâbî if he had not left his imprint on the conclusion of peace, no one would be enjoying such comfort.[59]

These poems presented a variety of status-associated virtues and metaphors and in that sense continued the earlier tradition of rank-conscious distribution of praises in Ottoman poetry. However, the panegyrists attributed Râmi Mehmed these qualities not only for their rhetorical value. What Râmi Mehmed's panegyrists prioritized were his knowledge about the main tenets and principles of the political system, his reputation in the public sphere for the actual consequences of political acts, the subtlety of his meaning, and the correctness of his writing and speech – qualities that had a bearing on the actual running of political affairs. These 'political skills' outweighed the infinite possibilities of the gifts and graces, and of the delights of *meclis* conversation that had defined 'classical' Ottoman panegyrics and in that sense demarcated the 'scribal panegyrics' within the genre.

These praiseful verses reveal the rhetorics at use in celebrating a scribe's rise to power, but at the same time they delineate the limits of that rhetorical world. Luckily, there are other sources that can help us understand how the arguments that were formulated in panegyric terms became explicitly political and claimed the seat of the grand vizier for a mere scribe. The *Anonymous History* covering the period between 1099–1116/1688–1704 offers some clues about the type of vizierial conduct that Râmi Mehmed idealized.[60] The author

---

57 "Sensin ol nüsḫa-i pâkîze ki yoḳdur sende/Noḳṭa-i sehv ü ḥurûf-ı galaṭ u lâfẓ-ı seḳām." Ergun, *Râmi Paşa*, 58.
58 "Zamân-ı devleti ṭab'-ı bülendin şimdi sulṭânım/Bi-Ḥamdillah revâc-efzâ-yi bâzâr-ı faṣâḥatdır." Ergun, *Râmi Paşa*, 65.
59 "Müşkil-i devleti hep andan ederlerdi sû'âl/Gerek eslâf-ı kirâm ve gerek eṣnâf-ı ümem/Dehrde anlamayub bilmediği ola meğer/Ṭama' u buġż u nifâḳ u ḥased ü ġadr ü sitem/Ḫalḳ bu râḥatı rü'yâda bile görmez idi/Basmasa re'y-i ḥâkim-i ḫıred-i ṣulḥa ḳadem." Ergun, *Râmi Paşa*, 57.
60 The earliest and most detailed account of his biography can be found in an anonymous chronicle, which covered the period between 1688 and 1704. See Özcan, *Anonim, passim*.

of this chronicle describes himself as a member of Râmi Mehmed's entourage and probably was a scribe himself.[61] It is in the sections where the anonymous author praises the grand vizierate of his patron that he divulged on the ideas on proper vizierial conduct. In that respect, the chronicle reifies Râmi Mehmed's idealization in the panegyric space and helps us locate it in a concrete historical context. In the first instance, he provides a long description of an imperial council (*dîvân*) meeting that took place on Thursday, Ramazan 8, 1114/26 January 1703.[62] It was Râmi Mehmed Pasha, who oversaw the *dîvân-ı hümâyûn* as the grand vizier. According to the anonymous author, Râmi Mehmed's *dîvân* was the best *dîvân* in Ottoman history.

> Everyone's petitions were read in the proper way. On matters related to land grants (*tımâr* and *zeâmet*), ancient laws (*kanun-ı kadîm*) were abided by. People could not compare any preceding councils to this one. In other instances, at times like this, there used to be so many people and such overcrowding that even if the *dîvân* session lasted until the evening, there would still be people and work undone. The reason is: Rookie grand viziers. People would seize each other's bread and land. They were addicted to obsolete cases and vain quarrels. What they witnessed at Râmi Mehmed Pasha's council was this: The petitioners with a case requiring legal (*şer'î*) treatment were referred to the judges, appointment officers, legion commanders and rulers. One could not appoint an arbitrator (*müvellâ*) through bypassing a judge. Seeking an appeal was not allowed. One could not write a subpoena from a distance. Unless every item was handled according to *şeriat* or customary law (*kanun*), the council did not function. There was no deferring of cases to the director of finances (*defterdar*) or others, so that the accused could find the opportunity for self-defence. Only a reply to solve the problem was given, if it worked it worked, if it did not, then the case was rejected, and could not come up to the council again. Unless it was vacant, not a single *akçe* was let out of either state property or the public endowments. In due place grace was given, in due place punishment. Unless there was a situation requiring dismissal, or in case of death, there would not be any changes in appointed positions. People got their replies in three to four days, for a case requiring daily treatment, the council convened for one to two hours per day, officials were present in the petition room until the evening, the

---

61   Özcan, *Anonim*, xvi, xvii.
62   Özcan, *Anonim*, 197.

director of finances, the chief sergeant and others studied and gauged the issue. Other times, they spent their time dealing with important issues and the state of the country. In their spare time, they occupied themselves with reading the *Siyer-i Kebîr* and other books.

The young and the old, everyone prayed for the State.
How swell, the world has found a fresh life
The word has filled with the sound of justice.[63]

Just as Tıflî emphasized Şâmîzâde's adeptness in running the 'affairs of the state' to set him apart from the 'others', the anonymous historian distinguished Râmi Mehmed from the other grand viziers by praising his skills in running the imperial council. Due to his previous experience as a council scribe, Râmi Mehmed was furnished with the knowledge of the intricate details about the procedures that had to be followed while running the imperial council. However, what was more important than Râmi Mehmed's knowledge of the procedures is his introduction of an academic/intellectual aspect to the workings of the imperial council. The anonymous historian claimed that the imperial sessions headed by Râmi Mehmed were always guided by the literature of *siyar*.[64] According to the anonymous author, the council officials in their spare time, studied *Kitâb-ı Siyer el-Kebîr*, the famous work on the Islamic law of nations, attributed to the Hanafi jurist Muḥammad al-Shaybānī (b.132/750) and widely known through Al-Saraḥsī's (b.483/1101) commentary on it.[65]

The author also claimed that he recorded what he heard from 'some erudite people' (*ukalâ*) about the proper grand vizierial etiquette.[66] He wrote

---

63   Özcan, *Anonim*, 197.
64   The Arabic word *siyar* is the plural of *sira* which means conduct, comportment, demeanour, behaviour, way of life, attitude, position, reaction, way of acting, (in singular or plural) biography, history, in plural campaigns. See Hans Wehr, *A Dictionary of Modern Written Arabic*, edited by J. Milton Cowan, 3rd edn (Ithaca, NY: Spoken Language Services, 1976), 447. Al-Saraḥsī's definition of *siyar* is as follows: "[*Siyar*] described the conduct of the believers in their relations with the unbelievers of enemy territory as well as the people with whom the believers had made treatises, who may have been temporarily (*musta'mins*) or permanently (*dhimmis*) in Islamic lands; with apostates, who were the worst of the unbelievers, since they abjured after they accepted [Islam]; and with rebels (*baġy*), who were not counted as unbelievers, though they were ignorant and their understanding [of Islam] was false." Shaybani, *The Islamic Law of Nations: Shaybānī's Siyar*, translated by Majid Khadduri (Baltimore: JHU Press, 1966), 40.
65   Shaybani, *Islamic*, 40–3.
66   Özcan, *Anonim*, 37.

that there were many books written in Arabic, Persian, and Turkish about the requirements of vizierate, and what he would say next on the subject was only an index of these. Most of what the anonymous author listed as essential knowledge for the grand vizier concerned the principles of running an empire, from making sure that janissaries got paid on time to guarding the pilgrimage routes and the pilgrims. Even though this register consist of items that can be called classical grand vizierial duties, there are some hints that the person dictating these had a different set of priorities for the vizierial office. For instance, among the requirements that the anonymous author heard from the erudite people, is the necessity to know the exact terms of peace treaties with the 'infidel states' and abiding by them during the times of peace. Based on all these, there is no reason not to assume that Râmi Mehmed was one of the *ukalâ* who dictated these fundamentals to the anonymous author. After all, Râmi Mehmed not only undertook the Karlowitz peace negotiations, but he also gave a detailed account of them in his *Sulhnâme*.

The section that most clearly disguises the identity of the vizier as someone with scribal sensitivities is the one about running a smooth *dîvân*.[67] According to the anonymous author, council posts (*menâsıb-ı dîvâniyye*) must be distributed to specialized people in turns. Trespassing the *dîvân* with a petition in hand should not be allowed. Petitions with marginal notes and involving disputes should be kept aside to be studied after the *dîvân*. The *dîvân* should have a recess not more than once a week. A specialist should be sought for issues requiring special treatment. Otherwise if the post of a master *dîvân* scribe was given to a shoemaker, he would not carry out the job given to him, and worse, all the other shoemakers would become the enemy of the grand vizier who made the appointment![68]

Şâmîzâde Mehmed and Râmi Mehmed both belonged to the 'middling literati strata' who populated the bureaucracies of the early modern empires.[69] The household networks of the grandees that facilitated Şâmîzâde's rise and made his survival possible in the first half of the seventeenth century continued

---

67  Özcan, *Anonim*, 38, 39.
68  Özcan, *Anonim*, 39.
69  Muzaffar Alam and Sanjay Subrahmanyam use this term in their study on the eighteenth-century Mughal scribes and prose writers (*munshi*). They argued that in the Mughal political and literary domain it was in the eighteenth century that the scribes made "a truly protean quality, to use their scribal profession as a point of departure to embark on the conquest of a number of new horizons". See Muzaffar Alam and Sanjay Subrahmanyam, "Witnesses and Agents of Empire: Eighteenth-Century Historiography and the World of the Mughal Munshi", *JESHO* 53 (1–2), 2009, 397.

to be a part of political life in the second. The politics of the grandee households were as important in Râmi Mehmed's time as they were in Şâmîzâde Mehmed's. Again, the literary status of panegyric poetry had long been sealed as the primary discursive tool that announced the arrival of well-qualified contesters at the political scene. In spite of these continuities, the sense of a scribal community and the political ideals and aspirations that bonded its members were not as tenable in Şâmîzâde Mehmed's time as they would be during Râmi Mehmed's tenure. The most important factor that distinguished the case of Şâmîzâde Mehmed and others from that of Râmi Mehmed is that the claim for being more qualified than others had not yet been fully elaborated. The panegyric poems written by Tıflî and others in the first half of the seventeenth century reflect only a vague notion of qualification.

The skills that formed the basis of an Ottoman scribal identity gained a sharper definition in the rhetorical world that surrounded Râmi Mehmed's image. The most basic sets of skills comprised 'scribal literacy', that is the knowledge of letters and numbers, correct grammar and orthography, calculation, and the rules of calligraphy (*hat*), prose writing and epistolography (*inşâ*). These skills created a range of identifications from the rather formulaic definition of the scribes as being the *ehl-i kalem* (masters of the pen) and *sâhib-i rakam* (possessors of scripture) to a more literary/philological recognition as being *fasîh* and *belîg*. Beyond these skills lay a wider intellectual horizon that was shared by the majority of the Ottoman political elite, but more intently claimed by the scribal community in the second half of the seventeenth century.

The anonymous account is not the only gateway to Râmi Mehmed's intellectual world. One particular work that Râmi Mehmed commissioned during his governorship in Egypt – *The Best Lines for the Stories of the Barmakids* (*Ahsenü'l-Mesâlik li Ahbâri'l-Berâmik*) – offer an important insight about his vision of the Ottoman politics and how he thought scribes would fit therein.[70] The Barmakid family produced famous secretaries, who served the Abbasid Caliphs (750–1258) as administrators and grand viziers. Their story is emblematic of the rise and demise of the secretarial classes in early Islamic history.[71]

---

70   Yūsuf b. Muḥammad Milāvī, *Aḥsanu'l-Masālik lī Aḥbāri'l-Barāmik*, MS 585, Reisülküttab, SK; idem, *Aḥsanu'l-Masālik lī Aḥbāri'l-Barāmik*, autograph copy dated 1706, MS 2616 Ahmed III, TSMK. See also Franz Rosenthal, "From Arabic Books and Manuscripts", *JAOS* 83 (4), 1963), 452–7. Rosenthal identified a certain Yūsuf b. Muḥammad, known as "Ibn al-Wakīl al-Milāwī" as the author.

71   See Tayeb El-Hibri, *Reinterpreting Islamic Historiography, Harun al-Rashid and the Narrative of the 'Abbasid Caliphate* (New York: CUP, 1999); Hugh Kennedy, "The Barmakid

Râmi Mehmed's gesture in selecting this famous secretarial/vizierial family as the subject of a work that he commissioned offers us important insights at the ideological level. This commissioning gesture, at least, shows that Râmi Mehmed wanted to learn what possibilities were available for them at higher echelons of power. Of course, his occupation of the grand-vizierial seat must have enabled Râmi Mehmed to pool resources – cultural or otherwise – to an extent that would have been impossible for Şâmîzâde to achieve.[72] Still, Râmi Mehmed clearly represented a different – a more mature, better endowed and more clearly stated – phase of the transformation of the Ottoman scribal identity.

The preliminary survey offered in this article is by no means enough to understand the breath and uniqueness of the scribal discourses formulated around Râmi Mehmed's patronage. Neither does it address the historical circumstances that accommodated the emergence of the scribal discourses at the time. The second half of the seventeenth century seems at first to be a calmer period characterized by the stern, yet stabilizing rule of the Köprülü grand viziers, who also proved to be impressive political and cultural patrons. This period also witnessed the concentration of many novel administrative measures concerning public policy that led the Köprülü era to be branded a 'restoration'. On the other hand, the extended period of campaigns and warfare in the Mediterranean and on the Habsburg frontiers, Mehmed IV's decision to take up residence in Edirne and the resulting absence of a political authority in Istanbul disrupted the apparent stability. The prolonged international conflicts created a war-weary political elite, which was inclined towards the

---

Revolution in Islamic Government", in Charles Melville (ed.), *History and Literature in Iran: Persian and Islamic studies in honour of P. W. Avery* (London: British Academic Press, 1990), 89–98.

72   A public endowment record from Cemâziyelevvel 1113/October–November 1701 lists the waqfs of the then grand vizier Râmi Mehmed. See MS Haremeyn Defteri no. 736, Sy. 167, Sıra 79 at VGMA. The properties certified as public endowments included a classroom (*muallimhâne*), a prayer room (*mescid*), and a fountain (*çeşme*) in the Nişancı district of Eyüp. The endowment deed also mentioned four villages and two fields in the Aleppo district as being granted as *mülk* to Râmi Mehmed in return for his service at the Karlowitz negotiations as the *reîsülküttâb*. Also mentioned in the deed is the appointment of an instructor (*muallim*) for a daily income of fifteen *akçe*s to teach students the Quran, and an assistant (*hilâfe-i mekteb*) for daily income of six *akçe*s. Most importantly, Râmi Mehmed added to the deed of his *vakıf* the appointment of a calligraphy teacher (*meşk hocası*) to instruct students in calligraphy (*resm-i hat*). He was to receive ten *akçe*s per day.

rapid secession of hostilities.[73] The Treaty of Karlowitz in 1699 ended a century stricken with warfare and the scribes like Râmi Mehmed, who once wrote accounts of conquest, became composers of peace treaties or members of border commissions settling the borders and the terms of peace. It might be the case that penholders were perhaps more aware than at any other time of their function as negotiators and treaty makers on the one hand and as formulators and implementers of these administrative experiments on the other. In this context, it is not surprising that rhetorical, linguistic and related philological skills were fully mobilized by the scribal corps and eventually gained an additional significance emphasizing their indispensable place in politics.

Râmi Mehmed and the scribal community around him never totally recovered from the 1703 Edirne rebellion and did not gain a similar opportunity to present itself as a viable political class. However, his political career was critical in producing the hallmarks of the *kalemiyye* ethos that would continue to define Ottoman political culture in the eighteenth century.[74]

## Bibliography

### *Primary Sources*
Devlet Arşivleri Genel Müdürlüğü Osmanlı Arşivi (DOA)
Cevdet Dahiliye 7226.
Cevdet Evkaf 12988.
İbnülemin Tevcihat 2141.
Evkaf Mektubi 02735.00055.
Evkaf Mektubi 00346.00004.

---

[73] Amcazâde Hüseyin Pasha (1644–1702), who served as the grand vizier from 1697 to 1702 was especially known for his aversion to warfare and inclination towards diplomacy. Amcazâde Hüseyin Pasha's tenure as the grand vizier came right after this heavily war-stricken period and the belligerent environment must have left a strong mark on the generation of Ottoman statesmen and lesser bureaucrats. See the Introduction for the discussion of Naîmâ's account as the main source for first Lewis V. Thomas and later Rifa'at Abou El-Haj's conclusions about the existence of peace and war camps within the Ottoman administration during this time. For a contemporary European perspective on Amcazâde's pro-peace policies, see John Stoye, *Marsigli's Europe, 1680–1730: The Life and Times of Luigi Ferdinando Marsigli, Soldier and Virtuoso* (New Haven: Yale University Press, 1994), 164.

[74] For a discussion of the development of the *kalemiyye* identity in Ottoman politics in the eighteenth and the nineteenth centuries, see Carter V. Findley's *Ottoman Civil Officialdom: A Social History* (Princeton, NJ: Princeton University Press, 1989), *passim*.

Evkaf Mektubi 00812.00066.
Evkaf Mektubi 00812.00065.
Evkaf Mektubi Cihat Kalemi 00396.00168.
Evkaf Müfettişliği 00638.00099.
Evkaf Müfettişliği 00643.00040.

### Vakıflar Genel Müdürlüğü Arşivi (VGMA)
Vakıflar Genel Müdürlüğü Defter 00480.00141.
Vakıflar Genel Müdürlüğü Haremeyn Defteri 736.

### Süleymaniye Kütüphanesi Library (SK)
Masrafzâde Şefik Mehmed Efendi. *Kitâb-i Şefîknâme-i 'İbret-me'al ve Mâfih min el-Makalât ve'l-Emsâl* (*Şefîknâme*). MS no. 2307. Esad Efendi, Süleymaniye Kütüphanesi.

[Râmî Mehmed Paşa] *Sulhnâme*. MS no. 685. Reşid Efendi. Süleymaniye Kütüphanesi.

Yūsuf b. Muḥammad Milāvī. *Aḥsanu'l-Masālik lī Aḥbāri'l-Barāmik*. MS no. 585. Reisülküttab, Süleymaniye Kütüphanesi.

### Topkapı Sarayı Müzesi Kütüphanesi Library
Yūsuf b. Muḥammad Milāvī. *Aḥsanu'l-Masālik lī Aḥbāri'l-Barāmik*. MS no. 2616. Ahmed III, Topkapı Sarayı Müzesi Kütüphanesi.

### Millet Kütüphanesi Library
Ahmed Resmî. *Sefînetü'r-Rüesâ*. MS no.720. Ali Emiri. Millet Kütüphanesi.

### İstanbul Üniversitesi Kütüphanesi Library
[Râmî Mehmed Pasha] *Sulhnâme*. MS Ty 407. İstanbul Üniversitesi Kütüphanesi.

### Published Primary Sources
Cantemir, Dimitrie. *The History of the Growth and Decay of the Othman Empire. Part I. Containing the Growth of the Othman Empire, from the Reign of Othman the Founder, to the Reign of Mahomet IV*. Translated by N. Tindal. London: Printed for James, John, and Paul Knapton, MDCCXXXIV[1734].

Defterdar Sarı Mehmed Paşa. *Zübde-i vekayiât: tahlil ve metin (1066–1116/1656–1704)*, edited by Abdülkadir Özcan. Ankara: TTK, 1995.

de Hammer, J. *Histoire de l'Empire ottoman depuis son origine jusqu'à nos jours; ouvrage puisé aux sources les plus authentiques et rédigé sur des documents et des manuscrits la plupart inconnus en Europe*. Translated by J. J. Hellert. 19 vols. Paris: Béthune et Plon, 1835–43.

Evliya Çelebi. *Evliya Çelebi Seyahatnâmesi: 3. Kitap: Topkapı Sarayı Bağdat 305 Yazmasının Transkripsiyonu-Dizini*, edited by Seyit Ali Kahraman and Yücel Dağlı. Istanbul: Yapı Kredi Yayınları, 1999.

Evliya Çelebi. *Evliya Çelebi Seyahatnâmesi: 6. Kitap: Topkapı Sarayı Kütüphanesi Revan 1457 Numaralı Yazmanın Transkripsiyonu-Dizini*, edited by Seyit Ali Kahraman and Yücel Dağlı. Istanbul: Yapı Kredi Yayınları, 2002.

İpekten, Haluk. *Naili-i Kadim Divanı*. Istanbul: Milli Eğitim Basımevi, 1970.

İsazade. *İsazade Tarihi (Metin ve Tahlil)*. Edited by Ziya Yılmazer. Istanbul: İstanbul Fetih Cemiyeti İstanbul Enstitüsü Yayınları, 1996.

Kaplan, Mahmut. *Neşati Divanı*. Izmir: Akademi Kitabevi, 1996.

Mermer, Ahmed. *XVII.yy, Divan Şairi Vecdi ve Divançesi*. Ankara: Milli Eğitim Basımevi, 2002.

Mirzazâde Sâlim Mehmed Emin Efendi. *Tezkiretü'ş-Şuarâ Sâlim Efendi, Mirzazâde Sâlim Mehmed Emin Efendi, 1156/1743*, edited by Adnan İnce. Ankara: Atatürk Kültür Merkezi Yayınları, 2005.

Mustafa Na'îmâ Efendi. *Tarih-i Naîma: Ravzatü'l-Hüseyn fî Hulâsati Ahbâri'l-Hâfikayn*, edited by Mehmet İpşirli, 4 vols. Ankara: TTK, 2007.

Mustafa Safâyî. *Tezkire-i Safâyî (Nuhbetü'l-Asar Min Feva'idi'l-Eş'ar) İnceleme-Metin-İndeks*, edited by Pervin Çapan. Ankara: Atatürk Kültür Merkezi Yayınları, 2005.

Müminzade Seyyid Ahmed Hasibî Efendi. *Ravzatü'l-Küberâ: Tahlil ve Metin*, edited by Mesut Aydıner. Ankara: TTK, 2003.

Osmanzade Ahmed Taib. *Hadîkatü'l-Vüzerâ*. Istanbul: Cerîde-i Havâdis Matbaası, 1271/1854.

Özcan, Abdülkadir (ed.), *Anonim Osmanlı tarihi, 1099–1116 (1688–1704)*. Ankara: TTK, 2000.

Silahdâr Fındıklılı Mehmed Ağa. *Nusretnâme*, edited by İsmet Parmaksızoğlu. Ankara: Milli Eğitim Bakanlığı, 1962.

Şeyhî Mehmed Efendi. *Veka'yü'l-Fudâlâ, Şâkâyık-i Numâniye ve Zeyilleri*, edited by Abdülkadir Özcan. 5 vols. Istanbul: Çağrı Yayınları, 1989.

Uşşakizade İbrahim Efendi. *Uşşakizade Tarihi*, edited by Raşit Gündoğdu. Istanbul: Çamlıca Basım Yayın A. Ş., 2005.

## Secondary Sources

Abou-El-Haj, Rifa'at. "The Reisü'l-küttab and Ottoman Diplomacy at Karlowitz". Ph.D. dissertation. Princeton University, 1963.

Abou-El-Haj, Rifa'at. "The Formal Closure of the Ottoman Frontier in Europe: 1699–1703". *Journal of the American Oriental Society* 89 (3) 1969, 467–75.

Abou-El-Haj, Rifa'at. "The Ottoman Vezir and Paşa Households 1683–1703: A Preliminary Report". *Journal of the American Oriental Society* 94 (4) 1974, 438–47.

Ahıskalı, Recep. *Osmanlı Devlet Teşkilatında Reisülküttablık (XVIII. yüzyıl)*. İstanbul: Tarih ve Tabiat Vakfı Yayınları, 2001.

Alam, Muzaffar and Sanjay Subrahmanyam. "Witnesses and Agents of Empire: Eighteenth-Century Historiography and the World of the Mughal Munshi". *Journal of the Economic and Social History of the Orient* 53 (1–2), 2009, 393–423.

Andreasyan, Hrand. "Balatlı Georg'a gore Edirne Vak'ası". *İstanbul Üniversitesi Edebiyat Fakültesi Dergisi* 11 (15) 1960, 47–64.

Barkan, Ömer Lütfi. "H.933–934 (M.1527–28) Mali Yılına Ait Bütçe Örneği". *İstanbul Üniversitesi İktisat Fakültesi Mecmuası* 15 (1–4), 1953/4, 238–329.

Camariano, Nestor. *Alexandre Mavrocordato: Le Grand Drogman, Son Activité diplomatique (1673–1709)*. Thessaloniki: Institute for Balkan Studies, 1970.

Çınar, Bekir. "Tıfli Ahmed Celebi, Hayati, Edebi kişiliği, Eserleri ve Divanının Tenkitli Metni". Ph.D. dissertation, Fırat University, 2000.

Dankoff, Robert. *The Intimate Life of an Ottoman Statesman: Melek Ahmed Pasha (1588–1662): As Portrayed in Evliya Çelebi's Book of Travels (Seyahatname)*. Albany: State University of New York Press, 1991.

El-Hibri, Tayeb. *Reinterpreting Islamic Historiography, Harun al-Rashid and the Narrative of the 'Abbasid Caliphate*. New York: Cambridge University Press, 1999.

Ergun, Saadettin Nüzhet. *Rami Paşa Hayatı ve Eserleri*. İstanbul: Kanaat Kütüphanesi, 1933.

Findley, Carter V. "Patrimonial Household Organization and Factional Activity in the Ottoman Ruling Class". In Halil İnalcık and Osman Okyar (eds). *Türkiye'nin Sosyal ve Ekonomik Tarihi 1071–1920*. Ankara: Meteksan Limited, 1980, 227–35.

Findley, Carter V. *Ottoman Civil Officialdom: A Social History*. Princeton, NJ: Princeton University Press, 1989.

Hathaway, Jane. "The Military Household in Ottoman Egypt". *International Journal of Middle East Studies* 27 (1) 1995, 39–52.

İnalcık, Halil. "Reîsülküttâb". *IA*, vol. 9. Ankara, 1964.

Kennedy, Hugh. "The Barmakid Revolution in Islamic Government". In Charles Melville (ed.), *History and Literature in Iran: Persian and Islamic Studies in Honour of P. W. Avery*. London: British Academic Press, 1990, 89–98.

Kunt, Metin. "The Köprülü Years 1656–1661". Ph.D. dissertation, Princeton University, 1971.

Kunt, Metin. "Naima, Köprülü and the Grand Vezirate". *Bosphorus University Journal-Humanities* 1 (1973), 57–63.

Meservey, Sabra. "An Ottoman Şeyhülislam". Ph.D. dissertation. Princeton University, 1965.

Molnar, Monika. "Karlofça Antlaşması'ndan sonra Osmanlı-Habsburg Sınırı 1699–1701." In Güler Eren (ed.) *Osmanlı*. Ankara: Yeni Türkiye Yayınları, 1999, vol. 1, 472–9.

Molnar, Monica. "Venezia e la questione turca nella prima metà della guerra dei quindici anni secondo i memoriali romani di un diplomatico veneziano". *Nuova Corvina* 6 (1999), 167–76.

Munson, William Bruce. "The Peace of Karlowitz". Ph.D. dissertation. University of Illinois, 1940.

Neumann, Christoph K. "Political and Diplomatic Developments". In Suraiya N. Faroqhi (ed.) *The Cambridge History of Turkey*, vol.3: *The Later Ottoman Empire, 1603–1839*. New York: Cambridge University Press, 2006, 44–62.

Nizri, Michael. "The Kapı in Ottoman Society: The Household of Şeyhülislam Feyzullah Efendi, 1695–1703 [in Hebrew]". Ph.D. dissertation. Tel-Aviv University, 2009.

Nizri, Michael. "The Memoirs of Şeyhülislam Feyzullah Efendi (1638–1703), Self, Family and Household". In Yavuz Köse and Ralf Elger (eds) *Ego-Documents: Arabic, Persian, Turkish (14th–20th Century)*. Wiesbaden: Harrassowitz Verlag, 2010, 29–38.

Özcan, Abdülkadir. "300.Yılında Karlofça Antlaşması". *Akademik Araştırmalar Dergisi* 2 (4–5) 2000, 237–57.

Popović, Michajlo R. *Der Friede von Karlowitz* (Paderborn: EGV, 2012; reprint of 1893 edition).

Rosenthal, Franz. "From Arabic Books and Manuscripts". *Journal of the American Oriental Society* 83 (4), 1963, 452–7.

Shaw, Stanford J. *History of the Ottoman Empire and Modern Turkey*, vol. 1. New York: Cambridge University Press, 1976.

Shaybani. *The Islamic Law of Nations: Shaybānī's Siyar*, translated with an introd., notes, and appendices by Majid Khadduri. Baltimore: Johns Hopkins University Press, 1966.

Stoye, John. *Marsigli's Europe, 1680–1730: The Life and Times of Luigi Ferdinando Marsigli, Soldier and Virtuoso*. New Haven: Yale University Press, 1994.

Tezcan, Baki. *The Second Ottoman Empire Political and Social Transformation in the Early Modern World*. New York: Cambridge University Press, 2010.

Turek, Ahmet and F. Çetin Derin (eds). "Feyzullah Efendi'nin Kendi Kaleminden Hal Tercümesi". *İstanbul Üniversitesi Edebiyat Fakültesi Tarih Dergisi* 23 (1969, 205–18).

Tuşalp-Atiyas, E. Ekin. "Political Literacy and the Politics of Eloquence: Ottoman Scribal Community in the Seventeenth Century." Ph.D. dissertation, Harvard University, 2014.

Uzunçarşılı, İsmail Hakkı. *Osmanlı Tarihi*, vol.3 kısım 1. Ankara: TTK, 1995; reprint of 1951 edition.

Wehr, Hans. *A Dictionary of Modern Written Arabic*. Edited by J. Milton Cowan, 3rd edition. Ithaca, NY: Spoken Language Services, 1976.

Woodhead, Christine. "Research on the Ottoman Scribal Service, c.1574–1630". In Christa Fragner and Klaus Schwarz (eds). *Festgabe an Josef Matuz: Osmanistik-Turkologie-Diplomatik*. Berlin: Klaus Schwarz Verlag, 1992, 311–28.

Yöntem, Ali Canib Yöntem. "Rami Mehmed Paşa'nın Sulhnâmesi". In *IV. Türk Tarih Kongresi: Kongreye Sunulan Tebliğler* [*Türk Tarih Kongresi (IV: 1948: Ankara)*], 346–53. Ankara: TTK, 1952.

CHAPTER 11

# The Compass and the Astrolabe: Empiricism in the Ottoman Empire

*B. Harun Küçük*

In 1991, an Ottoman astrolabe from the early-eighteenth century surfaced in a Sotheby's auction. It was originally a medieval instrument that a Turkish craftsman had updated, possibly under the direction of a *muvakkit*. Among the strange features of the item were an added disc with sub-equatorial latitudes, misspellings of Arabic names and verbatim reproductions of Maghribi astronomical terminology. The astrolabe also had other curiosities. The craftsman had retained miscalculated coordinates for Istanbul, perhaps as an antiquarian curiosity, and had installed a magnetic compass on the frame – ill-considered and redundant, according to David A. King.[1] If one were to pick a single object to tell the story of early modern Ottoman science, this astrolabe would be it.

We know precious little about who made the instrument and when. There are no names or dates on the device, but King's periodization seems correct. The early-eighteenth century was just the time when an Ottoman naturalist would install a compass on his astrolabe to check one against the other. This instrument was not the only place where the traditional instruments of Islamic astronomy and a modern contender met.[2] One could find compass roses on many Ottoman maps from the late-seventeenth and early-eighteenth centuries. Compasses and clocks were so fashionable that, in the 1720s, Damad İbrâhim Pasha had patronized a prayer rug with a built in compass and a book that showed how to reckon prayer times using a modern clock.[3]

---

[1] David A. King, "An Ottoman Astrolabe Full of Surprises", in N. Sidoli and G. Van Brumelen (eds). *From Alexandria, through Baghdad: Surveys and Studies in the Ancient Greek and Medieval Mathematical Sciences in Honor of J. L. Berggren* (Berlin: Springer Verlag, 2014), 329–42.

[2] David A. King and Richard Lorch, "Qibla Charts, Qibla Maps, and Related Instruments", in J. B. Harley and David Woodwards (eds). *The History of Cartography*, vol. 2, bk. 1: *Cartography in Traditional Islamic and South Asian Societies* (Chicago: Chicago University Press, 1992), 189–205.

[3] Ekmeleddin İhsanoğlu et al., *Osmanlı Astronomi Literatürü Tarihi*, 2 vols. (Istanbul: IRCICA, 1997), vol. 1, 396.

However, using a compass for determining the qibla was also the subject of some controversy. In 1730, two parties, one led by İbrâhim Müteferrika and another composed of various *muvakkits*, met in Bebek to determine the qibla for the new Kaymak Mustafa Pasha mosque. While the astronomers (*ehl-i raṣad*) read one direction on their astrolabes, the compass pointed in a wildly different direction. Müteferrika did not win the debate and had to go back to the drawing board and write about the magnetic compass at least twice in 1732. Today, we live in a world where the compasses or, rather, smartphones with GPS chips tell us which direction the qibla is. And, we now believe that many mosques, including those built by Sinan, were not perfectly aligned with the qibla. Whatever seems true to us was at best suspect in the early-eighteenth century. In the early-eighteenth century, the qibla was wherever the astrolabe said the qibla was.[4]

Although the astrolabe and the compass seem comparable in their function, they actually point to two qualitatively different types of knowledge.[5] The astrolabe was an object of medieval Islamic origin and numbered among the entrenched elements in Ottoman astronomical practices.[6] It also symbolized a highly theoretical and technical way to deal with both time and space. A craftsman had to painstakingly inscribe centuries of astronomical observation and modelling onto the astrolabe. And, operating such an expensive device meant to deduce new practical knowledge from a seemingly timeless theoretical model. Its results were exact and authoritative. The astrolabe represented some of the best features of high Islamic culture and, the finest astrolabes continue to amaze and delight any spectator who may chance upon one at a museum.

The compass, by contrast, was the product of a far lower culture – that of sailors. It was hardly the symbol of accuracy. As early as the sixteenth century, Seydî Ali Reis (d.1562) felt the need to develop an empirical protocol, using at least two compasses against one another as 'witnesses', to improve the

---

4 Hacı Halife Mustafa b. Abdullah Katib Çelebi, *Kitab-ı Cihannüma li-Katib Çelebi*, edited by İbrâhim Müteferrika (Istanbul: Darü't-Tıbaati'l-Âmire, 1145/1732), 66.

5 On the compass, see Jim Bennett, "Mechanical Arts", in Katharine Park and Lorraine Daston (eds) *The Cambridge History of Science*, vol. 3: *Early Modern Science* (Cambridge: CUP, 2006), 673–95. On the magnetic philosophy of William Gilbert, see the works of Stephen Pumfrey, as shown in https://www.lancaster.ac.uk/history/about/people/stephen-pumfrey (retrieved on 13 April 2019).

6 See İhsanoğlu, *Osmanlı Astronomi* 1, *passim*. Over the seventeenth and eighteenth centuries, the majority of the Ottoman treatises on astronomy were in Turkish and served as how-to manuals for instruments.

instrument's reliability.[7] The compass, unlike the astrolabe, was also an empirical device. It arguably pointed due north for an inexplicable reason and yielded instant and sensory information. Like most other navigational instruments, the compass was agnostic about religion, language or class. Anyone could pick it up and use it without much trouble. While an astrolabe could be used in several different locations, it gained its universality through an additive process.[8] Someone would have to inscribe and calculate each of the locations where the device might be used. The compass, however, was free of such trouble and arguably worked equally well everywhere. The compass was easy to build, too. İbrâhim Müteferrika could list at least three different and very convenient ways to build a compass within a paragraph.[9] This device was *basse classe* through and through: it was easy, cheap, only somewhat functional and not particularly beautiful.[10] In other words, it was not the kind of device on which one could stake his faith or his qibla. Müteferrika tried to imbue the compass with some authority when he said that the first appearance of the device was when the Khan of China gave it as a gift to ambassadors from Cochinchina and thus, successfully saved himself the trouble of assigning them a guide to get them back to their country.[11] Yet, we can hardly assume that this piece of lore was the kind of credential that would have been sufficient for his opponents in Bebek.

Over the eighteenth century, the compass acquired a more scientific character when Müteferrika translated an entire volume showcasing how reliable the combination of the horizontal and the vertical compass could be. Within a few years, in 1738, Petros Baronyan built on the newfound credibility of the instrument and constructed a staggeringly ornate kiblenuma that used the

---

[7] Himmet Büke, "Seydi Ali Reis-Kitabü'l-Muhit" (Master's thesis, Pamukkale University, Denizli, 2010), 84.
[8] King, "Ottoman Astrolabe", 335–6.
[9] İbrâhim Müteferrika, *Füyûzât-ı Mıknâtısiyye* (Istanbul: Darü't-Tıba'ati'l-'Âmire, 1145/1732), 4r.
[10] On the early Islamic compasses, see David A. King, "al-Ṭāsa", in $EI^2$ 10, 312–13; and Eilhard Wiedemann, "The Compass" (under Maghnāṭīs) in $EI^2$ 5, 1168–9.
[11] Müteferrika, *Füyûzât-ı Mıknâtısiyye*, fol. 3r. "According to the works and the testimony of these travellers, the Khan of China had received ambassadors from the Khan of Cochinchina. After the processions and the ceremonies, as the ambassadors the Khan of China gave for their return, among other precious gifts, a qibla device inlaid with precious stones and a compass showing the four directions and with etchings indicating the names of the winds. It is reported that the Khan of China said, in a civil idiom and attitude that was appropriate to the social standing of the ambassadors, since the country to which the ambassadors were to the south of China, that they could follow the direction of this compass without needing any guides. It is also reported that the people of China have mastered properties of the magnet two thousand and five hundred years ago."

compass as the centrepiece.[12] By this point, it was hard to tell whether the knowledge and the credibility of the instrument came from the European or the Ottoman experiences. From the very beginning of the seventeenth century onward, the compass was also an object of some philosophical interest. Since William Gilbert's *De magnete* (1600), countless authors from René Descartes to Edmund Halley had tried to crack its mystery. The compass was part of Europe's high intellectual culture and the English Senate was considering taking what the compass read as the truth – though they eventually decided in favour of John Harrison's chronometer after some forty years of deliberation.[13] Müteferrika's *Magnetic Effluvia* had introduced a highly inflected version of the European accounts of the compass, but the discussion within which he placed the instrument was wholly Ottoman.

1      The High and the Low in the Eighteenth Century

The crucial question is, what made room for the compass on that astrolabe? After all, compasses had been used by Ottoman merchants and sailors since the fifteenth century, but they never made it into a theoretical or *ʿilmī* text until Müteferrika provided a possible explanation for them. How was it that the high Islamic culture of the *ulema* had room for a lowly gadget that was used almost exclusively by soldiers and merchants? How could experience find a place in the purely rational enterprise that was Islamic mathematics?

The type of hybridity – juxtaposing the high against the low, the rational against the experiential, the scholarly against the mercantile, and occasionally, the Islamicate against the European – arising out of negotiation was so ubiquitous in the eighteenth century that this might as well serve to characterize what Ottoman science was. In this sense, *tıbb-ı cedîd*, or new medicine, serves as a paradigm for many other disciplines. Authors who were part of this movement sought to synthesize the alchemy of Jābir ibn Ḥayyān with Paracelsian drug recipes, the new pathology of Jean Fernel with the Galenic understanding of disease, imported mineral ingredients with local herbs, merchants' drachms with *şerʿî dirhem*s, terminologies drawn from Arabic, Persian, Greek, Latin

---

12    İhsanoğlu, *Osmanlı Astronomi* 1, 410. For a brief treatment, also see David A. King, *World-Maps for Finding the Direction and Distance to Mecca* (Leiden: Brill, 1999), 101. There are many copies of this *iblenümā*, some well-known copies are in Kandilli Rasathanesi, Topkapı Müzesi, Türk-İslam Eserleri Müzesi and Museo Civico Correr di Venezia.

13    For a comprehensive treatment of magnetism in the seventeenth and eighteenth centuries, see A. R. T. Jonkers, *Earth's Magnetism in the Age of Sail* (Baltimore: JHU Press, 2003).

and Turkish into a coherent body of knowledge and practices.[14] Early modern Ottoman geography and cartography were equally heterogenous in their sources and practices. Recent studies reveal the ubiquity of the uneasy combinations of Mercatorian and Islamicate cartographic projection techniques, of modern European and medieval Islamic geographical knowledge and of European atlases with local portolans.[15] Among other heterogenous practices were the use of European ephemerides within the context of Islamic *hey'et* tradition – a trend that continued well into the eighteenth century.[16]

This compass framing the astrolabe was the aggregate picture that arose out of conflict, not closure. The 1730 incident in Bebek suggests that combining the high and the low did not point to a compromise position where Ottoman science rested – this was not the repose of the syncretist. Whoever installed that compass on the astrolabe was not thinking that both devices provided the one true direction of the qibla. It was precisely because they signified qualitatively different types of knowledge that yielded quantitatively different results that both the compass and the astrolabe went together. It was not a compass and an astrolabe, it was a compass framing and qualifying the astrolabe, putting parentheses around the Islamic tradition as precisely that, a tradition. More importantly, however, we can also read a social dynamic into the hybrid nature of Ottoman science of the eighteenth century – namely, artisanal and mercantile culture as well as European knowledge framing the high theoretical world of *ulema*.

---

14   On *ıbb-ı cedīd*, see Natalia Bachour's excellent *Oswaldus Crollius und Daniel Sennert im frühneuzeitlichen Istanbul: Studien zur Rezeption des Paracelsismus im Werk des osmanischen Arztes Ṣāliḥ b. Naṣrullāh Ibn Sallūm al-Ḥalabī* (Freiburg: Centaurus, 2012). On the dirhem controversy, see Hayatizâde Mustafa's *Düstūrü'ṭ-Ṭabīb fī Mīzānü'l-Terkib*, MS 3602, Nuruosmaniye, SK.

15   In addition to Gottfried Hagen's work, *Ein osmanischer Geograph bei der Arbeit. Entstehung und Gedankenwelt von Katib Celebis Gihannüma* (Berlin: Schwarz, 2003), see Sonja Brentjes, "Patchwork: The Norm of Mapmaking Practices for Western Asia in Catholic and Protestant Europe as well as in Istanbul between 1550 and 1750?" in Feza Günergun and Dhruv Raina (eds), *Science between Europe and Asia* (Dordrecht: Springer Verlag, 2011), 77–102; John J. Curry, "An Ottoman Geographer Engages the Early Modern World: Katip Çelebi's Vision of East Asia and the Pacific Rim in the Cihānnümā", OA 40 (2012), 221–57.

16   Ekmeleddin İhsanoğlu. "Introduction of Western Science to the Ottoman World: A Case Study of Modern Astronomy (1660–1860)", in *idem* (ed.)*Transfer of Modern Science and Technology to the Muslim World* (Istanbul: IRCICA, 1992), 67–120.

## 2  Locating Empirical Science in the Ottoman Empire

In Europe, what mediated between the compass and the astrolabe, between the terrestrial and the empirical on the one hand, and the heavenly and the mathematical on the other was natural philosophy. By claiming the right of say in philosophical matters, figures such as Galileo Galilei and Robert Boyle leveraged the higher status attached to natural philosophy to legitimize their empirical enterprises.[17] Modern science, consequently, took over the role of natural philosophy.[18] However, because empirical knowledge was at odds with the methodology and scope of natural philosophy, early modern science also represented a union of artisanal ways of knowing and highly theoretical speculations about the fundamental structure of the universe. In this scheme, natural philosophy was a 'trading zone', where theologians, physicians, astronomers, philosophers, travellers and artisans who attached different meanings to words and things could communicate with one another using a creole language.[19] Since natural philosophy was arguably a freestanding discipline by the seventeenth century, it was occasionally possible to argue about it without touching theological matters. Although the Ottoman medrese appears to have been fundamentally similar to the European university, there was one important difference between the two, especially as it pertains to the career of science. There was no comparable trading zone in the Ottoman Empire, which made the academic rapprochement between the astrolabe and the compass difficult.

The absence of natural philosophy was a generic feature of the medrese.[20] When Mehmed II (d.1481) organized the empire's medreses, he placed *kelâm*, that is Islamic theology, at the foundation of education. In the fifteenth century, *kelâm* would have meant philosophical or speculative *kelâm*, which, in itself would serve as an entire course in the liberal arts – standard manuals,

---

17  On Galileo, see Mario Biagoli, *Galileo, Courtier: The Practice of Science in the Culture of Absolutism* (Chicago: Chicago University Press, 1993); Steven Shapin and Simon Schaffer, *Leviathan and the Air Pump: Hobbes, Boyle and the Experimental Life* (Princeton, NJ: Princeton University Press, 1993).

18  Peter Dear, "Historiography of Not So Recent Science", *History of Science* 50 (2) 2012, 197–211.

19  Peter Galison has coined the term 'trading zone' in his *Image and Logic* (Chicago: Chicago University Press, 1997), where he used it to describe how modern physicists and engineers managed to interact with one another although they worked within different 'paradigms'.

20  None of the surviving treatises on medrese curricula list an independent treatise on natural philosophy. See Cevat İzgi's *Osmanlı Medreselerinde İlim*, 2 vols. (Istanbul: İz Yayıncılık, 1997). It is noteworthy that İzgi primarily considered mostly the exact sciences under natural philosophy.

such as Nāṣīr al-Dīn al-Ṭūsī's *Tecrīdü'l-'Aḳā'id* included large amounts of logic, rhetoric, mathematics, natural philosophy and metaphysics in addition to sacred doctrine.[21] In the late-fifteenth century, Ali Kuşçu made the attempt to sever astronomy from its physical foundations, pushing natural philosophy further towards *kelâm*, though we cannot readily assume that he was completely successful in this enterprise.[22] In the sixteenth century, Süleyman I's (d.1566) medical medrese included no books on natural philosophy in the Aristotelian sense, which reinforced the century-old trend.[23] Although Taşköprülüzâde listed the most important books on natural philosophy in his *Mevẓū'ātü'l-'Ulūm*, none of the books that he listed was on the curriculum of any medrese whatsoever.[24] Natural philosophy only existed as part of *kelâm*. This suggests that the 'philosophy as the handmaiden of theology' model that was prevalent in the medieval and, to a certain extent, the early modern university was also a structural component of medrese training.

By the end of the seventeenth century, two separate movements had gone far towards liberating natural philosophy from simply being the handmaiden of theology in Europe. The first was the Paduan Aristotelians' push to remove metaphysics from the arts faculty in the sixteenth century.[25] A second, perhaps more important, development was the anti-academic and anti-clerical sentiments that were very prevalent among the various Protestant movements, especially among the Puritans of England and the Pietists of Prussia. And, I would argue that the Ottoman Empire was home to similar dynamics. I have argued elsewhere that Paduan Aristotelianism was an important feature of Istanbul's intellectual life in the eighteenth century because of the Ottoman Greeks' ties with Padua. One may expand the demographic basis of Ottoman Paduanism by including Jewish medicine as well.[26]

---

21  Oliver Leaman and Sajjad Rizvi, "The Developed Kalām Tradition", in Tim Winter (ed.) *The Cambridge Companion to Classical Islamic Theology* (Cambridge: CUP, 2008), 77–96. On the foundational role of al-Ṭūsī's theological work and its commentaries in the fifteenth century, see İsmail Hakkı Uzunçarşılı, *Osmanlı Devletinin İlmiye Teşkilatı* (Ankara: TTK, 1965), 11, 21.

22  F. Jamil Ragep and Alī al-Qūshjī, "Freeing Astronomy from Philosophy: An Aspect of Islamic Influence of Science", *Osiris* 16 (2001), 49–64, 66–71.

23  Nil Sarı, "Educating the Ottoman Physician", *Yeni Tıp Tarihi Araştırmaları* 1 (1995), 11–54.

24  Taşköprüzâde. *Mevẓū'ātü'l-'Ulūm*, 2 vols. (Istanbul: Asitane, 2000), vol. 1, 629.

25  For a summary, see B. Harun Küçük, "Natural Philosophy and Politics in the Eighteenth Century: Esad of Ioannina and Greek Aristotelianism at the Ottoman Court", *OA* 41 (2013), 125–59.

26  David B. Ruderman, *Jewish Thought and Scientific Discovery in Early Modern Europe* (New Haven: Yale University Press, 1995), 100–17.

As for the anti-academic and anti-clerical sentiment, the Ottoman Empire provides plenty of evidence from very different quarters. As early as 1581, bureaucrat Gelibolulu Mustafa Âlî viewed the medrese as a regressive institution and considered the *ulema* to be a rotten lot.[27] In the mid-seventeenth century, Kâtib Çelebi lamented the gradual disappearance of philosophical disciplines from the medrese curriculum in favour of a narrow legal training.[28] Many sultans in the eighteenth century tried to institute a mechanism of examinations to boost the quality of education and to ensure a certain standard of learning among those bearing the title *learned*. In other words, the formal learned establishment did not command universal respect by a long shot.

A significant element in Ottoman anti-clericalism was the Kadızâdeli movement of the seventeenth century, which putatively drew on the writings of Birgivî Mehmed, the sixteenth-century religious reformer. One of the foundational texts of the influential Kadızâdeli movement of the seventeenth century was *Ṭarîkat-ı Muḥammediyye*, a canonical text in Ottoman and later, Turkish Islam.[29] Therein, Birgivî commended against speculative philosophy of both the physical and the metaphysical kind. Halil İnalcık has provided the dominant reading of this phenomenon when he defined the entirety of the Kadızâdeli as the 'triumph of fanaticism' that signalled the end of *ʿulûm-i ʿakliyye* or the rational sciences. Recently, Khaled el-Rouayheb and Derin Terzioğlu made the case that logic, arithmetic, mathematical astronomy and dialectic were notable exceptions to this trend. Rouayheb has gone so far as to show that logic especially witnessed a veritable efflorescence, especially in the eighteenth century.[30] However, logic was an essential component of legal methodology and mathematics was part of legal practice. None of this suggests anything at all about natural philosophy, which seems to have disappeared without a trace from Ottoman intellectual life in the seventeenth century.

---

27 Andreas Tietze (ed.), *Mustafa Ali's Counsel for Sultans of 1581: Edition, Translation, Notes*, vol. 1 (Vienna: Verlag der Österreichischen Akademie der Wissenschaften, 1979), 66, 75, 77.

28 Seyfi Kenan, "Doğruyu Dengede Tutmak: Mīzānü'l-Hak Çerçevesinde Kātip Çelebi 'nin Bilgi ve Eğitim Anlayışı", in Said Öztürk (ed.) *Vefatının 350. Yılında Katip Çelebi* (Istanbul: İstanbul Büyükşehir Belediyesi, 2007), 87–91. As Kenan notes, Kâtib Çelebi's remarks were not universally applicable to all medreses, but still pointed to a fundamental change in Istanbul's major educational institutions.

29 Bernd Radtke, "Birgiwīs *Ṭarīqa Muḥammadiyya*: Einige Bemerkungen und Überlegungen", *JTS* 26 (2), 2002, 159–74.

30 Khaled el-Rouayheb, "The Myth of 'the Triumph of Fanaticism' in the Seventeenth-Century Ottoman Empire", *WIS* 48 (2) 2008, 196–221; Derin Terzioğlu, "Where 'İlm-I Ḥal Meets Catechism: Islamic Manuals of Religious Instruction in the Ottoman Empire in the Age of Confessionalization", *PP* 220 (2013), 79–114.

Since natural philosophy existed as part of theological discourse, it is also worthwhile to ask whether the formulaic articulations of the medrese sciences, such as the rational (*'aklî*) and the historical (*naklî*) sciences were truly applicable to this discipline. If free debate in matters pertaining to nature also meant challenging orthodoxy, which Birgivî implied, it is hard to call natural philosophy a purely rational undertaking. In fact, there are good historical reasons to question such distinctions for other parts of philosophy as well. Many of the early modern Islamic discussions of *hikmet* centred on questions of metaphysics and religion. Furthermore, İbn Sînâ's texts, when they were taught at the medrese, were subject to the same system of diplomas (*icâzets*) and *isnâds* (ascription of Islamic tradition) that was typical of *naklî* sciences.[31] That is, even philosophy was not necessarily subject solely to scrutiny that is often taken to constitute the *'aklî* status of a discipline. Thus, we have no reason to assume that the methods an Islamic scholar (*'âlim*) used for comprehending an exegetical text were any different from those he used for a naturalistic text.

Sociologist Robert K. Merton formulated the thesis that modern experimental science and Puritan sentiments – something historians have come to associate with the Kadızâdelis – were compatible, if not also mutually reinforcing.[32] As Steven Shapin has noted, the one important qualifier is that 'sentiment' here refers to a general climate rather than a particular type of 'cultural expression'.[33] While the thesis has been painstakingly qualified by Merton, one simple version is that experimentalism and Puritan sentiment were mutually dependent. The Puritans, who eschewed the incursion of the church and of the grand metaphysical theses, severed their ties with scholastic discourse. In this context, experimental knowledge – science of those facts that had been produced at a particular time and a particular place – that had useful ends gained a new kind of religious legitimacy.

The Merton thesis, *mutatis mutandis*, may be worth discussing in the Ottoman case because a number of historians have successfully deployed the vocabulary of European Protestantism and Puritanism in their analyses of

---

31  Gerhard Endress, "Reading Avicenna in the Madrasa: Intellectual Genealogies and Chains of Transmission of Philosophy and the Sciences in the Islamic East", in James E. Montgomery (ed.) *Arabic Theology, Arabic Philosophy, From the Many to the One: Essays in Celebration of Richard M. Frank* (Leuven: Peeters, 2006), 371–424.

32  Robert K. Merton, "Science, Technology and Society in Seventeenth Century England", *Osiris* 4 (1938), 360–632.

33  Steven Shapin, "Understanding the Merton Thesis", *Isis* 79 (4), 1988, 594–605.

the Kadızâdeli movement.[34] Marinos Sariyannis invoked Max Weber's thesis about capitalism and Protestantism as he made the case for the compatibility between mercantile ethics and the Kadızâdeli movement.[35] However, how the Kadızâdelis have affected the content of science, aside from putatively encouraging an austere piety, is something that scholarship has hardly explored. In piecing together what may be called 'Kadızâdeli' science, it is useful to post some signs to establish the comparability of Puritanism and science. For one, both the Kadızâdelis and the Puritans placed great emphasis on religious education. Proponents of both movements considered literary education unprofitable and the study of scholastic philosophy a pernicious undertaking that led away from God.[36] Both movements were sceptical of metaphysics because it provided an alternative, non-scriptural means to understanding God, which could be, at the same time, completely reliant on the abilities of human reason.[37] Furthermore, metaphysics had the unique ability to lead one away from the true faith as it had with Muhyiddin İbnü'l-Arabî's philosophy. In the Ottoman case, as in the European one, one may surmise that anti-scholasticism

---

34   The classic study of the Kadızâdelis is Madeline Zilfi's *Politics of Piety: The Ottoman Ulema in the Post-Classical Age* (Minneapolis: Bibliotheca Islamica, 1988). See also Tijana Krstić, *Contested Conversions to Islam: Narratives of Religious Change and Communal Politics in the Early Modern Ottoman Empire* (Stanford: SUP, 2011), 13, 117; Terzioğlu, "*İlm-i Hal*", passim. Although Krstić always uses the word 'Puritan' in quotations marks, I believe that Terzioğlu's suggestion that there indeed may have been some interaction between Christian and Muslim religious dynamics in the early modern period is worth serious consideration. For example, Niyazi Berkes, "İbrâhim Müteferrika", *EI2*, vol. 3 (Leiden: E. J. Brill, 1971), 996–8 pointed out the intrinsic commensurability between the Unitarian faith and Islam. Pierre Lambert de Saumery's five-volume *Mémoires et aventures secrètes et curieuses d'un voyage du Levant* (Liège: Kints, 1732) is filled with stories of confessional deviance among the Christians living in the Levant. De Saumery's curious account deserves a more extensive treatment. By the same token, I see no reason why the Puritans may not be called the Kadızâdelis of England. For example, the opponents of Socinianism usually called attention to the fact that Socinian doctrines resembled those of Islam. Edhem Eldem has made some use of this work in his *French Trade in Istanbul in the Eighteenth Century* (Leiden: Brill, 1999).

35   Marinos Sariyannis, "The Kadızâdeli Movement as a Social and Political Phenomenon: The Rise of a Mercantile Ethic?" in A. Anastasopoulos (ed.) *Political Initiatives from the Bottom – Up in the Ottoman Empire: Halcyon Days in Crete VII, A Symposium Held in Rethymno, 9–11 January 2009* (Rethymno: Crete University Press, 2012), 263–89.

36   Mehmed Birgivî, *Tekmile-i Terceme-i Ṭarīḳat-ı Muḥammediyye*, translated by Vedadi (Istanbul: Ali Rıza Karahisari Matbaası, 1278/1861), 39. Here, Birgivî warned that unscrupulously engaging in *kelâm* was a sure path to false beliefs; Merton, "Science, Technology", 427–8.

37   Francis Robinson, "Ottomans-Safavids-Mughals: Shared Knowledge and Connective Systems", *JIS* 8 (2) 1997, 151–84.

had both doctrinal and sociopolitical modalities. It was metaphysics that made Ottoman religion flexible and thus, amenable to Sufi influences.[38] Second, the Ottoman medrese shared its curriculum with Safavid Iran, which was Shiite.[39] Furthermore, the inclusion of technical, scholastic metaphysics in high natural discourse excluded the non-*ulema*, those who were not schooled at the medrese, from religious discourse altogether. It is therefore not surprising, Birgivî and many other Kadızâdelis commended against *taḵlīd* – a slavish imitation of one's forebears or superiors – and argued, much like the Puritans of England, that each individual must discover his own faith.[40] However, including the laity in the indoctrination of the entire empire was of paramount importance to many seventeenth-century Ottoman preachers, who advocated a simpler type of faith, one of orthopraxy rather than orthodoxy. Hence, avoiding *hikmet* or metaphysics at large as part of the doctrinal apparatus. Despite the fact that Birgivî engaged with scholastic disciplines, he generally believed the medrese to be a corrupt institution. In his last will and testament, he commended – albeit to unknown effect – to avoid formal schooling in general and to focus on those sciences that were conducive to commonweal:

---

38   Birgivî, *Ṭarîkat-ı Muḥammediyye*, 39–40, 43. Birgivî also associated the study of both speculative *kelâm* and astrology with epistemic pride, namely the notion that human reason could grasp the true causes of things.

39   Mehmed Birgivî, *Ṭarîkat-ı Muḥammediyye*, edited by Muhammed Hüsnî Mustafâ, Mehmet Fatih Güney and A. Faruk Beşikçi (Istanbul: Kalem Yayınevi, 2004), 39. According to Birgivî, the kind of *kelâm* that was *farẓ-ı kifâye* was the kind that helped defend one's *mezheb*. It is not clear how helpful Fakhr al-Dīn al-Rāzī (d.1209), Nāṣīr al-Dīn al-Ṭūsī (d.1274), Sayyid al-Sharīf al-Djurdjānī (d. 1413) or Muhammad b. ʿAbdullah al-Idjī (d.1500) would have been in drawing a confessional life, especially between Sunnis and Shiites. The *kelâm* book that did become popular in the seventeenth century was Saʿdüddîn Mesʿûd Teftâzânî's (d.1390) commentary on Nasafi's ʿAḳaʾid. Teftâzânî, as is well known, belonged to the Hanafi *mezheb*.

40   Radtke, "Birgiwi", 167–8. Compare Radtke's account of *keşf ḥissi* with the following passage from Thomas Sprat's *History of the Royal Society*: "[Christian revelation has] all bin prov'd to him his own way. Had not the appearance of Christ bin strengthen'd by undeniable signs of almighty Power, no age nor place had bin oblig'd to believe his Message. And these Miracles with which he asserted the Truths that he taught (if I might be allow'd this boldness in a matter so sacred). I would even venture to call Divine Experiments of his Godhead." Cited in Peter Dear, "Miracles, Experiments and the Ordinary Course of Nature", *Isis* 81 (4), 1990, 663–83. One may also find an echo of Sprat's sentiments in Yirmisekiz Mehmed's *Semeretüʾş-Şecere*. See Küçük, "Natural Philosophy and Politics", p. 129. This brings up the question of the relationship between empiricism and miracles or *keramât* in the Ottoman Empire, which deserves further study. However, it is noteworthy that one of the most popular non-*kelâm* naturalistic texts, Kazvînî's *ʿAcāʾibüʾl-Maḫlūkāt ve Garāʾibüʾl-Mevcūdāt* is filled with examples where the author asks whether an alleged miracle could not be explained away by reference to natural causes alone.

It is my last will to my sons that they should avoid being a student at the medrese. Nor should they become a client to the Kadıasker or willingly join the household of a judge or a lord. Instead, they should submit to God and busy themselves with the study of and writing about those sciences that are conducive to commonweal and with avoiding sins.[41]

These sciences not only included the teaching of the Quran and the '*ilm-i ḥāl* (catechism), but also medicine.[42]

It was not simply the Puritans, but also Sufis who placed emphasis on non-traditional and utilitarian knowledge. In this regard, too, there is some comparability between English Puritanism and the Ottoman Kadızâdeli movements – they both encouraged a certain type of pious sentiment without, at the same time, institutionalizing or monopolizing this kind of faith. For example, none other than the famous Niyâzî-i Mısrî, the bête noire of the arch-Kadızâdeli Vanî Mehmed Efendi, related that Abdülkadir-i Geylânî appeared to him in a dream and told him to engage with the world of appearances only for the purpose of *nâfiʿ ʿamel* or works that are conducive to commonwealth.[43]

There is an additional analytical advantage that English Puritanism of the Restoration provides, especially for the reign of Ahmed III (d.1736), not as a template but as a cognitive metaphor. Mid-seventeenth century, English Puritanism was a movement that was best defined as an eclectic grouping of people who had a problem with the institutional structure of the Church of England.[44] In the Ottoman Empire, too, a common contempt for the *ilmiyye* establishment could be found among as wildly divergent individuals as *Şeyhülislâm* Feyzullah Efendi in Istanbul or Abd al-Ghani al-Nabulsi in Damascus.[45] Second, much like post-1660 Puritanism, Kadızâdeli and later,

---

41  Birgivî Mehmed, *Vasiyyet-name: Dil İncelemesi, Metin, Sözlük, Ekler İndeksi, ve Tıpkıbasım*, edited byMusa Duman (Istanbul: R Yayınları, 2000), 126.
42  Birgivî, *Ṭarīḳat-ı Muḥammediyye*, 41.
43  Mustafa Aşkar, "Niyazi-i Mısri", DIA 33, 166–9. Other interesting examples of Sufis engaged in useful knowledge include the seventeenth-century physician Derviş Siyahi Lārendevi (fl.1615) and alchemist Ömer Şifai (fl.1720).
44  Michael Winship, "Defining Puritanism in Restoration England: Richard Baxter and Others Respond to a Friendly Debate", *The Historical Journal* 54 (3) 2011, 689–715.
45  On Feyzullah Efendi, see Michael Nizri's excellent biography, *Ottoman High Politics and the Ulema Household* (New York: Palgrave Macmillan, 2014). On Nabulsi's complicated engagement with the Ottoman legal establishment, see Martha Mundy, "Ethics and Politics in the Law: On the Forcible Return of the Cultivator", in Seyfi Kenan (ed.) *İSAM Konuşmaları: Osmanlı Düşüncesi, Ahlak, Hukuk, Felsefe-Kelam* (Istanbul: İSAM, 2013),

*müceddidī*, faiths were essentially absolutist enterprises.[46] According to the letters Sheikh Murād al-Bukhārī, the renewer of the faith would be none other than the sultan himself. Combined with the general tendency to indoctrinate even lay individuals over the seventeenth century, one may surmise that the *müceddidī* faith served as the consummation of the ancient dictum, *Cuius regio, eius religio*.[47]

However, it is also worthwhile to consider whether the institutional weakening of natural philosophy ultimately proved to be beneficial to naturalism in some other way. A parallel between English and Ottoman Puritanisms is that many of the people who were involved in naturalism in the eighteenth century, such as chief physician Nûh bin Abdülmennân, chief physician Ömer el-İznikî, Damad Ali Pasha who patronized several naturalistic works, Damad İbrâhim Pasha who was perhaps the most prominent patron of the sciences in early modern Ottoman history as well as Yirmisekiz Mehmed Çelebi and a host of others subscribed to the *müceddidi* creed of Sheikh Murād al-Bukhārī. Were these people pious royalists who believed in the superiority of utilitarian experimentalism?

The connection between Puritanism and science in the English case is easy to establish because we have the philosophy of Francis Bacon, who was the figurehead of royalist and utilitarian experimental philosophy and whose philosophy was adopted by Puritan naturalists.[48] On the other hand, there was no Bacon for the Ottoman naturalists. Or was there? We have circumstantial evidence about the Ottoman awareness of Francis Bacon. For one, Alexandros Mavrokordatos had a set of Francis Bacon's essays in his library. Most importantly, according to Miltos Pechlivanos, Mavrokordatos had penned an essay called *On Studies and Reading Books*, where he argued that experiential knowledge was on an equal footing with book learning, if not also somewhat

---

51–76. On his well-known anti-*ulema* sentiment, see Elizabeth Sirriyeh, *Sufi Visionary of Ottoman Damascus: 'Abd al-Ghani al-Nabulusi, 1641–1731* (London: Routledge, 2014).

46　For a discussion of Ottoman absolutism, see Baki Tezcan, *The Second Ottoman Empire: Political and Social Transformation in the Early Modern World* (Cambridge: CUP, 2012).

47　Butrus Abu-Manneh, "Sheikh Murād al-Bukhārī and the Expansion of the Naqshbandī-Mujaddidī Order in Istanbul", *WIS* 53 (1) 2013, 1–25. Also noteworthy is the fact that religious discussion between the *ulema* and the administrators, including publicly voicing disagreement on matters of faith, became a fixture of Ottoman religious culture over the eighteenth century. See Ebül'ula Mardin, *Huzur Dersleri*, 3 vols (Istanbul: İstanbul Üniversitesi, 1951–66).

48　Theodore K. Rabb, "Puritanism and the Rise of Experimental Science in England", *Journal of World History* 7 (1962), 46–67.

superior.[49] Mavrokordatos's observations about Ottoman naturalism in the early-eighteenth century also laments the lack of a solid empirical philosophy that could organize the otherwise occult occupations of the naturalists.[50]

Regardless of whether the Ottoman readers were in fact acquainted with Bacon, the kind of useful experimental science that we traditionally associate with his philosophy was present in the Ottoman Empire, particularly among the physicians. Physicians as advocates of empiricism were also a common feature of Renaissance medicine, making Bacon's philosophy only one of the many routes to high empiricism in early modern Europe.[51] While experiential medicine was one of the mainstays of the Greek tradition and had earlier roots than Galen, the dean of the physicians himself considered the empirics with some disdain. İbn Sînâ's *Kānûn* also stipulated a dual character for medicine – as an honourable and experimental art (*fenn-i şerîf*) and as a rational branch (*fürû'*) of natural philosophy. However, what was novel about the empiricism of Ottoman physicians was that they considered experiential knowledge to be superior to theoretical knowledge. We have ample anecdotal evidence from Evliya Çelebi to this effect.[52] More importantly, however we have textual evi-

---

49  Miltos Pechlivanos, "Bacon auf Altgriechisch. Erfahrungswissen und Buchwissen im griechischsprachigen Osmanischen Reich" (lecture, Freie Universität Berlin, Wissensbewegungen – Bewegliches Wissen: Wissenstransfer im Historischen Wandel, 12 February 2014). Pechlivanos draws his research from two main sources – Johannes Henricus Boecler, *Bibliographia historico-politico-philologica curiosa* (Frankfurt a. Main, 1677); and Nicholas Mavrocordato, "Peri grammatōn spoudēs kai Bibliōn anagnōseōs", unpublished essay in Kyrillos Athanasiades (ed.) *Hermeneia eis tus anabathmus tēs oktōēchu* (Jerusalem: Taphos, 1862). I would like to thank Professor Pechlivanos for sharing his knowledge of the Greek engagement with experimental science.

50  A second, far more tenuous, but also far more colourful, connection that is worth exploring was Ferenc II Rákóczi (d.1735), who engaged with alchemy at his court. Early in the twentieth century, theosophists made the claim that Rákóczi was a reincarnation of Francis Bacon. See Francis Udny, *Later Incarnations of Francis Bacon* (London: Edson, 1926). I would like to thank Tülay Artan for pointing out this connection.

51  See Dimitri Gutas, "The Empiricism of Avicenna", Oriens 40 (2) 2012, 391–436; Hiro Hirai, *Medical Humanism and Natural Philosophy: Renaissance Debates on Matter, Life and the Soul* (Leiden: Brill, 2011). This, it seems, was different from İbn Sînâ's own notion of experience; Gianna Pomata and Nancy G. Siraisi (eds), *Historia: Empiricism and Erudition in Early Modern Europe* (Cambridge: MIT Press, 2005).

52  ECS 3, 363: "Next to the Bayezid Han mosque is a hospital set in a heavenly garden. There, one also finds a medical medrese. Its cloisters are filled with students, expert physicians (*hükemâ-i hâzikî*) and perfect surgeons, who dispute about divine Plato, Hippocrates, Socrates, Aristotle, Galen and Pythagoras the Monotheist all day. Their methods are many times superior to that of Aristotle himself. The prophet has said: 'Science, it is two: first comes the science of bodies, and then comes the science of religions.' All of them

dence about how such an arrangement would work in action, that is in placing experiential knowledge above ancient authority from Hayatîzâde Mustafa Feyzi, the chief physician to Mehmed IV:

> This book seeks to offer health and wise counsel on the differences between hypochondria (*merâkiyye*) and melancholy hypochondria (*sevdâ-i merâkiyye*). The difficulties in telling these two diseases apart is well-known. Arab and Persian physicians have not recognized the differences between these two diseases and have lumped them together in miscellanies without proof or observation. As a consequence, I, a poor old man, have sieved the books, the ancient treatises and the works of virtuous Latin physicians at my disposal *through my true experiences with the afflicted men* ... to reach an abstract and judicious understanding of these two diseases.[53]

In this passage, and in many others, Hayatîzâde makes the claim that experience is the ultimate arbiter of knowledge, regardless of its source. The idea that true knowledge was useful and practical was staggeringly common among the Ottoman physicians. One way they captured this idea was in a well-known fabricated hadith – *Al-'ilmu 'ilmāni, 'ilmu'l-abdāni wa 'ilmu'l-adyāni* (science 'tis two: science of bodies and science of religions).[54] Many Ottoman physicians in the early-eighteenth century also made the case that their art was also a perfect way to theorize about nature, and that they deserved a higher status in society and within the *'ilmiyye* as a result. We know that these ideas had some

---

religiously study the time-honoured books in the science of medicine, and try to find a cure for the ailments of the son of man." For an exposition of experimental philosophy and its relation to the *tıbb-ı cedîd* movement, see B. Harun Küçük "New Medicine and the *Hikmet-i Tabiiyye* Problematic in Eighteenth-Century Istanbul", in Y. Tzvi Langermann and Robert G. Morrison (eds), *Texts in Transit in the Medieval Mediterranean* (University Park, PA: PSU Press, 2016), 222–42.

53   Hayatîzâde Mustafa Feyzi, *Hamse*, MS 3512, Nuruosmaniye, SK.
54   I would like to thank Halit Özkan for confirming that this is indeed a fabricated hadith. On the long and complex history of this fabricated hadith among the physicians, see Bachour, *Ibn Sallum*, p. 67; For a different inflection on the same fabricated hadith, see Franz Rosenthal, *Knowledge Triumphant: The Concept of Knowledge in Medieval Islam* (Leiden: Brill, 2006), 244: "Abu Uthman al-Maghribi (d.373/983–84) felt no hesitation to praise ash-Shafi'i for what must have been very far from the latter's mind, namely, that "the knowledge of religions" was the knowledge of the true realities and of gnostic insight, while "the knowledge of the bodies" was the knowledge of the various ways of political (?) guidance, ascetic training, and mystic exercise (*as-siyasat wa-r-riyadat wa-l-mujahadat*)."

traction at the palace because, from the early-eighteenth century onwards, the *hekimbaşı* leaped from being a fairly modest station to being of equal rank with the *kazasker* of Rumelia.[55] However, the point that there was an experimental tradition and some value attached to empirical knowledge over the seventeenth century stands regardless of whether the Ottoman scholars had any engagement with Bacon or not.

A second route to empiricism was Ibn Khaldun, with whom the Ottoman scholars had a long-standing engagement. Most scholars attest to *Muḳaddime*'s empirical bent, but we hardly discuss how such empiricism would have played out in practice. One very good example is Pirizâde Sahib Mehmed's Turkish rendition of this book. Today, we consider *Muḳaddime* to be about the philosophy of history and about social theory. Ottoman readers had generally consulted it for political wisdom. By contrast, Pirizâde's annotations reveal that he also read this book as a work on geography and contested Ibn Khaldun's authority on factual matters. Could ancient Palestine's agricultural output sustain as large an army as is claimed in the Bible? Were the dark skinned peoples of Sudan and Ethiopia really incapable of exercising reason? One of Pirizâde's longest and most notable annotations is about geodesy:

> Let it be known that in geodesy, geometers and mathematicians are in conflict regarding the degrees and the distances of the Earth. The author of *Taḳvīmü'l-Buldān* [Ebu'l-Fida] has said that the great ancient philosopher Ptolemy and others have found flat lands without hills or vales, and took out a quadrant and an astrolabe, measured the altitude of the north pole, that is, they measured how high the star known as the north pole was from the edge of the sky using instruments. They erected a pole at that location, tied a rope to the pole and walked from the north to the south along the meridian, without wavering right or left. Whenever they ran out of rope, they erected other poles, tied more rope and thus traversed a great distance. They took the altitude of the north pole every time they reached the end of the rope and kept going until the difference in the altitude was greater than one degree. They measured each mile at 3000 *arşın* and they found a difference of one degree at a distance of sixty-six miles and two-thirds. Later, during the reign of Ibn Ma'mun, Banu Musa and other geodesists sought to verify such claims and found one degree of altitude to correspond to fifty-six miles, which is ten miles shorter than the ancient measurement. According to the number the

---

55  Küçük, "New Medicine", 222–42.

author has relayed from Ibn Khaldun, this distance is twenty-five leagues, which makes seventy-five miles. This claim is at odds with both of the prior claims.[56]

In the case of Pirizâde as well, we find that he followed a practical route to this knowledge and placed experiential knowledge above both rationalism and textual authority. In the late 1730s, he patronized Mehmed Said Efendi's *müsellesiye*, a geodesical instrument that combined a European telescope with an Islamic quadrant – an instrument that is somewhat similar to the astrolabe with the compass in terms of its hybrid quality.[57] That geodesy was also a utilitarian and empirical kind of natural knowledge hardly needs an argument in the eighteenth-century Ottoman Empire. To observe how the shift from a fortress-based understanding of borderlands to a geometrical understanding of linear borders emerged, one only needs to look at Ebu Sehl Numan's *Tedbīrāt-i Pesendīde*, where one can find a first-hand account of how Ottoman borders were drawn empirically à la mode.[58]

Now, all of this brings up the challenging task of finding a practical naturalist who was both a *müceddidî* and placed value on utilitarian, empirical knowledge. Was there someone who had these qualifications? It turns out there was and he is very well known to the students of the Ottoman Empire – Yirmisekiz Mehmed Çelebi. We are accustomed to drawing our knowledge on Yirmisekiz Mehmed from his famous *Sefâretnâme*, where he praised how the French had managed to make a paradise of this world – again, a patently Puritanical ideal – by changing the material conditions. The standard interpretation is that this work had a 'Westernizing' influence, that it made European science

---

56   İbn Haldûn, *Mukaddime-i İbn Haldûn*, translated and edited by Pirizâde Mehmed Sahib (Bulak: Matbaa-i Âmire, 1274/1858), vol. 1, 55. For an excellent overview of Pirizâde's translation, see Yavuz Yıldırım, "*Mukaddime*'nin Osmanlı Dönemi Türkçe Tercümesi", *Divan: İlmi Araştırmalar* 21 (2) 2006, 17–33. On p. 25, Yıldırım notes that at least one reader of Pirizâde's translation felt the need to note that experiential knowledge is for the person who has the experience.

57   On the *müsellesiye*, see Mustafa Kaçar and Atilla Bir, "Ottoman Engineer Mehmed Said Efendi and His Works on a Geodesical Instrument (*Müsellesiye*)", in Ekmeleddin İhsanoğlu, Kostas Chatzis and Efthymios Nicolaïdis (eds) *Multicultural Science in the Ottoman Empire* (Turnhout: Brepols, 2003), 71–90.

58   Ebu Sehl Numan Efendi, *Tedbīrāt-i Pesendīde (Beğenilmiş Tedbirler)*, edited by Ali İbrahim Savaş (Ankara: TTK, 1999). A methodologically useful article on borders and territoriality is Chandra Mukherji, "The Territorial State as a Figured World of Power: Strategics, Logistics, and Impersonal Rule", *Sociological Theory*, 28 (4), 2010, 402–24.

fashionable.[59] However, this reading hardly takes Yirmisekiz Mehmed's career as a practical naturalist into account and, more importantly, masks what 'European science' might have meant in eighteenth-century Istanbul. Surely, Mehmed did not come back with a copy of Newton's *Mathematical Principles of Natural Philosophy*, which was slowly becoming fashionable in Paris. Nor did he bring with him the works of Descartes, the centrepiece of early-eighteenth-century natural philosophy in France. Instead, he filled his luggage with instruments, drawings and observations about how the French kept their country healthy, wealthy and orderly. In his earlier work as the translator of Şehrezūrī's *Şeceretü'l-İlāhiyye* (The Tree of Divinity), Yirmisekiz had used this otherwise *ishraqi* work to exalt his own views on natural knowledge.[60] This translation, titled *Semeretü'l-Şecere* (The Fruit of the Tree), was a partial rendition that focused on physics. For Yirmisekiz Mehmed, unlike Şehrezūrī, the highest form of knowledge was about nature, because it glorified God. Natural philosophy was the fruit of the tree of philosophy. He also went one step further; he argued that the practice of natural philosophy was more virtuous than theory, making alchemy, medicine and astrology the fruit of natural philosophy, thus suggesting that practical naturalism was the highest form of knowledge:

> The philosophers have said that 'for every theory (*'ilm*), there is a corresponding practice (*'amel*).' And the relationship of practice to theory is like the relationship of the fruit to the tree. Now, practice without theory is more beneficial (*hayr*) than theory without practice is. The fruit and the practice of natural science are the arts (*şınâ'at*) of alchemy, medicine and astrology.... He who studies natural science but does not study medicine wastes the fruit, which has greater dignity than the tree does. He who knows mathematical astronomy and the science of ephemerides, but does not know judicial astrology wastes the cleanest and the most delicious fruit of these sciences. While theory commands greater respect than practice does, practice nevertheless offers a unique pleasure to the

---

59 For the classic articulation of this thesis, see Fatma Müge Göçek, *East Encounters West: France and the Ottoman Empire in the Eighteenth Century* (Oxford: OUP, 1987).

60 For an overview of the book, see Bekir Karlığa, "Yirmisekiz Mehmet Çelebi'nin Yeni Bulunan Bir Fizik Kitabı Tercümesi ve On Sekizinci Yüzyılın Başlarında Osmanlı Düşüncesi", *Bilim- Felsefe-Tarih* 1 (1991), 277–311. For a preliminary study and partial translation, see Kemal Sözen, "Şehrezûrî'nin *El-Şeceret El-İlahiyye* İsimli Eseri ve Türkçe Tercümesi *Semeret El-Şecere*" (Master's thesis, Marmara University, 1989).

virtuous mind (*'akl*). And, the virtuous soul (*nefs*) is naturally drawn to practice.[61]

For Yirmisekiz Mehmed, an honest and practical engagement with nature was a sign of strong faith, because it exalted God's creation. A purely textual and imitative engagement, on the other hand, had no other explanation than a weak faith. There was also considerable harmony between the beliefs and the practices of Yirmisekiz Mehmed. Prior to becoming *defterdar* and later, envoy to France, he had served as a practical naturalist: He was the Master of the Mint during the coinage reform of Ahmed III, and he had also served as the Master of the Foundry. Since the mint was already mechanized by the early-eighteenth century, it is not surprising that he was most knowledgeable about and most attentive to the operation of machinery in France. None other than Saint Simon, the court chronicler of Louis XV, attests to this and Mehmed's impressively detailed descriptions of the famous Machine de Marly and Canal du Midi suggest as much.[62] My claim is not that Yirmisekiz was doing what he was doing merely because of their religious convictions, but I would argue that the Kadızâdeli movement was instrumental in vacating a space for non-scholastic naturalism, thus creating an environment where empirical knowledge, which was of lower status, could take the lead.

Vernacularity reinforced the values of usefulness and empiricism of natural knowledge, that is more people could take part in it and they could have their own voice without having to master an existing body of Islamic philosophy. Books written or translated into Turkish invariably invoked the enhanced usefulness (*nâfi'*) of vernacular texts and occasionally brought in non-*ulema* values to bear on true knowledge (*'ilm*), such as experience (*tecrübe*) or manual skill (*hazakat*), where the author also became the authority – again, quite distinct from the *ulema*'s understanding of knowledge.

---

61   [Yirmisekiz Çelebi Mehmed], *Semeretü'l-Şecere*, MS 526 fol. 119r–v. The relationship between theory and practice may also relate to Yirmisekiz Mehmed's interest in Murad al-Bukhari's *müceddidī* interpretation of Sufism, which focused not on religious knowledge but on religious practice. On the reception of the *müceddidī* branch of the Nakşbendi order in Istanbul in the eighteenth century, see Abu-Manneh, "Sheikh Murād al-Bukhārī", 1–25.

62   Mehmed Efendi, *Le Paradis des Infidèles: Un Ambassadeur Ottoman en France Sous la Regence*, translated by Julien-Claude Galland, with an introduction by Gilles Veinstein (Paris: Maspero, 1981), 226.

## 3 Ottoman Science and the Question of Westernization

The preceding examples illustrate how naturalists framed the Islamic tradition. They point to the rise of a more or less Baconian practical naturalism, which was compatible with Kadızâdeli and *müceddidî* sentiment. However, they also reveal something about a trend that has often been viewed as Westernization. While European sources show up with increasing frequency in Ottoman works, the reception of European knowledge was only a small part of this larger epistemic and social dynamic – one that was about a lower status empirical knowledge pushing for a higher theoretical status, and a lower class individual pushing for royal patronage. Jane Murphy has already studied the association with practical naturalism and social mobility in Egypt, and showed that the space that so-called modern Western knowledge filled had already been created long before Napoleon set foot in Egypt.[63] The introduction of Western knowledge was not the cause, but rather one of the many effects after the *ilmiyye* and the Islamic tradition lost its monopoly on naturalism.

Even the most cursory glance at scientific texts from the seventeenth and eighteenth centuries reveals that the authors of Turkish texts did not wholly associate either with the Islamic past or with the European present. Many had a strong grasp of the Islamic texts, but they recognized tradition as only one of many ways leading to knowledge. Some of them were deeply aware of the European developments – some were Europeans who had converted to Islam – but they did not, at the same time, read European works on (modern) European terms. For example, in the middle of the eighteenth century, Ottoman physician Abbas Vesim was convinced that Descartes was not an early-seventeenth-century French philosopher, but a late-seventeenth-century Dutch anatomist.[64] İbrâhim Müteferrika, on the other hand, read his Descartes through Edmond Pourchot's *Institutiones philosophicae*, the only Cartesian textbook that had Louis XIV's approval for university instruction. Peter the Great's aggressive expansionism was enormously influential in inflecting the Ottoman appreciation of the transformative power of science and technology.[65] The dominance of Padua-trained Greeks among the Ottoman power elite made

---

63  Jane Murphy, "Aḥmad al-Damanhūrī (1689–1778) and the Utility of Expertise in Early Modern Ottoman Egypt", *Osiris* 25 (1) 2010, 85–103. Murphy conceptualizes her understanding of expertise around '*ulūm al-gharāʾib*.
64  Quoted in İzgi, *İlim* 2, 37.
65  Adil Şen, *İbrahim Müteferrika ve Usulü'l-Hikem fi Nizami'l-Ümem* (Istanbul: Diyanet Vakfı, 2013), *passim*. It is towards the end of *Nizamü'l-Ümem* that Müteferrika brings up Russia as the prime example of how especially geography and technology leads to progress, especially military progress.

Istanbul, Budapest and Ioannina some of the last bastions of Renaissance Aristotelianism. Jewish physician Israel Conegliano relates that the courtiers in Edirne anxiously awaited a copy of Johann Helfrich Jüncken's *Vernünftiger und erfarner Leibartzt* (1699).[66] Yet, there is not a single piece of modern scholarship that treats this book on self-diagnosis as part of the European narrative. This feeds into a larger point that needs to be made about the Ottoman engagement with both European and Islamic science. What Ottoman naturalists deemed worthy about early modern European science was at odds with the canonical history of the Scientific Revolution. The Ottoman engagement with the Islamic tradition was also complex, if not mangled at the hands of lay practitioners. In other words, Ottoman science was, in many ways, Islamicate but not Islamic and Europeanate but not European – this was what it meant to be Ottoman in the early-eighteenth century.

In terms of 'Westernization', the Ottoman Empire was the photographic negative of the comparable Russia, where the 'Europeanness' of European knowledge was unmistakable. In Istanbul, the knowledge of the Latins often had a lower status than the knowledge of the Arabs and Persians. The typical agent of European knowledge in the Ottoman capital was invisible.[67] He had been rendered invisible through conversion, his name had been surgically removed from translations, or at best, he had worked under a front man, an 'Ottoman', such as Ebubekir Behram el-Dimaşkî or İbn Sallum who took and continues to take the entire credit for the resultant work. This began to change only after 1730, when someone such as Petros Baronyan could proudly put his name on the books and translations he prepared for Hekimoğlu Ali Pasha or presume to teach Muslims where their true qibla was. İbrâhim Müteferrika could give credit to both an Armenian artisan, Mıgırdiç of Galata, and a French scholiast, Edmond Pourchot, in a book that essentially challenged the *ulemas'* authority in the exact sciences. By contrast, Peter the Great almost literally imported European science, by establishing the St Petersburg Academy, by filling its halls with mostly German scholars, publishing its proceedings in Latin and by completely shutting it off to native Russians. He even went so far as to teach European civility to Russian courtiers, which would have been unimaginable in the Ottoman Empire.[68]

---

66  David Kaufmann. *Dr Israel Conegliano und seine Verdienste um die Republik Venedig bis nach dem Frieden von Carlowitz* (Budapest: Alkalay, 1895), xcvii.
67  Steven Shapin, "The Invisible Technician", *American Scientist* 77 (6) 1989, 554–63.
68  Michael D. Gordin, "The Importation of Being Earnest: The Early St Petersburg Academy of Sciences", *Isis* 91 (1) 2000, 1–31. Also noteworthy is the fact that, prior to Peter the Great, there was another academy that was far more cosmopolitan in nature. See Nikolaos Chrissidis, "A Jesuit Aristotle in Seventeenth-Century Russia: Cosmology and the Planetary

In the eighteenth century, the best the Ottoman empiricist could do was to frame and criticize the Islamic tradition, which led a long and flourishing career until the twentieth century. The people engaged in the types of activities we would today call science – a direct engagement with nature, unmediated through texts – had neither the financial nor the social resources that natural philosophers in Europe enjoyed; nor did it have the epistemic authority of the *ulema*. In other words, the practitioners did not enjoy a moral economy of science where they could readily gain credibility through experimental protocol, or exchange their knowledge in return for social status. They could only convert their intellectual labours into truth, income or status through patronage. It is, therefore, only reasonable that the career of Ottoman science is entangled in the story of state-building. Thus, it is hardly surprising that naturalism in the early modern Ottoman Empire was generally a royalist, centralizing and also sporadic enterprise – that is where the money and the power were when they were there at all.

Nevertheless, whether knowing was the entelechy of the *ulema* or whether *nazarî 'ilm* truly was the true knowledge of a thing, or whether the *ulema* had any say at all on natural knowledge became contested issues. In this sense, we can truly speak of an early modern Ottoman science where conflict rather than closure was the rule, and where the outcome of the conflict was uncertain. Early modern Ottoman science was not necessarily an embryonic version of the types of scientific discussion we find in the nineteenth century.[69] Nevertheless, if we define the two main groups as state-sponsored practical naturalists and self-empowered *ulema*, it is impossible not to draw at least some parallels. The eighteenth century was a theatre of competition, conflict and accommodation between these two groups with no closure in sight. The result was a heterogeneity that was typical to the Ottoman Empire and, in many ways, that merits the title *early modern*.

---

System in the Slavo-Greco-Latin Academy", in Marshall Poe and Jarmo Kotilaine (eds), *Modernizing Muscovy: Reform and Social Change in Seventeenth-Century Russia* (London: Routledge Curzon, 2004), 391–416.

69  Baki Tezcan, "Some Thoughts on the Politics of Early Modern Ottoman Science", in Donald Quataert and Baki Tezcan (eds), *Beyond Dominant Paradigms in Ottoman and Middle Eastern/North African Studies: A Tribute to Rifa'at Abou-El-Haj*, OA 36 (2010), 135–56.

## Acknowledgements

I would like to thank the Max Planck Institute for the history of science for its generous support, and the participants of the Institute for Turkish Studies, Georgetown seminar for their feedback.

## Bibliography

### Primary Sources
Süleymaniye Kütüphanesi Library (SK)

Hayatizâde Mustafa Feyzi. *Hamse*. MS no. 3512. Nuruosmaniye, Süleymaniye Kütüphanesi.

Hayatizâde Mustafa Feyzi. *Düstūrü't-Ṭabīb fī Mizānü'l-Terkib*. MS no. 3602. Nuruosmaniye, Süleymaniye Kütüphanesi.

[Yirmisekiz Çelebi Mehmed]. *Semeretü'l-Şecere* [translation of Şehrezūrī's *Şeceretü'l-İlāhiyye*]. MS no. 526, Hekimoğlu, Süleymaniye Kütüphanesi.

### Published Primary Sources

Birgivî, Mehmed. *Tekmile-i Terceme-i Tarîkat-ı Muhammediyye*, translated by Vedâdî. Istanbul: Ali Rıza Karahisarî Matba'ası, 1278/1861.

Birgivî, Mehmed. *Vasiyyet-name: Dil İncelemesi, Metin, Sözlük, Ekler İndeksi, ve Tıpkıbasım*, edited by Musa Duman. Istanbul: R Yayınları, 2000.

de Saumery, Pierre Lambert. *Mémoires et aventures secrètes et curieuses d'un voyage du Levant*. 5 vols. Liège: Kints, 1732.

Evliya Çelebi. *Evliya Çelebi Seyahatnâmesi: 3.Kitab: Topkapı Sarayı Bağdat 305 Yazmasının Transkripsiyonu-Dizini*, edited by Seyit Ali Kahraman and Yücel Dağlı. Istanbul: Yapı Kredi Yayınları, 1999.

Ebu Sehl Numan Efendi. *Tedbîrât-ı Pesendîde (Beğenilmiş Tedbirler)*, edited by Ali İbrahim Savaş. Ankara: TTK B, 1999.

Hacı Halife Mustafa b. Abdullah Katib Çelebi. *Kitab-ı Cihannüma li-Katib Çelebi*, edited by İbrâhim Müteferrika. Istanbul: Darü't-Tıbaati'l-Âmire, 1145/1732.

İbn Haldûn. *Mukaddime-i İbn Haldûn*, translated and edited by Pirizâde Mehmed Sahib, 2 vols. Bulak: Matba'a-i Âmire, 1274/1858.

İbrâhim Müteferrika. *Füyûzât-ı Mıknâtısiyye*. Istanbul: Darü't-Tıba'ati'l-'Âmire, 1145/1732.

Mehmed Efendi. *Le Paradis des Infideles: Un Ambassadeur Ottoman en France Sous la Regence*, translated by Julien-Claude Galland, with an introduction by Gilles Veinstein. Paris: Maspero, 1981.

Şen, Adil. *İbrahim Müteferrika ve Usulü'l-Hikem fi Nizami'l-Ümem*. Istanbul: Diyanet Vakfı, 2013.

Taşköprüzâde. *Mevzū'ātü'l-'Ulūm*, 2 vols. Istanbul: Asitane, 2000.

### Secondary Sources

Abu-Manneh, Butrus. "Sheikh Murād al-Bukhārī and the Expansion of the Naqshbandī-Mujaddidī Order in Istanbul". *Die Welt des Islams* 53 (1) 2013, 1–25.

Aşkar, Mustafa. "Niyazi-i Mısri." In *DIA*, vol. 33. Istanbul, 2007.

Bachour, Natalia. *Oswaldus Crollius und Daniel Sennert im frühneuzeitlichen Istanbul: Studien zur Rezeption des Paracelsismus im Werk des osmanischen Arztes Ṣāliḥ b. Naṣrullāh Ibn Sallūm al-Ḥalabī*. Freiburg: Centaurus, 2012.

Bennett, Jim. "Mechanical Arts". In Katharine Park and Lorraine Daston (eds) *The Cambridge History of Science*, vol. 3: *Early Modern Science*. Cambridge: Cambridge University Press, 2006, 673–95.

Berkes, Niyazi. "İbrâhim Müteferrika". *Encyclopaedia of Islam*. 2nd Edition. Vol. 3 (Leiden: E. J. Brill, 1971), 996–8.

Biagoli, Mario. *Galileo, Courtier: The Practice of Science in the Culture of Absolutism*. Chicago: Chicago University Press, 1993.

Boecler, Johannes Henricus. *Bibliographia historico-politico-philologica curiosa*. Frankfurt a. Main, 1677.

Brentjes, Sonja. "Patchwork: The Norm of Mapmaking Practices for Western Asia in Catholic and Protestant Europe as well as in Istanbul between 1550 and 1750?" In Feza Günergun and Dhruv Raina (eds). *Science between Europe and Asia*. Dordrecht: Springer Verlag, 2011, 77–102.

Büke, Himmet. "Seydi Ali Reis: Kitabü'l-Muhit". Master's thesis, Pamukkale University, Denizli, 2010.

Chrissidis, Nikolaos. "A Jesuit Aristotle in Seventeenth-Century Russia: Cosmology and the Planetary System in the Slavo-Greco-Latin Academy". In Marshall Poe and Jarmo Kotilaine (eds). *Modernizing Muscovy: Reform and Social Change in Seventeenth-Century Russia*. London: Routledge Curzon, 2004, 391–416.

Curry, John J. "An Ottoman Geographer Engages the Early Modern World: Katip Çelebi's Vision of East Asia and the Pacific Rim in the Cihānnümā". *Journal of Ottoman Studies* 40 (2012), 221–57.

Dear, Peter "Miracles, Experiments and the Ordinary Course of Nature". *Isis* 81 (4), 1990, 663–83.

Dear, Peter. "Historiography of Not So Recent Science". *History of Science* 50 (2) 2012, 197–211.

Eldem, Edhem. *French Trade in Istanbul in the Eighteenth Century*. Leiden: Brill, 1999.

Endress, Gerhard. "Reading Avicenna in the Madrasa: Intellectual Genealogies and Chains of Transmission of Philosophy and the Sciences in the Islamic East". In James E. Montgomery (ed.) *Arabic Theology, Arabic Philosophy, From the Many to the One: Essays in Celebration of Richard M. Frank.* Leuven: Peeters, 2006, 371–424.

Galison, Peter. *Image and Logic.* Chicago: Chicago University Press, 1997.

Göçek, Fatma Müge. *East Encounters West: France and the Ottoman Empire in the Eighteenth Century.* Oxford: Oxford University Press, 1987.

Gordin, Michael D. "The Importation of Being Earnest: The Early St Petersburg Academy of Sciences". *Isis* 91 (1) 2000, 1–31.

Gutas, Dimitri. "The Empiricism of Avicenna". *Oriens* 40 (2) 2012, 391–436.

Hagen, Gottfried. *Ein osmanischer Geograph bei der Arbeit. Entstehung und Gedankenwelt von Katib Celebis Gihannüma.* Berlin: Schwarz, 2003.

Hirai, Hiro. *Medical Humanism and Natural Philosophy: Renaissance Debates on Matter, Life and the Soul.* Leiden: Brill, 2011.

İhsanoğlu, Ekmeleddin. "Introduction of Western Science to the Ottoman World: A Case Study of Modern Astronomy (1660–1860)". In *idem* (ed.) *Transfer of Modern Science and Technology to the Muslim World.* Istanbul: Research Centre for Islamic History, Art and Culture (IRCICA), 1992.

İhsanoğlu, Ekmeleddin, et al. *Osmanlı Astronomi Literatürü Tarihi,* 2 vols. Istanbul: Research Centre for Islamic History, Art and Culture (IRCICA), 1997.

İzgi, Cevat. *Osmanlı Medreselerinde İlim,* 2 vols. Istanbul: İz Yayıncılık, 1997.

Jonkers, A. R. T. *Earth's Magnetism in the Age of Sail.* Baltimore: Johns Hopkins University Press, 2003.

Kaçar, Mustafa and Atilla Bir. "Ottoman Engineer Mehmed Said Efendi and His Works on a Geodesical Instrument (*Müsellesiye*)". In Ekmeleddin İhsanoğlu, Kostas Chatzis and Efthymios Nicolaïdis (eds). *Multicultural Science in the Ottoman Empire.* Turnhout: Brepols, 2003, 71–90.

Karlığa, Bekir. "Yirmisekiz Mehmet Çelebi'nin Yeni Bulunan Bir Fizik Kitabı Tercümesi ve On Sekizinci Yüzyılın Başlarında Osmanlı Düşüncesi". *Bilim Felsefe-Tarih* 1 (1991), 277–311.

Kaufmann, David. *Dr Israel Conegliano und seine Verdienste um die Republik Venedig bis nach dem Frieden von Carlowitz.* Budapest: Alkalay, 1895.

Kenan, Seyfi. "Doğruyu Dengede Tutmak: Mīzānü'l-Hak Çerçevesinde Kātip Çelebi 'nin Bilgi ve Eğitim Anlayışı". In Said Öztürk (ed.) *Vefatının 350. Yılında Katip Çelebi.* Istanbul: İstanbul Büyükşehir Belediyesi, 2007, 87–91.

King, David A. *World-Maps for Finding the Direction and Distance to Mecca.* Leiden: Brill, 1999.

King, David A. "Al-Ṭāsa". In *Encyclopedia of Islam,* 2nd edn, vol. 10. Leiden, 2000.

King, David A. "An Ottoman Astrolabe Full of Surprises". in N. Sidoli and G. Van Brumelen (eds). *From Alexandria, through Baghdad: Surveys and Studies in the Ancient Greek and Medieval Mathematical Sciences in Honor of J. L. Berggren*. Berlin: Springer Verlag, 2014, 329–42.

King, David A. and Richard Lorch. "Qibla Charts, Qibla Maps, and Related Instruments". In J. B. Harley and David Woodwards (eds). *The History of Cartography*, vol. 2, bk. 1: *Cartography in Traditional Islamic and South Asian Societies*. Chicago: Chicago University Press, 1992, 189–205.

Krstić, Tijana. *Contested Conversions to Islam: Narratives of Religious Change and Communal Politics in the Early Modern Ottoman Empire*. Stanford: Stanford University Press, 2011

Küçük, B. Harun. "Natural Philosophy and Politics in the Eighteenth Century: Esad of Ioannina and Greek Aristotelianism at the Ottoman Court". *Journal of Ottoman Studies* 41 (2013), 125–59.

Küçük, B. Harun. "New Medicine and the *Hikmet-i Tabiyye* Problematic in Eighteenth-Century Istanbul." In Y. Tzvi Langermann and Robert G. Morrison (eds), *Texts in Transit in the Medieval Mediterranean*. University Park, PA: Penn State University Press, 2016, 222–42.

Leaman, Oliver and Sajjad Rizvi. "The Developed Kalām Tradition." In Tim Winter (ed.) *The Cambridge Companion to Classical Islamic Theology*. Cambridge: Cambridge University Press, 2008, 77–96.

Mardin, Ebül'ula. *Huzur Dersleri*. 3 vols. Istanbul: Istanbul Universitesi, 1951–66.

Mavrocordato, Nicholas. "Peri grammatōn spoudēs kai Bibliōn anagnōseōs". Unpublished essay in Kyrillos Athanasiades (ed.) *Hermeneia eis tus anabathmus tēs oktōēchu*. Jerusalem: Taphos, 1862.

Merton, Robert K. "Science, Technology and Society in Seventeenth Century England". *Osiris* 4 (1938), 360–632.

Mukherji, Chandra. "The Territorial State as a Figured World of Power: Strategics, Logistics, and Impersonal Rule", *Sociological Theory*, 28 (4), 2010, 402–24.

Mundy, Martha. "Ethics and Politics in the Law: On the Forcible Return of the Cultivator". In Seyfi Kenan (ed.) *İSAM Konuşmaları: Osmanlı Düşüncesi, Ahlak, Hukuk, Felsefe-Kelam*. Istanbul: TDV ISAM, 2013, 51–76.

Murphy, Jane. "Aḥmad al-Damanhūrī (1689–1778) and the Utility of Expertise in Early Modern Ottoman Egypt". *Osiris* 25 (1) 2010, 85–103.

Nizri, Michael. *Ottoman High Politics and the Ulema Household*. New York: Palgrave Macmillan, 2014.

Pechlivanos, Miltos. "Bacon auf Altgriechisch. Erfahrungswissen und Buchwissen im griechischsprachigen Osmanischen Reich". Lecture, Freie Universität Berlin, Wissensbewegungen – Bewegliches Wissen: Wissenstransfer im Historischen Wandel, 12 February 2014.

Pomata, Gianna and Nancy G. Siraisi (eds). *Historia: Empiricism and Erudition in Early Modern Europe*. Cambridge: MIT Press, 2005.

Rabb, Theodore K. "Puritanism and the Rise of Experimental Science in England". *Journal of World History* 7 (1962), 46–67.

Radtke, Bernd. "Birgiwīs *Ṭarīqa Muḥammadiyya*: Einige Bemerkungen und Überlegungen". *Journal of Turkish Studies* 26 (2) 2002, 159–74.

Ragep, F. Jamil and Alī al-Qūshjī. "Freeing Astronomy from Philosophy: An Aspect of Islamic Influence of Science". *Osiris* 16 (2001), 49–71.

Robinson, Francis. "Ottomans-Safavids-Mughals: Shared Knowledge and Connective Systems". *Journal of Islamic Studies* 8 (2) 1997, 151–84.

Rosenthal, Franz. *Knowledge Triumphant: The Concept of Knowledge in Medieval Islam*. Leiden: Brill, 2006.

el-Rouayheb, Khaled. "The Myth of 'the Triumph of Fanaticism' in the Seventeenth-Century Ottoman Empire". *Die Welt des Islams* 48 (2) 2008, 196–221.

Ruderman, David B. *Jewish Thought and Scientific Discovery in Early Modern Europe*. New Haven: Yale University Press, 1995.

Sarı, Nil. "Educating the Ottoman Physician". *Yeni Tıp Tarihi Araştırmaları* 1 (1995), 11–54.

Sariyannis, Marinos. "The Kadızadeli Movement as a Social and Political Phenomenon: The Rise of a Mercantile Ethic?" In A. Anastasopoulos (ed.) *Political Initiatives from the Bottom – Up in the Ottoman Empire: Halcyon Days in Crete VII, A Symposium Held in Rethymno, 9–11 January 2009*. Rethymno: Crete University Press, 2012, 263–89.

Shapin, Steven. "Understanding the Merton Thesis", *Isis* 79 (4), 1988, 594–605.

Shapin, Steven. "The Invisible Technician." *American Scientist* 77 (6), 1989, 554–63.

Shapin, Steven and Simon Schaffer. *Leviathan and the Air Pump: Hobbes, Boyle and the Experimental Life*. Princeton, NJ: Princeton University Press, 1993.

Sirriyeh, Elizabeth. *Sufi Visionary of Ottoman Damascus: 'Abd al-Ghani al-Nabulusi, 1641–1731*. London: Routledge, 2014.

Sözen, Kemal. "Şehrezûrî'nin *El-Şeceret El-İlahiyye* İsimli Eseri ve Türkçe Tercümesi *Semeret El-Şecere*". Master's thesis, Marmara University, 1989.

Terzioğlu, Derin. "Where *'Ilm-I Ḥal* Meets Catechism: Islamic Manuals of Religious Instruction in the Ottoman Empire in the Age of Confessionalization". *Past and Present* 220 (2013), 79–114.

Tezcan, Baki. "Some Thoughts on the Politics of Early Modern Ottoman Science". In Donald Quataert and Baki Tezcan (eds). *Beyond Dominant Paradigms in Ottoman and Middle Eastern/North African Studies: A Tribute to Rifa'at Abou-El-Haj*. Osmanlı Araştırmaları 36 (2010), 135–56.

Tezcan, Baki. *The Second Ottoman Empire: Political and Social Transformation in the Early Modern World*. Cambridge: Cambridge University Press, 2012.

Tietze, Andreas (ed.) *Mustafa Ali's Counsel for Sultans of 1581: Edition, Translation, Notes*, 2 vols. Vienna: Verlag der Österreichischen Akademie der Wissenschaften, 1979–82.

Udny, Francis. *Later Incarnations of Francis Bacon*. London: Edson, 1926.
Uzunçarşılı, İsmail Hakkı. *Osmanlı Devletinin İlmiye Teşkilatı*. Ankara: TTK, 1965.
Wiedemann, Eilhard. "The Compass" (under Maghnāṭīs). In *Encyclopedia of Islam*, 2nd edn, vol. 5. Leiden, 1986.
Winship, Michael. "Defining Puritanism in Restoration England: Richard Baxter and Others Respond to a Friendly Debate". *The Historical Journal* 54 (3) 2011, 689–715.
Yıldırım, Yavuz. *"Mukaddime'*nin Osmanlı Dönemi Türkçe Tercümesi". *Divan: İlmi Araştırmalar* 21 (2) 2006, 17–33.
Zilfi, Madeline. *Politics of Piety: The Ottoman Ulema in the Post-Classical Age*. Minneapolis: Bibliotheca Islamica, 1988.

# PART 3

*Law, Religion and Political Thought*

∴

CHAPTER 12

# In Search of the Ancient Law or *Kānûn-i Kadîm*: Some Notes on Seventeenth-Century Ottoman Political Thought

*Mehmet Öz*

At the end of the sixteenth century Ottoman territories extended from northern Hungary in the west to Iran in the east and from the Ukraine in the north to the Indian Ocean in the south. Despite losses in central and south-eastern Europe for centuries, the Ottoman presence in the three continents lasted until the early twentieth century.

The second half of the sixteenth century witnessed fundamental changes that required the Ottomans to adapt their so-called classical structures to the new circumstances. There were a variety of factors affecting this process, ranging from geographical discoveries and the influx of American silver to population pressure, the spread of firearms and their diverse effects in the empire. While the Ottomans tried hard to minimize the adverse effects of the change in international trade roads, they also had to cope with the new, infantry-based military system in Europe. These in turn necessitated changes in the military and financial spheres due to the increasing need for cash for the treasury, as the state increased the number of paid soldiers; naturally enough, this brought about a shift from the *tımâr* to the tax-farming (*iltizam*) system, whereby the government farmed out certain revenue units to tax farmers. Yet another change in the classical system involved the gradual abolition of the *devşirme* levy, as sons of the members of the ruling class and purchased slaves of Caucasian origin entered, in increasing numbers, among the sultan's servants from the last quarter of the sixteenth century onwards.[1]

Such factors as population pressure, economic difficulties and the long wars against Iran and Austria between 1578 and 1606 worsened the situation, especially in Anatolia, and, under the leadership of former low-ranking military commanders, a series of rebellions known as the *Celâlî* uprisings broke out, causing large-scale destruction of the countryside and towns. Only through

---

1   For some general assessments of the changes in the classical system, see footnotes 3 and 4. A summary of political developments can be found in Michael Allan Cook (ed.), *A History of the Ottoman Empire to 1730* (Cambridge: CUP, 1976).

the use of brute force did the central government manage to neutralize to some extent the threat posed by the *Celâlî* bands around 1610.[2] On the other hand, the Peace of Zsitvatorok signed to end the Ottoman-Habsburg War meant the end of Ottoman supremacy vis-à-vis the Habsburg Empire, as it stipulated that the emperor and sultan were of equal status and that the Ottomans gave up their previous claim of taking tribute from the Habsburgs.

However, internal problems increased, especially after the death of Ahmed I (1603-17), and the reform attempt by his young and inexperienced successor ended in failure: Osman II was the first Ottoman sultan to be killed by rebellious soldiers. Now a new pattern was emerging in the power struggle in the capital, and in this process alliances among the Servants of the Gate (*kapıkulları*), the *ulema* and Imperial Harem played a decisive role.[3] One of the most striking features of the post-classical era was the change in succession, namely the renunciation of sending young princes to provinces and confining them to a restricted life in a *kafes* (cage) in the Imperial Palace. Although they refrained from practising the law of fratricide in the traditional manner from the accession to throne of Ahmed I onwards, the princes, now leading a sort of prisoner's life, were always anxious for their lives, and largely because of these conditions the seventeenth century saw two mentally ill Ottoman sultans. By the eighteenth century, however, the principle of senioratus was firmly established and, with the loosening of the conditions in the palace life, future sultans had more opportunities to prepare themselves for the future.

In 1683, when the Ottoman power still seemed overwhelming by any criteria, an Ottoman-Turkish army under the command of Merzifonlu Kara Mustafa Pasha, son-in-law of the famous grand vizier Köprülü Mehmed Pasha, marched to Vienna. However, this expedition turned into a disaster and, from then on, the Ottomans remained on the defensive. Even though they continued to nurture hopes of recovering their losses whenever they saw the circumstances in

---

2   For the *Celâlî* uprisings, see Mustafa Akdağ, *Türk Halkının Dirlik ve Düzenlik Kavgası-Celali İsyanları* (Ankara: Bilgi, 1975); Karen Barkey, *Bandits and Bureaucrats-The Ottoman Route to State Centralization* (Ithaca: Cornell University Press, 1994); William Griswold, *The Great Anatolian Rebellion* (Berlin: Klaus Schwarz Verlag, 1983). For an evaluation of the scale of the destruction caused by these uprisings in an Anatolian sub-district, based on Ottoman population and fiscal surveys, see Oktay Özel, "Changes in Settlement Patterns, Population and Society in Rural Anatolia: A Case Study of Amasya (1576-1642)" (Ph.D. dissertation, University of Manchester, 1993).

3   The Imperial Harem has long been a focus of popular as well as scholarly attention. For an excellent study on the Harem, see Leslie Penn Peirce, *The Imperial Harem: Women and Sovereignty in the Ottoman Empire* (New York: OUP, 1993). The Turkish translation is titled *idem, Harem-i Hümayun: Osmanlı İmparatorluğu'nda Hüküminranlık ve Kadınlar*, translated by Ayşe Berktay (Istanbul: TAV, 1996).

their favour, it proved impossible for them to reverse their retreat. This state of affairs had a deep impact on the overall structure of the empire, largely because the institutions and traditions built up for an aggressive and expanding state proved to be entirely inappropriate for an empire forced to live within fixed or even shrinking boundaries in a changing world. This should, however, not make us overlook another side of the coin: it appears that a very striking achievement of the Ottoman state, even during the so-called period of decline, was the longevity of the imperial framework. Ottoman central as well as provincial order undoubtedly proved, at least to a considerable degree, resilient and flexible against external and internal changes and assaults.[4]

In summary, then, the Ottomans had entered a new phase in the history of their empire by the end of the sixteenth century, the nature of which has been subject to controversy ever since: was it an era of stagnation to be followed by that of recession, that is a period of decline, or was it a period of crisis and change in which the Ottomans had to overcome new challenges?

## 1    A Brief Look at Classical Ottoman Political Thought

The problem of the so-called Ottoman decline was taken up by Ottoman intellectuals and statesmen in the sixteenth century by eminent figures such as Gelibolulu Mustafa Âlî, the bureaucrat and historian Hasan Kâfi Akhisârî of Bosnia, Koçi Bey, Kâtib Çelebi (Hacı Kalfa) and Hezarfen Hüseyin Efendi. Although they differed about the reasons, nature and results of the situation, they all approached the problem from the assumption that there was a 'decline' in the structure of the Ottoman state and society, and they largely explained it within the framework and conceptual instruments of traditional Turco-Islamic political thought.[5]

---

4  For a collective work dealing, through critical assessment, with the so-called golden age of the Ottoman empire, see Metin Kunt and Christine Woodhead (eds), *Süleyman the Magnificent and His Age: The Ottoman Empire in the Early Modern Age* (London: Longman, 1995).

5  There is an extensive literature on this issue; for some general assessments see, Pál Fodor, "State and Society, Crisis and Reform in 15th–17th Century Ottoman Mirror for Princes", *AOH* 40 (2–3) 1986, 217–40; M. Tayyib Gökbilgin, "XVII. Asırda Osmanlı Devleti'nde Islahat İhtiyaç ve Temayülleri ve Kâtip Çelebi", in *Kâtip Çelebi: Hayatı ve Eserleri Hakkında İncelemeler* (Ankara: TTK, 1957), 196–220; Douglas A. Howard, "The Ottoman Historiography and the Literature of 'Decline' of the Sixteenth and Seventeenth Centuries", *Journal of Asian History* 22 (1988), 52–77; Bernard Lewis, "Ottoman Observers of Ottoman Decline", *Islamic Studies* 1 (1) 1962, 71–87; Mehmet Öz, *Osmanlı'da 'Çözülme' ve Gelenekçi Yorumcuları* (Istanbul: DergâhYayınları, 1997) [revised and enlarged second edn Istanbul: Dergâh Yayınları, 2005).

To appreciate better the criticisms of Ottoman advice, let us take a brief look at the general features and basic concepts of Ottoman classical political thinking. At the centre of Ottoman political thought lay the idea that there has to be a leader/ruler to keep order in a community, even in the case of a gang. Ottoman writers such as Kınalızâde Ali Efendi presented the sultanate as the only form of government that met the need for social organization and political association. In brief, human societies could not exist in harmony and order without a sultanate.[6] In the case of a society, a ruler is expected to maintain *nizâm-ı âlem*, literally the order of the world but also meaning the public order in a given state.[7] To support the order, the ruler must be just (*âdil*) because justice is the foundation of the realm, country, or sovereignty (*mülk*). As is well-known, the circle of equity, *dâire-i adliyye*, an ancient formula defining the concept of just government, presupposes the interdependence of the four main elements – *mülk*, army, treasury and justice. It is thanks to a just administration that the tax-paying population (the *reâyâ*, entrusted to and placed under the safe-keeping of the ruler by the Creator) will be able to undertake production activities in a secure atmosphere and will prosper, which in turn will help fill the coffers of the imperial treasury. A strong treasury is required to maintain a powerful and efficient army, which in its turn supports the *mülk*.[8] Under the framework of the Four Pillars (the *erkân-ı erbaa*) the order of the society was founded on an equilibrium among its main constituents, namely the holders of the sword (the military administrators and army), the men of the pen (the *ulema* and *kadıs*), the craftsmen and merchants, and the peasants (cultivators). So long as the boundaries among these are clearly defined and not transgressed illegally, it is possible to maintain the order of the realm.

Ottoman political writers, in the second half of the sixteenth and throughout the seventeenth century, based their criticisms on the principles of this concept inherited from the previous Islamic and Turco-Islamic states. Recently, Hüseyin Yılmaz argued that while the idea that Ottoman political thought was inherited from the earlier Turco-Islamic states with additional contributions from the Byzantine state holds true as far as the origins of the Ottoman political thought are concerned, when applied to the whole corpus of the genre

---

6 Hüseyin Yılmaz, "The Sultan and the Sultanate: Envisioning Rulership in the Age of Suleyman the Lawgiver (1520–1566)" (Ph.D. dissertation, Harvard University, 2005), 146–7.
7 The concept of *nizâm-ı âlem* has, in my view, two meanings, both connoting the order of the world at large, and the order of a specific country, in this case the Ottoman lands. This concept is sometimes employed in place of the concept of world domination; although there is a connection between the two, they are not synonymous.
8 On this topic, see for example, Halil İnalcık, *Osmanlı'da Devlet, Hukuk ve Adâlet* (Istanbul: Eren Yayıncılık, 2000), *passim*.

of political thought in the Süleymanic age, "the Ottoman experience in government and the creativity of Ottoman authors" should also be added to this explanation as other components. We are reminded that, in the sixteenth century, such factors as geographical expansion and increasing contacts with the outside world, struggles for succession and factional rivalries among princes, and the engagement of the *ulema* acquainted with the Islamic political literature, all had their effects on Ottoman political thought.[9]

More importantly, Yılmaz underlines that a paradigmatic change occurred in four aspects of Ottoman political thought – (i) the replacement of moralism in government by legalism, (ii) the loss of appeal of historical understanding of the caliphate and its replacement by a new concept defining it "as a cosmic rank between Man and God, ... the result of a fusion between esoteric teachings of sufism and the conventional conceptions of rulership expressed in mainstream political theories", (iii) a shift in political thinking from the personality of ruler to the existing government and its institutions, and (iv) the replacement of the sultan by the grand vizier as the centre of government. He concludes that, "in contrast to the moralistic, idealistic, personality-oriented and sultan-centric paradigm in political reasoning, this realist and empirical approach to the question of rulership promoted such ideas as 'government by law' and 'institutional continuity of the state' as primary objectives of rulership."[10]

## 2  The Decline Paradigm Revisited

Undoubtedly, these elements played a significant role in the way the Ottoman elite perceived the events and changes in the sixteenth and seventeenth centuries. At first glance, it appears that authors of political writings from the second half of the sixteenth century onwards interpreted any deviance or flaw in the ideal order of the four pillars as the sign of a deep-rooted decline connected with the decay of the administration due to injustice, bribery and nepotism. Their views have been shared by some modern historians at least with respect to the notion that there 'was an Ottoman decline', but the latter differed from the former by claiming that what the Ottoman *nasihat* writers saw as the 'causes' of decline should be considered as its symptoms and or results.[11] Until the 1970s, modern historians were inclined to attribute the so-called Ottoman

---

9   Yılmaz, "The Sultan", 146–7.
10  Yılmaz, "The Sultan", 1–3.
11  See for example Lewis, "Ottoman Observers", 71–87.

decline to such factors as a price revolution, the discovery of the Americas and other geographical findings, and technological changes that occurred in the sixteenth century. It was argued that, organized according to the needs of an ever-expanding territorial empire, the Ottomans were unable to comprehend the nature of these changes, and did not have the mental capacity to adapt to them.[12]

However, in the 1970s, some historians and intellectuals started to express their doubts about the notion of approximately three centuries of decline, criticized the Euro-centric viewpoint behind it, and argued that it was perhaps more appropriate to use the terms 'crisis' or 'change' to define the problems encountered by the Ottomans towards the end of the sixteenth century. The following period should be considered one of change or adaptation to new developments rather than a decline. This approach has obviously been based on empirical studies on the one hand, and theoretical assessments on the other. Ottoman institutions and socio-economic life are then seen in a different way. For example, contrary to the previous perceptions on the character of the Ottoman sultanate in the seventeenth century, younger generation Ottomanists tend to define it as an era in which the Ottoman state formation underwent a significant transformation[13]

It should also be pointed out that in the last three decades there have been significant changes in the topics chosen by Ottoman historians; the seventeenth and eighteenth centuries, previously unpopular among Ottomanists, have been put under close scrutiny to understand the so-called post-classical period of the Ottoman empire. Thus, Ottoman historians are now much more concerned with those mechanisms that enabled the empire to overcome the first great crisis in Ottoman state and society than its disappearance from the political arena. This approach, they argue, is much more fruitful for understanding the Ottoman state and society as it frees us from the restraints of a Euro-centric approach.[14]

---

12   See for instance, H. A. R. Gibb and H. Bowen, *Islamic Society and the West*, vol. 1 pt.1 (London: OUP, 1950); Halil İnalcık, *The Ottoman Empire: The Classical Age, 1300–1600*, translated by Norman Itzkowitz and Colin Imber (London: Weidenfeld and Nicolson, 1973); Bernard Lewis, *The Emergence of Modern Turkey* (London: Oxford University, 1961).

13   This argument is extensively dealt with in Rifa'at Ali Abou-el-Haj, *Formation of Modern State: The Ottoman Empire, Sixteenth to Eighteenth Centuries* (Albany, NY: SUNY Press, 1991).

14   One can detect the first signs of a different approach to the new era which the Ottomans entered in the seventeenth century; the monumental work of Marshall G. S. Hodgson is an example. Though not a specialist on Ottoman history, he was aware of the fact that it was absolutism that declined in that period. He also pointed out that many institutions were adversely affected in the process, but the Ottomans were able to replace them by

However, we must re-emphasize that, despite all these arguments, it was the Ottomans themselves who spoke of a 'decline' in their polity, starting at least from the last quarter of the sixteenth century. Therefore, one must consider their attitude towards this concept and its implications when attempting to understand the changes in the seventeenth-century Ottoman state and society.

## 3  Ottoman Bureaucrat-Intellectuals and the Perception of Decline

Starting as early as the second half of the sixteenth century, members of the *ulema*, statesmen, and poets began to voice their complaints about the various troubles and signs of corruption in the Ottoman society and administration. As a matter of fact, this kind of complaint could be seen in previous times, though for different reasons and/or on different occasions. A typical example of such concerns was the complaint raised against the so-called 'land reform' of Mehmed II by an eminent chronicler of the time, Âşıkpaşazâde.[15] However, the nature of the complaints put on the agenda in the second half of the sixteenth century differed from previous ones in many regards. This period witnessed the appearance of a variant of the classical Islamic mirrors for princes, *siyaset* names, based theoretically and structurally on them but putting more emphasis on the actual problems in political and social life and on how to

---

new ones; thus, it seems to me that the roots of the views raised by some Ottoman historians in the 1980s and 1990s regarding the ability of the Ottomans to adapt themselves to new conditions can be traced in his work. See Marshall G. S. Hodgson, *The Venture of Islam: Conscience and History in a World Civilization*, vol. 3 (Chicago: University of Chicago Press, 1974), 126 ff. Another earlier study, İ. Metin Kunt's, *The Sultan's Servants: The Transformation of Ottoman Provincial Government, 1550–1650* (New York: Columbia University Press, 1983) on provincial administration takes up another dimension of the change and sheds light on the new responses developed by the Ottomans to the new conditions. Other historians have made significant contributions to this subject, including Linda Darling, *Revenue-Raising and Legitimacy: Tax-Collection and Finance Administration in the Ottoman Empire, 1560–1660* (Leiden: Brill, 1996); Suraiya Faroqhi, "Crisis and Change", in H. İnalcık and D. Quataert (eds) *An Economic and Social History of the Ottoman Empire* (Cambridge: CUP, 1994), 411–636; Halil İnalcık, "Military and Fiscal Transformation in the Ottoman Empire, 1600–1800", *AO* (1980), 283–337; Rhoads Murphey, "Continuity and Discontinuity in Ottoman Administrative Theory and Practice during the Late Seventeenth Century", *Poetics Today* 14 (2) 1983, 419–43.

15   For an article that emphasizes that this reform of Mehmed II was based on military and financial considerations and had nothing to do with a land reform, see Oktay Özel, "The Limits of the Almighty: Mehmed II's 'Land Reform' Revisited", *JESHO* 42 (2) 1999, 226–46.

remedy them, which were called *as nasihatnâme* (book of counsel, mirror for princes), *ıslâḥat layihası* (reform treatise) and so on.[16]

Though one can mention much earlier examples such as Prince-governor Korkud, son of Bayezid II, and Lütfi Pasha, the grand vizier, who expressed their views before the second half of the sixteenth century, it seems much more appropriate to date the criticisms directed against the changes or the breakdown of the traditional order from the last quarter of the century. However, it must immediately be recalled that by this we do not mean that there had been a static, unchangeable order prior to this time. The point here is that, having reached the limits of its geographical expansion as some historians put it, the Ottoman Empire entered a new phase in its long history. Now the Ottomans had to cope with a series of problems resulting from such diverse factors as geographical discoveries, inflation, devaluation, population rise, diffusion of firearms, and the military revolution. Even those modern historians who deem the views of the Ottoman *nasihat* writers as partial, biased, and products of a mentality unaware of the developments in the west, agree that the last quarter of the sixteenth century was a turning point in Ottoman history. But the heart of the matter is the nature of what happened at the time and how to interpret these 'changes'.[17]

According to contemporary Ottoman statesmen and scholars writing on the issue, the Ottoman state and society entered a period of disorder, the beginnings of which could be traced back to the midst of the reign of Süleyman the Magnificent. They argued that, until that time, the administrators had carefully observed the established ancient law or *kānūn-i kadîm*, stuck to the age-old dictum that 'justice is the foundation of the *mülk*'; they also maintained that during the times of the previous sultans all offices and posts would be given on the basis of merit. By contrast, since the mid-sixteenth century the *kānūn-i kadîm* was gradually neglected and bribery and nepotism began to play the most important role in the promotions and appointments of state officials. On this basis, it can be argued that the *nasihat-ıslâḥat* (reform treatises) literature of the seventeenth century was mainly constructed on this dichotomy. Of course, there are some differences in their writings, which stem from various factors such as their professional experience, character and so forth. For example, as C. Fleischer underlines in his excellent monograph on Mustafa

---

[16] For these, see Agah Sırrı Levend, "Siyasetnâmeler", *Türk Dili Araştırmaları Yıllığı-Belleten* (1962), 167–94; Ahmet Uğur, *Osmanlı Siyâsetnâmeleri* (Kayseri: Kültür ve Sanat Yayınları, 1987).

[17] A recent study on this subject uses the term 'the second empire' to define the post-sixteenth century Ottoman state. See Baki Tezcan, *The Second Ottoman Empire: Political and Social Transformation in the early Modern World* (New York: CUP, 2012).

Âlî, despite his consistent and even rigid emphasis on the notion of *ḳānūn* he sometimes manipulated or interpreted it in his own interest.[18]

More importantly, however, as opposed to Koçi Bey and the like, the authors of such works as *Hırzü'l-Mülûk* (The Amulet of the Kings/Sovereigns) and *Kitâbu Mesâlihi'l-Müslimîn ve Menâfi'i'i-Mü'minîn* (The Book on the Affairs of the Muslims and Benefits of the Faithful) adopted a somewhat distinct and critical approach to the concept of the *kānûni kadîm* or ancient law.[19] Even in the time of Selim I (1512–20), we come across a clear-cut criticism of the customary law in a poem attributed to the reigning sultan himself. When he asked the religious approval of the *ulema* before launching the war against the Safavids in 1514, they demanded that they should examine the matter according to the established law. The sultan, in reply, tells them that what they call the law and regulations are not the words of God descending from the heaven; nor are they the traditions (*sünnet*) of the prophet. He maintains that whatever a ruler institutes during his reign it undoubtedly becomes his law;[20] this idea is clearly related to the Turco-Mongol concept of rulership. In any case, the existence of contradictory views on the ancient law, in my view, demonstrates that, although they were not innovative in terms of theoretical analysis, the Ottoman statesmen and *ulema* writing on these matters were able to put diverse ideas and standpoints about the problem of the so-called decline. As Kafadar argues, "they never lost their analytical and critical perspective" and "none of the rulers and grandees of the classical age, from Mehmed the Conqueror to Süleyman the Magnificent, escaped their censure."[21]

---

18  Cornell Fleischer, *Bureaucrat and Intellectual in the Ottoman Empire: The Historian Mustafa Ali, 1540–1600* (Princeton, NJ: Princeton University Press, 1986).

19  For these works and the *Kitâb-ı Müstetâb*, see Yaşar Yücel (ed.), *Osmanlı Devlet Teşkilâtına Dair Kaynaklar* (Ankara: TTK, 1988). I have consulted the following editions of other reform treatises used in this chapter. Aziz Efendi, *Kanûnnâme-i Sultânî li 'Azîz Efendi (Introduction, English translation, transcription and facsimile)*, translated and edited by Rhoads Murphey and Şinasi Tekin (Cambridge: Harvard University Press, 1985); Defterdar Sarı Mehmed Pasha, *Devlet Adamlarına Öğütler /Nesâyihü'l-Vüzerâ ve'l-Ümerâ*, edited by Hüseyin Ragıp Uğural (Ankara: Türkiye ve Ortadoğu Amme İdaresi Enstitüsü, 1969; Mehmet İpşirli, "Hasan Kâfî el-Akhisarî ve Devlet Düzenine Ait Eseri-Usûlü'l-hikem fî Nizâmi'l-Âlem", *ITD* 10–11 (1979–80), 239–78; Kâtib Çelebi, *Düsturü'l-amel li-Islahi'l-halel* (Istanbul: Tasvir-i Efkâr Matbaası, 1280); Koçi Bey, *Koçi Bey Risâlesi*, edited by Ali Kemali Aksüt (Istanbul: Vakit Matbaası, 1939); Andreas Tietze (ed.), *Mustafa Ali's Counsel for Sultans of 1581: Edition, Translation, Notes*, 2 vols. (Vienna: Verlag der Österreichischen Akademie der Wissenschaften, 1979).

20  Uğur, *Osmanlı*, 106 fn.49.

21  Cemal Kafadar, "The Question of Ottoman Decline", *Harvard Middle Eastern and Islamic Review* 4 (1997/8), 63.

For instance, the anonymous author of *Kitâbu Mesâlih* openly criticizes the adherence to the customary laws and points out that what some people called the *kānûn-i kadîm* were actually created by such previous viziers as Hersekzâde Ahmed Pasha or Karagöz Pasha, during the reigns of Bayezid II (1481–1512) and Selim I (1512–20). He also stresses that these laws and regulations were neither *farz*, obligatory deeds for Muslims, nor *sünnet*, the traditions of the Prophet with which Muslims should comply. In his words, "it is no use to say that this has not been a rule from the olden times. At that time the present evils were absent.... It is better to do everything in accordance with the circumstances of its time."[22] Again, though less forcefully than the author of *Kitâbu Mesâlih*, the anonymous author of the *Hırzü'l-Mülûk* argues that behind the achievements of such sultans as Mehmed II (1451–81) and Selim I (1512–20) lay the fact that they did not see the ancient law as unchangeable and were conscious of the fact that whatever the sultans do becomes *kānûn* (*bu kānûn-i Osmânî'ye muhâlifdir dimeyüb hemân icra idüb Selâtin-i İzâm her ne iderlerse kānûn olur*).[23]

However, we must admit that despite the modifications made by the Ottomans in existent laws and regulations, respect for the ancient law, or what Fleischer called *kānûn* consciousness, was one of the most emphasized ideas in the Ottoman reform treatises even as late as the 1790s when a new reform attempt was undertaken by Selim III (1789–1807).[24] Starting from Mustafa Âlî, most Ottoman *nasihat* writers stuck to the concept of an idealized ancient law. For instance, the author of *Kitâb-ı Müstetâb* (The Pleasant Book) believes that the restoration of the order rested on the revival of the Law of the House of Osman, which he describes as a path laid down by *hikmet* or wisdom.[25] In this context, he puts special emphasis on the well-known two institutions of the old order – the *tımâr* and *kul* systems. He does not defend the *kānûn* blindly and provides us with the wisdom (*hikmet*) behind the ancient law. For example, he complains that, contrary to the established custom, the real *devşirme* boys were not recruited to the inner palace any more since they had been replaced by young men of urban (*şehir oğlanı*), Turkish, Kurdish, Armenian or gypsy

---

22  Yücel, *Kaynaklar*, 46–7. Although dated by Yücel to 1640, Baki Tezcan convincingly argued that this work belonged to the last years of Süleyman the Magnificent (1520–66). See Baki Tezcan, "II. Osman Örneğinde İlerlemeci Tarih ve Osmanlı Tarih Yazıcılığı", in Güler Eren, Kemal Çiçek and C. Oğuz (eds), *Osmanlı*, vol. 7 (Ankara: Yeni Türkiye Yayınları, 1999), 658–68.

23  "They should not say that this is contrary to the Ottoman Law, and immediately implement it since whatever the great Sultans do becomes law". Yücel, *Kaynaklar*, 175.

24  See Enver Ziya Karal, "Nizâm-ı Cedide Dair Lâyihalar", *Tarih Vesikaları* 1 (1942), 411–25; 2 (1942/3), 104–11, 324–51, 424–32.

25  Yücel, *Kaynaklar*, 16–17.

origins. The author gives a detailed analysis of why the *iç-oğlans*, pages in the inner palace, were chosen among the *devşirme*, pointing out that nobody knew their former status and they did not have any tie with the people outside the inner palace.[26]

This line of argumentation reached its peak in the treatises of the famous Koçi Bey, an Albanian *devşirme*, during the reign of the iron-handed Murad IV (1623–40). He was an uncompromising defender of the *kānûn-i kadîm*, who provided his audience (notably the sultan) with a very clear analysis of the golden age of the empire; when the sultans had been personally dealing with the affairs of state and society, no foreigner (that meant outsiders with respect to a certain career line according to the law) could claim a revenue-grant holding (*tımâr* or *zeâmet*) and no person of *reâyâ* status (namely tax-paying subjects) could enter the ranks of the *kul*s, the servants of the sultan. This well-organized order started to break down when certain statesmen overlooked, or failed to comply with, the rules of the ancient law.[27] The increase in the number of Servants of the Gate (*kapıkulları*), criticized as early as the first half of the sixteenth century by Lütfi Pasha, was a recurrent theme in the works of advice writers, including Koçi Bey.[28] They underlined the delicate balance between the *kapıkulları* and the *timariot*s and argued that the increase in the number of the former was an important factor in the disorder of the time.[29]

Apart from the overarching idea that the disintegration of the public order (*nizâm-ı âlem*) resulted from the attitudes of statesmen that went contrary to the ancient law, another main issue dealt with by the Ottoman intellectuals of the sixteenth and seventeenth centuries was bribery,[30] which they considered to be one of the prime causes of the so-called decline. They maintained that it was bribery that lay behind the negligence of the ancient law and lack of resourcefulness in the administration. As the administrative machine degenerated from the top-down, all the positions came to be sold through bribery to

---

26  Yücel, *Kaynaklar*, 26–7.
27  Koçi Bey, *Risâle*, 27 ff.
28  According to this view their numbers should be limited and they should be obedient. Aziz Efendi puts great emphasis on the increase of the numbers of the *kapıkulları* and considers it as contrary to the ancient law. Since the new recruits were coming from among the tax-paying subjects and their share had to be paid by the remaining taxpayers of their villages, this practice aggravated the tax burden of the peasants. See Aziz Efendi, *Kanûnnâme*, 30–3.
29  Aziz Efendi, *Kanûnnâme*, 31–2.
30  On the place and effects of bribery in the Ottoman state and society, see Ahmet Mumcu, *Osmanlı Devletinde Rüşvet (Özellikle Adlî Rüşvet)* (Ankara: Ankara Üniversitesi Hukuk Fakültesi Yayınları, 1969).

those not deserving these posts on the basis of merit.[31] Particularly important was the case of provincial administrators who, to compensate for the amount they had given as a bribe, always tried to extract illegal dues and taxes from the people in their areas. This in turn caused the depopulation of the villages as the tax-paying peasants found it unbearable to meet both the legal and illegal tax demands. Besides, bribery was also the main factor behind the usurpation of former *tımâr* lands, which were to be given to influential people as *arpalık* (additional incomes allotted to high-ranking persons for their extra expenses or as pensions), *pashmaklik* (revenue-grants allocated to female members of the imperial family) or *mülk* (private property).[32] Under these circumstances, the once mighty army of *timariot*s gradually weakened, becoming unable to balance the increasing power of the *kapıkulları*.

## 4   By Way of a Conclusion: The Contribution of Ottoman *Nasihat* Literature to Ottoman Political Thought

There are, of course, many other factors and elements highlighted by the reform literature with respect to the decline of the Ottoman state and society, but we are content to focus on the main framework for understanding and interpreting this phenomenon. At this point, it appears appropriate to provide a general picture of their way of thinking. As is known, these political treatises owed their theoretical framework to the classical Islamic political thinkers and their works. With its roots reaching back to such different but interrelated traditions as ancient Greek, Indian and Persian traditions, Islamic political theory underlined the necessity of, and obedience to, a ruler for the order of a society, the notion of justice expounded in the concept of *dâire-i adliyye* or circle of equity, the principle of meritocracy and so on. This political thought was inherited by the Ottomans through translations to be followed by

---

31  It was emphasized that the grand vizier should be *perhizkâr*, that is he should abstain from unlawful things and be a sober person without any inclination towards bribery. On the effects of bribery in the provincial administration and *tımâr* system. see for example, Hırzü'l-Mülûk (Yücel, *Kaynaklar*, 185–9). Koçi Bey sees bribery as the primary reason behind all the disorder, mischief and sedition (*fitne vü fesâd*) and territorial losses in Muslim lands. "Since the year 990 (AD 1582) all the imperial posts have been given to the undeserved persons through bribery. And the revenue-grant holdings (*tımâr* and *zeamet*s) that are the (legal) rights of the people of war (*erbab-ı mukatele*) have been usurped by the provincial grandees and their real holders have [become] impoverished" (Koçi Bey, *Risâle*, 49).

32  See Koçi Bey, *Risâle*, 47–8.

original works.[33] Although some have argued that it is difficult to mention a noteworthy contribution by the Ottomans to this heritage, we must concede that they were very skilful in developing concrete proposals for a wide range of political, social, financial and military problems. We do not, of course, forget about those writers who reiterated traditional formulae or previous works, but even most of those were able to put forward some sort of practical proposals about the problems in their areas of specialization.[34] For example, one can explain the relatively long space Defterdar Mehmed Pasha, who follows in a great deal of matters his predecessors such as Lütfi Pasha and Koçi Bey, allocates to the office of treasury *defterdar* and officials of the Imperial Council, to his own field of specialization. However, Abou-el-Haj attributes this to the problems caused by the government's increasing need for cash income.[35] It is easy to demonstrate the pragmatic and practical approach of the Ottoman reform treatises. These, for example, include the special place given by Hasan Kâfî Akhisârî, who lived on the western border of the empire, to the new weapons developed by the enemy;[36] Aziz Efendi's treatment of false claimants to descent from the Prophet (*müteseyyid*s) and the Kurdish tribal chieftains whom the Ottomans appointed as hereditary district governors;[37] and

---

33  See Halil İnalcık, "Kutadgu Bilig'de Türk-İran Siyaset Nazariye ve Gelenekleri", *Reşit Rahmeti Arat İçin* (Ankara: Türk Kültürünü Araştırma Enstitüsü Yayınları, 1966), 259–71. See also, Fodor, "State and Society", 220 ff.; Ahmet Yaşar Ocak, "Düşünce Hayatı: XIV–XVII. Yüzyıllar", in Ekmeleddin İhsanoğlu (ed.) *Osmanlı Devleti ve Medeniyeti Tarihi* (Istanbul: IRCICA, 1998), vol. 2, 164–73; Uğur, *Osmanlı*, 106 fn.49.

34  While accepting Fodor's views regarding the link between the Near Eastern political tradition and the Ottoman *nasihatnâme*s, Howard draws attention to the importance in the works of Ottoman writers of social and political criticisms and the concept of *kānûn*. As he put it (Howard, "Historiography", 55–6), "these Ottoman writers intended more than to give advice on how to rule. They presented a critical analysis of Ottoman society.... In the development of the Ottoman decline genre, a second influence is discernible in addition to the Near Eastern 'mirrors', that of the centrality of *qanun*, the regulations that comprised traditional Ottoman dynastic law."

35  Abou-el-Haj states that *Defterdar*'s new recommendation of collecting taxes through the salaried agents (*emin*s) amounted to the prototype of a ministry of taxation in a modern state, but at the time this would have entailed a substantial increase in the numbers of the members of the financial bureaucracy. See Abou-el-Haj, "The Ottoman Nasihatname as a Discourse over 'Morality'", in Abdeljelil Temimi (ed.) *Mélanges Professeur Robert Mantran* (Zaghouan: Publications du Centre d'Etudes et de Recherches Ottomanes, Morisques, de Documentation et d'Information, 1988), 22–3.

36  İpşirli, "Hasan Kâfi", 268 ff.

37  Aziz Efendi, *Kanûnnâme*, 12–20 (English translation) and 33–9 (transliteration from Ottoman Turkish).

Koçi Bey's detailed descriptions of the small and medium-sized revenue-grant holders (*timariots* and *zâims*).

Yet another distinctive feature of the Ottoman reform treatises is that the Ottomans sought the causes of decline in the negligence of the established rules of their classical system rather than attributing it to external factors (as argued by some modern historians).[38] They were aware of some new developments regarding military technology, at least in the case of Hasan Kâfî, and cannot be assumed to be ignorant of the effects of economic and social factors. Bribery, corruption and nepotism were the most important reasons for the breakdown of the order of the world (*nizâm-ı âlem*) in their analysis. With the exception of Kâtib Çelebi, who adopted the İbn Haldûnian cyclical theory about the fates of empires,[39] they all believed that the revival of the old order was possible provided that an able, trustworthy and pious grand-vizier was appointed by the sultan (here we must remember that the figure of grand vizier had become the centre of government in Ottoman political thought by the mid-sixteenth century). Whether or not we define the situation faced by the Ottomans at the turn of the sixteenth century as decline, crisis or change, we must especially emphasize a point: as some Ottoman historians have rightly pointed out during the last two decades, while some western historians studying Ottoman state and society assumed that Ottoman institutions had represented a static oriental system vis-à-vis the changing and improving western structures, the central role of mentally-ill and/or powerless rulers was, as Murphey pointed out, emphasized by Turkish historiography in the republican period.[40] Be that as it may, if one approaches seventeenth-century Ottoman history from a different perspective it may be argued that "the Ottoman sultanate underwent a gradual but permanent change from a polity ruled by a charismatic leader ... to a polity ruled by law and bureaucratic tradition: a kind of depersonalized institutional monarch."[41]

---

38  İpşirli points out that while writers of reform treatises adhered to traditional formulae in explaining political and social matters and did not pay attention to external factors, the Ottoman statesmen adopted a pragmatic and practical approach as they had to cope with the day-to-day problems of the state and society. See Mehmet İpşirli, "Osmanlı Esas Yapısının Bozulması ve Islahı Çalışmaları Üzerine Bazı Gözlemler", in Hasan Celal Güzel, Kemal Çiçek and Salim Koca (eds), *Türkler* (Ankara: Yeni Türkiye Yayınları, 2002), vol. 9, 839–46.

39  Kâtib Çelebi or Haji Khalifa, a follower of İbn Haldûn, believed that the Ottomans could overcome the crisis in his time through some effective measures and might thus prolong the phase of stagnation. See Kâtib Çelebi, *Düstur*, 123, 139.

40  Murphey, "Continuity and Discontinuity", 420–1.

41  Murphey, "Continuity and Discontinuity", 425.

Consequently, it is apparent that, whether we call it a decline, transformation or change, what occurred at the turn of the sixteenth century onwards was not taken up by contemporary Ottoman political thought with all its dimensions; the Ottomans seems to have concentrated basically on administrative measures. It is also apparent that the Ottoman statesmen of the period were reluctant to heed the advice of the *nasihat* writers, which mostly urged a return to the ancient customary rules; instead, they preferred to adapt to the changing conditions of the time. Meanwhile, it is generally agreed that 'Ottoman mirrors for princes' did not attain the philosophical depth of their Islamic predecessors,[42] which might be attributed to the pragmatic nature of Ottoman political thought. In conclusion, then, one may ask to what extent Ottoman political thought can be considered 'political'. The main feature of this thought, in our view, is that it interprets all political, social and economic issues from a bureaucratic standpoint. It is then quite natural that Ottoman *nasihat* writers should have concentrated more on practical administrative, military and financial issues than on the philosophical or socio-cultural dimensions of the problems of the post-classical era. Last but not the least, although most writers of reform treatises or the like held the so-called *kānûn-i kadîm* in great esteem and seemed to have yearned for the 'golden age' of the earlier sultans, almost all of them adopted a practical and pragmatic approach in their proposals regarding the rectification of the disorders of their time, not to mention those openly criticizing the established sultanic laws or the *kānûn-i kadîm*.

## Bibliography

### Primary Sources

Aziz Efendi. *Kanûnnâme-i Sultânî li ʿAzîz Efendi (Introduction, English translation, transcription and facsimile)*, translated and edited by Rhoads Murphey and Şinasi Tekin. Cambridge, MA: Harvard University Press, 1985.

---

42   Fodor points out that "in comparison with their Islamic predecessors, the Ottoman mirrors for princes are much more practical in their outlook, ... most of them are concerned with concrete phenomena. What in the final analysis links them to the 'classics' is that the spiritual approach to the problems is the same at either end of the centuries-wide span, and they also wish to resolve the crisis with the traditional formulae." See Fodor, "State and Society", 239.

Defterdar Sarı Mehmed Paşa. *Devlet Adamlarına Öğütler /Nesâyihü'l-Vüzerâ ve'l-Ümerâ*, edited by Hüseyin Ragıp Uğural. Ankara: Türkiye ve Ortadoğu Amme İdaresi Enstitüsü, 1969.

Karal, Enver Ziya. "Nizâm-ı Cedide Dair Lâyihalar". *Tarih Vesikaları* 1 (1942), 411–25; 2 (1942/3), 104–11, 324–51, 424–32.

Kâtib Çelebi. *Düsturü'l-amel li-Islahi'l-halel*. Istanbul: Tasvir-i Efkâr Matbaası, 1280/1863.

Koçi Bey. *Koçi Bey Risâlesi*. Edited by Ali Kemali Aksüt. Istanbul: Vakit Matbaası, 1939.

### Secondary Sources

Abou-el-Haj, Rifa'at Ali. "The Ottoman Nasihatname as a Discourse over 'Morality'". In Abdeljelil Temimi (ed.) *Mélanges Professeur Robert Mantran*. Zaghouan: Publications du Centre d'Etudes et de Recherches Ottomanes, Morisques, de Documentation et d'Information, 1988, 17–30.

Abou-el-Haj, Rifa'at Ali. *Formation of Modern State: The Ottoman Empire, Sixteenth to Eighteenth Centuries*. Albany, NY: State University of New York Press, 1991.

Akdağ, Mustafa. *Türk Halkının Dirlik ve Düzenlik Kavgası-Celali İsyanları*. Ankara: Bilgi, 1975.

Barkey, Karen. *Bandits and Bureaucrats: The Ottoman Route to State Centralization*. Ithaca: Cornell University Press, 1994.

Cook, Michael Allan (ed.) *A History of the Ottoman Empire to 1730*. Cambridge: Cambridge University Press, 1980.

Darling, Linda. *Revenue-Raising and Legitimacy: Tax-Collection and Finance Administration in the Ottoman Empire, 1560–1660*. Leiden: Brill, 1996.

Faroqhi, Suraiya. "Crisis and Change". In H. İnalcık and D. Quataert (eds). *An Economic and Social History of the Ottoman Empire*. Cambridge: Cambridge University Press, 1994, 411–636.

Fleischer, Cornell. *Bureaucrat and Intellectual in the Ottoman Empire: The Historian Mustafa Ali, 1540–1600*. Princeton, NJ: Princeton University Press, 1986.

Fodor, Pál. "State and Society, Crisis and Reform in 15th–17th Century Ottoman Mirror for Princes". *Acta Orientalia Academiae Scientiarum Hungaricae* 40 (2–3) 1986, 217–40.

Gibb, H. A. R. and Harold Bowen. *Islamic Society and the West*. vol. 1 part 1. London: Oxford University Press, 1950.

Gökbilgin, M. Tayyib. "XVII. Asırda Osmanlı Devleti'nde Islahat İhtiyaç ve Temayülleri ve Kâtip Çelebi". In *Kâtip Çelebi: Hayatı ve Eserleri Hakkında İncelemeler*. Ankara: TTK, 1957, 196–220.

Griswold, William. *The Great Anatolian Rebellion*. Berlin: Klaus Schwarz Verlag, 1983.

Hodgson, Marshall G. S. *The Venture of Islam: Conscience and History in a World Civilization*, vol.3. Chicago: University of Chicago Press, 1974.

Howard, Douglas A. "The Ottoman Historiography and the Literature of 'Decline' of the Sixteenth and Seventeenth Centuries". *Journal of Asian History* 22 (1988), 52–77.

İnalcık, Halil. "Kutadgu Bilig'de Türk-İran Siyaset Nazariye ve Gelenekleri". In *Reşit Rahmeti Arat İçin*. Ankara: Türk Kültürünü Araştırma Enstitüsü Yayınları, 1966, 259–71.

İnalcık, Halil. *The Ottoman Empire: The Classical Age, 1300–1600*, translated by Norman Itzkowitz, Colin Imber. London: Weidenfeld and Nicolson, 1973.

İnalcık, Halil. "Military and Fiscal Transformation in the Ottoman Empire, 1600–1800". *Archivum Ottomanicum* (1980), 283–337.

İnalcık, Halil. *Osmanlı'da Devlet, Hukuk ve Adâlet*. Istanbul: Eren Yayıncılık, 2000.

İpşirli, Mehmet. "Hasan Kâfî el-Akhisarî ve Devlet Düzenine Ait Eseri-Usûlü'l-Hikem fî Nizâmi'l-Âlem". *İstanbul Üniversitesi Edebiyat Fakültesi Tarih Dergisi* 10–11 (1979–80), 239–78.

İpşirli, Mehmet. "Osmanlı Esas Yapısının Bozulması ve Islâhı Çalışmaları Üzerine Bazı Gözlemler". In Hasan Celal Güzel, Kemal Çiçek and Salim Koca (eds). *Türkler*. Ankara: Yeni Türkiye Yayınları, 2002, vol. 9, 839–46.

Kafadar, Cemal. "The Question of Ottoman Decline". *Harvard Middle Eastern and Islamic Review* 4 (1997/8), 30–75.

Kunt, Metin, *The Sultan's Servants: The Transformation of Ottoman Provincial Government, 1550–1650*. New York: Columbia University Press, 1983.

Kunt, Metin, and Christine Woodhead (eds). *Süleyman the Magnificent and His Age: The Ottoman Empire in the Early Modern Age*. London: Longman, 1995.

Levend, Agah Sırrı. "Siyasetnâmeler". *Türk Dili Araştırmaları Yıllığı-Belleten* (1962), 167–94.

Lewis, Bernard. *The Emergence of Modern Turkey*. London: Oxford Universit Press, 1961.

Lewis, Bernard. "Ottoman Observers of Ottoman Decline". *Islamic Studies* (1) 1962, 71–87.

Mumcu, Ahmet. *Osmanlı Devletinde Rüşvet (Özellikle Adlî Rüşvet)*. Ankara: Ankara Üniversitesi Hukuk Fakültesi Yayınları, 1969.

Murphey, Rhoads. "Continuity and Discontinuity in Ottoman Administrative Theory and Practice during the Late Seventeenth Century". *Poetics Today* 14 (2) 1983, 419–43.

Ocak, Ahmet Yaşar. "Düşünce Hayatı: XIV–XVII. Yüzyıllar" In Ekmeleddin İhsanoğlu (ed.) *Osmanlı Devleti ve Medeniyeti Tarihi*. Istanbul: Research Centre for Islamic History, Art and Culture (IRCICA), 1998, vol. 2, 164–7.

Öz, Mehmet. *Osmanlı'da 'Çözülme' ve Gelenekçi Yorumcuları*. Istanbul: Dergâh Yayınları, 1997 (revised and enlarged 2nd edition Istanbul: Dergâh Yayınları, 2005).

Özel, Oktay. "Changes in Settlement Patterns, Population and Society in Rural Anatolia: A Case Study of Amasya (1576–1642)". PhD dissertation, University of Manchester, 1993.

Özel, Oktay. "The Limits of the Almighty: Mehmed II's 'Land Reform' Revisited". *Journal of the Economic and Social History of the Orient* 42 (2) 1999, 226–46.

Peirce, Leslie Penn. *The Imperial Harem: Women and Sovereignty in the Ottoman Empire*. New York: Oxford University Press, 1993.

Peirce, Leslie P. *Harem-i Hümayun: Osmanlı İmparatorluğu'nda Hükümranlık ve Kadınlar*, translated by Ayşe Berktay. Istanbul: Türkiye Ekonomik ve Toplumsal Tarih Vakfı, 1996.

Tezcan, Baki. "II. Osman Örneğinde İlerlemeci Tarih ve Osmanlı Tarih Yazıcılığı", in Güler Eren, Kemal Çiçek and C. Oğuz (eds). *Osmanlı*. Ankara: Yeni Türkiye Yayınları, 1999, vol. 7, 658–68.

Tezcan, Baki. The Second Ottoman Empire: Political and Social Transformation in the Early Modern World. New York: Cambridge University Press, 2012.

Tietze, Andreas (ed.) *Mustafa Ali's Counsel for Sultans of 1581: Edition, Translation, Notes*. 2 vols. Vienna: Verlag der Österreichischen Akademie der Wissenschaften, 1979–82.

Uğur, Ahmet. *Osmanlı Siyâsetnâmeleri*. Kayseri: Kültür ve Sanat Yayınları, 1987.

Yılmaz, Hüseyin. "The Sultan and the Sultanate: Envisioning Rulership in the Age of Suleyman the Lawgiver (1520–1566)". Ph.D. dissertation, Harvard University, 2005.

Yücel, Yaşar (ed.) *Osmanlı Devlet Teşkilâtına Dair Kaynaklar*. Ankara: TTK, 1988.

CHAPTER 13

# Between a 'Brilliant Retreat' and a 'Tragic Defeat': Ottoman Narratives of the 1529 and 1683 Sieges of Vienna

*N. Zeynep Yelçe*

"Kara Mustafa Pasha's retreat from Vienna has been a very grievous and bloody affair. It is true that one and a half century ago the Turkish army had retreated from the [gates] of Vienna; but the difference between that brilliant retreat and this tragic defeat was tremendous."[1] This is how the romanticizing historian Ahmet Refik (Altınay, d. 1937) starts his epoch-naming work, *The Tulip Age*. Judging from the book on the 1529 campaign, however, it is hard to say that Sultan Süleyman's soldiers would have agreed with Ahmet Refik. In either case, both campaigns followed a similar trajectory and were concluded in a similar manner. Depending on which side of the coin one is looking at, it is possible to say that both campaigns ended in a failed siege, or that both resulted in a successful manifestation of devastation and terror imposed on the enemy.

This chapter is an attempt to decontextualize the two sieges in order to see the tree for itself, perhaps initially at the expense of the forest. While examining works of art, art historians sometimes feel the need to isolate themselves from the context and concentrate on the stylistic features of the work itself. Following their lead, I take the two campaigns as individual works on the art of war. Trying to alienate myself from the debates and paradigms dominating the periods concerned, including those on decline and on military revolution, I shall look at the two campaigns on their own to delineate their basic underlying motives and dynamics as projected by contemporary Ottomans. Detaching the two historical events from the intellectual and theoretical baggage of periodization that they have long carried, I believe, gives one an opportunity not only to take a fresh look at these events but also to question some conventional assumptions about periodization.

1  Ahmed Refik [Altınay], *Lâle Devri*, 2nd edn (Istanbul: Muhtar Hâlid Kitabhânesi, 1331/1912), 2. "Ḳara Muṣṭafa Paşa'nın Viyana önünden ric'atı pek elem verici ve pek ḳanlı olmuşdı. Vâḳı'a, bir buçuḳ 'aṣır evvel Süleymân-ı Ḳānûnî ordusı da Viyana önünden çekilmişdi; faḳaṭ ol şâhâne ric'atla bu zelîlâne hezîmet beyninde pek büyük farḳ vardı."

Contemporary Ottoman narratives, written nearly a hundred and fifty years apart, present an almost identical trajectory for the two campaigns. With the names of the actors removed, first-time readers could easily confuse which of the two campaigns they are reading about. The overall narrative follows a basic action flow: the arch-enemy, namely the Austrians, conspires against the Ottomans to get hold of Hungary.[2] The rightful king of Hungary asks for Ottoman support to protect his dominion and people. The Ottoman army sets out on the road to defend the Hungarians against the oppressor and to teach the arch-enemy a lesson. As the campaign progresses, the Ottoman army devastates the lands of the enemy and decides to go as far as Vienna to capture the enemy king. In the end, the enemy king is not to be found in Vienna and the campaign season comes to an end. Lifting the siege, the army retreats without capturing the city. The typical narrative diverges at this point. The accounts of the 1529 campaign do not dwell much on the retreat, whereas the retreat is a major point of focus and discussion in the accounts of the 1683 campaign. While the grand vizier and general commander of the former is rewarded for his success and adds to his reputation, the grand vizier and general commander of the latter is condemned to death and held responsible for the evil yet to come. In the longer run, the 1529 retreat does not hamper the Ottoman presence in central Europe, while the 1683 retreat leads to the gradual elimination of that presence. While it is not my aim to elaborate on the reasons why, it is necessary to deconstruct some of the main aspects of each campaign comparatively, so that we can actually ask why and try putting the context into the narratives – rather than contextualizing the narratives.

Played out against a backdrop of a deep-rooted French-Habsburg conflict and in a region marked by confessional conflict, both campaigns feature a people stuck between two strong, quasi-absolutist and ideologically and politically hostile dynastic powers. Defensive strategies seem to merge with aggressive expansionist tactics in both cases as each faction claims legitimacy for its acts and accuses its opponent of being the faulty party. In either case, independent of the validity of any one party's claims and/or accusations, the two campaigns prove to be turning points in the competition for domination over Central Hungary. The Ottoman narrative in both events revolves around a Hungarian nobleman, a hero fighting for a noble cause, as the Ottomans venture to make him the rightful king of the Hungarian realm. The figure of the ambitious grand vizier takes front stage in both stories. While one comes to be hailed as

---

2  The term "Austrians" is used to signify the Ottoman *Nemçe* for lack of a better word. This usage is for convenience only and should not suggest any anachronistic – or nationalist – parallels with the modern day Republic of Austria.

a hero, the other becomes the loser, if not the villain, of the story. The glorious appearance of 1529, regardless of the eventual retreat, turns to shame in 1683.

The 1529 and 1683 campaigns both seem to confirm 'the radius of action theory' suggested by Géza Perjés. Based on statistical data such as distances, marching pace, and seasonal conditions, Perjés calculated what he calls the 'radius of operation' of the Ottoman army. According to his calculations, "it was precisely in Hungary that the sphere of Ottoman machinery of conquest reached its outer limit."[3] Given the Habsburg rivalry and the proximity of Vienna, maintaining Buda – let alone Vienna itself – by direct control from Istanbul had never been a feasible option. The dilemma of the Ottomans lay in the fact that they could neither annex all of Hungary nor leave it to the Habsburgs. Therefore, having control over Buda not only had several advantages, but was vital to the control of the Danube and Habsburg attacks thereon. The city, situated midway between Vienna and Transylvania, would serve as an obstacle to a possible Habsburg advance to the Ottoman realm. As such, according to Perjés, keeping Hungary as a buffer zone against Habsburg power was much more feasible than establishing direct control at Buda.[4] As the Ottomans found in Hungary, a buffer zone was needed to keep the Habsburgs away, but "the Habsburg Empire also need[ed] the Hungarian Kingdom, first of all as a buffer state against potential Ottoman onslaught."[5] Although Perjés's theory found more opponents than allies in Hungarian scholarship,[6] Ottoman

---

3 Géza Perjés, *The Fall of the Medieval Kingdom of Hungary: Mohacs 1526–Buda 1541* (Boulder, CO: Atlantic Research and Publications, 1989), 50.
4 Perjés, *Fall of The Medieval Kingdom*, especially 50–3.
5 Géza Pálffy, "The Impact of the Ottoman Rule on Hungary", *Hungarian Studies Review* 28 (1–2) 2001, 124. Pálffy, in a later work in a more nationalist strand, goes a step further in arguing that in the sixteenth and seventeenth centuries "the surviving Hungary had indeed become Central Europe's bulwark or bastion of defense" and that since "the Habsburgs were legitimate kings of Hungary all along, and therefore the Austrian, German and Bohemian lands were supporting not an alien buffer state, but an important and organic unit of the monarchy." Géza Pálffy, "The Bulwark and Larder of Central Europe (1526–1711)", in Ernő Marosi (ed.) *On the Stage of Europe: The Millennial Contribution of Hungary to the Idea of European Community* (Budapest: Research Institute for Art History of the Hungarian Academy of Sciences – Balassi, 2009), 108.
6 Ferenc Szakály, for example, refutes Perjés on the grounds that Ottomans actually fought in further zones. See, Ferenc Szakály, "The Hungarian – Croatian Border Defense System and its Collapse", in János Bak and Béla K. Király (eds), *From Hunyadi to Rakoczi: War and Society in Late Medieval and Early Modern Hungary* (Brooklyn: Brooklyn College Press, 1982), 141–58. Ottoman accounts of various campaigns, on the other hand, suggest that these further operations were raids with a view to destroy, terrorize, and obtain booty rather than organized action with long-term intentions. Accounts on return decisions of various campaigns often attribute the decision to the difficulty involved in going further due to logistic and climatic concerns, which show some degree of awareness regarding the range of

offensives against Vienna both in 1529 and 1683 appear to be punitive or even vindictive moves rather than a firm attempt actually to take the city. Accounts of the devastating effects of the surroundings before, during and after the siege of Vienna support contemporary claims of intended destruction and harm rather than outright conquest. Describing how violently the surroundings of Vienna were destroyed, Bostan evaluates the devastation as "revenge taken from the mentioned accursed [Ferdinand]."[7] Foreign reports not only provide vivid accounts of women and children being sent away from Vienna for security, but they also emphasize the destruction of the Austrian countryside during the 1529 campaign.[8] An anonymous compilation of the events of Süleyman's reign until 1533 reports that Süleyman "ruined the province of Austria using all possible cruelty", and turned it into a desert.[9] Comments on destruction and devastation during the 1683 campaign are similar to those made for 1529.[10] The campaign chronicle lists the castles and fortifications the Ottoman army acquired after the Rába passage and dwells on the devastation between Buda and Vienna.[11]

The discursive justification of both campaigns revolves around two main themes – the breach of the peace agreement by the Habsburgs and the protection offered to the Hungarian king. These two themes are embedded in two main arguments strongly stressed in the accounts. The first argument is based on the Ottoman right to Hungary; in other words, Hungary is Ottoman territory by right of conquest. The second argument underlines the rightful cause of the Hungarian people in resisting Habsburg domination. In both cases, the Habsburg party is accused of attacking Ottoman territory and of oppressing

---

operations. Furthermore, the proclamation of victory of the 1541 conquest of Buda clearly states that the reason for granting Zápolya kingship of Hungary was the distance and difficulty in establishing direct control there. Feridun Ahmed Bey, *Münşeatü's-Selâtin*, (Istanbul: Darü't-Tıbaati'l-Âmire, 1274/1858), vol.1, 551. *"Engürüs vilâyetinin dârü'l-mülki olan Budin taḫtı ki ol zamânda memâlik-i İslâmiyye'den ba'îd ve żabṭı 'asîr olub."*

7  Bostan Mehmed Çelebî, *Târîh-i Sultân Süleyman Hân*, MS 18350, fol.92b, Gedik, AIHK.
8  Marino Sanuto, *I Diarii di Marino Sanuto*, vols. 51 and 52 (Bologna: Forni Editore, 1970), vol. 51, 475, 478–9, vol. 52, 40–2.
9  Anonymous, "I Fatti di Solimano dopo la Presa di Rhodi fino all'anno XDXXXIII", in Francesco Sansovino (ed.) *Dell'Historia Universale dell'origine et imperio de'Turchi parte prima(-terza)* (Venetia, 1560–61), vol. 2, 127.
10 Mustafa Na'îmâ Efendi, *Tarih-i Naîma: Ravzatü'l-Hüseyn fi Hulâsati Ahbâri'l-Hâfikayn*, edited by Mehmet İpşirli (Ankara: TTK, 2007), vol. 1, 44; Râşid Mehmed Efendi and Çelebizade İsmail Asım Efendi, *Târîh-i Râşid ve Zeyli*, edited by Abdülkadir Özcan et al. (Istanbul: Klasik Yayınları, 2013), vol. 1, 242, 243, 246.
11 Mehtap Yılmaz, "Vekayi'name (Vekayi-i Bec)", (Master's thesis, Marmara University, 2006), 72–3. Also see, Defterdar Sarı Mehmed Pasha, *Zübde-i vekayiât: tahlil ve metin (1066–1116/1656–1704*, edited by Abdülkadir Özcan (Ankara: TTK, 1995), 151.

the Hungarians. Thus, the narrative is woven around a double-layered justification implying protection and punishment rather than expansive territorial action. The main actors behind the narratives of the 1529 and 1683 campaigns are John Zápolya and Imre Thököly, respectively. Ottoman narratives present Zápolya and Thököly as legitimate kings who come to ask for support from the sultan. This conception works in two ways. On one hand, the 'legitimate' king of Hungary becomes dependent on the sultan. On the other hand, by undertaking to provide protection and support to the 'legitimate' king of Hungary, the sultan emerges as a king-maker, thus proving one of his most important honorifics, *pâdişâh-ı 'âlem-penâh* – refuge of the universe.[12]

The roots of the 1529 campaign can be found in the aftermath of the death of Lajos II following the battle of Mohács. The Hungarian throne became an object of rivalry between pro-Habsburg and anti-Habsburg factions within the Hungarian nobility. While the more powerful aristocracy tended to rally around Ferdinand of Habsburg, the lesser nobility supported John Zápolya. This theatre of conflict was performed on slippery grounds, as Lajos II's court chaplain György Szerémi's words suggested: "The Hungarians have reached the point where if a family has two growing sons, they encourage one to join the cause of Ferdinand, the other the party of King János [John]."[13] The dual election process ended up with Ferdinand I's claim based on heredity and support from powerful Hungarian magnates and the claim of the ban of Transylvania John Zápolya based on the support of a majority of lesser Hungarian nobility.[14] Unable to resist Ferdinand I's attacks on Buda, Zápolya found the solution in requesting Ottoman help in return for his obedience and alliance. Zápolya's approach was most likely a welcome opportunity for Sultan Süleyman to increase his influence in Hungary and to prevent strong Habsburg dominion in the region.[15] It can also be interpreted as a welcome excuse to launch an attack on Ferdinand I while keeping up appearances.

Sixteenth-century chronicles cite as immediate reasons of the 1529 campaign the occupation of Buda and the invasion of Hungarian territory by Ferdinand I

---

12   For a discussion on Zápolya's case, see Nevin Zeynep Yelçe, "Ottoman Reception and Perception of Janos Szapolyai in 1529", in Robert Born and Sabine Jagodzinski (eds) *Türkenkriege und Adelskultur in Ostmitteleuropa vom 16.–18. Jahrhundert* (Leipzig: Thorbecke Jan Verlag, 2014), 141–54.

13   Quoted in Leslie S. Domonkos, "The Battle of Mohacs as a Cultural Watershed", in János Bak and Béla K. Király (eds), *From Hunyadi to Rakoczi: War and Society in Late Medieval and Early Modern Hungary* (Brooklyn: Brooklyn College Press, 1982), 213.

14   For a brief chronological overview of the dual election process extending from November 1526 to 1529, see Ferenc Szakály, *Ludovico Gritti in Hungary: 1529–1534* (Budapest: Akadémiai Kiadó, 1995), 42.

15   Perjés, *Fall of the Medieval Kingdom*, 124–5.

whom they identify as the target. The official aim cited in the campaign diary is "to drive Ferdinand away from Buda."[16] Ottoman authors condemn Ferdinand's actions for two main reasons. First, Hungary, especially Buda, belonged to the sultan by the right of the sword. Second, the sultan bestowed its kingship on King John (*Yanoş Kral*). Celâlzâde Mustafa (d.1567), chancellor of Süleyman I, attributes the 1529 campaign to Ferdinand's 'invasion' (*istîlâ*) of the Hungarian territory (*Engürüs vilâyetleri*). According to the brief background information given by the author, the sultan "granted the kingship of Hungary to King John – who was the ban of Transylvania – after the battle of Mohács."[17] Ottoman authors further justify this decision through an explanation of John's election as king according to Hungarian custom (10 November 1526),[18] and his right to the Hungarian throne by blood.[19] In his account of the 1526 campaign, Ottoman statesman Kemalpaşazâde (d.1534) underlines Zápolya's refusal to participate in the battle of Mohács. According to Kemalpaşazâde's version of the story, Transylvania (*Erdel*) was under the rule of a 'wise man of sound foresight' (*pîr-i sâ'ib-tedbîr*) 'who tended towards prudence' and chose the proper course and did not respond to the calls of the king, unlike the rest of the over-proud commanders. Kemalpaşazâde attributes Zápolya's decision not to an act of treason to the Hungarian king, but to his awareness that "he would not be able to match the ghazis on the battlefield."[20] That he is presented as a prudent and reasonable commander who knows his limits brings further justification to the support given to him in 1529. According to Lütfi Pasha (d.1564), who was governor of Damascus at the time, Süleyman was not pleased with Ferdinand's presence in Buda, so he set off with his army upon Zápolya's appeal for support.[21] Bostan Mehmed Çelebi (d.1569), a member of the religious establishment, attributes Süleyman's decision to take military action to Ferdinand's refusal to offer tribute in return for the Hungarian territories he occupied.[22] This is again taken as a violation of Süleyman's right of conquest. As

---

16   Feridun, *Münşeat*, 566.
17   Celâlzâde Mustafa, *Tabakâtü'l-Memâlik ve Derecâtü'l-Mesâlik* (*Geschichte Sultan Süleyman Kanunis von 1520 bis 1557*), edited by Petra Kappert (Wiesbaden: Franz Steiner Verlag, 1981), 183a. "Muḳaddemâ Engürüs-i menḥûs ile ṣaḥrâ-yı Mohaç'da uğraşdan ṣonra Engürüs ḳrallığı Erdel bânı olan Yanoş Kral'a iḥsân eylemişlerdi".
18   Bostan, *Târîḫ*, fol. 85b; Celâlzâde, *Tabakât*, 183a; Matrakçı Nasûh Silâhî b. Karagöz Bosnavî, *Dâstân-ı Sultân Süleymân*, MS R.1286, fol. 148a, TSMK.
19   Lütfi Pasha, *Tevârih-i Âl-i 'Osman*. Edited by Kayhan Atik (Ankara: Kültür Bakanlığı, 2001), 266 ff.
20   Kemalpaşazade, *Tevârih-i Al-i Osman X. Defter*, edited by Şerafettin Turan (Ankara: TTK, 1991), 340.
21   Lütfi Pasha, *Tevârih*, 265.
22   Bostan, *Târîḫ*, fol. 85b.

soldier himself, Matrakçı Nasuh (d.1563), on the other hand, emphasized that Ferdinand occupied Buda and forced 'Yanoş Kral' out of the city.[23] Described by Celâlzâde as the possessor of the German and Czech territories nearby and the brother of the 'Kaiser of Spain' (*İspanya Çesârı*), Ferdinand I is accused of coveting the lands of Hungary. As 'King John' (*Yanoş Ḳral*) did not have enough power to resist Ferdinand's attacks, he had to let go of Buda. According to Celâlzâde, Ferdinand's actions signified open hostility towards Süleyman.[24]

All these legitimizing motives are projected in the proclamation of victory sent to Venice following the 1529 campaign[25] – Süleyman's right of disposal on Hungary on the basis of conquest; Ferdinand's usurpation of the country and the crown defying the rights of conquest of Süleyman; and Süleyman's granting kingship to Zápolya. Written in the first person, the proclamation reads: "And I have donated the kingdom of Hungary to the Prefect János, according to the custom of my very great Majesty, with all its places and lands." After clearly delineating these points, it is announced that the main intention of the sultan was not to chase these things, but to find Ferdinand who tried to usurp Hungary and then ran away. Having followed Ferdinand with his army and taken all the strongholds on the way up to the German border, Süleyman was informed that Ferdinand had escaped. Not knowing whether he was dead or alive, the sultan sent his men to devastate Ferdinand's realm.[26] Celâlzâde attributes a preemptive defensive motive to the 1529 campaign, as he asserts that Ferdinand's assaults could extend into the borders of Süleyman's protected domains (*memâlik-i mahrûse-i hâkāniyye*). While introducing Ferdinand, the author mentions that European rulers (*selâtîn-i Frenk ve havâkîn-i küfr-âyin*) were proud of him and he was often victorious against his enemies. According to Celâlzâde, encouraged by these Ferdinand desired to be emperor (*çesâr*). As such, the author asserts that 'imperial protection' (*ḥamiyet-i cihânbânî*) required that Süleyman destroy Ferdinand's 'valour and might' (*şevket ü şehâmet*). Thus, Süleyman decided to proceed to Vienna.[27] Celâlzâde's explanations add yet another motive for the 1529 campaign – rivalry for universal rulership. Our author's employment of the term *çesâr*, which basically means emperor, taken within the context of Ferdinand's insistent efforts at the time

---

23    Matrakçı Nasûh Silâhî b. Karagöz Bosnavî, *Dâstân-ı Sultân Süleymân*, fol. 148b, MS R.1286, TSMK.
24    Celâlzâde, *Tabakât*, 183a.
25    For the letter of proclamation dated 13 November, from Belgrade, see Sanuto, *Diarii* 52, 370–2.
26    For some examples of the devastation, see for example, Sanuto, *Diarii* 52, 93, 160–1.
27    Celâlzâde, *Tabakât*, 183a–b.

to acquire the title of King of Romans, also sheds light on the contemporary power struggles and balancing attempts.

Kemalpaşazâde's account of the 1526 campaign was completed in early 1529, making Zápolya an already familiar figure. According to Lütfi Pasha, who was the governor of Damascus at the time, Zápolya approached Süleyman after Ferdinand captured Buda and drove him out. Upon this, Zápolya sent an envoy to the Ottoman court offering the sultan an annual tribute (haraç) of one thousand pieces of gold in return for intervening on his behalf to drive Ferdinand out and give the country to him instead. Süleyman was not pleased with Ferdinand's presence in Buda, so he set off with his army.[28] Foreign correspondence shows that Süleyman had been in communication with Zápolya from early on. The news from Hungary dated 20 June 1527 reports the presence of an Ottoman envoy at Buda. He is said to have dined with Zápolya and the barons on his arrival. He is also said to have had conversed with Zápolya in private and left immediately afterwards, which was taken as a sign that Zápolya had come to an agreement with the sultan.[29] By June, Venetian vice bailo Piero Zen's reports from Istanbul, as well as various rumours, were demonstrating the intention on Süleyman's part to support Zápolya.[30] Zen reports the arrival of an envoy from Zápolya on 28 January 1528, asking for help against Ferdinand with the offer to become tributary to the sultan. Zen notes that this was the fourth envoy sent by Zápolya to Süleyman's court. The first two were said to be robbed and the third killed. The offer seems to have been accepted as troops were ordered to assist Zápolya who instructed them not to engage in battle until the Rumelian troops had arrived.[31] Piero Zen's letters dated 6 and 11 May, as he saw the Ottoman army leave Istanbul in 1529, report that the sultan left the city with the wish of "putting [making] King János the voivode in the kingdom of Hungary".[32]

Zápolya was not alone in approaching the Ottoman sultan. Ferdinand sent Johann Hoberdanacz and Sigismund Weichselberger to Istanbul in 1528 to negotiate the Hungarian issue.[33] Piero Zen reports that the envoys arrived in April and were first accepted by Grand Vizier Damad İbrâhim Pasha (Pargalı) to whom they presented a silver cup with gold worth 300 ducats before being admitted for an audience with the sultan. Zen mentions İbrâhim Pasha's fury

---

28  Lütfi Pasha, Tevârih, 265.
29  Sanuto, Diarii 45, 360–1.
30  Sanuto, Diarii 45, 511, 580–1.
31  Sanuto, Diarii 47, 46–7. On the envoy and preparations, also see, Sanuto, Diarii 47, 100, 118–19, 380.
32  Sanuto, Diarii 50, 471.
33  Szakály, Gritti 49, passim.

over Ferdinand being addressed as the King of Hungary.[34] Zen's letter from Constantinople in early June 1528 reports on the audience given to Ferdinand's envoys. While the envoys asked for peace and were even ready to settle for a truce, Süleyman seems to have made their job harder by setting two conditions. As he asked Ferdinand to hand over Hungary to Zápolya and to have Emperor Charles V make peace with France and Venice, he already seems to have sent decrees to the provinces to assist the 'voivode'.[35] In early October, the envoys were still in Istanbul. Not only had they failed to obtain any favours from the sultan, but they were also detained because they incessantly kept asking for the Hungarian fortresses, thus evoking even more anger on the part of Sultan Süleyman. Zen reports that the sultan was so furious that he did not even hide his intention to undertake a Hungarian campaign aiming to penetrate far into *Alemagna*. Such openness of intention seems to have surprised Zen who emphasizes that this was contrary to the customs of previous sultans.[36]

By 1683, the issue of universal kingship seemed to have come to a stalemate and appeared no more to be a matter of competition, but political and territorial hostility remained. Chroniclers of the 1683 campaign acknowledge Leopold I (d.1705) as *çesâr* although a horrible one. While Râşid Mehmed addresses Leopold as 'the insidious emperor' (*çesâr-ı mekkâr*),[37] Fındıklılı Silâhdar defines the direction of the campaign as Hungary (*Engürüs*) with the intention of revenging the Austrian emperor (*intikâm-ı çesâr-ı Nemçe*).[38] The figure of Imre Thököly seems to have replaced Zápolya in 1683. Imre Thököly has often been characterized as a rebel, or, as John Stoye put it, as "the Magyar leader in rebellion against Habsburg authority in Christian Hungary, that part of the country which the Turks themselves did not occupy".[39] Early-eighteenth-century Ottoman chroniclers, on the contrary, regard Thököly as the king of a people under religious oppression. Silâhdar provides an account of the conflict between Thököly and Leopold I, presenting the latter as the emperor (*çesâr*) who forced the people of Upper Hungary (*Orta Macar*) to worship idols. According to the author, Hungarians are divided into two sects. While one sect worships idols,

---

34  Sanuto, *Diarii* 48, 131.
35  Sanuto, *Diarii* 48, 200.
36  Sanuto, *Diarii* 49, 182. The envoys were finally permitted to leave at the end of November 1528. Petervarad appears among the requested castles in Zen's report dated 28 November. Sanuto, *Diarii*, 370.
37  Râşid Mehmed Efendi and Çelebizade İsmail Asım Efendi, *Târîh-i Râşid ve Zeyli*, edited by Abdülkadir Özcan et al. (Istanbul: Klasik Yayınları, 2013), vol. 1, 231.
38  Nazire Karaçay Türkal, "Silahdar Fındıklılı Mehmed Ağa: Zeyl-i Fezleke (1065–c.1106/ 1654–7 Şubat 1695)" (Ph.D. dissertation Marmara University, 2012), 792.
39  John Stoye, *The Siege of Vienna: The Last Great Trial Between Cross and Crescent* (New York: Pegasus Books, 2007), 1.

the other refuses to have them in its churches, let alone worship them. It is this second group, according to the author, that the Austrian emperor (*Nemçe çesârı*) forced to worship idols. When they refused to do so, they were brutally suppressed. Thököly is called by the people upon his father's death to fight the oppressors and defend the people. Thököly, knowing that their own forces would be inadequate to fight the empire , turns to the Ottomans for help and submits to the sultan.[40] Thököly is justified through his return to command the Hungarians upon their demand. His appeal to Ottoman support is based on the general consensus of the Hungarian nobility: "We no longer have our former strength and might. Our country is in the hands of the enemy. Let us appeal to the Ottoman sultan for refuge and help, and submit to his service."[41] The alleged consensus helps transform the whole affair into one of voluntary submission in return for protection, thus legitimizing Ottoman involvement.

Contemporary accounts underline Ottoman support for Thököly, first diplomatically, then through military action.[42] Thököly is identified as "*Tökeli İmre* who has been bestowed with the Kingship of Middle Hungary." Although Thököly's initial appeals and offers were not accepted,[43] his envoys were received at Plovdiv by the grand vizier.[44] According to Silâhdar, the first refusal had come from Vizier Kasım Pasha: "Those who have been involved in the affairs of your kind have lost their heads and lives. And this would mean sowing sedition between the Ottoman Empire and Austria, causing further bloodshed for no right reason."[45] Thököly was ceremonially received at the Ottoman camp with a protocol similar to that with which Zápolya was received in 1529.[46] While Thököly sent envoys and eventually presented himself at the camp, Leopold, too, sent envoys to clear the situation. However, his envoys did not find a warmer reception than those of Ferdinand found in 1528. The imperial envoy was received by the grand vizier, but not presented with the customary robe of honour: "When an ambassador is given leave on whose

---

40 Türkal, "Silahdar", 769–71.
41 Türkal, "Silahdar", 770.
42 Râşid, *Târîh-i Râşid* 1, 230–1.
43 Defterdar Sarı Mehmed Pasha, *Zübde-i Vekayiât*, 125; Türkal, "Silahdar", 770.
44 Yılmaz, "Vekayi'name", 30. Yılmaz's thesis includes both the transcription and the facsimile of the manuscript at TSMK, with archive number R. 1310. Also see, Türkal, "Silahdar", 796.
45 Türkal, "Silahdar", 770. "Sizin gibi müteḥarriklerin arasına girenler baş ve cândan çıka gelmişlerdir. Bi'l-âḫire Devlet-i ʿAliyye ile Nemçe beynine nifâḳ düşürüb, nâ-ḥaḳḳ niçe ḳan dökülmeğe bâʾisdir."
46 For Zápolya's reception in 1529, see Yelçe, "Ottoman reception", *passim*.

king a campaign directed, he is not given [the] robe of honour. This means, be ready to your end."[47]

Some contemporary Ottoman chroniclers claimed that it was Zápolya who provoked Süleyman into attacking Vienna in revenge.[48] According to Nasuh, it was actually Yahyâpaşazâde Bâlî Bey's idea to take Vienna once the siege started. Nasuh mentions that, since the castle did not fall after nineteen days, the siege was lifted. The author failed to see this as a failure on the grounds that 'German' territories were destroyed and burned down in the meanwhile.[49] Ottoman accounts regarding the lifting of the siege of Vienna because of the absence of Ferdinand attest to the target of the attack as being Ferdinand. Bostan, for example, attributes the decision to mount the siege to the presumption of Ferdinand's presence in the castle, and its lifting to the realization that he was not.[50] The campaign diary also attributes the lifting of the siege to Ferdinand's absence. Although a final assault was planned and announced, according to the diary, on the designated day Süleyman learned that Ferdinand was not in the fortress; therefore, he decided to grant pardon to the city and have the soldiers retreat.[51] By September, it was common knowledge that Ferdinand was not in Vienna. While Venetian reports pointed Linz as the whereabouts of Ferdinand I,[52] an account from within the Ottoman camp shows that Ottomans were quite informed about Ferdinand's actions as well and believed him to travelling to Germany to procure help.[53] The prisoners taken along the way to Vienna also seem to have provided information about Ferdinand's location.[54] The decision to retreat in 1529 was accompanied by a war council in no way different from any other post-victory occasion. Along with this decision, the janissaries were rewarded a thousand aspers each. The

---

47   Yılmaz, "Vekayi'name", 56.
48   Nasuh, *Dâstân*, fol. 156a. See also Lütfi Pasha, *Tevârih*, 267.
49   Nasuh, *Dâstân*, 163a–165a.
50   Bostan, *Târîh*, fol. 92a. Also see Sanuto, *Diarii 52*, 361–2. The author of the letter, Maximo Leopardi, says that the Ottoman army left Vienna on learning from two high-level German prisoners that Ferdinand was not there but at Linz.
51   Feridun Bey, *Münşe'at* 1, 574. The agent of Marc Antonio Contarini, who left Vienna on 18 September, reports an Ottoman ambassador arriving in Vienna on 17 September. Sanuto, *Diarii* 52, 7.
52   Sanuto, *Diarii* 51, 331–2, 240.
53   For the report of Alvise Gritti's men sent to Istanbul from the camp, see Sanuto, *Diarii* 52, 59. For Ottoman awareness of Ferdinand's expectation of German help, also see Celâlzâde, *Tabakât*, 188a.
54   Nasûh, *Dâstân*, 159b. In a following poem (161a–b), Nasuh relates how Ferdinand escaped first to Linz [*Lança*], then further to Prague [*Brâga*], as he heard of Süleyman's march. Also see Feridun Bey, *Münşe'at* 1, 571.

commanders kissed the sultan's hand and were awarded robes of honour. Grand vizier İbrâhim Pasha was rewarded with a sword, four gowns, and five sacks of coins, while the other viziers were presented with two gowns apiece.[55] İbrâhim's reputation seems to be untarnished by the retreat as he was once again given general command of the army in 1532. Giving an account of this campaign, Celâlzâde cannot praise İbrâhim enough.[56]

The retreat in 1683, on the other hand, was an exigency prompted by the appearance of allied enemy forces. While the other chroniclers put the blame of the Vienna decision on Grand Vizier Mustafa who refused to heed the objections of experienced frontier commanders,[57] the campaign diary tells a different story. Accordingly, a war council was held near Székesfehérvár (Stolni Belgrad) with the participation of the Crimean Khan Murad Giray, Vizier Hüseyin Pasha, Kara Mehmed Pasha, Silistre governor Mustafa Pasha, Rumelian and Anatolian governors-general, the janissary chief commander and some experienced troop commanders. This war council determined the target to be Vienna.[58] While Naîmâ attributes the retreat to the "sudden appearance of the infidels from the mountains like lightening,"[59] Sarı Mehmed Pasha blames Merzifonlu Kara Mustafa Pasha for not being prepared for the enemy attack.[60] The disorganized and shattered nature of retreat in this case seems to have required a scapegoat. And Ottoman authors of the siege found the scapegoat in Grand Vizier Kara Mustafa Pasha.

Silâhdar foreshadowed this from the beginning of his account by blaming the grand vizier who opted for war instead of renewing the peace. Silâhdar described the grand vizier as a "provocative, aggressive, contemptuous, greedy, obstinate, unthankful and arrogant Turk who wished for the destruction of the state." As such, according to the author, he prevented the renewal of the peace agreement. Conspiring with the janissary commander, he convinced the sultan that the janissaries had complained about remaining idle and wished to go to war. As an experienced man who looked ahead, the sultan did not give in before asking for the informed opinions of the frontier commanders. Mustafa Pasha, however, threatened them into providing false letters and succeeded in convincing the sultan to wage war. Silâhdar's account emphasized Mustafa Pasha's malice more than once. The grand vizier was warned by a dream in which a seven-headed dragon appeared as he was trying to put on a new pair

---

55  Feridun Bey, *Münşe'at* 1, 574. Also see, Celâlzâde, *Tabakât*, 192a.
56  Celâlzâde, *Tabakât*, 211a.
57  Sarı Mehmed, *Zübde-i Vekayiât*, 146–7.
58  Yılmaz, *Vekayi'name*, 67.
59  Na'îmâ, *Târih-i Nâ'ima*, 44.
60  Sarı Mehmed Pasha, *Zübde-i Vekayiât*, 158.

of boots. The boots are interpreted as the campaign, and the dragon as the emperor, as "he has seven kings under his command." The bad omen seemed to have had little effect on Silâhdar's contemptuous grand vizier, for he summoned experienced warriors from the Buda frontier who were well informed about 'German affairs' for advice. They, too, warned him against a campaign into Austria, only to be dismissed in a furious manner.[61]

At the end of the day, we are left with one glorious retreat that is still commemorated, one praised sultan, one praised grand vizier, as well as one tragic and shameful retreat and one cursed grand vizier. Within the framework of the narrative presented by Ottoman sources, a comparative reading of contemporary – or near-contemporary – accounts of the 1529 and 1683 campaigns highlights three main common elements – the justification of the campaign decision; the perception of the Hungarian issue along with the reception and representation of John Zápolya and Imre Thököly; and the decision of targeting Vienna and the presentation of the retreat. So, why the sense of glory in one and the sense of failure in the other? If what is celebrated is the presence of the Ottoman army at the gates of Vienna, why do we produce and sell T-shirts featuring 1529 and Sultan Süleyman, and not 1683 and Sultan Mehmed IV? The answer seems to lie not in the sieges *per se* but in the aftermath.

The immediate aftermath of neither of the sieges brought a definite resolution of the conflict between the parties involved. Following the 1529 campaign, Ferdinand I did not abandon his claims in Hungary and on Buda. Buda was once more occupied by Habsburg forces in 1531. Having been retaken with large scale support from Ottoman troops stationed in Rumelia, the occupation nonetheless led to an imperial campaign into the depths of German territory. Led by the sultan himself, the 1532 campaign appears punitive and intended as a show of might and a quest to intimidate rather than a campaign with a specific target or solid intention of territorial gain. Thereafter, the conflict over Hungarian territory continued in the shape of smaller scale battles and border skirmishes until Buda was officially appropriated and turned into an Ottoman province in 1541, following the death of John Zápolya in 1540. Although the Ottoman-Habsburg conflict did not come to an end and resurfaced in long periods of war and border battles, the balance of power remained relatively similar. Although castles changed hands several times, the territorial make-up of both parties remained relatively stable[62] – at least until the late-seventeenth century when the status quo began changing to the detriment of the Ottomans.

61  Türkal, "Silahdar", 784.
62  For a balanced discussion of the Ottoman-Habsburg frontier during the period under focus, see Gabor Agoston, "Macaristanda Osmanlı-Habsburg Serhaddı (1541–1699), Bir

The defeat at Vienna, rather than the lifting of the siege, seems to have been the trigger to what was yet to come. The immediate aftermath resembled previous occasions when hostilities resumed after the Ottoman army had left. Skirmishes between Ottoman troops, mainly those under Rumelian commanders, and Habsburg forces on the way back was not uncommon in the sixteenth century. Thus, losing some troops and cannons, or even castles, on the way back would probably not scandalize the Ottoman audience of the time. What was scandalous, on the other hand, was the loss of Buda three years later in 1686. Losing Buda meant losing the main centre of operation and defence in the border zone. Once Buda fell, the rest followed in rapid succession until the Peace of Karlowitz in 1699. The treaty marked not only the first large-scale territorial loss of the Ottoman Empire, but also the dissolution of the longstanding equilibrium between the two powers. As Rhoads Murphey put it:

> The era of the Christian counteroffensive against the Ottomans, lasting from the inauguration of the *sacra ligua* in 1684 until its dissolution in 1699, is usually regarded as a period of exceptional instability and crisis in the Ottoman Empire. The fall of such important strategic fortresses as Buda (1686) and Azov/Azak (1696) increased the empire's vulnerability to external threat, while a variety of internal disturbances, ranging from tribal unrest to military rebellions, also destabilized the empire.[63]

Under these circumstances, I find the Holy League to be a decisive factor in the outcome of the following years of war. The siege of Vienna for a second time and the following retreat of the Ottoman army in a matter of a few hours in the face of a joint attack seems to have prompted and encouraged the institution of the Holy League in 1684. The ability to form an anti-Ottoman alliance and to preserve it for several years seems to have had some effect in the long run. The 1529 siege had also given pace to peace initiatives among European powers. As the Ottoman army was on the move in 1529, even before the siege of Vienna, the treaty of Barcelona was signed between the emperor and the pope on 29 June. Based on the mutual intention to unite against the *Turk* and against heresy, Charles V recognized papal claims to Ravenna, Cervia, Modena, Reggio and Rubiera in return for the Kingdom of Naples. A few weeks later, the Peace of Cambrai was signed on 3 August by Margaret of Austria, the regent of

---

Mukayese", in Güler Eren, Kemal Çiçek and Cem Oğuz (eds), *Osmanlı* (Ankara: Yeni Türkiye Yayınları, 2000), vol. 1, 443–51.

63  Rhoads Murphey, "Continuity and Discontinuity in Ottoman Administrative Theory and Practice during the Late Seventeenth Century", *Poetics Today* 14 (2) 1993, 436.

the Netherlands and Charles's aunt, and Louise of Savoy, mother of the French King Francis I. Charles V renounced his claims to Burgundian lands, while Francis I recognized Charles's rights to Flanders and Artois and renounced his own on Milan, Genoa and Naples. A marriage was negotiated between Francis and Charles's sister Eleanor.[64] The anti-Ottoman bonding efforts in Europe continued with Francis I laying out an anti-Ottoman war plan involving 60,000 men, cavalry and artillery before Charles's ambassadors, along with the promise of support in October 1529. The natural commander of the offensive would of course be the emperor, while Francis himself would lead the vanguard. Though he would be unable to provide financial support since he owed a lot to England, as imposed by the Treaty of Cambrai, he claimed that he would be happy to meet Charles in Italy and help plan the campaign.[65] On 21 January 1530, a group of English envoys was commissioned "to treat with the Pope, the Emperor, the kings of France, Portugal, Denmark and Scotland, the doge of Venice, and the dukes of Milan and Ferrara, for a general peace, and for resisting the *Turk*."[66] German princes who were reluctant to get involved so far seem to have decided to direct some attention to the calls for support after 1529. In the Diet of Augsburg, the Hungarian issue was one of the three main items on the agenda recorded in the summons dated 21 January 1530, along with the religious question and the government of Germany.[67] Unlike the case in 1684, these efforts failed to produce any long-term alliance and commitment against the Ottomans. Power holders in Europe, it seems, still had their own issues to resolve. In this sense, Süleyman I never faced the well-orchestrated cooperative resistance that his successor would face in the joint forces of the Holy Roman Empire, Poland, Venice and Russia, backed by the papacy.[68]

In this chapter, I have tried to take a first step towards decontextualizing the campaigns of 1529 and 1683 in order to bring forth the basics of a large-scale

---

64  Roy Strong, *Art and Power: Renaissance Festivals, 1450–1650* (Woodbridge, Suffolk: Boydell Press, 1984), 78.
65  Karl Brandi, *The Emperor Charles V: The Growth and Destiny of a Man and of a World-Empire*, translated by C. V. Wedgwood (London: Jonathan Cape, 1939), 281.
66  John Sherren Brewer (ed.), *Letters and Papers, Foreign and Domestic, of the Reign of Henry VIII* (London: Longman, 1867–75), vols 3–4, 2748.
67  Brandi, *Emperor Charles V*, 306–7. Charles wrote to his wife on 8 July 1530: "the propositions were divided into three heads. The first and most important is the religious question. The second deals with Hungary and the Turkish trouble. The third concerns the government of Germany." For an examination of the agenda, see Gottfried G. Krodel, "Law, Order, and the Almighty Taler: The Empire in Action at the 1530 Diet of Augsburg", *Sixteenth Century Journal* 13 (2) 1982, 75.
68  For a brief overview of the Holy League, see Peter H. Wilson, *German Armies: War and German Politics, 1648–1806* (London: Routledge, 1998), 71–4.

military campaign aimed in a particular direction, ending with a particular target, and resulting in retreat. While the first campaign apparently failed to reduce Ottoman claims to universal kingship, the second one seems to have set in motion a serious abandonment of such claims. This transformation can only be understood through looking at the aftermath of both campaigns. Methodologically, the divergence in the long-term aftermath of two almost identical campaigns makes it necessary to put the context back in.

## Bibliography

### Primary Sources
Topkapı Sarayı Müzesi Kütüphanesi Library
Matrakçı Nasûh Silâhî b. Karagöz Bosnavî. *Dâstân-ı Sultân Süleymân*. MS R.1286, Topkapı Sarayı Müzesi Kütüphanesi.

Afyon Gedik Ahmed Paşa İl Halk Kütüphanesi Library
Bostan Mehmed Çelebî, *Târîh-i Sultân Süleyman Hân*. MS 18350, Gedik, Afyon Gedik Ahmed Paşa İl Halk Kütüphanesi.

### Published Primary Sources
Anonymous. "I Fatti di Solimano dopo la Presa di Rhodi fino all'anno XDXXXIII". In Francesco Sansovino (ed.) *Dell'Historia Universale dell'origine et imperio de'Turchi parte prima(-terza)*. 3 vols. Venetia: 1560–1561.

Brewer, John Sherren (ed.) *Letters and Papers, Foreign and Domestic, of the Reign of Henry VIII*. 20 vols. London: Longman, 1867–75.

Celâlzâde Mustafa. *Tabakâtü'l-memâlik ve derecâtü'l-mesâlik (Geschichte Sultan Süleyman Kanunis von 1520 bis 1557)*. Edited by Petra Kappert. Wiesbaden: Franz Steiner Verlag, 1981.

Defterdar Sarı Mehmed Paşa. *Zübde-i Vekayiât: Tahlil ve Metin, 1656–1704*. Edited by Abdülkadir Özcan. Ankara: TTK, 1995.

Feridun Ahmed Bey. *Münşeatü's-Selâtin*. 2 vols. Istanbul: Darü't-Tıbaati'l-Âmire, 1274/1858.

Kemalpaşazade. *Tevârih-i Âl-i Osman. X. Defter*. Edited by Şerafettin Turan. Ankara: TTK, 1991.

Lütfi Paşa. *Tevârih-i Âl-i 'Osman*. Edited by Kayhan Atik. Ankara: Kültür Bakanlığı, 2001.

Mustafa Naîmâ Efendi. *Tarih-i Naîma: Ravzatü'l-Hüseyn fi Hulâsati Ahbâri'l-Hâfikayn*. Edited by Mehmet İpşirli. 4 vols. Ankara: TTK, 2007.

Râşid Mehmed Efendi and Çelebizade İsmail Asım Efendi. *Târîh-i Râşid ve Zeyli*. Edited by Abdülkadir Özcan et al. 3 vols. Istanbul: Klasik Yayınları, 2013.

Sansovino, Francesco. *Dell'Historia Universale dell'origine et imperio de'Turchi parte prima(-terza)*. 2 vols. Venetia, 1560–61.

Sanuto, Marino. *I Diarii di Marino Sanuto*. 59 vols. Bologna: Forni Editore, 1969–70.

*Secondary Sources*

Agoston, Gabor. "Macaristanda Osmanlı-Habsburg Serhadı (1541–1699): Bir mukayese". In Güler Eren, Kemal Çiçek and Cem Oğuz (eds). *Osmanlı*. Ankara: Yeni Türkiye Yayınları, 2000, vol. 1, 443–51.

Ahmed Refik [Altınay]. *Lale Devri*. 2nd edn. Istanbul: Muhtar Halid Kitabhanesi, 1331/1912.

Bak, János and Béla K. Király (eds). *From Hunyadi to Rakoczi: War and Society in Late Medieval and Early Modern Hungary*. Brooklyn: Brooklyn College Press, 1982.

Brandi, Karl. *The Emperor Charles V: The Growth and Destiny of a Man and of a World-Empire*. Translated by C. V. Wedgwood (London: Jonathan Cape, 1939).

Domonkos, Leslie S. "The Battle of Mohacs as a Cultural Watershed". In János Bak and Béla K. Király (eds). *From Hunyadi to Rakoczi: War and Society in Late Medieval and Early Modern Hungary*. Brooklyn: Brooklyn College Press, 1982, 203–24.

Krodel, Gottfried G. "Law, Order, and the Almighty Taler: The Empire in Action at the 1530 Diet of Augsburg". *Sixteenth Century Journal* 13 (2) 1982, 75–106.

Murphey, Rhoads. "Continuity and Discontinuity in Ottoman Administrative Theory and Practice during the Late Seventeenth Century". *Poetics Today* 14 (2) 1993, 419–43.

Pálffy, Géza. "The Impact of the Ottoman Rule on Hungary". *Hungarian Studies Review* 28 (1–2) 2001, 110–32.

Pálffy, Géza. "The Bulwark and Larder of Central Europe (1526–1711)". In Ernő Marosi (ed.) *On the Stage of Europe: The Millennial Contribution of Hungary to the Idea of European Community*. Budapest: Research Institute for Art History of the Hungarian Academy of Sciences – Balassi, 2009, 100–24.

Perjés, Géza. *The Fall of the Medieval Kingdom of Hungary: Mohacs 1526 Buda 1541*. Boulder, CO: Atlantic Research and Publications, 1989.

Stoye, John. *The Siege of Vienna: The Last Great Trial Between Cross and Crescent*. New York: Pegasus Books, 2007.

Strong, Roy. *Art and Power: Renaissance Festivals, 1450–1650*. Woodbridge, Suffolk: Boydell Press, 1984.

Szakály, Ferenc. "The Hungarian-Croatian Border Defense System and Its Collapse". In János Bak and Béla K. Király (eds). *From Hunyadi to Rakoczi: War and Society in Late Medieval and Early Modern Hungary*. Brooklyn: Brooklyn College Press, 1982, 141–58.

Szakály, Ferenc. *Ludovico Gritti in Hungary: 1529–1534*. Budapest: Akadémiai Kiadó, 1995.

Türkal, Nazire Karaçay. "Silahdar Fındıklılı Mehmed Ağa: Zeyl-i Fezleke (1065–c.1106/ 1654–7 Şubat 1695)". Ph.D. dissertation, Marmara University, 2012.

Wilson, Peter H. *German Armies: War and German Politics, 1648–1806*. London: Routledge, 1998.

Yelçe, Nevin Zeynep. "Ottoman Reception and Perception of János Szapolyai in 1529". In Robert Born and Sabine Jagodzinski (eds). *Türkenkriege und Adelskultur in Ostmitteleuropa vom 16.–18. Jahrhundert*. Leipzig: Thorbecke Jan Verlag, 2014, 141–54.

Yılmaz, Mehtap. "Vekayi'name (Vekayi-i Bec)". Master's thesis, Marmara University, 2006.

CHAPTER 14

# *Bidʿat*, Custom and the Mutability of Legal Judgments: The Debate on the Congregational Performance of Supererogatory Prayers in the Seventeenth-Century Ottoman Empire

*Derin Terzioğlu*

"You want to get rid of all innovations whether they be good or bad. It is also an innovation to wear underpants. Will you also abolish them?" asked one of the refined ones, who had reservations about the [Kadızâdeli] sheikhs.

"Yes, we shall also abolish them. Let them wear waistcloths instead," answered Turk Ahmed.

"Eating with a spoon is also an innovation. What will you do about that?" asked the same man.

"We shall also abolish it. Let them eat with their hands. It is not poison! What harm will it do to have food smeared on their hands?"

The refined man was astounded and retorted with a laugh: "Now, effendis, you want to strip the people and dress them like bare-bottomed Bedouins!"

Another man in their company added: "O my sultan, how will spoon-makers make a living, if you forbid spoons?"

Turk Ahmed answered: "Let them make toothpicks and rosaries and make a living thus."

The refined man challenged Turk Ahmed: "If you have the Turks of Gerede and Taraklı make toothpicks and rosaries, then by what trade will the poor ones of the two holy sanctuaries [Mecca and Medina] support themselves?"[1]

∴

---

1 Mustafa Naîmâ Efendi, *Târih-i Naʿîmâ* (*Ravzatü'l-Hüseyn fî Hulâsati Ahbâri'l-Hâfikayn*), edited by Mehmet İpşirli (Ankara: TTK, 2007), vol. 4, 1710.

© DERIN TERZIOĞLU, 2021 | DOI:10.1163/9789004442351_016
This is an open access chapter distributed under the terms of the CC BY-NC 4.0 license.

This humorous verbal exchange between a supporter and two critics of the Sunni revivalist movement of the Kadızâdelis reveals a central tension that underlay the seventeenth-century Ottoman debates on Islamic orthopraxy: Was it possible, or even desirable, to purge the living practice of Muslims of all *bid'at*s, innovations that had infiltrated it since the time of the Prophet? Could one pursue such a campaign oblivious of local customs or of social, political, and economic exigencies? Was the status of controversial practices to be determined by the yardstick of the 'ancients' (*selef*) alone, or could one also take into consideration the 'changing conditions of the times'?

While this chapter is concerned specifically with the ways Ottoman scholars grappled with these questions in the seventeenth century, the question of legal change has been raised by Muslims at multiple points in the course of history and it became particularly pertinent in the modern era. To understand these debates, it is essential to keep in mind that even although the word 'sharia' is commonly translated into English as 'Islamic law', it has historically been a broader concept signifying religious and moral as well as legal norms. As Baber Johansen has elucidated, in the premodern Hanafi jurisprudential tradition, the religious and moral norms comprised under the rubric of the sharia addressed relations between believers and God, and evaluated human behaviour from the perspective of 'religiosity' (*diyāna*), while the legal norms (*aḥkām*, plural of *ḥukm*) regulated human relations in the here and now. The legal norms were concerned only with the external manifestations of human acts, while religious and moral norms also took into consideration questions of intention. *Kadıs* judged mainly in accordance with legal norms, whereas depending on the issue in question muftis had to juggle both sets of norms. Johansen has shown that throughout the history of Islamic religio-legal deliberation these two sets of norms coexisted in a state of dynamic (and sometimes tension-ridden) equilibrium until the attempts to broaden the scope of *aḥkām* and to make legal judgments coterminous with 'religion and morality' in the late-eighteenth century.[2] This chapter will show that some of these tensions were in fact already being played out in the debates about religious worship and social custom in the seventeenth-century Ottoman Empire.

---

2  Baber Johansen, "Die sündige, gesunde Amme: Moral und gesetzliche Bestimmung (*Ḥukm*) im Islamischen Recht", in Baber Johansen, *Contingency in a Sacred Law: Legal and Ethical Norms in the Muslim Fiqh* (Leiden: Brill, 1999), 172–88; for a discussion of how earlier western scholarship has reckoned with the religious and ethical dimensions of the sharia, see also *idem*, "Introduction", ibid., 42–72.

A second general point that needs to be made before going into the seventeenth-century debates concerns the mutability of Islamic legal judgments. As the voluminous scholarship on the history of Islamic law has amply demonstrated, the vast corpus of religio-legal deliberations known as the sharia came into being as a result of the intellectual efforts of generations of Muslim scholars, and continued to evolve in various ways after the 'formative period' of the Islamic jurisprudential tradition. Yet, because the sharia is, like all religio-legal traditions, conservative by definition, its practitioners have not always been able to recognize its mutability, but neither was it completely unrecognized. Recent scholarship has documented for us a number of instances in which premodern Muslim jurists recognized legal change as both a fact and a *necessity*, and expressed this insight with the words, "legal judgments change in accordance with the change of time."[3] At the same time, however, pre-modern Muslim scholars wanted to limit the variability of legal judgments. It became the norm from the thirteenth century onwards for (Sunni) jurists to adhere to one of the four (Sunni) schools of law (*mezheb*).[4] It was also around this time that scholars began to allude to the 'closing of the gates of *ijtihad*' or 'independent reasoning', though views on this matter have differed from *mezheb* to *mezheb* and within each *mezheb*.[5]

In the Hanafi legal school, which was the official school of law in the Ottoman Empire, adherence to *mezheb* consensus was particularly valued. Still, this did not prevent the Hanafi jurists in the Mamluk sultanate in the fifteenth century and in the Ottoman Empire in the sixteenth century from rethinking certain aspects of Hanafi jurisprudence to meet the changing needs

---

3  Kevin Reinhart, "When Women Went to Mosques: al-Aydini on the Duration of Assessments", in Muhammad Khalid Masud, Brinkley Messick and David S. Powers (eds) *Islamic Legal Interpretation: Muftis and their Fatwas* (Cambridge, MA: HUP, 1996), 116–28. See also Wael B. Hallaq, "The Jurisconsult, the Author-Jurist and Legal Change", in *idem, Authority, Continuity and Change in Islamic Law* (Cambridge: Cambridge University Press, 2001), 166; Marion Holmes Katz, "The 'Corruption of the Times' and the Mutability of the Shari'a", *Cardozo Law Review* 28 (1) 2006, 171–85.

4  On the formation and consolidation of the schools of law, see Mohammed Fadel, "The Social Logic of *Taqlīd* and the Rise of the *Mukhtaṣar*", *ILS* 3 (2) 1996, 193–233; Christopher Melchert, *The Formation of the Sunni Schools of Law, 9th–10th Centuries CE* (Leiden: Brill, 1997); Ahmed El Shamsy, *The Canonization of Islamic Law: A Social and Intellectual History* (New York: CUP, 2013).

5  Wael B. Hallaq, "Was the Gate of *Ijtihad* Closed?" *IJMES* 16 (1984), 3–41; *idem*, "From *Fatwās* to *Furūʿ*: Growth and Change in Islamic Substantive Law", *ILS* 1 (1) 1994, 29–65; *idem, A History of Islamic Legal Theories* (Cambridge: CUP, 1997), Chs 4 and 5; *idem*, "The Jurisconsult", 166–235.

of the state as well as the wider public.[6] In the Ottoman context, the political authorities also played an active role in this process both by promulgating new laws (*kanun*) and by setting up an imperial hierarchy of *ulema*. It was the top-ranking members of this newly established learned hierarchy, in turn, who reinterpreted Hanafi jurisprudential thought on such matters as the land tax and cash waqfs, and who, in cooperation with the political authorities, helped achieve a greater degree of harmony with the state laws and customs in the lands of Rum (Anatolia and the Balkans).[7]

Predictably, the Ottoman brand of Hanafism that was thus fashioned also had its critics. Dissenting voices were heard particularly among the non-state appointed scholars in the former Mamluk provinces,[8] but they were not absent among the state-appointed scholars in the core lands of the Ottoman Empire, either. The Rumi scholars who questioned the compatibility of time-honoured practices of Ottoman Muslims with Islamic law included even a one-time

---

6  Baber Johansen, *Islamic Law on Land Tax and Rent: The Peasants' Loss of Property Rights as Interpreted in the Hanafite Legal Literature of the Mamluk and Ottoman Periods* (London: Croom Helm, 1988); *idem*, "Legal Literature, and the Problem of Change: The Case of the Land Rent", in Johansen, *Contingency*, 446–64; and Martha Mundy and Richard Saumarez Smith, *Governing Property, Making the Modern State: Law, Administration and Production in Ottoman Syria* (London: I. B. Tauris, 2007).

7  On the developments in Hanafi law in the early modern Ottoman context, see, in addition to the sources cited in fn.6, Guy Burak, "Faith, Law and Empire in the Ottoman Age of Confessionalization (Fifteenth-Seventeenth Centuries), The Case of 'Renewal of Faith'", *Mediterranean Historical Review* 28 (1) 2013, 1–23; and *idem*, *The Second Formation of Islamic Law: The Hanafī School in the Early Modern Ottoman Empire* (Cambridge: CUP, 2015); Snjezana Buzov, "The Lawgiver and His Lawmakers: The Role of Legal Discourse in the Change of Ottoman Legal Culture", Ph.D. dissertation (Chicago University, 2005); Hülya Canbakal, "Vows as Contract in Ottoman Public Life (17th–18th Centuries)", *ILS* 18 (1) 2011, 85–115; Haim Gerber, *State, Society, and Law in Islam: Ottoman Law in Comparative Perspective* (Albany: SUNY, 1994); Colin Imber, *Ebu's-Suʿud: The Islamic Legal Tradition* (Stanford: SUP, 1997); Jon E. Mandaville, "Usurious Piety in the Ottoman Empire: The Cash Waqf Controversy", *IJMES* 10 (1979), 289–308.

8  While scholars have mostly dwelled on the tensions between the Rumi and Arab *ulema*, some recent scholars have presented a more nuanced view. For the first approach, see Reem Meshal, "Antagonistic *Sharīʿas* and the Construction of Orthodoxy in Sixteenth-Century Ottoman Cairo", *JIS* 21 (2) 2010, 183–212; Abdul Karim Rafeq, "The Syrian ʿUlamāʾ, Ottoman Law, and Islamic Sharīʿa", *Turcica* 26 (1994), 9–32; *idem*, "The Opposition of the Azhar ʿUlamāʾ to Ottoman Laws and its Significance in the History of Ottoman Egypt", in Brigitte Marino (ed.) *Études sur les villes du Proche-Orient XVIᵉ et XIXᵉ siècle: Hommage à André Raymond*, (Damascus: Institut français d'études arabes de Damas, 2001), 43–54; for more nuanced treatments, see Burak, *Second Formation*, especially chapters 3–5; and Helen Pfeifer, "Encounter After the Conquest: Scholarly Gatherings in 16th-century Ottoman Damascus", *IJMES* 47 (2015), 219–39.

şeyhülislâm, Çivizâde Muhyiddin Mehmed Efendi (d.1547), but perhaps the most influential of the Rumi critics over the long run was the more modestly ranked Birgivî Mehmed Efendi (d.1573), who, from his post as *müderris* in the small town of Birgi in western Anatolia, boldly challenged the opinions of the influential *Şeyhülislâm* Ebüssuûd (d.1574) on such issues as the legal status of cash waqfs, payment for religious services and land ownership.[9]

Yet, it was only in the seventeenth century that this internal critique of the Ottoman Sunni-Hanafi orthopraxy found greater support. This was, significantly, a time of crisis for the Ottoman state, shaking the confidence of many in the existing order, and increasing inter-elite competition and conflict. It was also a time when both the Ottomanization of the Arab provinces and the Sunnitization of the lands of Rum reached a certain level of maturity, and when intellectual exchange between scholars in different regions became greater. All these developments created a fertile ground for the outbreak of a series of new debates about Sunni-Hanafi orthopraxy in the Ottoman Empire.

One of the distinguishing features of the seventeenth-century debates was that they were no longer confined to the *mevâlî*, the fully-fledged scholars who served as *müderrises* and *müftis*, but were also overtaken and popularized by the *meşâyih*, Sufi and non-Sufi mosque preachers. One such preacher was Kadızâde Mehmed Efendi of Balıkesir (d.1635), who was a student of a student of Birgivî Mehmed Efendi and who later gave his name to the Kadızâdeli movement. The Kadızâdeli preachers used their sermons and public lectures to mobilize the ordinary men and ruling powers alike to 'command the right and forbid the wrong' (*emr bi'l-ma'rûf ve nehy 'an il-münker*) and to put an end to the 'blameworthy innovations' that were rampant in Ottoman lands. The practices they targeted as *bid'at* covered a wide range from coffee, coffeehouses and smoking to the use of ritual music and dance at Sufi gatherings, and from

---

9 Mehmet Gel, "XVI. Yüzyılın İlk Yarısında Osmanlı Toplumunun Dinî Meselelerine Muhalif Bir Yaklaşım: Şeyhülislam Çivizâde Muhyiddin Mehmed Efendi ve Fikirleri Üzerine Bir İnceleme", Ph.D. thesis (Gazi Üniversitesi, 2010); Katharina Anna Ivanyi, "Virtue, Piety and the Law: A Study of Birgivī Mehmed Efendi's al-Ṭarīqat al-Muḥammadiyya", Ph.D. dissertation (Princeton University, 2012); idem, "'And the Question of Lands is Very Confusing': Birgivî Mehmed Efendi (d.981/1573) on Land Tenure and Taxation", in Marinos Sariyannis (ed.) *Political Thought and Practice in the Ottoman Empire, Halcyon Days in Crete IX*, a symposium held in Rethymno, 9–11 January 2015 (Rethymno: Crete University Press, 2019), 137–47; Ahmet Kaylı, "A Critical Study of Birgivî Mehmed Efendi's Works and Their Dissemination in Manuscript Form" (MA thesis, Boğaziçi Üniversitesi, 2010); Mandaville, "Usurious Piety"; Huriye Martı, *Birgivî Mehmed Efendi* (Ankara: Türkiye Diyanet Vakfı Yayınları, 2008); Emrullah Yüksel, *Mehmed Birgivî'nin (929–981/1523–1573) Dinî ve Siyasî Görüşleri* (Ankara: Türkiye Diyanet Vakfı Yayınları, 2011).

asking for intercession at the tombs of the saints to the melodic recitation of the Quran and *ezân*.

In the secondary literature, the Kadızâdelis have been characterized variously as 'Sunni revivalists', 'fundamentalists', 'Muslim puritans', and 'salafis' *avant la lettre*.[10] As scholars have looked more closely at the religio-legal literature of the time, however, it has become clear that the Kadızâdelis actually shared a lot with other members of the Ottoman learned establishment and the learned Sufis, who often opposed them. We now know, for instance, that far from being crypto-Hanbalis, the Kadızâdeli leaders were just as deeply steeped in the Hanafi tradition as their adversaries.[11] But this realization has also come

10   Marc David Baer, *Honored by the Glory of Islam: Conversion and Conquest in Ottoman Europe* (Oxford: OUP, 2008); Michael Cook, *Commanding Right and Forbidding Wrong in Islamic Thought* (Cambridge: CUP, 2000), 323–30; Semiramis Çavuşoğlu, "The Ḳāḍīzādeli Movement: An Attempt of *Şerī'at*-minded Reform in the Ottoman Empire", Ph.D. dissertation (Princeton University, 1990); Ahmet Yaşar Ocak, "XVII. Yüzyılda Osmanlı İmparatorluğu'nda Dinde Tasfiye (Püritanizm) Teşebbüslerine Bir Bakış: Kadızadeliler Hareketi", *Türk Kültürü Araştırmaları* 1–2 (1983), 208–225; Marinos Sariyannis, "The Kadızadeli Movement as a Social Phenomenon: The Rise of a 'Mercantile Ethic'?" in Antonis Anastasopoulos (ed.) *Political Initiatives 'from the Bottom up' in the Ottoman Empire, Halcyon Days in Crete VII, 9–11 Jan. 2009*. Rethymno: Crete University Press, 2012, 263–89; E. Ekin Tuşalp Atiyas, "The 'Sunna-Minded' Trend", in Marinos Sariyannis (ed.) *A History of Ottoman Political Thought up to the Early Nineteenth Century* (Leiden, Boston: Brill, 2019), 233–78; Madeline C. Zilfi, "The Kadızadelis: Discordant Revivalism in Seventeenth-Century Istanbul", *Journal of Near Eastern Studies* 4 (1986), 251–71; idem, *The Politics of Piety: The Ottoman Ulema in the Postclassical Age (1600–1800)* (Minneapolis: Bibliotheca Islamica, 1988).

11   On the Hanafi framework of Birgivî and his Kadızâdeli followers, see Ivanyi, "Virtue, Piety and the Law", 76–82; Ömer Faruk Köse, "The Fatwa Collection of an Ottoman Provincial Mufti, Vani Mehmed Efendi (d.1685)" (MA thesis, Boğaziçi Üniversitesi, 2015), Chapter 3; Bernd Radtke, "Birgiwīs *Ṭarīqa Muḥammadiyya*: Einige Bemerkungen und Überlegungen", *JTS* 26 (1) 2002. This same article also appears in Jan Schmidt (ed.), *Essays in Honour of Barbara Flemming* (Cambridge, MA: Department of Near Eastern Languages and Civilizations, Harvard University, 2002), 159–74; Khaled El-Rouayheb, "From Ibn Ḥajar al-Haytamī (d.1566) to Khayr al-Dīn al-Ālūsī (d.1899): Changing Views of Ibn Taymiyya amongst Sunni Islamic Scholars", in S. Ahmed and Y. Rapoport (eds), *Ibn Taymiyya and His Times* (Oxford: OUP, 2010), 303–5. For scholars who continue to see the influence of Ibn Taymiyya in the writings of some Kadızâdelis, see Yahya Michot's Introduction to Ahmed el-Akhisari, *Against Smoking: An Ottoman Manifesto*, edited and translated by Yahya Michot (Leicestershire: Kube Publishing: 2010); Mustapha Sheikh, *Ottoman Puritanism and its Discontents: Aḥmad al-Rūmī al-Aqḥiṣārī and the Qāḍīzādelis* (Oxford: OUP, 2016); idem, "Taymiyyan Influences in an Ottoman-Ḥanafī Milieu: The Case of Aḥmad al-Rūmī al-Aqḥiṣārī", *The Royal Asiatic Society* 3 (2014), 1–20. For a reconsideration of the question of Taymiyyan influences in the early modern Ottoman context, see Caterina Bori, "Transregional Spaces of Reading and Reception", *The Muslim World*, 108 (1) 2018, 87–123; Derin Terzioğlu, "Ibn Taymiyya, *al-Siyāsa al-Sharʿiyya* and the Early Modern Ottomans", in

at the cost of obscuring what it was that set the Kadızâdelis apart. It has also led to a new tendency to downplay the doctrinal differences between the contending sides and to privilege instead the social and professional animosities that propelled the conflict. Ultimately, however, what needs to be done is to analyse the debates *both doctrinally and contextually*. What was it that led the Kadızâdeli preachers to oppose certain changes in the practices of Muslims, and not others? What was it that led their critics to come to the defence of some of these changes, and not others?

This chapter suggests some partial answers to these questions in the context of the debate on the congregational performance of supererogatory prayers, and particularly the popular nocturnal prayers of Raghā'ib, Barā'at and Qadr. Although this was one of some two dozen items of debate between the Kadızâdelis and their adversaries, it has not attracted much attention until now. This is, in a sense, understandable, for unlike coffee, coffeehouses and smoking, which had been introduced to the Ottoman capital in the mid-sixteenth and early-seventeenth centuries respectively,[12] the congregational performance of supererogatory prayers was a long-standing 'innovation'. The popular Raghā'ib, Barā'at and Qadr prayers had been around for centuries, and were seen by many to be an integral part of Islamic piety. But this is also what makes the debate about them particularly interesting and potentially even more revealing about the competing understandings of Islamic law and piety, and normative change in the seventeenth-century Ottoman Empire.

## 1 Debate on the Congregational Performance of the Raghā'ib, Barā'at and Qadr Prayers

To a modern, secular observer, a debate about whether or not to perform supererogatory prayers in congregation might not seem like a weighty issue that merits much attention. Yet, this was actually one of the more divisive issues

---

Tijana Krstić and Derin Terzioğlu (eds). *Historicizing Sunni Islam in the Ottoman Empire, c.1450–c.1750* (Leiden: Brill, 2020).

[12] On coffee, coffeehouses and smoking as well as the religio-legal debates about them, see James Grehan, "Smoking and 'Early Modern' Sociability: The Great Tobacco Debate in the Ottoman Middle East (Seventeenth to Eighteenth Centuries)", *American Historical Review* 111 (December 2006), 1352–77; Ralph Hattox, *Coffee and Coffeehouses: The Origins of a Social Beverage in the Medieval Near East* (Seattle: University of Washington Press, 1985); Cemal Kafadar, "How Dark is the History of the Night, How Black the Coffee and How Bitter the Tale of Love: The Measure of Leisure and Pleasure in Early Modern Istanbul", in Arzu Öztürkmen and Evelyn Birge Vitz (eds), *Medieval and Early Modern Performance in the Eastern Mediterranean* (Turnhout: Brepols, 2014), 243–69.

being debated by Muslims in the seventeenth century. Writing around 1656, the Ottoman bureaucrat and intellectual Kâtib Çelebi described with clear disapproval how some fanatical men sometimes walked out on the congregation in protest at the communal performance of the nocturnal supererogatory prayers.[13] But walking out on the congregation was still a mild reaction, considering that in 1703 madrasa students opposed to the practice physically attacked the people who performed the popular Qadr prayer in congregation in the Ulucami (Great Mosque) in Bursa, killing one and wounding several. The incident prompted a hastily summoned court case, the execution and banishment of a few of the perpetrators and heated discussion about the whole affair for long afterwards.[14]

Why did this issue provoke such strong feelings among Ottoman Muslims at the time? What was at stake in the debates about the congregational performance of supererogatory prayers? To answer these questions, it is first necessary to review some basic information about the legal stipulations concerning ritual worship. According to all four Sunni *mezheb*s, the primary obligatory prayers for Muslims are the five daily prayers, whereas supererogatory prayers (*nāfila*, plural *nawāfil*) are those extra prayers that they may perform either before or after the obligatory prayers. The latter should be undertaken on a voluntary basis and out of devotion to God. While the religious authorities thought that such voluntary acts of piety were, in principle, good, they also wanted to distinguish them clearly from obligatory acts of worship. They worried that ordinary Muslims could mistakenly believe these supererogatory prayers to be obligatory, or else engage in them to show off their piety rather than to perfect their devotion to God. Hence, the insistence of most early authorities that Muslims perform supererogatory prayers in the privacy of their homes rather than in congregation in mosques. An exception was made only for those prayers that were considered *sunna mu'akkada*, that is sanctioned by

---

13    Katib Çelebi, *The Balance of Truth*, translated with an Introduction and Notes by G. L. Lewis (London: George Allen and Unwin Ltd, 1957), 98–9.

14    The incident is reported in a slightly different way in two different hagiographical accounts covering the lives and deeds of the dervishes of the Mısrî branch of the Halvetî *tarikat* – Gazzîzâde 'Abdüllatif, *Menâkıb-ı Gazzî*, fol. 57a–59a, MS 1042, Orhan, Bursa Eski Yazma ve Basma Eserler Kütüphanesi; and Râkım İbrahim, *Vâkı'ât-ı Pîr-i Rûşen*, 17–18, MS 790, İzmir, SK. The attack and the subsequent court course case are also discussed in several different works by the Celveti sheikh İsmâil Hakkı Bursevî (d.1725). See İsmâil Hakkı Bursevî, *Kitâbü'n-Netîce: Bursevî'nin Vâridatı ve Şerhleri*, edited by Ali Namlı (Istanbul: TYEKBY, 2019), 743; İhsan Kara, "İsmail Hakkı Bursevi'nin *Tuhfe-i Hasekiyyesi* (3. Bölüm)", MA thesis (Marmara Üniversitesi, 1997), 135; Ali Namlı, *İsmâil Hakkı Bursevî: Hayatı, Eserleri, Tarikat Anlayışı* (Istanbul: İnsan Yayınları, 2001), 79–81.

the Prophet's own example, such as the *tarāwīkh* prayers performed during the nights of Ramadan.[15] The latter could be performed in congregation, just like the five daily prayers, the prayers of the two canonical religious festivals (*ʿīd al-fiṭr* and *ʿīd al-aḍḥā*) as well as a few other special prayers, such as the funeral prayer, the prayer of the eclipse, and the prayer for rainfall.[16]

As might be expected, the actual practices of ordinary believers did not always fit the prescriptive framework of the early authorities. Indeed, a series of new public forms of supererogatory worship sprang up in the course of the ninth, tenth and eleventh centuries along with a whole lore of stories and traditions that invested the corresponding days in the Islamic calendar with liturgical significance. The first of these days in the Islamic calendar was the twelfth day of the month of Rabīʿ al-awwal, celebrated as the birthday (*Mawlid*) of the Prophet Muhammad. Then came the Night of Raghāʾib, or Benefits, which fell on the first Friday of the month of Rajab, and which was widely believed to be the night on which the Prophet was conceived. The 27th night in the month of Rajab was celebrated as the Night of Miʿrāj, or Ascension, on which Muhammad was believed to have undertaken a nightly journey from Mecca to Jerusalem and ascended to Heaven. The Night of Barāʾat, or Forgiveness, on which God was believed to forgive a great number of sinners, was associated with the night preceding the fifteenth day of the month of Shaʿbān. Last but not least, the twenty-seventh night of the month of Ramadan was celebrated as the Night of Power (*laylat al-Qadr*), which is mentioned in the ninety-seventh chapter of the Quran, though without associating it with a particular date, as the night on which the Quran was revealed (97:1), and as being "more auspicious than a thousand months" (97:3).

The introduction and popularization of a plethora of commemorative practices on the above-mentioned days took place by popular demand as well as with the support of the political authorities. As for the religious authorities, they widely conceded that the celebrations in question were, as we might say, 'invented traditions', but while some vehemently opposed them as 'reprehensible innovations' (*bidʿa makrūha*), others were willing to accommodate them as 'good' or 'permissible innovations' (*bidʿa ḥasana*), and yet others tried to set some limits on the kinds of celebration and worship that people undertook on these occasions. The debates about these practices were particularly heated in

---

15  Some present-day *salafīs* also question the *sunna muʾakkada* status of the *tarāwīkh* prayers and object to their congregational performance.

16  For an overview of Islamic strictures on canonical ritual prayer, see Marion Holmes Katz, *Prayer in Islamic Thought and Practice* (Cambridge: CUP, 2013).

Ayyubid and Mamluk Syria, where critics were bothered by the resemblances between these commemorative practices and those of Shiites and Christians on their own holy days. The critics also maintained that investing specific days of the calendar with religious significance in the absence of Prophetic sanction was a particularly dangerous form of innovation, as ordinary believers commonly mistook the performance of supererogatory forms of worship on these occasions to be a 'shortcut to salvation'. People who participated enthusiastically in these public celebrations, it was argued, were often lax or negligent about observing their daily obligatory prayers and other forms of canonical worship.[17]

It must be remarked, however, that scholars did not oppose all these 'innovations' with equal vehemence. Among the five non-canonical nocturnal public celebrations described above, the celebration of Mawlid, the Prophet's birthday, was considered less objectionable as "it was based not on blatantly spurious hadith but on a historical event of widely accepted religious significance."[18] Scholarly opinion was similarly more favourable about the commemoration of the Prophetic Ascension. By contrast, a good deal of polemic revolved around the congregational performance of supererogatory prayers on the nights of Raghā'ib, Barā'at and Qadr,[19] which would also be the main item contested by seventeenth-century Ottoman scholars.

Even though a detailed study of the spread of these popular celebrations in Anatolia and the Balkans is still a desideratum, the available evidence indicates that Rumi Muslims also honoured these five nights with a variety of supererogatory acts of worship from at least the fourteenth century onwards.[20] As for the

---

17  On the popular practices conducted on the five 'meritorious' days and the religio-legal debates about them in the medieval Islamic context, see Marion Holmes Katz, *The Birth of the Prophet Muhammad: Devotional Piety in Sunni Islam* (Abingdon: Routledge, 2007), especially 143–68; Daniella Talmon-Heller, *Islamic Piety in Medieval Syria: Mosques, Sermons and Cemeteries under the Zangids and Ayyūbids (1146–1260)* (Leiden: Brill, 2007), 61–6; Daniella Talmon-Heller and Raquel Ukeles, "The Lure of a Controversial Prayer: Ṣalāṭ al-Raghā'ib (The Prayer of Great Rewards) in Medieval Arabic Texts and from a Socio-Legal Perspective", *Der Islam* 89 (2) 2012, 141–66.

18  Katz, *The Birth of the Prophet*, 153. See also Jonathan Brown, "Even If It's Not True It's True: Using Unreliable Ḥadīths in Sunni Islam", *ILS* 18 (2011), 21–3.

19  Katz, *The Birth of the Prophet*, 153.

20  An early reference to the celebration of the Prophet's birthday and the 'blessed nights in the three months' (namely the months of Rajab, Sha'bān and Ramadan) in the Rum geography comes up in the 1323 endowment deed of Asporça Hatun, the Greek-born wife of the second Ottoman ruler Orhan. The original deed, however, is not extant. What we have at hand is a copy made in 1555 from the original in the kadı court of Bursa. For the facsimile, Arabic transcription and (a rather loosely made) Turkish translation of this copy,

performance of supererogatory prayers in congregation, the practice seems to have been so well established among Rumi Muslims that in the fifteenth and sixteenth centuries the non-canonical congregations on the nights of Raghā'ib, Barā'at and Qadr were often mentioned in the same breath as the congregations for the canonical prayers. For instance, the *vakfiye* of Karamanoğlu Ali Bey, drafted in 1415, asks that the imam of his newly founded madrasa in Niğde lead not just the five daily prayers but also the Raghā'ib, Barā'at, *tarāwīkh* and Qadr prayers 'in congregation according to Islamic custom'.[21] Likewise, in both the late-fifteenth and late-sixteenth-century copies of the endowment deed of Mehmed II, the responsibility of the imams of the mosque of Mehmed II was defined as leading the congregation during "the five obligatory daily prayers, the *tarāwīkh* prayers, the prayer of the night of Raghā'ib and other prayers similar to these that are performed in congregation."[22] It is worth stressing that madrasa-trained religious experts were involved in the preparation of these endowment deeds. Clearly, not just the common folk or laymen at large, but also a broad cross-section of the *ulema* viewed the popular nocturnal prayers as part of canonical worship in the lands of Rum.

The widespread acceptance of the congregational performance of supererogatory prayers among the Rumi *ulema* of the fifteenth and sixteenth centuries is perhaps not that surprising, considering that the vast majority of them were Hanafis, who were known for their more accommodating stance towards popular customs. However, not *all* the Hanafi authorities were comfortable with the congregational performance of supererogatory prayers. One Hanafi authority who had raised his voice against the practice at a fairly early point

---

see Sezai Sevim and Hasan Basri Öcalan (eds), *Osmanlı Kuruluş Dönemi Bursa Vakfiyeleri* (Bursa: Osmangazi Belediyesi, 2010). For articles that provide glimpses into the Ottoman celebrations of the said five nights, see Halide Aslan, "Osmanlı İmparatorluğu'nda Mübarek Gün ve Gecelerden Kandiller", *İslam San'at, Tarih, Edebiyat ve Mûsikîsi Dergisi* 7 (13) 2009, 199–231; M. Tayyib Okic, "Çeşitli Dillerde Mevlitler ve Süleyman Çelebi 'nin Mevlid'inin Çevirileri", *Atatürk Üniversitesi İlahiyat Fakültesi Dergisi* 1 (1976), 17–78.

21  For the Arabic text, its Turkish translation and facsimile, see İsmail Hakkı Uzunçarşılı, "Niğde'de Karamanoğlu Ali Bey Vakfiyesi", *Vakıflar Dergisi* 2 (1942), 45–69, especially 51. It is worth emphasizing that the endowment deed has come down to our time in the originally drafted 1415 version.

22  For a copy of the Arabic endowment deed, dated 1496, see Tahsin Öz (ed.), *Zwei Stiftungsurkunden des Sultans Mehmed II. Fatih* (Istanbul: Devlet Matbaası, 1935), 113–14; for a copy drawn up in Turkish in the late-sixteenth century copy, see [Mehmed II, 'Fatih'], *Fatih Sultan Mehmet Vakfiyeleri* (Istanbul: T. C. Başbakanlık Vakıflar Genel Müdürlüğü, 2003), 249–50. For the dating of the endowment deed and its variant versions, see Çiğdem Kafescioğlu, *Constantinopolis/Istanbul: Cultural Encounter, Imperial Vision, and the Construction of the Ottoman Capital* (University Park, PA: PSU Press, 2009), 243–4, fn.118.

was the Khwarezmian scholar Ibn al-Bazzāzī (d.1424), who was also widely known and respected in the Ottoman lands. In fact, it was by citing Bazzāzī that the Aleppan-born Ottoman Hanafi scholar İbrahim Ḥalabī (d.1549) refuted the legitimacy of the same prayers in the long version of his manual on ritual ablution and prayer titled *Ghunyat al-Mutamallī* (Companion for the Worshipper), also known as *Ḥalabī Kabīr* (The Long Ḥalabī). Possibly, however, Ḥalabī did not feel he had much of a chance of winning this battle, as he concluded his refutation with the remark, "the majority of the common people in Rum believe that these prayers are obligatory, and do not abandon them even when they abandon their obligatory prayers."[23] This might explain why he did not include this polemical discussion in the shorter, and by all indications more popular, version of his manual, *Mukhtaṣaru Ghunyat al-Mutamallī* (The Abbreviated Companion for the Worshipper), also known as *Ḥalabī Ṣaghīr* (The Short Ḥalabī). Instead, he simply pointed out that it was 'better' to perform supererogatory prayers other than *tarāwīkh* and *taḥiyyat al-masjid* in the privacy of one's home rather than in congregation.[24]

It seems, however, that Ḥalabī was not alone in trying to dissuade Rumi Muslims from performing these nocturnal prayers in congregation. Between the years 1526 and 1534, the *şeyhülislâm* İbn Kemal (d.1534) also issued several fatwas against the congregational performance of the nocturnal prayers of Raghā'ib, Barā'at and Qadr. From one of these fatwas we learn that a scholar generically identified as 'Zeyd the scholar' (perhaps Ḥalabī?) had read out the *şeyhülislâm*'s fatwa against the practice from the pulpits of mosques; as a result, 'most imams' had ceased to perform these prayers in mosques, but 'some other imams' had not. It seems, however, that İbn Kemal was unwilling to push the matter further, because when asked what to do about the non-conforming imams, he merely stated that 'they become sinners' (*âsim olurlar*).[25]

In any case, by the mid-sixteenth century, the Ottoman learned establishment had overcome its short-lived aversion to this long-standing innovation. When Ebüssuûd became *şeyhülislâm* in 1545, he defended the congregational

---

23   İbrahim Ḥalabī, *Ḥalabī Kabīr* (Istanbul: Arif Efendi Matbaası, 1325/1907–8), 432–4.
24   İbrahim Ḥalabī, *Tam Kayıtlı Halebî-i Sagîr ve Tercemesi (Taharet ve Namaz Bölümleri)*, translated by Hasan Ege (Istanbul: Salah Bilici Kitabevi, 1982), 237–8.
25   For variant copies of these fatwas, see İbn Kemal, Fetava, MS. 118, fol. 5b–6a, Darülmesnevi, SK; MS. 1967, fol. 119b–120a, Nuruosmaniye; Nushî el-Nâsıhi/Mustafa b. Hamza b. İbrahim b. Veliyüddin. *al-Ḥayāt Sharḥ Shurūṭ al-Ṣalāṭ*, MS 971, fol. 3b, Carullah, SK. The fatwas are also cited in İbn Kemal, *Şeyhülislâm İbn Kemal'in Fetvaları Işığında Kanûnî Devrinde Osmanlı'da Hukukî Hayat*, edited by Ahmet İnanır (Istanbul: Osmanlı Araştırmaları Vakfı, 2011), 56.

performance of supererogatory prayers on the nights of Raghā'ib, Barā'at and Qadr in multiple fatwas. His rationale was that these prayers were simply too popular to be prohibited: 'the people at large honour' (*âmme-i nâsın itibarları vardır*) the congregational performance of supererogatory prayers on the nights of Raghā'ib, Barā'at and Qadr; therefore, 'it is not permissible to prohibit them', the *şeyhülislâm* ruled. Interestingly, his only caveat was that the imam should not keep the communal performance of the supererogatory *tasbīḥ* prayer excessively long, and unduly burden the congregation.[26]

Of course, the Sunna-minded criticisms directed at the congregational performance of these nocturnal prayers continued despite Ebüssuûd's defence of the practice. In his *Jalā' al-Qulūb*, completed in 1564, the *şeyhülislâm*'s foremost critic, Birgivî Mehmed Efendi, condemned those who persist in the performance of the Raghā'ib, Barā'at and Qadr prayers, 'especially in congregation', and pointed out that such scholars as Ibn al-Jawzī (d.1201) and Ibn al-Bawwāb (?) had revealed these prayers to be based on spurious hadiths.[27] In his *al-Ṭarīqat al-Muḥammadiyya*, written in 1572, Birgivî further stressed that innovations in worship come right after innovations in belief in their level of harmfulness and he urged Muslims to perform their canonical forms of worship in public while keeping their supererogatory acts of worship private. He did not, however, explicitly mention the congregational performance of the Raghā'ib, Barā'at and Qadr prayers in this specific instance.[28] All in all, his position on these prayers can be said to have been clearly critical but also devoid of excessive polemical overtones.

Evidence indicates that the objections to the congregational performance of these prayers assumed a new urgency after the celebration of the five 'blessed nights' – Mawlid, Raghā'ib, Mi'rāj, Barā'at and Qadr – was given new imperial sanction, and as a result became both more ostentatious and more institutionalized in the late-sixteenth century. While I have been unable to ascertain the factual basis of the traditions that ascribe a leading role to Selim II (r.1566–74)

---

26  Ebussuûd, *Şeyhülislâm Ebussuûd Efendi Fetvaları Işığında 16. Asır Türk Hayatı*, edited by Ertuğrul Düzdağ (Istanbul: Enderun Kitabevi, 1983), 61, fatwas numbered 201 and 202.

27  Birgivî Mehmed, *Jalā' al-Qulūb*, edited by 'Āmir Sa'īd al-Zībārī (Beirut, 1995), 64. I thank Evren Sünnetçioğlu for directing me to this passage.

28  For a succinct discussion of Birgivî's views on this matter as he lays them out in his *al-Ṭarīqat al-Muḥammadiyya*, see Ivanyi, "Virtue, Piety", 99, 144–5. Another treatise that is misattributed to Birgivî and that critiques the performance of the Raghā'ib, Barā'at and Qadr prayers in congregation is the *Risāla fī'l-Dhikr al-Jahrī* (Treatise on vocal *zikr*). This treatise, however, has been shown by Kaylı to be the work of Ahmed Rumî el-Akhisarî instead (Kaylı, "Critical Study", 72–8).

in this regard, a variety of contemporary sources attest to the role played by his son and successor, Murad III (r.1574–95), in promoting the public celebration of the Prophet's birthday. Selânikî Mustafa Efendi (d.1600), for instance, reports that in Rabīʿ al-awwal 996/February 1588, Murad III issued an imperial edict, ordering a public celebration of the Prophet's birthday throughout the empire. The sultan specifically ordered that *mevlids* (versified narratives about the birth of the Prophet) be recited in all mosques and *masjid*s, that the 'sinful umma' (*günâhkâr ümmet*) ask for the Prophet's intercession and occupy themselves with ritual prayer and that the minarets of all mosques be illuminated with oil lamps "as on the nights of Raghā'ib and Barā'at."[29]

As is evident from the wording of this order, as well as from the extant *vakfi-yes*, the custom of illuminating houses and mosques on the nights of Raghā'ib and Barā'at in the lands of Rum actually went back considerably further and, to judge by the testimony of the Meccan scholar Jār Allāh Muḥammad b. Fahd (d.1547), it had already been customary in 'the lands of Rum' in 1524 to illuminate the minarets of mosques with candles throughout the nights of Ramadan.[30] It would seem, nevertheless, that mosques began to be illuminated on a more lavish scale on all the five 'holy' nights as well as on Ramadan nights in the late-sixteenth century.[31] Though no one to date has established the exact chronology, it is tempting to think that the affixing of the generic name of *kandil* (literally oil lamp) to the nights of Mawlid, Raghā'ib, Miʿrāj, Barā'at and Qadr in modern Turkey also has its roots in the institutionalization of these celebrations around this time.

There were a number of factors that prompted the Ottomans to invest greater significance in these nocturnal celebrations during the reign of Murad III. First, Murad had a strong interest in Sufism and cultivated close links with a number of Sufi sheikhs to fashion himself as a saintly ruler, who

---

29  Selânikî Mustafa, *Tarih-i Selânikî*, edited by Mehmet İpşirli (Istanbul: Edebiyat Fakültesi Basımevi, 1989), vol. 1, 197–8.
30  Jār Allāh Muḥammad b. Fahd, *Nukhbat Bahjat al-Zamān bi-ʿImārat Makka li-Mulk Banī ʿUthmān*, edited by Qays Kāẓīm al-Janabī (Beirut: Dār al-Kutub al-Ilmiyya, 2010). I thank Guy Burak for this reference.
31  For a description of the illumination of mosques by a German priest who visited Istanbul in the 1570s, see Salomon Schweigger, *Ein newe Reyssbeschreibung auss Teutschland nach Constantinopel und Jerusalem* (Nurnberg, 1608; reprinted Graz: Akademische Druck- u. Verlagsanstalt, 1964), 192–3; for a fascinating discussion of the new trends in the illumination of mosques in a broader social and cultural context, see Kafadar, "How Dark is the History of the Night", 256–7.

combined in his person the highest spiritual *and* temporal authority.[32] He even seems to have entertained thoughts about being the *kutb* or pole, an inheritor of the spiritual legacy of Muhammad and, as such, it must have made a good deal of sense for him to promote the public celebration of Muhammad's birthday as well as other popular celebrations associated with the latter's life cycle. Second, Murad's reign was also a time of renewed warfare with the Safavids, as well as of intensified Ottoman efforts to promote Sunnism. What distinguished this phase of Ottoman Sunnitization was the increasingly active role played by sharia-abiding Sufis, who used their popular appeal not just to galvanize support for the Ottoman dynasty but also to promote a new 'Sunni-Sufi synthesis' as the heart of Ottoman religious orthodoxy.

There is evidence that some of these sharia-abiding, 'Sunnitizing' Sufi dervishes also actively encouraged Murad to endorse and promote the popular nocturnal Mawlid, Raghā'ib, Mi'rāj, Barā'at and Qadr celebrations as part of an imperial campaign of piety. One such Sufi was the Halveti sheikh and preacher İbrâhim b. Hakk Mehmed el-Kırımî (d.1593), also known as 'Tatar Sheikh'. In the letters he wrote to Murad in the late 1580s and early 1590s, Kırımî repeatedly reminded the sultan of the blessings of various months and days in the Islamic calendar, including Mawlid and Mi'rāj, as well as Raghā'ib and Barā'at, and urged him to honour them by having candles and oil lamps lit throughout his realms and by ordering his Muslim subjects to occupy themselves with prayer and fasting, as well as with acts of good work, on these dates. According to Kırımî, particular vigilance was needed in this matter as they were living in bad times (*yaramaz zaman*), a theme that would also surface in the defence of these celebrations in the seventeenth century, as we shall see further below.[33]

---

32  On Murad's preoccupation with Sufism and its political uses, see John J. Curry, '"The Meeting of the Two Sultans': Three Sufi Mystics Negotiate with the Court of Murād III", in John J. Curry and Erik S. Ohlander (eds), *Sufism and Society: Arrangements of the Mystical in the Muslim World, 1200–1800* (London: Routledge, 2012), 223–42; Özgen Felek, "(Re)creating Image and Identity: Dreams and Visions as a Means of Murād III's Self-Fashioning", in Özgen Felek and Alexander D. Knysh (eds), *Dreams and Visions in Islamic Societies* (Albany: SUNY, 2012), 249–72.

33  The letters that Kırımî sent to Murad III remained forgotten until the mid-eighteenth century, when they were rediscovered and recopied but also misascribed to another famous Sufi of his time, Aziz Mahmud Hüdâ'î. For a correction of the authorship and analysis of the political contents of the letters, see Derin Terzioğlu, "Power, Patronage, and Confessionalism: Ottoman Politics as Seen through the Eyes of a Crimean Sufi, 1580–1593", in Marinos Sariyannis (ed.), *Political Thought and Practice in the Ottoman Empire*, Halcyon Days in Crete IX: A Symposium Held in Rethymno, 9–11 January 2015 (Rethymno: Crete University Press, 2019), 149–86. For the passages on the nocturnal celebrations, see

This reference to the corruption of the age, coming from a Sufi sheikh deeply implicated in the nitty-gritty of imperial politics, should not be taken as just a timeless topos of moral decline. This was, after all, a time when military and civic disturbances were becoming more common in Istanbul and beyond, and when mosques were emerging as spaces where crowds would gather to express discontent and even to plan collective modes of action against specific policies and their architects.[34] In this connection, it made sense for the palace to reclaim the mosques as imperial spaces, and the imperialization of the already popular nocturnal prayers must have been seen as a particularly effective way to do so.

At the same time, however, the imperialization of these popular celebrations also prompted some men of religion to critique these practices in a more public fashion. An early instance of such criticism occurred during the reign of Mehmed III (1595–1603), when Sun'ullâh Efendi, shortly after being appointed şeyhülislâm in 1599, spoke out against serving candy and sherbet to the grandees (ekâbir ü a'yân) who gathered in royal mosques to listen to the recitation of the Prophet's nativity poem on the twelfth night of Rabī' al-awwal. Sun'ullâh deemed the practice an 'ugly innovation' (çirkin bid'at), as well as wasteful, and called for the money of royal endowments to be spent instead on 'feeding the poor and the righteous' in madrasas and soup kitchens.[35] Clearly, however,

---

Mustafa Salim Güven (ed.), "Çeşitli Yönleriyle Azîz Mahmûd Hüdâyî'nin Mektupları", MA thesis (Marmara Üniversitesi, 1992), 25–6, 30, 47, 74, 97, 115, 130, 146–8. From these letters we also learn that Kırımî planned to write a treatise about the mysteries associated with the months of Şaban and Ramazan (p. 30), and that he had already written a treatise about the spiritual qualities of the night of Qadr and sent it to the sultan. (130–1).

34 For examples of political grievances being expressed in royal mosques during the 1590s, see Derin Terzioğlu, "Sunna-minded Sufi Preachers in Service of the Ottoman State: The Naṣīḥatnāme of Hasan Addressed to Murad IV", AO 27 (2010), 252–4; and Baki Tezcan, *The Second Ottoman Empire: Political and Social Transformation in the Early Modern World* (Cambridge: CUP, 2012), 6. For the rebellion of 1687, see 122–3. Royal mosques would play an even more critical role in the numerous political rebellions that punctuated Istanbul's history in the course of the seventeenth century.

35 Selânikî, *Tarih-i Selânikî*, vol. 2, 826. If Sun'ullâh expressed this opinion in the form of a fatwa, I could not locate it in his fatwa collection. However, I was able to locate another fatwa of his that deems it reprehensible (mekrûh) to serve food in masjids 'on some nights' (ba'zı leyâlîde). This indicates that Sun'ullâh objected to the serving of food and drinks in mosques categorically rather than to their being served to the grandees alone. For the relevant fatwa, see Sun'ullâh Efendi, *Fetâvâ-yi Sun'ullâh Efendi*, MS 502 fol.65b, Hasan Hüsnü Pasha, SK. For a slightly different reading of the Selânikî passage, see Gülru Necipoğlu, *The Age of Sinan: Architectural Culture in the Ottoman Empire* (Princeton: Princeton University Press, 2005), 516.

Sunʿullâh's admonition was not heeded, and the custom of serving food and drink (including coffee) to members of the congregation on major feast days continued throughout the seventeenth century. Likewise, the celebration of the Prophet's birthday was further imperialized in the reign of Ahmed I (1603–17), when it became a royal custom to commemorate it in the newly built mosque of Sultan Ahmed in the presence of all the high and mighty.[36]

When controversy truly flared up about innovations in religious worship in the 1620s and 1630s, it was not about serving food and drink in mosques on the occasion of the Mawlid, or on other occasions, but about the congregational performance of supererogatory prayers on the nights of Raghāʾib, Barāʾat and Qadr. Indeed, all the major figures associated with the Kadızâdeli movement, such as Kadızâde Mehmed Efendi of Balıkesir, Ahmed Rumî el-Akhisarî (d.1632), Üstüvânî Mehmed Efendi (d.1661) and Vanî Mehmed Efendi (d.1685), condemned the congregational performance of supererogatory prayers on these three nights as a blameworthy innovation.[37] It is unclear why the Kadızâdeli preachers were so opposed to the Raghāʾib, Barāʾat and Qadr prayers, but said nothing about the Miʿrāj or Mawlid ceremonies. Perhaps their accommodating stance on the Mawlid ceremonies stemmed from a reluctance to go against the imperial will on this matter; or perhaps, they were simply following the traditionalist scholars of thirteenth-century Syria and Egypt in going after only those ceremonies that were being legitimated with 'blatantly spurious hadiths'.

Indeed, such 'spurious hadiths' were at the forefront of the objections raised to the Raghāʾib and Barāʾat prayers by a Meccan scholar of Herati origin, ʿAlī al-Qārī (d.1605), at the turn of the sixteenth century. Like Çivizâde Muhyiddin Mehmed Efendi (d.1547), Ḥalabī and Birgivî before him, Qārī was a Hanafī scholar with a traditionalist bent, but unlike them, he was also a complete outsider to the Ottoman learned establishment, and had never held an official appointment, supporting himself instead as a calligrapher. While Qārī penned treatises in various branches of the Islamic sciences, he was particularly famous for his work on hadith criticism. It was also in a work on inauthentic hadiths that he debunked a number of traditions that were frequently cited to legitimize the Raghāʾib, and Barāʾat prayers.[38] It is worth noting that at

---

36  On the imperialization of the Mawlid ceremonies, see Necipoğlu, *The Age of Sinan*, 516.

37  For an exposition of the views of Kadızâde Mehmed, Üstüvânî Mehmed and Vanî Mehmed on the matter, see Çavuşoğlu, "The Ḳāḍīzādeli Movement", 248–52; for the views of Akhisarî, see Sheikh, *Ottoman Puritanism and its Discontents*, 131–6.

38  ʿAlī al-Qārī, *al-Asrār al-Marfūʿat fī l-Akhbār al-Mawḍūʿat*, edited by Muhammad b. Lutfī Sabbāgh (Beirut: Dār al-Amāna, 1971), 459–62; for more on his life and thought, see

least one of the hadiths that the Meccan scholar debunked, which attributed to the Prophet the words, "Rajab is the month of God, Shaʿbān is my month and Ramadan is the month of my community", was also frequently referenced in the letters of İbrâhim-i Kırımî to Murad III.[39] Could Qārī have articulated his criticism in response to the promotion of such spurious traditions by the likes of Kırımî? This is a distinct possibility, considering that there was a constant flow of scholars and Sufis as well as lay pilgrims between Istanbul and Mecca, relaying information orally as well as in writing. Considering the intellectual affinity between Qārī and the Kadızâdelis and the fact that the former's works are amply represented in the manuscript collections of Istanbul libraries, it would be worth investigating whether this Meccan scholar's objections to the said hadiths also provided an early spark for the seventeenth-century controversy about the popular nocturnal prayers.

Whatever the case may be with Qārī, there are other reasons to think that the outburst of polemic against the congregational performance of the Raghāʾib, Barāʾat and Qadr prayers in Istanbul during the 1630s was inspired, at least in part, by the objections raised to these prayers somewhat earlier in the Arab provinces of the empire. In a tract he penned to refute the legitimacy of the Raghāʾib, Barāʾat and Qadr prayers, Kadızâde Mehmed of Balıkesir claimed to have read more than one hundred works on the topic and to have conversed about it with the "*ulema* of Mecca, Medina, Jerusalem, Cairo, Damascus, Aleppo, the Maghrib, [lands of the] *Özbek* and India", and reported on their authority that they all considered the practice inadmissible.[40] Even though Kadızâde Mehmed did not indicate where he had these conversations, one of

---

Patrick Franke, "The Ego of the Mullah: Strategies of Self-Representation in the Works of the Meccan Scholar ʿAlī al-Qārī (d.1606)", in Ralf Elger and Yavuz Köse (eds), *Many Ways of Speaking About the Self: Middle Eastern Ego-Documents in Arabic, Persian, and Turkish (14th–20th century)* (Wiesbaden: Harrassowitz Verlag, 2010), 185–200; Cağfer Karadaş, "Ali el-Kârî'nin Akaide Dair Eserleri ve Bazı İtikadi Görüşleri", MA thesis (Marmara Üniversitesi, 1991); idem, "Ali el-Kârî'nin Hayatı, Selef Akîdesine Dönüş Çabası ve Eserleri", *Uludağ Üniversitesi İlahiyat Fakültesi Dergisi* 5 (5) 1993, 287–99; Fikret Soyal, "Celâleddin ed-Devvânî'nin Firavun'un İmânı Konusundaki Görüşleri ve Ali el-Kârî'nin Eleştirisi", MA thesis (Istanbul Üniversitesi, 2004).

39  See, for instance, Güven, "Çeşitli Yönleriyle", 47, 115, 146–8.
40  Kadızâde Mehmed, [Untitled treatise], MS 5563, fol. 44b–47b, esp. 45b, Yazma Bağışlar, SK. The treatise is recorded under various titles such as *Risâle-i Kâdızâde, Risâle-i Salât*, and *Risâle fî Îmân ve İslâm*. For a recent discussion of this treatise, see Baki Tezcan, "A Canon of Disenchantment: Birgivi, Rumi and Kadızade", in idem, *A Gift for the Turks: Studies on Islam and Its Early Modern Transformation in the Ottoman Empire*. Istanbul: ISIS Press, forthcoming 2020.

these venues was probably Cairo, a city that regularly attracted scholars from the said lands and that the Rumi preacher himself had visited at least once, in 1611/12.[41]

That Cairo was an early venue for debates on the congregational performance of supererogatory prayers is also clear from the *Mebâhisü's-Salât* (Discourses on Ritual Prayer), a detailed handbook on ritual ablution and prayer. The author of this work, Mustafa bin Hamza bin İbrahim bin Veliyüddin, who went by the penname of Nushî el-Nâsıhî, was originally from Bolu, but had either relocated to or frequently visited Cairo. He was also living in that city in 1624/5, when a debate erupted in that town about the legitimacy of the congregational performance of supererogatory prayers.[42] It might be worth pointing out that although Nushî dates this debate to 1624/5, the text in which he presents his views on the topic was the product of a later period. Nushî writes that he compiled the material for his handbook over the course of some two decades, finished the task of compilation and translation in 1633/4, and made a clean copy of the work in 1635/6.[43] Since the author was still in Cairo in 1635/6, it might seem that he was basically responding to the debate in that specific city rather than the one raging in the principal cities of Rum.[44] That he chose to bring up this issue only in his Turkish-language compendium on ritual prayer and not in the Arabic version, however, suggests that the intended audience of his remarks on the congregational performance of supererogatory prayers was first and foremost the Turcophone Muslims of Rum. This does not of course preclude the fact that the Rumis who participated in this debate were scattered across the Ottoman territories, and that some lived, like Nushî, in smaller Rumi communities surrounded by non-Rumis in such cosmopolitan centres as Cairo.

---

41  For Kadızâde Mehmed's time in Cairo, and his contact with Arab scholars, there, see Baki Tezcan, "The Portrait of the Preacher as a Young Man: Two Autobiographical Letters by Kadızade Mehmed from the Early Seventeenth Century", in Marinos Sariyannis (ed.) *Political Thought and Practice in the Ottoman Empire*, Halcyon Days in Crete IX: A Symposium Held in Rethymno, 9–11 January 2015 (Rethymno: Crete University Press, 2019), 202–3.

42  Nushî, *Mebâhisü's-Salât*, MS 948, fol. 151b–155a, 181a–187b. For a preliminary discussion of Nushî's identity, see Derin Terzioğlu, "Where *'Ilm-i Ḥāl* Meets Catechism: Islamic Manuals of Religious Instruction in the Ottoman Empire in the Age of Confessionalization", *PP* 220 (2013), 88. For the identification of his full name, see Tezcan, "The Portrait", 228–9.

43  Nushî, *Mebâhisü's-Salât*, MS 948, fol. 2b–3a, 111a.

44  For his whereabouts in that year, see Nushî, *al-Ḥayāt Sharḥ*, 136b–137a.

## 2 In Defence of the Congregational Performance of Supererogatory Prayers

For the rest of this chapter, I will dwell mainly on the arguments made by Nushî and another early seventeenth-century scholar, 'Abdülkerim Sivâsî, in defence of the congregational performance of supererogatory prayers on the nights of Raghā'ib, Barā'at and Qadr, as they offer interesting perspectives on the question of religious custom and change. Before turning to these arguments, however, it might be helpful to first locate these scholars a bit more precisely in the social and religious landscape of the early-seventeenth-century Ottoman Empire.

Who, or what kind of a Muslim was Nushî, and what was his relationship to the Kadızâdelis, if any? Since the author does not appear in any of the principal biographical dictionaries of the time, we can answer this question only in the light of his own writings. Nushî describes himself as belonging to 'the lowest ranks of the *ulema*' (*ednâ-i zümre-i 'ulemâ*), but he also writes of being the only person in his time to hold a certificate of transmission (*sened*) handed down across twenty-three generations from the founding father of the Hanafi legal school, Abū Ḥanīfa (d.767)[45] Even although Nushî does not provide any further information about his occupation, his use of the honorific 'Sheikh' and his penname 'Nushî', meaning 'advice-giver', suggest that he made his living as a preacher.[46] Such an occupation would also be consonant with the kinds of works he penned. Of the six works that we can attribute to Nushî, two are in Turkish, and the rest in Arabic, but all are basically handbooks written with the aim of enlightening ordinary men and women about the fundamentals of Islamic faith and practice.[47] In these works, Nushî pres-

---

45  Nushî, *Mebâhisü's-Salât*, 1a.
46  Ibid., 237b.
47  One of these works is a Turkish *'ilmihâl* titled *Mebâhisü'l-Îmân* or *Mebhas-ı Îmân*, which was written sometime between 1633 and 1636, and is discussed in Terzioğlu, "Where *'Ilm-i Ḥāl* Meets Catechism", 89–107. The other Turkish work is *Mebâhisü's-Salât*, discussed above. The remaining texts are in Arabic, and comprise *al-Ḥayāt Sharḥ Shurūṭ al-Salāt*, and *Manqūlat al-Dalā'il*, both which also deal with issues of ritual ablution and prayer, *Sharḥ Waṣiyyat al-Imām al-Aẓam*, which is a commentary on the famous creed attributed to Abū Ḥanīfa, and which was written in 1638/9, *al-Risālat al-Umniya l-Muhimma fī Bayāni'l-Udhiya 'alā l-Umma*, which deals with ritual animal sacrifice, and which was written in 1638, and *Risāla fī Dhikri A'immati l-Arba'a l-Mujtahidīn wa-Ba'aḍi'l-Masā'ili l-Fiqhiyya*, which deals with the founding fathers of the four Sunni legal schools and some legal issues. For a discussion of the authorship of these last five works, see Mustafa

ents himself as basically a 'compiler' (*câmi', musannif*) of religious knowledge, someone who culled, translated and reorganized key passages from 'reputable books' (*kütüb-i mu'tebere*) for the benefit of laymen and women. In contrast to Kadızâde Mehmed, who often used the works of others without acknowledgment, Nushî was extremely careful to identify his sources and included in each of his compendia a separate list of 'reputable books'. As one might expect from a Rumi scholar, most of his sources were by Hanafi-Maturidi scholars, and in his Turkish *'ilmihâl*, he directed his readers to consult, in addition to the many Arabic creeds and legal compendia, the Turkish *'ilmihâl*s of Birgivî Mehmed and Ahmed Rumî el-Akhisarî.

There is evidence that at least one work of Nushî's, the above-mentioned Turkish *'ilmihâl*, was popular in Kadızâdeli circles, so much so that in quite a few codices the text is misattributed to Kadızâde Mehmed and in some other codices, selections from it are reconfigured in the form of an independent treatise attributed to the latter.[48] The mix-up between the two men is actually quite understandable in the light of their many similarities: both men greatly valued the writings of Birgivî Mehmed; both were strongly Sunna-minded and objected to such popular pastimes as smoking and frequenting coffeehouses as well as the Sufi practices of ritual music and dance and the melodic chanting of the names of God as 'blameworthy innovations'; and yet, both were at the same time Sufis themselves, and even adherents of the same, Nakşbendi, *tarikat*, which stood out among the various Sufi *tarikat*s for the sobriety of its rituals and the especially high regard of its adherents for the sharia.[49]

As we shall see below, Nushî and Kadızâde Mehmed did not think alike on all issues: they actually took the opposite sides in the debate on the congregational performance of supererogatory prayers. There is even reason to believe that Nushî deferred on that issue to someone who may have been affiliated

---

İsmail Dönmez, "Kuşadalı Mustafa bin Hamza ve '*Netâicü'l-Efkâr fi Şerhi'l-İzhâr*' Adlı Eseri (İnceleme ve Tahkik)", Ph.D. dissertation, Marmara Üniversitesi, 2013, 27  30.

48   For example, see Nushî el-Nâsıhi/Mustafa b. Hamza b. İbrahim b. Veliyüddin, *Mebhas-ı Îmân* MS 5563, fol. 59a–137a, Yazma Bağışlar, SK. For an early example of the short *risâle* version of the same text, see Kadızâde Mehmed, MS TY 3529, fol. 116b–121a, TY, IUK. We can confidently rule out the authorship of *Mebhas-ı Îmân* by Kadızâde Mehmed, as the said work is explicitly referenced in *Mebâhisü's-Salât* (10a), and as the author clearly identifies himself by name in the latter work.

49   While Nushî's Sufi identity comes out the most clearly in his *'ilmihâl*, he is identified as a Nakşbendi in the manuscript copies of several other works. For one such copy of his *Mebâhisü's-Salât* in Cairo, see *Fihris Makhtūtāt al-Turkiya al-'Uthmāniyya*, vol. 4, 19, no. 4192. For Kadızâde Mehmed's Nakşbendi affiliation, see Tezcan, "The Portrait of the Preacher", 202.

with the Kadızâdelis' arch-enemies. Nushî writes that when he first heard of the objections to the congregational performance of supererogatory prayers, he wanted the opinion of a master jurist on the issue. Thus, he turned to ʿAbdülkerim Sivâsî, whom he describes as a "verifying scholar, a meticulous man of religion, a perfected man of virtue, a practising ascetic, and a second Abū Yūsuf". As far as I could ascertain, the only ʿAbdülkerim Sivâsî who lived in this time period and who could fit the profile given by Nushî was a younger brother of the famous Halveti sheikh ʿAbdülmecid Sivâsî (d.1639), who was the foremost adversary of Kadızâde Mehmed of Balıkesir. In the vita of Şemseddin Sivâsî, written by Receb Sivâsî sometime during the reign of Ahmed I (1603–17), Abdülkerim Sivâsî is mentioned as working as a preacher in a Friday mosque in Zile in north-central Anatolia.[50] Unfortunately, I have been unable to find any trace of this ʿAbdülkerim in later years, so if he were the same person as the scholar who issued the fatwa in answer to Nushî's question, it is impossible to tell whether he, too, was in Cairo at the time, or whether Nushî sought him out by writing him a letter. Neither do we know whether ʿAbdülkerim Sivâsî was also affiliated to the Sivâsî branch of the Halveti *tarikat*, but even if he had been, this need not have prevented Nushî from honouring him, for, as Dina Le Gall has pointed out, there was no categorical animosity between adherents of these two brotherhoods at the time.[51] It would thus not have been strange for Nushî and ʿAbdülkerim Sivâsî to think similarly on various issues.

---

50   Receb Sivâsî, *Necmü'l-Hüdâ fî Menâkıbi'ş-Şeyh Şemseddîn Ebi's-Senâ*, MS 694/2, fol. 40a, Lala İsmail, SK. It has been published as *Hidâyet Yıldızı: Şems-ed-dîn-i Sivâsî Hazretlerinin Menkıbeleri*, translated by Hüseyin Şemsi Güneren and edited by Fatih Güneren (Istanbul: n.d.), 73. Astonishingly, this rich source on the Halveti-Sivâsî sheikhs has been remarkably underutilized by modern scholars. This is a serious shortcoming in that some of the basic information contained in this work contradicts the information given by the later biographers, and which is often repeated uncritically in the secondary literature. For instance, we learn from this text that Receb Sivâsî did not die in 1599 or 1600, as was claimed by the later biographers, but was still alive during the reign of Ahmed I (1603–17), when, he says, finished his vita of Şemseddin Efendi. We also learn that ʿAbdülmecid Sivâsî himself was still based in Zile at the time Receb Sivâsî was writing his vita. Clearly, it would be important to verify all these dates against archival evidence, a task that lies outside the scope of this chapter. For the standard biographical narrative on ʿAbdülmecid Sivâsî, based overwhelmingly on the later biographical sources, see Cengiz Gündoğdu, *Bir Türk Mutasavvıfı Abdülmecîd Sivâsî (971/1563–1049/1639): Hayatı, Eserleri ve Tasavvufi Görüşleri* (Ankara: Kültür Bakanlığı, 2000), 39–85, 134–47; *idem*, "Sivâsî, Abdülmecid", DİA 37 (Istanbul, 2009), 286–7.

51   Dina Le Gall, "Kadızadelis, Nakşbendis, and Intra-Sufi Diatribe in Seventeenth-Century Istanbul", *The Turkish Studies Association Journal* 28 (1–2) 2004, 1–28; *idem*, *A Culture of Sufism: Naqshbandīs in the Ottoman World, 1450–1700* (Albany, NY: SUNY Press, 2005),

This having been said, the arguments that Nushî and ʿAbdülkerim Sivâsî presented in defence of the congregational performance of supererogatory prayers were complementary, but not identical. More as a compiler of juridical opinions than as a master jurist, Nushî launches the discussion of the Raghāʾib, Barāʾat and Qadr prayers by restating the conventional Sunni-Hanafi view that "it is better to perform supererogatory prayers at home and then go to the mosque." However, right after, he qualifies this remark with the words "but it has been said that *in our time* it is better to perform supererogatory prayers in mosques and masjids than at home" (my emphasis).[52] Perhaps because it was no light matter to argue that sharʿi judgments could change over time, Nushî himself does not elaborate on this line of argument, but defers instead to the expert opinion of ʿAbdülkerim Sivâsî on this matter.

The fatwa issued by Sivâsî, and reproduced, seemingly in full, in the *Mebâhisü's-Salât*, begins by unequivocally stating that "it is not permissible to prohibit the (congregational performance of the supererogatory) prayers of Raghāʾib and Qadr."[53] Even so, however, Sivâsî acknowledges that the said prayers are an instance of 'innovations in religious worship'. He also concedes that the earliest Muslim authorities strongly disapproved of such innovations. He, then, gives the example of Ibn ʿAbbās, a cousin of the Prophet Muhammad and an important early transmitter of hadiths. Accordingly, when Ibn ʿAbbās saw some Muslims form a circle and perform *zikr* in the mosque of the Messenger of God, he beat them with a stick and expelled them from the mosque, because they were indulging in a liturgical act that was not based on the example of the Prophet. Clearly, Sivâsî considered the precedent set by Ibn ʿAbbās to constitute the basis of all the later indictments of such innovations as the Raghāʾib, Barāʾat and Qadr prayers, and in the rest of his answer, he strives to show why this judgment of Ibn ʿAbbās can no longer apply 'in our time'.

Sivâsî builds his counterargument by citing the juridical principle that *'sharʿi* judgments change with the change of times'. He also illustrates why it would not serve the interests of religion to apply the prohibition of Ibn ʿAbbās to the case of the Raghāʾib and Qadr prayers in his own time. The gist of his argument is that the Muslims of his time are not only less pious and righteous

---

chapter 6. For a prominent Nakşbendi who polemicized *against* the Kadızâdelis, see Barbara Rosenow von Schlegell, "Sufism in the Ottoman Arab World: Shaykh ʿAbd al-Ghanī al-Nābulusī (d.1143/1731)", Ph.D. dissertation (University of California, Berkeley, 1997).

52  Nushî, *Mebâhisü's-Salât*, 149b–150a.

53  Ibid., 153a–154b. For the modern Turkish transliteration and English translation of the text, see Appendix.

than the first three generations of Muslims, but are also exposed to many more worldly temptations from wine-houses to coffeehouses and even to brothels. In such a context, the only remedy can be to encourage people to go to mosques and masjids, even if the acts of worship they perform in these places are not entirely free of abomination (kerâhet). It is interesting that Sivâsî also mentions the illumination of mosques and masjids with candles and oil lamps among the practices that would have been foreign to the austere piety of the earliest Muslims. In this manner, he reminds his opponents that they would have to object to many more features of devotional life, if they were to be logically consistent and insist on absolute adherence to the example of the Prophet and the earliest Muslims. He also drives home the same point by asking a hypothetical opponent: "O ignorant one, is there any worship in our own time that is free of abomination?" In Sivâsî's esteem, to insist on a rigid and narrow application of the Sunna at this point in time was not only infeasible but was also bound to be counterproductive, depriving Muslims of valuable channels to orient themselves towards God.

Reading Sivâsî's argument, one is immediately reminded of Baber Johansen's argument about the complex relationship between the religio-moral and legal dimensions of the shariah. Indeed, one could say that Sivâsî's fatwa represents an excellent example of how a premodern mufti could negotiate the productive tension between religio-moral and legal norms. There is no doubt that Sivâsî's argument foregrounded what he considered to be the higher dictate of 'religiosity' over strict adherence to an earlier legal ruling. Without denying the moral authority of the first generations of Muslims, who had formulated the legal ruling against performing supererogatory prayers in congregation, Sivâsî highlighted the impossibility of replicating their ways in the changed circumstances of his own times. Rather than trying to adhere blindly to the letter of the pronouncements of the *selef*, who lived in a significantly different context, he argued, it is important to figure out how to realize the essence of their call and live a life of piety and godliness in these more complex and challenging times.

It is clear from his presentation of the fatwa that Nushî agreed with Sivâsî on this matter. Interestingly, however, in the rest of the text, Nushî defends the congregational performance of supererogatory prayers on more technical grounds and with reference to its being rooted in local customs. The early authorities that ruled against the practice, Nushî argues, were actually targeting only those cases in which a special call to prayer preceded the congregational performance of supererogatory prayers. However, since no such special call to prayer precedes the congregational performance of supererogatory prayers in the lands of Rum, the earlier condemnations cannot apply to their case, he reasons.[54]

Nushî also takes care to stress that the Muslims of Rum who have long been performing their supererogatory prayers in congregation have done so with the backing of a substantial corpus of texts. Not surprisingly, most of what he cites in this connection are juridical works by Hanafi scholars, including both such well-established texts of the Transoxanian tradition as the *Ziyādāt* of Muḥammad al-Shaybānī (d.805), *al-Yawāqīt fī'l-Mawāqīt* of Najm al-Dīn al-Nasafī (d.1142), *Tajnīs Majmūʿ al-Nawāzil* of Aḥmad b. Mūsā al-Kashshī (d.after 1155), *al-Muḥīṭ* of Burhān al-Dīn Maḥmūd al-Bukhārī (d.1174) and more recent works of the Mamluk and Ottoman lands such as an unspecified work by the Mamluk scholar of Ayntabi origin, Abū Muḥammad b. Maḥmūd Badr al-Dīn al-ʿAynī (d.1451), Commentary on the *Nuqāya* by Abdülvâcid Muhammed el-Meşhedî el-Kütahyavî (d.1434), the *Dürer* and *Gurer* by Molla Hüsrev (d.1480) and the *Fetâvâ* of Ebüssuûd. The Shafiʿi tradition is represented with a lone work, *al-Fatāwā al-ʿAbbādī* by Abū ʿĀṣim Muḥammad al-ʿAbbādī (d.1066).

In addition, Nushî also cites three works that are not so much juridical works as works on devotional piety from a Sufi perspective, namely, Abū Ḥāmid al-Gazzālī's (d.1111) *Iḥyā ʿUlūm al-Dīn*, Abū Ṭālib al-Makkī's (d.996) *Qūt al-Qulūb* and Faḍlallāh b. Muḥammad b. Ayyūb's (d.1267/8) *Fatāwā al-Ṣūfiyya*.[55] The use of such Sufi or Sufi-inspired religious handbooks to justify contested religious practices was actually both common and bitterly contested in this period, with learned Sufis and Sufi-inclined scholars citing them as sources of authority and strictly legalist, traditionalist scholars contesting their use.[56]

The third and last category of works that Nushî cites consists of the canonical hadith collections of Muḥammad b. Ismāʿīl Bukhārī (d.870), Muslim b. Ḥajjāj (d.875) as well as *Jāmiʿ al-Uṣūl li-Aḥādith al-Rasūl* of Ibn al-Athīr (d.1210), which is a collation of the hadiths found in the six canonical hadith collections. He also cites a hadith (not found in any one of these six canonical

---

54   Ibid., 151b–153a, 181a–b.
55   Ibid., 154b–155a, 181a–186b.
56   For the biography of the author of *al-Fatāwā al-Ṣūfiyya*, see Faḍlallāh b. Muḥammad b. Ayyūb, *al-Fatāwā al-Ṣūfiyya fī Ṭarīqiʾl-Bahāʾīya*, 1–3, MS 957, Carullah, SK. For Birgivî's objections to *al-Fatāwā al-Ṣūfiyya*, see Birgivî Mehmed, *Rasāʾil al-Birkawī*, edited by Aḥmad Hādī al-Qaṣṣār (Beirut: Dār al-Kutub al-ʿIlmīya, 2011), 79–80. I thank Yavuz Aykan and Şükrü Özen for these references. For similar objections by Aydınî, see fn.63. For Vanî's objections to the use of Gazzālī's *Iḥyā ʿUlūm al-Dīn* and *Qīmiyā-i Saʿādat* along with a score of other 'books of the Sufi sheikhs' (*kütüb-i meşâyih-i tarîkat*) as jurisprudential sources (*kütüb-i fıkh-ı şerîf ve şerʿ-i latîf*), see Vanî Mehmed, *Muhyî's-Sünnet Müʾmitüʾl-Bidʿat*, fol. 2a, MS 663, Kasidecizade, SK.

compilations) – "What the Muslims see as praiseworthy is also praiseworthy in the eyes of God." (*Li-en mâ re'ehu'l-muslimûne hasenen fe-hüve 'ind'Allâhi hasenun.*)[57]

Nushî actually cites this last hadith not once but twice, as it is central to his argument that jurists must make an allowance for customs that are widespread among the Muslims when they are not expressly against the principles of Islamic law. It is for this reason that the author emphasizes that supererogatory prayers have long been performed in congregation "in Anatolia and its villages, in Constantinople and the surrounding areas, in Edrene (modern Edirne) and the villages of Rumelia, ... and in the lands of the Tatars ... and in Bukhara, Samarkand and India."[58] Thus, the author points to a vast geographical expanse in which the congregational performance of supererogatory prayers was a deeply ingrained custom, comprising not just the lands of the Ottomans but many of the eastern lands of Islamdom, where Hanafism was the dominant legal school.

However, it is in defence of the Ottoman/Rumi practice of Islam that the author turns out to be the most emphatic. Indeed, not content merely to defend the congregational performance of supererogatory prayers by Ottoman Muslims, Nushî goes fully on the offensive, and imputes politically subversive motives to those who condemn these practices as a 'grievous error' (*dalâlet*). He writes:

> In particular, the rulers of the House of Osman, who are sultans of the Arabs and the Acem and servants of the two holy sanctuaries (may God extend their lives till the end of times), together with their mothers and fathers and glorious ancestors, have long performed these prayers. Hence the (true) intent of those who say that it is a grievous error (*dalâlet*) to perform these prayers is to call the sultan of the House of Osman and his sons people of error. May God preserve us from such an error! May the Lord (praise be to Him and Exalted be He!) preserve the sultans of the House of Osman from error! Amen! And another intent of those who call the people who perform these prayers people of error is to slander and attack the viziers of the House of Osman, the *ulema* of the House of Osman and the sheikhs of the House of Osman as people of error.[59]

---

57    Nushî, *Mebâhisü's-Salât*, 186b. For this hadith, see Ahmad b. Ḥanbal, *Musnad*, vol. 1, 379; Ṭabarānī, *Mūjam al-Awṣaṭ*, vol. 4, 58; and Ḥākim, *Mustadrak*, vol. 3, 83.
58    Nushî, *Mebâhisü's-Salât*, 186b–187a.
59    Ibid., 187a–b.

What Nushî argues here is essentially that the congregational performance of superegotary prayers has the backing of Ottoman royal authority. Remarkably, however, he evokes the authority of 'the House of Osman' not just with reference to the Ottoman dynasty, but also with reference to the greater state edifice, extending from the sultans and the female and male members of the royal family to the viziers, the *ulema* and all the way down to the sheikhs. As such, this passage stands out as a rather early articulation of a more extended and corporate as well more bureaucratic notion of the state in the Ottoman lands.[60] The inclusion of the *meşâyih* in this state edifice is particularly significant, and is in line with the increased visibility of the sheikhs in the political imaginations of seventeenth-century Ottomans, and further illustrates the self-identification of at least some members of the *meşâyih* with the Ottoman state. This is a point of no little relevance to the wider debates about who could legitimately claim to be arbiters of orthodoxy/praxy in the Ottoman lands. It appears from this passage that Nushî not only considered the norm-setting functions of Ottoman royal authority to be self-evident and widely accepted, but also derived a degree of juridical authority from it himself via being a small cog in the state edifice.

It is worth noting, however, that even as Nushî was attacking opponents of the congregational performance of supererogatory prayers as enemies of the Ottoman social, political and moral order, criticism of the popular nocturnal prayers (and other controversial 'ancient customs') was no longer confined to non-Ottoman, non-Rumi and non-Hanafi Muslims, but was also spreading among the '*ulema* and sheikhs of the House of Osman'. It might be appropriate, then, to end this section with a brief consideration of the counterarguments made by one such Rumi Hanafi critic, Mehmed b. Hamza el-Aydınî (d.after 1706). Aydınî was a provincial scholar, who wrote most of his works in the last decade of the seventeenth and the first decade of the eighteenth century, and who was regarded by some of his contemporaries as a 'second Birgivî'. This epithet was not without reason, as Aydınî was opposed to many of the same 'innovations' as Birgivî and the Kadızâdelis, and he articulated his opinions about them in more than sixty treatises. In one of these treatises, entitled *Risâle fî*

---

60   On the emergence of a more bureaucratic and impersonal concept of the state in Ottoman political thought between the sixteenth and eighteenth centuries, see Marinos Sariyannis, "Ruler and state, state and society in Ottoman political thought", *Turkish Historical Review* 4 (2013), 83–117. For explorations of the social and political dynamics behind this conceptual change, see Rifa'at 'Ali Abou-El-Haj, *Formation of the Modern State: The Ottoman Empire, Sixteenth to Eighteenth Centuries* (New York: SUNY Press, 1991); Tezcan, *The Second Ottoman Empire, passim.*

*Beyâni Kerâhati't-Tahrîmiyye ve't-Tenzîhiyye* (Treatise on the clarification of permissible and impermissible abomination), he also touched on the debate on the congregational performance of supererogatory prayers.[61]

It is not certain, but quite probable that Aydınî wrote this treatise in rebuttal of the arguments presented in the *Mebâhisü's-Salât*. Though Aydınî never mentions Nushî or Sivâsî by name, he writes in scathing terms of "certain authors of deficient knowledge in our times [who] compile books by assembling bits and pieces from a variety of other books as if they are collecting wood at night". He critiques these writers for misquoting and misinterpreting their sources. He also objects to the interpretation of Quranic verses and hadiths by these writers on the grounds that the latter are basically *mukallid* scholars and are qualified only to 'imitate' the opinions of the master jurists of the past. He criticizes, among others things, how these writers have interpreted the hadith. "What the Muslims see as praiseworthy is also praiseworthy in the eyes of God." He argues that 'the Muslims' (*el-Müslimûn*) in this hadith are not Muslims in general but the *selef*, and cannot at any rate include the 'people of *bid'at*'. Hence, he concludes, the hadith cannot be used to justify such popular but abominable practices as the congregational performance of supererogatory prayers, as the author of the *Fatāwā al-Ṣūfiyya* (and following him, Nushî) had done. As if in direct response to Nushî's evocation of Rumi/Ottoman customs, Aydınî also retorts that even if many 'virtuous' people of Rum continue to perform supererogatory prayers in congregation, many other 'virtuous' people in the Hijaz, Sham, Egypt, Maghreb, Yemen, Samarkand, Bukhara, Hind and Sind have been giving them up. How, then, can one rule that the Muslims of Rum are more 'virtuous' than the rest? In such instances of disagreement, what needs to be done is to decide in accordance with the Book and the Sunna, and when and where there is doubt, it is necessary to err on the side of caution and prohibit any practice that is suspected of being an abomination.[62]

Even though Aydınî's arguments summarized above may seem primarily to target the arguments of Nushî, aspects of his arguments can be seen as an indirect response to Sivâsî's more historically and rationally grounded arguments as well. Aydınî makes it clear that he considers 'abominations' in ritual worship (*'ibâdet*) to be far worse than 'abominations' in human relations (*mu'âmelât*), and he explicitly criticizes those who advocate lenience towards the former. Although Sivasî in the fatwa discussed above did not argue that 'abominations'

---

61  On Aydınî and his works, the most comprehensive work is that of Recep Cici, *Bir Osmanlı Fakihi: Âlim Muhammed b. Hamza'nın Fıkıh Risâleleri* (Bursa: Emin Yayınları, [2006?]).

62  This discussion is based on the detailed summary given in ibid., 39–46.

in ritual worship should be tolerated as a matter of principle, he had, after all, argued that in a world teeming with sinful temptations, religious practices involving some degree of 'abomination' represented the lesser of two evils and had to be allowed.

Significantly, however, the more central aspect of Sivâsî's argument was that the rejection of the performance of supererogatory prayers in congregation by the Prophet's cousin Ibn 'Abbās was no longer applicable in later times, and Aydınî seemingly has nothing to say about that. It is worth dwelling a bit more on this silence, as Aydınî himself was no stranger to the legal maxim about the mutability of legal assessments over time. Quite to the contrary, in another treatise, he himself brings up the same principle, explaining that legal judgments of earlier authorities have to be revised when the underlying reasons (*'illet*) change. One of the examples he discusses in this context is the shift in juridical opinion concerning the attendance of women in mosques. Whereas the Prophet had explicitly forbidden fellow Muslims from banishing women from mosques, Aydınî argues, later authorities had found it necessary to change his ruling and to banish first younger and then, also older women from mosques, seeing that each successive generation had become more corrupted than the previous and considering that the presence of women posed a graver moral danger to the (male) congregations in these corrupted times.[63]

It is worth stressing that both Aydınî and Sivâsî shared the Sunni Muslim belief in the moral corruption of Muslims over time, but whereas Sivâsî advocated fighting this corruption by introducing new elements into the repertoire of Muslim piety from the realm of popular practice, Aydınî thought that the corruption would be best fought by the introduction of ever stricter strictures, intended to keep people (in this case, women, construed to be morally and socially inferior) in check. Ultimately, it seems, it was the individual scholars' social and political priorities and commitments that determined how they interpreted the religio-legal tradition and how they applied its insights to their own surroundings and times.

## 3      Conclusion

This chapter has been an attempt to tackle the question of the mutability of *shar'i* judgments through the debate about the permissibility of the

---

[63]   For an annotated Arabic edition, English translation and analytical discussion of this treatise, see Cici, *Bir Osmanlı Fakihi*, 33; see also Reinhart, "When Women Went", 116–28.

congregational performance of supererogatory prayers. I have tried to show that the debate about the congregational performance of supererogatory prayers actually touched on many of the central questions that Ottoman scholars (and some laymen) debated in the course of the sixteenth and especially, seventeenth centuries: are all innovations in worship categorically bad, or can some be deemed useful and therefore permissible? Is it permissible to root out 'innovations' that have become part of 'local custom'? Do the religio-legal pronouncements of the Prophet, the Companions and the Successors always bind later generations of Muslims, or can they be revised on the grounds of the juridical principle that 'shar'i judgments change with the change of times'?

We have seen above that the Ottoman scholars who defended the congregational performance of supererogatory prayers in general and the Raghā'ib, Barā'at and Qadr prayers in particular often did so on the grounds that these prayers were deeply rooted in 'local custom'. This was the position of various scholars from Şeyhülislâm Ebüssuûd in the mid-sixteenth century to Sheikh Nushî and Kâtib Çelebi in the early and mid-seventeenth century respectively. Yet, this position did not directly address the problem of the traditionalist objections that were directed at the practice in the first place. This was precisely what 'Abdülkerim Sivâsî attempted in the fatwa cited by Nushî. Evoking the juridical principle 'shar'i judgments change with the change of times', Sivasî argued that the strict prohibition by the Companions and Followers of even the smallest innovation in matters of worship could not be held to apply automatically to the rather different conditions of their own times. In a world that was infinitely more complex and that teemed with so many more opportunities for sin, innovations that attracted people to a life of piety could no longer be prohibited. This was a powerful line of argument that contained in itself the possibility of a more radical critique of Sunni traditionalism. It was also an argument that could be deployed, at least in theory, to defend not only the congregational performance of supererogatory prayers but also a whole set of other popular religious practices from the melodic recitation of the Quran to the Sufi rituals of vocal *zikr, semâ'* and *devrân*.[64]

Strangely, this line of argument does not seem to have been widely utilized by the Rumi scholars. It is true that the gentlemen whose conversations with

---

64   This is not to say that all critics of the Kadızâdelis wanted to defend *all* these practices. As we have seen, Nushî, for one, opposed the *semâ'* ceremonies as *bid'at*. Whether or not Sivâsî agreed with him on this particular matter, what is important is that Sivâsî's argument against traditionalist objections to the congregational performance of supererogatory prayers could be extended also to other items of debate.

the Kadızâdelis were cited at the beginning of this chapter poked fun at the unreasonableness (as they saw it) of the Kadızâdeli demands that they live like Muslims in the day of the Prophet. However, theirs was hardly a jurisprudential argument, and was probably made half in jest. The closest analogue that I could find to Sivâsî's historically- and rationally-grounded critique of Sunni traditionalism in the wider Ottoman literature is Kâtib Çelebi's *Mîzânü'l-Hakk fi İhtiyâri'l-Ehakk* (Balance of Truth for Choosing the Most True), and this tellingly is also the work of a non-specialist. Kâtib Çelebi, after all, was neither a jurist nor even a member of the *ulema* proper, but was rather a largely self-taught bureaucrat, who had, on his own initiative, attended the circles of some madrasa professors, and who wrote his work in Turkish for the benefit of laymen as much as scholars.

In the prologue to this work, Kâtib Çelebi makes an extensive case for the use of reason and the rational sciences and highlights their importance for the correct interpretation and application of religio-legal principles. Always keen to take into consideration both sides of an issue, he also acknowledges that the Companions of the Prophet had initially opposed the study of the rational sciences and the Greek books because they were worried about the infiltration of non-Islamic ideas into their newly adopted Islamic faith. However, after the Muslims had codified all the principal Islamic sciences, they had felt safe enough to study the rational sciences and lifted the ban on them in the time of the Umayyads and Abbasids. Hence, Kâtib Çelebi argues, it behooves the intelligent Muslims of the present times to follow the examples of these scholars and not reject the use of reason.[65] He also illustrates with some concrete examples how a mufti with insufficient grounding in the rational sciences is likely to err when deliberating on *shar'i* matters.

The rest of Kâtib Çelebi's book can be read as an illustration of the methodology he advocates in the preface. In chapter after chapter, he presents what he considered the most reasonable and balanced line on the principal issues of religio-legal controversy in his own time, using both proofs from the Quran, hadiths and various authoritative juridical sources, and rational argumentation. In chapters devoted to some of the primary participants in these debates, Kâtib Çelebi also critiques Birgivî and Kadızâde Mehmed for being insufficiently grounded in rational thought. According to Kâtib Çelebi, Birgivî had

---

65   Katib Çelebi, *Balance of Truth*, 21–32, esp. 24–5. For an analysis of Kâtib Çelebi's views on this matter, also see Seyfi Kenan, "Doğruyu Dengede Tutmak: *Mîzânü'l-Hak* Çerçevesinde Kâtip Çelebi'nin Bilgi ve Eğitim Anlayışı". In Said Öztürk (ed.) *Vefatının 350. Yılında Kâtip Çelebi* (Istanbul: İstanbul Büyükşehir Belediyesi, 2007), 87–91.

been proficient in logic but not in the other rational sciences, and he had been especially ignorant of history, which, if he had studied it, would have taught him the importance of 'local custom'. Kâtib Çelebi was even more dismissive of Kadızâde Mehmed in this matter, deeming the latter's knowledge of the rational sciences to be quite 'rudimentary and superficial'.[66]

It would be inaccurate, however, to say that the seventeenth-century Ottoman debate on *bid'at* was essentially a replay of the old conflict between 'rationalists' and 'traditionalists'. In his recent forays into the study of logic and *kelâm* in the seventeenth-century Ottoman Empire, Khaled El-Rouayheb has cast doubt on the once widely-accepted view that the rise of the Kadızâdelis was accompanied by a decline of interest in the rational sciences.[67] As far as the jurisprudential literature is concerned, too, the picture seems to have been a good deal more complex. Just as Sunni traditionalism was not only the monopoly of the Kadızâdelis but was also embraced by many Sufis,[68] neither was systematic legal reasoning the monopoly of the anti-Kadızâdelis. Among the Kadızâdelis (and like-minded scholars) Ahmed Rumî el-Akhisarî comes to mind as a strongly traditionalist scholar, who also boldly defended the ability of the scholars of his time to practise *ijtihad*.[69] Another scholar who combined strict adherence to the Sunna with systematic legal reasoning was Mehmed b. Hamza el-Aydınî, whose arguments against the congregational performance of supererogatory prayers as well as against the attendance of women in mosques have been discussed above. Interestingly, like Sivâsî, Aydınî also acknowledged the principle that legal judgments change with the change of time, but allowed such reassessments only if they were more stringent than previous ones, helping to keep in check those forces that he considered posed a threat to the moral integrity of the Islamic community.

Ultimately, what distinguished Aydınî from Sivâsî was less their positions on rational argumentation and more their approaches to the religio-moral dimensions of the sharia. Whereas Sivâsî saw no harm in relaxing legal judgments and admitting religious innovations into the practices of Muslims if he thought they served the purpose of reorienting people towards God and piety, Aydınî was far less tolerant of practices about which there was the slightest doubt

---

66  Katib Çelebi, *Balance of Truth*, 130, 136–7.
67  Khaled el-Rouayheb, *Islamic Intellectual History in the Seventeenth Century: Scholarly Currents in the Ottoman Empire and the Maghrib* (Cambridge: CUP, 2015), 13–59.
68  Derin Terzioğlu, "Sunna-minded Sufi Preachers", *passim*.
69  For Akhisarî's views on *ijtihād*, see Ahmed el-Akhisarî, *Against Smoking: An Ottoman Manifesto*, edited and translated by Yahya Michot (Leicestershire: Kube Publishing: 2010), 67–70.

of illegitimacy; and he would allow legal reassessments only if they reduced rather than expanded the scope of religious, moral and legal ambiguity. For him, as for many modern Muslims, adhering as strictly as possible to the law was at all times the best way to safeguard religion and morality.

To the extent that it is possible to generalize from this specific debate to the larger seventeenth-century Ottoman debates about the Sunna, one could perhaps say the following: Although the Kadızâdelis (and like-minded scholars) were not quite the forerunners of the Wahhabis they have been made out to be, they did share with the traditionalist, Sunni revivalist movements of the late-eighteenth and nineteenth centuries a decreasing 'tolerance for ambiguity', as well as a narrower understanding of the sharia as Islamic *legal* normativity.[70]

While it exceeds the scope of this chapter to probe the reasons for this epistemic shift, if one may call it that, suffice it to note that the Kadızâdelis themselves drew on the scholarship of a small but distinguished group of hadith scholars and jurists who had sought to cleanse the Islamic 'Tradition with a capital T' of spurious traditions and 'blameworthy innovations' since the twelfth century.[71] In a more direct way, they were also the product of at least a century of 'orthodoxizing' moves by the Ottoman learned establishment and the imperial state. As we have seen above, some early-sixteenth-century Ottoman scholars such as Ḥalabī and Ibn Kemâl had also advocated a similarly stringent position on such 'innovations' as the congregational performance of supererogatory prayers, albeit without capturing the imagination of a broader cross-section of the urban populace, as did the Kadızâdelis a century later.

Of course, it is questionable how successful the Kadızâdelis themselves were in the push for disambiguation, and in their effort to cleanse the living practice of Muslims of all *bidʿat*s. For the fact is that even as few middle and high-ranking *ulema* followed the example of Nushî, Sivâsî or Kâtib Çelebi in putting forth a rationally and historically grounded defence of local customs in the face of Sunni traditionalist objections; when it came to actual practice, it was the defenders of the mutating local customs who carried the day. Just

---

[70] On the growing hegemony of law and legalism at the expense of other discursive traditions in modern Muslim conceptions of Islam and on the consequent withering away of the earlier Islamic 'culture of ambiguity', see Shahab Ahmed, *What is Islam? The Importance of Being Islamic* (Princeton: Princeton University Press, 2016); Thomas Bauer, *Die Kultur der Ambiguität: Eine andere Geschichte des Islams* (Berlin: Verlag der Weltreligionen im Insel Verlag, 2011). On the modern tendency to reduce sharia normativity to legal judgments, see Johansen, "Die sündige, gesunde Amme", *passim*.

[71] Jonathan Berkey, "Tradition, Innovation and the Social Construction of Knowledge in the Medieval Near East", *PP* 146 (1995), 38–65; Brown, "Even If It's Not True It's True", 1–52.

as coffeehouses, smoking and the various forms of Sufi music and dance survived the bans of the imperial state and the sermonizing of the preachers, so did the congregational performance of the Raghā'ib, Barā'at and Qadr prayers survive the objections and bickering of the Sunni vigilantes and their lay supporters, and continued to provide vast numbers of Muslim mosque-goers with an important platform for piety *and* sociability for centuries to come.

## Appendix

*Excerpt from* **Mebâhisü's-Salât**, *153a–154b*

İy mü'minler kaçankim bir mes'ele bilinmese ve yahud ol mes'elede 'ulemâ ihtilâf itse esahh-ı akvâl bilmek içün fetvâ çıkarurlar ve anuñla 'amel iderler. Biñ otuz dört senesinde Mısr-ı Kâhirede nâfile namâzlar hakkında ihtilâf vâki'[72] olmagın bu 'abd-ı fakîr ilâ rahmeti rabbihi'l-kadîr istiftâ eyledüm. Sûret-i fetvâ budur.

'Âlim-i muhakkık ve hibr-i[73] müdakkik ve fâzıl-ı kâmil (153b) ve zâhid-i 'âmil ve Ebû Yûsuf-ı sânî 'Abdü'l-Kerîm es-Sivâsî hazretleri cevâb virüp buyurur ki: "*El-hamdü lillâhi esahhu'l-akvâl ellezî edînu Allâhe Te'âlâ bihi 'ademu'l-i'tirâzi 'alâ'l-'âbidi fî hâzâ*. 'Avâm-ı nâs[1] men' câ'iz degüldür salât-ı Regâ'ibden ve salât-ı Kadirden. Ammâ İbn 'Abbâs hazretlerinüñ mescid-i Resûlullâhda halka ile zikr idenleri cirîd ile darb idüp mescidden ihrâc itmesi ol evvel zamânda idi. Ve ol zamânda kahve içilmezdi ve duhân içilmezdi ve câmi'lerde kanâdîl asılmazdı ve mumlar yanmazdı, tegannî vü terennüm nâs beyninde yok idi ve mesâlih-i müslimîn nâ-ehile virilmezdi ve 'avâm-ı cehleye menâsıb-ı 'ulemâ virilmezlerdi ve cühelâ'i re'îs itmezlerdi." Ba'de eyitdi: "Kaçankim 'avâm-ı nâs çarşularda ve bâzâr(154a)larda zikr ider görseyidiñiz ve namâzı kerâhatle kılur görseyidiñüz. Fî zamâninâ men' câ'iz degüldür." *Sümme kâle*: "*Sübhânallâh, el-'acebu kulle'l-'acebi*. Hürmet[i] delîl-i kat'î ile sâbit olanı söylemeyüp sükût iderler. Zinâ ve livâtadan ve şurb-ı hamr ve şurb-ı duhândan men' itmezler ve tavla ve satrancdan men' itmezler. Muhassal-ı kelâm fî zamâninâ halkı 'ibâdâtdan men' câ'iz olmaz, zîrâ ahkâm-ı şer'iyye tegayyür-i zamânla mütegayyir olur. Ve eger ol gicelerde me'âbid-i ilâhî[yi] kaparsak, ya'nî câmi'ler ve mescidler kapusın kaparsak me'âbid-i şeyâtîn kapuları açukdur, ya'nî kahvehâneler ve bozahâneler ve meyhâneler ve bâbülhâneler açukdur, ekser halk anda giderler ve fisk iderler. Halkuñ sulehâ nâmında olanları (154b)

---

72  In the manuscript this sentence actually reads as "*vâki' oldı olmagın*".
73  In the manuscript, this word is actually written as "*hayr*".

ednâ mertebe kahvehâneye girerler ve gıybet ü mesâvî iderler ve duhân içerler ne'ûzu billâhi te'âlâ. Kaçankim müftî halkı bu beliyyelerde görse ehven-i beliyyeteyn ile fetvâ virmek gerekdür ve ehven-i beliyyeteyn câmi'leri ve mescidleri ta'mîr itmekdür, anda bir zarar varsa dahî." *Sümme kâle:* "İy câhil fî zamânınâ kerâhatden hâlis hiçbir 'ibâdet bulunur mı? Ol sen didügüñ sahâbe ve tâbi'în ve tâbi'-i tâbi'în zamânı idi. Mezheb-i mu'temed budur." *İntehâ fetvâ 'Abdü'l-Kerîmi's-Sivâsî.*

### English Translation

O believers, whenever [the religio-legal status of] a matter is unknown or whenever the *ulema* disagree on [the religio-legal status of] a matter, to reach the soundest opinion, they seek a fatwa and act in accordance with it. In the year 1034 (1624/5 CE), when there was a dispute about supererogatory prayers, this slave, this poor one in need of the mercy of God Almighty, sought a fatwa about it. This is the copy of the fatwa:

The verifying scholar, meticulous man of religion, perfected man of virtue, practising ascetic, and a second Ebû Yûsuf, 'Abdülkerîm es-Sivâsî, has answered as follows:

Praise be to God! The soundest of opinions, about which I submit to God Almighty, is not interfering with the worshipper on this matter. It is not permissible to prohibit the common folk from [the congregational performance of] the prayers of Regaib and Kadir. It was in the bygone times that Ibn 'Abbās beat with a stick those who formed a circle and performed *zikr* in the mosque of the Messenger of God and expelled them from the mosque. In that age, people did not drink coffee or smoke tobacco; mosques were not illuminated with oil lamps and candles; people did not even know of singing and humming; the affairs of the Muslims were not given to the incapable, and the positions of the *ulema* were not given to the ignorant among the commoners, and they did not appoint the ignorant as leaders." Then he said: [In that bygone time], you could never see the commoners among the people perform *zikr* in shops and in the marketplace or make blameworthy blunders while performing their ritual prayers. In our time, it is not permissible to prohibit [the congregational performance of the supererogatory prayers of Regaib and Kadir]. Then he said: Praise be to God! This is a most wondrous thing: They keep quiet about those matters that are prohibited by incontrovertible proofs [and they make objections to those that are not]. They do not try to prevent people from committing adultery and sodomy, drinking alcohol and smoking tobacco, or playing backgammon and chess. In short, it cannot be permissible in our time to prevent the people from performing acts of worship, because legal judgments change with the changing times. If on those nights we close down the divine temples – namely, mosques and masjids, the temples of Satan – namely, coffeehouses, boza stalls, wine-taverns and brothels [literally, Houses of Babel], will be still open; and most people will go to them and engage in mischief. Even the people who are deemed to be righteous at the very least go to coffeehouses, where they talk behind others and smoke. We seek refuge in God Almighty! When the jurisconsult finds the people to be in a state of such affliction, he should rule for the lesser of the two afflictions and the lesser affliction is to support [going to] mosques and masjids, even if there is some harm in that. Then he said: O ignorant one, is there any worship in our own time that is free of abomination? That which you speak about was true for the time of the Companions, Successors and Successors of the Successors. This is the trusted path. The fatwa of 'Abdülkerîm es-Sivâsî ends.

### Note on Transcription

All Turkish names and titles, including Arabic citations in Turkish texts, have been rendered according to a simplified form of Turkish transcription. Arabic titles and the names of authors who wrote exclusively in Arabic have been transcribed according to Brill's transliteration system for Arabic. Terms shared by Arabic and Turkish speakers have been rendered according to the conventions of the language used in the specific context discussed in this chapter.

### Acknowledgements

This chapter is dedicated to Professor Metin Kunt as an expression of gratitude for his exemplary scholarship. It is based on research funded by the European Research Council under the European Union's Seventh Framework Programme (FP/2015–2020)/ERC Grant Agreement 648498, "The Fashioning of a Sunni Orthodoxy and the Entangled Histories of Confession-Building in the Ottoman Empire, 15th–17th Centuries". I would like to thank Ahmet Kaylı, Çiğdem Kafesçioğlu, Evren Sünnetçioğlu, Guy Burak, Tijana Krstić and Yavuz Aykan as well as the editors of this volume for their insightful comments and criticisms. Naturally, I remain solely responsible for any mistakes that this chapter may contain.

## Bibliography

### Unpublished Primary Sources

Gazzîzâde Abdüllatif. *Menâkıb-ı Gazzî*. MS 1042. Orhan, Bursa Eski Yazma ve Basma Eserler Kütüphanesi.

Kadızâde Mehmed. [Untitled treatise]. MS 5563, 44b–47b. Yazma Bağışlar, Süleymaniye Kütüphanesi.

Kadızâde Mehmed. [Untitled Treatise], MS TY 3529, fol. 116b–121a, Türkçe Yazmalar. İstanbul Üniversitesi Kütüphanesi.

Nushî el-Nâsıhî/Mustafa b. Hamza b. İbrahim b. Veliyüddin. *al-Ḥayāt Sharḥ Shurūṭ al-Ṣalāṭ*, MS 971, 1a–137a. Hacı Mahmud Efendi, Süleymaniye Kütüphanesi.

Nushî el-Nâsıhî/Mustafa b. Hamza b. İbrahim b. Veliyüddin. *Mebhas-ı Îmân*. MS 5563, 59a–137a. Yazma Bağışlar, Süleymaniye Kütüphanesi.

Nushî el-Nâsıhi/Mustafa b. Hamza b. İbrahim b. Veliyüddin. *Mebâhisü's-Salât*. MS 948. Hacı Mahmud Efendi, Süleymaniye Kütüphanesi.

Râkım İbrahim. *Vâkıʿât-ı Pîr-i Rûşen*. MS 790. İzmir, Süleymaniye Kütüphanesi.

Sivâsî, Receb. *Necmü'l-Hüdâ fî Menâkıbi'ş-Şeyh Şemseddîn Ebi's-Senâ*. MS 694/2. Lala İsmail, Süleymaniye Kütüphanesi.

Sunʿullâh Efendi. *Fetâvâ-yi Sunʿullâh Efendi*. MS 502. Hasan Hüsnü Paşa, Süleymaniye Kütüphanesi.

Vanî Mehmed. *Muhyî's-Sünnet Müʾmitü'l-Bidʿat*. MS 663. Kasidecizade. Süleymaniye Kütüphanesi.

### Published Primary Sources

el-Akhisarî, Ahmed. *Against Smoking: An Ottoman Manifesto*, edited and translated by Yahya Michot. Leicestershire: Kube Publishing, 2010.

Birgivî Mehmed. *Tarîkat-ı Muhammediyye*, edited by Muhammed Hüsnî Mustafâ, Mehmet Fatih Güney and A. Faruk Beşikçi. Istanbul: Kalem Yayınevi, 2004.

Birgivî Mehmed. *Jalāʾ al-Qulūb*, edited by ʿĀmir Saʿīd al-Zībārī. Beirut, 1995.

Ebussuûd. *Şeyhülislâm Ebussuûd Efendi Fetvaları Işığında 16. Asır Türk Hayatı*, edited by Ertuğrul Düzdağ. Istanbul: Enderun Kitabevi, 1983.

Ḥalabī, İbrahim. *Ḥalabī Kabīr*. Istanbul: Arif Efendi Matbaası, 1325/1907–8.

Ḥalabī, İbrahim. *Tam Kayıtlı Halebî-i Sagîr ve Tercemesi (Taharet ve Namaz Bölümleri)*, translated by Hasan Ege. Istanbul: Salah Bilici Kitabevi, 1982.

İbn Kemal. *Şeyhülislâm İbn Kemal'in Fetvaları Işığında Kanûnî Devrinde Osmanlı'da Hukukî Hayat*. Edited by Ahmet İnanır. Istanbul: Osmanlı Araştırmaları Vakfı, 2011.

İsmâil Hakkı Bursevî. *Kitâbü'n-Netîce: Bursevî'nin Vâridatı ve Şerhleri*, edited by Ali Namlı. Istanbul, 2019.

Jār Allāh Muḥammad b. Fahd. *Nukhbat Bahjat al-Zamān bi-ʿImārat Makka li-Mulk Banī ʿUthmān*, edited by Qays Kāẓim al-Janabī. Beirut: Dār al-Kutub al-Ilmiyya, 2010.

Katib Çelebi. *The Balance of Truth*, edited and translated by Geoffrey L. Lewis. London: George Allen and Unwin Ltd, 1957.

[Mehmed II, 'Fatih']. *Fatih Sultan Mehmet Vakfiyeleri*. 3 vols. Istanbul: T.C. Başbakanlık Vakıflar Genel Müdürlüğü ve Çamlıca Kültür ve Yardım Vakfı, 2003.

Mustafa Naîmâ Efendi. *Târih-i Naʿîmâ (Ravzatü'l-Hüseyn fî Hulâsati Ahbâri'l-Hâfikayn)*. Edited by Mehmet İpşirli, 4 vols. Ankara: TTK, 2007.

Öz, Tahsin (ed.) *Zwei Stiftungsurkunden des Sultans Mehmed II. Fatih*. Istanbul: Devlet Matbaası, 1935.

al-Qārī, ʿAlī. *Al-Asrār al-Marfūʿat fī l-Akhbār al-Mawḍūʿat*, edited by Muḥammad b. Lutfī Sabbāgh. Beirut: Dār al-Amāna, 1971.

Schweigger, Salomon. *Ein newe Reyssbeschreibung auss Teutschland nach Constantinopel und Jerusalem*. Nurnberg: Lantzenberger, 1608; reprinted. Graz: Akademische Druck- u. Verlagsanstalt, 1964.

Selânikî Mustafa. *Tarih-i Selânikî*, edited by Mehmet İpşirli, 2 vols. Istanbul: Edebiyat Fakültesi, 1989.

Sevim, Sezai and Hasan Basri Öcalan (eds). *Osmanlı Kuruluş Dönemi Bursa Vakfiyeleri*. Bursa: Osmangazi Belediyesi, 2010.

Sivasî, Receb. *Hidâyet Yıldızı: Şems-ed-dîn-i Sivâsî Hazretlerinin Menkıbeleri*, translated by Hüseyin Şemsi Güneren and edited by Fatih Güneren. Istanbul, n.d.

Uzunçarşılı, İsmail Hakkı. "Niğde'de Karamanoğlu Ali Bey Vakfiyesi", *Vakıflar Dergisi* 2 (1942), 45–69.

### Secondary Sources

Abou-El-Haj, Rifaʿat ʿAli. *Formation of the Modern State: The Ottoman Empire, Sixteenth to Eighteenth Centuries*. New York: State University of New York Press, 1991.

Ahmed, Shahab. *What is Islam? The Importance of Being Islamic*. Princeton: Princeton University Press, 2016.

Aslan, Halide. "Osmanlı İmparatorluğu'nda Mübarek Gün ve Gecelerden Kandiller". *İslam Sanʿat, Tarih, Edebiyat ve Mûsikîsi Dergisi* 7 (13) 2009, 199–231.

Baer, Marc David. *Honored by the Glory of Islam: Conversion and Conquest in Ottoman Europe*. Oxford: Oxford University Press, 2008.

Bauer, Thomas. *Die Kultur der Ambiguität: Eine andere Geschichte des Islams*. Berlin: Verlag der Weltreligionen im Insel Verlag, 2011.

Berkey, Jonathan. "Tradition, Innovation and the Social Construction of Knowledge in the Medieval Near East". *Past and Present* 146 (1995), 38–65.

Birgivî Mehmed, *Rasāʾil al-Birkawī*, edited by Aḥmad Hādī al-Qaṣṣār. Beirut: Dār al-Kutub al-ʿIlmīya, 2011.

Bori, Caterina. "Transregional Spaces of Reading and Reception". *The Muslim World* 108 (1) 2018, 87–123.

Brown, Jonathan. "Even If It's Not True It's True: Using Unreliable Ḥadīths in Sunni Islam," *Islamic Law and Society* 18 (2011), 1–52.

Burak, Guy. "Faith, Law and Empire in the Ottoman Age of Confessionalization (Fifteenth-Seventeenth Centuries): The Case of 'Renewal of Faith'". *Mediterranean Historical Review* 28 (1) 2013, 1–23.

Burak, Guy. "The Second Formation of Islamic Law: The Post-Mongol Context of the Ottoman Adoption of a School of Law". *Comparative Studies in Society and History* 55 (3) 2013, 579–602.

Burak, Guy. *The Second Formation of Islamic Law: The Hanafī School in the Early Modern Ottoman Empire*. Cambridge: Cambridge University Press, 2015.

Buzov, Snjezana. "The Lawgiver and His Lawmakers: The Role of Legal Discourse in the Change of Ottoman Legal Culture." Ph.D. dissertation, Chicago University, 2005.

Canbakal, Hülya. "Vows as Contract in Ottoman Public Life (17th–18th Centuries)". *Islamic Law and Society*, 18 (1) 2011, 85–115.

Cici, Recep. *Bir Osmanlı Fakihi: Âlim Muhammed b. Hamza'nın Fıkıh Risâleleri*. Bursa: Emin Yayınları, [2006].

Cook, Michael. *Commanding Right and Forbidding Wrong in Islamic Thought*. Cambridge: Cambridge University Press, 2000.

Curry, John J. "'The Meeting of the Two Sultans': Three Sufi Mystics Negotiate with the Court of Murād III". In John J. Curry and Erik S. Ohlander (eds). *Sufism and Society: Arrangements of the Mystical in the Muslim World, 1200–1800*. London: Routledge, 2012, 223–42.

Çavuşoğlu, Semiramis. "The Ḳāḍīzādeli Movement: An Attempt of *Şerīʿat*-minded Reform in the Ottoman Empire". Ph.D. dissertation, Princeton University, 1990.

Dönmez, Mustafa İsmail. "Kuşadalı Mustafa bin Hamza ve '*Netâicü'l-Efkâr fi Şerhi'l-İzhâr*' Adlı Eseri (İnceleme ve Tahkik)". Ph.D. dissertation, Marmara Üniversitesi, 2013.

Fadel, Mohammed. "The Social Logic of *Taqlīd* and the Rise of the *Mukhtaṣar*". *Islamic Law and Society* 3 (2) 1996, 193–233.

Felek, Özgen. "(Re)creating Image and Identity: Dreams and Visions as a Means of Murād III's Self-Fashioning". In Özgen Felek and Alexander D. Knysh (eds). *Dreams and Visions in Islamic Societies Dreams and Visions in Islamic Societies*. Albany: State University of New York Press, 2012, 249–72.

Franke, Patrick. "The Ego of the Mullah: Strategies of Self-Representation in the Works of the Meccan Scholar ʿAlī al-Qārī (d.1606)". In Ralf Elger and Yavuz Köse (eds), *Many Ways of Speaking About the Self: Middle Eastern Ego-Documents in Arabic, Persian, and Turkish (14th–20th century)*. Wiesbaden: Harrassowitz Verlag, 2010, 185–200.

Gel, Mehmet. "XVI. Yüzyılın İlk Yarısında Osmanlı Toplumunun Dinî Meselelerine Muhalif Bir Yaklaşım: Şeyhülislam Çivizâde Muhyiddin Mehmed Efendi ve Fikirleri Üzerine Bir İnceleme". Ph.D. thesis, Gazi Üniversitesi, 2010.

Gerber, Haim. *State, Society, and Law in Islam: Ottoman Law in Comparative Perspective*. Albany: State University of New York Press, 1994.

Grehan, James. "Smoking and 'Early Modern' Sociability: The Great Tobacco Debate in the Ottoman Middle East (Seventeenth to Eighteenth Centuries)". *American Historical Review* 111 (December 2006), 1352–77.

Gündoğdu, Cengiz. *Bir Türk Mutasavvıfı Abdülmecîd Sivâsî (971/1563–1049/1639): Hayatı, Eserleri ve Tasavvufî Görüşleri*. Ankara: Kültür Bakanlığı, 2000.

Cengiz Gündoğdu. "Sivâsî, Abdülmecid". *DİA*, vol. 37. Istanbul, 2009.

Güven, Mustafa Salim (ed.) "Çeşitli Yönleriyle Azîz Mahmûd Hüdâyî'nin Mektupları". MA thesis, Marmara Üniversitesi, 1992.

Hallaq, Wael B. "Was the Gate of *Ijtihad* Closed?" *International Journal of Middle East Studies* 16 (1984), 3–41.

Hallaq, Wael B. "From *Fatwās* to *Furūʿ*: Growth and Change in Islamic Substantive Law". *Islamic Law and Society* 1 (1) 1994, 29–65.

Hallaq, Wael B. *A History of Islamic Legal Theories*. Cambridge: Cambridge University Press, 1997.

Hallaq, Wael B. "The Jurisconsult, the Author-Jurist and Legal Change". In *idem, Authority, Continuity and Change in Islamic Law*. Cambridge: Cambridge University Press, 2001, 166–235.

Hattox, Ralph. *Coffee and Coffeehouses: The Origins of a Social Beverage in the Medieval Near East*. Seattle: University of Washington Press, 1985.

Imber, Colin. *Ebu's-Su'ud: The Islamic Legal Tradition*. Stanford: Stanford University Press, 1997.

Ivanyi, Katharina Anna. "Virtue, Piety and the Law: A Study of Birgivī Mehmed Efendi's al-Ṭarīqat al-Muḥammadiyya". Ph.D. dissertation, Princeton University, 2012.

Ivanyi, Katharina Anna. "'And the Question of Lands is Very Confusing': Birgivî Mehmed Efendi (d.981/1573) on Land Tenure and Taxation". In Marinos Sariyannis (ed.) *Political Thought and Practice in the Ottoman Empire, Halcyon Days in Crete IX*, a symposium held in Rethymno, 9–11 January 2015. Rethymno: Crete University Press, 2019, 137–47.

Johansen, Baber. *Islamic Law on Land Tax and Rent: The Peasants' Loss of Property Rights as Interpreted in the Hanafite Legal Literature of the Mamluk and Ottoman Periods*. London: Croom Helm, 1988.

Johansen, Baber. "Die sündige, gesunde Amme: Moral und gesetzliche Bestimmung (*Ḥukm*) im Islamischen Recht", in *idem, Contingency in a Sacred Law: Legal and Ethical Norms in the Muslim Fiqh* (Leiden: Brill, 1999), 172–88

Johansen, Baber. *Contingency in a Sacred Law: Legal and Ethical Norms in the Muslim Fiqh*. Leiden: Brill, 1999.

Kafadar, Cemal. "How Dark is the History of the Night, How Black the Coffee and How Bitter the Tale of Love: The Measure of Leisure and Pleasure in Early Modern Istanbul". In Arzu Öztürkmen and Evelyn Birge Vitz (eds), *Medieval and Early Modern Performance in the Eastern Mediterranean*. Turnhout: Brepols, 2014, 243–69.

Kafesçioğlu, Çiğdem. *Constantinopolis/Istanbul: Cultural Encounter, Imperial Vision, and the Construction of the Ottoman Capital*. University Park, PA: Pennsylvania State University Press, 2009.

Kara, İhsan. "İsmail Hakkı Bursevi'nin *Tuhfe-i Hasekiyyesi* (3. Bölüm)," MA thesis, Marmara Üniversitesi, 1997.

Karadaş, Cağfer. "Ali el-Kârî'nin Akaide Dair Eserleri ve Bazı İtikadi Görüşleri". MA thesis, Marmara Üniversitesi, 1991.

Karadaş, Cağfer. "Ali el-Kârî'nin Hayatı, Selef Akîdesine Dönüş Çabası ve Eserleri". *Uludağ Üniversitesi İlahiyat Fakültesi Dergisi* 5 (5) 1993, 287–99.

Katz, Marion Holmes. "The 'Corruption of the Times' and the Mutability of the Sharīʿa". *Cardozo Law Review* 28 (1) 2006, 171–85.

Katz, Marion Holmes. *The Birth of the Prophet Muhammad: Devotional piety in Sunni Islam*. Abingdon: Routledge, 2007.

Katz, Marion Holmes. *Prayer in Islamic Thought and Practice*. Cambridge: Cambridge University Press, 2013.

Kaylı, Ahmet. "A Critical Study of Birgivî Mehmed Efendi's Works and their Dissemination in Manuscript Form". MA thesis, Boğaziçi Üniversitesi, 2010.

Kenan, Seyfi. "Doğruyu Dengede Tutmak: *Mîzânü'l-Hak* Çerçevesinde Kâtip Çelebi'nin Bilgi ve Eğitim Anlayışı". In Said Öztürk (ed.) *Vefatının 350. Yılında Kâtip Çelebi*. Istanbul: İstanbul Büyükşehir Belediyesi, 2007, 87–91.

Köse, Ömer Faruk. "The Fatwa Collection of an Ottoman Provincial Mufti, Vani Mehmed Efendi (d.1685)". MA thesis, Boğaziçi Üniversitesi, 2015.

Krstić, Tijana. *Contested Conversions to Islam: Narratives of Religious Change in the Ottoman Empire*. Stanford: Stanford University Press, 2011.

Le Gall, Dina. "Kadızadelis, Nakşbendis, and Intra-Sufi Diatribe in Seventeenth-Century Istanbul". *The Turkish Studies Association Journal* 28 (1–2) 2004, 1–28.

Le Gall, Dina. *A Culture of Sufism: Naqshbandīs in the Ottoman World, 1450–1700*. Albany, NY: State University of New York Press, 2005.

Mandaville, Jon E. "Usurious Piety in the Ottoman Empire: The Cash Waqf Controversy". *International Journal of Middle East Studies* 10 (1979), 289–308.

Martı, Huriye. *Birgivî Mehmed Efendi*. Ankara: Türkiye Diyanet Vakfı Yayınları, 2008.

Melchert, Christopher. *The Formation of the Sunni Schools of Law, 9th–10th Centuries CE*. Leiden: Brill, 1997.

Meshal, Reem. "Antagonistic *Sharī'as* and the Construction of Orthodoxy in Sixteenth-Century Ottoman Cairo." *Journal of Islamic Studies* 21 (2) 2010, 183–212.

Mundy, Martha and Richard Saumarez Smith. *Governing Property, Making the Modern State: Law, Administration and Production in Ottoman Syria*. London: I. B. Tauris, 2007.

Namlı, Ali. *İsmâil Hakkı Bursevî: Hayatı, Eserleri, Tarikat Anlayışı*. Istanbul: İnsan Yayınları, 2001.

Necipoğlu, Gülru. *The Age of Sinan: Architectural Culture in the Ottoman Empire*. Princeton: Princeton University Press, 2005.

Ocak, Ahmet Yaşar. "XVII. Yüzyılda Osmanlı İmparatorluğu'nda Dinde Tasfiye (Püritanizm) Teşebbüslerine Bir Bakış: Kadızadeliler Hareketi". *Türk Kültürü Araştırmaları* 1–2 (1983), 208–25.

Okic, M. Tayyib. "Çeşitli Dillerde Mevlitler ve Süleyman Çelebi'nin Mevlid'inin Çevirileri". *Atatürk Üniversitesi İlahiyat Fakültesi Dergisi* 1 (1976), 17–78.

Pfeifer, Helen. "Encounter After the Conquest: Scholarly Gatherings in 16th-century Ottoman Damascus." *International Journal of Middle East Studies* 47 (2015), 219–39.

Radtke, Bernd. "Birgiwīs *Ṭarīqa Muḥammadiyya*: Einige Bemerkungen und Überlegungen". *Journal of Turkish Studies* 26 (1) 2002. This same article also appears in Jan Schmidt (ed.), *Essays in Honour of Barbara Flemming*. Cambridge, MA: Department of Near Eastern Languages and Civilizations, Harvard University, 2002, 159–174.

Rafeq, Abdul Karim. "The Syrian 'Ulamā', Ottoman Law, and Islamic Sharī'a". *Turcica* 26 (1994), 9–32.

Rafeq, Abdul Karim. "The Opposition of the Azhar 'Ulamā' to Ottoman Laws and its Significance in the History of Ottoman Egypt" In Brigitte Marino (ed.) *Études sur les villes du Proche-Orient XVI$^e$ et XIX$^e$ siècle: Hommage à André Raymond*. Damascus: Institut français d'études arabes de Damas, 2001, 43–54.

Reinhart, Kevin. "When Women Went to Mosques: al-Aydini on the Duration of Assessments". In Muhammad Khalid Masud, Brinkley Messick and David S. Powers (eds). *Islamic Legal Interpretation: Muftis and Their Fatwas*. Cambridge, MA: Harvard University Press, 1996, 116–28.

Repp, Richard C. *The Müfti of Istanbul: A Study in the Development of the Ottoman Learned Hierarchy*. London: Ithaca Press, 1986.

El-Rouayheb, Khaled. "From Ibn Ḥajar al-Haytamī (d.1566) to Khayr al-Dīn al-Ālūsī (d.1899): Changing Views of Ibn Taymiyya amongst Sunni Islamic Scholars". In S. Ahmed and Y. Rapoport (eds). *Ibn Taymiyya and His Times*. Oxford: Oxford University Press, 2010, 69–318.

El-Rouayheb, Khaled. *Islamic Intellectual History in the Seventeenth Century: Scholarly Currents in the Ottoman Empire and the Maghrib*. Cambridge: Cambridge University Press, 2015.

Sariyannis, Marinos. "The Kadızadeli Movement as a Social Phenomenon: The Rise of a 'Mercantile Ethic'?" In Antonis Anastasopoulos (ed.) *Political Initiatives 'from the Bottom up' in the Ottoman Empire, Halcyon Days in Crete VII, 9–11 Jan. 2009*. Rethymno: Crete University Press, 2012, 263–89.

Sariyannis, Marinos. "Ruler and State, State and Society in Ottoman Political Thought". *Turkish Historical Review* 4 (2013), 83–117.

Schlegell, Barbara Rosenow von. "Sufism in the Ottoman Arab World: Shaykh ʿAbd al-Ghanī al-Nābulusī (d. 1143/1731)". Ph.D. dissertation University of California, Berkeley, 1997.

El-Shamsy, Ahmed. *The Canonization of Islamic Law: A Social and Intellectual History*. New York: Cambridge University Press, 2013.

Sheikh, Mustapha. *Ottoman Puritanism and its Discontents: Aḥmad al-Rumī al-Aqḥiṣārī and the Qāḍizādelis*. Oxford: Oxford University Press, 2016.

Sheikh, Mustapha. "Taymiyyan Influences in an Ottoman-Ḥanafī Milieu: The Case of Aḥmad al-Rūmī al-Aqḥiṣārī". *The Royal Asiatic Society* 3 (2014), 1–20.

Soyal, Fikret. "Celâleddin ed-Devvânî'nin Firavun'un İmânı Konusundaki Görüşleri ve Ali el-Kârî'nin Eleştirisi". MA thesis, Istanbul Üniversitesi, 2004.

Talmon-Heller, Daniella. *Islamic Piety in Medieval Syria: Mosques, Sermons and Cemeteries under the Zangids and Ayyūbids (1146–1260)*. Leiden: Brill, 2007.

Talmon-Heller, Daniella and Raquel Ukeles. "The Lure of a Controversial Prayer: Ṣalāt al-Raghā'ib (The Prayer of Great Rewards) in Medieval Arabic Texts and from a Socio-Legal Perspective". *Der Islam* 89 (2) 2012, 141–66.

Terzioğlu, Derin. "Sunna-minded Sufi Preachers in Service of the Ottoman State: The Naṣīḥatnāme of Hasan Addressed to Murad IV". *Archivum Ottomanicum* 27 (2010), 241–312.

Terzioğlu, Derin. "Where ʿIlm-i Ḥāl Meets Catechism: Islamic Manuals of Religious Instruction in the Ottoman Empire in the Age of Confessionalization". *Past and Present* 220 (2013), 79–114.

Terzioğlu, Derin. "Power, Patronage, and Confessionalism: Ottoman Politics as Seen through the Eyes of a Crimean Sufi, 1580–1593". In Marinos Sariyannis (ed.), *Political Thought and Practice in the Ottoman Empire: Halcyon Days in Crete IX*, A symposium held in Rethymno, 9–11 January 2015. Rethymno: Crete University Press, 2019, 149–86.

Terzioğlu, Derin. "Ibn Taymiyya, *al-Siyāsa al-Sharʿiyya* and the Early Modern Ottomans". In Tijana Krstić and Derin Terzioğlu (eds). *Historicizing Sunni Islam in the Ottoman Empire, c.1450–c.1750*. Leiden: Brill, 2020.

Tezcan, Baki. *The Second Ottoman Empire: Political and Social Transformation in the Early Modern World*. Cambridge: Cambridge University Press, 2012.

Tezcan, Baki. "The Portrait of the Preacher as a Young Man: Two Autobiographical Letters by Kadızade Mehmed from the Early Seventeenth Century". In Marinos

Sariyannis (ed.) *Political Thought and Practice in the Ottoman Empire*, Halcyon Days in Crete IX: A Symposium Held in Rethymno, 9–11 January 2015. Rethymno: Crete University Press, 2019, 187–249.

Tezcan, Baki. "A Canon of Disenchantment: Birgivi, Rumi and Kadızade". In *idem, A Gift for the Turks: Studies on Islam and its Early Modern Transformation in the Ottoman Empire*. Istanbul: ISIS Press, forthcoming 2020.

Tuşalp Atiyas, E. Ekin. "The 'Sunna-Minded' Trend". In Marinos Sariyannis (ed.) *A History of Ottoman Political Thought up to the Early Nineteenth Century*. Leiden: Brill, 2019, 233–78.

Yüksel, Emrullah. *Mehmed Birgivî'nin (929–981/1523–1573) Dinî ve Siyasî Görüşleri*. Ankara: Türkiye Diyanet Vakfı Yayınları, 2011.

Zilfi, Madeline C. "The Kadızadelis: Discordant Revivalism in Seventeenth-Century Istanbul". *Journal of Near Eastern Studies* 4 (1986), 251–71.

Zilfi, Madeline C. *The Politics of Piety: The Ottoman Ulema in the Postclassical Age (1600–1800)*. Minneapolis: Bibliotheca Islamica, 1988.

CHAPTER 15

# The *Sicil*s of Karaferye (Veria) in the Eighteenth Century: A Case of Transformation?

*Antonis Anastasopoulos*

In recent years, historians have made extensive use of *kadı* registers (Islamic court records, *kadı sicilleri*) from across the former Ottoman territories as sources for the study of Ottoman society, economy and administration. The focus here is on the registers as such, and attention is drawn to deviations from what a 'typical' register is expected to be in terms of structure and content. More specifically, I focus on the general absence of trials and contracts from the *kadı* registers of the town of Karaferye in the second half of the eighteenth century. As explained below, at this stage of research, it is difficult to determine if this phenomenon, which seems to extend beyond Karaferye, either reflects changes in record-keeping practices and in the functioning of the court of law itself in relation to the earlier period, or only particular series of registers, namely those predominantly containing incoming correspondence and tax-related entries, were preserved.

## 1 Karaferye and Its *Sicil*s

Karaferye is the Ottoman name of the town of Veria, which lies at a distance of roughly sixty-five kilometres west-southwest of Thessaloniki (O. Selânik) in northern Greece. In the Ottoman period, Karaferye was the centre of a district (*kaza*) that belonged to the sub-province (*sancak*) of Selânik.

*Kadı* registers are among the most important sources for studying the history of Karaferye under Ottoman rule. Karaferye *kadı* registers are located in three countries. The largest collection, which consists of 129 volumes, is kept at the Imathia branch of the Greek General State Archives, in Veria.[1] Twelve registers are kept in Turkey – four at the Balıkesir Public Library (Balıkesir İl Halk

---

1 The Veria *kadı* registers are accessible online through the website "Archeiomnimon" of the Greek General State Archives: http://arxeiomnimon.gak.gr/browse/resource.html?tab=01&id=175573 (accessed 16 July 2015).

Kütüphanesi) and eight at the DOA in Istanbul.[2] Two more volumes are kept at the Institute for the Near and Middle East (Institut für den Nahen und Mittleren Osten) in Ludwig Maximilian University of Munich, Germany.[3] From a chronological point of view, the surviving Karaferye registers (*sicil*s) in Veria cover the period from 1602 to 1890 (H. 1011–1308). Those in Turkey cover the period from 1682 to 1831 (H. 1093–1247), and those in Munich several years between 1705 and 1786 (H. 1117–1200).[4] The registers kept in the three countries partly overlap in terms of the years they cover, but one would need to juxtapose them in order to ascertain if registers of the same years in Greece, Turkey and Germany were parts of the same original volume that at some point in time was broken into two, or if they had always been separate volumes.

In fact, things are even more complicated. The registers in Veria had not always totalled 129. An inventory taken in 1921 cites fifty-six volumes. A scholar who visited Veria ten years later, in 1931, reported that he saw fifty-six volumes and two bundles of unbound folios of various dates, which, he estimated, could make up fifteen more volumes of the size of the bound ones. The volumes had been kept in a chest for years, and when that was opened in 1949, fifty-four volumes were counted as well as three bundles of folios randomly put together. It was assumed that the two volumes that had been missing in 1931 had been included in the three bundles. At least until 1980, reports from the Veria archive kept referring to fifty-four volumes. The first mention of 129 volumes – that is the current number of *sicil*s – is to be found in an inventory that is still used today in the local archive as a catalogue. The covering letter accompanying the inventory was signed by the then director of the Historical Archive of Macedonia, Professor Vassilis Demetriades, and was dated 2 May 1984. In other words, the Karaferye *kadı* registers as we have them today were put together in

---

2   I would like to thank my colleague Professor Vehbi Günay of Ege Üniversitesi and Mr Mustafa Birol Ülker, the ISAM Library and Documentation director, for kindly providing this information. The ISAM Library in Istanbul holds digital copies of these volumes, as well as of those in Veria. In 2003, the volumes in Turkey were kept at the Balıkesir Public Library and the AMKT. See Vehbi Günay, "Balkan Şehir Tarihleri Kaynağı Olarak Şer'iye Sicillerinin Envanter ve Kataloglarının Tespiti Hakkında", *Tarih İncelemeleri Dergisi* 18 (2) 2003, 76–7.

3   On these registers, see Margareta Lindner, "Die Rückwirkungen des osmanisch-venezianischen Krieges auf den Gerichtssprengel Karaferya (Veroia) in den Jahren 1715 und 1716 (nach dem Protokollbuch des Kadiamtes)" (Master's thesis, Ludwig Maximilian University, Munich, 1987), 19–22; Marianne Kathrin Neumann, "Die Rückwirkungen des osmanisch-russischen Krieges auf den Gerichtssprengel Qaraferya (Veroia) im Jahre 1771 (nach dem Protokollbuch des Kadiamtes)" (Master's thesis, Ludwig Maximilian University, Munich, 1987/88), 1–6. I would like to thank Dr Anna Vlachopoulou of the Institute for the Near and Middle East for confirming that the *sicil*s are still kept there, at the Faculty of Turkish Studies (Fachbereich Türkische Studien).

4   According to information kindly provided by Mustafa Birol Ülker, the two Munich registers cover the Islamic years 1117, 1127–29, 1138–40, 1167–68, 1175, 1184–87, and 1199–1200.

the early 1980s.[5] As a result, many registers are in reality fragments that contain few or very few folios. There are no more than fifty-five registers in good condition and half of them come from the years after 1780, and more specifically from the nineteenth century. According to the archive catalogue, the *sicil*s have 5351 folios in total, which gives an average of almost forty-two folios per volume.

## 2    Contents of the Eighteenth-Century Karaferye *Sicil*s

If we judge them by today's standards, the Ottoman Islamic judges (*kadı*s) fulfilled, as is well established in literature, three functions: they were judges, notaries and administrative officials. The *kadı* court was where Ottoman subjects would bring their disputes, record their transactions and conduct other legal business, while it also served as a point of contact between the state and the local population (mostly through decrees and petitions, respectively) and as the place where negotiations would take place in order to settle fiscal and other affairs of the public sphere.[6]

The *kadı* registers are expected to reflect this triple role of the Ottoman judges and their courts. As a result, on the one hand, they provide information on various aspects of local life and, on the other, they document the inclusion and functioning of a region within the Ottoman administrative and fiscal setup. This double nature of the *sicil*s is expressed in locally produced entries on contested and non-contested issues such as trials, contracts, legal statements, and the recording and distribution of estates among heirs, in entries that copy incoming correspondence, usually decrees from higher authorities, as well as lists on the apportionment of taxes, fees and other payments among the local communities.

What we may call a 'typical' Karaferye *sicil* contains, as elsewhere in the Ottoman Empire, two parts – a first part with documents like title deeds and other certificates (*hüccet*s), judicial decrees (*i'lâm*s) and probate inventories (*tereke defter*s), and a second part with correspondence and registers

---

5   For a more detailed account, see Antonis Anastasopoulos, "Οι οθωμανικοί ιεροδικαστικοί κώδικες (σιτζίλ) της Βέροιας: προβλήματα ταξινόμησης [The Ottoman Court Registers (*Sicil*s) of Veria: Classification Problems]", *Imeros* 1 (2001), 149–69.

6   There is abundant literature on the Ottoman *kadı*s and their courts. Among them, Rossitsa Gradeva, "A *Kadı* Court in the Balkans: Sofia in the Seventeenth and Early Eighteenth Centuries", in Christine Woodhead (ed.) *The Ottoman World* (London: Routledge, 2012), 57–71; Halil İnalcık and Carter V. Findley, "Maḥkama – 2. The Ottoman Empire", *EI2* 6, 3–11; Ronald C. Jennings, "Kadi, Court, and Legal Procedure in 17th C. Ottoman Kayseri: The Kadi and the Legal System", *Studia Islamica* 48 (1978), 133–72; İlber Ortaylı, "Some Observations on the Institution of Qadi in the Ottoman Empire", *Bulgarian Historical Review* 10 (1) 1982, 57–68.

concerning the distribution of taxes and other forms of expenditure in the local population (*tevzi defters*).[7] For instance, volume No. 49 of the Veria archive, which covers the years 1707 to 1709, contains ten pages of *hüccets*, then seventeen pages of *tereke defters* followed by a note by the *kadı* that this was the end of that section. Then there are two blank pages followed by four pages of mixed content and then twenty-two pages with correspondence and *tevzi defters* related to the incoming orders. The next four pages contain certificates (*temessüks*) on the farming of various public revenues (*mukataas*) in the context of the tax-farming system (*iltizam*) and the last four are dedicated to officially fixed prices (*narh*). Likewise, volume No. 52, of the years 1711 to 1713,[8] contains nineteen pages with *hüccets* and *tereke defters* followed by twenty-two pages of incoming orders and *tevzi defters* compiled in response to them.

However, it is remarkable that the Veria *sicils* from the second half of the eighteenth and early nineteenth centuries contain mostly incoming orders, lists of items related to provincial expenditures (*masarif-i vilayet defters*), *tevzi defters* and *tereke defters*, and a few *hüccet*-type entries. Consequently, we have rather limited information on local life at the family level, or with regard to the social and economic statuses and relationships of private individuals, since most of the data that one can obtain from the *kadı* registers are on administrative, military and fiscal issues, or on local tensions in which the state was asked to intervene. For that period, sources such as the *Rumeli Ahkâm Defterleri*, which are kept at the DOA in Istanbul, rather than the Karaferye *sicils*, are the type of archival material in which the private litigations of Karaferye inhabitants are to be found, whereas there are few or no records of non-disputed matters, such as transactions.

More specifically, according to the inventory of the Veria archive, *sicils* with *hüccets* ceased to exist in 1736, but reappeared in 1825. According to another, more detailed, catalogue of the *kadı sicils* of the Veria archive, the gap was narrower between 1766 and 1814.[9] This information seems to be confirmed by the publication in Greek of selected entries of the Veria *sicils* in the 1940s and 1950s: while the selected entries of the period up to the end of the seventeenth century include a fair number of *hüccets* and *ilâms*, the entries for the later period are almost exclusively imperial decrees or firmans, orders by provincial governors (*buyruldus*), official letters (*mektubs*), and *masarif-i vilayet defters*. With the exception of very few reports by *kadıs* to higher authorities and one

---

7   Cf. Suraiya Faroqhi, "Sidjill – 3. In Ottoman Administrative Usage", *EI2* 9, 539–40.
8   In fact, this volume covers the period up to March 1712 except for a short note from 1713 on the first page.
9   Both the inventory and the catalogue are available locally, and remain unpublished. However, one may find brief information about the contents of the Veria *sicils* on "Archeiomnimon" (see fn.1 above).

*hüccet*, the only recurrent type of locally-produced entry is the recording of conversions to Islam.[10]

To illustrate this change in the surviving eighteenth-century *sicil*s of Karaferye, I will refer below in greater detail to the contents of registers of 1710, 1746–48, 1765, 1780, and 1812, that is, volumes that cover a period of just over a century.[11]

The thirty-two pages of *sicil* No. 51 of the Veria archive contain eighty-one entries, which cover the period from the beginning of February to the beginning of September 1710, with the exception of one dated 24 September 1708/9 Receb 1120. Of these entries, sixty-eight are *hüccet*s, twelve are *tereke defter*s and one is a note recording the amount of the bridal gift (*mehr*) in a marriage. Even though the section concerning incoming orders and *tevzi defter*s is missing, what is important in the context of our discussion is that still at this date one may find many *hüccet*s in the Veria registers.

The next register to consider is one kept in Turkey, which Vehbi Günay has studied.[12] The introductory entry in Arabic of this *sicil* of 1746 is dated 24 March/1 Rebîülevvel 1159, but the volume contains entries that cover the period from February to October, and also two decrees, a *berat* (sultanic writ of appointment) and a firman of 1745, which were recorded in the register in 1746. The first three entries concern the appointment of Mevlânâ Mustafa Efendi as *kadı* and *kassâm-i askerî*, or trustee authorized to divide the estates of deceased members of the ruling class of Karaferye. Then, up to page 32 it contains *hüccet*s, which dominate, though not without exceptions such as five *tereke defter*s and two *tevzi defter*s. From page 32 to 44 most entries are *tereke defter*s. From page 45 to 93 it includes incoming orders, principally firmans and *buyruldu*s, that occupy most of the space; a number of entries of different sorts (such as *berat*s, *mektub*s, *mürâsele*s, that is, official letters issued by the *kadı*, *temessük*s, *kefalet*s (sureties), an *ifta kâğidi*, or document containing an Islamic legal opinion or fatwa) refer to appointments, state-related or not. Eight blank pages follow, and the last entry, on page 102, is a *narh* entry. This division of the material, locally originating entries in the first half and incoming correspondence in the second, makes this register fit the description of a 'typical' *kadı* register as described above.

---

10   Ioannis K. Vasdravellis (ed.), Ιστορικόν Αρχείον Βεροίας. Εκλογαί [Historical Archive of Veria: A selection] (Thessaloniki: Etaireia Makedonikon Spoudon, 1942); idem, ed., Ιστορικά αρχεία Μακεδονίας. Β'. Αρχείον Βεροίας – Ναούσης, 1598–1886 [Historical archives of Macedonia. II. Archive of Veria – Naoussa, 1598–1886] (Thessaloniki: Etaireia Makedonikon Spoudon, 1954).

11   My analysis is based on the microfilms of the registers. The numbering of the registers, and sometimes the arrangement of the sets of folios that make up a volume, are different on "Archeiomnimon".

12   Vehbi Günay, "H. 1159 (M. 1746) Tarihli Karaferye Kazası Şer'iye Sicili (Transkripsiyon ve Değerlendirme)", (Master's thesis, Ege University, 1993).

A register that partly coincides chronologically with the one that Günay studied is *sicil* No. 72 at the archive of Veria. It is one that has been preserved in its original form, has 137 pages (seven of them left blank), and covers the period from the end of May 1746 to the middle of July 1748, with one entry dated 7 November 1748/16 Zilkade 1161. The way this register has been organized is very different from that of the one above. It starts with a few brief entries that are more like notes, a *narh* entry, entries about the appointment of the *kadı*, more *narh* entries, and then entries of incoming correspondence (such as firmans, *berat*s, *buyruldu*s, *mektub*s) and those of a fiscal-administrative nature (such as land survey registers known as *mesâha defter*s, *tevzi defter*s, and *temessük*s), interspersed with *hüccet*s and *tereke defter*s. The register ends with brief entries like the ones on its opening page. Overall, it is possible to count sixty-six incoming decrees and letters (thirty-one *ferman*s, eight *berat*s, twenty-three *buyruldu*s, and four *mektub*s), to which one may add at least some of the twenty tax or income-related *temessük*s. However, if we treat the *temessük*s as fiscal documents, we may add to them the eight *tevzi defter*s and the three *mesâha defter*s of the register, as well as one tax-related collective pledge. Furthermore, there are three outgoing reports towards the central government and four *müráseles*. Against them, the number of twenty-four *hüccet*s, twenty-two *tereke defter*s, and a few *narh* entries and notes is relatively small. Furthermore, it needs to be stressed that, as noted above, contrary to the practice observed in the register that Günay studied, there are no separate sections for incoming entries and locally-produced documents in register No. 72. On the other hand, it is important to note that there is still a decent, even if not too large a number of *hüccet*s and *tereke defter*s to be found in the register, because this seems to change in *sicil*s of the later period.

A *kadı* register of almost twenty years later, the *sicil* No. 85 in Veria, covers, according to the original label on its front cover, the period from late November 1764 to the middle of April 1766. This is a register that was apparently put together using loose fragments, which may or may not have belonged to the same original register, and certainly with gaps. Of a total of sixty-four entries, thirty-nine are *firman*s, *berat*s, and *buyruldu*s, and two more *arzuhal*s (petitions), recorded together with the brief note written in response to them, most likely by the council (*dîvân*) of the governor of Thessaloniki. Of the remaining twenty-three entries, fourteen are tax-related (*tevzi defter*s, *temessük*s, a letter and a *tezkere*), three concern the appointment of the new *kadı*-cum-*kassâm-i askerî*, three are *tereke defter*s, four record conversions to Islam (one of them also the marriage of the convert woman), one concerns *narh* and another a *kefalet* (some peasants guarantee that their fellow villagers, who are accused of robbery, will appear in court when summoned). The earliest entries are two *berat*s dated 2–11 May 1764/evail-i Zilkade 1177, apparently entered in the *sicil* at a later date, and the latest is a receipt (*izin tezkeresi*) for the payment of the appropriate customs duty for tobacco, dated 6 December 1765/22 Cemâziyelâhir 1179.

The limited number of surviving folios does not allow definite conclusions, but there is an indication that, as with *sicil* No. 72, there is no clear pattern of organization of different types of entries in sections in the folios of *kadı* register No. 85. In other words, one of the three *tereke defter*s is followed by a firman, which is followed by another *tereke defter*, which is in its turn followed by a *temessük*. The third *tereke defter* is found between two *tevzi defter*s. This means that at least these three *tereke defter*s have not been entered in a section specifically reserved for them. It is also noteworthy that, contrary to the registers discussed above, there are no *hüccet*s or *i'lâm*s in the folios of which *sicil* No. 85 is composed, with the exception of the entries that are typical of the first and final pages of each *kadı* register (brief, note-like entries such as the ones recording conversions to Islam, sureties and official price setting).

*Sicil* No. 98 of the Veria archive is, unlike No. 85, but like No. 72, another one that has been preserved in its original form. It includes 170 pages, and its entries cover the period from the beginning of September 1780 to mid-August 1782,[13] with a few entries bearing earlier dates, the earliest being a pious endowment, or waqf, donation of 29 April 1778. The register opens with a page of notes, followed by the information about the appointment of the *kadı*. From page three onwards it almost exclusively contains incoming correspondence and tax-related entries with very few other locally-produced documents copied in-between. More specifically, I have counted sixty-five firmans, thirteen *berat*s, eighty-seven *buyruldu*s, of which twenty-seven are short notes accompanied by the *arzuhal*s that provoked them, two *mektub*s, one *mürâsele*, eighteen *temessük*s, twelve *tevzi defter*s, two *müfredat defter*s (fiscal inventories), five other tax-related entries, and six notes about the arrival of firmans and *buyruldu*s. Up to page 160, one can also find in the register two *hüccet*s, three *vakfiye*s (waqf trust deeds), nine *tereke defter*s, two entries about the appointment of the *kadı* as *kassâm-ı askerî* and the appointment of a *nâib*, or substitute judge, and a *narh* entry, the last one on page 157. The eleven last pages of the register, from 160 to 170, have been reserved for recording *narh* and other guild-related entries, conversions to Islam, *kefalet*s, *taahhüd*s or official contracts, and another five *hüccet*s. In other words, the register is almost exclusively dedicated to matters of public interest and correspondence with authorities outside Karaferye. The number of locally-produced entries is much smaller than in registers Nos 51 and 72 or the register that Günay studied.

---

13   The date Zilkade 1196 that a *temessük* on p. 90 bears must be a mistake for an earlier date.

Sicil no. 103 in Veria has lost an unspecified number of folios, but still preserves sixty-five pages and its front and back cover. Its entries cover the period from mid-January 1812 to mid-June 1813, with one entry dated 3 December 1811/17 Zilkade 1226 and another 11 May 1809/26 Rebîyülevvel 1224, but this might be a mistake for 1227. The general picture is similar to that of the *kadı* registers of the second half of the eighteenth century – twenty-eight firmans and six *buyuldu*s in full or summarized form, a summary of a firman and a *buyruldu*, a note about the arrival of a *buyruldu*, nine *berat*s, one *mektub*, six *mürâsele*s, five *tevzi defter*s, one *temessük*, interspersed with only four *hüccet*s, thirteen *tereke defter*s, and two *vakfıye*s. The first two pages of the register contain a few brief entries, while the last five pages, 61–5, contain *narh* and other guild-related entries, as well as the record of a conversion to Islam.

## 3  Conclusion

Is it a coincidence that the *kadı sicilleri* of the second half of the eighteenth and early-nineteenth century that are kept in Veria contain few *hüccet*s and *i'lâm*s, or does their limited number reflect a change, a transformation, not only in the registers, but also, and more importantly, in record-keeping practices, or even in the function of the local court of law that produced the *sicil*s?

As explained above, many of the registers in Veria have not been preserved in their original form, but are volumes that were put together in the late-twentieth century and consist mainly of unbound sets of folios. This means that it is possible that only the section containing the incoming orders and tax lists survived, though we have seen that some of the registers with a majority of incoming orders and other entries of an administrative-fiscal nature contain *tereke defter*s and other locally-produced entries. It may also mean that different registers were kept concurrently for judicial and notarial cases (or private matters), on the one hand, and administrative-fiscal affairs (or matters of public interest), on the other, even though there is no clear evidence of such a practice having existed in Karaferye.[14] If that were the case, such a possibility would entail a process of consciously preserving only one specific type of register, since it is unlikely that it was by pure chance that no registers with a majority of locally-produced entries have survived.

What seems unlikely is that the local court of law had ceased to try cases or to provide notarial services. That the members of the local society continued

---

14  There are a few specialized seventeenth-century registers (for example, on credit relations), but no evidence of systematically keeping such special *sicil*s in Karaferye. Cf. Gradeva, "*Kadı* Court", 59.

to have disputes among themselves is self-evident. However, if evidence of that were needed, one may find ample in the incoming orders recorded in the Karaferye *sicil*s, which deal with disputes among local people or disputes in which the local population was involved, as well as in the copies of such decrees in the *Rumeli Ahkâm Defterleri*.

Furthermore, the orders issued in response to *arzuhal*s usually required the *kadı* of Karaferye to hear the cases in question in his court.[15] Some refer to the petitioners having already made use of the services of the local court of law,[16] and others include the request of the petitioners that their case is not heard at the provincial courts of law but in Istanbul by the central authorities.[17]

Karaferye's case is not necessarily unique, but further research is needed before one can speak of parallel phenomena in other localities. Rossitsa Gradeva has noted about three surviving eighteenth-century *kadı* registers from Hacıoğlu Pazarcık (present-day Dobrich, north-east Bulgaria) that also mostly contain orders from higher authorities and relatively few locally-produced documents. The explanation she gives is that different registers possibly existed for different types of documents, such as for those related to the local waqfs.[18] Bruce McGowan has remarked, too, that the types of entries found in the *kadı* registers of Manastır (present-day Bitola, south-west North Macedonia) change over time, with a tendency for the *sicil*s gradually to become "more public in nature [because] the volume of interpersonal, local and small scale transactions diminished over time". But, unlike Karaferye,

---

15  See, for instance, *Rumeli Ahkâm Defteri* no. 24, entry no. 623 (23 September–2 October 1768), DOA: "iḥḳāḳ-ı ḥaḳḳ olunmaḳ bâbında ḥükm-i hümâyûn ricâ etmeğin maḥalinde şer'le görülmek içün yazılmışdır"; *Karaferye Kadı Sicili* no. 98, p. 24, entry no. 1 (15 January 1781), "ta'yîn olınan mübâşir ma'rifetiyle ḥużûr-ı şer'e iḥżâr ve terâfu'-yı şer' ve iḥḳāḳ-ı ḥaḳḳ eyl-eyesiz deyü".

16  For three examples, see *Rumeli Ahkâm Defteri* No. 14, entry no. 978 (26 June–5 July 1759); *Rumeli Ahkâm Defteri* No. 15, entry no. 71 (15–24 August 1759); *Rumeli Ahkâm Defteri* No. 27, entry no. 319 (22 June–1 July 1773), DOA. In the second case, the decree is addressed to the *kadı*s of Karaferye and the neighbouring district of Platamona, and does not make clear in which of the two courts the case had been heard previously. In the third case, the decree is addressed to the *kadı* of Karaferye and the *mütesellim* of Selânik, and it is the latter who is ordered to resolve the issue "şer' ve ḳānûn üzere". This may be read in relation to Boğaç Ergene's argument about the weakening of the judicial authority of the *kadı*s of Çankırı, that is discussed below. See Boğaç A. Ergene, *Local Court, Provincial Society and Justice in the Ottoman Empire: Legal Practice and Dispute Resolution in Çankırı and Kastamonu (1652–1744)* (Leiden: Brill, 2003), 32–56.

17  *Rumeli Ahkâm Defteri* no. 15, entry no. 141 (4–13 September 1759), DOA.

18  Rossitsa Gradeva, "The Activities of a Kadi Court in Eighteenth-Century Rumeli: The Case of Hacıoğlu Pazarcık", *Oriente Moderno* 79 (1), 1999, 187.

McGowan situates this phenomenon in the nineteenth rather than the eighteenth century in the case of the registers of Manastır.[19]

Furthermore, Boğaç Ergene juxtaposed the *kadı* registers of Çankırı and Kastamonu (both in northern Anatolia) from the mid-seventeenth to the mid-eighteenth century, and remarked that the former consistently contained a significantly smaller percentage of locally-composed documents than the latter, and that their 'administrative' character became stronger over time. Ergene notes that he cannot fully explain this discrepancy, but that it may be attributed to factors such as the smaller size of Çankırı compared with Kastamonu and the weakening of the judicial authority of the local *kadı* in favour of other official and unofficial loci of power that the local people felt were more effective in the resolution of their disputes. In this respect, he argues that the *kadıs* of Çankırı might have been more useful to local society because of their administrative functions, especially the authority to forward petitions and applications to higher authorities. He also points out that, even though decrees issued in response to *arzuhal*s of the local people against state officials often ordered the *kadıs* of Çankırı to hear these cases in their court, there are very few records of such hearings in the *sicil*s. Ergene interprets this as a possible sign of general lack of effectiveness of the petitioning procedure, and implies that it may be seen as an indication of the weakening of the credibility of the local court as a centre of dispute resolution between the powerful and the weaker members of local society.[20] This is, I believe, an interesting line of thinking that is worth pursuing in reference to Karaferye.

However, before doing so, it is necessary not only systematically to examine all the eighteenth-century Karaferye registers kept in Greece, Turkey, and Germany, but also to juxtapose them with those of the seventeenth century. This will allow us both to obtain a comprehensive, more accurate, picture of their contents, and to determine if 'typical' registers, as described above, prevailed in any period. There are many possibilities: for instance, it may be that indeed there were parallel series of *kadı sicilleri* or specialized sections of registers that have been lost. It may also be that in the eighteenth century the local people made greater use of other local authorities than in the past, to the detriment of the *kadı* court: one may think of the *voyvoda*, that is, the tax farmer and collector who must have acted as the *de facto* governor of the town, or of the local – informal from the point of view of the state – communal institutions (including the Church in the case of the Christians) or other informal

---

19   Bruce McGowan, *Economic Life in Ottoman Europe: Taxation, Trade and the Struggle for Land, 1600–1800* (Cambridge: CUP, 1981), 124–7. The quotation is from p. 126.

20   Ergene, *Local Court, Provincial Society*, 32–56. See also 170–88 for alternative centres of dispute resolution.

settlement mechanisms. Appealing to the provincial governors of Thessaloniki or Rumelia or even to the sultan in Istanbul was not out of the question either. The *Rumeli Ahkâm Defterleri* of the second half of the eighteenth century contain a fair number of orders addressed to the *kadı* of Karaferye, sometimes at a rate of one or more cases per month.

However, the problem with this last possibility is that, as noted above, the provincial and central authorities often referred the cases back to the *kadı* in Karaferye. Therefore, there must have been *sicil*s with records of these hearings, unless Ergene is right in his suggestion that the effectiveness of such orders is debatable. Another important problem is with the non-contested cases. Where, for instance, could one record a contract, sale, settlement, or the value and distribution of an estate among its legal heirs, if not in the register of practically the only official authority that could do so, namely, the local court of law? It seems illogical that people no longer needed to record such matters there, since this is what they had done in the past and such entries – albeit very few as noted above – do exist in the surviving registers of the second half of the eighteenth century in Veria.

Finally, it is also possible that we will never be able to reach a definite answer, given the state of the archival material, namely the relatively small number of fully preserved original registers, as well as the general lack of alternative, narrative sources about life in Karaferye of that era. The modest aim of this chapter has been simply to raise the issue of a possible transformation in record-keeping practices in the court of law of Karaferye and to provide information and evidence that may prove useful on a wider plane and a comparative basis.

## Acknowledgement

This chapter is partly based on work I did for the "Ottoman Qadi Court Records Workshop" organized by Harvard University Center for Middle East Studies and Middle East Social and Cultural History Association (18–20 May 2001).

## Bibliography

### *Primary Sources*
Devlet Arşivleri Genel Müdürlüğü Osmanlı Arşivi (DOA)
*Rumeli Ahkâm Defterleri*. Volumes 14, 15, 24, 27.

Greek General State Archives – Imathia Branch, Veria, Greece
*Karaferye Kadı Sicilleri*. Volumes 49, 51, 52, 72, 85, 98, 103.

## Secondary Sources

Anastasopoulos, Antonis. "Οι οθωμανικοί ιεροδικαστικοί κώδικες (σιτζίλ) της Βέροιας: προβλήματα ταξινόμησης [The Ottoman Court Registers (*Sicils*) of Veria: Classification Problems]". *IMEros* 1 (2001), 149–69.

Ergene, Boğaç A. *Local Court, Provincial Society and Justice in the Ottoman Empire: Legal Practice and Dispute Resolution in Çankırı and Kastamonu (1652–1744)*. Leiden: Brill, 2003.

Faroqhi, Suraiya. "Sidjill – 3. In Ottoman Administrative Usage". In *Encyclopaedia of Islam*, 2nd edn, vol. 9. Leiden, 1997.

Gradeva, Rossitsa. "The Activities of a Kadi Court in Eighteenth-Century Rumeli: The Case of Hacıoğlu Pazarcık". *Oriente Moderno* 79 (1) 1999, 177–90.

Gradeva, Rossitsa. "A *Kadı* Court in the Balkans: Sofia in the Seventeenth and Early Eighteenth Centuries". In Christine Woodhead (ed.) *The Ottoman World*. London: Routledge, 2012, 57–71.

Günay, Vehbi. "H. 1159 (M. 1746) Tarihli Karaferye Kazası Şer'iye Sicili (Transkripsiyon ve Değerlendirme)". Master's thesis, Ege University, 1993.

Günay, Vehbi. "Balkan Şehir Tarihleri Kaynağı Olarak Şer'iye Sicillerinin Envanter ve Kataloglarının Tespiti Hakkında". *Tarih İncelemeleri Dergisi* 18 (2) 2003, 71–82.

İnalcık, Halil, and Carter V. Findley. "Maḥkama – 2. The Ottoman Empire." In *Encyclopaedia of Islam*, 2nd edn, vol. 6. Leiden, 1991.

Jennings, Ronald C. "Kadi, Court, and Legal Procedure in 17th C. Ottoman Kayseri: The Kadi and the Legal System". *Studia Islamica* 48 (1978), 133–72.

Lindner, Margareta. "Die Rückwirkungen des osmanisch-venezianischen Krieges auf den Gerichtssprengel Karaferya (Veroia) in den Jahren 1715 und 1716 (nach dem Protokollbuch des Kadiamtes)". Master's thesis, Ludwig Maximilian University, Munich, 1987.

McGowan, Bruce. *Economic Life in Ottoman Europe: Taxation, Trade and the Struggle for Land, 1600–1800*. Cambridge: Cambridge University Press, 1981.

Neumann, Marianne Kathrin. "Die Rückwirkungen des osmanisch-russischen Krieges auf den Gerichtssprengel Qaraferya (Veroia) im Jahre 1771 (nach dem Protokollbuch des Kadiamtes)". Master's thesis, Ludwig Maximilian University, Munich, 1987/8.

Ortaylı, İlber. "Some Observations on the Institution of Qadi in the Ottoman Empire." *Bulgarian Historical Review* 10 (1) 1982, 57–68.

Vasdravellis, Ioannis K. (ed.) *Ιστορικόν Αρχείον Βεροίας. Εκλογαί* [Historical Archive of Veria: A Selection]. Thessaloniki: Etaireia Makedonikon Spoudon, 1942.

Vasdravellis, Ioannis K. (ed.) *Ιστορικά αρχεία Μακεδονίας. Β΄. Αρχείον Βεροίας – Ναούσης, 1598–1886* [Historical archives of Macedonia. II. Archive of Veria – Naoussa, 1598–1886]. Thessaloniki: Etaireia Makedonikon Spoudon, 1954.

CHAPTER 16

# Ottoman Legal Change and the *Şeriat* Courts in the Long Nineteenth Century

*Iris Agmon*

This chapter discusses the transformation of the Ottoman *şeriat* (sharia) court system during the long nineteenth century as part of a broader project of Ottoman legal modernization. Conventionally, the process of legal change occurring during the nineteenth-century Ottoman reforms has been conceived in terms of the binary of religious versus secular courts and legal spheres.[1] This binary was entrenched in a teleological perception of socio-legal change in the Ottoman Middle East. By framing the process of legal modernization in terms of 'secularization', the sharia courts were deemed 'religious courts' and thus considered immaterial to the process of legal modernization. In addition to this conceptual weakness, historians have neither discussed the meanings of the terms 'religious' and 'secular' in the discourse on Ottoman reforms, nor have they questioned the explanatory value of these terms for analysing the process of Ottoman legal change.[2]

In recent years, a growing body of revisionist studies on Ottoman law employing socio-legal approaches to Ottoman history has gradually changed

---

[1] Avi Rubin, "Ottoman Judicial Change in the Age of Modernity: A Reappraisal", *HC* 7 (2009), 119–40.

[2] Rubin, "Judicial Change", 4–5. A critical analysis of discussions on the modernization of Islamic law in terms of secularization may be found in Talal Asad, *Formations of the Secular: Christianity, Islam, Modernity* (Stanford: SUP, 2003). Asad's erudite study offers significant insights on 'the secular' as an epistemic category, on 'secularism' as political doctrine, and their interrelations (Asad, *Formations*, 1). Particularly relevant to my criticism above is Asad's focus on the complex dynamics of Islamic legal modernization in colonial Egypt discussed in the last chapter of his book (Asad, *Formations*, 205–56). His perspective there may be described as follows: 'secularism' was culturally constituted in Egypt under British colonial rule through a variety of socio-legal dynamics. In order to follow the changing meanings of 'secularism' it is necessary to explore "precisely what is involved when conceptual changes in a particular country make 'secularism' thinkable" (Asad, *Formations*, 209). In other words, instead of forcing an abstract and rigid meaning on terms like 'religious' and 'secular' when investigating modernizing societies, Asad deconstructs the changing use of these terms through exploring 'secularism' as a process.

our understanding of several dimensions of Ottoman legal change.[3] However, to date almost none of these studies has focused on late Ottoman sharia courts from a socio-legal perspective. Hence, it seems that the religious – secular binary has remained as influential as it has been among students of Ottoman history. There are several theoretical and historical reasons to question the characterization of the sharia courts as 'religious courts', and the religious – secular binary as an adequate explanatory tool for analysing late Ottoman legal change, as a whole.[4] I am going to discuss these issues in depth and offer alternative categories of analysis for historicizing Ottoman legal reforms in my larger work (in progress) on the sharia courts during the First World War and its aftermath.[5] Therefore, I will not elaborate on the brief criticism above that serves here as a vantage point for the following discussion.

---

3   See, for example, Iris Agmon, *Family and Court: Legal Culture and Modernity in Late Ottoman Palestine* (New York: Syracuse University Press, 2006); Iris Agmon and Ido Shahar, "Shifting Perspectives in the Study of *Shari'a* Courts: Methodologies and Paradigms", *ILS* 15 (2008), 1–19; Ebru Aykut Türker, "Alternative Claims on Justice and Law: Rural Arson and Poison Murder in the 19th-Century Ottoman Empire" (Ph.D. dissertation, Boğaziçi University, 2011); Boğaç A. Ergene, *Local Court, Provincial Society and Justice in the Ottoman Empire: Legal Practice and Dispute Resolution in Çankırı and Kastamonu (1652–1744)* (Leiden: Brill, 2003); Huri İslamoğlu, "Property as a Contested Domain: A Reevaluation of the Ottoman Land Code of 1858", in Roger Owen (ed.) *New Perspectives on Property and Land in the Middle East* (Cambridge, MA: Harvard University Press, 2000), 3–61; Noémi Lévy and Alexandre Toumarkine (eds), *Osmanlı'da Asayiş, Suç ve Ceza: 18–20 Yüzyıllar* (Istanbul: Tarih Vakfı Yurt Yayınları, 2007); Ruth A. Miller, *Legislating Authority: Sin and Crime in the Ottoman Empire and Turkey* (New York: Routledge, 2005); Omri Paz, "Crime, Criminals, and the Ottoman State: Anatolia Between the Late 1830s and the Late 1860s" (Ph.D. dissertation, Tel Aviv University, 2011); Leslie Peirce, *Morality Tales: Law and Gender in the Ottoman Court of Aintab* (Berkeley: University of California Press, 2003); Avi Rubin, *Ottoman Nizamiye Courts: Law and Modernity* (London: Palgrave MacMillan, 2011); Kent F. Schull, *Prisons in the Late Ottoman Empire: Microcosms of Modernity* (Edinburgh: Edinburgh University Press, 2014); Ehud R. Toledano, *As If Silent and Absent: Bonds of Enslavement in the Islamic Middle East* (New Haven: Yale University Press, 2007). These are but a few socio-legal studies. The body of literature in the field has been growing fast recently. More socio-legal studies will be referred to in the following notes. It should be noted that with regard to the nineteenth-century reforms, socio-legal studies have focused so far mostly on the development of the civil and criminal legal spheres. The reforms in the sphere of family law and the sharia courts have not attracted much attention among socio-legal scholars.
4   One such historical reason is the fact that the sharia courts were not described as 'religious courts' in Ottoman bureaucratic discourse.
5   The research for my broader work in progress, on the sharia courts in the First World War and its aftermath, was supported by grants from the Israel Science Foundation, and from the Gerda Henkel Stiftung. I am grateful to both foundations, as well as to Tel Aviv University and St Antony's College, for the Oxford Israeli Visiting Scholarship I received for the purpose of my research.

The focus of the main part of this chapter is on the actual changes that Ottoman reformers introduced to the sharia court system with the emphasis on the interrelations between those changes and the reforms in the Ottoman legal system as a whole. My presupposition is that the Ottoman judicial reforms in the long nineteenth century were about turning the judicial system, as a whole, into a modern centralized state judicial system. I argue that, from the outset, the sharia courts were part and parcel of the refashioning of the judicial system. Furthermore, efforts to introduce changes into the various judicial forums, including the sharia courts, with the aim of improving their work as branches of a comprehensive state system, continued until the very end of the empire following the First World War.

After a brief discussion of the issue of periodization and the concept of the 'long nineteenth century', the main part of this chapter is devoted to the three dimensions of the Ottoman judicial system – its structure; legislation and codification; and judiciary and legal education – that underwent profound changes during the long nineteenth century, and their effects on the sharia courts. Some concluding remarks end the discussion.

## 1  The Periodization of Ottoman Legal Reforms: 'The Long Nineteenth Century'

The notion of reforming and adjusting the state administration to changing realities was not new to the Ottomans. It was part and parcel of Ottoman ruling traditions. Thus, the reorganization of the Ottoman administration and ruling methods during the long nineteenth century constituted, in part, a continuation of the top-down tradition of change. Yet, it also differed from past reforms, mainly in terms of three characteristics. First, the nineteenth-century reforms were part of a broader trend of state reforms initiated by rulers and political elites in empires and states all over the globe. This trend may be seen as the culmination of a longer process of the emergence of the world economic system. Hence, the nineteenth-century Ottoman reforms may be considered part of the first globalization.[6] Second, they accompanied a broader modernization process in which the empire introduced brand new notions of statehood and

---

[6] See, for example, Jane Burbank and Frederick Cooper, *Empires in World History: Power and the Politics of Difference* (Princeton, NJ: Princeton University Press, 2010), 219–50; Huri İslamoğlu, *Ottoman History as World History* (Istanbul: Isis Press, 2007); Rubin, *Nizamiye Courts*, 4–8. On the Ottoman Empire and the paradigm of the world economy, see Immanuel Wallerstein, "The Ottoman Empire and the Capitalist World-Economy: Some Questions for Research", *Review* 2 (1979), 389–98.

interrelations between rulers and ruled. In the process, subjects were – at least potentially – becoming citizens.[7] Finally, in terms of time span, nineteenth-century reforms were the longest and, in retrospect, the most comprehensive reorganization project in Ottoman history, enduring serious external pressures and several major political upheavals and crises.

Until the late-twentieth century, the historiography on nineteenth-century Ottoman reforms focused on the official reorganization (*Tanzimat*). The *Tanzimat* began in 1839 with the Imperial Edict of the Rose Chamber (*Hatt-ı Şerif-i Gülhane*), ended in 1876 with the first Ottoman constitution, and was divided into two sub-periods by the end of the Crimean War and the announcement of a second imperial edict on resuming the reforms (*Islahat Fermanı*) in 1856. The early reforms initiated by Sultan Selim III (r. 1789–1807) and his successor, Sultan Mahmud II (r. 1808–39) were considered precursors of the Tanzimat, whereas the rule of Sultan Abdülhamid II (r. 1876–1908) was depicted as a reaction to the Tanzimat. In line with this narrative, the rule of the 'Young Turks', who revolted against Abdülhamid and took over the Ottoman government (1908–1919/23), was depicted as a prelude to the Turkish nation-state.[8] In this way, the last quarter of the nineteenth century was excluded from the discussion on the reforms, and the early twentieth century was deemed as the last breath of the 'sick man of Europe', leading to the inevitable fall of the Ottoman Empire and its succession by the Turkish Republic.

In the last few decades, however, historians studying the late Ottoman Empire have revisited some of the presuppositions underlying this periodization. Studies around the turn of both the nineteenth and the twentieth centuries have shown that reforms were conducted long before and well after the Tanzimat, and that, despite certain unique features of the Tanzimat period, it is possible to trace a long chain of reforms from the late-eighteenth century to the dissolution of the Ottoman Empire, which allow one to see that period as one era, 'the long nineteenth century'. The time of Abdülhamid II was revealed as particularly significant for the continuation and expansion of

---

[7] See, for example, Michelle U. Campos, *Ottoman Brothers: Muslims, Christians, and Jews in Early Twentieth-Century Palestine* (Stanford: SUP, 2011); Karen M. Kern, *Imperial Citizen: Marriage and Citizenship in the Ottoman Frontier Provinces of Iraq* (New York: Syracuse UP, 2011); Donald Quataert, *The Ottoman Empire, 1700–1922*, 2nd edn (Cambridge: CUP: 2005), 65–8.

[8] See, for example, Niyazi Berkes, *The Development of Secularism in Turkey* (Montreal: McGill University Press, 1964); Roderic H. Davison, *Reform in the Ottoman Empire, 1856–1876* (Princeton, NJ: Princeton University Press, 1963); Bernard Lewis, *The Emergence of Modern Turkey* (London: OUP, 1966).

the legal reforms.[9] Furthermore, studies on the actual implementation of the reforms and on their outcomes throughout the empire during the late Ottoman period provided a better understanding of the culture of Ottoman reform.[10] Consequently, the concept of 'the long nineteenth century' describing the period that began before and ended after the calendric nineteenth century has proved useful. According to this periodization, the thirty-seven years of Tanzimat are considered part of a longer chain of reforms from the late-eighteenth century until the dissolution of the Ottoman Empire following its defeat in the First World War.[11]

## 2      Dimensions of Legal Change

Given the goals of this chapter and its limited space, the discussion on the judicial reforms is structured thematically, while skipping the painstaking efforts of Ottoman reformers to bring about changes, typically through trial and error, and the struggles among them along the way.

---

9    Rubin, *Nizamiye Courts*, 3–4, 31–37, 79–80. Carter Findley challenged much earlier the conventional periodization of Ottoman reforms. See Carter V. Findley, *Bureaucratic Reform in the Ottoman Empire: The Sublime Porte, 1789–1922* (Princeton, NJ: Princeton University Press, 1980).

10   See, for example, Marc Aymes, *A Provincial History of the Ottoman Empire: Cyprus and the Eastern Mediterranean in the Nineteenth Century*, translated by Adrian Morfee (New York: Routledge, 2014); Carter V. Findley, Ottoman Civil Officialdom: A Social History (Princeton, NJ: Princeton University Press, 1989); Michael E. Meeker, *A Nation of Empire: The Ottoman Legacy of Turkish Modernity* (Berkeley: University of California Press, 2002); Bülent Özdemir, *Ottoman Reforms and Social Life: Reflections from Salonica, 1830–1850* (Istanbul: Isis Press, 2003); Mahmoud Yazbak, Haifa in the Late Ottoman Period, 1864–1914: A Muslim Town in Transition (Leiden: Brill, 1998).

11   Originally, it was historian Erik Hobsbawm who coined the term 'the long nineteenth century' for the age of revolution and nationalism in Europe beginning with the French Revolution (1789) and ending with the end of the First World War. The suggestion of scholars of Middle East history to borrow the term for the purpose of revisiting the periodization of Ottoman history is based on a wide range of detailed research findings on the length and depth of Ottoman reforms. A broader discussion on this topic, however, goes beyond the scope of this chapter. On the beginning of the long nineteenth century and the rule of Selim III, see Seyfi Kenan (ed.) *Nizam-ı Kadim'den Nizam-ı Cedid'e: III. Selim ve Dönemi* [Selim III and his Era: From Ancién Regime to New Order] (Istanbul: ISAM, 2010).

## 2.1 Redefinition of Legal Spheres and Restructuring the Judicial System

The Ottomans had already begun to introduce reforms in certain spheres, including the legal system, by the end of the eighteenth century. In the judicial system, however, the earliest meaningful reforms began in the late 1830s and continued successively, despite political obstacles and crises, until the Ottoman Empire ceased to exist. The Ottoman reformers made substantial efforts to turn the judicial system into a multi-court system. The reformed system comprised several judicial forums, each specializing in certain legal spheres. Both the definitions of legal spheres (as criminal, civil, commercial, and family law) and the division of labour among the various judicial forums according to these definitions represented significant change. During the process of restructuring the judicial system, the sharia court system that had been the backbone of the Ottoman pre-modern state judicial system,[12] became one among several judicial forums in the new multi-court system. During the 1840s and 1850s, the Ottoman government gradually developed a mixed civil and criminal system based on sharia courts and new administrative-judicial councils.[13] The reorganization of the provincial system since the mid-1860s, following the legislation of the Provincial (*vilâyet*) Reform Law in 1864, marked a further step in the institutionalization of the multi-court system. Alongside

---

12   Another judicial forum that existed prior to the legal reforms, beside the sharia courts, was that of the consular courts. Originally, these courts conducted legal proceedings involving foreign merchants under the protection of the sultan. This protection was part of the capitulations (*imtiyazat*) that the sultan awarded certain European countries to encourage the economic activities of their subjects in the Ottoman domains. Gradually, however, these rights were used by consuls of European powers to expand the foreign communities under their jurisdiction by awarding the same legal rights to any citizen of their countries and, ultimately, also to Ottoman citizens, mostly to members of the non-Muslim communities. Consequently, the Ottoman government considered the consular courts a challenge to its sovereignty. Tackling this challenge was one of the motivations behind the Ottoman reformers for introducing the *nizamiye* commercial courts. Consistent Ottoman efforts during the nineteenth century to abolish the capitulations were yet another means to deal with this situation. See Feroz Ahmad, "Ottoman Perceptions of the Capitulations 1800–1914", *JIS* 11 (2000), 1–20; Edhem Eldem, "Capitulations and Western Trade", in Suraiya N. Faroqhi (ed.) *The Cambridge History of Turkey*, vol. 3: *The Later Ottoman Empire, 1603–1839* (Cambridge: CUP, 2006), 283–335; Maurits H. van den Boogert, *The Capitulations and the Ottoman Legal System: Qadis, Consuls and Beraths in the 18th Century* (Leiden: Brill, 2005).

13   Aykut, "Alternative Claims", *passim*; Omri Paz, "Documenting Justice: New Recording Practices and the Establishment of an Activist Criminal Court System in the Ottoman Provinces (1840-late 1860s)", *ILS* 21 (2014), 81–113; Milan V. Petrov, "Everyday Forms of Compliance: Subaltern Commentaries on Ottoman Reform, 1864–1868", *Comparative Study of Society and History* (2004), 730–59.

the implementation of the *Provincial Reform Law*, Ottoman reformers redefined the jurisdiction of the sharia courts and the provincial councils. The latter were integrated into a new hierarchy of *nizamiye* ('organized', or 'reformed') courts.[14] The *nizamiye* system comprised two branches – one for civil cases, and the other for criminal ones. In certain towns (mostly, but not exclusively, port cities), there were also commercial courts.

Administratively, both the civil and criminal branches of the *nizamiye* court system belonged to the Ministry of Justice, and its establishment represented yet another significant dimension in the restructuring of the legal system. In both branches of the *nizamiye* system, the institutional hierarchy had three levels, the two higher ones of which served as instances of appeal. Yet, with regard to statutes, legal procedure, and personnel, the two branches developed in different directions. In certain respects, the *nizamiye* civil courts interacted with the sharia courts more closely than with the *nizamiye* criminal ones, particularly at the lower-level sub-district (*kaza*) and district (*sancak*) courts. While they remained the responsibility of the chief mufti (*şeyhülislâm*),[15] and family law was the main legal sphere under their jurisdiction, the sharia courts also tried civil cases, much like the civil *nizamiye* courts. Procedurally, until the adoption of a new procedural *nizamiye* code in 1879, both the sharia and civil *nizamiye* courts followed the shar'i law of procedure. The *Mecelle* (*Mecelle-i Ahkâm-ı Adliye*), a new code of shar'i civil law compiled between 1869 and 1876, was enforced by both the *nizamiye* and sharia courts. Furthermore, at the lower levels, shar'i judges presided over the *nizamiye* civil courts as well.[16] The *nizamiye* criminal courts, by contrast, developed in a different direction.

---

14  Rubin, *Nizamiye Courts*, 27–31. On the development of the provincial councils, see Jun Akiba, "The Local Councils as the Origin of the Parliamentary System in the Ottoman Empire", in Tsugitaka Soto (ed.) *Development of Parliamentarism in the Modern Islamic World* (Tokyo: Toyo Bunko, 2009), 178–84.

15  Except for three years (1917–20), during which the administration of the sharia courts was transferred from the authority of *Şeyhulislâm* to that of the Ministry of Justice, *Ceride-i İlmiye* 31 (1335H/1917), 875; *Ceride-i İlmiye* 61 (1338H/1920), 1907/8. I assume that this step was taken (in March 1917) in preparation for the legislation of the *Family Code* in October 1917 (see below). I am currently examining this issue as part of my research in progress. I tend to interpret the legislation and the transfer of the sharia courts to the Ministry of Justice as part of the continuous efforts by the Ottoman government to improve the work of the multi-court system and not, as some historians claim, as an effort to weaken *Şeyhülislâm*. See Berkes, *Development of Secularism*, 415–17.

16  Jun Akiba, "From *Kadi* to *Naib*: Reorganization of the Ottoman Sharia Judiciary in the Tanzimat Period", in Colin Imber and Keiko Kiyotaki (eds) *Frontiers of Ottoman Studies: State, Province, and the West* (London: I. B. Tauris, 2005), vol. 1, 53–4.

In terms of substantive law, legal procedure, and legal administration, the borrowing from continental models, the French in particular, was more evident in the criminal system than in the civil one.[17]

The reasons for these differences were twofold: from the outset, the state of the legal sphere defined by modern terms as 'criminal law' was less institutionalized in the early-modern structure of the Ottoman legal system than the sphere of 'civil law'. Serving as the main judicial framework of the Ottoman state, the pre-Tanzimat sharia courts were designed for hearing mostly private legal cases, even when the offence on trial was severe, belonging by shar'i terminology in the category of offences against God (*hadd*). The ideas underlying modern criminal systems were alien to the sharia court culture and shar'i law (as they were to other pre-modern judicial systems). Granted, the early-modern Ottoman legal culture was heavily shaped by the presence of the state. Hence, the significant role of sultanic legislation (*kānûn*), the judicial functions of the Imperial Council, the elevated position of *Şeyhülislâm* in the Ottoman administration, and the involvement of provincial governors in trying and punishing offenders, to mention but a few examples.[18] However, the notion that 'the state' is an entity that actively takes to court offenders who allegedly violated the body, the property, or the morality of certain individuals or institutions; that such offences are considered crimes against the interest of 'the public'; and that this public is epitomized by the state (a notion

---

17  For instance, the reformers borrowed from the French legal system the position of the public prosecutor and introduced it into the Ottoman criminal judicial system. At the same time, like in other cases of Ottoman legal borrowing, the reformers adjusted the new position to the characteristics and needs of the Ottoman legal system. In his discussion on the institution of public prosecution, Avi Rubin shows the development of the borrowed position within the Ottoman reformed judicial system and the important role it played in the civil legal sphere in addition to the criminal one. See Rubin, *Nizamiye Courts*, 133–52. On the criminal codes, see below.

18  Paz, "Documenting Justice", 90–8. See, for example, Yavuz Aykan, "Les acteurs de la justice à Amid et dans la province du Diyarbekir d'après les sicil provinciaux du 18ᵉ siècle" (Ph.D. dissertation, École des Hautes Études en Sciences Sociales, Paris, 2012); James E. Baldwin, "Islamic Law in an Ottoman Context: Resolving Disputes in Late 17th/Early 18th Century Cairo" (Ph.D. dissertation, New York University, 2010); Rositsa Gradeva, "On Judicial Hierarchy in the Ottoman Empire: The Case of Sofia, Seventeenth – Beginning of Eighteenth Century", in Muhammad K. Masud, Rudolph Peters and David S. Powers (eds) *Dispensing Justice in Islam: Qadis and Their Judgments* (Leiden: Brill, 2006), 271–98; Michael Ursinus, *Grievance Administration in an Ottoman Province: The Kaymakam of Rumelia's 'Record Book of Complaints' of 1781–1783* (New York: Routledge Curzon, 2005); Eyal Ginio, "The Administration of Criminal Justice in Ottoman Selanik (Salonica) During the Eighteenth Century", *Turcica* 30 (1998), 185–209.

developed in nineteenth-century European law), was not part of Ottoman legal culture.[19] Centralizing the Ottoman Empire and turning it into a modern intervening state, however, were significant goals of the Ottoman reformers. An enhanced criminal system of the kind that had not been part of the early-modern Ottoman legal culture was just what they needed to achieve that goal. At the same time, developing this type of criminal system was not merely a means for achieving an end; it was a major aspect of that end.[20]

The reorganization of the judicial system affected the sharia courts not only in terms of the distribution of jurisdiction and interrelations with other judicial forums, but also in terms of their internal organization. In the seventeenth and eighteenth centuries, the sharia court system underwent a process of decentralization. Whereas senior judges were appointed at the imperial capital to judicial positions in the main provincial centres, junior judges and judicial deputies were often appointed to courts in more marginal provincial locations by senior judges using the practice of 'farming out' judicial positions. Furthermore, judges were paid from the court's revenues.[21] Institutionally, the sharia court system was structured vertically. All the courts were of the same level without instances of appeal (various mechanisms for challenging court decisions, such as petitions to the sultan, were available to and employed by Ottoman subjects, but these were not built-in elements of the court system).

Beginning in 1855, the shar'i judiciary system was reorganized in a new hierarchy of five ranks of *nâib*s. They were appointed in the capital and placed on the imperial payroll. In addition, as part of the implementation of the Provincial Reform Law in the provinces, the entire sharia court system (except for the lowest tier, that is county [*nahiye*] level) was reorganized into a centralized hierarchy. At the same time, appeal instances were gradually introduced into the sharia court system.[22] In addition, to facilitate top-down supervision of the judicial work at courts in the provinces, *Bab-ı Meşîhat* (the office of *Şeyhülislâm*) introduced practices to the sharia courts for documenting court cases in detail and regulations for summoning the records for review at the capital.[23]

---

19   Miller, *Legislating Authority*, *passim*; Rubin, *Nizamiye Courts*, 137–8.
20   Omri Paz explains this process as a transformation of the pre-modern Ottoman judicial system from a reactive system to proactive one. See Paz, "Documenting Justice", *passim*.
21   Akiba, "From Kadı to Naib", 44–6; Ergene, *Local Court*, 23–31. See also a detailed analysis of local court fees, in the sixteenth to eighteenth centuries, Ergene, *Local Court*, 76–98.
22   Jun Akiba, "A New School for Qadis: Education of Sharia Judges in the late Ottoman Empire", *Turcica* 35 (2003), 125–63; *idem*, "From Kadı to Naib", 47–53; *Düstur*² 5, 352–61.
23   Iris Agmon, "Text, Court, and Family in Late-Nineteenth-Century Palestine", in Beshara Doumani (ed.) *Family History in the Middle East: Household, Property, and Gender* (Albany:

Another institutional innovation introduced into the sharia courts was the attachment of officials appointed as directors of local orphan funds (*Eytam Sandıkları*) to the personnel of local courts. The orphan funds functioned under the new Authority for Supervision of Orphan Properties (*Emval-i Eytam Nezareti*) established at the *Meşîhat* during the reforms. This authority was in charge of managing property inherited by minors and other dependent family members whose natural guardians (in most cases, their fathers) had died leaving an inheritance. The directors of local orphan funds were assigned to help local shar'i judges fulfil their traditional responsibility of regulating the actions taken by relatives of the deceased in the management of property inherited by orphans.[24] The establishment of the Authority for Supervision of Orphan Properties and the network of orphan funds demonstrates two major aspects of Ottoman reforms – first, the aspirations of the reformers to involve the Ottoman state in spheres in which it had not interfered in the past, like family relations;[25] and second, their perception of the sharia courts as an integral part of the reformed state legal system.

## 2.2 Legislation and Codification

Another major aspect of legal change was legislation – the promulgation of new codes inspired by continental law, the codification of shar'i laws, and the circulation of numerous imperial edicts and decrees for the administration of the legal system. In fact, the first code inspired by continental law, the penal code, was legislated in 1840 prior to the establishment of criminal courts. The implementation led to the initial experiments with the mixed shar'i and criminal judicial forums of the early 1840s.[26] This code was followed by numerous new codes and amendments of existing ones, which the Ottoman legislator introduced to all legal spheres until the last day of the empire.[27] While all these

---

SUNY Press, 2003), 201–28; *idem*, "Recording Procedures and Legal Culture in the Late Ottoman *Shari'a* Court of Jaffa", *ILS* 11 (3) 2004, 333–77.

24  Agmon, *Family and Court*, 147–58; İlhami Yurdakul, *Osmanlı İlmiye Merkez Teşkilatı'nda Reform, 1826–1876* (Istanbul: İletişim Yayınları, 2008), 178–90.

25  There are several other indications for the state's tendency to interfere in family relations during this period. A relatively early example (1838) of such interference is the measures taken by the Sublime Porte to prevent child abortion in order to boost population growth. See Tuba Demirci and Selçuk Akşin Somel, "Women's Bodies, Demography, and Public Health: Abortion Policy and Perspectives in the Ottoman Empire of the Nineteenth Century", *Journal of the History of Sexuality* 17 (3) 2008, 377–420.

26  Paz, "Documenting Justice", 92.

27  For instance, Code of Commerce, 1850; Land Code, 1858; Penal Code, 1858; Code of Civil Procedure, and Code of Criminal Procedure, 1879; to mention but a few.

codes were inspired by laws from various European continental legal systems (mostly, but not exclusively, the French one), none of them represented a pure transplantation of a European code in its entirety into the Ottoman legal system. The reformers invested a great deal of effort in adjusting continental laws to their goals and the changing conditions of the Ottoman legal system, thereby creating a unique amalgam of Ottoman and continental laws.

The very act of codification, however, represented an adoption of modern continental legal practice (which was also new in European legal systems).[28] Codification of shar'i laws, in particular, signified a substantial change. The function and logic of legal codes are very different from those of shar'i law. Given the basic perception that shar'i law was sacred, its framework gave judges a wide range of legal interpretations and judicial precedents, which provided a pool of legal alternatives for shaping concrete court decisions. Such a judicial method may seem arbitrary to an outside observer, particularly one whose legal thinking has been shaped by modern continental law. A deeper examination of this practice, however, may reveal that it was embedded in a matching legal culture, and, most importantly, in a broader notion of law as a moral habitus.[29] Legal codes, by contrast, are meant to provide judges with a complete set of rules that predetermine rulings for any specific case, a ready-made law. They are intended to be operational, hence the simple and imperative nature of their wording. Legal codes represented nineteenth-century trends of standardization of law and its extensive use by rulers, bureaucrats, and the emerging middle classes in various societies all over the world.

Thus, when codifying shar'i laws, Ottoman jurists changed both the form and organization of the law books consulted by judges and other court personnel during the judicial process. The change of form also set in motion a gradual yet substantial transformation of the content of shar'i law, and of the notion of law and socio-legal relations, as a whole. In Talal Asad's words, "what happens to the *shari'a* is best described not as curtailment but as transmutation. It is rendered into a subdivision of legal norms (*fıkıh*) that are authorized and maintained by the centralizing state."[30]

In practical terms, the codification of shar'i laws required a nuanced selection of rules and major simplification of their wording, which meant ruling

---

28   Avi Rubin, "Modernity as a Code: The Ottoman Empire and the Global Movement of Codification", *JESHO* 59 (5) 2016, 828–56.

29   Asad, *Formations*, 241.

30   Asad, *Formations*, 227. It should be noted that Asad's depiction of the implications of the codification of shar'i law is rather different from that of some legal historians whose approach to it may be defined as idealistic (Asad, *Formations*, 219–21).

out many legal options. Legal historians often stress the innovativeness demonstrated by the practice of selecting certain rules for creating shar'i codes. With regard to the last Ottoman codification, the *Family Code* (*Hukuk-i Aile Karanamesi*, 1917), which is presented shortly in some detail, that the legislators incorporated rules from legal schools other than the official Ottoman Hanafi school and from customary law (*örf*) is particularly highlighted. The significance of this inclusive tendency notwithstanding, it should be noted that the selection of rules from such a variety of legal sources might have involved implementing non-Hanafi rules that had existed in the legally-pluralistic Ottoman judicial system. Furthermore, the selection of one set of rules from such a wide range of alternatives (even within the Hanafi school) necessarily meant the exclusion of all those other alternatives that had been available – at least, potentially – until the codification. It is, therefore, important to note that codification entailed weakening certain features of legal pluralism present in Ottoman law and substantially restricted the discretion of judges.

A striking example of the codification of shar'i law was the promulgation of the *Mecelle*, a selection of Hanafi civil and procedural laws reshaped and structured as a modern law book.[31] The *Mecelle* was prepared by a special committee in the years 1869–76. By then, Ottoman reformers had acquired rich codification experience. The original model for codification worldwide (Europe included), namely the French *code civil* of 1804, had by that time turned into one among many sources for legal borrowing.[32] The *Mecelle* was designed to serve as a law code in both sharia and *nizamiye* civil courts, and indeed it was used in both forums, thus demonstrating that they were parts of the same system.[33]

The *Family Code*, one of the most significant projects of Ottoman legal modernization, was yet another example of the codification of shar'i law.[34]

---

31  *Düstur*, 1st edn, vol. 3, 38–148; *Düstur*, 1st edn, vol. 4, 93–115.
32  Rubin, "Modernity as a Code", *passim*.
33  Agmon, *Family and Court*, 155, fn.26. Following the reforms, court records included detailed documentation of court cases. But they did not include references to the legal sources on which the court's rulings were based. In the court records of Haifa and Jaffa, however, every now and then, a certain article of the *Mecelle* would be mentioned during the deliberations by one of the parties (often by a lawyer) to sustain the claim in question and then it would be recorded.
34  *Düstur*, 2nd edn, vol. 9, 762–81. It should be noted that together with the *Family Code*, the Ottoman legislator promulgated a *Code of Procedure for the Şeriat Courts*, *Düstur*, 2nd edn, vol. 9, 783–94. The conventional translation of the family code's title is *Ottoman Law of Family Rights* (OLFR). I prefer a different translation, namely *The Family Code*. Labelling the code as 'Ottoman' was apparently the outcome of discussions on post-Ottoman family

Misinterpretation of this code seems to be widespread in the conventional historiography on the late Ottoman period. Consequently, its historical significance was hardly studied.[35] Being a major theme of my research in progress, I will not elaborate on this issue here. For the sake of the current discussion, however, it may be noted that the idea of employing the concepts of the *Mecelle* for the codification of a family law was not new in the Ottoman reformist discourse. Yet, before this direction was finally chosen, the Ottoman legislator had promulgated two imperial decrees (*irade-i seniyye*) sanctioning an expert legal interpretation (in Turkish *ictihad*) that had permitted sharia courts to accept, under certain circumstances, the requests of wives to terminate their marriage.[36] Issuing legal opinions (fatwa, Turkish *fetva*) by Şeyhülislâm on pressing questions was not a new practice in the Ottoman politico-religious tradition. In this case, the legal opinions offered certain relief for women trapped in intolerable marriages by slightly opening the door for change in the strict Hanafi rules on the matter. By turning the legal opinion into an imperial decree, a regulation of shar'i family law became, formally, statute law. The significance of this step notwithstanding, this practice was not useful for a comprehensive treatment in the sphere of family law in the broader spirit of Ottoman legal reform.

Shortly after the promulgation of those imperial decrees in March 1916, a committee for drafting the new family code was appointed by the Minister of Justice.[37] The family code that the committee created was highly significant for a variety of reasons. In the context of the current discussion, two aspects of the code's significance need to be highlighted: the code signified a step forward in the process of creating a unified state judicial system; and the sharia

---

codes that were based on the 1917 *Family Code*. Obviously, such addition is redundant in this chapter. The word '*hukuk*' in Arabic and Ottoman meant both 'laws' and 'rights'. However, the code in question includes a set of laws dealing with the creation of families (marriage) and the termination thereof (divorce), not with 'rights' of the institution of the family (the discourse of 'rights' that was so central to the development of continental law in the nineteenth century was among the aspects of modern law that Ottoman reformers had not borrowed). The term 'code' expresses both the content (family laws) and form (code) of the legislation – hence, the *Family Code*.

35 Due to the consequences of the First World War, the Family *Code* was never fully implemented in the Ottoman Empire. This is probably one of the reasons why it did not attract much scholarly attention. Only very few studies have analysed its content. See, for example, M. Akif Aydın, *İslam-Osmanlı aile hukuku* [Islamic-Ottoman Family Law] (Istanbul: Marmara Üniversitesi, 1985); Robert H. Eisenman, *Islamic Law in Palestine and Israel: A History of the Survival of Tanzimat and Shari'a in the British Mandate and the Jewish State* (Leiden: Brill, 1978).
36 *Düstur* 2nd edn, vol. 8 (no. 305), 478–82; (no. 390), 853–57.
37 DOA ŞD. 2836/29.

courts were intended to play an important role in that process. A strong state judicial system is a major characteristic of modern states. The Ottoman judicial reforms aimed to achieve that end. On the eve of the First World War, the Ottoman judicial system was well into that process through refashioning its structure and through codification. At that point, only the sphere of family law was not codified. The *Family Code* and accompanying legislation (procedural law, administrative regulations) complemented previous reforms in the sharia courts and reshaped their position within the reformed judicial system.

### 2.3 The Judiciary and Legal Education

Finally, the transformation of the legal system was sustained by a profound reorganization of the judiciary and establishment of new institutions for higher legal training. Efforts to centralize the judiciary of the sharia courts in the provinces began even before the official announcement of the Tanzimat, in 1838. These early reforms tackled the prevailing methods of recruitment of junior judges titled 'deputies' (*nâib*) by senior ones (*kadı*) through 'farming out' judgeship positions to lower-ranking courts in the provinces. The goal was to reduce the dependency of junior judges on senior ones and to shift control over the former to the imperial centre as an initial step towards reorganizing the judiciary. More systematic reorganization began in the mid-1850s. The hierarchy of the judiciary was reorganized according to a set of uniform criteria, such as the judge's level of training and grades. All judges were appointed by a special committee at the Office of Şeyhülislâm and were placed on the state payroll. This reorganization resulted in a tendency to define the lion's share of shar'i judges as *nâibs* rather than *kadıs*. The implementation of the *Provincial Reform Law* in the mid-1860s reinforced the institutionalization of the reformed judiciary and enhanced interrelations between the sharia and the new *nizamiye* court systems.[38]

In 1855, a college for shar'i judges (*Muallimhâne-i Nüvvab*) was established in Istanbul, and it gradually became a major pool for the recruitment of new appointees in sharia courts all over the empire. In the years following its establishment, the curriculum and character of the college underwent gradual

---

[38] Akiba, "From *Kadi* to *Naib*", *passim*. Some of these rules were revised during the course of the reforms. For instance, the title *kadı* was restored in 1913; the restrictions concerning the length and number of terms of service in the same court became more flexible, *Düstur*, 2nd edn, vol. 5, 352–61. But the main features of the reforms, namely creating a unified hierarchic judicial system subordinated to the central government in Istanbul, remained.

changes that strengthened its reputation as a modern institution for training professional judges and scribes for the reformed judicial system. That throughout the entire period, shar'i judges headed the adjudicating councils of civil *nizamiye* district courts was reflected in the curriculum of the college by the growing number of courses focusing on the various codes and legal procedures legislated for in the *nizamiye* courts.[39] At the same time, the curriculum of the new law school for training professional jurists for the *nizamiye* system established in Istanbul in 1878 included courses on Islamic jurisprudence (*fıkıh*) in its curriculum.[40]

## 3   Concluding Remarks

Two features stand out from the above discussion on the transformation of the Ottoman judicial system – a redistribution of labour among various judicial forums; and the unification of the judicial system, thus strengthening its features as a state system. These two trends may seem mutually exclusive but in fact they complemented each other. The process of redistributing judicial labour among the various courts did not aim to create isolated judicial forums. Rather, it was meant to enhance the competency of each judicial forum while improving coordination with other judicial forums. In other words, the constant modifications of the distribution of labour among different judicial forums were linked to the effort to modernize and further institutionalize the judicial system as a whole.

This is not to say that the reforms were without internal contradictions. Many contradictions, overlaps, confusions, and compromises in the judicial system resulted from the prolonged reforms. There were also numerous political struggles and ideological debates on reform policies over the years. Moreover, jurisdictional conflicts and contradictions resulting in justice being compromised to some degree can be found in any modern judicial system. However, certain features of the Ottoman reforms that contemporary observers and – later – historians saw as contradictions or failures of the reformers were neither contradictions nor failures.[41] They represented the path taken consistently by the

---

39   Akiba, "A New School for Qadis", *passim*.
40   Rubin, *Nizamiye Courts*, 79.
41   See, for example, Berkes, *Secularism*, 417–18; Avi Rubin, "British Perceptions of Ottoman Judicial Reform in the Late Nineteenth Century: Some Preliminary Insights", *Law and Social Inquiry* 37 (4) 2012, 991–1012.

reformers, despite changing political trends – a legal modernization that was deeply rooted in Ottoman legal culture while being strongly influenced and inspired by legal modernization trends in continental law.

During the long period of reforms, all the judicial forums that formed the modern Ottoman judicial system underwent substantial changes. The sharia courts constituted the only institutionalized judicial forum among them that continued from the pre-modern Ottoman legal system into the modern one. The other courts were created from scratch during the nineteenth century. Thus, at first glance, it seems that the reforms were only about creating new judicial forums and removing various spheres of jurisdiction from the old one, the sharia court system, and distributing them among the new courts. Described in this way, the expected conclusion about the sharia courts would be that they were either marginalized or on their way to being abolished. Moreover, if the discussion on the reforms is conceptualized in terms of a religious-secular binary, such a description might be seen to infer that the Ottoman reformers intended to weaken or eliminate the 'religious' sharia courts.

A closer look at the complex process of Ottoman legal change, however, reveals that such conclusion stands on weak factual and interpretive grounds. The sharia courts were not depicted by the Ottoman reformers as a liability, to begin with. They put a great deal of effort into refashioning and strengthening the sharia court system, much like they did with the other judicial forums. While removing certain legal spheres from the jurisdiction of the sharia courts they expanded their responsibilities by adding new judicial activities and positions. Moreover, while members of the new Ottoman reformist elite were fascinated by modern European legal concepts and practices, the legal culture that shaped their visions for legal modernization was the one that had prevailed in and been nurtured by the sharia courts for centuries.

The nineteenth century was indeed long and fraught with profound changes. Several generations of reformers lived consecutively during that period. The ideas, political context, and agendas that motivated different generations of reformers changed substantially along the way. Yet, the codification that turned out to be the last, the *Family Code* promulgated in October 1917, shows that the last generation of Ottoman reformers followed in the footsteps of their predecessors. The codification and the ensuing legal administrative activities are indicative of an intention to develop further the unique multi-court system and to assign the sharia courts new roles in it.

## Bibliography

### Primary Sources
Devlet Arşivleri Genel Müdürlüğü Osmanlı Arşivi (DOA)
Şura-yı Devlet 2836/29.

### Published Primary Sources
*Ceride-i İlmiye* (official periodical for publishing fatwas and other religious opinions).
*Düstur* (official periodical for publishing law codes).

### Secondary Sources
Agmon, Iris. "Text, Court, and Family in Late-Nineteenth-Century Palestine". In Beshara Doumani (ed.) *Family History in the Middle East: Household, Property, and Gender*. Albany: State University of New York Press, 2003, 201–28.

Agmon, Iris. "Recording Procedures and Legal Culture in the Late Ottoman *Shari'a* Court of Jaffa". *Islamic Law and Society* 11 (3) 2004, 333–77.

Agmon, Iris. *Family and Court: Legal Culture and Modernity in Late Ottoman Palestine*. New York: Syracuse University Press, 2006.

Agmon, Iris and Ido Shahar. "Shifting Perspectives in the Study of *Shari'a* Courts: Methodologies and Paradigms". *Islamic Law and Society* 15 (2008), 1–19.

Ahmad, Feroz. "Ottoman Perceptions of the Capitulations 1800–1914". *Journal of Islamic Studies* 11 (2000), 1–20.

Akiba, Jun. "A New School for Qadis: Education of Sharia Judges in the late Ottoman Empire". *Turcica* 35 (2003), 125–63.

Akiba, Jun. "From *Kadi* to *Naib*: Reorganization of the Ottoman Sharia Judiciary in the Tanzimat Period". In Colin Imber and Keiko Kiyotaki (eds). *Frontiers of Ottoman Studies: State, Province, and the West*. London: I. B. Tauris, 2005, vol. 1, 43–60.

Akiba, Jun. "The Local Councils as the Origin of the Parliamentary System in the Ottoman Empire". In Tsugitaka Soto (ed.) *Development of Parliamentarism in the Modern Islamic World*. Tokyo: Toyo Bunko, 2009, 176–204.

Asad, Talal. *Formations of the Secular: Christianity, Islam, Modernity*. Stanford: Stanford University Press, 2003.

Aydın, M. Akif. *İslam-Osmanlı aile hukuku* [Islamic-Ottoman Family Law]. Istanbul: Marmara Üniversitesi, 1985.

Aykan, Yavuz. "Les acteurs de la justice à Amid et dans la province du Diyarbekir d'après les sicil provinciaux du 18ᵉ siècle". Ph.D. dissertation, École des Hautes Études en Sciences Sociales, Paris, 2012.

Aykut Türker, Ebru. "Alternative Claims on Justice and Law: Rural Arson and Poison Murder in the 19th-Century Ottoman Empire" Ph.D. dissertation, Boğaziçi University, 2011.

Aymes, Marc. *A Provincial History of the Ottoman Empire: Cyprus and the Eastern Mediterranean in the Nineteenth Century*. Translated by Adrian Morfee. New York: Routledge, 2014.

Baldwin, James E. "Islamic Law in an Ottoman Context: Resolving Disputes in Late 17th/Early 18th Century Cairo". Ph.D. dissertation, New York University, 2010.

Berkes, Niyazi. *The Development of Secularism in Turkey*. Montreal: McGill University Press, 1964.

Burbank, Jane and Frederic Cooper. *Empires in World History: Power and the Politics of Difference*. Princeton, NJ: Princeton University Press, 2010.

Campos, Michelle U. *Ottoman Brothers: Muslims, Christians, and Jews in Early Twentieth-Century Palestine*. Stanford: Stanford University Press, 2011.

Davison, Roderic H. *Reform in the Ottoman Empire, 1856–1876*. Princeton NJ: Princeton University Press, 1963.

Demirci, Tuba and Selçuk Akşin Somel. "Women's Bodies, Demography, and Public Health: Abortion Policy and Perspectives in the Ottoman Empire of the Nineteenth Century". *Journal of the History of Sexuality* 17 (3) 2008, 377–420.

Eisenman, Robert H. *Islamic Law in Palestine and Israel: A History of the Survival of Tanzimat and Shari'a in the British Mandate and the Jewish State*. Leiden: Brill, 1978.

Eldem, Edhem. "Capitulations and Western Trade". In Suraiya N. Faroqhi (ed.) *The Cambridge History of Turkey*, Vol. III: *The Later Ottoman Empire, 1603–1839*. Cambridge: Cambridge University Press, 2006, 283–335.

Ergene, Boğaç A. *Local Court, Provincial Society and Justice in the Ottoman Empire: Legal Practice and Dispute Resolution in Çankırı and Kastamonu (1652–1744)*. Leiden: Brill, 2003.

Findley, Carter V. *Bureaucratic Reform in the Ottoman Empire: The Sublime Porte, 1789–1922*. Princeton, NJ: Princeton University Press, 1980.

Findley, Carter V. *Ottoman Civil Officialdom: A Social History*. Princeton, NJ: Princeton University Press, 1989.

Ginio, Eyal. "The Administration of Criminal Justice in Ottoman Selanik (Salonica) During the Eighteenth Century". *Turcica* 30 (1998), 185–209.

Gradeva, Rositsa. "On Judicial Hierarchy in the Ottoman Empire: The Case of Sofia, Seventeenth – Beginning of Eighteenth Century". In Muhammad K. Masud, Rudolph Peters and David S. Powers (eds). *Dispensing Justice in Islam: Qadis and Their Judgments*. Leiden: Brill, 2006, 271–98.

İslamoğlu, Huri. "Property as a Contested Domain: A Reevaluation of the Ottoman Land Code of 1858". In Roger Owen (ed.) *New Perspectives on Property and Land in the Middle East*. Cambridge, MA: Harvard University Press, 2000, 3–61.

İslamoğlu, Huri. *Ottoman History as World History*. Istanbul: Isis Press, 2007.

Kern, Karen M. *Imperial Citizen: Marriage and Citizenship in the Ottoman Frontier Provinces of Iraq*. New York: Syracuse University Press, 2011.

Kenan, Seyfi (ed.) *Nizam-ı Kadim'den Nizam-ı Cedid'e: III. Selim ve Dönemi* [Selim III and his Era: From Ancién Regime to New Order]. Istanbul: TDV ISAM, 2010.

Lewis, Bernard. *The Emergence of Modern Turkey*. London: Oxford University Press, 1966.

Lévy, Noémi and Alexandre Toumarkine (eds). *Osmanlı'da Asayis, Suç ve Ceza: 18–20 Yüzyıllar*. Istanbul: Tarih Vakfı Yurt Yayınları, 2007.

Meeker, Michael E. *A Nation of Empire: The Ottoman Legacy of Turkish Modernity*. Berkeley: University of California Press, 2002.

Miller, Ruth A. *Legislating Authority: Sin and Crime in the Ottoman Empire and Turkey*. New York: Routledge, 2005.

Özdemir, Bülent. *Ottoman Reforms and Social Life: Reflections from Salonica, 1830–1850*. Istanbul: Isis Press, 2003.

Paz, Omri. "Crime, Criminals, and the Ottoman State: Anatolia Between the Late 1830s and the Late 1860s". Ph.D. dissertation, Tel Aviv University, 2011.

Paz, Omri. "Documenting Justice: New Recording Practices and the Establishment of an Activist Criminal Court System in the Ottoman Provinces (1840–late 1860s)". *Islamic Law and Society* 21 (2014), 81–113.

Peirce, Leslie. *Morality Tales: Law and Gender in the Ottoman Court of Aintab*. Berkeley: University of California Press, 2003.

Petrov, Milen V. "Everyday Forms of Compliance: Subaltern Commentaries on Ottoman Reform, 1864–1868". *Comparative Study of Society and History* (2004), 730–59.

Quataert, Donald. *The Ottoman Empire, 1700–1922*. 2nd edn. Cambridge: Cambridge University Press, 2005.

Rubin, Avi. "Ottoman Judicial Change in the Age of Modernity: A Reappraisal". *History Compass* 6 (2008), 1–22.

Rubin, Avi. *Ottoman Nizamiye Courts: Law and Modernity*. London: Palgrave Macmillan, 2011.

Rubin, Avi. "British Perceptions of Ottoman Judicial Reform in the Late Nineteenth Century: Some Preliminary Insights". *Law & Social Inquiry* 37 (4) 2012, 991–1012.

Rubin, Avi. "Modernity as a Code: The Ottoman Empire and the Global Movement of Codification". *Journal of the Economic and Social History of the Orient* 59 (5) 2016, 828–56.

Schull, Kent F. *Prisons in the Late Ottoman Empire: Microcosms of Modernity*. Edinburgh: Edinburgh University Press, 2014.

Toledano, Ehud R. *As If Silent and Absent: Bonds of Enslavement in Islamic Middle East*. New Haven: Yale University Press, 2007.

Ursinus, Michael. *Grievance Administration in an Ottoman Province: The Kaymakam of Rumelia's 'Record Book of Complaints' of 1781–1783*. New York: Routledge Curzon, 2005.

van den Boogert, Maurits H. *The Capitulations and the Ottoman Legal System: Qadis, Consuls and Beraths in the 18th Century*. Leiden: Brill, 2005.

Wallerstein, Immanuel. "The Ottoman Empire and the Capitalist World-Economy: Some Questions for Research". *Review* 2 (1979), 389–98.

Yazbak, Mahmoud. *Haifa in the Late Ottoman Period, 1864–1914: A Muslim Town in Transition*. Leiden: Brill, 1998.

Yurdakul, İlhami. *Osmanlı İlmiye Merkez Teşkilatı'nda Reform, 1826–1876*. Istanbul: İletişim Yayınları, 2008.

CHAPTER 17

# Transformation through Constitution: Young Ottomans and the *Kānûn-i Esâsî* of 1876

*Cemil Koçak*

The aim of this chapter is to provide an overview of the historical and political circumstances leading up to the promulgation of the first Ottoman constitution (*Kānûn-i Esâsî*), along with a description of the ideological concepts and actors associated with it. The declaration of the Ottoman constitution emerged from attempts by a small group of young oppositional bureaucrats among the political elite to modernize the Ottoman Empire, a process boosted by Muslim public reaction to the Imperial Edict of 1856, which many saw as a surrender to the Christian West by Tanzimat statesmen such as Âlî Pasha and Fuad Pasha. The group of oppositional bureaucrats took full advantage of the Muslim public's reaction as they opportunistically played out their elite-level power politics. The final outcome of this political conflict was the institution of the Ottoman parliament. Though of short duration, this first experience of parliamentary life had lasting consequencess for the era following the Young Turk Revolution of 1908.

The declaration of the Imperial Edict of the Rose Chamber on 3 November 1839, which is known to have promoted the reorganization of the state and legal reforms and thus initiated the so-called *Tanzimat* (or reorganization) era, signified a shift of power from the sultan and his cabal to the reformist Sublime Porte (*Babıâli*) bureaucracy. The political domination of the Sublime Porte happened while Mustafa Reşid Pasha (d.1858) was playing the major political. At the end of the Crimean War (1853–56), the Ottoman Reform Edict, issued on 18 February 1856, led to another political earthquake. This edict, which was issued when Âlî Pasha (d.1871) and Fuad Pasha (d.1869) were in control of the administration, guaranteed legal equality between Muslims and non-Muslims, thus terminating the traditional hegemony of one community over the others. For Muslims, this was a highly controversial issue; many even saw it as a state sell-out of the well-earned bloodshed of their ancestors to the 'infidels'. It triggered a major rupture in nineteenth-century Ottoman society and caused internal division among the bureaucratic elite. The emergence of the Young Ottoman movement (*Genç Osmanlılar/Yeni Osmanlılar*) was a crucial outcome of this crisis. These young candidates for the governing elite, who were critical of the *Tanzimat* modernization programme, particularly of the Reform Edict, and had substantial reservations about the political and cultural proposals surrounding the process, formed an opposition within the Ottoman pro-modernization team.[1]

Contrary to general assumptions, the political views of the Young Ottomans were hardly typical of a homogenous political group, for they were neither well-formulated nor clearly defined. Rather than a movement, they constituted more a set of divergent political and cultural proposals developed by a group of young elites. It is also impossible to talk about a group that displayed a notable degree of organizational solidarity. They were effectively aspirant bureaucrats eager to join the Ottoman ruling elite, whose relations with one another were sometimes close and sometimes distant.[2]

## 1  The Young Ottomans: Continuities and Breakpoints in Ottoman Turkish Political Thought

A glimpse at the biographical backgrounds and political characteristics of some outstanding members of the Young Ottomans might provide us with a better idea of the nature of this movement. These include names such as İbrâhim Şinâsi, Nâmık Kemal, Ziyâ Pasha, Ali Suâvî, Mustafa Fâzıl Pasha, and Midhat Pasha.

The first person to be associated with the Young Ottomans, İbrâhim Şinâsi (d.1871), had an unusual political career; until fleeing to France in 1862, he expressed his political activism through oppositional journalism, but then moved on to a more scholarly approach. He deliberately distanced himself from the Young Ottomans who arrived in Paris a few years after he did, and maintained this distance even after his return to Istanbul shortly before his death. However, whether this was a reflection of Şinâsi's personality or of his political views, it in fact was characteristic of actual relations between the movement's founding members. For example, the contrast between Şinâsi's style of writing in plain, understandable Turkish and Ziyâ's flowery, elaborated

---

1  Butrus Abu-Manneh, "The Roots of the Ascendancy of Âli and Fuad Paşas at the Porte (1855–1871)", in *idem, Studies on Islam and the Ottoman Empire in the 19th Century* (Istanbul: Isis Press, 2001), 115–24; Roderic Davison, *Reform in the Ottoman Empire 1856–1876* (Princeton, NJ: Princeton University Press, 1963), 57–77; Halil İnalcık, "Sened-i İttifak ve Gülhane Hatt-ı Hümâyunu", in *idem, Osmanlı İmparatorluğu. Toplum ve Ekonomi* (Istanbul: Eren Yayıncılık, 1993), 343–59; Şerif Mardin, *The Genesis of Young Ottoman Thought: A Study in the Modernization of Turkish Political Ideas* (Princeton, NJ: Princeton University Press, 1962).

2  Kemal Beydilli, "Yeni Osmanlılar", *DIA* 43, 431–2; Mardin, *Genesis*, 78–80.

prose, was an obvious example of their difference of style. In fact, Şinâsi's conspicuous rationalism set him apart from many of the other Young Ottomans.[3]

Without any doubt, Şinâsi was an intellectual pillar of the Young Ottoman movement. Under the patronage of Grand Vizier Mustafa Reşid Pasha, he spent his formative years in France where he studied finance. Had conditions remained the same, he might easily have risen high in the bureaucracy, but Mustafa Reşid Pasha's fall from power had a deleterious effect on his career. The new grand vizier Âlî Pasha, himself a former protégé of Reşid Pasha, became rivalrous and effectively blocked any career opportunities for Şinâsi.[4]

On experiencing Âlî Pasha's attitude as unjust, arbitrary and authoritarian, Şinâsi decided to move into a field hitherto unknown to Ottoman Muslims. In 1860, in collaboration with Çapanzâde Agâh Efendi, who belonged to a notable family from Central Anatolia and was disaffected by the centralizing policies of the *Tanzimat*, Şinâsi published the first private and independent Turkish newspaper, *Tercüman-ı Ahvâl* (Interpreter of Conditions). This was an early attempt to mobilize oppositional views and develop Ottoman Turkish public opinion through the print medium. Consequently, the emergence of the Young Ottoman movement was to an important extent related to independent journalism and, two years later, Şinâsi began to publish his own newspaper, *Tasvir-i Efkâr* (the Illustration of Opinion). While the effects of these newspapers, which propagated the principles of a parliamentarian system in a mostly illiterate society, should not be overemphasized, the excessive response of the Sublime Porte suggests that they were more effective than assumed. Upon Şinâsi's sudden departure for France for unknown political reasons in 1865, Nâmık Kemal, as we shall see below, took over the running of the newspaper. When a few years later Nâmık Kemal also fled from Istanbul to Paris, on meeting Şinâsi again he was surprised to discover that his former comrade, whose activism he had previously so admired, had moved away from politics and was mainly engaged in an academic life. By this point it was apparent that Şinâsi's Young Ottoman days were over.[5]

Until the mid-1850s Şinâsi had been an aspirant member of the Ottoman ruling elite. One might assume that his political horizon at this early stage was probably fairly similar to those of the reformist elite, who pursued a policy of reorganizing the state and society from top to bottom. However, when Şinâsi's

---

3 Ziyad Ebüzziya, *Şinasi*, edited by Hüseyin Çelik (Istanbul: İletişim Yayıncılık, 1997), 275–313; Âlim Kahraman, "Şinasi", DIA 39, 168; Bedri Mermutlu, *Sosyal Düşünce Tarihimizde Şinasi* (Istanbul: Kaknüs Yayınları, 2003), 187–91.
4 Ebüzziya, *Şinasi*, 90–1, 103–33; Mermutlu, *Sosyal Düşünce*, 27–38.
5 Ebüzziya, *Şinasi*, 164–227, 275–9; Mardin, *Genesis*, 253–4, 259–64.

bureaucratic career prospects came to a sudden end, his journalistic activities began to reflect a political position that was clearly different from those of the *Tanzimat* reformists. In the very first issue of *Tercüman-ı Ahvâl* it was declared that people had certain rights to be respected by the administration.[6] Şinâsi's separation from the ruling elite signified a split in the commitment to Ottoman modernization that had hitherto been monopolized by elitist government officials.

One might argue that Şinâsi's views about the rights that people hold in relation to their responsibilities was a reflection of Western political thinking. There is no doubt that his emphasis on people's rights was a major political statement of the period. However, Şinâsi's concept of people (or society) has remained vague; he never specified what exactly he meant by 'people'.[7] This vagueness might have been related to the political conditions of his time. The careful nature of his writing is reflected in his discussions of other political concepts. For example, for Şinâsi there was no political freedom, as understood in liberal systems, but he emphasized the idea of equality before the law as the foundation of justice. Despite the traditional Sunni Islamic view that the sultan is only held responsible at the time of eternal judgement, Şinâsi believed that the sultan was also responsible for man-made laws, thus implying a limit to sultanic authority. According to him, the grand vizier was the authority who could both implement this limitation and make laws. The notion of an authority other than the sultan being able to make laws was completely outside any traditional Islamic political understanding, since, according to classical Sunni Islam, the law is the law of God, namely sharia, and only implemented by the sultan.[8]

One point at which he displayed clarity was when he emphasized the importance of reason, as in rationalism. As opposed to the traditional Islamic understanding of belief coming first and reason following it, he placed reason before belief. In this respect, he differed radically from the other members of the Young Ottoman movement.[9]

One of the best-known Young Ottomans was Nâmık Kemal (d.1888), who was renowned for being a passionate poet of freedom and patriotism.[10]

---

6  Ebüzziya, *Şinasi*, 171–3, 175–6; Mardin, *Genesis*, 263, 266, 273.
7  Mardin, *Genesis*, 273.
8  Ebüzziya, *Şinasi*, 175, 180–3, 374–5, 377–9; Mardin, *Genesis*, 259, 260, 267–8, 268–9, 271–2; Mermutlu, *Sosyal Düşünce*, 351–63.
9  Ebüzziya, *Şinasi*, 374–5, 377–9; Mardin, *Genesis*, 266–8, 275.
10  Ömer Faruk Akün, "Namık Kemal ", *DIA* 32, 361–78; Mithat Cemal Kuntay, *Namık Kemal. Devrinin İnsanları ve Olayları Arasında*, 2nd edn, 2 vols (Istanbul: Türkiye İş Bankası Kültür Yayınları, 2009/10); Mardin, *Genesis*, 283–336.

Although with social origins within the traditional Ottoman governing elite, his family had lost its status and wealth, partially as a result of state modernization. His mother died while he was still an infant and he was raised by his grandfather. However, because of his grandfather's frequent appointments as a provincial administrator, Nâmık Kemal's schooling was limited, but he was nonetheless heavily influenced by traditional scholars in the provinces and, at the age of seventeen, he began his bureaucratic career by entering the translation office of the Sublime Porte (*Babıâli Tercüme Odası*), which was where well-educated, promising young individuals with a broad intellectual orientation could find work. By becoming a clerk at this institution, Nâmık Kemal encountered Western cultural and political influences and, through this broadening of his intellectual horizons, he became aware of the writings of Şinâsi. In 1862, Nâmık Kemal started to write for *Tasvir-i Efkâr*, and through this connection, he and Şinâsi formed a friendship.[11] On taking over the editorship of the newspaper in 1865, his involvement in oppositional politics became stronger. In the same year, a group of like-minded young civil servants, among them Nâmık Kemal, formed the nucleus of the so-called *Meslek* (Mission) or *İttifak-ı Hamiyyet* (Patriotic Alliance), which later became known as the Young Ottomans. This group perceived the rule of reformist *Tanzimat* statesmen such as Âlî and Fuad Pashas not only as despotic and corrupt, but also as extremely lenient towards the political demands of powers such as France and Britain, and felt that they were too ready to give political concessions to non-Muslim communities. Despite significant political differences among them, this group agreed to kill Âlî and Fuad Pashas and to set up a parliament.[12]

This secret network of young civil servants, which included some members of the Ottoman dynasty such as Crown Prince Murad and Prince Abdülhamid, became widely known through Mustafa Fâzıl Pasha's public quarrel with the Ottoman government, discussed in more detail below. When Nâmık Kemal's articles became more critical of state policies, he was assigned the post of assistant governor of Erzurum as a means of removing him from the capital. However, Fâzıl Pasha's generous financial support for the Young Ottomans enabled Nâmık Kemal and his friends to flee to France in 1867. In Paris and then London, Nâmık Kemal and Ziyâ published the oppositional newspaper *Hürriyet* (Liberty), which propagated Young Ottoman political ideas. When

---

11   Akün, "Namık Kemal ", 361–4; Ebüzziya, *Şinasi*, 213–15; Kuntay, *Namık Kemal* 1, 1–65.
12   M. Kaya Bilgegil, "Türkiye'de Bazı Yeni Osmanlılarla Yeni Osmanlı Tarafdarlarının Bir Millet Meclisi Kurma Teşebbüsleri", in *idem*, *Yakın Çağ Türk Kültür ve Edebiyatı Üzerinde Araştırmalar I. Yeni Osmanlılar* (Erzurum: Atatürk Üniversitesi Yayınları, 1976), 355–6, 400–1; Mardin, *Genesis*, 10–24, 26; Ebuzziya Tevfik, *Yeni Osmanlılar. İmparatorluğun Son Dönemindeki Genç Türkler*, edited by Şemsettin Kutlu (Istanbul: Pegasus Yayınları, 2006), 70.

their main enemies, Fuad and Âlî Pashas died in 1869 and 1871 respectively, the Young Ottomans, already worn out by petty disagreements, rapidly disintegrated, and most of them, including Nâmık Kemal, returned to Istanbul in 1871. Remaining highly critical of the Sublime Porte, Nâmık Kemal edited the *İbret* (Lesson) newspaper between 1872 and 1873, in which he developed and refined his political views.[13]

However, his overall oppositional activities and, in particular, his secret relations with the Crown Prince, resulted in the deportation of Nâmık Kemal and his associates to remote fortresses. Between 1873 and 1876, Nâmık Kemal remained at the fortress of Famagusta, where he mainly produced literary works. On 30 May 1876, the former grand vizier Midhat Pasha and Hüseyin Avni Pasha, commander-in chief of the Ottoman armed forces orchestrated a *coup d'état* in which Sultan Abdülaziz was deposed, and a swift amnesty to all Young Ottoman prisoners followed. Nâmık Kemal and Ziyâ then enjoyed a short period of political influence as palace secretaries and members of the Council of State, where they took part in the formulation of the first Ottoman constitution – a situation that ended with Sultan Abdülhamid's consolidation of power in 1877. Young Ottomans who refused to cooperate with the new regime, or were considered dangerous, were removed from Istanbul. In the final stage of his life, Nâmık Kemal served as governor of the Aegean islands of Rhodes, Mytilene and Chios.[14]

Nâmık Kemal stands out from the other Young Ottomans because he tried to develop a political theory that would consolidate Islamic and Western political thought. The need to define an alternative modernization project inevitably had to address the issue of Western civilization, or at least certain aspects of it. This problem was not confined to Ottoman intellectuals, for numerous other non-Western societies were having to come to terms with the political and cultural impact of the West. Examples of Asian journalists-cum-politicians with comparable concerns in the late nineteenth century include names such as Fukuzawa Yukichi (d.1901) in Japan and Yu Kil-chun (d.1914) in Korea.[15]

---

13    Christiane Czygan, *Zur Ordnung des Staates: Jungosmanische Intellektuelle und ihre Konzepte in der Zeitung Hürriyet (1868–1870)* (Berlin: Klaus Schwarz Verlag, 2012), 64–104; Kuntay, *Namık Kemal* 1, 79, 90, 93–7, 257–9; Bernard Lewis, *The Emergence of Modern Turkey*, 2nd edn (London: OUP, 1968), 153–8; Mardin, *Genesis*, 44–67; Mustafa Nihat Özön, *Namık Kemal ve İbret Gazetesi: İnceleme*, 2nd edn (Istanbul: Yapı Kredi Yayınları, 1997), passim.

14    Akün, "Namık Kemal", 368–71; Lewis, *Emergence*, 158–63; 169–74.

15    Alastair Bonnett, "Makers of the West: National Identity and Occidentalism in the Work of Fukuzawa Yukichi and Ziya Gökalp", *Scottish Geographical Journal* 118 (3) 2002, 165–82; Yeonsik Choi, "Yu Kil-chun's Moral Idea of Civilization and Project to Make All People Gentlemen", *Asian Philosophy* 24 (2) 2014, 103–20.

For Nâmık Kemal, concepts such as the rule of law, equality, and freedom, were crucial for preserving the geographical integrity of the Ottoman Empire. In fact, these three concepts should be regarded as integral to the *Tanzimat* reformists' policy of building a rational state. In his opinion, this formula would boost the idea of an 'Ottoman fatherland', which the different ethnic and religious communities shared. Similarly, his support for the principle of 'freedom of thought' arose from a concern to keep the different elements within the empire together. Another optimistic expectation was that such an integrative approach would bring the 'Eastern Question' and foreign interventions to an end. In this context, Ottoman and Islamic history had to be re-evaluated from the viewpoint of the assumed relative harmony of the past coexistence of various religious communities within the Islamic framework. For him, history provided an important foundation on which to build his political views.[16]

As noted above, a sign of the birth of Young Ottoman political activity was the emergence of independent journalism. One could say that Nâmık Kemal's journalism was closely related to his mission to promote and mobilize Ottoman Turkish public opinion, even though literacy among the masses was low. In fact, underlying Nâmık Kemal's literary approach might have been a wish to propagate ideas and persuade the public of certain political causes. For him, newspapers served the function of supervising the government on behalf of the public. Also, printed material could also be used to educate the public, for he himself was probably also aware that public opinion was still too weak to fulfil the supervisory mission that he and Şinâsi considered a necessity.[17]

For Nâmık Kemal, the concept of political freedom implied direct participation in politics, so its political mechanisms had to be set up. From his point of view, aside from governing in the form of a republic, which would be desirable under ideal conditions, only a constitutional monarchy, as opposed to despotic governance (*istibdat*), would be feasible within the Ottoman context. His model of a constitutional monarchy included guaranteeing the holy rights of the sultan, the caliphate and the Ottoman dynasty, which appears controversial in comparison with other liberal examples of a constitutional monarchy.[18]

According to his point of view, Western liberal political philosophy was, in essence, in harmony with original Islamic governing principles. In fact, they were more than just in tune with one another because classical Islam already

---

16  Czygan, *Ordnung*, 227–8; Nazan Çiçek, *The Young Ottomans: Turkish Critics of the Eastern Question in the Late Nineteenth Century* (London: I.B. Tauris, 2010), 140–1, 153; Mardin, *Genesis*, 36–7, 326–31; Mümtaz'er Türköne, *Siyasî İdeoloji Olarak İslâmcılığın Doğuşu*, 2nd edn (Istanbul: İletişim Yayınları, 1994), 96–7.
17  Akün, "Namık Kemal", 372–6; Özön, *İbret*, 45, 120–3, 130–8, 171–8, 214–20.
18  Lewis, *Emergence*, 172–173; Mardin, *Genesis*, 288, 293–7.

contained in itself the Western political way of thinking, as well as its principles and theory. The problem was in the application rather than the theory in that it entailed remembering a past that had been forgotten. His attempt to harmonize Western and Islamic political thought became apparent through his discussions of the functions of parliament. He saw parliament, which he called the 'Assembly of the Council of the Community' (*Meclis-i Şurâ-yı Ümmet*), as an organ for representing the public and supervising the government. For Nâmık Kemal, it was the practical application of the method of consultation (*meşveret*), as specified in the Quran. While *meşveret* was considered an essential component of Islamic political thought, the Ottoman state was at its most powerful when consultation was effectively applied. Likewise, Nâmık Kemal compared the European political notion of the separation of powers with pre-reform Ottoman history in which the sultan and his viziers were the executive, the *ulema* the legislative, and the janissaries or 'people in arms' the popular controllers of the executive. The notion of a social contract was being considered as commensurate with the concept of pledging obeisance to the sultanic authority (*biat*). Since all these notions were present in Islamic law, to abide by the rules of the sharia would promote their realization. The sultan was responsible for implementing the rules of the sharia and for providing justice, which in turn would shape the ideal gracious, generous state (*kerim devlet*).[19]

In trying to formulate a political framework through harmonizing Western political ideas taken from Locke, Hobbes, Montesquieu and Rousseau with Islamic political ideas, Nâmık Kemal possibly intended to free those theories, concepts or organizations from being defamed as foreign imports. Young Ottoman attacks on the *Tanzimat* reformists for supposedly unconditionally accepting Western policies should be understood within this conceptual background.

Nâmık Kemal's writings are worth considering insofar as they contain the basic principles of a constitutional regime. This rather eclectic political theory, possibly a first attempt of its kind, is meaningful in that it forged organic ties with daily politics, and constituted a basis for a new political tradition. In presenting traditional Islamic/Ottoman political philosophy in a Western theoretical framework, Nâmık Kemal was actually striving to present the traditional in a modern guise. However, his attempt to combine Islamic political traditions based mainly on religious principles with European political notions based mostly on the Enlightenment was bound to be defective and to contain

---

19   Niyazi Berkes, *Türkiye'de Çağdaşlaşma* (Istanbul: Doğu-Batı Yayınları, 1978), 283–8; Mardin, *Genesis*, 289–310; Türköne, *Siyasî İdeoloji*, 110–12, 116–18, 122–3.

logical inconsistencies.[20] To insist on developing a political theory that lacked the consistency it needed to defend certain political positions and to show no wish to do the opposite, emerged as a heritage of political thinking for the coming generations in Turkey.

The life story of another Young Ottoman, Ziyâ Pasha (d.1880), seemed remarkably like that of Şinâsi. He too was rising in the bureaucracy under the protection of Mustafa Reşid Pasha and could have had a brilliant future had the loss of his protector not cast a shadow over his official career. Compared with other Young Ottomans, he was a relatively senior bureaucrat. Following a brief period as palace secretary to Sultan Abdülaziz in 1861, he became a pasha in 1862 when he was made governor (*mutasarrıf*) of Cyprus, followed by membership of the Sublime Council (*Meclis-i Vâlâ*), and appointment as minister of justice (*deâvi nazırlığı*) in 1863. However, Âlî Pasha insisted on keeping Ziyâ far away from Istanbul by appointing him to the governorships of Amasya and Canik (present-day Samsun) (1863–65). Ziyâ Pasha's sense of bitterness towards Âlî Pasha turned him into an arch enemy of the grand vizier and led him to move close to the Young Ottomans and to write oppositional articles for the *Muhbir* (Informant). Like other Young Ottomans, he fled to France in 1867 and, with Nâmık Kemal, published the *Hürriyet*. Following his return to Istanbul after 1871, Ziyâ worked as a senior functionary in the Council of Judicial Regulations (*Divan-ı Ahkâm-ı Adliyye*). After the 1876 coup, he helped to compile the first Ottoman constitution. Even before the dissolution of the parliament by Abdülhamid II, Ziyâ Pasha had been removed from the capital by being appointed governor of Syria, then Konya and finally Adana (1877–80), where he died.[21]

Ziyâ's experiences in his professional career greatly affected his ideas about political reform. His position as a palace official, in particular, sensitized him to the political function of a sultan. The main focus of his political thinking was on controlling and limiting the power of the grand vizier and bureaucracy, positions he considered prone to corruption and arbitrary rule. To counterbalance this tendency, Ziyâ attributed critical importance to the authority of the sultan. Issues such as the political participation of citizens and the formation of a representative parliament were of only secondary importance to him. For Ziyâ, a parliament should have mainly consultative functions with only

---

20 Berkes, *Çağdaşlaşma*, 283–5; Mardin, *Genesis*, 289–317.
21 Mustafa Apaydın, *Türk Hiciv Edebiyatında Ziya Paşa* (Ankara: T. C. Kültür Bakanlığı Yayınları, 2001); M. Kaya Bilgegil, *Ziya Paşa Üzerine Bir Araştırma* (Erzurum: Atatürk Üniversitesi Yayınları, 1970); Önder Göçgün, Ziya Paşa'nın Hayatı, *Eserleri, Edebî Kişiliği, Bütün Şiirleri ve Eserlerinden Açıklamalı Seçmeler* (Ankara: T. C. Kültür Bakanlığı Yayınları, 2001); Abdullah Uçman, "Ziya Paşa", *DIA* 44, 475–9.

limited powers, which was a view close to traditional Islamic political thinking. Ziyâ assumed that a sultan following sharia would be a just and efficient ruler, and be able to prevent any bureaucratic tendency towards despotism and corruption. As he saw it, the corruption and despotism in Âlî and Fuad Pashas' administrations arose from Westernization and a growing deviation from the sharia.[22]

Among the Young Ottomans, Ali Suâvî (d.1878) stood apart from the others as both an intellectual and an activist. He was born in Istanbul to a humble family and, after graduating from a government secondary school (*rüşdiyye*), he entered the bureaucracy as a minor clerk. Meanwhile, he took various mosque courses to learn Islamic sciences. Between 1856 and 1865, he worked as a *rüşdiyye* instructor and as a clerk in various provincial towns. Around 1858 he went on a pilgrimage to Mecca. After returning to Istanbul he began to preach at the Şehzâdebaşı Mosque while building his general cultural capital by attending intellectual gatherings at the mansions of certain pashas. During this period, Ali Suâvî acquired a public reputation for his mosque sermons and knowledge of the Islamic sciences. In 1867, he began to write articles for the *Muhbir*, in which he harshly criticized the government. In these articles he used simple Turkish to reach a wider public. When his mentor Mustafa Fâzıl Pasha publicly criticized the Sublime Porte, the government deported him, along with various other oppositional writers, to different parts of the empire, in his, Ali Suâvî's case, to Kastamonu. However, with generous support from Mustafa Fâzıl Pasha, he was able to flee from the empire and join Nâmık Kemal and Ziyâ Pasha. Although the Young Ottomans assigned Ali Suâvî the task of publishing an oppositional newspaper in London, the *Muhbir*, Nâmık Kemal and Ziyâ found the political content of the early issues unacceptable, which forced them into publishing the alternative *Hürriyet*. When Fâzıl Pasha's subsidies stopped in late 1868, he had no option but to close down the *Muhbir*. He then moved to Paris to publish the *Ulûm* (Sciences), which carried articles on culture, history, theology, philosophy, pedagogy, and economics. While the Franco-Prussian War brought the publication of this newspaper to an end in 1870, Ali Suâvî had effectively cut his ties with the Young Ottomans and remained in France until 1876, where he continued to produce the occasional pamphlet or almanac on cultural issues. When Sultan Abdülhamid II invited him to return to Istanbul, Ali Suâvî did so, but despite the sultan's attempts to make use of him by appointing him to join an abortive 'association of translators' or to become the director of the elite *Mekteb-i Sultânî* high school

---

22   Apaydın, *Türk Hiciv*, 176–250; Mardin, *Genesis*, 337–59; Türköne, *Siyasî İdeoloji*, 68–70, 79–80.

(present-day Galatasaray Lycée), Ali Suâvî proved to be too independent a personality to be controlled by Abdülhamid; in fact, he started to conspire against the sultan. While Russian troops were occupying San Stefano (present-day Yeşilköy near Atatürk Airport) following the disastrous Russo-Ottoman War of 1877/8, and parliament had been dissolved, Ali Suâvî arranged for a large group of Balkan Muslim refugees to free former Sultan Murad v from his confinement at the Çırağan Palace with a view to reinstating him. However, the local guards resisted this operation and Ali Suâvî was killed during the confrontation.[23]

Ali Suâvî's modest social origins had set him apart from other Young Ottomans and, while his religious education had not been profound, he had more or less been regarded as a member of the *ulema* and grounded his main political ideas on religious arguments. He had, however, been highly critical of Nâmık Kemal's attempt to synthesize Islamic and Western political concepts. For him, it would have been a serious mistake to have considered the West a model worth emulating. Like other Young Ottomans, Ali Suâvî saw constitutional monarchy as a natural result of Islamic political philosophy, but thought that the idea of popular sovereignty was against Islamic principles. According to him, sovereignty belonged only to God, and God was the only source of ethics and justice. On earth, the sultan and other responsible officials appointed by God represented God's sovereignty. The public, he had felt, ought to keep a check on the sultan and other responsible administrators, and the people had the right to oppose an illegitimate or despotic ruler. Crucially, Ali Suâvî had stated that the claim of a universal caliphate made by the Ottoman sultans was invalid in terms of classical Islam. Thus, he had stripped the Ottoman dynasty of any sort of sanctity. Like Nâmık Kemal and Ziyâ, Ali Suâvî considered sharia to be the foundation of all laws, to which the sultans were to comply. For him sharia and politics were not separate realms. However, he saw sharia not as a set of unchangeable and inflexible rules but open to interpretation and modifications depending on historical necessities. A thorough application of the sharia by an administration would, he felt, lead to just rule.[24]

---

23  Hüseyin Çelik, *Ali Suavi ve Dönemi* (Istanbul: İletişim Yayınları, 1994); Mehmet Erdül, *Başveren İnkılapçı Ali Suavi* (Istanbul: Toplumsal Dönüşüm Yayınları, 2002); Necmi Günel, *II. Meşrutiyet Öncesi Fikir Akımları ve Ali Suavi* (Istanbul: Feyziye Mektepleri Vakfı, 2011); Mithat Cemal Kuntay, *Sarıklı İhtilâlci Alî Suavi* (Istanbul: Ahmet Halit Kitabevi, 1946); Abdullah Uçman, "Ali Suavi", DIA 2, 445–8; Seyit Battal Uğurlu, "Eklektik Bir Tanzimat Aydını: Ali Suavi Efendi", *History Studies: International Journal of History* 2 (2) 2010, 207–21.

24  Süleyman Hayri Bolay, "Tanzimat'tan Cumhuriyet'e Türk Düşünce Tarihi", in Hasan Celâl Güzel, Kemal Çiçek and Salim Koca (eds), *Türkler* (Ankara: Yeni Türkiye Yayınları, 2002), vol. 14, 526–8; Çelik, *Ali Suavî*, 557–96; Kuntay, *Sarıklı*, 70–2; Türköne, *Siyasî İdeoloji*, 118–22.

On the other hand, an effective realization of sharia required the presence of a capable stratum of *ulema* being able to exert control over the administrators. However, to develop a sufficiently capable stratum, Ali Suâvî stressed, would require a reform of medrese education. While underlining the importance of Islam and the sharia, Ali Suâvî seemed indecisive about the scope of the political community he was discussing. While in some of his writings, in a rather pan-Islamic manner, he considered the world Muslim community as the main political reference point, in others he narrowed the scope of his preferred political community to ethnic Turks and emphasized Turkish nationalism and the importance of Central Asian Turkic history.[25]

When Young Ottomans are the subject matter, Mustafa Fâzıl Pasha (d.1875) deserves a mention, for without the protection of this Egyptian prince, Young Ottomans would have been unable to operate in Europe. Mustafa Fâzıl was a grandson of Kavalalı Mehmed Ali Pasha and heir apparent to İsmail Pasha, his elder brother and governor of Egypt. Having been educated by private tutors in Cairo, Mustafa Fâzıl entered the Sublime Porte bureaucracy in 1845 and, from 1851 onwards, was involved in Ottoman state affairs as a member of the Sublime Council, and was promoted first to the Ministry of Education (1862) and then to the Ministry of Finance (1863). During this period he quarrelled with Âlî and Fuad Pasha, and this prompted him to establish secret contacts with oppositional journalists later known as the Young Ottomans. When Fâzıl Pasha complained to Sultan Abdülaziz about Fuad Pasha's problematic financial policies, he was dismissed from his ministerial post. Because İsmail Pasha saw him as a powerful rival and forbade his return to Egypt, he was forced to move to France (1866). Shortly afterwards, following repeated urgings from his elder brother, the Sublime Porte approved a major change in the succession system of the governorship of Egypt, which would henceforth be based on primogeniture rather than Agnatic seniority, thus effectively abrogating Fâzıl Pasha's right to future governorship. Embittered by this vital blow, in 1867 he launched a comprehensive press campaign in France and Belgium against Abdülaziz and the *Tanzimat* statesmen, which denounced widespread corruption and misrule within the empire and called for a constitutional regime. While doing so, Fâzıl Pasha declared his patronage for an oppositional group called *les Jeunes Turques*. When the Sublime Porte took active measures against the Young Ottomans, he provided the material means for them to flee to France. With his financial support, exile newspapers like *Muhbir* and *Hürriyet* were published in London and Paris. Although Fâzıl Pasha received imperial

---

25  Çelik, *Ali Suavî*, 557–62, 603–6, 616–42, 650–6; Mardin, *Genesis*, 368, 370–2, 379; Türköne, *Siyasî İdeoloji*, 118–19, 283–9.

mercy from Abdülaziz during his official visit to France, he continued to support the Young Ottomans, at least until 1871. Following his return to Istanbul he was appointed Minister of Justice and then Minister of Finance (1870/1).[26]

Mustafa Fâzıl Pasha's political vision was reflected in his press declarations of 1867. According to him, the solution to the problems in the empire lay not in further centralizing the state and thus increasing bureaucratic pressure on the society, but in reducing it by founding a political order based on freedom in which Muslims and Christians shared equal rights and responsibilities. He attributed the corruption of the sultan's absolute power not to the ruler's personality, but to the failure of the governing elite surrounding him to provide reliable information to the monarch. The authoritarianism of the bureaucratic elite could only be eliminated by forming a responsible government. However, this project was limited to forming a consulting body rather than a fully-fledged liberal constitutional monarchy.[27]

Young Ottomans came to consider Midhat Pasha (d.1884) their natural leader, particularly after 1872.[28] Since this statesman provided the crucial link between Young Ottomans and constitutionalism, he ought to be discussed at this point. Born in Istanbul, his father was a lower *ulema* working as a minor clerk in the Ministry of Pious Foundations and also held appointments as a substitute judge (*nâib*), which was why the family subsequently moved to Vidin and Lovec, both in present-day Bulgaria. Having received a traditional Islamic education, Midhat entered the Sublime Porte bureaucracy as an assistant secretary, and served as a clerk in various Anatolian and Syrian towns (1842–48). His appointment as a civil servant in the Sublime Council opened opportunities for a rapid rise in his career; his successful investigations between 1852 and 1857 of corruption at the provincial level earned him the support of crucial statesmen such as Mustafa Reşid, Âlî Pasha, and Fuad Pasha. While conducting these investigations, he gained in-depth knowledge of conditions in the provinces. In 1858, he spent six months developing his French skills in Paris, London, Brussels and Vienna. He distinguished himself as a bureaucrat during his highly successful governorships of the provinces of Nish and Danube (1861–68), where the new *vilayet* (province) system was being applied in an efficient manner. With infrastructural developments and an equitable administration,

---

26  M. Kaya Bilgegil, "Mustafa Fâzıl Paşa'nın Abdülazîz'e Yazdığı Mektup ve Bunun Şimdiye Kadar Bilinmeyen Karşılığı", in idem, *Yakın Türk Kültür ve Edebiyatı Üzerinde Araştırmalar I. Yeni Osmanlılar* (Erzurum: Atatürk Üniversitesi Yayınları, 1976), 5–105; Ş. Tufan Buzpınar, "Mustafa Fazıl Paşa", *DIA* 31, 300–1; Kuntay, *Namık Kemal* 1, 200, 277–91, 311–28, 348–56.
27  Bilgegil, *Ziya Paşa*, 91–4; Buzpınar, "Mustafa Fazıl Paşa", 301.
28  Beydilli, "Yeni Osmanlılar", 432.

a significant portion of the local Serb and Bulgar population, previously prone to separatism, was won back to the Ottomanist cause.[29]

Midhat Pasha became a major political actor upon his appointment to the presidency of the newly formed legislative body, the Council of State (Şûrâ-yı Devlet) in 1868. He then had disagreements of a political and personal nature with the grand vizier, Âlî Pasha, and this resulted in his removal from the capital to take on the governorship of Baghdad Province (1869–72). Developments in the capital interrupted his successful tenure there when Âlî Pasha died in 1871 and his successor Mahmud Nedim Pasha (d.1883) radically purged the civil service, which effectively disrupted the functioning of the Ottoman state. In protest against these developments, Midhat Pasha resigned from the governorship of Baghdad and returned to Istanbul. Since he had become a point of attraction for the Young Ottoman opposition, Mahmud Nedim Pasha attempted to remove him from Istanbul; however, Midhat outsmarted him by persuading Sultan Abdülaziz to dismiss Mahmud Nedim and appoint him instead as grand vizier (1872). However, because of political disagreements and his undiplomatic attitude towards Abdülaziz, his tenure lasted less than three months. After his dismissal, Midhat Pasha was appointed minister of justice twice (in 1873 and 1875); then, having compiled a report in favour of founding a representative parliament, he was appointed governor of Thessaloniki (1873/4). After 1875, he developed ties with various oppositional groups that were attempting to establish a constitutional regime. With support from the army and the *ulema*, Midhat Pasha staged a *coup d'état* that deposed Abdülaziz in favour of his nephew Crown Prince Murad, who was known to have sympathies for the Young Ottoman political ideals (1876). However, a chain of violent events, including ongoing revolts in Herzegovina and Bulgaria; increasing foreign diplomatic interventions; European reactions to the previous declaration of a moratorium by Mahmud Nedim Pasha; the unexplained violent death of Abdülaziz; and a deadly attack on a cabinet meeting by a military officer seeking revenge for the alleged murder of the deposed sultan, shattered the new sultan's already delicate mental equilibrium, and Murad V effectively became incapable of performing the functions of a monarch. After three months, he

---

29  Gökhan Çetinsaya and Ş. Tufan Buzpınar, "Midhat Paşa", DIA 30, 7–8; Ali Haydar Midhat, *The Life of Midhat Pasha: A Record of His Services, Political Reforms, Banishment, and Judicial Murder* (London: John Murray, Albemarle Street, W., 1903), 1–47; İlber Ortaylı, "Midhat Paşa'nın Vilayet Yönetimindeki Kadroları ve Politikası", in *Uluslararası Midhat Paşa Semineri: Bildiriler ve Tartışmalar. Edirne, 8–10 Mayıs 1984* (Ankara: TTK, 1986), 227–33; Skender Rizaj, "Midhat Paşa'nın Rumeli'de Vilayetler Kurulmasındaki Rolü", in *Uluslararası Midhat Paşa Semineri*, 59–69.

had to be deposed in favour of his younger brother, Abdülhamid II (1876). Midhat Pasha became grand vizier once again and worked tirelessly towards preparing for the first Ottoman constitution. However, his rigid and uncompromising attitude towards the new sultan, who had his own political visions, ended in his suspension from office and forcible banishment abroad (1877). This event might be considered the biggest irony in Midhat Pasha's life; he was sent into exile under a clause that Abdülhamid had insisted on including in article 113 of the constitution and that Midhat had not opposed – a clause that empowered the sultan to deport individuals outside imperial borders if they were considered a threat to the security of the state. This clause, which enabled extrajudicial action against the head of the executive, signified a substantial regression from the ideals of the rule of law as envisaged by the Edict of the Rose Chamber. During the Russo-Ottoman War of 1877/8, Midhat Pasha toured the European capitals trying to lobby political support for the empire in Western political circles.[30]

The final chapter of his life began in late 1878 when Abdülhamid allowed Midhat Pasha to return to the empire, and appointed him governor of the provinces of Syria (1878–80) and then of Aydın (1880/1). However, given Midhat Pasha's former role in the dethronements of both Abdülaziz and Murad V, Abdülhamid's distrust of Midhat Pasha did not subside. In addition, Midhat's political enemies in the capital were starting to scheme against him by renewing the question of the suspicious circumstances surrounding Abdülaziz's death, and questioning the medical report that had declared it to be a suicide. In 1881, a special investigating commission sent from Istanbul arrested Midhat Pasha in Izmir and transferred him to the capital. A controversial tribunal at the Yıldız Palace sentenced him to death for participating in the murder of Abdülaziz. However, Abdülhamid commuted the sentence to life imprisonment and Midhat Pasha was deported to Taif fortress (near Mecca in present-day Saudi Arabia), where he was strangled in 1884.[31]

---

30   Cevdet Pasha, *Ma'rûzât*, edited by Yusuf Halaçoğlu (Istanbul: Çağrı Yayınları, 1980), 213–40; *idem*, *Tezâkir 40-Tetimme*, edited by Cavid Baysun, 2nd edn (Ankara: TTK, 1986), 94, 120–70; Mahmud Celâleddin Pasha, *Mir'ât-ı Hakîkat: Târihî Hakîkatların Aynası. Cilt I–II–III*, edited by İsmet Miroğlu (Istanbul: Berekât Yayınları, 1983), 92–163, 171–9, 202–7, 212–18, 228–9, 237–42; Çetinsaya and Buzpınar, "Midhat Paşa", 8–9; Midhat, *Life*, 47–171; Bilâl N. Şimşir, "Midhat Paşa'nın İkinci Sadrazamlığı ve İngiltere", in *Uluslararası Midhat Paşa Semineri*, 237–9; Yaşar Yücel, "Midhat Paşa'nın Bağdat Vilâyetindeki Alt Yapı Yatırımları", in *Uluslararası Midhat Paşa Semineri*, 175–83.

31   Zeki Arıkan, "Midhat Paşa'nın Aydın Valiliği (Ağustos 1880–Mayıs 1881)", in *Uluslararası Midhat Paşa Semineri*, 127–64; Cevdet Pasha, *Tezâkir*, 209–14; Çetinsaya and Buzpınar, "Midhat Paşa", 9–10; Midhat, *Life*, 173–256; Shimon Shamir, "Midhat Pasha and the

Midhat Pasha, like many Young Ottomans, had a mainly Islamic education, and his European experiences were limited. Since he worked mostly outside Istanbul until his fifties, he never developed his political and diplomatic skills. Consequently, his individual successes in provincial administration gave him an exaggerated feeling of self-worth, which emboldened him in Sublime Porte political manoeuvres and which led to a series of political blunders. Midhat's idea of reform consisted of three points – promoting loyalty to the sultan and state among Muslims and non-Muslims by introducing the notion of equal citizenship; the necessity of a constitutional regime; and administrative decentralization. However, Midhat Pasha was more a political activist than a political theoretician, and administrative experience played an important role in the development of his political ideas.[32]

## 2   The Young Ottomans: Modernization, Power and Opposition

The Young Ottomans have to be considered part of the *Tanzimat* modernization process, even although most of them were opposed to certain aspects of it. According to them, the modernization project had to be reviewed and its pitfalls avoided. It should on no account mimic Europe, which they claimed would be wrong and, since factors such as the existing physical geography and society needed to be taken into account and redefined. The Young Ottomans agreed that not only cultural and political values, but also the traditions of the East and of Islam needed to be accorded the importance they deserved in this redefinition.

Looking at the origins of Ottoman modernization, which can be traced back as early as the first decades of the eighteenth century, the predominant concern was military reform. For the Ottoman ruling elite of that period, military complications produced vital weaknesses in the state and society, which immediately had to be corrected. This narrow focus on a solely military dimension of modernization continued until the early-nineteenth century. In fact, until the New Order (*Nizâm-ı Cedid*) (1792–1807) of Selim III (d.1808) came

---

Anti-Turkish Agitation in Syria", *MES* 10 (2) 1974, 115–41; İsmail Hakkı Uzunçarşılı, *Midhat Pala ve Tâif Mahkûmları* (Ankara: TTK, 1950); idem, *Midhat Paşa ve Yıldız Mahkemesi*, 2nd edn (Ankara: TTK, 2000).

32   Berkes, *Çağdaşlaşma*, 302; Çetinsaya and Buzpınar, "Midhat Paşa", 10.

into being, which itself ended in popular rebellion and failure, it is impossible to talk about a comprehensive modernization project that included Westernization.[33]

The former Ottoman ruling elite appears not to have seriously considered a wholesale modernization project along the lines of the Petrine modernization of Russia. Instead, Ottoman modernization displayed highly pragmatic features; it took shape in response to challenging events and immediate threats to the empire, through the supplementation of a variety of ideas and proposals, some loosening and some gaining priority, by trial and error.[34] For this reason, the Ottoman modernization process contains inconsistencies and eclectic features. Ottoman reformist elites possibly approved of the jelly-like shape of the project, because it gave them flexibility they needed to manoeuvre during struggles for political power.

The political features of the Young Ottomans were contradictory. While on the one hand, their intellectual development had been shaped by traditionalism, on the other they were groping in the dark to grab hold of something new, something modern. Another feature they had in common was that, as promising young candidates for the governing elite, they had to obey the rules to climb the bureaucratic ladder, yet at the same time they were adopting an oppositional political stance. Although defending tradition, they were also looking for ways of breaking from it. In effect, this inner contradiction was a common characteristic of the Ottoman/Turkish reformist ruling elite. While supposedly protecting tradition, some values had to be abandoned and these

---

33 For a general overview of Ottoman-Turkish modernization from the perspective of modernization theory, see Feroz Ahmad, *The Making of Modern Turkey* (London: Routledge, 1993); Berkes, *Çağdaşlaşma, passim*; Lewis, *Emergence, passim*; Stanford J. Shaw and Ezel Kural Shaw, *History of the Ottoman Empire and Modern Turkey*, vol. 2: Reform, Revolution, and Republic: The Rise of Modern Turkey, 1808–1975 (Cambridge: CUP, 1977). For a Kemalist perspective, see Yusuf Hikmet Bayur, *Türk İnkılâbı Tarihi*, 3rd edn, 3 vols (Ankara: TTK, 1983); and Enver Ziya Karal, *Osmanlı Tarihi*, 2nd edn, vols 5–8 (Ankara: TTK, 1976–83). For alternative perspectives on Ottoman-Turkish modernization, see Carter Vaughn Findley, *Turkey, Islam, Nationalism, and Modernity: A History, 1789–2007* (New Haven: Yale University Press, 2010); M. Şükrü Hanioğlu, *A Brief History of the Late Ottoman Empire* (Princeton, NJ: Princeton University Press, 2008); Erik J. Zürcher, *Turkey. A Modern History* (London: I. B. Tauris, 1993).
34 Berkes, *Çağdaşlaşma*, 163–245; Stanford J. Shaw, *Between Old and New: The Ottoman Empire under Sultan Selim III (1789–1807)* (Cambridge, MA: Harvard University Press, 1971).

were carefully measured, calculated, identified, and separated from what they considered new and useful.[35]

The huge inconsistencies in the political ideas of Nâmık Kemal and his friends suggest that political theory *per se* was an unimportant starting point. On the contrary, the general aim was to create political theories that would offer solutions that could be validated and legitimized in relation to existing political problems, bearing in mind that many of the solutions to those problems were predetermined. Instead of political theory determining policy, it was everyday politics that determined the theory. Since somehow or other solving the problem was what mattered, the inner consistency of the theory was unimportant. The important point was that the theory should show and even prove that the problem could be solved.

The fact that Şinâsi, Nâmık Kemal and Ziyâ Pasha were civil servants for an important part of their lives and considered themselves in the service of the state, placed them among the candidates to become members of the ruling elite. Their bureaucratic status, on the other hand, deprived them of a meaningful tie with other social groups in the empire. As officials of the state, Nâmık Kemal and Ziyâ were always guaranteed an arena in which to pursue their political struggles, irrespective of whether or not they had the confidence of the palace, or had been exiled to distant places. Although forced to flee to France because of their oppositional stances, they were nonetheless still enjoying the patronage of an agent who himself was part of the ruling elite and engaged in a struggle for power, a power the Young Ottomans inevitably served, for he was the patron paying their salaries. In turn, the dependence of the Young Ottomans on their patron pashas limited their political autonomy. The conflicts and searches for compromise among the belligerent higher ranks would always affect and determine the line of development of the Young Ottoman opposition. It is known that possible compromises and alliances between different political fronts and patrons sometimes left Young Ottomans in the cold, which created major frustrations among them. Despite this, there was no significant resistance among them to such betrayals.[36]

In these aspects, the Young Ottoman opposition was radically different from that of contemporary Western Europe. Whereas the former limited itself to 'saving the state', the opposition in Western Europe was mainly a concrete reflection of – occasionally bloody – struggles for power that took place between social classes during the revolutions of 1830 and 1848, as well as in

---

35  Berkes, *Çağdaşlaşma*, 265–77; Mardin, *Genesis*, 81–132; Türköne, *Siyasî İdeoloji*, 93–9.
36  Bilgegil, *Ziya Paşa*, 81–116, 256–68; Ebüzziya, *Şinasi*, 103–274; Kuntay, *Namık Kemal* 1, *passim*; Mardin, *Genesis*, 398.

the Paris Commune (1871). Their political and ideological framework, however, was not intended to protect the existing political system, but rather to destroy the state institutions.[37]

Let us look at some of the distinguishing features of prominent Young Ottomans. Although their educational backgrounds differed considerably, many shared the education they received at the translation office attached to the Sublime Porte, for it provided them with a window to the Western world, proficiency in at least one foreign language and, from the detailed articles that appeared in European newspapers and reports, a close knowledge of world affairs. These advantages gave them opportunities for comparatively fast promotion through the hierarchy of the governing elite.[38] Another common feature of the Young Ottomans was their close tie with and loyalty towards Mustafa Reşid Pasha. When referring to Reşid Pasha's pivotal role at the declaration of the Edict of the Rose Chamber, Şinâsi, went so far as to proclaim that his patron had "liberated the people while being under the captivity of oppression" (*ettin âzâd bizi olmuş iken zulme esir*), was "president of the virtuous people" (*eyâ ahâli-yi fazlın reîs-i cumhûru*), and the "prophet of civilization" (*medeniyyet resûlü*).[39] When Reşid Pasha fell from power and Âlî and Fuad Pasha rose to positions of political decision-making, the young civil servants hitherto protected by Reşid and expecting future promotions lost any hope of joining the governing elite. It should also be stated that the Edict of Reforms, granting legal equality and liberty to non-Muslims, produced deep-seated resentment among a wide spectrum of Muslims ranging from common people at the popular level to reformists like Reşid Pasha and his clients. It was this resentment of Âlî and Fuad Pasha, combined with the perception of a sellout of vital imperial interests to foreign powers that brought these enraged and disappointed individuals together.[40]

Whether in power or in opposition, the primary concern of the Young Ottomans was to save 'their state'. This might give the impression that they were worried about modernization threatening the future existence of the state, but

---

37  For a general perspective on revolutions in the nineteenth century, see David Armitage and Sanjay Subrahmanyam, *The Age of Global Revolutions in Global Context, c.1760–1840* (Houndmills: Palgrave Macmillan, 2010); E. J. Hobsbawm, *The Age of Revolution, 1789–1848* (New York: Vintage Books, 1996); Theda Skocpol, *Social Revolutions in the Modern World* (Cambridge: CUP, 1994).
38  Ali Akyıldız, "Tercüme Odası", *DIA* 40, 504–6; Carter V. Findley, *Bureaucratic Reform in the Ottoman Empire: The Sublime Porte, 1789–1922* (Princeton, NJ: Princeton University Press, 1980), 132–9, 158.
39  Ebüzziya, *Şinasi*, 377, 378.
40  Davison, *Reform*, 52–80, 172–86.

that could not be further from the truth. The Young Ottomans were definitely not against modernization *per se*, but against the way it was being perceived. As we have seen above, there were some Young Ottomans who tried to reconcile Islamic political traditions with Western political thought. However, the crucial question concerned the 'coordinates of power', or in what position the relevant parties found themselves placed in the power game. Even Mustafa Reşid Pasha, the main architect of the *Tanzimat* era, switched sides when Âlî Pasha and Fuad Pasha gained power and he blamed them for drafting the Edict of Reforms.[41] However, it is difficult to tell whether the Young Ottomans were opposing the increasing bureaucratic hegemony of the Sublime Porte or just the authority of Âlî and Fuad Pasha. Had everything gone well and had Reşid Pasha remained in power with his own political team promoted to the key political posts, the Young Ottoman movement would most likely have included some very different names.

At this point, we may examine the nature of the struggle among Ottoman political elites in the late *Tanzimat* era. Both sides were members of the state and both agreed on the need to preserve the existence of the state. However, they disagreed over the ways and means of saving it. In fact, on this point the Young Ottomans even disagreed among themselves. While Ali Suâvî, the most radical of them, saw revolution and the resistance of ordinary people as a political tool, others supported a more conservative approach. The main tendency among the Young Ottoman prospective governing elite who had climbed the traditional Ottoman political career ladder with the help of a patron, was exactly the opposite of that of Ali Suâvî. If, accordingly, the only problem was on the level of the ruling elites, then the solution would be determined at that level itself, within the framework of a political and personal struggle, sponsored and supported by their patrons. The Young Ottomans' short-term European adventures could not have taken place without such political patronage. The intra-dynastic conflict between Mustafa Fâzıl and Khedive İsmâil on the one side, and Khedive İsmâil's manoeuvres to extend the autonomy of Egypt from the Sublime Porte on the other, produced a power struggle with Abdülaziz, the Khedive, Âlî and Fuad on one side, and Fâzıl Pasha and his Young Ottoman clients on the other.[42]

---

41  Kemal Beydilli, "Mustafa Reşid Paşa", *DIA* 31 (Istanbul: 2006), 348–50; Cevdet Pasha, *Tezâkir 1–12*, 67–86.

42  Bilgegil, *Ziya Paşa*, 22–33, 88–116, 126–39, 220–53; Çelik, *Ali Suavî*, 28–84, 374–89, 557–62; Ebüzziya, *Şinasi*, 57–79, 101–44; Kuntay, *Namık Kemal, passim*; Mardin, *Genesis*, 107–32; Tevfik, *Yeni Osmanlılar, passim*.

The oppositional movement against the hegemony of Âlî and Fuad first took shape through Şinâsi publishing independent newspapers like *Tercüman-ı Ahvâl* and *Tasvir-i Efkâr*. The Young Ottoman organization formed in 1865, which called itself Mission and later Patriotic Alliance, was able to draw attention to itself at the beginning of 1867 when Fâzıl Pasha's political declarations were published in the European press. The group immediately translated them from French to Ottoman Turkish and secretly distributed them among the common people. Meanwhile, in exile, Ali Suâvî was publishing the *Muhbir*, and Nâmık Kemal and Ziyâ were editing the *Hürriyet*. Nâmık Kemal then continued his oppositional activities in Istanbul by editing the *İbret* newspaper. All these developments show how modern mass media, such as newspapers, came to be used for the first time in the central Ottoman lands in the course of an essentially traditional type of intra-elite political struggle. This suggests that, despite the highly elitist nature of these political confrontations, Young Ottomans felt a strong urge to mobilize the support of the Muslim masses and many of their literary activities were geared towards that end. The arrival of the first Ottoman Turkish novels, changes in the content of poetry, efforts to simplify the written language, and the advent of theatre were all offshoots of that attempt. However, from the beginning, all these endeavours were seen and perceived as platforms for political activity, rather than as literary or aesthetic creations.[43]

## 3  The Young Ottomans: Their Understanding of Political Struggle and The Constitution Project

In one of his articles, Ziyâ Pasha set out a political agenda that at least one important faction of the Young Ottomans supported. Ziyâ, who was at that time in exile, presented his ideas in the form of a dream in which he met Sultan Abdülaziz alone in his palace. In his dream, he took that golden opportunity to tell the sultan everything that nobody had yet told him, or had deliberately withheld from him – in other words, the 'truth'. This was the only way to free Abdülaziz of the prejudices he harboured after years of disinformation. Once Abdülaziz became aware of 'the reality' his country faced, he would naturally

---

43  Bilgegil, "Millet Meclisi Kurma", 352–71; Çelik, *Ali Suavî*, 634–49; Ebüzziya, *Şinasi*, 339–69; Mardin, *Genesis*, 10–80; Joseph G. Rahme, "Namık Kemal's Constitutional Ottomanism and Non-Muslims", in *Islam and Muslim-Christian Relations* 10 (1) 1999, 30–1; Ahmet Hamdi Tanpınar, *19. Asır Türk Edebiyatı Tarihi*, 10th edn (Istanbul: Çağlayan Kitabevi, 2003), *passim*; Tevfik, *Yeni Osmanlılar*, 15–77, 196–449.

try to look for a new political formula with which to lead the country out of its existing situation, which is what Young Ottomans had been doing through their newspapers in Europe. Hence, it was necessary to draw up a constitution and, contrary to general belief, no harm would come from doing so. On the contrary, it would be the only way of keeping the state and country together and thus saving the state. If, for once, leading members of the Young Ottoman movement could replace the sultan's entourage – and it went without saying that the sultan himself would take this decision – then there would no reason for anything to go wrong because now 'good' would have replaced 'evil'. Having been misled, the sultan would naturally be on the side of 'the good'.[44]

It is hard to say that there was perfect harmony between what the members of the Young Ottoman group defended and how they actually acted. When their attempts to persuade the sultan, either directly through people like Ziyâ, Fâzıl Pasha or Midhat, or through journalism, proved unsatisfactory, they started to discuss alternatives to absolutist sultanic rule. Since, with the exception of Ali Suâvî, their political theorists refrained from extending the struggle for power down to the masses, there remained but one option – turn to traditional Ottoman methods of altering the forces in power. The Young Ottomans thus expected first Murad V and then Abdülhamid II, both waiting to replace their uncle, to become determining names in this struggle. However, the eventual accession of the latter dealt a major blow to their political aspirations because, as previously with Fâzıl Pasha, on assumption of power, their patron immediately abandoned them. The Young Ottomans had learned that it was impossible to advance politically without a patron or patrons, but equally impossible to remain in power through trusting and depending on one's patrons.[45]

As already stated, the Young Ottomans thought that a constitutional regime would be the best way of saving the state. Their intellectual perspective on constitutionalism was largely shaped by traditional Islamic political theory, particularly as seen in Nâmık Kemal's ideas. At the same time, Western political thought also made an impact on certain Young Ottomans. Trying to reconcile these fundamentally different traditions did not overly bother them because attaining their political goals was of more urgent concern. There was little discussion on the fundamentals of Western political thought, such as questions on the separation of powers, parliament as a representative body, limits to parliamentary authority, delegation of power to the government, responsibilities

---

44   Ziya Pasha, "Rüya", in Şemsettin Kutlu (ed.), *Tanzimat Dönemi Türk Edebiyatı Antolojisi*, 2nd edn (Istanbul: Remzi Kitabevi, 1981), 123–30.
45   Celâleddin Pasha, *Mir'ât*, 92–131, 159–63, 237–9; Cevdet Pasha, *Tezâkir*, 153–70; Mardin, *Genesis*, 28–56.

and limits of the executive, and basic individual rights. Since the constitutionalists could find no example of a constitution from the classical Islamic era as a precedent on which to depend, they looked at contemporary constitutional models from countries in the West such as France, Belgium and Prussia, as well as at extant constitutional political systems within the greater Ottoman realm such the Danubian Principalities (1831/2; 1858; 1866), Serbia (1838; 1869), Tunis (1861), and Egypt (1866).[46]

Young Ottomans only really began to discuss the constitution in earnest after the 30 May 1876 coup, when they found themselves in power. Despite this obvious advantage, certain factors hampered the formulation of a truly liberal constitution. As stated, the Young Ottoman movement lacked a homogeneous political line and, due to differences of view, their political ideas were insufficiently clear. The deposition of Murad V after three months and the accession of Abdülhamid II, who was less liberal, created additional uncertainty. Most important, however, was the immense time pressure to which the Young Ottomans were subjected. Unlike constitutions that emerge from social movements and from balancing political forces, the designers of the first Ottoman constitution had to ensure the immediate diplomatic backing of external powers such as Britain and France against pressure from Russia and Austria-Hungary. From 1875 onwards, the latter two powers had been intervening on behalf of Serbian and Bulgarian rebels and were putting pressure on the Sublime Porte to initiate administrative reforms in the Balkans. For the new (post-May 1876) government, the promulgation of a constitution aimed to guarantee the political support of liberal powers against the interventions of the Russians and Habsburgs. The British and French needed to be convinced that the empire was reformable through internal means. The declaration of a liberal constitution would render the approaching Constantinople Conference (*Tersane Konferansı*) on the Balkan crisis superfluous.[47]

Whatever their reasons, the Young Ottomans in power felt an urgent need for a constitution – a need that did not originate from society itself, but from the state. Despite contradictory views among members of the Ottoman political

---

46  Berkes, *Çağdaşlaşma*, 321 fn.31; Celâleddin Pasha, *Mir'ât*, 126; Charles Jelavich and Barbara Jelavich, *The Establishment of the Balkan National States, 1804–1920* (Seattle: University of Washington Press, 1986), 58, 65–6, 90–2, 115–16, 122–3; Bernard Lewis, "Dustūr", *EI2* 2, 638–40, 642; Mardin, *Genesis*, 70–6, 289–323, 332–6; Recai G. Okandan, *Âmme Hukukumuzun Anahatları: Birinci Kitap (Osmanlı Devletinin Kuruluşundan İnkırazına Kadar)* (Istanbul: İstanbul Üniversitesi Yayınları, 1968), 138; Fritz Steppat, "Miṣr", *EI2* 7, 183; Syed Tanvir Wasti, "A Note on Tunuslu Hayreddin Paşa", *MES* 36 (1) 2000, 1–20.

47  Celâleddin Pasha, *Mir'ât*, 161–3, 171–6, 182–5, 192–207; Okandan, *Âmme Hukukumuzun*, 136–7, 139–40.

elite, numerous individuals considered the introduction of a constitution, or at least of a representative assembly, of paramount importance. The common belief of the proponents of a constitution was that the state would rise again.[48] If a constitution were ever needed, it was for this that it was needed – it could well have been left aside had it been a mere response to the political demands of various sections of the society.

At this point, one might ask if some sections of multi-religious, multi-ethnic Ottoman society actually wanted a constitution. However, given that Ottoman society was predominantly rural, illiterate and had limited experience of participatory politics, it is difficult to answer that question. Nonetheless, some parts of the realm had clearly experienced constitutional regimes, though not necessarily liberal ones. For example, the provisions contained in the Edict of Reforms of 1856 gave Greek, Armenian and Jewish *millet*s basic constitutional rights in core Ottoman regions. For instance, inspired by the French Revolution, Greek intellectuals such as Rigas Feraios (Velestinlis) (d.1798), came up with a democratic constitution for Ottoman lands and later, during the Greek War of Independence, most Greek intellectuals advocated a liberal constitution for an autonomous, sovereign Greece. It was only after the revolution of 1844, however, that Greece became a constitutional kingdom. Prior to the *Tanzimat* era, major Muslim notables (*âyân*) from Anatolia and the Balkans had, during a period of domestic and international strife, served a Deed of Agreement (*Sened-i İttifak*) (1808) on Sultan Mahmud II (d.1839), which limited his powers and acknowledged the right of notables to counter the actions of the grand vizier. However, the deed of agreement remained a dead letter because the sultan and ruling elites of Istanbul prevented its application. Although a rather rudimentary text, it was undeniably a constitutional document produced by provincial elites to curtail the hitherto unlimited powers of the imperial centre, so at least was an indication of the existence of a basic notion of a constitutional political system among rural elites prior to the era of Westernizing reforms.[49]

---

48    Nurullah Ardıç, "Islam, Modernity, and the 1876 Constitution", in Christoph Herzog and Malek Sharif (eds), *The First Ottoman Experiment in Democracy* (Würzburg: Ergon Verlag Würzburg, 2010), 94–7; Berkes, *Çağdaşlaşma*, 317; Abdulhamit Kırmızı, "Authoritarianism and Constitutionalism Combined: Ahmed Midhat Efendi Between the Sultan and the *Kanun-i Esasi*", in Herzog and Sharif, *The First Ottoman Experiment*, 55–7; Tevfik, *Yeni Osmanlılar*, 45–6.

49    Ali Akyıldız, "Sened-i İttifak'ın İlk Tam Metni", *İslâm Araştırmaları Dergisi* 2 (1998), 209–22; İnalcık, "Sened-i İttifak", 344–8; Jelavich, *Establishment*, 76, 81–2; Herkül Millas, *Yunan Ulusunun Doğuşu* (Istanbul: İletişim Yayınları, 1994), 102–9.

Members of the ruling elite who either rejected the idea of a constitution outright or accepted only some non-liberal or restricted version of it included conservatives like Hüseyin Avni Pasha (d.1876), Mütercim Rüşdü Pasha (d.1882), Mehmed Nâmık Pasha (d.1892), and Ahmed Cevdet Pasha (d.1895). For them, the reign of a benevolent, honest sultan was crucial to just rule,[50] which is rather reminiscent of Ziyâ Pasha's political ideas discussed earlier.

The Young Ottomans could have allied themselves with at least one major social group in the society to realize their constitutional project, which might have protected them against possible attack, but they clearly appear to have refrained from any such route to political power. In the absence of a civil political horizon, proponents of the constitutional project minimized the likelihood of the unexpected political consequences resulting from a constitutional regime. A crucial question in this respect was the authority of the future parliament and, as discussed below, the House of Representatives (*Heyet-i Mebusan*) was given minimal legislative and political powers. In fact, most Young Ottomans deemed it necessary to preserve the holy rights and authority of the sultan. In addition, factors such as international crises, time pressure and Abdülhamid's inflexibility over making concessions with regard to the absolute authority of the sultan, weakened the hand of the negotiators. In effect, the Young Ottomans were forced to agree to a system in which the traditional rights of the absolute monarch were constitutionally guaranteed. Although, ideally, a constitutional system should define and limit the authority of the political power, here the opposite was realized. The legal infrastructure that was set up enabled Abdülhamid to establish a constitutional autocracy.

The absence of political consensus among Young Ottomans was reflected in the emergence of separate constitutional drafts, some known to have been produced by Midhat Pasha, Ziyâ Pasha, and Nâmık Kemal. We learn from Ahmed Mithat Efendi's *Üss-i İnkılab* (Foundation of Revolution), an eye-witness account of political developments in the capital between 1876 and 1878, that nearly twenty draft texts were compiled.[51] Strikingly, while legal modernization in the *Tanzimat* era was mainly based on French legal models, the same was not true of compiling a constitution, probably because of the republican nature of the French constitution. According to one point of view, in the draft prepared by Midhat Pasha, the 1831 Belgian Constitution – which in turn was based on the 1814 French Constitution – was taken as a model. In addition, the

---

50  Berkes, *Çağdaşlaşma*, 303, 305–6; Celâleddin Pasha, *Mir'ât*, 111, 119, 126–7; Okandan, *Âmme Hukukumuzun*, 131, 140–1; Abdullah Saydam, "Namık Paşa", *DIA* 32, 379.

51  Berkes, *Çağdaşlaşma*, 314; Ahmed Mithat, *Üss-i İnkılâb*, edited by İdris Nebi Uysal (Istanbul: Dergâh Yayınları, 2013), 390–3, 460–87.

Prussian Constitutional Edict of 1850 was also taken into consideration. This draft was forwarded to a commission controlled by Abdülhamid and a new document drafted. The version finally accepted at the end of long negotiations was the text that was approved by the sultan, and that became known as the Constitution of 1876 (*Kānûn-i Esâsî*). In fact, the ultimate form included some articles added by the sultan himself. Therefore, the final constitution was a complex result of numerous texts and ideas.[52]

The constitution came into effect through an imperial edict and the sultan emerged as its sole legitimator. In this regard, the Ottoman constitution was similar to the Prussian one, whereas the Belgian one derived its legitimation from a constituent assembly representing the sovereign people.[53]

## 4  An Analysis of the 1876 Constitution from the Viewpoint of Constitutional Law

The *Kānûn-i Esâsî* consisted of 19 sections and 119 articles.[54] The first section defined the empire and its political system. Accordingly, the Ottoman state was an indivisible unit (*article 1*) and its capital Istanbul (*article 2*). The reign of the Ottoman sultan and the caliphate belonged to the Ottoman dynasty, while the oldest male member of the family would become the sultan (*article 3*). The sultan was both caliph and head of state; he was also sacrosanct and not responsible (*articles 4 and 5*). In a liberal constitution, the latter clause could

---

52  Berkes, *Çağdaşlaşma*, 302–3, 309, 320–3; Lewis, "Dustūr", 642.
53  Lewis, "Dustūr", 642.
54  For the original text of the 1876 Ottoman Constitution, see Suna Kili and Şeref Gözübüyük (eds), *Sened-i İttifak'tan Günümüze Türk Anayasa Metinleri*, 3rd edn (Istanbul: Türkiye İş Bankası Kültür Yayınları, 2006), 36–51; Friedrich von Kraelitz-Greifenhorst, *Die Verfassungsgesetze des Osmanischen Reiches. Osten und Orient. Vierte Reihe. Erste Abteilung. Erste Heft* (Vienna: Verlag des Forschungsinstitutes für Osten und Orient, 1919), 30–50. On the secondary literature discussing the *Kānûn-i Esâsî*, see Orhan Aldıkaçtı, *Anayasa Hukukumuzun Gelişmesi ve 1961 Anayasası*, 2nd edn (Istanbul: İstanbul Üniversitesi Hukuk Fakültesi Yayınları, 1973), 44–52; Robert Devereux, *The First Ottoman Constitutional Period*. (Baltimore: John Hopkins Press, 1963); Gotthard Jaeschke, "Die Entwicklung des Osmanischen Verfassungsstaates von den Anfängen bis zur Gegenwart", *WIS* 5 (1–2), 1917, 11–14; Suna Kili, "1876 Anayasasının Çağdaşlaşma Sorunları Açısından Değerlendirilmesi", in *Armağan. Kanun-u Esasi'nin 100. Yılı* (Ankara: Ankara Üniversitesi Siyasal Bilgiler Fakültesi Yayını, 1978), 192–4; Okandan, *Âmme Hukukumuzun*, 134–43; Mümtaz Soysal, *Anayasaya Giriş*, 2nd edn (Ankara: Ankara Üniversitesi Siyasal Bilgiler Fakültesi Yayını, 1969), 57–8; Tarık Zafer Tunaya, *Türkiye'de Siyasal Gelişmeler (1876–1938): (Birinci Kitap: Kanun-ı Esasi ve Meşrutiyet Dönemleri 1876–1918)* (Istanbul: İstanbul Bilgi Üniversitesi Yayınları, 2001), 7–9.

be accepted as a standard rule only if the absence of responsibility was tied to symbolic authority. However, what happened here was just the opposite: the sultan was both non-liable and equipped with extensive powers. As a caliph, he was the protector of Islam; as the sultan, he was the sultan and sovereign of his citizens (*article 4*). The legal rights of the Ottoman dynasty were guaranteed (*article 6*) and the official religion of the state was Islam (*article 11*).[55]

Articles related to the executive power granted major authority to the sultan, who was head of the executive organ. He appointed and dismissed the grand vizier and members of the government. The government was formed by the sultan, not by the grand vizier, who had no authority whatsoever on this issue (*articles 7 and 27*). Government decisions could only come into force with the sultan's approval (*article 27*). Each minister was responsible solely for his specific field, and there was no such thing as the common political responsibility of the government (*articles 29–31*). It was considered unnecessary for the government to get a vote of confidence from the parliament, because it was not responsible to parliament. As we shall see below, the House of Representatives (HR), which formed a wing of the parliament, could issue petitions of complaint against members of the government, but only in areas under their jurisdiction (*article 31*). In such a case, if two-thirds of the HR considered the petition of complaint justified, the grand vizier would inform the sultan and if the sultan also considered the complaint justified, the minister in question would be invited to the Supreme Court (*article 92–102*).[56]

The sultan was authorized to sign treaties with foreign countries, declare war and conclude peace. He commanded both the army and navy (*article 7*). He had the authority to call both wings of parliament, the HR and Senate (*Hey'et-i Âyân*), for session, and if the need arose, dissolve the HR and hold elections (*article 44*). If any government proposals were rejected twice in a row in the HR, the sultan would either dismiss the government, or dissolve the HR pending an election (*article 35*). If, at a given time, the parliament was not convening, decisions taken by the government would enter effect with the sultan's approval, as if they had been the parliament's decisions (*article 36*). Members of parliament (MPs) had the right to ask members of government questions and in this case, the minister in question could either personally answer the question or have somebody from his staff do so on his behalf. However, he also had the right to postpone answering, providing he took responsibility

---

[55] Aldıkaçtı, *Anayasa Hukukumuzun*, 52–3; Okandan, *Âmme Hukukumuzun*, 143–51; Soysal, *Anayasaya*, 60–1; Bülent Tanör, *Osmanlı-Türk Anayasal Gelişmeleri (1789–1980)*, revised 3rd edn (Istanbul: Afa Yayıncılık, 1996), 103; Tunaya, *Siyasal Gelişmeler*, 9–11.
[56] Okandan, *Âmme Hukukumuzun*, 143–65; Tanör, *Osmanlı*, 105–14.

(*articles 37–8*), but it was unclear what this responsibility involved. The supervisory mechanism of the legislative organ over the executive was rather limited.[57]

The parliament (*Meclis-i Umûmî*) as a legislative organ had two chambers – HR and Senate (*article 42*) – and both convened at the same time. The parliament assembled at the beginning of November with the sultan's permission and ended at the beginning of March (*article 43*). If needs be, it could start earlier and conclude later, but only with the sultan's permission (*article 44*).[58]

Members of the Senate were appointed directly by the sultan and their number could not exceed one-third of the members of the HR (*article 60*). Being a member of Senate was a lifetime appointment. Only 'reliable' people over the age of forty and experienced in state affairs qualified (*articles 61–2*). The members of the HR were elected from among Ottoman citizens by realizing a ratio of one MP for every 50,000 adult males (*article 65*). The constitution did not expound on the electoral system other than to stipulate that elections were to be made by secret ballot (*article 66*). MPs were elected for four years and re-election was possible (*article 69*). They were regarded as representative of the whole empire and not just of the region from which they were elected (*article 71*). An MP could not become a member of the government (*article 67*). To qualify as an MP required being a citizen of the Ottoman state, not in the service of a foreign country, proficient in Turkish, more than thirty years of age, and not in the personal service of any person. Other conditions for candidacy were related to commercial respectability and honesty (*article 68*). Voters elected their representatives from among the people in their electoral region (*article 72*) and meetings of the parliament were open to the public. However, a closed session could be held on request but only if the majority agreed (*article 78*). MPs enjoyed legislative immunity, apart from cases of criminality (*article 79*).[59]

The legislative authority that liberal constitutions could grant to parliaments was biased in favour of the sultan (*article 7*). The government, Senate and HR shared the authority to propose bills. While the government could propose bills on any subject, the HR and Senate could only do so within the scope

---

57   Aldıkaçtı, *Anayasa Hukukumuzun*, 53–4; Jaeschke, "Entwicklung", 14–20; Kili, "1876 Anayasasının", 194–209; Ahmet Mumcu, "Osmanlı Devletinde 1876 Anayasasına Değin Temel Hak ve Özgürlükler İle 1876 Anayasasının Temel Yapısı", in *Türk Parlamentoculuğunun İlk 100 Yılı (1876–1976), Kanun-u Esasinin 100. Yılı Sempozyumu (1976 Ankara)* (Ankara: Ajans-Türk Matbaacılık, [1977?]), 31–47; Okandan, *Âmme Hukukumuzun*, 151–61; Tanör, *Osmanlı*, 136–44; Tunaya, *Siyasal Gelişmeler*, 11. Sosyal, *Anayasaya*, 60.
58   Kili and Gözübüyük, *Sened-i İttifak'tan*, 41; Okandan, *Âmme Hukukumuzun*, 150; Tanör, *Osmanlı*, 105.
59   Kili and Gözübüyük, *Sened-i İttifak'tan*, 43–6; Tanör, *Osmanlı*, 104.

of some of their duties (*article 53*), regarding which no definition was given. To use even this limited authority to propose bills required the sultan's permission through the grand vizier. Once the sultan's approval had been obtained, the Council of State formulated a draft of the law, which was then discussed first in the HR and then in the Senate. If both chambers accepted it, the draft was presented to the sultan and could be enacted only if he ratified it. The sultan had the right to veto a law proposal (*articles 53–54*). A draft bill that was rejected could not be discussed again for the rest of the year. In both chambers of parliament, decisions were taken by majority vote. For a bill to be enacted, each article had to be voted on separately and accepted by the majority (*article 54*). The Senate could only examine a bill to ensure that it did not threaten religion, the sultan's rights, freedom, the constitution, the unity of the state, internal security, the defence of the country and common morals. If it did, it would reject the bill or send it back to the HR for alteration (*article 64*). The parliament conducted its discussions in Turkish (*article 57*).[60]

According to the *Kānûn-i Esâsî*, judicial courts were independent and covered both the Islamic and secular (*nizamiye*) courts. The religious courts based their verdicts on sharia law and handled cases related to private law, whereas the secular courts dealt with those covered by criminal and commercial laws. The Supreme Court handled cases involving members of the government, members of the Court of Cassation, or people who had committed crimes against the state or sultan (*articles 81–107*).[61] The issue of the judiciary is inseparable from that of basic rights and freedoms. Accordingly, whatever their religion or sect, subjects of the Ottoman state were considered to be Ottoman citizens (*article 8*) and legal equality was guaranteed (*article 17*). Nobody could be accused for reasons other than those specified by law (*article 10*). All religions and sects were free to exercise their creed as long as they respected public morals and did not threaten state security (*article 11*). Protection of life and property were guaranteed (*article 9*) as was residential immunity (*article 22*). Nobody could be tried anywhere other than in a court of law (*article 23*). Confiscation and forced labour were prohibited, and no taxation could be

---

60 Aldıkaçtı, *Anayasa Hukukumuzun*, 55–8; Ali İhsan Gencer, "İlk Osmanlı Anayasasında Türkçenin Resmi Dil Olarak Kabulü Meselesi", in *Armağan. Kanun-u Esasi'nin 100. Yılı*, 183–9; Mumcu, "Osmanlı Devletinde", 37–9; Okandan, *Âmme Hukukumuzun*, 161–5; Sosyal, *Anayasaya*, 59–60; Tanör, *Osmanlı*, 136–44; Tunaya, *Siyasal Gelişmeler*, 11–12.
61 Kili and Gözübüyük, *Sened-i İttifak'tan*, 46–9; Okandan, *Âmme Hukukumuzun*, 166–7; Tanör, *Osmanlı*, 108, 110, 112.

imposed without a law (*articles 24–5*). Torture and any kind of cruelty were outlawed (*article 26*).[62]

The scope of basic rights and freedoms was rather narrowly delineated. Rights to hold a meeting or found a civilian organization were non-existent and this effectively restricted political participation. Press freedom was defined by law (*article 12*). There was no notion of freedom of expression. Since all basic rights and freedoms were defined by laws subject to the sultan's approval, what actual form these rights and freedoms could take was left to the sultan's mercy. For example, at the last moment of bargaining, Abdülhamid succeeded in including a clause in article 113 empowering the sultan to deport individuals outside imperial borders if he considered them a threat to the security of the state. As mentioned earlier, Midhat Pasha himself became the first victim of this stipulation. This clause violated the *rechtsstaat* principle of due process. Any change in the constitution required the sultan's approval (*article 116*).[63]

To conclude, the first Ottoman constitution was not based on national sovereignty, but derived its legitimation from the will of the sultan. Fundamental rights and freedoms were limited and lacked judicial guarantees. A close look at the constitution indicates its rather eclectic nature. While certain individual rights of a liberal nature were put forward, stipulations pertaining to the state structure were mainly absolutistic. This eclecticism possibly reflected the wide variety of viewpoints expressed during the process of constitutional bargaining.[64]

## 5 Elections and the First Ottoman Parliament

Immediately after the constitution came into effect, an election was held to choose the members of the HR. However, the constitution stipulated that a special bill be enacted for this purpose. Since the same constitution stipulated that the HR was to be formed before a bill could be enacted, a temporary arrangement was accepted.[65]

---

62 Kili and Gözübüyük, *Sened-i İttifak'tan*, 37–8; Okandan, *Âmme Hukukumuzun*, 166–7; Tanör, *Osmanlı*, 110–11.

63 Kili and Gözübüyük, *Sened-i İttifak'tan*, 37, 50–1; Okandan, *Âmme Hukukumuzun*, 167–70; Tanör, *Osmanlı*, 107, 111, 112.

64 Aldıkaçt, *Anayasa Hukukumuzun*, 58–62; Mumcu, "Osmanlı Devletinde", 37–9; Okandan, *Âmme Hukukumuzun*, 166–71; Soysal, *Anayasaya*, 61–2; Tanör, *Osmanlı*, 112–16; Tunaya, *Siyasal Gelişmeler*, 13–14.

65 Servet Armağan, "Memleketimizde İlk Parlamento Seçimleri", in *Armağan. Kanun-u Esasi'nin 100. Yılı*, 151, 153–5; Bekir Sıtkı Baykal, "Birinci Meşrutiyete Dair Belgeler", *Belleten* 24 (96) 1960, 609–23; Kili and Gözübüyük, *Sened-i İttifak'tan*, 44; Tanör, *Osmanlı*, 116.

According to this temporary arrangement, dated 28 October 1876, indirect elections were to be held by applying a simple majority system to select eighty Muslim and fifty non-Muslim representatives. The age of eligibility for election was set at 25, and some new conditions were added, such as knowing Turkish, originating from the province in which one is elected, being an honourable person, and owning at least some property. For electoral purposes, the Ottoman lands were divided into two regions – Istanbul and the rest of the empire. In Istanbul, a total of forty secondary electors, elected by primary electors, would elect the MPs. Elections were also to be held in rural centres. However, the rural areas would not hold a separate election to choose the secondary electors; instead, people previously elected to the provincial councils would take on that role. Both to vote and to be elected, it was necessary to be male – women had no such rights. Two elections were held before the dissolution of the parliament.[66]

The first Ottoman parliament, which convened for two periods, did not function for a long time. The initial session of the HR's first period took place on 20 March 1877 and, in a little over three months, after fifty-six sessions, the HR ended its activities on 28 June 1877. Following new elections, parliament resumed its sessions on 13 December 1877, but operated for only two months, in which there were twenty-nine sessions, before Abdülhamid dissolved the HR on 14 February 1878.[67]

The first Ottoman constitutional experiment took place under rather exceptional conditions. Following the *coup d'état* of May 1876, the new power holders faced the Balkan crisis and political interventions from Russia and Austria-Hungary. For constitutionalists like the Young Ottomans and Midhat Pasha, the promulgation of an Ottoman constitution aimed to weaken the bureaucratic power of the *Tanzimat* and offer a certain amount of popular representation – including to non-Muslims – in the capital and thus propagate the image of an empire able to reform itself. The creation of such an image would help the government resist Russian and Habsburg demands for autonomy for Balkan Slavs and provide support for liberal powers like Britain and France. This already complex situation became even more so with the unexpected mental breakdown of Murad V and the accession of Abdülhamid

---

66   Aldıkaçtı, *Anayasa Hukukumuzun*, 57–9; Armağan, "Memleketimizde", 154–7; Devereux, *First Ottoman*, 123–52; Kili and Gözübüyük, *Sened-i İttifak'tan*, 44; Tanör, *Osmanlı*, 116–18; Tunaya, *Siyasal Gelişmeler*, 14–16.

67   Aldıkaçtı, *Anayasa Hukukumuzun*, 57–9; Armağan, "Memleketimizde", 161–7; Devereux, *First Ottoman*, 123–52; İlber Ortaylı, "İlk Osmanlı Parlamentosu ve Osmanlı Milletlerinin Temsili", in *Armağan. Kanun-u Esasi'nin 100. Yılı*, 173–6; Tanör, *Osmanlı*, 119; Tunaya, *Siyasal Gelişmeler*, 14–16.

II, whose commitment to the constitutionalist cause was uncertain. At the same time, representatives of the Great Powers were going to convene the Constantinople Conference on 23 December 1876 to discuss the Balkan crisis. All these factors, along with a race against time, determined the shape and character of the first Ottoman constitution, which was promulgated on the very same day as the conference opened.

Although the HR was designed to be a passive body, after an initial period of passivity, the MPs showed unexpected political will by developing a collective identity as representatives of the Ottoman people. When the Russo – Ottoman War of 1877/8 broke out following the failure of the Constantinople Conference, the HR became a hotbed of Ottoman patriotism. As the war turned into a major Ottoman defeat, numerous MPs questioned the government's military and political competence, as well as that of the army commanders. The arrival of Russian troops at St Stefano in early 1878 prompted MPs to demand the appearance of three ministers in the chamber to defend themselves against charges of incompetence and treason. This unprecedented development presented Abdülhamid and the ruling elite with a wholly unacceptable political challenge. The next day, Abdülhamid dissolved the HR, and forcibly sent the MPs back to their provinces. While the sultan's action technically conformed to the relevant article in the constitution, the parliament, which was due to meet again at the beginning of November, did not assemble for another thirty years.[68]

## 6 Epilogue: Legacy of 1876 Constitution

The assertion that Abdülhamid abolished the constitution is technically untrue, for the sultan was merely exercising his constitutional right. He just dissolved the HR and refrained from convening the assembly for thirty years.

---

68 For a collection of parliamentary debates during the two periods of the HR, see Hakkı Tarık Us (ed.), *Meclis-i Meb'usan Zabıt Ceridesi, 1293–1877*, 2 vols (Istanbul: Vakit, 1939/40), *passim*. On concrete examples of politically active deputies, see Bülent Bilmez and Nathalie Clayer, "A Prosopographic Study on some 'Albanian' Deputies to the First Ottoman Parliament", in Herzog and Sharif, *The First Ottoman Experiment*, 155–7, 164–8, 177–8; Elke Hartmann, "The 'Loyal Nation' and its Deputies: The Armenians in the First Ottoman Parliament", in Herzog and Sharif, *The First Ottoman Experiment*, 216–22; Malek Sharif, "A Portrait of Syrian Deputies in the First Ottoman Parliament", in Herzog and Sharif, *The First Ottoman Experiment*, 304–11. For general accounts, see Sina Akşin, "I. Meşrutiyet Üzerine Bazı Düşünceler", in *Uluslararası Midhat Paşa Semineri*, 27–9; Devereux, *First Ottoman*, 186–215; Lewis, *Emergence*, 167–9; Okandan, *Âmme Hukukumuzun*, 179–87; Tanör, *Osmanlı*, 118–21.

The constitution itself was printed as usual as the official yearbooks throughout the Hamidian era. While this action fell legally within the bounds of his authority, he nonetheless failed to keep his original promise of preserving the constitutional regime.[69]

The underground Young Turk opposition emerging from 1889 onwards secretly kept the political ideals of Nâmık Kemal and Ziyâ Pasha alive among the Ottoman intelligentsia. The Committee of Union and Congress (CUPR), or *İttihad ve Terakki Cemiyeti*, one of many secret organizations, succeeded in staging a military rebellion in the Macedonian mountains while mobilizing the local population with the demand to reconvene the parliament. Being unable to quell the rebellion, on 24 July 1908 Abdülhamid was forced to declare an imperial decree for opening the HR.[70]

The final decade of Ottoman political life, which began with the Young Turk Revolution and ended at the end of the First World War, was characterized by the predominance of the CUPR in imperial politics. Members of the CUPR consisted mainly of young military and civil government officials, and their political concerns were comparable to those of the previous Young Ottoman generation. Like the Young Ottomans, the CUPR initially saw the institution of the HR as a basic way of saving the state.[71] The suppression of the counter-revolutionary 31 March Incident (13–27 April 1909) and the deposition of Abdülhamid in favour of the politically passive Mehmed V provided an opportunity to liberalize the constitution. On 21 August 1909, constitutional amendments were made to shift political sovereignty away from the sultan and his grand vizier and towards the parliament. Certain authoritarian articles, including the notorious clause within article 113, were removed from the text. For that time, the Ottoman Empire became a truly constitutional regime.[72]

However, the CUPR's centralization policy created tensions with the political parties in the HR that were representing the interests and political liberalism of non-Turkish ethnic groups. With increasing authoritarianism, the CUPR tried to take legislative steps towards bolstering the power of the executive

---

69   M. Akif Aydın, "Kānûn-ı Esâsî", *DIA* 24, 330; Berkes, *Çağdaşlaşma*, 307; Celâleddin Pasha, *Mir'ât*, 161–2; Devereux, *First Ottoman*, 235–50.

70   Sina Akşin, *Jön Türkler ve İttihat ve Terakki* (Istanbul: Remzi Kitabevi, 1987), 21–78; Bayur, *Türk İnkılâbı Tarihi I-1* and *I-2*, *passim*; Lewis, *Emergence*, 187–209; M. Naim Turfan, *Jön Türklerin Yükselişi: Siyaset, Askerler ve Osmanlının Çöküşü*, translated by Mehmet Moralı (Istanbul: Alkım, 2003), 171–90.

71   Şerif Mardin, *Jön Türklerin Siyasi Fikirleri 1895–1908* (Istanbul: İletişim Yayınları, 1983), 219–23.

72   Akşin, *Jön Türkler*, 83–147; Lewis, "Dustūr", 643; Okandan, *Âmme Hukukumuzun*, 285–333; Tanör, *Osmanlı*, 147–51; von Kraelitz-Greifenhorst, *Verfassungsgesetze*, 54–62.

against the authority of the HR. It did this by introducing new constitutional amendments in 1911 to strengthen the authority of the sultan, who was believed to be easily manipulated by the CUPR, but the parliament successfully resisted these moves. When the military wing of the CUPR established a military dictatorship following the *coup d'état* of 23 January 1913, it created the conditions for the desired amendments of 1914 and 1916, which gave the sultan the right to dissolve the HR. In this sense, it meant a partial return to the 1876 text.[73]

The Ottoman defeat in the First World War and the demise of the CUPR regime was followed by the Allied occupation of Istanbul on 16 March 1920. On 11 April, Sultan Mehmed VI dissolved the HR. The Ottoman constitution, on the other hand, remained valid in occupied Istanbul as well as in Anatolian regions controlled by the government of the Grand National Assembly, formed in Ankara on 23 April 1920. It survived the abolition of the Ottoman sultanate on 1 November 1922 and the foundation of the Turkish Republic on 29 October 1923. The constitution of 1876 became null and void after a legal existence of forty-seven years when a new republican constitution was issued on 20 April 1924.[74] In terms of lifespan, it lasted longer than all later Turkish constitutions, including those of 1924, 1961, and 1982.

The constitution of 1876 is a document that signifies both continuity and transformation in the late Ottoman political system. Its proponents included the Young Ottomans, who tried to combine traditional Islam with Western political ideas. Although they stressed the political importance of public opinion in the context of Muslim reactions to the Reform Edict of 1856, their political action remained within the bounds of traditional intra-elite confrontations and patronage, without regard for social forces. For them, the main political function of the constitution was to save the state to which they felt they belonged. In its original form, the constitution was highly autocratic, leaving limited authority to the HR. Nonetheless, individual rights were for the first time clearly formulated in an Ottoman constitutional document. Strikingly,

---

[73] For the changes of the constitution in year 1909, 1914, 1915, 1916 and 1919, see Yavuz Abadan and Bahri Savcı, *Türkiye'de Anayasa Gelişmelerine Bir Bakış* (Ankara: Siyasal Bilgiler Fakültesi Yayınları, 1959), 45–6, 51–2, 54–6; Burhan Gündoğan, "İkinci Meşrutiyet Devrinde Anayasa Değişiklikleri", *Ankara Üniversitesi Hukuk Fakültesi Dergisi* 16 (1959), 91–105; Jaeschke, "Entwicklung", 20–56; Lewis, "Dustūr", 643; Soysal, *Anayasaya*, 62–7; Tarık Zafer Tunaya, "Osmanlı İmparatorluğundan Türkiye Büyük Millet Meclisi Hükümeti Rejimine Geçiş", in *Devletler Hususi Hukuku Ordinaryüs Profesörü Muammer Raşit Seviğ'e Armağan* (Istanbul: İstanbul Üniversitesi Hukuk Fakültesi, 1956), 373–94; Tanör, *Osmanlı*, 153–7; Mete Tunçay, "1293 Kanunu Esasisinin Son Tadilleri", in *Armağan. Kanun-u Esasi'nin 100. Yılı*, 249–55; von Kraelitz-Greifenhorst, *Verfassungsgesetze*, 54–62.

[74] Tanör, *Osmanlı*, 187–8, 239.

the MPs of the first two parliamentary periods refused to comply with the passive political role they were assigned; they even challenged the Sublime Porte, since they saw themselves as the representatives of the whole Ottoman nation. In this sense, the first Ottoman parliament was on the threshold of democratic action, and thus holding in itself the seeds of a political transformation. The dissolution of the parliament could not eradicate the memories of this period, a legacy that became a political goal for the Young Turk revolution. While the period between 1908 and 1918 saw the expansion of public political participation, most of the constitutional amendments of this era reflected a continuation of the elitist nature of Ottoman Turkish politics, a legacy that remained predominant until the end of the one-party period in 1950.

## Bibliography

### Published Primary Sources

Akyıldız, Ali. "Sened-i İttifak'ın İlk Tam Metni". *İslâm Araştırmaları Dergisi* 2 (1998), 209–22.

Baykal, Bekir Sıtkı. "Birinci Meşrutiyete Dair Belgeler". *Belleten* 24 (96), 1960, 601–36.

Celâleddin Paşa, Mahmud. *Mir'ât-ı Hakîkat: Târihî Hakîkatların Aynası. Cilt I–II–III*. Edited by İsmet Miroğlu. Istanbul: Berekât Yayınları, 1983.

Cevdet Pasha. *Ma'rûzât*. Edited by Yusuf Halaçoğlu. Istanbul: Çağrı Yayınları, 1980.

Cevdet Pasha. *Tezâkir 40-Tetimme*. Edited by Cavid Baysun. 2nd edn. Ankara: TTK, 1986.

Kili, Suna and Şeref Gözübüyük (eds). *Sened-i İttifak'tan Günümüze Türk Anayasa Metinleri*. 3rd edn. Istanbul: Türkiye İş Bankası Kültür Yayınları, 2006.

Mithat, Ahmed. *Üss-i İnkılâb*. Edited by İdris Nebi Uysal. Istanbul: Dergâh Yayınları, 2013.

Us, Hakkı Tarık (ed.) *Meclis-i Meb'usan Zabıt Ceridesi, 1293–1877*. 2 vols. Istanbul: Vakit, 1939/40.

### Secondary Sources

Abadan, Yavuz and Bahri Savcı. *Türkiye'de Anayasa Gelişmelerine Bir Bakış*. Ankara: Siyasal Bilgiler Fakültesi Yayınları, 1959.

Abu-Manneh, Butrus. "The Roots of the Ascendancy of Âli and Fuad Paşas at the Porte (1855–1871)". In idem. *Studies on Islam and the Ottoman Empire in the 19th Century*. Istanbul: Isis Press, 2001.

Ahmad, Feroz. *The Making of Modern Turkey*. London: Routledge, 1993.

Akşin, Sina. "I. Meşrutiyet Üzerine Bazı Düşünceler". In *Uluslararası Midhat Paşa Semineri. Bildiriler ve Tartışmalar. Edirne, 8–10 Mayıs 1984*. Ankara: TTK, 1986.

Akşin, Sina. *Jön Türkler ve İttihat ve Terakki*. Istanbul: Remzi Kitabevi, 1987.

Akün, Ömer Faruk. "Namık Kemal". *DIA*. Vol. 32. Ankara, 2006.
Akyıldız, Ali. "Tercüme Odası". *DIA*. Vol. 40. Istanbul, 2011.
Aldıkaçtı, Orhan. *Anayasa Hukukumuzun Gelişmesi ve 1961 Anayasası*. 2nd edn. Istanbul: İstanbul Üniversitesi Hukuk Fakültesi Yayınları, 1973.
Apaydın, Mustafa, *Türk Hiciv Edebiyatında Ziya Paşa*. Ankara: T. C. Kültür Bakanlığı Yayınları, 2001.
Ardıç, Nurullah. "Islam, Modernity, and the 1876 Constitution". In Christoph Herzog and Malek Sharif (eds). *The First Ottoman Experiment in Democracy*. Würzburg: Ergon Verlag Würzburg, 2010, 89-106.
Arıkan, Zeki. "Midhat Paşa'nın Aydın Valiliği (Ağustos 1880–Mayıs 1881)". In *Uluslararası Midhat Paşa Semineri. Bildiriler ve Tartışmalar. Edirne, 8–10 Mayıs 1984*. Ankara: TTK, 1986, 127-64.
Armağan, Servet. "Memleketimizde İlk Parlamento Seçimleri". In *Armağan, Kanun-u Esasi'nin 100. Yılı*. Ankara: Ankara Üniversitesi Siyasal Bilgiler Fakültesi Yayını, 1978, 147-68.
Armitage, David and Sanjay Subrahmanyam. *The Age of Global Revolutions in Global Context, c.1760–1840*. Houndmills: Palgrave Macmillan, 2010.
Aydın, M. Akif. "Kānûn-ı Esâsî". *DIA*. Vol. 24. Istanbul, 2001.
Bayur, Yusuf Hikmet Bayur. *Türk İnkılâbı Tarihi*. 3rd edn. 3 vols. Ankara: TTK, 1983.
Berkes, Niyazi. *Türkiye'de Çağdaşlaşma*. Istanbul: Doğu-Batı Yayınları, 1978.
Beydilli, Kemal. "Mustafa Reşid Paşa". *DIA*. Vol. 31. Istanbul, 2006.
Beydilli, Kemal. "Yeni Osmanlılar". *DIA*. Vol. 43. Ankara, 2013.
Bilgegil, M. Kaya. *Ziya Paşa Üzerine Bir Araştırma*. Erzurum: Atatürk Üniversitesi Yayınları, 1970.
Bilgegil, M. Kaya. "Mustafa Fâzıl Paşa'nın Abdülazîz'e Yazdığı Mektup ve Bunun Şimdiye Kadar Bilinmeyen Karşılığı". In *idem, Yakın Çağ Türk Kültür ve Edebiyatı Üzerinde Araştırmalar I. Yeni Osmanlılar*. Erzurum: Atatürk Üniversitesi Yayınları, 1976, 5-105.
Bilgegil, M. Kaya. "Türkiye'de Bazı Yeni Osmanlılarla Yeni Osmanlı Taraftarlarının Bir Millet Meclisi Kurma Teşebbüsleri". In *idem, Yakın Çağ Türk Kültür ve Edebiyatı Üzerinde Araştırmalar*. Erzurum: Atatürk Üniversitesi Yayınları, 1976, 309-407.
Bilmez, Bülent and Nathalie Clayer. "A Prosopographic Study on some 'Albanian' Deputies to the First Ottoman Parliament". In Christoph Herzog and Malek Sharif (eds). *The First Ottoman Experiment in Democracy*. Wuerzburg: Ergon Verlag, 2010, 151-85.
Bolay, Süleyman Hayri. "Tanzimat'tan Cumhuriyet'e Türk Düşünce Tarihi", in Hasan Celâl Güzel, Kemal Çiçek and Salim Koca (eds), *Türkler*. Ankara: Yeni Türkiye Yayınları, 2002, vol. 14, 515-66.

Bonnett, Alastair. "Makers of the West: National Identity and Occidentalism in the Work of Fukuzawa Yukichi and Ziya Gökalp". *Scottish Geographical Journal* 118 (3) 2002, 165–82.

Buzpınar, Ş. Tufan. "Mustafa Fazıl Paşa". *DIA*. Vol. 31. Ankara, 2006.

Choi, Yeonsik. "Yu Kil-chun's Moral Idea of Civilization and Project to Make All People Gentlemen". *Asian Philosophy* 24 (2) 2014, 103–20.

Czygan, Christiane. *Zur Ordnung des Staates: Jungosmanische Intellektuelle und ihre Konzepte in der Zeitung Hürriyet (1868–1870)*. Berlin: Klaus Schwarz Verlag, 2012.

Çelik, Hüseyin. *Ali Suavi ve Dönemi*. Istanbul: İletişim Yayınları, 1994.

Çetinsaya, Gökhan and Ş. Tufan Buzpınar. "Midhat Paşa". *DIA*. Vol. 30. Ankara, 2005.

Çiçek, Nazan. *The Young Ottomans: Turkish Critics of the Eastern Question in the Late Nineteenth Century*. London: I. B. Tauris, 2010.

Davison, Roderic. *Reform in the Ottoman Empire 1856–1876*. Princeton, NJ: Princeton University Press, 1963.

Devereux, Robert. *The First Ottoman Constitutional Period*. Baltimore: John Hopkins Press, 1963.

Ebüzziya, Ziyad. *Şinasi*. Edited by Hüseyin Çelik. Istanbul: İletişim Yayıncılık, 1997.

Erdül, Mehmet. *Başveren İnkılapçı Ali Suavi*. Istanbul: Toplumsal Dönüşüm Yayınları, 2002.

Findley, Carter V. *Bureaucratic Reform in the Ottoman Empire: The Sublime Porte, 1789–1922*. Princeton, NJ: Princeton University Press, 1980.

Findley, Carter V. *Turkey, Islam, Nationalism, and Modernity: A History, 1789–2007*. New Haven: Yale University Press, 2010.

Gencer, Ali İhsan. "İlk Osmanlı Anayasasında Türkçenin Resmi Dil Olarak Kabulü Meselesi". In *Kanun-u Esasi'nin 100. Yılı*, 183–9.

Göçgün, Önder. *Ziya Paşa'nın Hayatı, Eserleri, Edebî Kişiliği, Bütün Şiirleri ve Eserlerinden Açıklamalı Seçmeler*. Ankara: T. C. Kültür Bakanlığı Yayınları, 2001.

Gündoğan, Burhan. "İkinci Meşrutiyet Devrinde Anayasa Değişiklikleri". *Ankara Üniversitesi Hukuk Fakültesi Dergisi* 16 (1959): 91–105.

Gunel, Necmi. *II. Meşrutiyet Öncesi Fikir Akımları ve Ali Suavi*. Istanbul: Feyziye Mektepleri Vakfı, 2011.

Hanioğlu, M. Şükrü. *A Brief History of the Late Ottoman Empire*. Princeton, NJ: Princeton University Press, 2008.

Hartmann, Elke. "The 'Loyal Nation' and its Deputies: The Armenians in the First Ottoman Parliament". In Christoph Herzog and Malek Sharif (eds), *The First Ottoman Experiment in Democracy*. Wuerzburg: Ergon Verlag, 2010, 187–222.

Hobsbawm, E. J. *The Age of Revolution, 1789–1848*. New York: Vintage Books, 1996.

İnalcık, Halil. "Sened-i İttifak ve Gülhane Hatt-ı Hümâyunu". In *idem*, *Osmanlı İmparatorluğu: Toplum ve Ekonomi*. Istanbul: Eren Yayıncılık, 1993, 343–59.

Jaeschke, Gotthard. "Die Entwicklung des Osmanischen Verfassungsstaates von den Anfängen bis zur Gegenwart". *Die Welt des Islams* 5 (1–2), 1917, 5–56.

Jelavich, Charles and Barbara Jelavich. *The Establishment of the Balkan National States, 1804–1920*. Seattle: University of Washington Press, 1986.

Kahraman, Âlim. "Şinasi". *DIA*. Vol. 39. Ankara, 2010.

Karal, Enver Ziya Karal. *Osmanlı Tarihi*. 2nd edn, vols. 5–8. Ankara: TTK, 1976–83.

Kili, Suna. "1876 Anayasasının Çağdaşlaşma Sorunları Açısından Değerlendirilmesi". In *Armağan. Kanun-u Esasi'nin 100. Yılı*. Ankara: Ankara Üniversitesi Siyasal Bilgiler Fakültesi Yayını, 1978, 191–211.

Kırmızı, Abdulhamit. "Authoritarianism and Constitutionalism Combined: Ahmed Midhat Efendi Between the Sultan and the *Kanun-i Esasi*". In Christoph Herzog and Malek Sharif (eds) *The First Ottoman Experiment in Democracy* (Würzburg: Ergon Verlag, 2010), 53–65.

Kuntay, Mithat Cemal. *Sarıklı İhtilâlci Ali Suavi*. Istanbul: Ahmet Halit Kitabevi, 1946.

Kuntay, Mithat Cemal. *Namık Kemal: Devrinin İnsanları ve Olayları Arasında*. 2nd edn, 2 vols. Istanbul: Türkiye İş Bankası Kültür Yayınları, 2009/10.

Lewis, Bernard. *The Emergence of Modern Turkey*. 2nd edn. London: Oxford University Press, 1968.

Lewis, Bernard. "Dustūr". *Encyclopedia of Islam*. 2nd edn. Vol. 9, 1997.

Mardin, Şerif. *The Genesis of Young Ottoman Thought: A Study in the Modernization of Turkish Political Ideas*. Princeton, NJ: Princeton University Press, 1962.

Mardin, Şerif. *Jön Türklerin Siyasi Fikirleri 1895–1908*. Istanbul: İletişim Yayınları, 1983.

Mermutlu, Bedri. *Sosyal Düşünce Tarihimizde Şinasi*. Istanbul: Kaknüs Yayınları, 2003.

Midhat, Ali Haydar. *The Life of Midhat Pasha: A Record of His Services, Political Reforms, Banishment, and Judicial Murder*. London: John Murray, Albemarle Street, W., 1903.

Millas, Herkül. *Yunan Ulusunun Doğuşu*. Istanbul: İletişim Yayınları, 1994.

Mumcu, Ahmet. "Osmanlı Devletinde 1876 Anayasasına Değin Temel Hak ve Özgürlükler İle 1876 Anayasasının Temel Yapısı". In *Türk Parlamentoculuğunun İlk 100 Yılı (1876–1976): Kanun-u Esasinin 100. Yılı Sempozyumu (1976 Ankara)*. Ankara: Ajans-Türk Matbaacılık, [n.d.], 31–47.

Okandan, Recai G. *Âmme Hukukumuzun Anahatları: Birinci Kitap (Osmanlı Devletinin Kuruluşundan İnkırazına Kadar)*. Istanbul: İstanbul Üniversitesi Yayınları, 1968.

Ortaylı, İlber. "İlk Osmanlı Parlamentosu ve Osmanlı Milletlerinin Temsili". In *Armağan. Kanun-u Esasi'nin 100. Yılı*. Ankara: Ankara Üniversitesi Siyasal Bilgiler Fakültesi Yayını, 1978, 169–82.

Ortaylı, İlber. "Midhat Paşa'nın Vilayet Yönetimindeki Kadroları ve Politikası". In *Uluslararası Midhat Paşa Semineri. Bildiriler ve Tartışmalar. Edirne, 8–10 Mayıs 1984*. Ankara: TTK, 1986, 227–33.

Özön, Mustafa Nihat. *Namık Kemal ve İbret Gazetesi: İnceleme*. 2nd edn. Istanbul: Yapı Kredi Yayınları, 1997.

Rahme, Joseph G. "Namık Kemal's Constitutional Ottomanism and Non-Muslims". *Islam and Muslim-Christian Relations* 10 (1) 1999, 23–39.
Rizaj, Skender. "Midhat Paşa'nın Rumeli'de Vilayetler Kurulmasındaki Rolü". In *Uluslararası Midhat Paşa Semineri: Bildiriler ve Tartışmalar. Edirne, 8–10 Mayıs 1984*. Ankara: TTK, 1986, 59–69.
Saydam, Abdullah. "Namık Paşa". *DIA*. Vol. 32. Istanbul, 2006.
Shamir, Shimon. "Midhat Pasha and the Anti-Turkish Agitation in Syria". *Middle Eastern Studies* 10 (2) 1974, 115–41.
Sharif, Malek. "A Portrait of Syrian Deputies in the First Ottoman Parliament". In Christoph Herzog and Malek Sharif (eds). *The First Ottoman Experiment in Democracy*. Wuerzburg: Ergon Verlag, 2010, 285–311.
Shaw, Stanford J. *Between Old and New: The Ottoman Empire under Sultan Selim III (1789–1807)*. Cambridge, MA: Harvard University Press, 1971.
Shaw, Stanford J. and Ezel Kural Shaw. *History of the Ottoman Empire and Modern Turkey*. Vol. 2. *Reform, Revolution, and Republic: The Rise of Modern Turkey, 1808–1975*. Cambridge: Cambridge University Press, 1977.
Skocpol, Theda. *Social Revolutions in the Modern World*. Cambridge: Cambridge University Press, 1994.
Soysal, Mümtaz. *Anayasaya Giriş*. 2nd edn. Ankara: Ankara Üniversitesi Siyasal Bilgiler Fakültesi Yayını, 1969.
Steppat, Fritz. "Mişr". *Encyclopedia of Islam*. 2nd edn. Vol. 7 (1993).
Şimşir, Bilâl N. "Midhat Paşa'nın İkinci Sadrazamlığı ve İngiltere". In *Uluslararası Midhat Paşa Semineri Semineri. Bildiriler ve Tartışmalar. Edirne, 8–10 Mayıs 1984*. Ankara: TTK, 1986, 237–339.
Tanör, Bülent. *Osmanlı-Türk Anayasal Gelişmeleri (1789–1980)*. Revised 3rd edn. Istanbul: Afa Yayıncılık, 1996.
Tanpınar, Ahmet Hamdi. *19. Asır Türk Edebiyatı Tarihi*. 10th edn. Istanbul: Çağlayan Kitabevi, 2003.
Tevfik, Ebüzziya. *Yeni Osmanlılar. İmparatorluğun Son Dönemindeki Genç Türkler*. Edited by Şemsettin Kutlu. Istanbul: Pegasus Yayınları, 2006.
Tunaya, Tarık Zafer. "Osmanlı İmparatorluğundan Türkiye Büyük Millet Meclisi Hükümeti Rejimine Geçiş". In *Devletler Hususi Hukuku Ordinaryüs Profesörü Muammer Raşit Seviğ'e Armağan*. Istanbul: İstanbul Üniversitesi Hukuk Fakültesi, 1956, 373–94.
Tunaya, Tarık Zafer. *Türkiye'de Siyasal Gelişmeler (1876–1938): (Birinci Kitap: Kanun-ı Esasi ve Meşrutiyet Dönemleri 1876–1918)*. Istanbul: İstanbul Bilgi Üniversitesi Yayınları, 2001.
Tunçay, Mete. "1293 Kanunu Esasisinin Son Tadilleri". In *Armağan. Kanun-u Esasi'nin 100. Yılı*. Ankara: Ankara Üniversitesi Siyasal Bilgiler Fakültesi Yayını, 1978, 249–55.

Turfan, M. Naim. *Jön Türklerin Yükselişi: Siyaset, Askerler ve Osmanlının Çöküşü*. Translated by Mehmet Moralı. Istanbul: Alkım, 2003.

Türköne, Mümtaz'er. *Siyasî İdeoloji Olarak İslâmcılığın Doğuşu*. 2nd edn. Istanbul: İletişim Yayınları, 1994.

Uçman, Abdullah. "Ali Suavi". *DIA*. Vol. 2. Ankara, 1989.

Uçman, Abdullah. "Ziya Paşa". *DIA*. Vol. 44. Ankara, 2013.

Uğurlu, Seyit Battal. "Eklektik Bir Tanzimat Aydını: Ali Suavi Efendi". *History Studies. International Journal of History* 2 (2) 2010, 207–21.

Uzunçarşılı, İsmail Hakkı. *Midhat Pala ve Tâif Mahkûmları*. Ankara: TTK, 1950.

Uzunçarşılı, İsmail Hakkı. *Midhat Paşa ve Yıldız Mahkemesi*. 2nd edn. Ankara: TTK, 2000.

von Kraelitz-Greifenhorst, Friedrich. *Die Verfassungsgesetze des Osmanischen Reiches: Osten und Orient*. Vierte Reihe. Erste Abteilung. Erste Heft. Vienna: Verlag des Forschungsinstitutes für Osten und Orient, 1919.

Wasti, Syed Tanvir. "A Note on Tunuslu Hayreddin Paşa". *Middle Eastern Studies* 36 (1) 2000, 1–20.

Yücel, Yaşar. "Midhat Paşa'nın Bağdat Vilâyetindeki Alt Yapı Yatırımları". In *Uluslararası Midhat Paşa Semineri. Bildiriler ve Tartışmalar. Edirne, 8–10 Mayıs 1984*. Ankara: TTK, 1986, 175–83.

Ziya Paşa. "Rüya". In Şemsettin Kutlu (ed.), *Tanzimat Dönemi Türk Edebiyatı Antolojisi*, 2nd edn. Istanbul: Remzi Kitabevi, 1981.

Zürcher, Erik J. *Turkey: A Modern History*. London: I. B. Tauris, 1993.

*In Lieu of a Conclusion*

CHAPTER 18

# Repertories of Empire: How Did the Ottomans Last So Long in a Changing World?

*Karl K. Barbir*

Because of the Ottoman state's long life, it is easy to characterize the whole length of Ottoman history in a simplistic way – process of origins, growth, stasis, and decline, following more or less the pattern identified by Edward Gibbon for the Roman Empire. An alternative framework emphasizes the Ottomans' self-view during the seventeenth and eighteenth centuries, when they compared their time unfavourably with the supposed apogee of Ottoman power and wealth during the reign of Süleyman the Magnificent. Over the last few decades – although general works still stay with one or the other of these frameworks, or continue to take the nationalist approach that prevailed in much of the twentieth century – scholars of the Ottomans have grown increasingly dissatisfied with these approaches, none more so than the honoree of this book, Professor Metin Kunt. In one of his essays, he wrote that:

> students of Ottoman history have learned better than to discuss a 'decline' which supposedly began during the reigns of Süleyman's 'ineffectual' successors and then continued for centuries. Süleyman's sons and grandsons, as sultans, merely continued in the same detached imperial tradition that was first fashioned during Süleyman's long reign. As for broader institutional and social fluctuations and dislocations, these are properly to be seen as features of a *transition* [emphasis added] which eventually reached a new equilibrium in the seventeenth century. The 'time of troubles' may have seemed of millennial significance to Ottomans themselves; we should see its features rather as aspects of the Ottoman effort to confront the challenges of a changing and widening world, beyond their frontiers and experience.[1]

---

1  Metin Kunt, "Introduction to Part I", in Metin Kunt and Christine Woodhead (eds), *Süleyman the Magnificent and His Age: The Ottoman Empire in the Early Modern World* (London: Longman, 1995), 37–8.

Of course, this observation had been anticipated in an earlier work by Professor Kunt, one that introduced the concept of *transformation* as an alternative framework to decline.[2] Indeed, Leslie Peirce writes that "scholarship of the past [thirty] years has liberated the post-Süleymanic period from the straightjacket of decline in which every new phenomenon was seen as corruption of pristine 'classical' institutions."[3]

In this chapter, I attempt a modest reassessment of a question that has puzzled me for many years, namely, if the Ottomans were in such dire straits in the seventeenth and eighteenth centuries, how did they manage to last so long, surviving into the twentieth century? The question is hardly original, yet it persists. In a popular account of the empire's last century, Alan Palmer emphasizes not the successive early Ottoman conquests but, rather, "the way in which an astonishingly narrow ruling class imposed government on lands ... [on three continents]."[4] Palmer goes on to ask, "But how did it survive so long?"[5] Indeed, David Cannadine faults Gibbon's view of *Byzantine* (not Ottoman) decline, in Gibbon's words, as "a tedious tale of weakness and misery". Cannadine argues that "no empire could have lasted for more than a millenium being as corrupt, degenerate, and sclerotic, as infirm of purpose, or as wholly devoid of redeeming characteristics as the one [Gibbon] described in the second half of *The Decline and* Fall."[6] This observation might equally be applied to the Ottomans, who became to Europeans in modern times 'the terrible Turk'.[7]

This question of survival also must discomfort those who view the Ottoman past through the prism of modern nationalism, which in whatever form denies and negates that past, overlooking the many Ottoman peoples and cultures that lived together for so long.[8] Likewise, Şuhnaz Yılmaz and İpek K. Yosmaoğlu find another wrinkle to this dilemma:

---

2 İ. Metin Kunt, *The Sultan's Servants: The Transformation of Ottoman Provincial Government, 1550–1650* (New York: Columbia University Press, 1983), reviewed by this writer in *The Muslim World* 75 (3) 1985, 178.

3 Leslie Peirce, "Changing Perceptions of the Ottoman Empire: The Early Centuries", *Mediterranean Historical Review* 19 (1) 2004, 22.

4 Alan Palmer, *The Decline and Fall of the Ottoman Empire* (New York: Barnes and Noble, 1992), vii. The reader will note how closely Palmer follows the title of Gibbon's great work.

5 Palmer, *Decline*, vii.

6 David Cannadine, *The Undivided Past: Humanity Beyond Our Differences* (New York: Knopf, 2013), 26.

7 For an account of how this terminology persisted well beyond the First World War, see M. Hakan Yavuz, "Orientalism, the 'Terrible Turk' and Genocide", *Middle East Critique* 23 (2) (2014), 111–26.

8 This point is made forcefully by Christine Philliou, "The Paradox of Perceptions: Interpreting the Ottoman Past through the National Present", *MES* 44 (2008), 661–75.

denial of a place to the Ottoman past in the nation-state's historical and cultural legacy ... serves a larger purpose than distancing the self from the Turkish other; it also ensures that the complexities and hybridity contained in that legacy is safely packed away in a place where it cannot threaten the nation's genealogical purity. What taints the imperial past is not only the foreign rulers, but the experience of a communal existence that is anathema to the nation-state's exigency of clear boundaries and social purity.[9]

These authors are not alone in their view. Linda T. Darling writes: "For historians in the post-Ottoman states of Turkey, the Balkans, and the Arab world, countries whose national identities depended on no longer being Ottoman, a declining Ottoman Empire can safely be blamed for present-day political and socioeconomic difficulties."[10]

Here I argue that, following a very popular recent theoretical treatise on empire, the Ottomans employed various *repertories* that successfully allowed them to manage transitions in institutions and power balances among elite groups as well as the diversity of their populations.[11] I will first present the theoretical framework of Burbank and Cooper, then apply their insights to some of the salient features of the early modern Ottomans, ending in about the year 1800. At this point, readers should keep in mind that the explosion of publications in Ottoman Studies over the last forty years makes broad generalizations about the Ottomans harder than ever. In a comment on Virginia H. Aksan's "What's Up in Ottoman Studies",[12] Ehud Toledo contends that "it is impossible to do justice to what has become a huge and rapidly growing body of knowledge in a diversified and specialized field of scholarship." He adds:

> Although I believe that a case can be made for retaining the Ottoman Empire as an analytically useful unit of study, given the enormous diversity within the Empire and its long history, this is not an automatic

---

9   Şuhnaz Yılmaz and İpek Yosmaoğlu, "Fighting the Spectres of the Past: Dilemmas of Ottoman Legacy in the Balkans and the Middle East", *MES* 44 (2008), 677.
10  Linda T. Darling, *Revenue-Raising and Legitimacy: Tax Collection and Finance Administration in the Ottoman Empire, 1550–1560* (Leiden: Brill, 1996), 2.
11  Jane Burbank and Henry Cooper, *Empires in World History: Power and the Politics of Difference* (Princeton: Princeton University Press, 2010). Subsequent references are to Burbank and Cooper, who use the French, repertoires. This author prefers repertories for its clarity.
12  Virginia H. Aksan, "What's Up in Ottoman Studies?" *Journal of the Ottoman and Turkish Studies Association* 1 (1–2) 2014, 3–21. This is an attempt to survey a broad swath of recent scholarship.

presumption anymore. Rather, we need to justify why the history of Yemen in the second half of the nineteenth century and the history of Algiers in the seventeenth belong in the same area of study; or, for that matter, why Cemal Pasha's rule in Damascus during World War I has any commonalities with the Eyalet of Temeşvar in the late-sixteenth century.[13]

It is, nonetheless, desirable to examine both the repertories of empire and their transformations over time and space. As the late Donald Quataert observed: "The emerging new scholarship is revealing an Ottoman state (society and economy) in the process of continuous transformation, rather than a decline or fall from idealized norms of the past or a failure to successfully imitate the West."[14] He continued by suggesting that, "rather than looking for sultanic despotism as the norm and deviation from it as decline, scholarship is revealing a constantly shifting locus of power."[15]

Indeed, Burbank and Cooper emphasize both continuities and changes over time in the empires they study, including the Ottomans. While acknowledging that violence was one of the tools by which empires were constructed, they recognize that "successful empires ... had to manage their unlike populations, in process producing a variety of ways to both exploit and rule."[16] More importantly, they also "describe the ranges of ruling strategies that were imaginable and feasible in specific historical situations, the conflicts that emerged in different power structures, and the contentious relationships among empires that emerged at particular moments and over time drove world history."[17] Both out of habit and out of necessity, empires were pragmatic in facing new situations. "Recognizing imperial repertoires as flexible, constrained by geography and history but open to innovation, enables us to avoid the false dichotomy of continuity or change, contingency or determinism, and to look instead for actions and conditions that pushed elements into and out of empires' strategies."[18]

---

13   Ehud Toledano, "A Comment on Virginia H. Aksan's 'What's Up in Ottoman Studies?'" *Journal of the Ottoman and Turkish Studies Association* 2 (1) 2015, 219.
14   Donald Quataert, "Ottoman History Writing and Changing Attitudes Towards the Notion of 'Decline'", *HC* 1 (2003), 4.
15   Quataert, "Ottoman History Writing", 5. This is indeed the perspective of Baki Tezcan, *The Second Ottoman Empire: Political and Social Transformation in the Early Modern World* (Cambridge: CUP, 2010).
16   Burbank and Cooper, *Empires*, 2.
17   Burbank and Cooper, *Empires*, 3.
18   Burbank and Cooper, *Empires*, 3.

Contributing to this pragmatism was the recognition by imperial rulers of the clear 'politics of difference' that their populations presented. "The politics of difference in some empires could mean recognizing the multiplicity of peoples and their varied customs as an ordinary fact of life; in others it meant drawing a strict boundary between undifferentiated insiders and 'barbarian' outsiders."[19] Alternatively, "an empire could be an assemblage of peoples, practicing their religions and administering justice in their own way, all subordinated to an imperial sovereign."[20] This was clearly the Ottoman model: "recognition of difference – particularly of local leaders who could manage 'their' people – could enhance maintenance of order, collection of taxes or tribute, and military recruitment. Empire could profit from skills and connections developed by distinct communities. Difference could be a fact and an opportunity, not an obsession."[21] Furthermore, the varying repertoires employed could easily contribute to longevity.

One of the most important repertoires was the employment of intermediaries, an essential part of a successful imperial system. Burbank and Cooper

> emphasize a kind of political relationship that is often downplayed or ignored today – vertical connections between rulers, their agents, and their subjects.... The study of empires ... draws attention to people pushing and tugging on relationships with those above and below them, changing but only sometimes breaking the lines of authority and power.[22]

This helps to explain the frequent rebellions and disturbances noted in all parts of the Ottoman world, and their frequently orderly resolution. "It was perhaps the slow and uneven course of empire-building that gave a succession of Ottoman rulers and advisors the chance to reflect upon experience, to absorb tactics from others, and to take new initiatives that, once power was secured, allowed the Ottoman empire to last until 1922."[23]

---

19   Burbank and Cooper, *Empires*, 12. This observation is a reminder of Victor Turner's comment that the paradox of the European Middle Ages was "that it was at once cosmopolitan and more localized than either tribal or capitalist society". Victor Turner, *Dramas, Fields, and Metaphors* (Ithaca, NY: Cornell University Press, 1974), 183. Here Cooper and Burbank owe much to Karen Barkey, *Empire of Difference: The Ottomans in Comparative Perspective* (New York: CUP, 2008), although some readers caution that Barkey's conclusions are too strong: see Donald Quataert's review of this book in *American Historical Review* 114 (2009), 413–15.
20   Burbank and Cooper, *Empires*, 12.
21   Burbank and Cooper, *Empires*, 12.
22   Burbank and Cooper, *Empires*, 14.
23   Burbank and Cooper, *Empires*, 130.

Other repertories that Burbank and Cooper recognize as effective included, first, the *tımâr* land tenure system that kept the elites loyal, until the transformation that brought in tax farming and created a new elite of clients seeking Ottoman patronage. "A second principle was the impermanence of officeholding. The sultan could replace officials at will, rewarding loyal service, punishing incompetents. Appointments could also be used to make rebels part of the system."[24] In short, the Ottomans took advantage of the size of their empire (scattered across three continents): they "could not have a single way of ruling or controlling their intermediaries. Personalized authority facilitated flexibility, compromise, and pragmatism.... Co-optation into officialdom prevented consolidation of linkages outside the state. The system's most effective tool was its largesse: it paid to be an officeholder."[25] Seen from this angle, the constant competition among the Ottoman elites for preferment and advancement may be seen as normal, not the usually cynical view of those elites that prevailed in the past.

With this theoretical perspective in mind, one can identify three elements that enabled Ottoman longevity – the ability to deal with difficult communications and varying densities of population across the empire; varying methods of rule over time and space; and acceptance of pluralism as a governing norm.

It is still startling to be reminded of the geographic scope of this empire: maybe some three dozen provinces from the sixteenth century onwards, on three continents, with a total population estimated at a range from twenty-five to thirty-two million inhabitants around 1800.[26] Even this is misleading because of the slow but steady loss of territories, especially in the Balkans, that occurred over these middle centuries, 1500–1800. Also remarkable is the relatively low population density: in 1600, by one estimate, the Ottoman provinces in Asia (Turkey today) had a density of twenty persons per square mile, whereas for the European provinces that density was forty-one persons per square mile. This contrasted sharply with densities of fifty-six, eighty-six, ninety-seven, and one hundred and twelve for Britain, France, Italy, and the Low Countries in the same period.[27] The relatively low Ottoman population density probably was due to the very slow recovery (if there was one) from the demographic ravages of the Black Death of the fourteenth century. It was only in the nineteenth century that the density began to increase dramatically

---

24  Burbank and Cooper, *Empires*, 139.
25  Burbank and Cooper, *Empires*, 139–40.
26  Bruce McGowan, "The Age of the Ayans, 1699–1812", in Halil İnalcık and Donald Quataert (eds), *An Economic and Social History of the Ottoman Empire* (Cambridge: CUP, 1994), 646.
27  See Table I: 5 in İnalcık and Quataert, *Economic and Social History*, 31.

due to improved public health, more efficient transport and communications, along with greater efforts at governmental control of a modern type over a diverse population now stirred by the ideas of nationalism. Despite all these limitations before the nineteenth century, there is plenty of evidence that the Ottomans could respond quickly and efficiently to the demands of changing times. As Şevket Pamuk writes:

> Ottoman state and society were able to adapt to changing circumstances during the early modern era, well before the nineteenth-century reforms known as *Tanzimat*…. Pragmatism, flexibility, and negotiation enabled the central bureaucracy to co-opt and incorporate into the state the social groups that rebelled against it.[28]

This perspective sharply differs from that of non-specialists writing about the Ottomans, for example the famed economic historian David Landes, who describes "a centralized, monolithic entity lacking in internal dynamism and differentiation".[29]

This leads us directly to varying methods of rule over time and space. Once more, a recent change of perspective, based on new evidence, shows that Ottoman methods of rule varied considerably:

> The minutes of local judicial courts, complaints of provincial authorities, and the communication between the central and local authorities present a different picture and demonstrate the limits to centralization. In these sources local and central government appear to have enjoyed a relationship that was far more complex than the one-sided command-and-execute relationship put forward by historians in the past.[30]

The author of these words considers the empire's frontiers at two extremes, the northwest (Habsburgs) and the southeast (Safavids). He shows how at the perimeter, the Ottomans reverted to "earlier, pre-sixteenth century flexible administrative strategies" in newly conquered areas.[31] An innovation

---

28  Şevket Pamuk, "Institutional Change and the Longevity of the Ottoman Empire, 1500–1800", *Journal of Interdisciplinary History* 35 (2) 2004, 228.
29  Pamuk, "Institutional Change", 227.
30  Gábor Ágoston, "A Flexible Empire: Authority and Its Limits on the Ottoman Frontiers", *International Journal of Turkish Studies* 9 (1–2) 2003, 16.
31  Ágoston, "Flexible Empire", 18.

was the condominium, "the joint rule of the former power elite and the Ottoman authorities."[32]

Another method concerned the supply of grain and the collection of taxes for dedicated purposes. Maintaining the grain supply was essential to civil peace, especially in cities. One author has found that at times of food insecurity during the eighteenth century, Damascus supplied grain to the island of Rhodes and Egypt; and on another occasion, the governor of Tunis supplied grain to Damascus.[33] Likewise, this writer found long ago that governors of Damascus in the same period found alternative sources of taxation and had recourse to emergency taxation if given permission from Istanbul. In one instance, it took eleven days for the local governor's request to reach Istanbul and be approved, suggesting an efficient system of relay horses and riders.[34]

Given these random examples (and there are many more), what is remarkable is that the size of the Ottoman government was so limited. Linda Darling has found that the number of financial scribes in the seventeenth century ranged from 70 to 212, and post-1768 from 700 to 714.[35] An undated archival document describes the structure and functions of the central bureaucracy, probably in the late eighteenth century – seven bureaux at the *Babıâli* (Sublime Porte) and twelve for the treasury, but without giving any numbers.[36] Even if one were to add the clerks who staffed the provincial administrative offices, the empire-wide total was probably still very low. It was not until the nineteenth century that the Ottomans expanded their bureaucracy to deal with the wrenching economic change brought about by increased trade with Europe and to carry out reforms to keep the empire together.

We are still, however, left with the last piece of the puzzle of the Ottomans' longevity, namely, pluralism. European observers over these middle centuries looked to the neighbouring Ottoman Empire and saw the threat of Islam, something that had long helped Europeans to define themselves as Christendom: "the existence of the political power of Islam was a factor in prolonging the domination of Christendom as a political as well as a cultural concept."[37] But

---

32  Ágoston, "Flexible Empire", 23.
33  James Grehan, *Everyday Life and Consumer Culture in 18th-Century Damascus* (Seattle: University of Washington Press, 2007), 85.
34  Karl K. Barbir, *Ottoman Rule in Damascus, 1708–1758* (Princeton: Princeton University Press, 1980), 114 (using tax revenues from Urfa) and 158 (emergency local taxation). The evidence is found, respectively, in MS E. 3439, dated end Şaban 1155/late October 1742, and MS E. 3630, dated 1 Receb 1163/4 May 1753, at TSA. The latter notes approval for emergency taxation on 12 Receb 1163/15 May 1753.
35  Darling, *Revenue-Raising*, 59 (Table 2).
36  MS D. 3208, TSA.
37  M. E. Yapp, "Europe in the Turkish Mirror", *PP* 137 (1992), 138.

early modern Europeans also noticed something else, particularly if they had visited the Ottoman lands: although the Ottoman state was an Islamic state, the population was very diverse. As one scholar of literature and drama notes, Europeans viewed

> the Early Modern Turkish empire as singularly syncretistic, the threat it posed to states from England to Italy arising not just from the 'unity' that Islam displayed at a time of Christian 'Schism and Sect …,' but also from Ottoman society's *plurality*, from a relative openness to any number of religions and cultures, in marked contrast to the closures that typify state culture after [the Council of] Trent.[38]

The French political philosopher Jean Bodin, drawing on Richard Knolles's specialized knowledge of the Ottomans (the latter's *General Historie of the Turks* was published in 1603), wondered at the workings of the Ottoman system:

> The great emperour of the Turkes doth with as great devuotion as any prince in the world honour and obserue the religion by him received from his ancencestours, and yet detesteth he not the strange religions of others; but to the contrarie permitteth every man to live according to his conscience: yea and that more is, neere unto his palace at Pera, suffereth foure diuers religions, *viz.*, That of the Iewes, that of the Christians, that of the Grecians, and that of the Mahometans.[39]

It is ironic that Knolles, though an Oxford graduate probably born in the late 1540s, was a Roman Catholic who spent years in exile from England and wanted to overcome the divisions within Christendom. Several decades earlier, the king of France was departing from the traditional concept of Christendom by establishing diplomatic relations with the Ottomans:

> Süleyman and Francis formed an alliance … in opposition to the Habsburg Charles V, who was their common enemy.… But it was to the Habsburgs' advantage to emphasize the differences between the Ottomans and

---

38 Jacques Lezra, "Translated Turks on the Early Modern Stage", in Robert Henke and Eric Nicholson (eds), *Theatre Crossing Borders: Transnational and Transcultural Exchange in Early Modern Drama* (Aldershot, UK: Ashgate Press, 2008), 160–1.

39 Jean Bodin, *The Six Books of a Commonweale*, edited by Kenneth Douglas McRae (Cambridge, MA: HUP, 1962), 537. This is a facsimile edition of the 1606 English translation, with corrections. Richard Knolles was the translator. The language is as in the original translation.

Christian Europeans whether using medieval crusade ideology or the classically humanist ideology of Europe versus Asia.[40]

Ottoman pluralism was a fact and it certainly contributed to the longevity of the empire. Twentieth-century nationalist historiography – regardless of what successor state produced it – tended to obscure the long centuries when a dizzying number of ethnic and religious communities lived together. Otherwise, how could the Ottoman Empire have survived? By way of example, the late Bülent Ecevit, several times prime minister of the Turkish Republic, was also a poet who wrote these words:

> Only when homesick do you realize
> you have become brother to the Greek.
> When he hears a Greek melody abroad
> how transformed is the child of Istanbul.
> With pungent Turkish we have abused you
> to our heart's content.
> We have become mortal enemies.
> Still, there is affection within us,
> Hidden away during more harmonious days.[41]

Such sentimental feelings should not lead one to romanticize the early modern Ottoman era – far from it. But recent developments in the Middle East may make contemporary readers more appreciative of the Ottoman past. They should also be willing to change their perspective on the kinds of conflicts, rooted in religion, that have characterized the last two centuries in that area of the world. David Cannadine argues that "focusing only on such conflicts is rather like ignoring every other page while reading a book: the resulting account isn't just incomplete, but is misleading to the point of incoherence."[42]

He argues, further, that "for relatively few people of any faith is religion the be-all and end-all of existence. There are many facets of lives, activities, and identity, among both elites and common folk, not significantly explained by religious sentiment."[43] This suggests new areas for scholarly investigation into the nature of pluralism in Ottoman times.

---

40   Christine Isom-Verhaaren, *Allies with the Infidel: The Ottoman and French Alliance in the Sixteenth Century* (London: I. B. Tauris, 2011), 184.
41   Quoted in Vamık Volkan and Norman Itzkowitz, *Turks and Greeks: Neighbours in Conflict* (Huntingdon, UK: Eothen Press, 1994), 7.
42   Cannadine, *Undivided Past*, 36.
43   Cannadine, *Undivided Past*, 49.

The question of empire has recently been revisited by many authors. The Ottomans have had no shortage of chroniclers who have tended to emphasize the end of the Ottomans. It is no accident that a spate of books has been published recently marking the hundredth anniversary of the coming of the First World War to the Ottoman Empire. Other than that anniversary, there may be in the minds of the books' authors an unstated recognition that the impact of the Ottoman era on the Middle East, North Africa, and the Balkans and beyond extended well after the end of the empire. How else does one explain the Ukrainian revolution arising in Kiev at a place called *maydan*?[44] How else to account for the destruction of ancient ruins in Syria and Iraq (ruins that remained more or less intact through the Ottoman centuries), and the cruel destruction of peoples that history seemed to have forgotten? One might even be forgiven for venturing the bold statement that the Ottoman Empire did not fall in 1922 or 1923, but that it is finally falling now, today, before our very eyes![45] Recently, this writer put it another way to his students: the Ottomans ruled Iraq from 1638 to 1917. How did they do that, given what we know about Iraqi society, composed not just of Sunni, Shia, and Kurds, but Christians and Yazidis and many others, as well as consisting of multiple geographic regions? And why was the United States unable to manage Iraq between 2003 and 2011? The answer may lie in an unlikely place: an author who lived more than 250 years ago who astutely analysed the difficulties his country was having in controlling a number of colonies in North America. Edmund Burke was critical of the British government's heavy-handed treatment of the Americans. In his speech on conciliation with the American colonies, Edmund Burke made this remark to the House of Commons on 22 March 1775:

> In large bodies, the circulation of power must be less vigorous at the extremities. Nature has said it. The Turk cannot govern Egypt, and Arabia, and Kurdistan, as he governs Thrace; nor has he the same dominion in Crimea and Algiers which he has at Brusa and Smyrna. Despotism itself is

---

44   For fascinating perspectives, see Gábor Kármán and Lovro Kunčevič (eds), *The European Tributary States of the Ottoman Empire in the Sixteenth and Seventeenth Centuries* (Leiden: Brill, 2013).

45   Among the recent books on the end of the Ottoman Empire in the First World War by scholars and popular writers alike, are Daniel Allen Butler, *Shadow of the Sultan's Realm: the Destruction of the Ottoman Empire and the Creation of the Modern Middle East* (Washington, DC: Potomac Books, 2011); Michael A. Reynolds, *Shattering Empires: The Clash and Collapse of the Ottoman and Russian Empires, 1908–1918* (Cambridge: CUP, 2011); Eugene Rogan, *The Fall of the Ottomans: The Great War in the Middle East* (New York: Basic Books, 2015); and Kristian Coates Ulrichsen, *The First World War in the Middle East* (London: Hurst and Company, 2014).

obliged to truck and huckster. The Sultan gets such obedience as he can. He governs with a loose reign that he may govern at all; and the whole of the force and vigor of authority in his center is derived from a prudent relaxation in all his borders.[46]

Here, Burke recognizes the repertories of empire that this essay has identified. He was certainly very prescient about how the Ottomans survived in a changing world.

## Bibliography

### *Primary Sources*

Archival Material: Topkapı Saray Arşivi (TSA)

E. 3439, dated end Şaban 1155 (late October 1742); E. 3630, dated 1 Receb 1163 (4 May 1753); D. 3208 (undated).

### *Secondary Sources*

Ágoston, Gábor. "A Flexible Empire: Authority and its Limits on the Ottoman Frontiers". *International Journal of Turkish Studies* 9 (1–2) 2003, 15–31.

Aksan, Virginia H. "What's Up in Ottoman Studies?" *Journal of the Ottoman and Turkish Studies Association* 1 (1–2) 2014, 3–21.

Barbir, Karl K. *Ottoman Rule in Damascus, 1708–1758*. Princeton: Princeton University Press, 1980.

Barkey, Karen. *Empire of Difference: The Ottomans in Comparative Perspective*. New York: Cambridge University Press, 2008.

Bodin, Jean. *The Six Books of a Commonweale*. Edited by Kenneth Douglas McRae. Cambridge, MA: Harvard University Press, 1962.

Burbank, Jane and Henry Cooper. *Empires in World History: Power and the Politics of Difference*. Princeton: Princeton University Press, 2010.

Burke, Edmund. "Speech on Conciliation with the Colonies". In Isaac Kramnick (ed.) *The Portable Edmund Burke*. New York: Penguin Books, 1999.

Butler, Daniel Allen. *Shadow of the Sultan's Realm: the Destruction of the Ottoman Empire and the Creation of the Modern Middle East*. Washington, DC: Potomac Books, 2011.

---

46  Edmund Burke, "Speech on Conciliation with the Colonies", in Isaac Kramnick (ed.), *The Portable Edmund Burke* (New York: Penguin Books, 1999), 264.

Cannadine, David. *The Undivided Past: Humanity Beyond Our Differences*. New York: Knopf, 2013.
Darling, Linda T. *Revenue-Raising and Legitimacy: Tax Collection and Finance Administration in the Ottoman Empire, 1550–1560*. Leiden: Brill, 1996.
Grehan, James. *Everyday Life and Consumer Culture in 18th-Century Damascus*. Seattle: University of Washington Press, 2007.
Isom-Verhaaren, Christine. *Allies with the Infidel: The Ottoman and French Alliance in the Sixteenth Century*. London: I. B. Tauris, 2011.
Kármán, Gábor and Lovro Kunčevič (eds). *The European Tributary States of the Ottoman Empire in the Sixteenth and Seventeenth Centuries*. Leiden: Brill, 2013.
Kunt, İ. Metin. *The Sultan's Servants: The Transformation of Ottoman Provincial Government, 1550–1650*. New York: Columbia University Press, 1983.
Kunt, Metin. "Introduction to Part I". In İ. Metin Kunt and Christine Woodhead (eds). *Süleyman the Magnificent and His Age: The Ottoman Empire in the Early Modern World*. London: Longman, 1995, 37–8.
Lezra, Jacques. "Translated Turks on the Early Modern Stage". In Robert Henke and Eric Nicholson (eds). *Theater Crossing Borders: Transnational and Transcultural Exchange in Early Modern Drama*. Aldershot, UK: Asghate Press, 2008, 159–80.
McGowan, Bruce. "The Age of the Ayans, 1699–1812". In Halil İnalcık and Donald Quataert (eds). *An Economic and Social History of the Ottoman Empire*. Cambridge: Cambridge University Press, 1994.
Palmer, Alan. *The Decline and Fall of the Ottoman Empire*. New York: Barnes and Noble, 1992.
Pamuk, Şevket. "Institutional Change and the Longevity of the Ottoman Empire, 1500–1800". *Journal of Interdisciplinary History* 35 (2) 2004, 225–47.
Peirce, Leslie. "Changing Perceptions of the Ottoman Empire: The Early Centuries". *Mediterranean Historical Review* 19 (1) 2004, 6–28.
Philliou, Christine. "The Paradox of Perceptions: Interpreting the Ottoman Past through the National Present". *Middle Eastern Studies* 44 (2008), 661–75.
Quataert, Donald. "Ottoman History Writing and Changing Attitudes towards the Notion of 'Decline'". *History Compass* 1 (2003), 1–8.
Quataert, Donald. "Review of Karen Barkey, *Empire of Difference*". *American Historical Review* 114 (2009), 413–15.
Reynolds, Michael A. *Shattering Empires: The Clash and Collapse of the Ottoman and Russian Empires, 1908–1918*. Cambridge: Cambridge University Press, 2011.
Rogan, Eugene. *The Fall of the Ottomans: The Great War in the Middle East*. New York: Basic Books, 2015.
Tezcan, Baki. *The Second Ottoman Empire: Political and Social Transformation in the Early Modern World*. Cambridge: Cambridge University Press, 2010.

Toledano, Ehud. "A Comment on Virginia H. Aksan's 'What's Up in Ottoman Studies?'" *Journal of the Ottoman and Turkish Studies Association* 2 (1) 2015, 215–19.

Turner, Victor. *Dramas, Fields, and Metaphors.* Ithaca, NY: Cornell University Press, 1974.

Ulrichsen, Kristian Coates. *The First World War in the Middle East.* London: Hurst and Company, 2014.

Volkan, Vamık and Norman Itzkowitz. *Turks and Greeks: Neighbours in Conflict.* Huntingdon, UK: Eothen Press, 1994.

Yapp, M. E. "Europe in the Turkish Mirror". *Past and Present* 137 (1992), 134–55.

Yavuz, M. Hakan. "Orientalism, the 'Terrible Turk' and Genocide". *Middle East Critique* 23 (2) (2014), 111–26.

Yılmaz, Şuhnaz and İpek Yosmaoğlu. "Fighting the Spectres of the Past: Dilemmas of Ottoman Legacy in the Balkans and the Middle East". *Middle Eastern Studies* 44 (2008), 677–93.

# Glossary

*'adālet*   justice
*âdet*   custom
*âdil*   just
*adl*   justice
*ağa*   military commander or official
*ahdname*   agreement, pledge
*ahi*   fraternity or trade guild
*aḥkām*   legal norms (plural of *ḥukm*)
*akçe*   coins
*'akl*   reason, virtuous mind
*'aklî*   rational
*âlim (pl. ulemâ)*   scholar. learned man, religious-judicial hierarchy consisting of Muslim scholars
*'amel*   practice
*arpalık*   additional incomes allotted to high-ranking persons for their extra expenses or as pensions
*arzuhal*   petition
*asesbaşı*   chief policeman, capital of the guard
*ayan*   provincial warlords, notables
*Babıâli*   the Sublime Porte
*baġy*   acting wickedly and rebelliously
*beğ/bey*   prince, gentleman, ruler or notable
*belâgat*   eloquence
*berat*   appointment diploma, sultanic writ of appointment
*beylerbeyi*   governor-general
*beylikçi*   assistant to the chief scribe
*biat*   oath of allegiance, homage
*bid'at*   blameworthy innovations
*buyruldu*   order by provincial governors
*çelebi*   well-cultivated, educated, man of refinement, Ottoman gentleman
*dahil*   one of the advanced levels of medreses, education
*daire-i adliye*   circle of justice/equity
*dalâlet*   grievous error, corruption
*dânişmend*   advanced students in medrese
*Dârü'l-İslâm*   dominion of Islam
*deâvi nazırlığı*   minister of justice

*defter*    account book, register, inventory
*defterdar*    finance officer, treasurer
*devrân*    time, epoch
*devşirme*    recruiting of boys for the Janissary corps
*dhimmis*    non-Muslim subjects
*dîn ü düvel*    of the state and religion
*dirlik/dirlikli*    scribes with prebend
*dîvân*    imperial council
*dîvân efendisi*    the official secretary of vizier
*dîvânî*    calligraphy used in the imperial chancery
*Divan-ı Ahkâm-ı Adliyye*    Council of Judicial Regulations
*dönme*    converts or dönmeh
*Düzme*    impostor
*ehl-i hibre*    experienced master, expert
*ehl-i kalem*    masters of the pen
*ehl-i raşad*    astronomers
*ekâbir ü ayân*    grandees
*emin*    commissioner, salaried agent
*emîr (pl. ümerâ)*    prince, commander
*Emval-i Eytam Nezareti*    Authority for Supervision of Orphan Properties, Ministry of Property
*Enderun*    Palace School
*Engürüs vilâyetleri*    Hungarian territory
*Erdel*    Transylvania
*esnaf*    guilds
*evkaf defteri*    registers of pious foundations
*Eytam Sandıkları*    Eytam Chests, orphan funds
*faris*    knight, cavalier
*farz-ı kifaye*    a duty, the observance of which by some will absolve the rest
*fasâhat*    subtlety of meaning/articulateness
*fasîh*    articulate
*fesâd*    corruption, decay, decomposition
*fıkıh*    Islamic jurisprudence
*firman*    imperial edict, grant, permit
*fitne vü fesâd*    disorder, mischief and sedition
*fürû'*    branch, rational branch
*fütüvvet/futuwwa*    bravery, spiritual chivalry
*gazânâme*    literature of military expedition to promote Islam

*gazel*   lyric poems
*gedik*   set of artisansal rights and obligations
*Genç Osmanlılar/Yeni Osmanlılar*   Young Ottoman movement
*ghaza*   military expedition to promote Islam
*ghazi/gazi*   Muslim fighter against non-Muslims, honorific title
*hâbnâme*   literature of dreams
*hadd*   offences against God
*halîfe*   political or spiritual successor, substitute
*halife-i mekteb*   assistant, substitute teacher
*haraç*   annual tribute, head tax
*Haremeyn müfettişi*   inspector of the pious foundations in the two Holy Cities
*has*   crown lands with an annual income of more than 100,000 akçes
*hazakat*   manual skill
*hekimbaşi*   Palace doctor, head doctor
*Hey'et-i Âyân*   Senate
*Heyet-i Mebusan*   House of Representatives
*hikmet*   wisdom
*hirfet*   guilds
*Hırzü'l-Mülûk*   *Amulet of the Kings*
*hükemâ-i hâzikî*   expert physicians
*ḥukm*   legal norm
*hukuk*   laws, rights
*hürriyet*   liberty
*ibâdullah*   the people of God
*ibâdet*   ritual worship
*İbret*   Lesson
*icâzet*   diploma
*iç-oğlan*   pages in the inner palace
*ictihâd/ijtihâd*   expert legal opinion or interpretation, independent reasoning
*ifta kâğidi*   document containing an Islamic legal opinion
*ihtilâl*   revolution, disturbance of the public peace
*i'lâm*   judicial decree
*'illet*   reasons
*'ilm (pl. ulûm)*   science, true knowledge
*'ilmī*   scientific
*'ilm-i hal/ilmihâl*   catechism
*'ilmiyye*   the ulema/learned class
*ilmiyye kānûnnâmesi*   the regulation of the ulema class
*iltizam*   tax farming

*imtiyazat*   privileges, capitulations
*inkılâb*   transformation, reform, radical change, evolution
*inşâ*   chancery prose, belletristic
*insân al-kâmil*   the perfect man
*irade-i seniyye*   imperial decrees
*ishraqi*   illuminationist school in Islamic philosophy, gnosticism
*ıslāḥ*   improvement, amelioration, correction
*ıslāḥat layihası*   reform treatise
*ıslāḥ ve ilga*   transformation through nullification of the old
*ıslāḥ ve tanzim*   reform and reorganization
*istibdat*   despotic government
*İttifak-ı Hamiyyet*   Patriotic Alliance
*kadı*   judge
*kadı sicilleri*   Ottoman court records
*kadiaskers (kazaskers)*   highest-ranking members of the learned class
*kadılık*   profession of judge
*kâhya*   steward, caretaker, leader
*kalemiyye*   men of the pen, scribes, bureaucracy
*kandil*   special sacred nights in Ottoman tradition, oil lamp
*kanun/ḳānūn/qanun*   customary law or secular legislation
*Kanun-i Esasi*   Ottoman constitution
*ḳānûn-i kadîm*   ancient laws
*kapı*   household
*Kapıkulları*   Servants of the Gate
*kaside*   panegyric poetry
*kassâm-i askerî*   trustee of a will
*kaza*   township, district
*kefalet*   surety
*kefil*   guarantor
*kelâm*   Islamic theology
*kerâmet (pl. keramât)*   marvel, oracle
*keşf-i ḥissi*   sensual exploration
*kethüda*   leader, guild headman
*kevn ü fesâd*   existence and disintegration
*ḳıblenümā*   compass with the card that shows the direction of Mecca
*kul*   servant of the sultan
*lala*   tutor
*makâm*   rank, degree, station
*masjid/mescid*   prayer room, mosque

# GLOSSARY

*Mawlid*   Prophet Muhammad's birthday
*meclis*   council
*Meclis-i Umûmî*   parliament
*Meclis-i Vâlâ*   Sublime Council
*mecmua*   magazine, poetry anthologies
*medrese*   college for Islamic instruction
*mektub*   official letter
*memâlik-i mahrûse-i hâkāniyye*   imperial protected domains
*menâkıb*   spiritual deeds of a holy person, hagiography
*merhûm*   deceased
*mertebe*   rank
*meşâyih*   Sufi and non-Sufi mosque preachers
*Meşîhat*   Office of the Sheikh al-Islam after 1826
*meşk hocası*   calligraphy teacher
*mesnevī*   poem in rhymed couplets
*mevâlî*   fully-fledged scholars who served as *müderrise*s and *müfti*s
*mevleviyet*   major *kadı* posts in major centres like Istanbul, Mecca and Medina, Edirne, Bursa, Damascus, and Egypt
*mevleviyet kadılık*   dignitaries, same as *mevleviyet*
*mevlid*   versified narrative about the birth of the Prophet
*mezheb*   Muslim school of thought, legal school
*millet*   religious community, officially recognized religious community
*mirliva*   same as *sancakbeyi/sancak beyi/sancak beği*
*miskîn*   wretched, humble person
*molla*   teacher, doctor of Islamic law
*muallim*   instructor
*muâmelât*   secular and practical transactions according to Islamic law
*muhbir*   informant
*muhtesib*   market inspector
*Muḳaddime*   Ibn Khaldun's *Muqaddimah* (*Prolegomena*)
*mukallid*   imitator
*mukataa*   tax farm
*musâhib*   companion, associate
*muvaḳḳit*   timekeeper at a mosque
*musta'min*   non-Muslim foreigner temporarily in the Ottoman lands
*müderris/mudarris*   professor, teacher in medrese
*müfredat defteri*   fiscal inventory
*müfti/mufti*   official expounder of Islamic law. expert on the Islamic law officially recognized to issue legal opinions

*mülâzemet*   candidacy for a post
*mülâzım*   eligible candidate for a post
*mülk*   state, realm, sovereignty, private property
*mültezim*   tax farmer
*münşeat*   literary compositions, collections of official letters
*mürâsele*   a *kadı*'s letter of appointment, correspondence
*müteferrika*   member of elite palace corps of various origins, member of the retinue of a high official with various duties, miscellaneous
*nahiye*   county, township
*naib/nâib*   regent, substitute judge
*naklî*   historical, based on traditions
*narh*   officially-decreed prices
*nasihat*   advice
*nasihatnâme*   letters of advice, book of counsel, mirror for princes
*nazır*   financial entrepreneur, inspector of tax farms
*nezaret*   financial administrative unit
*nişan*   imperial monogram or sultan's stylized signature
*nişancı*   prince's chancellor
*nizam*   order, regulation, set of rules
*nizam-ı alem*   social order, public order in a given state
*Nizâm-ı Cedid*   New Order
*örf*   custom, customary law
*padişah*   sultan
*pençe*   official signature of high officials
*qanun*   regulations comprising traditional Ottoman dynastic law
*reaya/reâyâ*   masses, subjects, tax-paying population
*redif*   word repeated on every line of a poem
*re'isü'l-eṭṭibā*   head physician
*reîsülküttâb*   chief secretary to the divan, chief scribe
*Republica Christiana*   realms of Christianity
*ribat*   frontier military station
*risâle*   treatise
*rûznâmçe defteri*   day book of current financial transactions in a government office
*sahaf*   antiquarian, dealer in second-hand books
*salât*   prayer
*sancak*   sub-province
*sancakbeyi/sancak beyi/sancak beği*   provincial governor
*saray*   palace
*sayyid/seyyid*   a descendant of the Prophet Muhammad; honorific title

*şehzâde*   Ottoman prince
*sekbans*   peasant mercenaries, provincial militia equipped with firearms
*selef*   ancients, predecessors
*semâ*   whirling spiritual dance performed during a Mevlevi ritual
*Sened-i İttifak*   Deed of Agreement
*Siyasetname*   book of political advice intended for sultans or princes
*şeriat*   sharia, Islamic law
*seyfiyye*   men of the sword, military class in the Ottomans
*şer'î dirhem*   money earned through legitimate means
*şer' ve ḳānûn üzere*   in harmony with Islamic and sultanic law
*şeyhülislâm/Sheikh al-Islam*   chief mufti/müfti
*sicil (pl. siciller)*   record, register
*sinur*   border, limit
*sipahi*   cavalrymen
*sira (pl. siyar/siyer)*   conduct, comportment, demeanour, behaviour, way of life, attitude, position, reaction, way of acting, (in singular or plural) biography, history, in plural campaigns
*sünnet*   traditions, traditions related to the Prophet Muhammad
*tahrir defteri*   tax register
*takriz*   laudatory preface by a literary personality for another's work
*Tanzimat*   reforms, reorganization denoting a historical period between 1839 and 1876
*Tasvir-i Efkâr*   *Illustration of Opinion*
*tekke*   convent
*temāşāgāh-ı cihān*   a place of promenade for the world
*temessük*   certificate, bill, title deed
*tereke defteri*   probate inventory
*tevzi defteri*   provincial register specifying local taxes and expenditures of appointed officials
*tezkire*   memorandum, letter, petition, certificate
*tımâr/timar*   military fief assigned by the state to a cavalryman with an annual income of less than 20,000 akças
*tımâr defteri*   register containing the lists and incomes of local *tımâr*s
*timariots*   mounted cavalry
*tuğra*   signature or seal of a sultan affixed to official documents
*tülbend/tülbendcis*   manufacturers of fine cottons
*türbedâr*   tomb keeper
*uç beği*   frontier lord
*ukalâ*   erudite people

*'ulûm-i 'akliyye*   the rational sciences
*'ulūm al-ghara'ib*   occult sciences
*ümmet*   Islamic community, umma
*vakfiye*   pious endowment, trust deed of a pious endowment
*vakıf/waqf (pl. evkâf)*   pious foundation
*velî*   saint
*vilayet*   province
*voyvoda*   local official responsible for collecting revenues, provincial commander
*zâim*   holder of a *zeâmet*
*zâviye*   dervish lodge
*zeâmet*   prebend, land grant, military fief with an annual income between 20,000 and 100,000 akças
*zikr*   Sufi form of prayer consisting of the repetition of the divine names of God or of a verse of the Quran

# Index

Abbot of Theologos  42
Abdi, Abdurrahman  83
Abdi, Sarhoş (poet)  196
Abdülhamid II, Sultan  xxx, 382, 403–404, 407–408, 413, 420–421, 423–424, 428–431
Abdülkerim Sivâsî  342, 344–345, 352–358
Abdülmecid Sivasî  344
abomination (kerâhet)  346
Abou-El-Haj, R. A.  19–20
agency  9, 11–12, 176
    collective  9, 13
    female  20
    human  8
    see also human action
ahis  133
Ahmed Çelebi (see under Tiflî)  234
Ahmed Cevdet Pasha  15
Ahmed I  71–72, 99 n. 5 107 n. 30, 212 n. 43, 219, 229 n. 3, 235 n. 22, 288, 339, 344
Ahmed III  61 n. 16, 77, 141, 241, 268, 275
Ahmed Pasha  72 n. 45, 76
Akdağ, M.; see also historiography  15–16
el- Akhisarî, Ahmed Rumî  335 n. 28, 339, 343, 354
Aksan, V.  20, 443
Alaman seferi (German campaign)  165, 167, 175, 178–179
Albania  14, 39, 43–44
Albanians  225
Aleppo  72, 75–76, 124, 168, 172, 204, 206, 235, 250 n. 72, 340
Alexander the Great  220
Ali Bey (sancak beyi of Koppány)  191 n. 29
Âlî Pasha  399, 401, 403–404, 407–408, 410–412, 417–419
Altınay (Ahmet Refik)  92, 305
Amasya  71, 73 n. 4,6 166, 170, 176, 180, 407
amelioration  2
Anooshar, A.  22
appointment diploma  192–193
    fee  193 n. 39
    see also berat  191
Arabs  277, 348

Argyrokastron (Ottoman Turkish Ergiri, present-day Gjirokastër, Albania)  39 n. 4, 44
Aristotle  4, 270 n. 52
Armenians  17
army  13, 27, 47, 72 n. 44, 77 n. 63, 123, 175, 195, 208, 223, 236 n. 25, 272, 288, 290, 298, 305–307, 310–312, 316–318, 412, 425, 430
arpalık  298
Arslan (commissioner)  195
Artan, T.  25, 115
    see also historiography  22
artisan(s)  21, 25, 123–136, 138–143, 262, 277
    Muslims attempting to push non-Muslims out of their trades  138
arzuhal  41, 213
Asad, Talal  389
asesbaşı  224
Âşıkpaşazâde  293
astrolabe  28, 257–262, 272–273
Avlona (present-day Vlorë, Albania)  44
Awfi, Muhammad  168
ayans (notables)  29
    see also grandee
Ayas Pasha  167, 174, 178
Aydın  116, 413
el-Aydınî, Mehmed bin Hamza  347 n. 56, 349–351, 354
Aykan, Yavuz  347 n. 56, 358
Ayyubid  332
Aziz Efendi  297 n. 28, 299
Azmîzâde Haleti  202–203, 211–214
    takriz writing  202

Babinger, Franz  55, 86
Babur  22
Bachstrom, Johann Friedrich  54–55, 57–58, 60–64, 83–87
Baghdad  207, 226–227, 412
Balkans  xxxii, 15, 20, 45, 47, 64, 166, 326, 332, 421–422, 443, 446, 451
    Balkan Wars  14
Barkan, Ö. L.  16
    see also historiography  15

Barkey, K. 21
Bartov, O. 22
Báta 185
Bayezid, Prince 43, 165, 168–170, 172, 174–175, 179
Bayezid I XXIX, 24–25, 45, 155 n. 34, 162
Bayezid II 180, 294, 296
Bayezid Han mosque 270 n. 52
al-Bazza-zī, Ibn 334
Bedreddin, Şeyh Bedreddin 46
Bektaş Bey (*sancak beyi* of Szolnok) 195
Belgrade 77 n. 63, 167, 175, 184, 208, 236 n. 25,
*berat* 194, 371
see also appointment diploma 191
Berat 69
Berkes, Niyazi XXXIV, 17
*beşli* 186
*beylerbeyi*, of Buda 184, 190–191, 194
see also governor-general 185
*bid'at* 324, 327, 338, 350, 354
Birgivî Mehmed Efendi 264–265, 267, 327, 335, 339, 343, 349, 353
Black Death 446
Bodin, Jean 449
Bosnia 184 n. 5, 289
Bosnians 225
Bosphorus 111 n. 49, 113, 115
Bostan Mehmed Çelebi 308, 310, 315
Bourdieu, P. 8–9
Buda (O. Budin) 167, 184, 186–187, 190–191, 193–194, 196–197, 208, 307, 308 n. 6 309, 311–312, 317–318
Burbank, Jane 443–446
bureaucracy XXIX, XXXII, XXXIV, 13, 17, 124, 131, 135, 141, 143, 191, 208, 230, 232, 238 n. 31, 401, 407–408, 410–411, 447–448
  career lines 26–27, 203
  military 12, 27
  patrimonialism 17
  patronage networks XXVIII, XXX, 26
  political elites XXXII, XXXIV, 28, 231, 381, 418
  reformist elites 17, 415
  scribal 27, 80, 230–231, 238, 244–245, 248–251
  Sublime Porte 13, 399
  see also patronage

Burhan Efendi 185
Burke, Edmund 451–452
Bursa 25, 124, 130–131, 150 n. 7, 155 n. 40, 162, 204, 211–212, 330, 332 n. 20
Byzantines 45–47, 112 n. 51

Cairo 21, 124, 168, 204, 207, 340–341, 344, 410
Çankırı 376
Cannadine, David 442, 450
capitulations 64
*çavuşan ve bevvaban* 193 n. 39
*çavuşes* 193 n. 39
Celâlî 208, 210, 214
  bands 288
  uprisings 287
Celâlzâde Atâullah 168
Celâlzâde Mustafa 166–168, 170–172, 174–175, 180, 208, 310–311, 316
Celâlzâde Sâlih 26, 165–180
Central Asia 11
Chalkokandylas 48
change 17–18, 20–21, 24, 29, 142, 189, 191, 194, 205, 209, 215, 287, 289, 291–292, 300–301, 329, 345, 351–352, 358, 374–375, 381, 384, 389, 391, 428, 444, 447–448, 450
  legal 324–325
  social 14
  see also transformation
Charles V (of Habsburg) 313, 318, 449
child history, see also historiography 20
Christianity (*Republica Christiana*), see civilization 25
chronicler Sphrantzes 47
cities 124, 126–127, 129, 139–141, 173, 175, 179, 214, 341, 385, 448
citizenship 14, 30, 414
civilization 10, 417
civilization
  Christianity (*Republica Christiana*) 25
  civilizational spheres 25
  Islamic societies 6
  Oriental civilizations 6
  Western 5, 29, 404
code 8, 10, 210, 385, 388, 390–391
  family 391
  French code civil 390
  penal code 388

INDEX 465

codification   30, 381, 388–390, 392, 394
coffeehouses   327, 329, 343, 346, 356, 358
Cold War era   6
colonialism, age of   12
commissioner   195
  see also emin   187 n. 17
compass   257–262, 273
condominium (form of government)   448
Condorcet, Marquis de   6
Constantinople   48, 68, 80, 94, 313, 348, 421, 430
  siege of   64
Constitution (1876)   XXIX, 424, 432
constitutional   12, 13 n. 28, 14, 20, 30, 405–406, 409–412, 414, 420, 422–423, 428–432
Cook, J.   10
Cooper, Frederick   443–446
Corfu   44
correction   2
corruption (fesâd)   1
courts   22, 29–30, 369, 375, 379–380, 385, 387–388, 390, 392–394, 427, 447
  nizamiye   384 n. 12, 385, 390, 392–393, 427
  şeriat   232, 246, 379
  sharia   385
craft guilds   126–127, 133
  borders between   125
craft organization(s)   123, 135
  history of   125
crisis   4, 20, 24, 134, 143, 289, 292, 300, 318, 327, 399, 421, 423, 429
Csábrág (now Čabrad)   189
culture   8, 11, 19, 21–22, 25, 27, 75 n. 50, 78, 251, 258, 260–261, 383, 386, 389, 394, 408, 449
  cultural categories   10
  cultural history   19, 181
  cultural interactions   25
  see also historiography, social structure
Cüneyd Bey of Smyrna   46
customs   242 n. 44
  duty   184 n. 3
  fees   196
  houses   186
  stations   185

daily instalment   184
Dale, S. F.   22
Daltaban Mustafa   241
Damascus   72 n. 44, 124, 168, 204–206, 268, 310, 312, 340, 444, 448
Danilevsky, N.   5
Danube   47, 197, 236 n. 25, 307, 411
Darling, Linda   443, 448
Dávid, Géza   197
de Chassepol, François   66, 68, 71–78, 81
decay, decomposition (fesâd)   1, 9, 291
decentralization   XXXI, 1, 13, 18, 28–29, 414
decline   17–20, 26–28, 223–225, 240, 289, 291–293, 295, 297–298, 300–301, 305, 338, 354, 441–442, 444
decline
  organicist notion of Ottoman history   XXXI–XXXIV, 18
  see also historiography; Ibn Khaldun
defterdar   197, 207, 209, 224, 246, 275, 299
  see also finance director   191
Defterdar Mehmed Pasha   299
Delhi Sultanate   168
Delvinë   43
Demetriades, Vassilis   368
Deringil, S.   20
Derviş Pasha   XXXI–XXXII, 233
determinism   6, 8, 444
devrân   352
devşirme   XXIX–XXXIV, 69, 287, 297
diachronic   11
diplomacy   64, 251 n. 73
district governor   183, 185, 190–191
diversity   443
dönme   221
Doumani, Beshara   21
Droviani Monastery   39–40, 44
duality of structure, see also social structure   8
Duindam, J.   22
Dukaginzâde Osman   207, 211
Dukas   48
Durkheim, E.   7
Düzme Mustafa (impostor)   24, 40, 43, 45–50
  see also Mustafa Çelebi (the pretender)

early modern    12–13, 21–22, 25, 97 n. 1, 104
    n. 22, 127, 133, 177, 181, 231, 248, 257,
    261–263, 265, 269–270, 277–278, 443,
    447, 449–450
  period    12, 266 n. 34
Ebüssuûd Efendi    205, 207–209, 327,
    334–335, 347, 352
Ecevit, Bülent    450
economics    XXXI, 3 n. 5, 19, 408
  see also historiography    7
Edirne    43, 47, 49, 79 n. 69, 139–140, 142,
    166, 168, 172, 175, 179, 204, 236 n. 25,
    238 n. 30, 241, 250–251, 277, 348
  Incident    241 n. 43, 242
Eger (O. Eğri)    193, 195, 197, 221, 224
Egypt    241 n. 44, 21, 73, 127, 167–168, 210, 241,
    249, 276, 339, 350, 379 n. 2, 410, 418, 421,
    448, 451
election    309–310, 426, 428–429
emin    187 n. 17
  see also commissioner    195
Emîr Sultan    153 n. 26, 25, 162
empire(s)    1–3, 11–14, 16, 19–21, 24, 26, 28–30,
    77, 124, 127–128, 132, 137, 141, 155 n. 34,
    180, 198, 204, 238 n. 31, 248, 262, 287,
    289, 297, 299–300, 314, 318, 340, 381,
    405, 408, 410–411, 413, 415–416, 424,
    426, 429, 442–452
  Habsburg    22, 288, 307
  Islamic    12, 22
  Mongol    11
  organicist notion of the    15
  Ottoman    xviii, 1, 4, 12–13, 15, 17–19,
    21, 28–30, 59, 78, 132, 219, 223, 225,
    242, 262–264, 268, 270, 273, 277–278,
    289, 292, 318, 324–327, 329, 342, 354,
    369, 382, 384, 387, 405, 431, 443, 448,
    450–451
empiricism    28, 267 n. 40, 270, 272, 275
Emval-i Eytam Nezareti    388
Enlightenment    6–7, 13, 84, 406
environmental factors    7
Erdem, Y. H.    20
Ergene, Boğaç    376–377
erkân-ı erbaa    290
Ermiş, F.    23
Ernst, Archduke of Habsburg    186
Esztergom (O. Estergon)    193, 195, 197
  sancak of    189, 191

Evliya Çelebi    XXXIV, 111 n. 48, 64, 83,
    113–117, 139, 236, 238 n. 30, 239, 270
evolution    2–4, 16, 24
  see also transformation    23
execution    47–48, 104 n. 22, 113–115, 117, 142,
    174, 231–233, 237, 330

family    20, 45, 63, 68, 71, 82, 86, 125, 127–128,
    169, 173, 197, 207, 215, 298, 309, 349, 370,
    388, 391, 401, 408, 424
faris    186
farming out    387, 392
Faroqhi, Suraiya N.    25, 114
fatwa    334, 338 n. 35, 344–346, 350, 352,
    357–358, 371, 391
Fâzıl Ahmed    73, 76, 236 n. 25
Fâzıl Ahmed Pasha    76, 236–237
female    20
Ferdinand I (of Habsburg)    308–312,
    314–315, 317
Ferhad (ağa of the azabs of Pest)    187
Ferhad Pasha of Buda    193
fetva    391
Feyzullah Efendi    240–241, 242 n. 45,
    243 n. 51, 268
fıkıh    389, 393
finance director    184, 191
  see also defterdar
Findley, C. V.    20, 383 n. 9
First World War    5, 12, 124 n. 1, 380–381, 383,
    391 n. 35, 392, 431–432, 444, 451
Fleischer, Cornell    26, 294, 296
Földvár    185
food insecurity    448
Francis I, King    319
French Revolution    383 n. 11
Fuad Pasha    399, 403–404, 408, 410–411,
    417–419
Fülek (O. Filek)    186–188, 191, 196
fütüvvet/futuwwa    133

Ganchou, T.    46, 48
garden    113–114, 116–117, 270 n. 52
gardens    115
Gazi Giray    207 n. 23
Gazi Giray II, Khan of the Crimea    204,
    207, 211
Geertz, C.    8
Gelibolu    46–47

INDEX

gender studies, *see* historiography 19
General Archives of Greece 40
Genghis Khan 11
Genoese of New Phokaia 47–48
*ghaza* XXX, 20, 26–27, 161, 223–224
*ghazi* XXX, 20, 22, 162, 223
Gibbon, Edward 441–442
Giddens, A. 8
globalization 381
governor-general XXVIII–XXXIV, 107 n. 30
  of Eger 195
  *see also beylerbeyi* 168
Gradeva, Rossitsa 375
grandee 27, 249
  *see also ayans* 26
grand vizier 71–72, 75–77, 82, 136–137, 140,
  167, 174, 177–178, 185, 191, 195, 206,
  230–233, 235–237, 239, 241–243, 245,
  248, 251 n. 73, 288, 291, 294, 298 n. 31,
  300, 306, 314, 316–317
Greek Orthodox subjects 41
Greeks 17, 263, 276
Greek War of Independence 422
  *see also* revolution 14
guarantor, see also *kefil* 189
guilds 21, 25, 123, 125–127, 130–131, 133,
  141–142
Győr (O. Yanık) 195, 207

habitus 9
habitus, see social structure 389
*Hâbnâme* 219
Habsburg 59 n. 11, 236 n. 25
Habsburg(s) 21–22, 26, 29, 59, 86 n. 84, 128,
  165, 174–175, 179, 186, 196, 236 n. 25, 237,
  250, 288, 306–309, 313, 317–318, 421,
  429, 447, 449
Hacı Kalfa 289
Hacıoğlu Pazarcık 375
*hadd* 386
hadith 271, 332, 339, 347–348, 350, 355
Hafiz Ahmed Pasha 72
Halveti 337, 344
Hanafi 247, 324, 327–328, 333, 339, 343, 345,
  347, 349, 390–391
Hanafi, school 267 n. 39, 325, 342, 390
Hanbalis 328

Hanna, N. 21
*harmincad* (thirtieth) 184, 186
Hasan Kâfi Akhisârî 289, 299–300
Hasan Voyvoda, mosque (in Vác) 187
*has* estates (imperial crown lands) 187,
  191–193
*Hatt-ı Şerif-i Gülhane* 382
Hatvan 192
Hatvan, *sancak* of 193
Hawaiians 10
*Hayâl u Yâr* 203–207, 212
Hayreddin, Hâce Efendi 166, 172
Hegel, G. W. F. 6
heresy 318
Herodotus 4
Hersekzâde Ahmed Pasha 296
*Heyet-i Mebusan* 423
Heywood, Colin 46, 50
Hezarfen Hüseyin 289
Hezarpâre Ahmed Pasha 232, 237
*hikmet* (wisdom) 265, 296
historical events 8, 10, 19, 305
historiography 4, 19, 21–22, 25, 97 n. 123,
  300, 382, 391, 450
  agricultural history 16
  economic history 21
  gender studies 19–20
  history from below 16
  history of emotions 19–20
  history of medicine 19
  subaltern history 19–20
  *see also* decline; Ibn Khaldun; Kâtib
  Çelebi; modernization theory;
  organicist notion of Ottoman Empire;
  Orientalism; perceptions of history;
  world history 15
*Hırzü'l-Mülûk* 295–296
Ḥalabī, İbrahim 334, 339, 355
Hoberdanacz, Johann 312
Hobsbawm, Eric 383 n. 11
Hoca Mesud 233
Hoca, Süleyman 189
human action 7
human action, see also under agency 25
Hungary 26, 58, 59 n. 11, 66 n. 30, 85 n. 83,
  90, 184–188, 193, 196–197, 199–200, 207,
  287, 306–314, 317, 319 n. 67, 421, 429

Hungary (cont.)
   Hungarian   29, 55–58, 59 n. 11, 60,
      85 n. 83, 86 n. 84, 167, 184, 186, 190,
      196, 207, 306–309, 312, 314, 317, 319
   Hungarian, exiles   86
Hürrem (Süleyman's wife)   170, 176

İbn 'Abbās   345, 351
Ibn Battuta   158 n. 61, 133
Ibn Khaldun   XXXI, 2, 4, 5 n. 8, 15, 273
   see also decline
İbrâhim Efendi   242 n. 44
İbrâhim Kırımî   337, 340
İbrâhim Pasha   56 n. 7, 61 n. 16, 73, 75–76,
      132, 167, 173–174, 178, 236, 269, 312,
      316
İbrâhim Peçevî   64
İbrâhim, Sultan   229 n. 3, 232
İbşir Pasha   233, 235
*icmallü haslar, see also has* estates   191
*ilmihâl*   343
*ilmiyye*   27, 30, 205, 210, 268, 276
*iltizam*   370
   see also tax farm   287
Imperial Council   166, 183, 185 n. 8, 191, 193
   n. 38, 204, 211, 237, 299, 386
Imperial Harem   288
impostor(s)   25, 45, 56 n. 7, 63, 79, 82–83
improvement   2
İnalcık, Halil   18, 264
information flow   79, 81
*inkılâb*   2
innovation   2, 323, 329, 332, 334, 338–339,
      352, 388, 444, 447
institutional changes   XXIX, 1, 15, 26, 183
interregnum (1402–13)   24
Iranian   XXXII–XXXIII, 12, 16
*Islahat Fermanı*   382
Islam   247 n. 64, 25, 27, 29, 50, 60, 264, 276,
      348, 371–374, 402, 405, 409–410, 414,
      425, 432, 448–449
Islamic jurisprudence, see *fıkıh*   30, 393
Islamic law   129, 247, 325–326, 329, 348,
      379 n. 2, 406
   see sharia   324
Islamism   14
İsmâil Ma'şûkî   24, 113–114, 116–117
Istanbul   124 n. 3, 338 n. 34, 26, 29, 54–55,
      56 n. 7, 59–61, 63, 70–71, 73, 76, 77 n. 63,

      78, 80, 82, 84–85, 117, 124–126, 128–130,
      133, 135–137, 139–143, 162, 167, 175,
      179, 203–205, 208, 211, 213, 220–221,
      229 n. 3, 235, 238 n. 30, 241–242, 250,
      257, 263, 268, 274, 275 n. 61, 277, 307,
      312, 336 n. 31, 338, 340, 368, 370, 375,
      377, 392, 400–401, 404, 407–408,
      411–414, 419, 422, 424, 429, 432, 448,
      450
Izmit   59, 79
*ıslāḥ*   2
*ıslāḥ ve tanzim*   2

janissaries   13, 69, 72 n. 45, 132, 142, 224,
      229 n. 3, 232, 234 n. 16, 235 n. 22,
      241–242, 248, 315–316, 406
*Jawāmi' al-ḥikāyāt wa lawāmi' al-riwāyāt*
      168, 176
Jews   222
Jews, of Buda   187
judiciary   381, 387, 392, 427
justice (*'adālet*)   XXXII, 12, 14, 21, 29, 178, 221,
      226, 247, 290, 298, 393, 402, 406, 409,
      443, 445

*kadı*(s)   27, 29–30, 41, 43–45, 49, 126,
      129–130, 135–136, 138–141, 168, 170, 202,
      204, 207–212, 214, 219, 290, 367–377,
      392
   courts   29, 369, 376
   of Delvinon   42
Kadızâdelis   28–29, 264–266, 268, 275–276,
      323–324, 327–329, 339–340, 342–344,
      349, 352 n. 64, 353–355
Kadızâde Mehmed of Balıkesir   327,
      339–340, 343–344
Kafadar, Cemal   19, 295
*kafes* (cage)   288
*kâhya*   126
Kalaylıkoz Ali Pasha   190–191
*kalemiyye*   239, 251
*kalemiyye*, see scribes   27
*Kānūn-i Esāsī*   399, 424, 427
*kānūn-i kadīm*   28, 294–297, 301
Karagöz Pasha   296
Kara Mustafa Pasha   57 n. 9, 58 n. 10, 57, 288,
      305, 316
Karlowitz   240, 245, 248, 250 n. 72
   Treaty of   59, 240, 241 n. 42, 251, 318

INDEX  469

*kaside* 27, 167, 204, 207, 230, 234–235, 238, 243–244
Kasım Bey mosque 187
Kasım Pasha 314
Kasım Voyvoda Bey/Pasha 197
Kastamonu 376, 408
Kâtib Çelebi XXXIV, 2, 15, 195, 264, 289, 300, 330, 352–353, 355
*kaza* 70, 209, 367, 385
*kazasker* 205, 211
Kâzerûnî (dervish order) 26
Kâzerûnî, Ebû İshâk 26, 161–162
*kefil* 189
Kékkő (O. Kekköy) 189
Kemal, Nâmık 400–409, 416, 419–420, 423, 431
Kemalpaṛazāde Ahmed 166, 174, 310, 312
*kethüda* 126, 139, 187
Kınalızâde Ali Efendi 204–205, 207–208, 212, 290
Kınalızâde, family 202
Kınalızâde Hasan Efendi 205, 207, 210–211
*Kıssa-i Firuz Şah* 168
*Kitâbu Mesâlih* 295–296
Knolles, Richard 449
Koca-ili (in Bithynia) 46
Koçi Bey/Beğ XXXIV, 289, 295, 297, 299
Komárom 189
Kondratiev, N. 5
    Kondratiev waves 5
Köprülü, family 25, 55, 58, 60, 63–64, 66, 71, 82, 86, 230, 250
Köprülü, Fuad 15
Köprülü Mehmed, Grand Vizier 57, 68–69, 71, 82, 237
Köprülü Mehmed Pasha 71–73, 75–76, 83, 86, 231 n. 7, 233, 288
Köprülüzâde Fâzıl Ahmed Pasha 76
Korkud, Prince 294
Kundmann, Johann Christian 55, 61
Kunt, İbrahim Metin 1, 15, 18–19, 22, 161, 165, 181, 198, 231, 234 n. 16, 358, 441–442
Kütahya 170, 176, 180

Lajos II 309
Lala Mustafa Pasha 205–206
Lâmiî Çelebi 170–171
Landes, David 447
Larende 202, 204, 208, 210, 214
law 17, 30, 42, 221, 232, 246, 291, 294–297, 300, 325, 355, 367, 374–375, 377, 379, 389–390, 402, 405, 413, 427–428
    civil 384–386
    commercial 384, 427
    continental 391 n. 34, 388–389, 394
    criminal 384–386, 427
    family 380 n. 3, 384–385, 392
    Provincial (*vilâyet*) Reform 384, 387, 392
legal 14, 16, 23, 28, 132, 168, 173, 205, 246, 264, 298, 325, 327–328, 330, 346, 351–355, 357–358, 369, 371, 377, 382, 389–390, 393–394, 399, 417, 423, 425, 427, 432
    change 379–380, 383, 388, 394
    education 381, 392
    modernization 379, 390, 394, 423
    school (*mezheb*) 325, 342, 348
    system 30, 381, 384–386, 388, 392, 394
legislation 12, 381, 384, 386, 388, 392
Lemnos 46
Le Noble, Eustache 66, 68–69, 77–78, 81
Leopold I 58 n. 10, 90, 313–314
Lévi-Strauss, C. 8
Lewis, Bernard XXXIV, 17–18
*Leyla and Mecnun* 169
liberalism 431
Lieven, D. 22
linguistic structures, *see also* social structure 11
long nineteenth century xx, 379, 381, 383 n. 11
Long War (1593–1606) 194, 196
Lowry, Heath W. 19
Lütfi Pasha 294, 297, 299, 310, 312

Machiavelli, Niccolò 4
magnetism 62 n. 19, 260 n. 13
Mahmud II, Sultan 382, 422
Mahmud of Ghazni 22
*mahzar* 202–203, 211–214
Maksudyan, N. 20
Mamluk 127, 168, 325–326, 332, 347
Manastır 375
market inspector (*muhtesib*) 139

Marxist   6
Marx, K.   7
Matrakçı Nasuh   311
McGowan, Bruce   375
Mecca   76, 207, 323, 331, 340, 408, 413
*Mecelle-i Ahkâm-ı Adliye*   385, 390–391
*mecmua*   26, 165–167, 169–172, 174–180
medieval   12, 17, 19, 30, 73, 257–258, 261, 263, 450
medieval period   167
*medrese*   270 n. 52, 16, 28, 166–167, 172, 178–180, 202, 204–205, 207–208, 210, 212, 214, 225, 241, 243 n. 51, 262, 264–265, 267, 410
Mehmed (*kethüda* of Visegrád)   187
Mehmed Ağa (tax farmer)   188
Mehmed b. Mehmed   211
Mehmed I   46–47
Mehmed II (the Conqueror)   77, 155 n. 34, 167, 262, 293, 295–296, 333
Mehmed III   XXIX, 204 n. 7, 338
Mehmed IV   58 n. 10, 65, 72, 75–77, 78 n. 63, 79–80, 82, 229 n. 3, 230, 232, 234 n. 16, 239, 250, 271, 317
Mehmed VI   432
Melâmî-Bayramîs   114, 116–117
Melek Ahmed Pasha   83
Memi Bey (*sancak beyi* of Kirka)   192
memorandum   185, 190 n. 24, 191, 193 n. 39, 194
merchants   21, 29, 79, 229 n. 3, 260, 290, 384 n. 12
Merton, Robert K.   265
messianic kingship   167
methodology   6, 11, 262, 264, 353
  diachronic   8
  empirical   7, 28, 291
  interpretative sociology   8
  quantitative   7
  synchronic analysis   8
  textuality   8
  *see also* social sciences
methods of rule   446–447
Meylî (poet)   209, 211
*mezheb* (legal school)   267 n. 39
  *see also* legal school   357
Midhat Pasha   400, 404, 411–414, 420, 423, 428–429

Mikhail, Alan   21, 23
military   29, 44, 49, 76, 83, 128, 132, 134, 142, 167, 172, 175, 179, 183, 195–196, 202, 204–210, 229 n. 3, 276 n. 65, 287, 290, 294, 299–301, 305, 310, 314, 318, 320, 338, 370, 412, 414, 430–432, 445
  class   XXX, XXXII, 177
*millet*-system   12
Ministry of Justice   385
modernization   XXXI, XXXIII, 6 n. 13, 379 n. 2, 6, 13, 17–18, 29, 379, 381, 390, 394, 400, 402–404, 414–415, 417
  modernization theory   6
Mohács   78 n. 63, 186 n. 11
  battle of   77, 309–310
monarchy   307 n. 5, 405, 409, 411, 423
monastic archives   45
Mongol   12, 20, 167, 295
Moralı Defterdar   233
Moralı Hasan Pasha   241
mosque (*câmi, mescid*)   69, 111 n. 49, 168, 170, 197, 258, 327, 333, 339, 344–345, 356–357, 408
  illumination of   336, 346
Mount Ganos (present-day Işıklar Dağı, close to Tekirdağ)   47
Mpogkas, Evangelos   39–40, 48
*Muallimhâne-i Nüvvab*   392
*müderris*   202, 204–206, 208–209, 211–212, 214
*mukallid*   350
*mukataa*   187 n. 17, 188–189
  of Vác   184–189, 195–196
*mülk*   290, 294, 298
*mülk ü milel*   244
*mültezim*, see also tax farmer(s)   188
*Münşeat*   171, 202, 211–213, 219
Murad II   22, 24, 47–48, 50
Murad III   XXIX, 204 n. 7, 336–337, 340
Murad IV   68, 72–73, 76, 227, 229 n. 3, 297
Murad V   409, 412–413, 420–421, 429
Murphey, Rhoads   300, 318
Musa, Banu   272
Musa Çelebi   46
Musa, Emir   214
Musahib Mehmed   72 n. 43
Musâhib Mustafa Pasha   239
Muslim community   2, 410

Mustafa Âlî (Gelibolulu)   xxxiv, 64, 171, 206, 208, 264, 289, 295–296
Mustafa bin Hamza bin İbrahim bin Veliyüddin   341
Mustafa (cavalryman)   187
Mustafa Çelebi (the pretender)   24, 49 n. 45
   see Düzme Mustafa (impostor)   48, 50
Mustafa Fâzıl Pasha   400, 403, 408, 410–411, 418–420
Mustafa I   72, 132 n. 23, 227
Mustafa II   241
Mustafa Reşid Pasha   399, 401, 407, 411, 417–418
Mustafa (*sipahi*)   188
Mustafa, son of Bayezid I   40, 45
*müteferrika*   205
Müteferrika, İbrâhim   56, 60, 62, 86–87, 258–260, 276–277
Mystras (Peloponnese)   46

Nâbî (Yusuf Nâbî)   244
Nagykálló   194–195
*nahiye*   43, 188, 387
*nahiye* of Vagenetia   43
Nâilî-i Kadîm   238
Naîmâ, Mustafa   xxxi, xxxii, 83, 232, 316
Naîmâ, Mustafa, see also decline   15
Nakşbendi   275 n. 61, 343
*narh* (officially-decreed prices)   124, 142, 370–374
*nasihat-ıslâhat* (reform treatises)   294
*nasihatnâme*   219, 227, 294
nationalism   14, 383 n. 11, 410, 442, 447
nation-state   14, 382, 443
nation-state(s)   7, 15
*nazır*   189–190, 197
Neşātī   238
*nezarets*, of Belgrade   184
   of Vác   184–185, 194
Nógrád (O. Novigrad)   185, 190
   *sancak* of   188
non-Muslim communities   xxxii, 384 n. 12, 403
nostalgia   25
Nushî el-Nâsıhî   341–343, 345–350, 352, 355

Ömer Efendi (son of Hayali)   207
*örf*   390

organicist notion   18
   see decline   15
Orientalist   xxxiv, 6, 55, 61, 63, 64 n. 23, 84, 86
Oriental romances   66, 84–85
orphan funds   388
orthopraxy   267, 324, 327
Osman   73–76, 162, 183–184, 186–190, 296, 349
Osman Ağa (*çelebi/bey* of Hungary)   26, 184, 186–197
Osman Bey *medresesi*/mosque   197
Osman, House of   348–349
Osman II, Sultan   229 n. 3, 288
Osman Pasha *medrese*   210
Ottoman
   citizens   384 n. 12, 426–427
   constitution   382, 399, 404, 407, 413, 421, 424, 428–429
   elites   446
   Empire   xvii, 15, 19, 28, 124 n. 1, 155 n. 34, 257, 267 n. 40, 277, 294, 314, 318, 325, 358, 381 n. 6, 391 n. 35, 415
   literary language (*belagat*/belles-lettres/*münşeat*/rhetorics)   26, 171, 230, 245
   reforms   379, 381–383, 388, 393
   state   19, 24, 26, 41, 46, 60, 123 n. 1, 183, 219, 289, 292–294, 298, 300, 327, 386, 388, 410, 412, 426, 441, 444, 447, 449
   see under empire(s)   1
Ottoman–Habsburg War   288, 317
Ottomanism   14
Ottomano, Padre (Domenico)   73–76
Özdemiroğlu Osman Pasha   206, 209–210

Paks   185
palace (*saray*) of Edirne   47
Palestine   21, 272
Palmer, Alan   442
Pamuk, Şevket   447
panegyric poetry (*kaside*)   27, 230, 249
parliament   14, 30, 399, 403, 406–407, 409, 412, 420, 423, 425–433
Pasha Yiğit   44
patronage   xxviii, xxx, 26–27, 73 n. 46, 156 n. 45, 165, 167–168, 172, 180, 202, 206, 211, 230–232, 250, 276, 278, 401, 410, 416, 418, 432, 446
peasants   16, 21, 127, 290, 297 n. 28, 298, 372

Peirce, L. P.   20, 442
perceptions of history
    cyclical understanding of historical events, see perceptions of history   4
    linear history   5
    Orientalism   84
Perjés, Géza   307
Pest   167, 187, 195–196
Philliou, Christine   21, 23
pious foundations (*vakıf, evkâf*)   129, 411
Pirizâde Mehmed Sâhib   272–273
Plato   4, 270 n. 52
pluralism   390, 446, 448, 450
Polanyi, K.   7
political elites, see *under* bureaucracy   28
political legitimacy   24
politics   21, 29, 72, 75 n. 50, 76, 80, 82, 219, 229–230, 234 n. 16, 236, 239, 249, 251, 338, 399, 401, 403, 405–406, 409, 416, 422, 431, 433
    of difference   445
Polybius   4
population density   446
postmodern   8
post-mortem inventories   125
prayer, congregational performance of   330
prayer (*salât*)   29, 169, 221, 330–331, 333–337, 341, 346
prayer (*salât*), Berat   29
    canonical   331–333, 335
    congregational performance of   329, 332–335, 339–343, 345–346, 348–350, 352, 354–357
    *Kadir* (night of power)   29, 345, 357
    *mevlids*   336
    prayer (*salât*), nocturnal   329–330, 332–338, 340, 349
    Regaib   29, 357
    supererogatory (*nâfile, nevâfil*)   329–333, 335, 339, 341–343, 345–352, 354–355, 357
preacher(s)   166, 211, 223, 267, 327, 329, 337, 339, 341–342, 344, 356
preacher(s)   242 n. 44
progressivist understanding of history   6
Protestant   58 n. 10, 59, 61–63, 263
public monuments   24
Puritanism   263, 265–266, 268–269

al-Qāri, 'Ali   339–340
Quataert, Donald   18, 444
Quran   55, 62, 205, 222, 250 n. 72, 328, 331, 352–353

Ráckeve   185
Radziwiłł, Prince Michał   57, 86
Rákóczi, family   60, 63, 86
Rákóczi, Ferenc I   57–59
Rákóczi, Ferenc II   57, 59–61, 85–86, 270 n. 50
Rákóczi, György II   236 n. 25
Râmi Mehmed   27, 229–230, 239–251
Râşid Mehmed Efendi   83
Râşid Mehmed Efendi   244, 313
realms of Islam (*Dârü'l-İslâm*)   25
*reaya* (subjects)   XXXII, 13
Receb Pasha, Grand Vizier   72
Receb (son of Abdullah)   188
reformist elites, see *under* bureaucracy   17
registrar   188
*reîsülküttâb*   178, 204, 209, 224, 229, 232, 234, 239, 243–244, 250 n. 72
religious-secular binary   380, 394
renegade(s)   56, 69, 79
resistance   44, 59, 319, 416, 418
    to increasing the number of shops   137
resource dimension/resources   8–12, 18, 250, 278
    see *also* social structure   10–11
revolution   2, 4, 294, 305, 383 n. 11, 418, 422, 451
    American   14
    French   5, 14, 422
    Young Turk   14, 431, 433
Rhodes   167, 242, 404, 448
Rimaszombat (now Rimavská Sobota)   187
Romhány   195
royal courts   22
    Schönbrunn   22
    Topkapı Palace   22, 71
    Versailles   22
Rum   326–327, 332 n. 20, 333–334, 336, 341, 347, 350
*Rumeli Ahkâm Defterleri*   370, 375, 377
Rumeli Hisarı   111 n. 47, 113, 115, 117
Rumi   177, 326, 332–334, 341, 343, 348–350, 352

INDEX 473

Russian history 21
*rûznâmçe defteri* 188, 191–192, 194

Saadet Giray (Khan of Crimea) 172
Safavids 229 n. 3, 295, 337, 447
Şah Kulu medrese 205
Sahlins, M. 8, 10
Saint Augustine of Hippo 6
Saint Thomas Aquinas 6
Sajószentpéter 187
salafis 328, 331 n. 15
Şâmîzâde Mehmed 230–238, 244, 247–248, 250
*sancak beyi* 77, 192, 194, 197
 see also district governor 190
Sariyannis, M. 23, 266
Sarı Mehmed Pasha 316
schemas 8–10, 12, 14
 see also social structure 11
scribes (*kalemiyye*) 136, 141, 229, 231, 233, 237, 238 n. 31, 239, 242, 249, 251, 393, 448
 see also bureaucracy 42
secularization 17, 379
*şehir oğlanı* 242, 296
Şehrezūrī, Muhammed 274
*sekbans* 13
Selânikî Mustafa Efendi 64, 336
*selef* 324, 346, 350
Selim Giray (Khan of Crimea) 243
Selim I 166, 295–296
Selim III 125, 132, 296, 382, 383 n. 11, 414
*semâ* 113–114, 116, 352
Şemseddin, Efendi Sivāsī 344
Şemseddin, Kadızade Ahmed 205
*şeriat* 30
Serres 48
Şevkî Çelebi 150 n. 7
Sewell Jr, W. H. 8–12, 16
*seyfiyye* 27, 239
*şeyhülislām* 243 n. 51, 385 n. 15, 204, 240, 268, 327, 334–335, 338, 352, 386–387, 391–392
Seyyid Mehmed 184
Shafi'i 271 n. 54, 347
sharia 30, 114, 324–325, 337, 343, 354–355, 379, 381, 384, 390–392, 394, 402, 406, 408–410, 427
 courts 43, 379–381, 384–388, 392, 394
 see also *kadı*(s) courts 391

shar'i judgments 29, 345, 351–352
sheikh(s) 111 n. 48, 113–117, 126, 162, 223, 323, 336–338, 344, 348–349
Silahdâr Fındıklılı Mehmed Ağa 73, 242, 313–314, 316
Sima Qian 4
Şinâsi, İbrâhim 400–403, 405, 407, 416–417, 419
*sipahi*(s) 13, 16, 26, 188, 224
Sivāsī, Şeyh 211
*Siyer-i Kebîr* 247
*Siyer-i Veysî* 219
slavery 20
smoking 327, 329, 343, 356, 358
social change, see transformation 3
social mobility 27, 276
social sciences 7–8
 Annales School 7
 cultural anthropology 8
 interpretative sociology 8
 see also methodology 4
social structure 7, 10–11, 27
 economic base 7
 *habitus* 9
 linguistic structures 11, 20
 political superstructure 7, 28
 resource dimension 10–11
 resources 11
 schemas 28
socio-legal 379–380, 389
Sorokin, P. 5
state 2, 13, 16–17, 21, 24, 26, 30, 111 n. 49, 113–115, 117, 123–125, 128, 132–133, 135, 141, 183, 221–222, 224–225, 230, 235, 239, 244–247, 278, 287, 290–292, 297, 307, 316, 324, 326, 319, 355–356, 358, 369–371, 376, 381, 384, 389, 391–393, 399, 401, 403, 405–406, 411, 413–414, 416–418, 420–421, 424, 426–428, 431–432, 443, 446–447, 449–450
Streusand, D. E. 22
structure, see social structure 29
Suâvî, Ali 400, 408–410, 418–420
*subaşı* 224
Sublime Porte 388 n. 25, 401, 403–404, 408, 410–411, 414, 417–418, 421, 433, 448
 see also bureaucracy 399
Subrahmanyam, Sanjay 22, 248 n. 69
Sufi 114, 267, 327, 336–338, 343, 347, 352, 356

Süleyman Ağa   71 n. 43, 73, 232
Süleymaniye   169
   manuscript   165, 169–171, 176
   *medrese*   204
Süleyman Pasha   77 n. 63
Süleyman the Magnificent   xviii, 26,
   153 n. 26, 166–167, 171–173, 175, 178–179,
   263, 294–295, 296 n. 22, 305, 308–313,
   315, 317, 319, 441
sultan   xviii, 14, 41, 50, 60, 64, 67, 71–73,
   76–77, 78 n. 63, 82, 85 n. 83, 113–114,
   116, 123, 127, 132–133, 135–136, 142, 162,
   165, 167, 172, 174–180, 195, 197, 208, 211,
   214–215, 219, 226, 288, 291, 295, 300,
   309–310, 314, 317, 323, 336–337, 348,
   425
Sultan Ahmed mosque   339
sultan, see also royal court   269
Sunni   XXXII–XXXIII, 325, 327, 330, 337,
   345, 351–355, 358, 402, 451
   revivalist movement   324, 328, 355
Sun'ullâh Efendi   338–339
supererogatory prayers   329–330, 332–333,
   335, 339, 341–343, 345, 349–352,
   354–355, 357
synchronic analysis, *see under*
   methodology   8
Syria   14, 72, 125, 127, 332, 339, 407, 413, 451
Szabadka (O. Sobotka, Rimavská
   Sobota)   188
Szécsény (O. Seçen)   185, 189, 191–193
   *sancak beyi* of   192
   *sancak* of   184, 191–192
Székesfehérvár (O. İstolni Belgrad)   195, 316
Szerémi, György   309
Szikszó   187
Szolnok (O. Solnok)   193–194
   *bey* of   193
   *sancak beyi* of   194

*Tabakâtü'l-memâlik ve*
   *derecâtü'l-mesâlik*   170
Tab'i Süleyman Efendi   207, 209
*takriz*   202–203, 211–213
*Tanzimat*   30, 125, 382, 386, 392, 399,
   401–403, 405–406, 410, 414, 418,
   422–423, 429, 447
Tanzimat, reforms   30
*Târîh-i Feth-i Budun*   171

*Tasvir-i Efkâr*   295 n. 19, 302, 401, 403, 419
Tatar   195, 207
tax farm(s)   13, 139, 183, 186–188
   see also *iltizam*   185–186
   lifetime   128
   tax farmer(s)   13, 183–184, 186–187
   see also *mültezim*   187–189, 376
tax registers (*tahrir defteri*)   127
*tecdid*   2
Tezcan, Baki   13 n. 28, 20
*tezkire*   191, 209
Thököly, Imre   57–58, 61, 78–79, 86 n. 84,
   309, 313–314, 317
Thököly, family   86
Thrace   47, 49, 451
*timariots*   13, 69, 297–298, 300
time scales   7
Tıflî   234–235, 237–238, 244, 247, 249
*tımâr*   XXXI, XXXIII, 46, 71, 188, 194, 206,
   246, 287, 296–298
   *defteri*   194
   holder   187
   holders   39
   system   13, 18, 446
Timur   XXIX, 46
Tolna   185
Topkapı Palace Library   171
Toynbee, Arnold J.   5
trade   21, 64–65, 133, 136, 184 n. 3, 196, 287,
   323, 448
   in cattle in Ottoman Hungary   186
traditionalist   17, 339, 347, 352, 354–355
transformation   XXX–XXXIII, 1–3, 7–8,
   10–11, 13–14, 16, 18, 20, 25–26, 28–30,
   230 n. 4, 231, 250, 292, 301, 320, 374, 377,
   379, 387 n. 20, 389, 392–393, 432, 442,
   444, 446
   transformative action   9
   see also agency, evolution   24
transition   4, 24–25, 27, 239, 441
Transylvania   58 n. 10, 59 n. 11, 236 n. 25,
   88–89, 186, 236 n. 25, 307, 309–310
treasury   129, 183, 184 n. 5, 185, 232–233, 287,
   290, 299, 448
   of Buda   184
Tura   195
Turkish Republic   132, 382, 432, 450
Turkism   14
turning point   4, 294

*uç beği* (frontier lord)   44
ulema   XXIX, XXXII, 12–13, 17, 29, 326 n. 8,
    333, 340, 342, 348–349, 353, 355, 357
    *see also ilmiyye*   326
universal monarchy   167
Üsküb (present-day Skopje, Macedonia)   44, 70
USSR   21
Üstüvânî Mehmed   339

Vác (O. Vaç)   184–190, 194, 196–197
*vakfiye*   333
Vanî Mehmed Efendi   268, 339, 347 n. 56
Vecdî   231, 238
Veysî   XXXIV, 27, 212, 219–227
Vico, G.   5
Vienna   28, 57–58, 61, 80, 288, 305–307, 311, 315–318, 411
Vienna, siege of   58 n. 10, 308, 315, 318
*vilayet* (province)   39 n. 4
Visegrád (O. Vişegrad)   187
Víziváros (Watertown), *see* Buda   197
von Hagen, Mark   22
Vranoussis, Leandros   40
Vücûdî Mehmed Efendi   26, 202–203, 205, 207–216
Vücûdî Mehmed Efendi, as *zeâmet*
    holder   204, 206–207
    birthplace   204
    early career   202
    *kadı*   204
    patrons   205–206
    works   203

Wallachian voivode Mircea   46
Weber, Max   7, 266
Weichselberger, Sigismund   312
Weitz, E. D.   22
West   6–7, 399, 404, 406, 409, 421, 444
    Westernization   276–277, 408, 415
    *see also* civilization   25

Wittek, Paul   XXX, 20, 46
women   22, 27, 63, 72 n. 44, 73, 75, 82–83, 128, 131, 137, 179, 221, 308, 342, 351, 354, 391, 429
world history   19, 21–22, 444
    *see also* historiography   211

Yahyâ Efendi   111 n. 49, 204, 207, 209, 211
Yanık   195, 207, 236 n. 26
Yemen   14, 350, 444
Yirmisekiz Mehmed Çelebi   269, 273, 275
Yılmaz, Hüseyin   290–291
Yılmaz, Şuhnaz   442
Yosmaoğlu, İpek   442
Young Ottomans   14, 30, 399–412, 414–421, 423, 429, 431–432
Young Turks   14, 20, 382, 399, 431
    Committee of Union and Progress   14, 138
    Dashnagtsutyun   14
    Hunchakian Party   14
    Internal Macedonian Revolutionary Organization   14
Yûsuf, Frenk/Sinan Pasha   184, 193
Yûsuf, Frenk/Sinan Pasha   184 n. 5
Yûsuf, son of Abdullah   188

Zápolya, John   308 n. 6, 309–315, 317
*zeâmet*   188, 205–206, 233, 246, 297
*zeâmet*, holder   184, 190, 204, 207
Zenevessi, Gjin   44
Zen, Piero   312
*zikr*   345, 352, 356–357
Ziyâ Pasha   400, 403–404, 407–409, 416, 419–420, 423, 431
Zotos, B. D.   39–40, 49
Zrínyi, family   86
Zrínyi, Ilona   58 n. 10, 59–61, 63
Zsitvatorok, Peace of   288

Printed in the United States
by Baker & Taylor Publisher Services